Efficient and Flexible Reading

Efficient and Flexible Reading

Seventh Edition

Kathleen T. McWhorter
Niagara County Community College

PEARSON
Longman

New York • San Francisco • Boston
London • Toronto • Sydney • Tokyo • Singapore • Madrid
Mexico City • Munich • Paris • Cape Town • Hong Kong • Montreal

Vice President and Editor in Chief: Joseph Terry
Acquisitions Editor: Susan Kunchandy
Development Manager: Janet Lanphier
Development Editor: Leslie Taggart
Senior Marketing Manager: Melanie Craig
Senior Supplements Editor: Donna Campion
Media Supplements Editor: Nancy Garcia
Production Manager: Joseph Vella
Project Coordination, Text Design, and Electronic Page Makeup:
      Thompson Steele, Inc.
Design Manager/Cover Designer: John Callahan
Cover Images: Courtesy of PhotoDisc
Photo Researcher: Photosearch, Inc.
Manufacturing Buyer: Dennis J. Para
Printer and Binder: R.R. Donnelley and Sons, Harrisonburg
Cover Printer: Coral Graphic Services

For permission to use copyrighted material, grateful acknowledgment is made to the
copyright holders on pp. 601–612, which are hereby made part of this copyright page.

Library of Congress Cataloging-in-Publication Data
McWhorter, Kathleen T.
    Efficient and flexible reading / Kathleen T. McWhorter. — 7th ed
      p.   cm.
    Includes bibliographical references and index.
    ISBN 0-321-14607-7—ISBN 0-321-14609-3 (AIE) .
    1. Developmental reading—Handbooks, manuals, etc.   2. Reading (Higher education)—
Handbooks, manuals, etc.   I. Title.
LB1050.53.M38   2005
428.4′071′1—dc22   2004001148

Please visit us at http://www.ablongman.com/mcwhorter

ISBN 0-321-14607-7   (Student Edition)
ISBN 0-321-14609-3   (Annotated Instructor's Edition)

1 2 3 4 5 6 7 8 9 10—DOH—07 06 05 04

In memory of Harry Thompson,
a gentle and loving father

Brief Contents

Detailed Contents

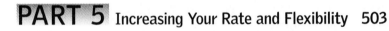

Disciplinary Readings*

Efficient and Flexible Reading, Seventh Edition, contains numerous and diverse academic readings, as well as 36 readings from popular press sources. The table below demonstrates this text's academic focus.

Academic Discipline	Number of Readings	Sample Topic	Page
Anatomy and Physiology	3	Head muscles	(Ch. 4. p. 271)
		Functions of the skin	(Ch. 4. p. 299)
		Principal parts of a hair root	(Ch. 9. p. 649)
Animal Science	1	The value of pet ownership	(Ch. 8. p. 623)
Anthropology	3	Study of fossils of prehistoric humans	(Ch. 4, p. 256)
		Urban population of developing countries	(Ch. 4, p. 284)
		Types of advisory groups	(Ch. 5, p. 364)
Archeology	2	Archaeological sites	(Ch. 3, p. 212)
		Evolution of Homo sapiens	(Ch. 7 p. 526)
Art	5	Texture through visual art	(Ch. 4, p. 250)
		Etching	(Ch. 5, p. 347)
		Printmaking	(Ch. 5, p. 389)
Astronomy	2	Constellations	(Ch. 5, p. 390)
		Bennet, et al. "Are We Alone in the Universe?"	(Ch. 7 p. 551)
Automotive Technology	1	Automotive technology	(Ch. 8, p. 594)
Biology	18	Molecule formation	(Ch. 4, p. 280)
		Alternative drug testing update	(Ch. 6, p. 487)
		Homeostasis	(Ch. 9. p. 667)
Business	4	Mortgages	(Ch. 4, p. 242)
		Work sharing	(Ch. 13, p. 259)
		Barriers to effective listening	(Ch. 4, p. 966)

*A complete list of readings organized by discipline appears in the Instructor's Manual.

Academic Discipline	Number of Readings	Sample Topic	Page
Health	3	Seasonal affective disorder	(Ch. 4, p. 244)
		Food irradiation	(Ch. 4, p. 244)
		External factors in obesity	(Ch. 5, p. 372)
History	3	African-American women as Writers	(Ch. 2, p. 86)
		Gerald Ford	(Ch. 14, p. 1012)
		Changes in the U.S. in the late '60s	(Ch. 14, p. 1015)
Literature	4	Stevens, "Anecdote of the Jar"	(Ch. 7 p. 514)
		Thurber, "A Dog's Eye View of Man"	(Ch. 7 p. 533)
		Terkel, "Working: People Talk About What They Do"	(Ch. 10, p. 741)
Marketing	7	Consumer "self-giving"	(Ch. 4, p. 261)
		People's evaluation of products	(Ch. 4, p. 270)
		Use of borrowed money	(Ch. 4, p. 298)
Nursing	1	Medical assisting	(Ch. 8. p. 594)
Philosophy	1	Existentialism	(Ch. 7 p. 517)
Physics	4	Why the sky is blue	(Ch. 3, p. 222)
		Radioactive dating	(Ch. 4, p. 254)
		Reflected light and color	(Ch. 8. p. 601)
Political Science	2	Profile of a terrorist	(Ch. 2, p. 123)
		Political background of segregation	(Ch. 5, p. 351)
Psychology	16	Effects of cultural nonverbal communication	(Ch. 4, p. 276)
		Forming self-concept	(Ch. 4, p. 278)
		Problem Solving	(Ch. 8. p. 610)
Sociology	29	Rules of etiquette for different societies	(Ch. 4, p. 257)
		Migration of people	(Ch. 4, p. 269)
		Television networks becoming more liberal	(Ch. 4, p. 276)
Zoology	1	Rods and cones of the eyes of mammals	(Ch. 7 p. 508)

Preface

To succeed in college, students must learn to understand a wide variety of reading material. Textbooks—the student's primary reading material—represent unique academic disciplines, each with it own style, content, and conceptual complexity. Many students are also required to read literature, supplementary assignments, reference materials, periodicals, manuals, handbooks, and study guides. Students also read online; the Internet is growing in importance, and many students regard it as a primary source of information and means of communication. Many instructors assign film, video, and computerized tutorials as well.

Each of these materials offers unique reading challenges, and even more important, the student's purpose for reading each is different. A student may read to prepare for a class lecture, make notes for a discussion, review for an exam, or locate information for a paper. To handle these diverse reading situations effectively, a student must develop reading flexibility, adjusting strategies and techniques to suit each reading situation.

College students face rigorous course requirements and must cope with time restraints created by jobs, family, and social activities. Reading and study must be accomplished within a realistic time frame and result in effective learning. Reading efficiency, then, is also vitally important. *Efficient and Flexible Reading* is designed to enable students to become efficient and flexible readers capable of meeting the challenging demands of college.

Goals and Themes

The primary goal of this text is to teach students how to accomplish reading tasks within an efficient and realistic framework. It guides students in developing reading flexibility—adjusting both comprehension and rate to suit the purpose, type and complexity of the material, as well as degree of familiarity. A second, more specific goal of the text is to encourage students to develop successful active academic reading strategies. To enable students to learn more efficiently from both print and electronic texts, this text focuses on the development of vocabulary, comprehension, study-reading, and critical analysis techniques. A third goal of the text is to encourage students to approach reading as a thinking process. Metacomprehension—the student's awareness of and control over the reading and learning process and its attendant thought processes—is a theme emphasized throughout.

Content Overview

Efficient and Flexible Reading, Seventh Edition, offers a blend of reading comprehension, retention, vocabulary development, critical reading, and rate building techniques that have proven essential for college students.

Reading Is for Everyone

This four-color feature emphasizes the importance and relevance of reading beyond the academic classroom. The feature highlights 14 popular press books that contain a wide range of useful and interesting information relevant to students' everyday lives. Each page of the feature highlights a specific book by providing a synopsis and quotations from readers. Topics include career planning and job hunting, credit card and debt management, health, and personal safety. The feature is intended to help students understand the value of reading in a visual and electronic age and to encourage students to become lifelong readers and learners.

Part 1 Developing a Basis for Reading and Learning

This part presents the organization and framework for the text, developing and explaining the concepts and principles of efficiency and flexibility and emphasizing reading as a thinking process. Strategies for active reading are presented, concentration and retention techniques are described, and basic vocabulary-building techniques are presented.

Part 2 Improving Your Comprehension

Methods for improving comprehension skills through knowledge and use of text structure is the focus of Part 2. The location of main ideas, the structure of paragraphs, the types of transitions, and the organization of ideas into thought patterns are described. Strategies for reading articles, essays, and scholarly journal articles are presented.

Part 3 Reading and Learning from College Texts

Part 3 is concerned with reading and learning from college textbooks. Graphic and visual literary skills are presented, and techniques for learning and retaining course material, including specialized and technical vocabulary, are emphasized. Other topics include SQ3R, highlighting, paraphrasing, outlining, mapping, and summarizing.

Part 4 Reading Critically

Critical reading skills are the focus of Part 4. Skills in making inferences, distinguishing fact and opinion, identifying the author's purpose, understanding tone, recognizing generalizations, and identifying bias are included. A separate chapter is devoted to reading and evaluating Internet sources. Students learn to locate reliable Web sites and to evaluate their purpose, content, accuracy, timeliness, and structure. Techniques for evaluating arguments and persuasive writing are emphasized, including recognizing types of evidence and identifying logical fallacies.

Part 5 Increasing Your Rate and Flexibility

Part 5 details specific techniques for improving reading rate and flexibility, including skimming, scanning, and techniques for reading faster. Some instructors may choose to teach this material earlier in the text.

Part 6 Multiple-Choice Questions for Even-Numbered Reading Selections

Even-numbered readings at the end of each chapter use open-ended vocabulary, comprehension, and critical-thinking questions to assess a student's mastery of the reading selection. Part 6 contains multiple-choice vocabulary, comprehension, and critical-thinking questions for those same readings. These may be used in lieu of the open-ended questions or as pretest or self-test before students complete the open-ended questions within the chapter.

Chapter Organization

The parts and chapters of *Efficient and Flexible Reading* are designed to be interchangeable, allowing the instructor to organize the course to suit his or her preferred skill sequence and to accommodate the particular needs of each class. Each chapter, however, follows a consistent pattern of organization:

- Chapter objectives
- Context and purpose for learning each skill
- Instruction and demonstration
- Guided practice using in-chapter exercises
- Critical thinking tip
- Interactive chapter summary
- Two longer reading selections with questions

Features

The following features enhance the text's effectiveness for both instructor and student:

Focus on Academic Reading Skills

The text provides the necessary instruction in literal and critical reading, vocabulary development, and study-reading skills to meet the demands of academic reading assignments.

Emphasis on Active Reading

The text encourages students to become active readers by enabling them to interact with the text by predicting, questioning, and evaluating ideas (Chapter 2).

Focus on Electronic Literacy

Because college students are increasingly required to use the Internet, reading electronic sources is a new emphasis in the text. Chapter 12 discusses how to locate and evaluate Internet sources and examines the new ways of reading and thinking required by electronic text.

Metacomprehension

Metacomprehension is the reader's awareness of his or her own comprehension processes. Mature and proficient readers exert a great deal of cognitive control over their reading; they analyze reading tasks, select appropriate reading strategies, and evaluate the effectiveness of those strategies. The text guides students in developing these metacognitive strategies and includes a Learning Style Questionnaire that enables students to assess how they learn and process information (Chapter 1).

Academic Thought Patterns

The text describes six primary thought patterns—chronological order/process, definition, classification, comparison-contrast, cause-effect, and enumeration—which are used in various academic disciplines to organize and structure ideas. Five additional patterns are also briefly discussed: statement and clarification, summary, generalization and example, addition, and spatial order/location. These patterns, presented as organizing schemata, are used to improve comprehension and recall of textbook material (Chapter 5).

Comprehensive Skill Coverage

The text addresses each of four major skill areas: vocabulary, literal and critical comprehension, study-reading, and rate and flexibility. Individual chapters offer instruction, demonstration, and guided practice. Reading selections provide skill interpretation and application.

High-Interest and Relevant Reading Selections

Each chapter concludes with two reading selections representative of the types of reading expected of college students. Included are numerous textbook excerpts, as well as articles and essays. These readings provide an opportunity for direct skill application as well as a means by which students can measure and evaluate their progress. The questions that follow each reading have been grouped into four categories: "**Checking Your Vocabulary,**" emphasizing context clues and word parts; "**Checking Your Comprehension,**" measuring literal and critical comprehension; "**Thinking Critically,**" requiring interpretive reading skills; and "**Questions for Discussion.**" Odd-numbered readings use a multiple-choice format; even-numbered readings feature open-ended questions for writing or group activities. Part 6 contains 14 sets of multiple-choice questions for the 14 even-numbered reading selections. These are provided for instructors who prefer objective evaluation or for students working independently.

New to the Seventh Edition

The primary thrust of this revision was to establish a focus on lifelong learning and reading, to update the text, and to provide additional exercises where students need more practice. Specific changes include the following:

Reading Is for Everyone

This four-color feature emphasizes the importance of literacy skills beyond the college classroom. By highlighting 14 popular press books, this section demonstrates that interesting, valuable, and useful information is available by reading. For each book, a synopsis is given as well as a photo of the book's cover. When available, quotations from other readers are included to affirm the books' utility and demonstrate that others do read and find it valuable. The feature begins *Efficient and Flexible Reading* with a positive, fun approach to reading as it promotes lifelong reading and learning.

Book titles include *What Color Is Your Parachute? 2004: A Practical Manual for Job Hunters & Career-Changers*, *What's So Great About America*, *The Hard Questions: 100 Essential Questions to Ask Before You Say "I Do,"* and *How to Talk So Kids Will Listen and Listen So Kids Will Talk*. Information on locating the books using the Internet, libraries, and bookstores appears on the inside of the back cover of the book.

Additional Coverage of Thought Patterns

Additional sample passages and new exercises have been added for each of the basic thought patterns covered in Chapter 5. For the five additional thought patterns presented (statement and clarification, summary, generalization and example, addition, and spatial order/location), paragraph examples of each have been added.

Expansion of Critical-Reading Chapters

Since students often have difficulty with critical-reading skills, additional practice exercises have been added on making inferences, distinguishing fact and opinion, and recognizing tone to Chapter 10.

Expanded Coverage of Paragraph Comprehension

Additional exercises have been added to Chapter 4, expanding coverage of topics, main ideas, details, implied main ideas, and transitions. The new exercises are intended to provide students will successful practice using approachable materials.

New Readings

New reading selections have been added on topics including workplace drug testing, volunteerism at a crisis hotline, and profiling a terrorist.

Reordering of Chapters in Part 3

Chapter 9, on graphic and visual literacy, (formerly Chapter 7) has been moved to follow Chapter 8, on techniques for learning textbook material, (formerly Chapter 9), providing a logical progression from reading textbooks to analyzing specific graphic and visual features within them.

The Teaching and Learning Package

Efficient and Flexible Reading comes with a full array of supplements designed to ensure that the course is rewarding for both students and instructors.

Book-Specific Supplements

The **Annotated Instructor's Edition (AIE)** is an exact replica of the student text, with the answers provided in the write-on lines in the text. (0-321-14609-3)

The **Instructor's Manual,** prepared by the author, offers teaching tips, sample syllabi, and other teaching resources. (0-321-14608-5)

The printed **Test Bank** for *Efficient and Flexible Reading* offers a series of skill and reading quizzes for each chapter, formatted for ease of copying and distribution (ISBN 0-321-14610-7). The **Longman Electronic Test Bank for Developmental Reading** is also available. The electronic test bank offers more than 3,000 questions in all areas of reading, including vocabulary, main idea, supporting details, patterns of organization, language, critical thinking, analytical reasoning, inference, point of view, visual aids, and textbook reading. With this easy-to-use CD-ROM, instructors simply choose questions from the electronic test bank, then print out the completed test for distribution. To order a copy of the electronic test bank, please contact your Longman sales consultant. A print version is also available.

For additional quizzes, readings, and Internet-based activities, be sure to visit *Efficient and Flexible Reading Online* at **http://www.ablongman .com/mcwhorter.** On this Web site you will find a series of PowerPoint Presentations for each chapter in the textbook, which can be downloaded and used for classroom presentations.

Instructors may choose to shrink-wrap *Efficient and Flexible Reading* with a free copy of **The Longman Reader's Journal.** This innovative journal provides students with a place to record their questions about, reactions to, and summaries of what they have read. Also included are a personal vocabulary log and additional pages for reflection. To preview the journal, please contact your Longman sales consultant.

The Longman Developmental Reading Package

In addition to the book-specific ancillaries discussed above, Longman offers many other supplements to instructors and students. All of these supplements are available either free or at greatly reduced prices.

For Additional Reading and Reference

The Dictionary Deal. Two dictionaries can be shrink-wrapped with any Longman Reading title at a nominal fee. *The New American Webster Handy College Dictionary* is a paperback reference text with more than 100,000 entries. *Merriam-Webster's Collegiate Dictionary,* Tenth Edition, is a hardback reference with a citation file of more than 14.5 million examples of English words drawn from actual use. For more details on ordering a dictionary with this text, please contact your Longman sales consultant.

Penguin Quality Paperback Titles. A series of Penguin paperbacks is available at a significant discount when shrink-wrapped with any Longman title. Some titles available are Toni Morrison's *Beloved,* Julia Alvarez's *How the Garcia Girls Lost Their Accents,* Mark Twain's *Huckleberry Finn,* Frederick Douglass's *Narrative of the Life of Frederick Douglass,* Harriet Beecher Stowe's *Uncle Tom's Cabin,* Dr. Martin Luther King Jr.'s *Why We Can't Wait,* and plays by Shakespeare, Miller, and Albee. For a complete list of titles or more information, please contact your Longman sales consultant, or log on to **http://www.ablongman.com/penguin**.

The Longman Textbook Reader. This supplement, for use in developmental reading courses, offers five complete chapters from Addison-Wesley and Longman textbooks: computer science, biology, psychology, communications, and business. Each chapter includes additional comprehension quizzes, critical-thinking questions, and group activities. For information on how to bundle the free *Longman Textbook Reader* with *Efficient and Flexible Reading,* please contact your Longman sales consultant.

Vocabulary Simplified. Instructors may choose to shrink-wrap *Efficient and Flexible Reading* with a copy of Vocabulary Simplified. This book, written by Kathleen McWhorter, works well as a supplemental text providing additional instruction and practice in vocabulary. Students can work through the book independently or units may be incorporated into weekly lesson plans. Topics covered include methods of vocabulary learning, contextual aids, word parts, connotative meanings, idioms, euphemisms, and many more interesting and fun topics. The book concludes with vocabulary lists and exercises representative of eleven academic disciplines. To preview this book, contact your Longman sales consultant for an examination copy.

Newsweek **Alliance.** Instructors may choose to shrink-wrap a 12-week subscription to *Newsweek* with any Longman text. The price of the subscription is 59 cents per issue (a total of $7.08 for the subscription). Available with the subscription is a free "Interactive Guide to *Newsweek*"— a workbook for students who are using the text. In addition, *Newsweek* provides a wide variety of instructor supplements free to teachers, including maps, Skill Builders, and weekly quizzes. For further information on the *Newsweek* Alliance, please contact your Longman sales consultant.

Florida Adopters: *Thinking Through the Test,* **by D. J. Henry.** This special workbook, prepared specially for students in Florida, has been updated to offer all new readings and practice exercises to help students prepare for the Florida State Exit Exam. To shrink-wrap this workbook free with your textbook, please contact your Longman sales consultant. Also available: two laminated grids (one for reading, one for writing) that can serve as handy references for students preparing for the Florida State Exit Exam.

Texas Adopters: *Texas Higher Education Assessment (THEA) Study Guide,* by Jeanette Harris (ISBN 0-321-27240-4). This study guide offers many features to help students prepare for and take the reading and writing sections of the THEA test.

New York Adopters: *Preparing for the CUNY-ACT Reading and Writing Test* edited by Patricia Licklider (0-321-19608-2). This booklet offers a variety of strategies and features to help lessen students' test-taking anxieties and to provide them with the information and practice needed to successfully complete the CUNY-ACT exams.

Electronic and Online Offerings

Reading Roadtrip. This innovative and exciting tool takes students on a tour of 15 cities and landmarks throughout the United States. Each of the 15 modules corresponds to a reading or a study skill (for example, finding the main idea, understanding patterns of organization, and thinking critically). All modules contain a tour of the location, instruction and tutorial, exercises, interactive feedback and mastery tests.

Vocabulary Site. Practice with hundreds of exercises in ten topics to strengthen and increase your vocabulary knowledge.

StudySkills Site. Review strategies for college success, learn time management and stress management skills, learn study strategies, and more.

Longman Writer's Warehouse. Get guided assistance for each stage of the writing process; create your own web-based writing portfolios; take diagnostic tests, exercises, and more.

Exercise Zone. Practice with over 2,500 exercises in ten topics of grammar, style, and punctuation.

Avoiding Plagiarism. Explore issues of plagiarism, take self-scoring tests, and view sample papers to learn ways of avoiding plagiarism.

Research Navigator. Access the *New York Times* archives as well as online research tools and thousands of print journals.

Online Solutions Student Access code for Longman Skills Solutions (0-321-26323-5). Online Solutions Instructor Access code for Longman Skills Solutions (0-321-26322-7).

Teaching Online: Internet Research, Conversation, and Composition, **Second Edition.** Ideal for instructors who have never surfed the Net, this easy-to-follow guide offers basic definitions, numerous examples, and step-by-step information about finding and using Internet sources. Free to adopters. (ISBN 0-321-01957-1)

New! *Research Navigator Guide for English,* by H. Eric Branscomb and Linda R. Barr (Student 0-321-20277-5). Designed to teach students how to conduct high-quality online research and to document it properly.

Research Navigator guides provide discipline-specific academic resources; in addition to helpful tips on the writing process, online research, and finding and citing valid sources. Free when packaged with any Longman text. Research Navigator guides include an access code to Research Navigator™, providing access to thousands of academic journals and periodicals, the *New York Times* Search by Subject Archive, Link Library, Library Guides, and more. FREE when packaged with a Longman textbook/ VALUEPACK ONLY.

For Instructors

CLAST Test Package, Fourth Edition. These two 40-item objective tests evaluate students' readiness for the CLAST exams. Strategies for teaching CLAST preparedness are included. Free with any Longman English title. (Reproducible sheets: ISBN 0-321-01950-4; Computerized IBM version: ISBN 0-321-01982-2; Computerized Mac version: ISBN 0-321-01983-0)

TASP Test Package, Third Edition. These 12 practice pre-tests and post-tests assess the same reading and writing skills covered in the TASP examination. Free with any Longman English title. (Reproducible sheets: ISBN 0-321-01959-8; Computerized IBM version: ISBN 0-321-01985-7; Computerized Mac version: ISBN 0-321-01984-9)

Acknowledgments

I wish to acknowledge the contributions of my colleagues and reviewers who provided valuable advice and suggestions, both for this edition and for previous editions:

Robyn Browder, Tidewater Community College; Jessica Stephens Bryant, Eastern Kentucky University; Denise G. Chambers, Normandale Community College; Carol Chesler, Kishwaukee Community College; Pat Cookis, College of DuPage; Marva Cooper-Cromer, Georgia Perimeter College; Linda S. Edwards, Chattanooga State College; Bertilda Garnica Henderson, Broward Community College; Paula Gibson, Cardinal Stritch College; Linda Gilmore, Carroll Community College; Simon Grist, Atlanta Metro College; Catherine Harvey, Grossmont College; Janice Hill-Matula, Moraine Valley Community College; Deborah Hunt, State Technical Institute at Memphis; Elizabeth Ince, U.S. Military Academy; Almarie Jones,

Gloucester County College; Maxine Keats, Framingham State College; Evelyn Koperwas, Broward Community College; Thomas W. Lackman, Temple University; Gary Laird, Lamar University; Pamela C. Leggat, NVCC; Barbara Levy, Nassau Community College; Caroline Lewis, West Valley College; Patricia Malinowski, Finger Lakes Community College; Steve Matthews, Wayne State University; Helen Muller, Essex County College; Susan Nnaji, Prarie View A & M University; Beth Parks, Kishwaukee Community College; Ann Perez, Miami-Dade Community College; Loraine Phillips, Blinn College; Jamses A. Rogge, Broward Community College; Jeanne Shay Schumm, University of Miami, Coral Gables; Mary D. Shelor, Pima Community College; Barbara Sherman, Liberty University; Jeanne C. Silliman, Ivy Tech State College; Pam Smith, Pellissippi State Technical College; Diane Starke, El Paso Community College; Margaret Triplett, Central Oregon Community College

The editorial staff of Longman Publishers deserves special recognition and thanks for the guidance, support, and direction they have provided. In particular I wish to thank Leslie Taggart, my development editor, for her valuable advice and assistance and Susan Kunchandy, Acquisitions Editor, for her enthusiastic support of the revision.

KATHLEEN T. MCWHORTER

Reading Is for Everyone

Reading IS NECESSARY ...

Reading is a necessary SURVIVAL SKILL in a variety of everyday living situations. You need to read maps and road signs if you are travelling by car. You need to read store advertisements and nutritional labels if you are grocery shopping. You need to read movie listings and TV schedules to choose an evening of entertainment. Reading is also a vital ACADEMIC SKILL—you need to read textbooks, read questions on exams, read sources to write research papers. The remainder of the book will focus on reading as an essential academic skill.

AND Reading IS FUN!

However, before we get started, let's consider reading as not only necessary, but FUN! Read through the following pages. I'll bet you will find books that spark your interest and that you'll want to read them. To locate any of these books, see the inside of the back cover.

Read ABOUT THE LATEST TECHNOLOGY . . .

The Cell Phone Buyer's Guide: Choosing Your Wireless Phone with Confidence! *by Penelope Stetz*

This easy-to-read book will help you choose a cell phone. It includes the three basic elements to consider when shopping for a phone, the top ten questions to ask, the jargon to master so you can talk the same language as the cell phone rep, and all the different features to think about before you get to the cell phone store.

Read ABOUT YOUR OWN PHYSIOLOGY . . .

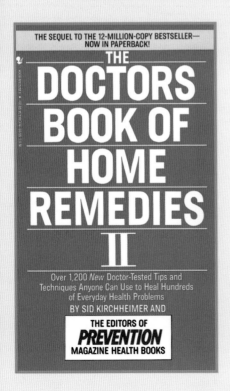

Doctor's Book of Home Remedies: Thousands of Tips and Techniques Anyone Can Use to Heal Everyday Health Problems *by the Editors of Prevention Health Magazine.*

"What do doctors do when they get sick? The editors of Prevention Magazine Health Books asked more than 500 of the nation's top specialists to recommend their best doctor-tested and easy-to-follow remedies for 138 illnesses and maladies. This complete, practical guide contains the distilled experience of health professionals who offer more than 2300 accessible healing tips for the most common medical complaints." (Rodale Press)

Read IF YOU'RE A VICTIM OF FASHION . . .

Fashion Victim: Our Love-Hate Relationship with Dressing, Shopping, and the Cost of Style *by Michelle Lee (former editor of fashion magazines Glamour and Mademoiselle)*

This book looks inside the fashion world and exposes the truth about shopaholics, sweatshops, and celebrity closets. Lee examines how our society is obsessed with fashion and style and how we rack up credit card debt to support our compulsive shopping habits.

Read IF BASS FISHING IS YOUR PASSION . . .

Knowing Bass: The Scientific Approach to Catching More Fish *by Dr. Keith A. Jones (a biologist and expert on fish research) and Paul C. Johnson.*

This book is about the science of bass fishing; it explains why bass behave as they do, what they can sense, how they respond to lures, and how they interact with anglers. It is intended to help you improve your chances of catching bass, no matter where or how you fish.

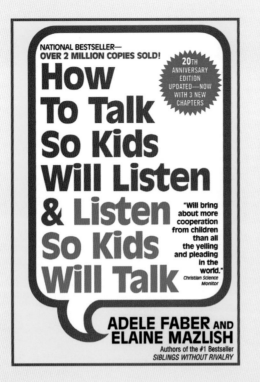

Read SO YOU'LL KNOW WHAT TO SAY . . .

How to Talk So Kids Will Listen & Listen So Kids Will Talk *by Adele Faber, Elaine Mazlish, and Kimberly Coe*

This book offers a step by step approach to improving family communication. It helps parents talk and problem-solve with their children The Los Angeles Times says the book is "designed to bring adults to the level of children, and children to the level of adults, so that this happy meeting ground can truly make for harmony in the home."

Read IF ROCK CLIMBING SEEMS LIKE PLAY . . .

How to Rock Climb! *by John Long*

This book is a "how-to" manual for beginning and intermediate rock climbers. It discusses equipment, technique, and training methods and includes sections on face climbing; crack climbing; ropes, anchors, and belays; getting off the rock; and sport climbing. The author is an experienced rock climber; his accomplishments include a one-day descent of El Capitan.

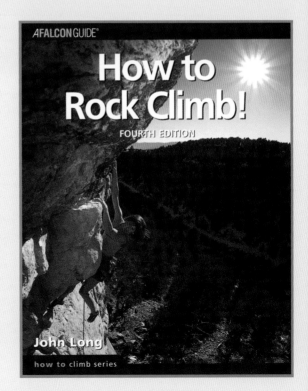

Read JUST FOR THE JOY OF BEING ALIVE...

Friendship: Celebration of Humanity (M.I.L.K.—<u>M</u>oments of <u>I</u>ntimacy, <u>L</u>aughter and <u>K</u>inship.)

In this book of photographs, photographers from around the world "depict the powerful connection of friendship that lights up life in both good times and bad." Photos include "tiny children going to school in Bali, picking huge banana leaves to shelter each other when tropical rain storms threaten their immaculate white shirts... . Two old men in Athens, so lost in their daily chess game that they were unaware of the traffic swirling around and tourists pushing past them... . Shoppers in New York clutching each other with excitement at the thought of the next bargain possibly around the next corner." (William Morrow)

Read PRACTICAL ADVICE ON HOW TO SURVIVE...

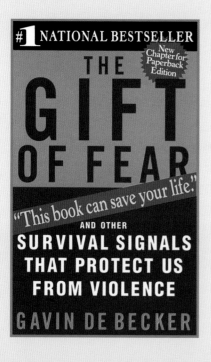

The Gift of Fear: Survival Signals that Protect Us from Violence *by Gavin de Becker*

Becker, a national expert on crime and violence, offers practical advice on how to stay safe and not become a victim of crime or violence. "De Becker...thinks most people are great victims because they ignore their fears and survival signals. ...De Becker believes every crime has a warning and a motive and that the code of predictable violence can be broken by trusting the phenomenon that he defines as 'knowing without knowing why.' If people believe in and are alert to the possibility of danger, they can reduce their risks and save themselves." —by Partricia Hassler, from Booklist, June 1 & 5, 1997, Copyright American Library Association. used with permission.

Read TO DECIDE WHAT YOU WANT TO ACHIEVE . . .

"What Color is Your Parachute? 2004: A Practical Manual for Job-Hunters and Career *by* Richard Nelson Bolles.*

This books walks you through the process of finding a job, considering both what you want to do and where you want to do it. This book has been in print for nearly 30 years and has been used by hundreds of thousands of people to find a job or make a career change.

Reprinted with permission from *What Color Is Your Parachute?* by Richard Bolles. Copyright 2003 Richard Bolles, Ten Speed Press, Berkely, CA.
Available from your local bookseller, by calling Ten Speed Press at 800-841-2665, or by visiting us online at www.tenspeed.com

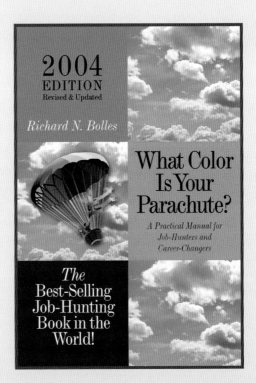

Read TO DISCOVER WHAT SOMEONE ELSE BELIEVES . . .

What's So Great About America by Dinesh D'Souza.

Written in the months following the September 11 terrorist attacks, D'Souza takes the position that America has "the best life the world has to offer." D'Souza, an immigrant from India, describes his first experiences in the United States. He also confronts important issues such as slavery, racism, and cultural permissiveness.

Read HOW YOU CAN HAVE MORE FOR LESS . . .

The Complete Tightwad Gazette: Promoting Thrift as a Viable Alternative Lifestyle *by Amy Dacyczyn.*

This book presents thousands of ideas for saving money, whether it's how much you spend on your electric bill, how much it costs you to move, or how many Christmas gifts you buy or make. Included along with the how-to tips are essays describing the philosophy behind being a tightwad. What do you value? How can you use your resources to meet your personal goals?

Read HOW TO GET YOURSELF OUT OF A MESS . . .

Credit Card & Debt Management: A Step-by Step How-To Guide for Organizing Debt & Saving Money on Interest Payments *by Scott Bilker*

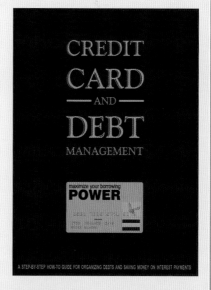

"If you ask single Americans in their 20s or early 30s what their biggest financial worry is, most will probably answer credit card debt. Bilker shows them the formulas for digging out of the credit-card hole—methodically, systematically, and with a minimum of confusion. Surprises abound, including Bilker's advice against cutting up one's credit cards—after all, one may need that credit line in case of emergency. He also advises against paying off one's credit card debt with savings, opting instead to use budgeting from salary and letting that savings grow untouched. If used correctly, this book could be a big help to those experiencing a rather common burden." —by Joe Collins, from *Booklist*, February 15, 1996. Copyright American Library Association. Used with permission.

Read TO FIND OUT WHAT QUESTIONS TO ASK . . .

The Hard Questions: 100 Essential Questions to Ask Before You Say "I Do"
Susan Piver

This book, intended for readers who are planr
to marry, raises important questions that enga
couples need to consider in order to avoid cor
or disappointment later in their relationship.
intended to help couples gain a deeper understanding of each other and build a lasting rela
ship. It focuses on issues such as money, work
sex, friends, spirituality, and family.

Read HOW TO GET OUT OF A DISASTER FAST . . .

The Worst –Case Survival Handbook *by
Joshua Piven and David Borgenicht*

Learn how to escape an avalanche, how to bu
fire without matches, what to do if your car i
sinking in water, how to wrestle an alligator,
how to deal with a carjacking, among other c
ters, in this illustrated how-to guide.

**To find out how to locate these and ot
books, see the inside of the back cover.**

Developing Your Efficiency and Flexibility

IN THIS CHAPTER YOU WILL LEARN:

1. To analyze your reading efficiency and flexibility.
2. To assess your learning style.
3. To understand factors that affect rate and comprehension.
4. The basic principles that govern efficiency and flexibility.

Y ou have heard about "fuel-efficient" cars. They use fuel "efficiently" and conserve energy. An "efficient" worker is one who does his or her job well and on time. Efficiency, then, is the ability to perform with the minimum amount of effort, expense, or waste.

Efficiency involves the effective use of time or resources to accomplish a specific task. As you think more about the concept of efficiency, you may begin to realize that it is a major objective in our work- and time-oriented society. For example, a mechanic who takes an hour to change a tire, a short-order cook who takes 25 minutes to prepare a cheeseburger, or a sales clerk who takes five minutes to package a purchase is not efficient.

Analyzing Your Reading Efficiency

As a college student, many heavy demands are placed on your time. Your course work, which includes reading textbook chapters, completing assignments, studying for exams, and writing papers, competes with part-time jobs and social, recreational, and housekeeping tasks. Each demands your valuable time. At times, college may seem like a balancing act in which

1

you are trying to do many things at once and trying to do all of them well. You are probably wondering if you will be able to keep up and how to get everything done. One of the best ways to handle the demands and pressures of college life is to become more efficient—to get more done in less time.

Many students think that the only way to become more efficient is to read faster. They believe that slow reading is poor reading. This is not true. *How* you read is more important than *how fast* you read. If you read a 12-page assignment in one hour but remember only 60 percent of what you read, you are not reading efficiently. Efficient reading involves adequate comprehension and recall within a reasonable time frame. Reading efficiency increases as you develop techniques that improve your comprehension and retention, which will enable you to use your time most economically.

The Efficiency Questionnaire below will help you assess whether you are an efficient reader. Answer *yes* or *no* to each question in the spaces provided. Be honest with yourself!

Efficiency Questionnaire

	Yes	No
1. Do you set goals and time limits for yourself at the beginning of each reading study session?	❏	❏
2. Do you have particular questions in mind as you begin to read an assignment?	❏	❏
3. Do you spend a few minutes looking over an assignment before you begin reading it?	❏	❏
4. When reading, do you try to predict or anticipate what the writer will say next?	❏	❏
5. When you finish reading an assignment, do you take a few minutes to review what you have read?	❏	❏
6. Are you on the alert for words and phrases that signal change or continuation in thought?	❏	❏
7. Do you sort out more and less important details as you read?	❏	❏
8. When you read a word you do not know, do you try to determine its meaning from the way it is used in the sentence?	❏	❏
9. Do you regularly use underlining, summary notes, and marginal notations to identify important information?	❏	❏
10. When reading nontextbook material, do you try to determine the author's purpose for writing?	❏	❏

If you answered *yes* to all or most of these questions, you are well on your way to becoming an efficient reader. If you answered *no* to some or many of the questions, you need to improve your efficiency.

In this chapter we discuss how you can become a more efficient and flexible reader by varying your reading techniques to suit the material and your purpose for reading it. You will learn more specific approaches as you proceed through the rest of the text.

Analyzing Your Learning Style

In college it is important that you take in information efficiently through reading, but it is equally important that you study and learn that information efficiently. You want to choose the learning strategies that will help you learn the largest amount of material in the least amount of time.

Not everyone learns in the same way, and not all reading and learning strategies are equally effective for everyone. Each person has his or her own unique way of learning, which is called *learning style*. Some students, for example, tend to be applied learners who prefer learning tasks that reflect practical, real-life situations. Other students may be conceptual learners who enjoy working with concepts and ideas; practical applications are unnecessary for understanding. Some students tend to be spatial learners who work well with visual material—charts, diagrams, maps, and so forth. Others tend to be verbal learners who work well with language. The following brief Learning Style Questionnaire will help you discover the features of your learning style.

Learning Style Questionnaire

Directions: Each item presents two choices. Select the alternative that best describes you. In cases in which neither choice suits you, select the one that is closest to your preference. Write the letter of your choice in the blank to the left of each item.

PART ONE

_____ 1. I would prefer to follow a set of
    a. oral directions.
    b. written directions.

_____ 2. I would prefer to
    a. attend a lecture given by a famous psychologist.
    b. read an article written by the psychologist.

_____ 3. When I am introduced to someone, it is easier for me to
remember the person's
a. name.
b. face.

_____ 4. I find it easier to learn new information by using
a. language (words).
b. images (pictures).

_____ 5. I prefer classes in which the instructor
a. lectures and answers questions.
b. uses films and videos.

_____ 6. To follow current events, I prefer to
a. listen to the news on the radio.
b. read the newspaper.

_____ 7. To learn how to operate a fax machine, I would prefer to
a. listen to a friend's explanation.
b. watch a demonstration.

Part Two

_____ 8. I prefer to
a. work with facts and details.
b. construct theories and ideas.

_____ 9. I would prefer a job involving
a. following specific instructions.
b. reading, writing, and analyzing.

_____ 10. I prefer to
a. solve math problems using a formula.
b. discover why the formula works.

_____ 11. I would prefer to write a term paper explaining
a. how a process works.
b. a theory.

_____ 12. I prefer tasks that require me to
a. follow careful, detailed instructions.
b. use reasoning and critical analysis.

_____ 13. For a criminal justice course, I would prefer to
a. discover how and when a law can be used.
b. learn how and why it became law.

_____ 14. To learn more about the operation of a high-speed computer printer, I would prefer to
   a. work with several types of printers.
   b. understand the principles on which they operate.

PART THREE

_____ 15. To solve a math problem, I would prefer to
   a. draw or visualize the problem.
   b. study a sample problem and use it as a model.

_____ 16. To best remember something, I
   a. create a mental picture.
   b. write it down.

_____ 17. Assembling a bicycle from a diagram would be
   a. easy.
   b. challenging.

_____ 18. I prefer classes in which I
   a. handle equipment or work with models.
   b. participate in a class discussion.

_____ 19. To understand and remember how a machine works, I would
   a. draw a diagram.
   b. write notes.

_____ 20. I enjoy
   a. drawing or working with my hands.
   b. speaking, writing, and listening.

_____ 21. If I were trying to locate an office on an unfamiliar campus, I would prefer
   a. a map.
   b. written directions.

PART FOUR

_____ 22. For a grade in biology lab, I would prefer to
   a. work with a lab partner.
   b. work alone.

_____ 23. When faced with a difficult personal problem I prefer to
   a. discuss it with others.
   b. resolve it myself.

_____ 24. Many instructors could improve their classes by
   a. including more discussion and group activities.
   b. allowing students to work on their own more frequently.

_____ 25. When listening to a lecture by a speaker, I respond more to the
   a. person presenting the ideas.
   b. ideas themselves.

_____ 26. When on a team project, I prefer to
   a. work with several team members.
   b. divide the tasks and complete those assigned to me.

_____ 27. I prefer to shop and do errands
   a. with friends.
   b. by myself.

_____ 28. A job in a busy office is
   a. more appealing than working alone.
   b. less appealing than working alone.

PART FIVE

_____ 29. To make decisions, I rely on
   a. my experiences and gut feelings.
   b. facts and objective data.

_____ 30. To complete a task, I
   a. can use whatever is available to get the job done.
   b. must have everything I need at hand.

_____ 31. I prefer to express my ideas and feelings through
   a. music, song, or poetry.
   b. direct, concise language.

_____ 32. I prefer instructors who
   a. allow students to be guided by their own interests.
   b. make their own expectations clear and explicit.

_____ 33. I tend to
   a. challenge and question what I hear and read.
   b. accept what I hear and read.

_____ 34. I prefer
   a. essay exams.
   b. objective exams.

_____   35. In completing an assignment, I prefer to
            a. figure out my own approach.
            b. be told exactly what to do.

To score your questionnaire, record the total number of *a*'s you selected and the total number of *b*'s for each part of the questionnaire. Record your totals in the scoring grid provided.

Scoring Grid

PARTS	TOTAL # OF CHOICE **a**	TOTAL # OF CHOICE **b**
Part One	_____ Auditory	_____ Visual
Part Two	_____ Applied	_____ Conceptual
Part Three	_____ Spatial	_____ Verbal
Part Four	_____ Social	_____ Independent
Part Five	_____ Creative	_____ Pragmatic

Now, circle your higher score for each part of the questionnaire. The word below the score you circled indicates a strength of your learning style. The next section explains how to interpret your scores.

Interpreting Your Scores

Each of the five parts of the questionnaire identifies one aspect of your learning style. These five aspects are explained here.

Part One: Auditory or Visual Learners

This score indicates whether you learn more effectively by listening (auditory) or by seeing (visual). If you have a higher score on auditory than visual, you tend to be an auditory learner. That is, you tend to learn more easily by hearing than by reading. A higher score on visual suggests strengths with visual modes of learning—reading, studying pictures, reading diagrams, and so forth.

Part Two: Applied or Conceptual Learners

This score describes the types of learning tasks and learning situations you prefer and find easiest to handle. If you are an applied learner, you prefer tasks that involve real objects and situations. Practical, real-life examples are ideal for you. If you are a conceptual learner, you prefer to work with language and ideas; you do not need practical applications for understanding.

Part Three: Spatial or Verbal Learners

This score reveals your ability to work with spatial relationships. Spatial learners are able to visualize or mentally see how things work or how they are positioned in space. Their strengths may include drawing, assembling, or repairing things. Verbal learners lack skills in positioning things in space. Instead they rely on verbal or language skills.

Part Four: Social or Independent Learners

This score reveals whether you like to work alone or with others. If you are a social learner, you prefer to work with others—both classmates and instructors—closely and directly. You tend to be people-oriented and enjoy personal interaction. If you are an independent learner, you prefer to work alone and study alone. You tend to be self-directed or self-motivated and often goal oriented.

Part Five: Creative or Pragmatic Learners

This score describes the approach you prefer to take toward learning tasks. Creative learners are imaginative and innovative. They prefer to learn through discovery or experimentation. They are comfortable taking risks and following hunches. Pragmatic learners are practical, logical, and systematic. They seek order and are comfortable following rules.

If you disagree with any part of the Learning Style Questionnaire, go with your own instincts rather than the questionnaire results. The questionnaire is just a quick assessment; trust your knowledge of yourself in areas of dispute.

Developing a Learning Action Plan

Now that you know how *you* learn, you are ready to develop an action plan for learning what you read. Suppose you discovered that you are an auditory learner. You still have to read your assignments, which is a visual task. However, to learn the assignment you should translate the material into an auditory form. For example, you could repeat aloud, using your own words, information that you want to remember, or you could tape

Table 1.1　Learning Styles and Reading/Learning Strategies

If Your Learning Style Is . . .	*Then the Reading/Learning Strategies to Use Are . . .*
Auditory	Discuss/study with friends. Talk aloud when studying. Tape record self-testing questions and answers.
Visual	Draw diagrams, charts, and/or tables. Try to visualize events. Use films and videos when available. Use CD-ROMs or software when available.
Applied	Think of practical situations to which learning applies. Associate ideas with their application. Use case studies, examples, and applications to cue your learning.
Conceptual	Organize materials that lack order. Use outlining. Focus on organizational patterns.
Spatial	Use mapping. Use outlining. Draw diagrams; make charts and sketches. Use visualization.
Verbal	Translate diagrams and drawings into language. Record steps, processes, and procedures in words. Write summaries. Write your interpretation next to textbook drawings, maps, and graphics.
Social	Form study groups. Find a study partner. Interact with the instructor. Work with a tutor.
Independent	Use computer-assisted instruction when available. Purchase review workbooks or study guides when available.
Creative	Ask and answer questions. Record your own ideas in the margins of textbooks.
Pragmatic	Study in an organized environment. Write lists of steps, procedures, and processes. Paraphrase difficult materials.

record key information and play it back. If you are also a social learner, you could work with a classmate, testing each other out loud.

　　Table 1.1 lists each aspect of learning style and offers suggestions for how to learn from a reading assignment. To use the table:

1. **Circle the five aspects of your learning style in which you received higher scores.** Disregard the others.

2. **Read through the suggestions that apply to you.**

3. **Place a check mark in front of suggestions that you think will work for you.** Choose at least one from each category.

4. **List the suggestions that you chose in the "Action Plan for Learning" box.**

5. **Experiment with these techniques, one at a time.** Continue using the techniques that you find work. Revise or modify those that do not. Do not hesitate to experiment with other techniques listed in the table as well.

Action Plan for Learning

Learning Strategy 1:_____

Learning Strategy 2:_____

Learning Strategy 3:_____

Learning Strategy 4:_____

Learning Strategy 5:_____

Learning Strategy 6:_____

EXERCISE 1-1

DIRECTIONS: The class should form two groups: concrete learners and abstract learners. Each group should discuss effective learning strategies that take into account this type of learning style.

EXERCISE 1-2

DIRECTIONS: Write a brief description of yourself as a learner based on the results of the Learning Style Questionnaire. Describe your strengths and weaknesses. Include examples from your own experience as a student.

Developing Reading Flexibility

Do you read the newspaper in the same way and at the same speed that you read a chemistry textbook? Do you read poetry in the same way and at the same speed that you read an article in *Time* magazine? Surprisingly, for many adults the answer to these questions is *yes*. Many adults, including college graduates, read everything in nearly the same way at the same rate.

Efficient and flexible readers, however, read the newspaper both *faster* and *differently* than the way they read a chemistry book because the newspaper is usually easier to read and because they have a different purpose for reading each. Flexible readers read poetry more slowly and in a different way than they read magazine articles. Your ability to adjust your reading rate and methods to suit the type of material you are reading and your purpose for reading is called *reading flexibility*.

To become a flexible reader, you make decisions about how you will read a given piece of material. *How* you read depends on *why* you are reading and *how much* you intend to remember. Rate and comprehension are the two most important factors. Think of them as weights on a balancing scale: as one increases, the other decreases. Your goal is to achieve a balance that suits the nature of the material and your purpose for reading. This chapter discusses how to achieve this balance.

Assessing Difficulty

The first step in determining how to read a given piece of writing is to assess its difficulty. Many features of the reading material itself influence how easily and how quickly you can read it. Here are a few important characteristics to consider:

1. **The format.** The physical arrangement of a page can influence how easily material can be read. For example, it is more difficult to read a page that is a solid block of print than it is to read a page on which the ideas are broken up by headings, spacing, and listing.

2. **Graphic and visual material.** The inclusion of maps, pictures, graphs, and charts also may influence your reading. Graphic elements present detailed information and require close, careful study.

3. **Typographical aids.** Features of print such as boldface, italics, colored type, and headings often make a page easier to read and understand. Headings announce the topic about to be discussed and together form an outline of ideas covered in the material. Words in italics, boldface, or colored type emphasize certain words and phrases.

4. **Language features.** Factors such as sentence length, paragraph length, and vocabulary level determine how difficult a piece of material is to read. Generally, the longer the sentences and paragraphs in a selection, the more difficult they are to read.

5. **Subject matter.** The type and number of ideas and concepts that an author presents influence difficulty. For instance, a passage that explains a complicated scientific theory or procedure requires close reading. Material that discusses everyday, newsworthy topics normally requires less careful attention. Also, a passage that explains one new idea is easier to read than a passage that presents three or four separate new ideas in the same amount of space.

6. **Length.** Long chapters, articles, and essays are often more difficult to read than shorter ones. Lengthy materials demand sustained concentration and require you to relate larger numbers of ideas and to maintain a broader focus and perspective.

7. **Organization.** Some materials progress in an orderly, logical fashion from point to point. Others are more loosely organized, and the writer's pattern of thought is more difficult to identify. As a general rule, the less clearly organized written material is, the more difficult it is to read.

The easiest way to assess the difficulty of a selection is to preread it. Prereading (see Chapter 2) reveals how well organized the material is and gives you a feeling for the difficulty of the language and content. Once you have made a quick estimate of the material's difficulty, you can adjust your reading rate accordingly.

No rule tells you how much to slow down or speed up. You must use your judgment and adjust your reading to the conditions at hand. For example, you can slow down if you encounter a passage with long, complicated sentences or an article that presents complex ideas or uses technical vocabulary. You can speed up if you come across simple, straightforward ideas and everyday vocabulary. In addition to adjusting your rate, you should alter the manner in which you read the material, using different techniques to suit different types of material. A major portion of this book discusses techniques designed to increase your efficiency and flexibility.

EXERCISE
1-3

DIRECTIONS: Use the seven characteristics described earlier to assess the difficulty of each reading selection that appears at the end of this chapter (pages 55–62). Then answer the following questions.

1. Which selection appears to be more difficult? List the features that make it appear difficult.

   _____

   _____

   _____

2. What features make the other selection seem easier to read?

   _____

   _____

   _____

EXERCISE 1-4

DIRECTIONS: Use the seven characteristics listed earlier to assess the difficulty of each textbook you have been assigned this semester. Also consider your interest, skills, and background knowledge for each discipline. Rank your texts from most to least difficult:

1. _____

2. _____

3. _____

4. _____

Defining Your Purpose

Your purpose for reading a particular piece should influence *how* you read it. Different situations require different levels of comprehension and recall. For example, you may not need to recall every fact when leisurely reading an article in the newspaper, but you *do* need a high level of comprehension when reading a contract that you plan to sign. When reading course assignments, your purpose may also vary. You might read a psychology assignment very closely in preparation for an objective exam. You might read or reread a portion of a chemistry text only to learn how to solve a particular problem. Your reading can range from paying careful, close attention to a very brief, quick reading for only main ideas. Then, as your comprehension varies, so does your reading rate. If close, careful comprehension is not required, you can read faster. You will generally find that as your comprehension decreases, your reading rate increases. Table 1.2 illustrates this relationship.

Table 1.2 The Relationship among Purpose, Rate, and Comprehension

Type of Material	Purpose in Reading	Desired Level of Comprehension	Approximate Range of Reading Rate
Poetry, legal documents, argumentative writing	Analyze, criticize, evaluate	Complete (100%)	Under 200 wpm
Textbooks, manuals, research documents	High comprehension recall for exams, writing research reports, following directions	High (90–100%)	200–300 wpm
Novels, paperbacks, newspapers, magazines	Entertainment, enjoyment, general information	Moderate (60–90%)	300–500 wpm
Reference materials, catalogs, magazines, nonfiction	Overview of material, locating specific facts, review of previously read material	Low (60% or below)	600–800 wpm or above

DIRECTIONS: Each day you read a wide variety of materials, and your purpose is slightly different for each. Make a list of materials you have read this week, and describe your purpose for reading each. (Don't forget such everyday items as labels, instructions, menus, etc.)

_____

_____

_____

_____

DIRECTIONS: For each of the following situations, define your purpose for reading and indicate the level of comprehension that seems appropriate. Refer to Table 1.2 if necessary.

1. You are reading a case study at the end of a chapter in your criminology textbook in preparation for an essay exam.

   Purpose: _____

   Level of Comprehension: _____

2. You are reading sample problems in a chapter in your mathematics text that you feel confident you know how to solve.

Purpose: _____

Level of Comprehension: _____

3. You are reading the end-of-chapter review questions in your economics text in preparation for an exam that is likely to contain similar questions.

Purpose: _____

Level of Comprehension: _____

4. You are reading a section of a chapter in your economics textbook that refers to a series of graphs and illustrations in the chapter; you can understand the information in the graphs easily.

Purpose: _____

_____

_____

Level of Comprehension: _____

5. You are reading a critical essay that discusses an e. e. cummings poem you are studying in a literature class in preparation for writing a paper on that poem.

Purpose: _____

Level of Comprehension: _____

Assessing Your Skills and Abilities

If you were a physics major, you would probably find a math or chemistry text easier to read than if you were a communications or art major. If you spent a long afternoon doing library research, you would likely have more difficulty completing a psychology reading assignment that evening than if you had spent the afternoon shopping. Thus you can see that the following characteristics and circumstances can affect your reading rate and comprehension:

Your Background Knowledge

The amount of knowledge you have about a topic influences how easily and quickly you will be able to read about it. Suppose you were asked to read an excerpt from an organic chemistry text. If you have completed several chemistry courses, the excerpt would be fairly easy to understand. If you had never taken a chemistry course, even in high school, the excerpt would be extremely difficult to read, and you would probably understand very little.

Your Physical and Mental State

How you feel, how much sleep you have had, whether you are recovering from a cold, and even whether you are happy or relaxed after enjoying dinner can all affect your ability to read and concentrate. Try to complete analytical or careful reading assignments when you are at your physical peak and can maintain a high level of concentration. (See Chapter 2 for suggestions on improving your concentration.)

Your Interest Level

Most people have little difficulty understanding and remembering material if the subject is highly interesting. Interest can improve comprehension and rate; a lack of interest or motivation can have a negative effect.

Your Reading Skills

Your ability to comprehend directly influences how well and how fast you are able to read a given page. Your vocabulary is also an important factor. If your vocabulary is limited, you will encounter numerous unfamiliar words that will impair your comprehension and slow your reading down. On the other hand, an extensive, well-developed vocabulary will enable you to grasp meanings accurately and rapidly.

Varying Your Rate and Comprehension

Materials should not all be read in the same way or with the same level of comprehension. You should select a level of comprehension appropriate for what you are reading and why you are reading it. For example, if you are reading a textbook chapter to pass an objective exam based on that chapter, your purpose is to learn all the important facts and ideas, and you need a very high level of comprehension and recall.

Try the following techniques in order to find the appropriate level of comprehension and recall.

1. **Clearly define your purpose for reading the material.** Is it an assignment? Are you reading for general information, for details, for entertainment, or to keep up with current events?

2. **Analyze what, if anything, you will be required to do after you have read the material.** Will you have to pass an exam, participate in

a class discussion, or summarize the information in a short paper? To pass an exam, you need a very high level of comprehension. To prepare for a class discussion, a more moderate level of comprehension or retention is needed.

3. **Evaluate the relative difficulty of the material.** Assess your background knowledge and experience with the subject.

Once you have established your purpose for reading and have selected a desired level of comprehension, you must develop a reading strategy that suits your purpose. The remaining chapters in this text present a variety of techniques that allow you to choose a specific level of comprehension.

EXERCISE 1-7

DIRECTIONS: For each of the following situations, identify the appropriate level of comprehension (low to high).

1. You are reading the classified ads to find an apartment to rent.

   _____

2. You are reading a friend's English composition to help him or her revise it.

   _____

3. You are reviewing an essay that you read last evening for a literature course.

   _____

4. You are reading your lab manual in preparation for a biology lab.

   _____

5. You are reading an article in *Newsweek* about trends in violent crime in America for a sociology class discussion.

   _____

EXERCISE 1-8

DIRECTIONS: Make a list of reading assignments your instructors expect you to complete in the next two weeks. Indicate the level of comprehension that you should achieve for each assignment.

Principles of Efficiency and Flexibility

Each of the following statements expresses one of the major principles on which the techniques presented in this book are built. Are you surprised by any of them? Do any of the statements seem to contradict what you have been taught previously? Because these are vital principles, a brief rationale for each follows:

1. **You do not always have to read everything.** In this text you will see that, depending on your purpose for reading, it may be perfectly acceptable and even advisable to skip portions of sentences, paragraphs, and articles.

2. **Not everything on a page is of equal importance.** Sentences, paragraphs, and longer selections each contain a mixture of important and less important information. You will learn to identify what is important and to see how the remaining parts of the sentence, paragraph, or article relate to it.

3. **Shortcuts can save valuable time and make reading or studying easier.** Reading is not simply a matter of opening a book and jumping in. There are specific techniques you can use before you begin reading, while you are reading, and after you have finished reading that will greatly increase your efficiency.

4. **You can increase your reading rate without losing comprehension.** Most students can increase their rate by applying techniques for improving their comprehension and retention. Of course, you cannot expect to double or triple your rate while maintaining a high level of comprehension, but a significant increase is usually noted.

5. **Not everything that appears in print is true.** An active reader must question and evaluate the source, authority, and evidence offered in support of statements that are not verifiable.

Throughout the rest of this book, each of these principles will be demonstrated and applied to a variety of reading situations.

Evaluating Your Rate and Flexibility

Now that you have read about rate and flexibility, you are probably wondering how fast and flexibly you read. Here is an easy method for estimating your reading rate for whatever material you are reading. (Use this method to complete Exercise 1–9.)

1. **After you have chosen a passage in a book or article, count the total number of words in any three lines.** Divide the total by three (3). Round off to the nearest whole number. This will give the average number of words per line.

2. **Count the number of lines on one page of the article or book.** Multiply the number of words per line by the total number of lines. This will give you a fairly accurate estimate of the total number of words.

3. **As you read, time yourself.** Record the hour, minute, and second of your starting time (for example, 4:20:00). Start reading when the second hand of the clock reaches 12. Record your finishing time. Subtract your starting time from your finishing time.

4. **Divide the total reading time into the total number of words.** To do this, round off the number of seconds to the nearest quarter of a minute and then divide. For example, if your total reading time was 3 minutes and 12 seconds, round it off to 3¼, or 3.25 minutes and then divide. Your answer will be your words per minute (WPM) score.

EXAMPLE:

Total number of words on 3 lines: 23

Divide by 3 and round off: 23 ÷ 3 = 7⅔ = 8

Total number of lines in article: 120

Multiply number of words per line by number of lines:

   8 × 120 = 960 (total words)

Subtract starting time from finishing time:
$$\begin{array}{r} 1:13:28 \\ -1:05 \\ \hline 0:08:28 \end{array}$$

Round off to nearest quarter minute: 8.5 minutes

Divide time into total number of words:

960 ÷ 8.5 = 112 + a fraction (your WPM score)

**EXERCISE
1-9**

DIRECTIONS: Measure how effectively you adjust your reading rate by reading each of the following materials for the purpose stated. Fill in your rate in the space provided, then compare your results with the rates given in Table 1.2.

1. Material: A portion of a legal document (insurance policy, financial aid statement, credit card agreement)

Purpose: Complete understanding

Rate: _____

2. Material: A three-page assignment in one of your textbooks

   Purpose: High comprehension—recall for an objective exam

   Rate: _____

3. Material: An article in a favorite magazine

   Purpose: Moderate comprehension—entertainment

   Rate: _____ ▬

Critical Thinking Tip #1

Developing Critical-Thinking Skills

An efficient and flexible reader is also a critical reader. Your college instructors expect you not only to understand and recall what you read, but also to interpret and evaluate it. They expect you to read and think critically. The word *critical,* when used in this context, does not mean being negative or finding fault. Instead, it means having a curious, questioning, and open mind. To get a better sense of what critical thinking involves, and to assess your current level of critical reading and thinking skills, complete the following mini-questionnaire.

When You Read, Do You . . .	Always	Sometimes	Never
1. Question the author's motives?	❏	❏	❏
2. Think about what the author *means* as well as what he or she *says*?	❏	❏	❏
3. Ask questions such as Why? or How? as you read?	❏	❏	❏
4. Pay attention to the author's choice of words and notice their impact on you?	❏	❏	❏
5. Evaluate the evidence or reasons an author provides to support an idea?	❏	❏	❏

If you answered *always* or *sometimes* to a number of the questions, you are well on your way to becoming a critical reader. If you answered *never,* you will learn more about these skills, as well as others, in the Critical Thinking boxes in each chapter.

**EXERCISE
1-10**

DIRECTIONS: Select one of the readings at the end of the chapter.

1. For the reading selected, choose a purpose for reading and a desired level of comprehension from Table 1.2 and record them here.

   Selection: _____

   Purpose: _____

   Desired Level of Comprehension: _____

2. Read the selection while keeping in mind the purpose you have chosen, then answer the questions that follow the reading.

3. Evaluate the difficulty of the reading and your approach to it by completing the checklist in Figure 1.1.

FIGURE 1.1   A Checklist to Evaluate Difficulty

Format
❏ helpful
❏ difficult to follow

Graphic/Visual Aids
❏ yes
❏ no

Typographical Aids
❏ yes
❏ no

Language Features
❏ short sentences and paragraphs
❏ long sentences and paragraphs

Vocabulary Level
❏ difficult vocabulary
❏ understandable vocabulary

Subject Matter
❏ complex
❏ understandable
❏ familiar

Length
❏ short
❏ moderate
❏ long

Organization
❏ strong
❏ moderate
❏ weak

Your Background Knowledge
❏ strong
❏ moderate
❏ weak

Your Physical/Mental State
❏ alert
❏ moderately alert
❏ distractible

Your Interest Level
❏ high
❏ moderate
❏ low

Summary

1. What is meant by reading efficiency and reading flexibility?

Reading efficiency and flexibility are vital concepts for college readers.
- Efficiency refers to the ability to accomplish tasks effectively within a reasonable period of time.
- Flexibility refers to the ability to adjust reading rates to the difficulty of the material, the purpose for reading, and the reader's skills and abilities.

2. What is learning style?

Learning style refers to each person's unique strengths and weaknesses as a learner.

3. What are the features of a piece of writing that can affect its level of reading difficulty?

Text features that affect difficulty include
- format
- graphics
- typographical aids
- language features
- subject matter
- length
- organization

4. What characteristics or circumstances can affect your reading rate and comprehension?

Reader characteristics that affect rate and comprehension are
- background knowledge
- physical and mental state
- interest
- reading skills

5. Why should you vary your reading rate and level of comprehension?

Since reading materials differ widely and your purpose for reading them varies, you should adjust your rate and comprehension to form a strategy for each different reading situation.

6. What are the five major principles behind the techniques presented in this book?

- You do not always have to read everything.
- Not everything on a page is of equal importance.
- Shortcuts can save valuable time and make reading and studying easier.
- You can increase your reading rate without losing comprehension.
- Not everything that appears in print is true.

Reading Selection 1

Careers: Planning

How to Brag About Yourself to Win and Hold a New Job

James E. Challenger
From *The Buffalo News*

Do you feel prepared for a job interview? Do you know how to sell yourself to a potential customer? This essay, written by the president of an international company that specializes in job placement, offers advice that will help you do well during a job interview.

— · —

1   For most people, boasting about oneself does not come naturally. It is not easy or comfortable to tell someone all the wonderful things you have accomplished. But that is exactly what you need to do if you are seeking a new job, or trying to hold on to the one you have.

2   Of course, there is a fine line between self-confidence and arrogance, so to be successful in winning over the interviewer you must learn to maximize your accomplishments and attributes without antagonizing the interviewer.

3   The natural tendency for most job seekers is to behave modestly in a job interview. Although humility is usually an attractive trait, it will work against you when job hunting and moving up the corporate ladder. If you do not tell a prospective employer how good you are, who will?

4   More than half of the people interviewing for jobs fail to win an offer simply because they failed to sell their accomplishments. More than likely you have the qualifications for the jobs for which you are interviewing. That should give you the confidence to tell the interviewer why your accomplishments make you the best person for the position.

5   Give yourself a fighting chance at the interview. Your resume might have helped you get the interview, but its usefulness has ended there.

It will not speak for itself. If it makes you feel more comfortable, take a step "outside yourself." This means to view yourself as someone else may view you. Rather than thinking that you are talking about yourself, pretend you are giving a recommendation of a good friend.

6   To do the best job of selling yourself in an interview, you have to be prepared in advance. As part of your job-hunting checklist, write

"If you do not tell a prospective employer how good you are, who will?"

down on a piece of paper your major job-related accomplishments. Commit them to memory. You will probably be pleasantly surprised to see in writing all that you have done.

7   By developing this list, you will have accomplished two things: the first is you will impress the interviewer by being able to talk confidently and succinctly about your accomplishments. You will not have to sit uncomfortably while you think of your successes. They will be at the tip of your tongue.

8   Secondly, rather than dwell on your own personality characteristics, such as how hard-working or creative you are, you can discuss hard facts, such as how you saved your employer money or an idea you developed that helped a customer make more money.

9   Let the interviewer know about the praise your accomplishments have won from your former supervisors. Make a point of mentioning any awards or honors you received in your work or a related field. If your job evaluations were consistently excellent, quote your supervisors' complimentary remarks.

10   When chronicling your accomplishments for the interviewer, take as much credit as you honestly can. If you were a key part behind a major group project, tell the interviewer. If you developed a specific idea without help from your supervisor, it is acceptable to say that. Remember, you are at that interview to sell yourself, not your former co-workers.

11   However, never criticize your former employer. Sharing your negative thoughts with the interviewer is an immediate turn-off and will only brand you as a complainer and gossip, whom no one likes or will hire.

12   Keep in mind that the most important part of a job interview is making the employer like you and presenting yourself as the person he or she wants you to be. Consciously or not, most employers tend to hire people who reflect their own values and standards.

13   One important thing to keep in mind while you are discussing your accomplishments: Do not tell the employer how to run his or her business. Just discuss your qualifications and the good things you have done and let the interviewer decide how you might fill the company's needs.

14   Once you get the job you want, boasting about your accomplishments does not stop. Although you may think all your successes and achievements are highly visible, remember that you are only one of many people in a company. Lack of recognition is cited by a majority of discharged managers as the most frequent complaint against the former employer.

15   Do not let it happen to you. Make a point to tell your supervisor what you have done. Even if not asked, write down what you have accomplished on a regular basis and give it to your supervisor so he or she knows what you are doing. A written report can also be referred to during performance and salary reviews to document your achievements.

16   To help make yourself more visible in the company, volunteer for additional assignments—both job-related and nonbusiness-related. These could include community relations or charitable activities in which your company is involved. These types of activities may enable you to have more time and access to top executives of the company to whom you may endear yourself. You might even have the opportunity to tell them what you are doing for the company, which can never hurt.

17   Remember, letting people know what you are doing and what you have accomplished is not a bad thing, whether you are interviewing for a new job or working your way up the corporate hierarchy. Your worklife is a constant sales job. You must sell yourself like a product to win a job. Once you have a job, you must continually promote yourself and your accomplishments to hold on to your job and move successfully through the corporate ranks.

James E. Challenger is president of Challenger, Gray & Christmas, Inc., an international outplacement consulting firm with 24 U.S. and foreign offices.

EXAMINING READING SELECTION 1

Checking Your Vocabulary

Directions: Using context, word parts, or a dictionary if necessary, circle the letter of the meaning for each word as it is used in the reading.

1. antagonizing (paragraph 2)
   a. rejecting
   b. humanizing
   c. impressing
   d. annoying

2. humility (paragraph 3)
   a. honesty
   b. modesty
   c. cunning
   d. frankness

3. chronicling (paragraph 10)
   a. presenting a record of
   b. explaining a cause or effect
   c. emphasizing
   d. comparing or contrasting

4. charitable (paragraph 16)
   a. profit making
   b. recreational
   c. honoring others
   d. helping the needy

5. hierarchy (paragraph 17)
   a. spatial arrangement
   b. chronological listing
   c. ranking according to status
   d. listing by age

Checking Your Comprehension

Directions: Circle the letter of the best answer.

6. This article is mostly about how to
   a. interview for a job.
   b. please your boss.
   c. get along with coworkers.
   d. get and keep a job.

7. Which of the following statements best expresses the central thought of this article?
   a. "More than likely you have the qualifications for the jobs for which you are interviewing."
   b. "Do not tell the employer how to run his or her business."
   c. "Make a point to tell your supervisor what you have done."
   d. "Your worklife is a constant sales job."

8. According to the reading, more than half of the people who interview for jobs don't get offered one because they
   a. are not qualified.
   b. appear arrogant or too self-confident.
   c. fail to sell their accomplishments.
   d. have no contacts within the company.

9. The author states that the one thing you should *never* do during an interview is
   a. criticize your former employer.
   b. promote your qualifications for the job.
   c. tell your potential boss about projects you've worked on.
   d. list your successes in previous jobs.

10. The author states that the most important part of a job interview is
    a. taking credit for your accomplishments and giving credit to your coworkers.
    b. showing your potential boss you have the initiative to do the job and will work hard.
    c. making your boss like you and appearing like the person he/she wants you to be.
    d. impressing your potential boss with your ideas for running his business.

11. The ideas in this selection are arranged
    a. by order of importance of advice, from most to least.
    b. chronologically, from finding to keeping a job.
    c. spatially, within an office environment.
    d. by causes and effects of employment.

Thinking Critically

12. The author provides his views on winning and holding a new job by
    a. offering suggestions.
    b. presenting facts and statistics.
    c. describing several situations.
    d. telling a story.

13. The author's primary purpose in writing the article is to
    a. criticize.
    b. inform.
    c. entertain.
    d. argue.

14. Based on the reading, which one of the following statements would the author think is best for you to make during a job interview for a sales position?
    a. "I'm the best person for the job because I am creative and hardworking."
    b. "You might want to hire me because of my background in sales and my ability to get along."
    c. "My present company increased sales by 25 percent this year as a result of an advertising campaign that I spear-headed."
    d. "I have played a part in helping the company to increase revenues over the last five years."

15. In light of his views on job interviews, the reader can conclude that the author is
    a. assertive.
    b. aggressive.
    c. humble.
    d. conceited.

Questions for Discussion

1. Some people worry that if they boast about themselves during a job interview, they'll appear to be conceited. Do you think this is true? Why or why not?

2. Do you agree that "your worklife is a constant sales job"? Justify your answer.

3. The author suggests that you should not tell the employer how to run his or her business. Do you agree or disagree? Why?

4. What other suggestions can you offer for success in getting and keeping a job?

Selection 1:			959 words
Finishing Time:	_____	_____	_____
	HR.	MIN.	SEC.
Starting Time:	_____	_____	_____
	HR.	MIN.	SEC.
Reading Time:		_____	_____
		MIN.	SEC.
WPM Score:			_____
Comprehension Score:		_____	%

READING SELECTION 2

SOCIOLOGY

TALKING A STRANGER THROUGH THE NIGHT

Sherry Amatenstein

From: *Newsweek* magazine

This reading first appeared in Newsweek *in November 2002. Read it to find out how one woman connected with another person in an impersonal city and saved a life.*

— · —

1   The call came 60 minutes into my third shift as a volunteer at the crisis hot line. As the child of Holocaust survivors, I grew up wanting to ease other people's pain. But it wasn't until after September 11 that I contacted Help Line, the nonprofit telephone service headquartered in New York. The instructor of the nine-week training course taught us how to handle a variety of callers, from depressed seniors to "repeats" (those who checked in numerous times a day).

2   We spent two sessions on suicide calls, but I prayed I wouldn't get one until I felt comfortable on the line. Drummed over and over into the 30 trainees' heads was that our role wasn't to give advice. Rather, we were to act as empathetic sounding boards and encourage callers to figure out how to take action.

3   My idealism about the hot line's value faded that first night, as in quick succession I heard from men who wanted to masturbate while I listened, repeats who told me again and again about their horrific childhoods, know-nothing shrinks and luckless lives, and three separate callers who railed about the low intellect of everyone living in Queens (my borough!). Sprinkled into the mix were people who turned abusive when I refused to tell them how to solve their problems.

4   I tried to remain sympathetic. If I, who had it together (an exciting career, great friends and family), found New York isolating, I could imagine how frightening it was for people so untethered they needed a hot line for company. That rationale didn't help. After only 10 hours, I no longer cringed each time the phone rang, terrified it signified a problem I wasn't equipped to handle. Instead I wondered what fresh torture this caller had up his unstable sleeve.

5   Then Sandy's (not her real name) quavering voice nipped into my ear: "I want to kill myself." I snapped to attention, remembering my training. Did she have an imminent plan to do herself in? Luckily, no. Sandy knew a man who'd attempted suicide via pills, threw them up and lived. She was afraid of botching a similar attempt. Since she was handicapped, she couldn't even walk to her window to jump out.

6   Sandy's life was certainly Help Line material. Her parents had disowned her 40 years before. She'd worked as a secretary until a bone-crushing fall put her out of commission. Years later she was working again and had a boyfriend who stuck with her even after a cab struck Sandy and put her back on the disabled list. They became engaged, and then, soap-opera like, tragedy struck again. Sandy's boyfriend was diagnosed with cancer and passed away last year. Now she was in constant pain, confined to a dark apartment, her only companion a nurse's aide. "There's nothing left," she cried. "Give me a reason to live."

7   Her plea drove home the wisdom of the "no advice" dictum. How could I summon the words to give someone else's life meaning? The best I could do was to help Sandy fan the spark that

had led her to reach out. I tossed life-affirming statements at her like paint on a canvas, hoping some would stick. I ended with "Sandy, I won't whitewash your problems. You've had more than your share of sorrow. But surely there are some things that have given you pleasure."

8   She thought hard and remembered an interest in books on spirituality. The downside followed immediately. Sandy's limited eyesight made it difficult for her to read. She rasped, "My throat hurts from crying, but I'm afraid if I get off the phone I'll want to kill myself again."

9   I said, "I'm here as long as you need me."

10   We spoke another two hours. She recalled long-ago incidents—most depressing, a few semi-joyful. There were some things she still enjoyed: peanuts, "Oprah," the smell of autumn. I again broached the topic of spirituality. My supervisor, whom I'd long ago motioned to listen in on another phone, handed me a prayer book. I read, and Sandy listened. After "amen," she said, "I think I'll be all right for the night."

11   Naturally, she couldn't promise to feel better tomorrow. For all of us, life is one day, sometimes even one minute, at a time. She asked, "When are you on again?"

12   I said, "My schedule is irregular, but we're all here for you, any time you want. Thanks so much for calling."

13   As I hung up, I realized the call had meant as much to me as to Sandy, if not more. Despite having people in my life, lately I'd felt achingly lonely. I hadn't called a hot line, but I'd manned one, and this night had been my best in a long time. Instead of having dinner at an overpriced restaurant or watching HBO, I'd connected with another troubled soul in New York City.

WRITING ABOUT READING SELECTION 2*

Checking Your Vocabulary

Directions: Complete each of the following items; refer to a dictionary if necessary.

1. Discuss the connotative meanings of the word *suicide.*

2. Define each of the following words:
   a. horrific (paragraph 3)

   b. rationale (paragraph 4)

   c. signified (paragraph 4)

   d. imminent (paragraph 5)

   e. dictum (paragraph 7)

3. Define the word *empathetic* (paragraph 2) and underline the word or phrase that provides a context clue for its meaning.

   _____

   _____

   _____

   _____

4. Define the word *botching* (paragraph 5) and underline the word or phrase that provides a context clue for its meaning.

   _____

   _____

   _____

_____
* Multiple-choice questions are contained in Part 6 (page 575).

5. Determine the meanings of the following words by using word parts:
   a. nonprofit (paragraph 1)

   _____

   b. untethered (paragraph 4)

   _____

   c. unstable (paragraph 4)

   _____

   d. spirituality (paragraph 8)

   _____

   e. irregular (paragraph 12)

   _____

Checking Your Comprehension

6. What main point does the author make?

   _____

   _____

7. Describe Sandy's life.

   _____

   _____

8. Describe the training the author received.

   _____

   _____

9. How and when was the author's idealism about the hot line shattered?

   _____

   _____

   _____

   _____

Thinking Critically

10. How did Sandy's call change the author's attitude toward the hotline?

    _____

    _____

    _____

11. Describe the organization of this selection. What organizational pattern predominates?

    _____

    _____

    _____

12. Cite several examples that suggest that the author was helpful to Sandy.

    _____

    _____

    _____

    _____

13. What is the author's purpose?

    _____

    _____

    _____

    _____

14. What can you infer about the author's lifestyle from information contained in the reading?

    _____

    _____

    _____

Questions for Discussion

1. Discuss why it is the hotline's policy not to offer advice.

2. Evaluate the level of training and supervision the hotline offered its volunteers.

3. Discuss situations in which you did something to help another person and it resulted in making you feel better about yourself.

4. Brainstorm a list of volunteer options on campus or in your community. Discuss potential rewards; try to anticipate potential problems.

Selection 2:			824 words
Finishing Time:	_____	_____	_____
	HR.	MIN.	SEC.
Starting Time:	_____	_____	_____
	HR.	MIN.	SEC.
Reading Time:		_____	_____
		MIN.	SEC.
WPM Score:			_____
Comprehension Score:			_____%

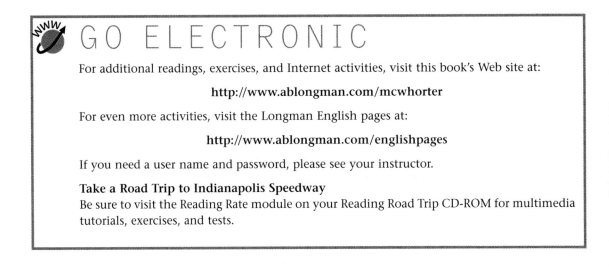

GO ELECTRONIC

For additional readings, exercises, and Internet activities, visit this book's Web site at:

http://www.ablongman.com/mcwhorter

For even more activities, visit the Longman English pages at:

http://www.ablongman.com/englishpages

If you need a user name and password, please see your instructor.

Take a Road Trip to Indianapolis Speedway
Be sure to visit the Reading Rate module on your Reading Road Trip CD-ROM for multimedia tutorials, exercises, and tests.

CHAPTER 2

Active Reading and Learning

IN THIS CHAPTER YOU WILL LEARN:

1. To read actively.
2. To develop critical thinking skills.
3. To improve your ability to concentrate.
4. To monitor your comprehension.
5. To preview and predict before reading.
6. To develop guide questions.

When reading and studying a textbook assignment, what could you do before reading to make the task easier? What could you do while you are reading to understand and remember more of the material? This chapter introduces numerous techniques that can mak⁰e a noticeable difference in how well you read and how much you remember. These techniques—active reading and thinking, assessing your learning style, prereading and predicting, forming guide questions, monitoring your comprehension, and building your concentration—can make an immediate, significant improvement in your reading efficiency. Each technique demands that you become actively involved in reading—thinking, anticipating, connecting, and assessing your performance.

Reading and Thinking Actively

College instructors expect their students to read actively and think critically. This section offers strategies for improving these skills.

Reading Actively

Reading at first may appear to be a routine activity in which individual words are combined to produce meaning. Consequently, many college students approach reading as a single-step process. They open the book, read, and close the book. Research shows that effective reading is not a single-step process but a complex set of skills involving activities before, during, and after reading. Here is a partial list of those skills:

BEFORE READING

1. Determine the subject of the material.
2. Determine how the material is organized.
3. Decide what you need to remember from the material.
4. Define your purpose for reading.

DURING READING

1. Identify what is important.
2. Determine how key ideas are supported.
3. Identify patterns of thought.
4. Draw connections between ideas.
5. Anticipate what is to come next.
6. Relate ideas to what you already know.

DURING AND AFTER READING

1. Identify the author's purpose for writing.
2. Analyze the writer's technique and language.
3. Evaluate the writer's competence or authority.
4. Ask critical questions.
5. Evaluate the nature and type of supporting evidence.

To better grasp the concept of active reading, consider a similar situation. Have you ever gone to a ball game and watched the fans? Most do not sit passively and watch the game. Instead they become actively involved; they direct players to make certain plays; they criticize calls, encourage players, and reprimand the coach. They feel and act as if it's *their* game, not just the players' game. Similarly, active readers get involved with the material they are reading. They think about, question, challenge, and criticize

Table 2.1   Active Versus Passive Reading

Active Readers . . .	*Passive Readers . . .*
Read each assignment differently	Read all assignments the same way
Analyze the purpose of an assignment	Read an assignment because it was assigned
Adjust their speed to suit their purpose	Read everything at the same speed
Question ideas	Accept whatever is in print as true
Compare and connect textbook readings with lecture content	Study each separately
Find out what an assignment is about before reading it	Check the length of an assignment before reading it
Keep track of their level of comprehension and concentration	Read until the assignment is completed
Read with pencil in hand, highlighting, jotting notes, and marking key vocabulary	Read

the author's ideas. They try to make the material *their* material. Table 2.1 lists examples of successful active reading strategies and contrasts them with passive (unsuccessful) approaches.

Throughout this chapter and the remainder of the text, you will learn numerous techniques and strategies for becoming a more active reader.

DIRECTIONS: Using Table 2.1, analyze how you read. Place check marks beside items that describe you. Are you an active or a passive reader?

DIRECTIONS: Consider each of the following reading assignments. Discuss ways to get actively involved in each assignment.

1.   Reading two poems by Walt Whitman for an American literature class

_____

_____

2. Reading the procedures for your next biology lab

_____

_____

3. Reading an article in *Time* magazine assigned by your political science instructor in preparation for a class discussion

_____

_____

**EXERCISE
2-3**

DIRECTIONS: Compile a list of active reading strategies you already use. Discuss new strategies that could be used with your instructor or classmates. Add these to your list.

_____

_____

_____

Table 2.2   Levels of Thinking

Level	Examples
Remembering: Recalling information; repeating information with no changes	Recalling definitions; memorizing dates
Understanding: Understanding ideas; using rules and following directions	Explaining a theory, recognizing what is important
Applying: Applying knowledge to a new situation	Using knowledge of formulas to solve a new physics problem
Analyzing: Seeing relationships; breaking information into parts; analyzing how things work	Comparing two essays by the same author
Evaluating: Making judgments; assessing value or worth of information	Evaluating the effectiveness of an argument opposing the death penalty
Creating: Putting ideas and information together in a unique way; creating something new	Designing a new computer program

Sources: Bloom, B., et al., eds., *Taxonomy of Educational Objectives.* New York: McKay, 1956 and Anderson, Lorin, et al. *Taxonomy for Learning, Teaching and Assessing: A Revision of Bloom's Taxonomy of Educational Objectives.* Boston: Allyn and Bacon, 2000.

Thinking Critically

Active reading requires critical thinking. To be an active reader, you must think beyond a factual, literal level. Instructors expect you to understand ideas, but they also expect you to apply, analyze, and evaluate information and to create new ideas.

Table 2.2 describes a progression of academic thinking skills ranging from basic to more complex.

When instructors assign papers, write exam questions, or conduct class discussions, they often ask you to do more than just remember and understand. Table 2.3 gives a few sample exam questions from a course in interpersonal communication.

Awareness of these levels of thinking will help you move beyond factual learning and focus your study on applying, analyzing, evaluating, and creating.

The following passage is taken from a human biology textbook. Read the passage and study the list of questions that follow.

COMMUNICATION AND THE SKIN

We generally think of communication as a matter of voice and gesture, but the skin is an important communicative organ. Animals communicate their moods and sometimes make threats by fluffing their fur or causing it to rise on the backs of their neck and shoulders; humans cannot do that. However, the patterns of human hair distribution and color do signal sex and age. Fair-complexioned people can also—involuntarily—change blood flow to the skin and blush to indicate embarrassment,

Table 2.3   Test Items and Levels of Thinking

Test Item	Level of Thinking Required
Define nonverbal communication.	Remembering
Explain how nonverbal communication works.	Understanding
Describe three instances in which you have observed nonverbal communication.	Applying
Study the two videotape segments and analyze the motives of each person.	Analyzing
Evaluate an essay whose major premise is: "Nonverbal communication skills should be taught formally as part of the educational process."	Evaluating
Read the short story and then create an alternative ending.	Creating

turn red with rage, and go pale with shock. In addition, we have considerable voluntary control over subcutaneous muscles in the face and neck, many of which attach to the skin to produce the stretchings and wrinklings of facial expressions.

An additional communicative role is served by the skin's apocrine sweat glands, particularly in adults. The substances they secrete have strong odors, especially after they have been worked on by the bacteria that dwell on the skin, and these glands are found in areas, such as the armpits, groin, and anal region, that have wicklike tufts of hair that can spread the odor into the air. Emotionally charged situations are likely to stimulate apocrine secretions, which may signal that a certain level of sexual readiness or fear or anxiety (emotional intensity) has been attained.

Rischer and Easton, *Focus on Human Biology.*

Remembering	What happens when fair-complexioned people blush?
Understanding	Why is the skin an important vehicle for communication?
Applying	Study two facial portraits and discuss how the people are using their skin to communicate.
Analyzing	How does stretching of the skin produce communication?
Evaluating	Why is it important to know that skin can communicate?
Creating	Write a set of guidelines for determining what messages can be sent by skin movement.

EXERCISE 2-4

DIRECTIONS: For each of the following activities or situations, identify which levels of thinking are primarily involved.

1. You are reading and comparing research from several sources to write a term paper for sociology.

_____

2. You received a "C" grade on an essay you wrote for your freshman composition course. Your instructor will allow you to revise it to improve your grade.

_____

3. You are translating an essay from Spanish to English.

_____

4. You are dissecting a frog in your biology class.

_____

5. You are bathing a patient as part of your clinical experience course in nursing.

_____

EXERCISE 2-5

DIRECTIONS: Read the following excerpt from a history textbook. Then read the questions that follow and identify the level of thinking that each requires.

AFRICAN-AMERICAN WOMEN AS WRITERS

Phillis Wheatley was a young, African-American slave who belonged to landowner John Wheatley in Colonial America. She was also a poet and the first African-American ever to publish a book. Her *Poems on Various Subjects, Religious and Moral* was printed in Boston in 1773, three years before the penning of the Declaration of Independence.

Early slaves were generally denied education (it was deemed dangerous), but Wheatley was allowed by her owner to study poetry, Latin, and the Bible, and by the time she reached her late teens she had written enough poetry to put together a slender book of verse. Even so, publication was difficult. Proper Bostonians, fearful of a hoax, forced her to submit to a scholarly examination by a board of educated men, including the colonial governor and the same John Hancock who later copied out the Declaration of Independence and signed it with a flourish. The board of judges questioned Wheatley extensively and ruled that she was literate enough to have written the book. Only then was publication permitted.

Wheatley may have been the first, but she was not the only slave to write a book during the growing days of the republic. Unfortunately, most of the early popular African-American writers have been all but forgotten in modern times. Until now. A Cornell professor, Henry Louis Gates, recently started a research project, looking into 19th-century African-American fiction and poetry. In the process, he uncovered numerous lost works, almost half of which were written by African-American women. In varied literary styles, the newly resurfaced manuscripts offered a rich repository of African-American culture, recreating, among other things, the early days of slavery and the importance of religion to people under subjugation.

The literary finds were important. So important, in fact, that 30 of the lost books were republished in the late 1980s by Oxford University Press. The newly reclaimed writers range from poet Wheatley to novelist Frances Harper, essayist Ann Plato, and outspoken feminist Anna Julia Cooper. Perhaps this time they won't be lost.

Merrill, Lee, and Friedlander, *Modern Mass Media.*

1. Who was the first African-American to publish a book?

   _____

2. Explain why Phillis Wheatley was forced to submit to a scholarly examination.

   _____

3. Name two writers who have been recently rediscovered.

   _____

4. Read two poems by Phillis Wheatley and compare them.

   _____

5. Why does the writer of this article hope the newly reclaimed work won't be lost?

   _____

6. Read a poem by Phillis Wheatley and explain what meaning it has to your life.

   _____

7. Critique one of Wheatley's poems; discuss its strengths and weaknesses.

   _____

8. Discuss the possible reasons Wheatley's owner allowed her to study.

   _____

9. Read five essays by Ann Plato, and develop a list of issues with which she is concerned.

   _____

10. Decide whether or not it was fair to ask Wheatley to submit to a scholarly examination.

   _____

Improving Your Concentration

Do you have difficulty concentrating? If so, you are like many other college students who say that poor concentration is the main reason they cannot read or study effectively. Concentration is the ability to focus on the task at hand. Most students find that improving their concentration can reduce their reading time and improve their learning efficiency.

Concentration Quiz

	Yes	No
1. Are you sitting on a comfortable chair or lying on a comfortable bed?	❏	❏
2. Is a television on nearby?	❏	❏
3. Are friends or family who are not studying in the room with you?	❏	❏
4. Do you wish you didn't have to read this chapter?	❏	❏
5. Are you reading this chapter only because it was assigned by your instructor?	❏	❏
6. Are you worried about anything or trying to make an important decision?	❏	❏
7. Are you tired, either physically or mentally?	❏	❏
8. Are you thinking about other things you have to do while you are reading?	❏	❏

Take the quiz above to assess your ability to concentrate. If your answer is *yes* to any of the questions, reading and studying this chapter will probably take you more time than it should. A *yes* answer indicates that you are not operating at your peak level of concentration.

Improving your concentration can best be achieved by controlling external distractions and increasing your attention span. Here are some suggestions for accomplishing these goals.

Control External Distractions

A phone ringing, a dog barking, friends arguing, or parents reminding you about errands can break your concentration and cost you time. Each time you are interrupted, you have to find where you left off, and it takes you a minute or two to refocus your attention.

Although you cannot eliminate all distractions, you can control many of them through a wise choice of time and place for study. For a week or so, analyze where and when you study. Try to notice situations in which you accomplished a great deal as well as those in which you accomplished very little. At the end of the week, look for a pattern. Where and when did you find it was easy to concentrate? Where and when was it most difficult? Use the information from your analysis along with the following suggestions to choose a regular time and place for study.

1. **Choose a place to study that is relatively free of interruptions.** You may need to figure out what types of interruptions occur most frequently and then choose a place where you will be free of them. For instance, if your home, apartment, or dorm has many interruptions such as phone calls, friends stopping by, or family members talking or watching TV, it may be necessary to find a different place to study. The campus or neighborhood library is often quiet and free of interruptions.

2. **Choose a place free of distractions.** Although your living room, for example, may be quiet and free of interruptions, you may not be able to concentrate there. You may be distracted by noises from the street, the view from a window, the presence of a TV, or a project you are working on.

3. **Do not study where you are too comfortable.** If you study sitting in a lounge chair or lying across your bed, you may find it difficult to concentrate.

4. **Study in the same place.** Once you have located a good place to study, try to study in this place regularly. You will become familiar with the surroundings and begin to form associations between the place and the activity you perform there. Eventually, as soon as you enter the room or sit down at the desk, you will begin to feel as though you should study.

5. **Choose a time of day when you are mentally alert.** Give yourself the advantage of reading or studying when your mind is sharp and ready to pick up new information. Avoid studying when you are hungry or tired because it is most difficult to concentrate at these times.

6. **Establish a fixed time for reading or studying.** Studying at the same time each day will help you fall into the habit of studying more easily. For example, if you establish, as part of a schedule, that you will study right after dinner, soon it will become almost automatic.

Increase Your Attention Span

Most people can keep their minds on one topic for only a limited period of time. This period of time represents their *attention span.* Your attention span varies from subject to subject, from book to book, and from speaker to speaker. It may also vary according to the time of day and place where you are studying. However, you can increase your attention span by using the following techniques:

1. **Set goals for yourself.** Before you begin to read or study, decide what you intend to accomplish during that session and about how much

time it will take. You might write these goals on paper and keep the list in front of you. By having specific goals to meet, you may find that you feel more like working. For an evening of reading or studying, you might write goals like this:

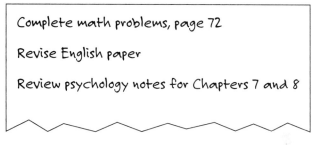

Complete math problems, page 72

Revise English paper

Review psychology notes for Chapters 7 and 8

2. **Read with a purpose.** If you are looking for specific information as you read, it will be easier to keep your attention focused on the material.

3. **Keep a distractions list.** As you are reading, often you will think of something you should remember to do. You might remember that you needed to call your sister or buy a Mother's Day card. An effective solution to this problem is to keep a "To Do" list. Keep a piece of paper nearby, and whenever something distracts you or you are reminded of something, jot it down on the paper. You will find that once you have written the item on paper it will no longer keep flashing through your mind. Your distractions list might look like this:

Call Sam

Buy lab manual for chemistry

Get tire fixed

4. **Vary your reading.** It is easy to tire of reading about a particular subject if you spend too long on it. To overcome this problem, work on several assignments in an evening rather than finishing one assignment completely. The variety in subject matter will provide a needed change and maintain your interest.

5. **Combine physical and mental activities.** Reading is primarily a mental activity. Because the rest of your body is not involved in the reading process, it is easy to become restless or feel a need to *do* something. Activities such as highlighting, underlining, making marginal

notes, or writing summary outlines provide an outlet for physical energy and supply useful study aids (see Chapter 7).

6. **Take frequent breaks.** Because your attention span is necessarily limited, take frequent breaks while you are reading. For instance, never decide to sit down and read for a solid three-hour block. After the first hour or so you will tire, begin to lose concentration, and accomplish less and less. For extremely difficult subjects such as foreign languages, take breaks more frequently and study for shorter periods.

7. **Approach your assignment positively.** If you think of a reading assignment as a waste of time, you will have difficulty concentrating. A negative mind-set almost guarantees poor comprehension and concentration. To overcome this, find some way to become interested in the subject. Question or challenge the authors as you read or try to develop questions about the material.

EXERCISE 2-6

DIRECTIONS: Now that you are aware of the factors that influence your concentration, answer the following questions about where and how you are reading this chapter. Your answers will give you an idea of how well you are controlling the factors that influence concentration.

1. Are you reading in a place relatively free of distractions and interruptions?

_____

2. Are you reading in the same place in which you usually read and study?

_____

3. Notice what time of day it is. Is this a high or low concentration period? Is it the same time that you usually study?

_____

4. What is your purpose for reading this chapter?

_____

5. How long do you expect to spend reading this chapter?

_____

6. How many times has your mind wandered while you were doing this exercise?

_____

Monitoring Your Comprehension

Have you ever read an assignment only to realize later, perhaps much later during an exam, that you did not really understand it? Or have you ever spent your time supposedly reading several pages or more, only to discover later that you really understood very little? If so, you can develop a very important and useful skill to overcome these problems. It is known as *cognitive monitoring,* and it means keeping track or being aware of what is happening mentally as you read. In cognitive monitoring you stay aware of your level of understanding by picking up clues or signals that indicate whether you are understanding what you are reading.

Think for a moment about what occurs when you read material you can understand easily. Then compare this feeling with what happens when you read complicated material that is difficult for you to understand. When you read certain material, does it seem that everything "clicks"? Do ideas seem to fit together and make sense? At other times is that "click" noticeably absent?

Read each of the following paragraphs. As you read, be alert to your level of understanding of each.

PARAGRAPH 1

Probably the major error beginning speakers make is to try to cover a huge topic in too short a time. The inevitable result is that nothing specific is covered; everything is touched on but only superficially. No depth is achieved with a broad topic, so all you can succeed in doing is telling the audience what it already knows. To be suitable for a public speech, a topic must be limited in scope; it must be narrowed down to fit the same constraints and to permit some depth of coverage.

DeVito, *The Elements of Public Speaking.*

PARAGRAPH 2

Large-quantity waste generators and SQGs must comply with the RCRA regulations, including obtaining an EPA identification (EPA ID) number, proper handling of the waste before transport, manifesting the waste (discussed in the next section), and proper record keeping and reporting. Conditionally exempt SQGs do not require EPA ID numbers. Appropriate pre-transport handling requires suitable packaging to prevent leakage and labeling of the packaged waste to identify its characteristics and dangers.

Nathanson, *Basic Environmental Technology.*

Most likely, as you read Paragraph 1, everything seemed to fit together and make sense. Ideas led from one to another; you could easily follow the author's train of thought. While reading Paragraph 2, you may have experienced difficulty and confusion. You realized that ideas weren't making sense. Unfamiliar terms were used and unfamiliar concepts were discussed; consequently, you could not see the flow of ideas.

Recognizing Comprehension Signals

The two examples were quite clear-cut: In one case understanding was easy; in the other it was difficult. In many situations, however, the distinction between understanding and the lack of it is not as clear. As you learned in Chapter 1, your comprehension depends on numerous factors; it may vary from high to low even with a single piece of material. In those cases, you have to pick up on more subtle clues or signals. Table 2.4 lists and compares some common signals that may assist you in monitoring your comprehension. Not all signals must appear at the same time, and not all signals work for everyone.

Table 2.4   Comprehension Signals

Positive Signals	Negative Signals
Everything seems to fit and make sense; ideas flow logically from one to another	Some pieces do not seem to belong; the material seems disjointed
You are able to see where the author is leading	You feel as if you are struggling to stay with the author and are unable to think ahead
You are able to make connections and see patterns of thought developing	You are unable to detect relationships; the organization is not apparent
You read at a regular pace without slowing down or rereading	You need to reread frequently and you make frequent regressions
You understand why the material was assigned	You do not know why the material was assigned and cannot explain why it is important
You feel comfortable and have some knowledge about the topic	The topic is unfamiliar, yet the author assumes you understand it
You recognize most words or can figure them out from context	Many words are unfamiliar
You can express the main ideas in your own words	You must reread and use the author's language to explain an idea
You read at a regular, comfortable pace	You often slow down or reread
You understand what is important	Nothing or everything seems important

EXERCISE 2-7

DIRECTIONS: Select a two- to three-page section from one of your textbooks or choose one of the readings at the end of the chapter. As you read it, monitor your level of understanding. After reading the material, answer the following questions.

1. In what sections was your comprehension strongest?

    _____

2. Did you feel at any time that you had lost, or were about to lose, comprehension? If so, go back to that section now. What made the section difficult to read?

    _____

3. Analyze any sections where you slowed down or reread. Why was this necessary?

    _____

4. How did you connect the content with your background knowledge and experience?

    _____

Correcting Incomplete Comprehension

Once you recognize clues that signal your level of understanding, you will find situations in which you are not comprehending as well as you should. When this happens, try the following:

1. **Analyze the time and place in which you are reading.** If you've been reading or studying for several hours, mental fatigue may be the source of the problem. If you are reading in a place with numerous distractions or interruptions, lack of concentration may contribute to comprehension loss.

2. **Rephrase each paragraph in your own words.** You might approach extremely complicated material sentence-by-sentence, expressing each in your own words.

3. **Read aloud sentences or sections that are particularly difficult.** Oral reading often provides auditory feedback signals that aid comprehension.

4. **Write a brief outline of the major points of the article.** This will help you to see the overall organization and progression of ideas in the material. (Chapter 7 discusses outlining and summary notes in greater detail.)

5. **Do not hesitate to reread difficult or complicated sections.** In fact, at times several rereadings are appropriate and necessary.

6. **Highlight important ideas.** After you've read a section, go back and think about and highlight what is important. Highlighting forces you to sort out what is important, and this sorting process facilitates overall comprehension and recall. (See Chapter 7 for suggestions about how to highlight effectively.)

7. **Slow down your reading rate if you feel you're beginning to lose comprehension.** On occasion simply reading more slowly will provide the needed boost in comprehension.

8. **Summarize.** Test your recall by summarizing each section after you have read it.

If none of these suggestions is effective, you may be lacking the necessary background knowledge that a particular writer assumes the reader has.

If you feel you are lacking background knowledge in a particular discipline or about a particular topic, take immediate steps to correct the problem. You might:

1. **Obtain a more basic text from the library that reviews basic principles and concepts.**

2. **Review several encyclopedia entries and other reference sources to obtain an overview of the subject.**

3. **Ask your instructor to suggest reference sources, guidebooks, or review books that will be helpful.**

Prereading and Predicting

Before reading an assignment, it is useful to discover what it is about—preread—and to anticipate what the material will cover—predict. Prereading is an active way to approach any reading assignment.

Prereading

What is the first thing you do as you begin reading a text assignment? If you are like many students, you check to see how long it is and then begin to read. Many students do not realize that they can use a technique before they begin to read that will improve their comprehension and recall. This technique, called prereading, is a way to familiarize yourself quickly with the organization and content of the material. It is one of the easiest techniques to use, and it makes a dramatic difference in your reading efficiency. Prereading involves getting a quick impression of what you are going to read before you read it. As a result, you will be able to read faster and follow the author's train of thought more easily. Prereading is similar to looking at a road map before you start out on a drive to an unfamiliar place. The road map, like prereading, gives you an idea of what lies ahead and how it is arranged.

How to Preread

When you preread you look only at those parts of the material that tell you what it is about or how it is organized. The portions to look at in reading a textbook chapter are listed here.

1. **Read the title.** Often the title functions as a label and tells you what the material is about. It identifies the overall topic or subject.

2. **Read the introduction or opening paragraphs.** The first few paragraphs of a piece of writing are usually introductory. The author may explain the subject, outline his or her ideas, or give some clues about his or her direction of thought. If the introduction is long, read only the first two or three paragraphs.

3. **Read each boldface heading.** Headings, like titles, serve as labels and identify the content of the material they head. Together, the headings form a mini-outline of the important ideas.

4. **Read the first sentence under each heading.** Although the heading often announces the topic that will be discussed, the first sentence following the heading frequently explains the heading and states the central thought of the passage. In the following sample selection, notice that many of the first sentences further explain the heading.

5. **Notice any typographical aids.** The typographical aids include all features of the page that make facts or ideas outstanding or more understandable. These include italics (slanted print), boldface type, marginal notes, colored ink, capitalization, underlining, and enumeration (listing).

6. **Notice any graphs or pictures.** Graphs, charts, and pictures are used for two purposes. First, they emphasize important ideas. Second, they clarify or simplify information and relationships. Therefore, they are always important to notice when you are prereading. The easiest way to quickly establish what important element of the text is being further explained by the graph or picture is to read the caption.

7. **Read the last paragraph or summary.** The last paragraph of a chapter often serves as a conclusion or summary. In some chapters, more than one paragraph may be used for this purpose. In some textbooks, these last few paragraphs may be labeled "Summary" or "Conclusion." By reading the summary before reading the chapter you will learn the general focus and content of the material.

Now preread the sample selection titled "Types of Nonverbal Cues." To illustrate how prereading is done, these pages have been specially marked. Everything that you should read has been shaded. After you have preread the selection, complete the quiz contained in Exercise 2–8.

TYPES OF NONVERBAL CUES

Let's look more closely at these cues that tell others about us or that tell us about them. Our own self-awareness and empathic skills will increase as we become more sensitive to different kinds of nonverbal cues. The broader our base of understanding, the more likely we are to be able to interpret the cues we perceive. But we know that nonverbal communication can be ambiguous, and we must be careful not to overgeneralize from the behavior we observe. We may feel hurt by the listless "Hi" we receive from a good friend unless we remember that the listlessness could have been brought on by a headache, lack of sleep, preoccupation, or some other factor we don't know about. We would be unwise to assume we are being personally rejected if this friend doesn't smile and stop to talk with us every single morning.

We should always be alert to *all* cues and try to get as much information as possible on which to base our conclusions. One way to organize our thinking about nonverbal communication is to think in terms of spatial cues, visual cues, and vocal cues. In considering each of these, we should not overlook the fact that any communication occurs in a specific environmental setting. This setting influences much of the nonverbal interaction that takes place. The weather can affect how we behave just as much as the actual setting—cafeteria, classroom, car, park bench, or wherever.

SPATIAL CUES

Spatial cues are the distances we choose to stand or sit from others. Each of us carries with us something called "informal space." We might think of this as a bubble; we occupy the center of the bubble. This bubble expands or contracts depending on varying conditions and circumstances such as the

Age and sex of those involved
Cultural and ethnic background of the participants
Topic or subject matter
Setting for the interaction
Physical characteristics of the participants (size or shape)

Attitudinal and emotional orientation of partners
Characteristics of the interpersonal relationship (like friendship)
Personality characteristics of those involved

In his book *The Silent Language,* Edward T. Hall, a cultural anthropologist, identifies the distances that we assume when we talk with others. He calls these distances intimate, personal, social, and public. In many cases, the adjustments that occur in these distances result from some of the factors listed above.

Intimate Distance

At an *intimate distance* (0 to 18 inches), we often use a soft or barely audible whisper to share intimate or confidential information. Physical contact becomes easy at this distance. This is the distance we use for physical comforting, love-making, and physical fighting, among other things.

Personal Distance

Hall identified the range of 18 inches to 4 feet as *personal distance*. When we disclose ourselves to someone, we are likely to do it within this distance. The topics we discuss at this range may be somewhat confidential, and usually are personal and mutually involving. At personal distance we are still able to touch each other if we want to. This is likely to be the distance between people conversing at a party, between classmates in a casual conversation, or within many work relationships. This distance assumes a well-established acquaintanceship. This is probably the most comfortable distance for free exchange of feedback.

Social Distance

When we are talking at a normal level with another person, sharing concerns that are not of a personal nature, we usually use the *social distance* (4 to 12 feet). Many of our on-the-job conversations take place at this distance. Seating arrangements in living rooms may be based on "conversation groups" of chairs placed at a distance of 4 to 7 feet from each other. Hall calls 4 to 7 feet the close phase of social distance; from 7 to 12 feet is the far phase of social distance.

The greater the distance, the more formal the business or social discourse conducted is likely to be. Often, the desks of important people are broad enough to hold visitors at a distance of 7 to 12 feet. Eye contact at this distance becomes more important to the flow of communication; without visual contact one party is likely to feel shut out and the conversation may come to a halt.

Public Distance

Public distance (12 feet and farther) is well outside the range for close involvement with another person. It is impractical for interpersonal communication. We are limited to what we can see and hear at that distance; topics for conversation are relatively impersonal and formal; and most of the communication that occurs is in the public-speaking style, with subjects planned in advance and limited opportunities for feedback. . . .

VISUAL CUES

Greater visibility increases our potential for communicating because the more we see and the more we can be seen, the more information we can send and receive. Mehrabian found that the more we direct our face toward the person we're talking to, the more we convey a positive feeling to this person. Another researcher has confirmed something most of us discovered long ago, that looking directly at a person, smiling, and leaning toward him or her conveys a feeling of warmth.

Facial Expression

The face is probably the most expressive part of the human body. It can reveal complex and often confusing kinds of information. It commands attention because it is visible and omnipresent. It can move from signs of ecstasy to signs of despair in less than a second. Research results suggest that there are ten basic classes of meaning that can be communicated facially: happiness, surprise, fear, anger, sadness, disgust, contempt, interest, bewilderment, and determination. Research has also shown that the face may communicate information other than the emotional state of the person—it may reveal the thought processes as well. In addition, it has been shown that we are capable of facially conveying not just a single emotional state but multiple emotions at the same time. . . .

Eye Contact

A great deal can be conveyed through the eyes. If we seek feedback from another person, we usually maintain strong eye contact. We can open and close communication channels with our eyes as well. Think of a conversation involving more than two people. . . .

The Body

The body reinforces facial communication. But gestures, postures, and other body movements can also communicate attitudes. They can reveal differences in status, and they can also indicate the presence of deception. With respect to attitudes, as noted previously, body movements also reveal feelings of liking between people.

According to some investigators, a person who wants to be perceived as warm should shift his or her posture toward the other person, smile, maintain direct eye contact, and keep the hands still. People who are cold tend to look around, slump, drum their fingers, and, generally, refrain from smiling. . . .

Personal Appearance

Even if we believe the cliché that beauty is only skin-deep, we must recognize that not only does our personal appearance have a profound effect on our self-image, but it also affects our behavior and the behavior of people around us. Our physical appearance provides a basis for first and sometimes long-lasting impressions. . . .

Weaver, *Understanding Interpersonal Communication.*

EXERCISE 2-8

DIRECTIONS: Complete this exercise after you have preread the selection titled "Types of Nonverbal Cues." For each item, indicate whether the statement is true or false by marking "T" or "F" in the space provided.

_____ 1. Spatial cues refer to the manner and posture in which we sit or stand.

_____ 2. Nonverbal communication is sometimes ambiguous or unclear.

_____ 3. The social distance is used for nonpersonal conversations.

_____ 4. Voices are slightly louder and higher pitched in the intimate distance.

_____ 5. The distance in which people are farthest apart is the social distance.

_____ 6. Hands are the most expressive part of the body.

_____ 7. The author discusses four types of distance.

_____ 8. Personal distance can affect the behavior of other people.

_____ 9. Visual cues are provided by facial expression, eye contact, personal appearance, and body movement.

_____ 10. Gesture and posture provide important nonverbal cues.

Did you score 80 percent or higher on the exercise? You may have noticed that it did not test you on specific facts and details. Rather, the questions provided a fairly accurate measure of your recall of the _main ideas_ of the selection. If you scored 80 percent or above, your prereading was successful because it acquainted you with most of the major ideas contained in the selection.

This exercise suggests that prereading provides you with a great deal of information about the overall content of the article before you read it. It allows you to become familiar with the main ideas and acquaints you with the basic structure of the material.

Adapting Prereading to Various Types of Materials

If the key to becoming a flexible reader lies in adapting techniques to fit the material and your learning style, the key to successful prereading is the same. You must adjust the way you preread to the type of material you are working with. A few suggestions to help you make these adjustments are summarized in Table 2.5.

Table 2.5 How to Adjust Prereading to the Material

Type of Material	Special Features to Consider
Textbooks	Title and subtitle Preface Table of contents Appendix Glossary
Textbook chapters	Summary Vocabulary list Review and discussion questions
Articles and essays	Title Introductory paragraphs Concluding paragraphs
Articles without headings	First sentences of paragraphs
Tests and exams	Instructions and directions Number of items Types of questions Point distribution
Internet Web site	Title Features listed on home page Links Sponsor

Why Prereading Is Effective

Prereading is effective because it

1. **Helps you become interested and involved with what you will read.**
2. **Gives you basic information about the organization and content of the article.**
3. **Focuses your attention on the content of the article.**
4. **Allows you to read somewhat faster because the material is familiar.**
5. **Provides you with a mental outline of the material.** You can anticipate the sequence of ideas, see relationships among topics, and follow the author's direction of thought. Also, reading becomes a process of completing or expanding the outline by identifying supporting details.

EXERCISE 2-9

DIRECTIONS: Working with another student, choose three of the materials from the following list. Discuss how you would adapt your prereading technique to suit the material.

1. a front-page newspaper article
2. a poem
3. a short story
4. a mathematics textbook
5. a newspaper editorial or letter to the editor
6. a new edition of your college catalog
7. a sales brochure from a local department store

EXERCISE 2-10

DIRECTIONS: Select a chapter from one of your textbooks and preread it, using the guidelines included in this chapter. Then answer the following questions.

Textbook title:_____

Chapter title:_____

1. What general subject does the chapter discuss?

    _____

2. How does the textbook author approach or divide the subject?

    _____

3. What special features does the chapter contain to aid you in learning the content of the chapter?

    _____

4. What are the major topics discussed in this chapter?

    _____

Predicting

When you see a movie preview, you make a number of judgments and predictions. You think about what the film will be about, how it will achieve its cinematic goals, and whether or not you want to see it. To do this, you anticipate or make predictions based on the preview. For example,

you may predict that the film will be violent and frightening or senti-
mental and romantic. You might also predict how the film will develop or
how it will end. You use your life experience and your experience with
other films to make those predictions.

Prereading is similar to watching a film preview. After prereading you
should be able to make predictions about the content and organization of the
material and make connections with what you already know about the topic.

Making Predictions

Predictions are educated guesses about the material to be read. For
example, you might predict an essay's focus, a chapter's method of development, or the key points to be presented within a chapter section. Table 2.6
presents examples of predictions that may be made.

You make predictions based on your experience with written language,
your background knowledge, and your familiarity with the subject. As you
work through remaining chapters in this text, you will become more
familiar with the organization of written materials, and your ability to
make predictions will improve.

To get started making predictions, keep the following questions in mind:

- What clues does the author give?
- What will this material be about?
- What logically would follow?
- How could this be organized?

**EXERCISE
2-11**

DIRECTIONS: Predict the content or organization of each of the following
textbook chapter headings taken from a sociology textbook.

1. Inequality in the United States

_____

_____

2. Nontraditional Marital and Family Lifestyles

_____

_____

3. The Development of Religious Movements

_____

_____

Table 2.6   Sample Predictions

Title	Prediction
Highlights of Marketing Research History	An overview of the history of market research will be presented.
Why Do Hot Dogs Come in Packs of Ten?	Packaging of products and profitability will be discussed.
A Sample Fast-Food Promotional Plan	A fast-food chain will be used as an example to show how fast-food restaurants promote (sell) their products.

Opening Sentence	Prediction
Marketers have been the objects of criticism from several consumer groups as well as from governmental agencies.	The section will discuss consumer groups' objections first, then governmental objections.
The situations and problems consumers face directly influence their purchasing behavior.	The section will give examples of situations and problems and explain why or how purchasing behavior is affected.
The key to determining a product's demand is the estimation of the total market and its anticipated share.	The section will explain this process.

4. Education and Change in the 1980s

_____

_____

5. The Automobile, the Assembly Line, and Social Change

_____

_____

6. Health Care Systems in Other Countries

_____

_____

7. Computers in the Schools

_____

_____

8. Sociology and the Other Sciences

_____

_____

9. The Consequences of Sexual Inequality

_____

_____

10. What Is Religion?

_____

_____ ▬

Making Connections

Once you have preread an assignment and predicted its content and organization, an important next step is to call to mind what you already know about the subject. Do this by making connections between the material to be read and your background knowledge and experience.

There are several reasons for making such connections:

1. **Learning occurs more easily if you can relate new information to information already stored.**

2. **Tasks become more interesting and meaningful if you can connect them to your own experience or to a subject you have already learned.**

3. **Material is easier to learn if it is familiar and meaningful.** For example, it is easier to learn a list of real words (sat, tar, can) than a list of nonsense syllables (sar, taf, cag). Similarly, it is easier to learn basic laws of economics if you have examples from your experience with which to associate them.

Search your previous knowledge and experience for ideas or information that you can connect the new material to in an assignment. You might think of this process as tying a mental string between already stored information and new information. As you pull out or recall old information you will find that you also recall new information.

Here are a few examples of the kinds of connections students have made:

- "This chapter section is titled Stages of Adulthood—it should be interesting to see which one I'm in and which my parents are in."

- "I'll be reading about types of therapy for treating mental problems. I remember hearing about the group therapy sessions my aunt attended after her divorce. . . ."

- "This chapter is titled "Genetics"—I wonder if it will discuss chromosome mapping or sickle-cell anemia."

To draw on your prior knowledge and experience for less familiar subjects, think about the subject using one of the following techniques:

1. **Ask as many questions as you can about the topic, and attempt to answer them.**
2. **Divide the subject into as many features or subtopics as possible.**
3. **Free-associate or write down anything that comes to mind related to the topic.**

Each of these techniques is demonstrated in Figure 2.1. Although the results differ, each technique forces you to think, draw from your experience, and focus your attention.

FIGURE 2.1 Techniques for activating your knowledge.

Topic: The Immune System	
Technique	Demonstration
Asking questions	How does the immune system work? What does it do? What happens when it does not work? Are there other diseases, similar to AIDS, yet undiscovered? Does stress affect the immune system? Does diet affect the immune system?
Dividing into subtopics	Diseases of immune system Operation Functions Effects Limitations
Free association	The immune system protects the body from disease and infection. It attacks body invaders and destroys them. When illness occurs the immune system has failed. AIDS is a disease affecting the immune system. Stress may affect the body's defenses.

Which technique you use depends on the subject matter you are working with and on your learning style. Dividing a subject into subtopics may *not* work well for an essay in philosophy but may be effective for reading about television programming. Likewise, free association may work well for a creative learner, while dividing into subtopics may be more effective for a more pragmatic learner.

DIRECTIONS: Assume you have preread a chapter in a sociology text on domestic violence. Discover what you already know about domestic violence by writing a list of questions about the topic.

DIRECTIONS:

STEP 1: Preread one of the readings at the end of the chapter. Activate your previous knowledge and experience by

1. dividing the subject into subtopics.
2. writing a list of questions about the topic.
3. writing for two minutes about the topic, recording whatever comes to mind.

STEP 2: Evaluate the techniques used in Step 1 by answering the following questions:

1. Which technique seemed most effective? Why?
2. Might your choice of technique be influenced by the subject matter with which you are working?
3. Did you discover you knew more about the topic than you initially thought?

DIRECTIONS: Connect each of the following headings, taken from a psychology text, with your own knowledge or experience. Discuss or summarize what you already know about each subject.

1. Pain and Its Control
2. Television and Aggressive Behavior
3. Problems of Aging
4. Sources of Stress
5. Eating Disorders

**EXERCISE
2-15**

ELECTRONIC
APPLICATION

DIRECTIONS: Locate a Web site for one of the following:

1. a college or university
2. a newspaper
3. a radio station or television network

Preview the site, and write a list of what you think the site offers.

Developing Guide Questions

When you order a hamburger, go to the bank, or make a phone call, you have a specific purpose in mind. In fact, most of your daily activities are purposeful; you do things for specific reasons to accomplish some goal.

Reading should also be a purposeful activity. Before you begin reading any article, selection, or chapter, you should know what you want to accomplish by reading it. Your purpose should vary with the situation. You might read a magazine article on child abuse to learn more about the extent of the problem. You may read a sociology text chapter to locate facts and figures about the causes, effects, and extent of child abuse. Your purpose for reading should be as specific as possible. One of the best ways to develop specific purposes is to form guide questions.

How to Develop Guide Questions

Guide questions can be formed by turning the chapter or essay titles and headings into questions that you try to answer as you read. For instance, for a chapter from a sociology text titled "Methods of Studying Society," you could ask, "What are the methods of studying society?" As you read the chapter, look for the answer. Here are a few other titles or headings and questions that you might ask:

Title:	Our Ten Contributions to Civilization
Question:	What are our ten contributions to civilization?
Title:	Bringing Science Under the Law
Questions:	How can science be brought under the law?
	Why should science be brought under the law?
Heading:	Unequal Distribution of Income
Question:	Why is income unequally distributed?

Heading: The Life Cycle of Social Problems
Questions: What are the stages in the life cycle of social problems?
                What social problems have a life cycle?

Heading: The Development of the Women's Movement
Questions: How did the women's movement develop?
                Why did it develop?

Asking the Right Guide Questions

To put guide questions to their best use, you must ask the right questions. Questions that begin with *what, why,* or *how* are useful because they usually require you to think or to consolidate information and ideas. Questions that begin with *who, when,* or *where* are less useful because they can often be answered in a word or two; they often refer to a specific fact or detail rather than to larger ideas or concepts. For a section titled "Treatment for Drug Abuse Conditions" you could ask, "Where does treatment take place?" or, "Who is treated for drug abuse?" Most likely these questions would not lead you to the main point of the section. However, a question such as "How is drug abuse treated?" would focus your attention on the main topic discussed.

EXERCISE 2-16

DIRECTIONS: For each of the following titles or headings, write a guide question that would be useful in guiding your reading of the material.

1. We Ask the Wrong Questions about Crime

   _____

2. The Constitution: New Challenges

   _____

3. Political Party Functions

   _____

4. The Thinking of Men and Machines

   _____

5. Ghana and Zimbabwe—A Study in Contrasts

   _____

6. Magnetic Fields and Lines of Force

_____

7. Comparing X-Rays and Visible Light

_____

DIRECTIONS: Select a chapter from one of your textbooks that you are about to read. Write a guide question for each title and major heading. After you have used these questions to guide your reading, identify the weak questions and rephrase them in a way that would have been more useful to you.

Critical Thinking Tip #2

Developing a Questioning Mind-Set

Guide questions help you identify what is important to learn and remember, but they are not the only type of questions you should ask. It is also useful to ask critical questions—questions that will help you analyze and interpret what you read. Here are a few critical questions that will help you develop a questioning mind-set.

1. What does the writer expect me to understand or believe after reading this?

2. What is the writer leading up to? (What ideas will come next?)

3. How much and what kind of evidence does the writer offer in support of his or her ideas?

4. Why is this idea important?

5. How does this information fit with other things I'm learning?

6. How can I use this information?

Summary

1. What is involved in reading and learning actively?

Reading and learning actively means becoming engaged in the material you are reading and studying. It involves the activities of reading, thinking, predicting, connecting, focusing your concentration, and assessing your performance.

2. What does active reading mean?

Active reading is a process of staying focused on the material you are reading before, during, and after reading it. It means participating consciously and directly in the reading process.

3. What academic thinking skills do your instructors expect you to possess?

Your instructors expect you to function at six different levels of thinking. They not only expect you to work with ideas that involve:

- Remembering—recalling information or facts
- Understanding—grasping the meaning of facts
- Applying—using knowledge in new situations
- Analyzing—seeing relationships among ideas and how things work
- Evaluating—making judgments about ideas
- Creating—putting ideas together to form something new

4. How can you improve your concentration?

Concentration can be improved by controlling external distractions and increasing your attention span.

5. What is the purpose of comprehension monitoring?

Comprehension monitoring helps you keep track of your comprehension while reading. By recognizing positive and negative comprehension signals, you will be aware of your level of comprehension and will be able to correct incomplete comprehension.

6. Why are prereading and predicting useful activities?

Prereading allows you to become familiar with the organization and content of the material before reading it, providing you with a "road map" to guide you through the material. Predicting helps you to discover what you already know about a topic and to connect this with the material to be read.

7. How are guide questions helpful?

Guide questions enable you to establish purposes for reading. They focus your attention and improve your retention.

8. What is involved in learning actively?

Learning actively involves an awareness of your level of concentration and your particular learning style. You can improve your concentration by controlling external distractions and increasing your attention span. Assessing your learning style will not only help you see how you learn best but can help you build an action plan for more effective learning.

READING SELECTION 3
POLITICAL SCIENCE

PROFILE OF A TERRORIST
Cindy C. Combs
From *Terrorism in the Twenty-First Century*

This political science textbook excerpt discusses the problem of terrorism. Activate your thinking by prereading and answering the following questions.

1. *Are all terrorists alike? Do they have similar motives?*
2. *What can we learn about terrorists that will enable us to defend ourselves against them?*

Nothing is easier than to denounce the evil doer; nothing is more difficult than to understand him.
—Fyodor Dostoyevsky

1   Why do people become terrorists? Are they crazy? Are they thrill seekers? Are they religious fanatics? Are they ideologues? Is there any way to tell who is likely to become a terrorist?

2   This final question provides a clue as to why political scientists and government officials are particularly interested in the psychological factors relating to terrorism. If one could identify the traits most closely related to a willingness to use terrorist tactics, then one would be in a better position to predict, and prevent, the emergence of terrorist groups.

Three Types of Terrorists

3   Unfortunately, identifying such traits is not easy. Just as not all violence is terrorism, and not all revolutionaries are terrorists, not all persons who commit acts of terrorism are alike. Frederick Hacker suggested three categories of persons who commit terrorism: *crazies, criminals,* and *crusaders.* He notes that an individual carrying out a terrorist act is seldom "purely" one type or the other but that each type offers some insights into why an individual will resort to terrorism.

4   Understanding the individual who commits terrorism is vital, not only for humanitarian reasons, but also to decide how best to deal with those individuals *while they are engaged in terrorist acts.* From a law enforcement perspective, for example, it is important to appreciate the difference between a criminal and a crusading terrorist involved in a hostage-taking situation. Successful resolution of such a situation often hinges on understanding the mind of the individual perpetrating the crime.

5   Let us consider the three categories of terrorists suggested by Hacker: crazies, criminals, and crusaders. For the purposes of this study, we need to establish loose descriptions of these three types. Hacker offers some useful ideas on what is subsumed under each label. **Crazies,** he suggest, are *emotionally disturbed individuals who are driven to commit terrorism "by reasons of their own that often do not make sense to anybody else."*

6   **Criminals,** on the other hand, *perform terrorist acts for more easily understood reasons: personal gain.* Such individuals transgress the laws of society knowingly and, one assumes, in full pos-

session of their faculties. Both their motives and their goals are usually clear, if still deplorable, to most of humanity.

7   This is not the case with the crusaders. These individuals commit terrorism for reasons that are often unclear both to themselves and to those witnessing the acts. Their ultimate goals are frequently even less understandable. Although such individuals are usually idealistically inspired, their idealism tends to be a rather mixed bag of half-understood philosophies. **Crusaders,** according to Hacker, *seek not personal gain, but prestige and power for a collective cause.* They commit terrorist acts in the belief "that they are serving a higher cause," in Hacker's assessment.

8   The distinction between criminals and crusaders with respect to terrorism needs some clarification. Clearly, when anyone breaks the law, as in the commission of a terrorist act, he or she becomes a criminal, regardless of the reason for the transgression. The distinction between criminal and crusader, though, is useful in understanding the differences in the motives and goals moving the person to commit the act.

A Trend Toward Crusaders

9   The majority of the individuals and groups carrying out terrorist acts in the world in the last decade of the twentieth and the beginning of the twenty-first century have been crusaders. This does not mean that there are not occasional instances in which individuals who, reacting to some real or perceived injury, decide to take a machine gun to the target of their anger or kidnap or destroy anyone in sight. Nor does it mean that there are not individual criminals and criminal organizations that engage in terrorist activities.

10   Nonetheless, the majority of individuals who commit modern terrorism are, or perceive themselves to be, crusaders. According to Hacker, the typical crusading terrorist appears to be normal, no matter how crazy his or her cause or how criminal the means he or she uses for their cause

may seem. He or she is neither an idiot nor a fool, neither a coward nor a weakling. Instead, the crusading terrorist is frequently a professional, well trained, well prepared, and well disciplined in the habit of blind obedience to a cause.

Negotiating with Terrorists

11 Table A indicates a few dramatic differences between the types of terrorists Hacker profiles. One is that crusaders are the least likely to negotiate a resolution to a crisis, both because such action can be viewed as a betrayal of a sublime cause and because there is little that the negotiator can offer, because neither personal gain nor safe passage out of the situation are particularly desired by true crusaders. Belief in the cause makes death not a penalty, but a path to reward and glory; therefore, the threat of death and destruction can have litter punitive value. What can a police or military negotiator offer to a crusader to induce the release of hostages or the defusing of a bomb?

12 In terms of security devices and training, the profiles become even more vital. The events of September 11, 2001, illustrate dramatically the consequences of training and equipping for the wrong type of perpetrators. The pilots of airlines in the United States had been trained to respond to attempts to take over flights as hostage situations and thus were engaged in trying to keep the situation calm and to "talk down" the plane, to initiate a hostage release without violence. But the individuals engaged in the takeover were crusaders, not criminals or crazies, who did not plan to live through the incidents. Only the passengers on the flight that crashed in Pennsylvania were able to offer substantial resistance—perhaps in part because they had not been trained to assume that a peaceful resolution could be negotiated with hostage takers.

13 This does not suggest that the pilots and crew were not vigilant and did not make every effort to save the lives of the passengers. But because the profile they had been trained to respond to did not match that with which they were confronted, they were unable to respond successfully to the demands of the situation. Thus, inaccurate profiling in pilot training was a serious contributing factor to the sequence of events on that day.

14 To political scientists, as will as to military, police, and other security an intelligence units

Table A Hacker's Typology of Terrorists

Type of Terrorist	Motive/Goal	Willing to Negotiate?	Expectation of Survival
Crazy	Clear only to perpetrator	Possible, but only if negotiator can understand motive and offer hope/understanding	Strong, but not based on reality
Criminal	Personal gain/profit	Usually, in return for profit and/or safe passage	Strong
Crusader	"Higher cause" usually (a blend of religious and political)	Seldom, because to do so could be seen as a betrayal of the cause	Minimal, because death offers reward in an afterlife

assigned the task of coping with terrorism, an understanding of the type of person likely to commit acts of terrorism is invaluable. As our understanding of a phenomenon increases, our ability to predict its behavior with some accuracy also increases. Thus, as we try to understand who terrorists are and what they are like, we should increase our ability to anticipate their behavior patterns, thereby increasing our ability to respond effectively and to prevent more often the launching of successful terrorist attacks.

═══════════

Examining Reading Selection 3

Checking Your Vocabulary

Directions: Using context, word parts, or a dictionary if necessary, circle the letter of the meaning for each word as it is used in the reading.

1. resolution (paragraph 4)
   a. conflicting opinion
   b. unpopular action
   c. satisfactory conclusion
   d. disagreeable situation

2. subsumed (paragraph 5)
   a. emphasized
   b. included
   c. determined
   d. regarded

3. perceive (paragraph 10)
   a. oppose
   b. detract
   c. wonder about
   d. think of

4. betrayal (paragraph 11)
   a. going against a promise
   b. revealing information
   c. discovering the truth
   d. opposing action

5. vigilant (paragraph 13)
   a. watchful and alert
   b. considerate and caring
   c. assertive and forceful
   d. oppressive and hateful

Checking Your Comprehension

Directions: Circle the letter of the best answer.

6. This reading is primarily concerned with
   a. causes of terrorism.
   b. ways to prevent terrorism.
   c. types of terrorists.
   d. the September 11th terrorist attacks.

7. The main point of this reading is that
   a. nothing can be done to control terrorism.
   b. the September 11th terrorist attacks should have been handled differently.
   c. crusader terrorists are more dangerous than criminal terrorists.
   d. Understanding and classifying terrorists may improve our ability to respond effectively to their attacks.

8. The author states that
   a. crusader terrorists are unlikely to be interested in negotiating.
   b. criminal terrorists have no known motives.
   c. the motives of terrorists are always easily understood by everyone involved.
   d. criminal organizations are never involved in terrorist activities.

9. Crusader terrorists
   a. do not regard death as a penalty.
   b. are poorly trained.
   c. are willing to listen to alternatives.
   d. seek personal gain.

10. According to the selection, the pilots in the September 11th attacks
    a. should have been more vigilant.
    b. should have recognized they were dealing with criminals.
    c. did not offer the terrorists acceptable alternatives.
    d. did not understand the type of terrorists they were dealing with.

11. The most important distinction between a criminal and a crusader is one of
    a. ethnic origin.
    b. funding.
    c. motive.
    d. damage.

Thinking Critically

12. The author is most likely to agree with which one of the following approaches to dealing with terrorists?
    a. placing weapons in the cockpit of all aircraft.
    b. decreasing airport surveillance.
    c. using large sums of money to encourage terrorists to retreat.
    d. training pilots to deal with crusader terrorists.

13. The tone of the article can best be described as
    a. distraught.
    b. imposing.
    c. frightening.
    d. analytical.

14. The author refers to the events of September 11th to
    a. show a practical application of creating profiles of terrorists.
    b. emphasize to terrorists that we understand their motives.
    c. reveal that the United States is ready to respond to future terrorist attacks.
    d. discourage future terrorist attacks within the United States.

15. Which one of the following can be inferred from the selection?
    a. The author believes that the risk of terrorism will decrease in the next decade.
    b. The author regards crusaders are the most difficult type to deal with.
    c. The author considers the United States to be the most vulnerable target for crusader terrorists.
    d. The author is opposed to negotiating with terrorists.

Questions for Discussion

1. Recall recent terrorist attacks that have occurred. What type of terrorist was responsible?

2. What further steps, beyond pilot training, need to be taken to curtail attacks by crusaders?

3. Was Hitler a terrorist? If so, what kind? Think of other historical figures or events that involved terrorism.

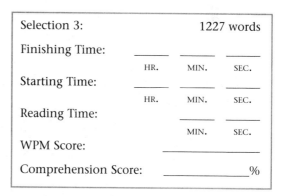

Selection 3:		1227 words
Finishing Time:		
	HR. MIN.	SEC.
Starting Time:		
	HR. MIN.	SEC.
Reading Time:		
	MIN.	SEC.
WPM Score:		
Comprehension Score:		%

READING SELECTION 4

LITERATURE: ESSAY

JUST WALK ON BY: A BLACK MAN PONDERS HIS POWER TO ALTER PUBLIC SPACE

Brent Staples

From *Harper's* magazine

Brent Staples, a well-known black writer, describes how others respond to him in a variety of situations. Activate prereading and then read the essay to answer the following questions.

1. *What stereotypes exist for black males?*
2. *How did Staples confront and overcome these stereotypes?*

— · —

1   My first victim was a woman—white, well dressed, probably in her early twenties. I came upon her late one evening on a deserted street in Hyde Park, a relatively affluent neighborhood in an otherwise mean, impoverished section of Chicago. As I swung onto the avenue behind her, there seemed to be a discreet, uninflammatory distance between us. Not so. She cast back a worried glance. To her, the youngish black man—a broad six feet two inches with a beard and billowing hair, both hands shoved into the pockets of a bulky military jacket—seemed menacingly close. After a few more quick glimpses, she picked up her pace and was soon running in earnest. Within seconds she disappeared into a cross street.

2   That was more than a decade ago. I was twenty-two years old, a graduate student newly arrived at the University of Chicago. It was in the echo of that terrified woman's footfalls that I first began to know the unwieldy inheritance I'd come into—the ability to alter public space in ugly ways. It was clear that she thought herself the quarry of a mugger, a rapist, or worse. Suffering a bout of insomnia, however, I was stalking sleep, not defenseless wayfarers. As a softy who is scarcely able to take a knife to a raw chicken—let alone hold it to a person's throat—I was surprised, embarrassed, and dismayed all at once. Her flight made me feel like an accomplice in tyranny. It also made it clear that I was indistinguishable from the muggers who occasionally seeped into the area from the surrounding ghetto. That first encounter, and those that followed, signified that a vast, unnerving gulf lay between nighttime pedestrians—particularly women—and me. And I soon gathered that being perceived as dangerous is a hazard in itself. I only needed to turn a corner into a dicey situation, or crowd some frightened, armed person in a foyer somewhere, or make an errant move after being pulled over by a policeman. Where fear and weapons meet—and they often do in urban America—there is always the possibility of death.

3   In that first year, my first away from my hometown, I was to become thoroughly familiar with the language of fear. At dark, shadowy intersections in Chicago, I could cross in front of a car stopped at a traffic light and elicit the *thunk, thunk, thunk, thunk* of the driver—black, white, male, or female—hammering down the door locks. On less traveled streets after dark, I grew accustomed to but never comfortable with people who crossed to the other side of the street rather than pass me. Then there were the standard unpleasantries with police, doormen, bouncers, cab drivers, and others whose business it is to screen out troublesome individuals *before* there is any nastiness.

4   I moved to New York nearly two years ago and I have remained an avid night walker. In central

Manhattan, the near-constant crowd cover minimizes tense one-on-one street encounters. Elsewhere—visiting friends in SoHo, where sidewalks are narrow and tightly spaced buildings shut out the sky—things can get very taut indeed.

5   Black men have a firm place in New York mugging literature. Norman Podhoretz in his famed (or infamous) 1963 essay, "My Negro Problem—And Ours," recalls growing up in terror of black males; they "were tougher than we were, more ruthless," he writes—and as an adult on the Upper West Side of Manhattan, he continues, he cannot constrain his nervousness when he meets black men on certain streets. Similarly, a decade later, the essayist and novelist Edward Hoagland extols a New York where once "Negro bitterness bore down mainly on other Negroes." Where some see mere panhandlers, Hoagland sees "a mugger who is clearly screwing up his nerve to do more than just *ask* for money." But Hoagland has "the New Yorker's quick-hunch posture for broken-field maneuvering," and the bad guy swerves away.

6   I often witness that "hunch posture," from women after dark on the warrenlike streets of Brooklyn where I live. They seem to set their faces on neutral and, with their purse straps strung across their chests bandolier style, they forge ahead as though bracing themselves against being tackled. I understand, of course, that the danger they perceive is not a hallucination. Women are particularly vulnerable to street violence, and young black males are drastically overrepresented among the perpetrators of that violence. Yet these truths are no solace against the kind of alienation that comes of being ever the suspect, against being set apart, a fearsome entity with whom pedestrians avoid making eye contact.

7   It is not altogether clear to me how I reached the ripe old age of twenty-two without being conscious of the lethality nighttime pedestrians attributed to me. Perhaps it was because in Chester, Pennsylvania, the small, angry industrial town where I came of age in the 1960s, I was

scarcely noticeable against a backdrop of gang warfare, street knifings, and murders. I grew up one of the good boys, had perhaps a half-dozen fist fights. In retrospect, my shyness of combat has clear sources.

8   Many things go into the making of a young thug. One of those things is the consummation of the male romance with the power to intimidate. An infant discovers that random flailings send the baby bottle flying out of the crib and crashing to the floor. Delighted, the joyful babe repeats those motions again and again, seeking to duplicate the feat. Just so, I recall the points at which some of my boyhood friends were finally seduced by the perception of themselves as tough guys. When a mark cowered and surrendered his money without resistance, myth and reality merged—and paid off. It is, after all, only manly to embrace the power to frighten and intimidate. We, as men, are not supposed to give an inch of our lane on the highway; we are to seize the fighter's edge in work and in play and even in love; we are to be valiant in the face of hostile forces.

9   Unfortunately, poor and powerless young men seem to take all this nonsense literally. As a boy, I saw countless tough guys locked away; I have since buried several, too. They were babies, really—a teenage cousin, a brother of twenty-two, a childhood friend in his mid-twenties—all gone down in episodes of bravado played out in the streets. I came to doubt the virtues of intimidation early on. I chose, perhaps even unconsciously, to remain a shadow—timid, but a survivor.

10   The fearsomeness mistakenly attributed to me in public places often has a perilous flavor. The most frightening of these confusions occurred in the late 1970s and early 1980s when I worked as a journalist in Chicago. One day, rushing into the office of a magazine I was writing for with a deadline story in hand, I was mistaken for a burglar. The office manager called security and, with an ad hoc posse, pursued me through the labyrinthine halls, nearly to my editor's door. I had no way of proving who I was. I could only

move briskly toward the company of someone who knew me.

11   Another time I was on assignment for a local paper and killing time before an interview. I entered a jewelry store on the city's affluent Near North Side. The proprietor excused herself and returned with an enormous red Doberman pinscher straining at the end of a leash. She stood, the dog extended toward me, silent to my questions, her eyes bulging nearly out of her head. I took a cursory look around, nodded, and bade her good night. Relatively speaking, however, I never fared as badly as another black male journalist. He went to nearby Waukegan, Illinois, a couple of summers ago to work on a story about a murderer who was born there. Mistaking the reporter for the killer, police hauled him from his car at gunpoint and but for his press credentials would probably have tried to book him. Such episodes are not uncommon. Black men trade tales like this all the time.

12   In "My Negro Problem—And Ours," Podhoretz writes that the hatred he feels for blacks makes itself known to him through a variety of avenues—one being his discomfort with that "special brand of paranoid touchiness" to which he says blacks are prone. No doubt he is speaking here of black men. In time, I learned to smother the rage I felt at so often being taken for a criminal. Not to do so would surely have led to madness—via that special "paranoid touchiness" that so annoyed Podhoretz at the time he wrote the essay.

13   I began to take precautions to make myself less threatening. I move about with care, particularly late in the evening. I give a wide berth to nervous people on subway platforms during the wee hours, particularly when I have exchanged business clothes for jeans. If I happen to be entering a building behind some people who appear skittish, I may walk by, letting them clear the lobby before I return, so as not to seem to be following them. I have been calm and extremely congenial on those rare occasions when I've been pulled over by the police.

14   And on late-evening constitutionals along streets less traveled by, I employ what has proved to be an excellent tension-reducing measure: I whistle melodies from Beethoven and Vivaldi and the more popular classical composers. Even steely New Yorkers hunching toward nighttime destinations seem to relax, and occasionally they even join in the tune. Virtually everybody seems to sense that a mugger wouldn't be warbling bright, sunny selections from Vivaldi's *Four Seasons*. It is my equivalent of the cowbell that hikers wear when they know they are in bear country.

Writing about Reading Selection 4*

Checking Your Vocabulary

Directions: Complete each of the following items; refer to a dictionary if necessary.

1. Discuss the connotative meanings of the word *victim* (paragraph 1).

2. Define each of the following words:
   a. errant (paragraph 2)

   _____

   _____

   b. elicit (paragraph 3)

   _____

---

* Multiple-choice questions are contained in Part 6 (page 576)

c. perilous (paragraph 10)

_____

d. cursory (paragraph 11)

_____

e. congenial (paragraph 13)

_____

3. Define the word *alienation* (paragraph 6) and underline the word or phrase that provides a context clue for its meaning.

_____

_____

4. Define the word *episodes* (paragraph 11) and underline the word or phrase that provides a context clue for its meaning.

_____

_____

5. Determine the meanings of the following words by using word parts:
   a. uninflammatory (paragraph 1)

_____

   b. unwieldy (paragraph 2)

_____

   c. unpleasantries (paragraph 3)

_____

   d. overrepresented (paragraph 6)

_____

   e. lethality (paragraph 7)

_____

_____

Checking Your Comprehension

6. Sumzmarize the problem the author is describing.

_____

_____

_____

7. Why was Staples unaware of this problem until the age of 22?

_____

8. In what sense does Staples use the word *victim*? In what sense is Staples himself a "victim"?

_____

_____

_____

_____

_____

_____

_____

_____

9. How has Staples altered his behavior in public?

_____

_____

_____

Thinking Critically

1. Discuss the meaning of the title. How does Staples alter public space? How has it affected his life?

   _____

   _____

   _____

   _____

   _____

   _____

   _____

   _____

2. Discuss Staples' attitude toward his "victims." Does he perceive them as rational or irrational? Is he sympathetic? angry?

   _____

   _____

   _____

   _____

Questions for Discussion

1. In what other situations can an individual alter public space?

2. What is your opinion of the behavior of Staples' "victims"?

3. Do you feel Staples should have altered his behavior in public? Would you do the same?

4. After reading only the first paragraph, what did you think was happening?

Selection 4:			1645 words
Finishing Time:	_____	_____	_____
	HR.	MIN.	SEC.
Starting Time:	_____	_____	_____
	HR.	MIN.	SEC.
Reading Time:		_____	_____
		MIN.	SEC.
WPM Score:		_____	
Comprehension Score:		_____%	

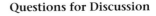 GO ELECTRONIC

For additional readings, exercises, and Internet activities, visit this book's Web site at:

http://www.ablongman.com/mcwhorter

For even more activities, visit the Longman English pages at:

http://www.ablongman.com/englishpages

If you need a user name and password, please see your instructor.

Take a Road Trip to Bourbon Street, New Orleans
Be sure to visit the Active Reading module on your Reading Road Trip CD-ROM for multimedia tutorials, exercises, and tests.

CHAPTER 3

Strengthening Your Word Power

IN THIS CHAPTER YOU WILL LEARN:

1. To expand your vocabulary.
2. To determine a word's meaning from its context.
3. To use word parts to figure out meanings of new words.
4. How the index card system can expand your vocabulary.
5. How to select and use the best vocabulary reference sources.

Are you constantly looking for new words that can expand your vocabulary? To provoke your "word awareness," try the following quiz. Answer each item as either true or false.

_____ 1. There are 135 different meanings for the word *run*.

_____ 2. If you read an unfamiliar word in a textbook, the first thing you should do is look it up in the dictionary.

_____ 3. If *psycho* means mind and *-osis* means diseased or abnormal condition, then a psychosis is a disease of the mind.

_____ 4. Memorizing a list is the most effective way to learn new vocabulary.

_____ 5. An unabridged dictionary is more complete than a pocket dictionary.

_____ 6. If you were taking a psychology course and were having difficulty distinguishing between the terms *drive* and *motive*, the most detailed reference source to consult would be a collegiate dictionary.

_____ 7. The statement, "as the crow flies," means to flap one's wings like a crow.

73

Now, check your answers on page 75.

These questions illustrate important topics covered in this chapter: expanding your vocabulary, using context to determine the meaning of unfamiliar words, using word parts to analyze word meanings, systems for learning new vocabulary, using reference sources, and understanding idioms.

Expanding Your Vocabulary

Your vocabulary can be one of your strongest assets or one of your greatest liabilities. It defines and describes you by revealing a great deal about your level of education and your experience. Your vocabulary contributes significantly to that all-important first impression people form when they meet you.

A strong vocabulary provides both immediate academic benefits and long-term career effects. This portion of the chapter offers numerous suggestions for directing and developing your vocabulary so that it becomes one of your most valuable assets.

Read Widely and Diversely

One of the best ways to improve your vocabulary is to read widely and diversely, sampling many subjects and styles of writing. Through reading you encounter new words as well as new uses for already familiar words. You may also notice words used in contexts in which you had never thought of them being used.

In addition to reading widely, being motivated to expand your vocabulary is critical to dramatically improving it. You must be interested in expanding your vocabulary and willing to spend time and effort working at it. In other words, a powerful vocabulary doesn't just happen; you have to *make* it happen. In each of your courses, you encounter new words each day through reading text assignments and listening to lectures. Now is the ideal time to begin expanding your vocabulary.

Use Words to Remember Them

Regardless of how much time you spend recording and looking up words, most likely you will remember only those you use fairly soon after you learn them. Forgetting occurs rapidly after learning unless you take action to use and remember what you have learned.

Answer Key

1. True. Yes! There are 135 meanings. One way you can expand your vocabulary is to learn additional meanings for already familiar words.

2. False. The first thing you should do is keep reading and try to figure out the word from the way it is used in the sentence (its context), as described in this chapter.

3. True. This item illustrates how knowledge of word parts can help you figure out unfamiliar words. Common word parts are discussed in this chapter.

4. False. List learning is ineffective; this chapter suggests a more effective index card system.

5. True. This chapter describes a variety of dictionaries, each designed for a different purpose.

6. False. A more detailed source is a subject-area dictionary (see p. 102).

7. False. The statement is an idiom. It means to fly in a straight line.

Be Selective

An unabridged (most complete) dictionary lists approximately 600,000 words. But be realistic: you'll never learn them all—no one ever has. Your first task is to decide what to learn—to be selective. Some words are more useful to you than others, depending on a range of factors including your major, your career goals, and your social and recreational preferences. If you are a computer science major and plan to get a job in a major corporation, your effective working vocabulary should be different than if you are a biology major planning a career in genetic research.

Use What You Already Know

Most people think they have one vocabulary and that it is either weak or strong, good or bad. Actually, you have four different vocabulary levels—one each for reading, writing, listening, and speaking. Although they share a common core of basic operational words, they range widely in both size and content. For example, you recognize and understand certain words as you read, but you never use them in your own writing. Similarly, you understand certain words while listening, but you don't use them as part of your speaking vocabulary. Most likely your listening and reading vocabularies are larger than your speaking and writing vocabularies. In other words, you already know a large number of words that you are not using. Read the following list of words. You may know or have heard each word, but you probably do not use them in your own speech or writing.

conform	congeal
congenial	contour
congenital	contrite
contort	cosmopolitan
cosmic	cosmos

You can begin to strengthen your vocabulary by experimenting with words you already know but do not use. Make a point of using one of these words each day, in both speaking and writing.

Work on Vaguely Familiar Words

One of the best groups of words to begin to learn are those that are vaguely familiar—those that you have heard or seen before but cannot precisely or accurately define. These are words that you see regularly but have never felt comfortable using. Such words might include:

polemic	prodigy
pragmatism	profuse
precept	prototype

As you notice these words in your reading or hear them in class lectures, mark them or jot them down in the margin; later check their meanings in a dictionary.

Learn Multiple Word Meanings

When you took the word awareness quiz, were you surprised to learn that the word *run* has a total of 135 meanings? You probably thought of meanings such as to *run* fast, a home *run*, and a *run* in a stocking, but the word has so many meanings that the entry requires nearly an entire dictionary page. You certainly have heard the word used in the following ways: to *run* the store, *run* upstream, *run* a machine, *run* a fever. On the other hand, you may not have known that *run* is a term used in billiards meaning a series of uninterrupted strokes or that in golf, *run* means to cause the ball to roll.

Most words in the English language have more than one meaning. Just open any standard dictionary to any page and glance down one column of words. You will see that more than one meaning is given for most words. Also, you can see that there is considerable opportunity to expand your vocabulary by becoming aware of additional meanings of words you already know.

DIRECTIONS: Each of the following sentences uses a relatively uncommon meaning of the underlined word. After reading each sentence, write a synonym or brief definition of the underlined word. You may need to check a dictionary to locate a precise meaning.

1. Investors should keep at least a portion of their assets <u>fluid</u>.

   _____

2. The speech therapist noted that the child had difficulty with <u>glides</u>.

   _____

   _____

3. The prisoner held a <u>jaundiced</u> view of life.

   _____

4. The two garden hoses could not be connected without a <u>male</u> fitting.

   _____

5. The outcome of the debate was a <u>moral</u> certainty.

   _____

   _____

DIRECTIONS: The Internet offers a variety of vocabulary improvement programs. Do a Web search to discover what online aids to vocabulary improvement are available. Share your findings with your classmates. ▬

Using Contextual Aids

The following tests are intended to demonstrate an important principle of vocabulary development. Before continuing with this section, try these vocabulary tests. Complete *both* tests before checking your answers, which appear in the paragraph following test B. While working on the second test *do not* return to the first test to change any answers.

Test A: Words without Context

Directions: For each item, choose the word that is closest in meaning to the first word. Write the letter of your answer in the space provided.

_____ 1. verbatim
    a. word for word
    b. using verbs
    c. idea by idea
    d. using abbreviations
    e. using an outline

_____ 2. sedentary
    a. very routine
    b. dull and boring
    c. quiet
    d. exciting
    e. involves sitting

_____ 3. thwarted
    a. initiated
    b. blocked
    c. controlled
    d. disagreed
    e. imposed

_____ 4. renounced
    a. gave up
    b. kept
    c. transferred
    d. criticized
    e. applied for

_____ 5. audacity
    a. patience
    b. boldness
    c. good sense
    d. courtesy
    e. understanding

_____ 6. disparaging
    a. encouraging
    b. questioning
    c. sincere
    d. logical
    e. belittling

_____ 7. capricious
    a. changeable
    b. dependable
    c. rational
    d. unusual
    e. puzzling

_____ 8. periphery
    a. outside
    b. focus
    c. inside
    d. edge
    e. middle

_____ 9. indigenous
    a. natural
    b. fertile
    c. native
    d. adaptations
    e. mutations

_____ 10. abject
  a. cruel
  b. low and miserable
  c. frightening

  d. difficult to commit
  e. illogical

Number Correct: _____

Test B: Words in Context

Directions: For each item, choose the word that is closest in meaning to the underlined word. Write the letter of your answer in the space provided.

_____ 1. It is more efficient to take lecture notes in your own words than to try to record the lecture <u>verbatim</u>.
  a. word for word
  b. using verbs
  c. idea by idea
  d. using abbreviations
  e. using an outline

_____ 2. Office work is quite <u>sedentary</u>, while in factory work you are able to move around more.
  a. very routine
  b. dull and boring
  c. quiet
  d. exciting
  e. involves sitting

_____ 3. Joe's parents <u>thwarted</u> his efforts to get a student loan; they refused to cosign for him.
  a. initiated
  b. blocked
  c. controlled
  d. disagreed
  e. imposed

_____ 4. Despite his love of the country, he <u>renounced</u> his citizenship when the war broke out.
  a. gave up
  b. kept
  c. transferred

  d. criticized
  e. applied for

_____ 5. The woman had the <u>audacity</u> to return the dress to the store after wearing it several times.
  a. patience
  b. boldness
  c. good sense
  d. courtesy
  e. understanding

_____ 6. Despite her husband's <u>disparaging</u> remarks, the woman persisted in her efforts to find a full-time job.
  a. encouraging
  b. questioning
  c. sincere
  d. logical
  e. belittling

_____ 7. As evidence of his wife's <u>capricious</u> behavior, the husband described how frequently she shifted from one extreme to another.
  a. changeable
  b. dependable
  c. rational
  d. unusual
  e. puzzling

_____ 8. In certain societies, young children are always on the <u>periphery</u>, instead of in the center of family life.
  a. outside

b. focus
c. inside
d. edge
e. middle

_____ 9. Most types of pine trees are <u>indigenous</u> to North America, but many ornamental shrubs were brought here from other continents.
a. natural
b. fertile
c. native
d. adaptations
e. mutations

_____ 10. Matricide, the killing of one's mother, is one of the most contemptible and <u>abject</u> crimes.
a. cruel
b. low and miserable
c. frightening
d. difficult to commit
e. illogical

Number Correct: _____

Now score each test. The answers to both tests are the same. They are (1) a, (2) e, (3) b, (4) a, (5) b, (6) e, (7) a, (8) d, (9) c, (10) b. You most likely had more items correct on test B than on test A. Why did your scores differ when the words and choices were the same on both tests? The answer is that test B was easier because the words were presented *in context;* the words around the underlined word provide clues to its meaning. Test A, on the other hand, had no sentences in which the words were used, and it provided no meaningful clues at all.

The purpose of these tests, as you can see, is to demonstrate that you can often figure out the meaning of an unknown word by looking for clues in the sentence or paragraph in which it appears. In the rest of this section we show how to use the four most common clues that context can provide about the meaning of an unknown word.

Definition Clues

Many times a writer directly or indirectly defines a word immediately after its use. The writer usually does this when he or she suspects that some readers may be unfamiliar with the new term or concept. Sometimes a writer includes a formal definition like you might find in a dictionary. In these cases, the meaning of the word will be stated directly. At other times a writer may informally restate the idea or offer a synonym, a word that means the same thing. Here are a few examples of each type of definition clue:

FORMAL DEFINITIONS

1. **Horology** is the <u>science of measuring time</u>.

2. **Induction** refers to the <u>process of reasoning from the known to the unknown</u>.

3. **Metabolism** refers to the <u>rate at which the body's cells manufacture energy from food or produce new cells</u>.

Notice that in each example the boldface word is clearly and directly defined (by the underlined part of the sentence). In fact, each sentence was written for the sole purpose of defining a term.

Indirect Definitions

1. **Hypochondria**, <u>excessive worry over one's health</u>, afflicts many Americans over forty.

2. There was a **consensus**, or <u>agreement</u>, among the faculty to require one term paper for each course.

3. <u>Referring to the ability to "see" without using the normal sensory organs</u>, **clairvoyance** is being studied at the Psychic Research Center.

4. **Middle age** (<u>35 years to 65 years</u>) is a time for strengthening and maintaining life goals.

In each of these examples, a meaning is also provided for the boldface term. A complete definition is not given, but sufficient information (underlined) is included to give you a general idea of the meaning so that you can continue reading without stopping to check a dictionary. These definitions are usually set apart from the main part of a sentence by commas or parentheses, or they are expressed in a phrase or clause that further explains the sentence's core parts.

EXERCISE 3-3

DIRECTIONS: In each sentence underline the portion that gives a definition clue for the boldface term.

1. **Chemical reactivity**, the tendency of an element to participate in chemical reactions, is an important concept in combining elements.

2. The **effectiveness adjustment**, the process by which an organism meets the demands of its environment, depends on many factors.

3. **Deductive thinking** involves drawing a conclusion from a set of general principles.

4. **Interrogation**, or questioning, can be psychologically and emotionally draining.

5. The boy was **maimed**, or disfigured, as a result of the accident.

Example Clues

A second way to determine the meaning of an unknown word is to look for examples that explain or clarify it. Suppose you do not know the meaning of the word "trauma," and you find it used in the following sentence:

Diane experienced many **traumas** during early childhood, including injury in an auto accident, the death of her grandmother, and the divorce of her parents.

This sentence gives three examples of **traumas,** and from the examples given you can conclude that "trauma" means a shocking or psychologically damaging experience. Here are a few other examples of sentences that contain example clues:

Toxic materials, such as arsenic, asbestos, pesticides, and lead, can cause permanent bodily damage.

Unconditioned responses, including heartbeat, blinking, and breathing, occur naturally in all humans.

Crickets, grasshoppers, and cockroaches, for example, are **Orthopterans** and thrive in damp conditions.

You may have noticed in these sentences that the examples are signaled by certain words or phrases. "Such as" and "including" are used here. Other common signals are "for example," "for instance," and "to illustrate."

EXERCISE 3-4

DIRECTIONS: Read each sentence and write a definition or synonym for each boldface word or phrase. Use the example clue to help you determine the meaning of the word or phrase.

1. Because of their **metallic properties** such as thermal and electrical conductivity, luster, and ductility (ability to be shaped into thin pieces), copper and lead are used for electrical wiring.

   _____

2. Perceiving, learning, and thinking are examples of **cognitive** processes.

   _____

3. Many **debilities** of old age, including loss of hearing, poor eyesight, and diseases such as arthritis, can be treated medically.

   _____

4. **Phobias** such as fear of heights, fear of water, or fear of crowds can be eliminated through conditioning.

   _____

5. Humans have built-in **coping mechanisms;** we shout when we are angry, cry when we are sad, and tremble when we are nervous.

____

Contrast Clues

It is sometimes possible to determine the meaning of an unknown word from a word or phrase in the context that has an opposite meaning. In the following sentence, notice how a word opposite in meaning from the boldface word provides a clue to its meaning.

> During the concert the audience was quiet, but afterward the crowd became **boisterous**.

Although you may not know the meaning of **boisterous,** you know that the audience was quiet during the concert and that afterward it acted differently. The word "but" suggests this. You know, then, that the crowd became the opposite of quiet (loud and noisy). Here are a few additional examples of sentences containing contrast clues:

> I **loathe** cats even though most of my friends love them.
>
> Although the cottage appeared **derelict**, we discovered that a family lived there on weekends.
>
> Pete, through long hours of study, successfully passed the exam; on the other hand, Sam's efforts were **futile.**

In these examples, you may have noticed that each contains a word or phrase that indicates that an opposite or contrasting situation exists. The signal words used in the examples were "even though," "although," and "on the other hand." Other words that also signal a contrasting idea include "however," "despite," "rather," "while," "yet," and "nevertheless."

EXERCISE 3-5

DIRECTIONS: Read each sentence and write a definition or synonym for each boldface word. Use the contrast clue to help you determine the meaning of the word.

1. Al was always talkative, whereas Ed remained **taciturn.**

____

2. The microwave oven is becoming **obsolete;** the newer microwave-convection oven offers the user more cooking options.

____

3. My brother lives in the **remote** hills of Kentucky so he seldom has the opportunity to shop in big cities.

_____

4. One of the women shoppers **succumbed** to the temptation of buying a new dress, but the others resisted.

_____

5. Most members of Western society marry only one person at a time, but in other cultures **polygamy** is common and acceptable.

_____

Inference Clues

Many times you can determine the meaning of a word you do not know by guessing or figuring it out. This process is called "drawing an inference." From the information that is given in the context you can infer the meaning of a word you are not familiar with. For instance, look at the following sentence:

My father is a **versatile** man; he is a successful businessman, sportsman, author, and sports car mechanic.

You can see that the father is successful at many types of activities, and you could reason that "versatile" means capable of doing many things competently. Similarly, in the following example the general sense of the context provides clues to the meaning of the word *robust:*

At the age of 77, Mr. George was still playing a skillful game of tennis. He jogged four miles each day and seldom missed his daily swim. For a man of his age he was extremely **robust.**

From the facts presented about Mr. George, you can infer that "robust" means full of health and vigor.

Sometimes your knowledge and experience can help you figure out the meaning of an unknown word. Consider, for instance, the following sentence:

After tasting and eating most of seven different desserts, my appetite was completely **satiated.**

Your own experience would suggest that if you ate seven desserts, you would no longer feel like eating. Thus you could reason that "satiated" means full or satisfied.

**EXERCISE
3-6**

DIRECTIONS: Read each sentence and write a definition or synonym for each boldface word. Try to figure out the meaning of each word by using information provided in the context.

1. Although my grandfather is 82, he is far from **infirm;** he is active, ambitious, and healthy.

   _____

2. My **unscrupulous** uncle tried to sell as an antique a rocking chair he bought just last year.

   _____

3. My sister's lifestyle always angered and disappointed my mother; yet she **redeemed** herself by doing special favors for my mother's friends.

   _____

4. The wind howling around the corner of the house, the one rumored to have ghosts, made an **eerie** sound.

   _____

5. We burst out laughing at the **ludicrous** sight of the basketball team dressed up as cheerleaders.

   _____

**EXERCISE
3-7**

DIRECTIONS: The meaning of the boldface word in each of the following sentences can be determined from the context. Underline the part of the sentence that contains the clue to the meaning of that word. Then write a definition or synonym for the boldface word.

1. Tremendous **variability** characterized the treatment of the mentally retarded during the Medieval Era, ranging from treatment as innocents, toleration as fools, and persecution as witches.

   _____

2. A citizen review panel **exonerated** the public official of any possible misconduct or involvement in the acceptance of bribes.

   _____

3. The **tenacious** residents living near the polluted landfill responded vehemently to the court's recommended settlement, while the chemical industry immediately agreed to the court settlement.

   _____

4. The economy was in continual **flux**; inflation increased one month and decreased the next.

_____

5. The short story contained a series of **morbid** events: the death of the mother, the suicide of the grandmother, and the murder of a young child.

_____

6. Certain societies practice the custom of **levirate**, the required remarriage of a widow to her deceased husband's brother.

_____

7. Contrasted with the corporation, the risk and liability of a privately owned **proprietorship** are much higher.

_____

8. Many cultural systems are **dynamic**; they change with environment, innovations, and contact with other groups.

_____

9. Personality is the **configuration** of feelings and behaviors created in a person throughout the process of growing up.

_____

10. A **cornucopia** of luxury and leisure-time goods, designed to meet the requirements of the upper-middle-class standard of living, has flooded the economic market.

_____

EXERCISE 3-8

DIRECTIONS: Select a chapter in one of your textbooks and identify at least five words whose meanings can be understood by using context clues. Write definitions for each of these words and list the types of context clues you used to arrive at their meanings.

Analyzing Word Parts

Many words in the English language are made up of word parts called *prefixes, roots,* and *suffixes.* You might think of these as the beginning, middle, and ending of a word. These word parts have specific meanings and when added together can provide strong clues to the meaning of a particular word.

The prefixes, roots, and suffixes listed in the following tables (see Tables 3.1 to 3.3, pages 89–91) occur in thousands of words. For instance, suppose you do not know the meaning of the word *pseudonym.* However, if you know that *pseudo* means false and *nym* means name, you can add the two parts together and realize that a pseudonym means a false name.

Before you begin to use these tables to figure out new words, you need to know a few things:

1. Words do not always have a prefix or suffix.

2. Roots may vary in spelling when they are combined with certain prefixes.

3. Some roots are commonly found at the beginnings of words, others at the end, and still others can be found in either position.

4. In certain situations, you may recognize a group of letters but find that it does not carry the meaning of a prefix or root. For example, the word internal has nothing to do with the prefix *inter* meaning between.

5. Words can have more than one prefix, root, or suffix.

DIRECTIONS: Use the list of common prefixes (Table 3.1) to determine the meaning of each of the following words. Write a brief definition or synonym for each. If you are unfamiliar with the root, you may need to check a dictionary.

1. misinformed   _____

2. rephrase   _____

3. interoffice   _____

4. circumscribe   _____

5. irreversible   _____

6. substandard   _____

7. supernatural   _____

8. telecommunications _____

9. unqualified   _____

10. subdivision   _____

11. transcend   _____

12. hypercritical   _____

13. pseudointellectual _____

14. contraception   _____

15. equivalence   _____

EXERCISE 3-10

DIRECTIONS: Use the list of common prefixes (Table 3.1), the list of common roots (Table 3.2), and the list of common suffixes (Table 3.3) to determine the meaning of each of the following words. Write a brief definition or synonym for each, checking a dictionary if necessary.

1. chronology   _____

2. photocomposition   _____

3. introspection   _____

4. biology   _____

5. subterranean   _____

6. captivate   _____

7. conversion   _____

8. teleprompter   _____

9. monotheism   _____

10. exportation   _____

Table 3.1   Common Prefixes

Prefix	Meaning	Sample Word
ad	to, at, for	adhere, advocate, adhesive
anti	against	antiwar, antiseptic, antioxidant
circum	around	circumvent, circumnavigate, circumstellar
com/col/con	with, together	compile, collaborate, conjunction
contra	against, opposite	contradict, contraband, contrary
de	away, from	deport, detach, derail
dis	apart, away, not	disagree, disband, disavow
equi	equal	equidistant, equinox, equitable
ex/extra	from, out of, former	ex-wife, exclude, exhale
hyper	over, excessive	hyperactive, hypercharge, hyperextension
in/il/ir/im	in, into, not	illogical, irrevocable, impossible
inter	between	interpersonal, interfaith, intercoastal
intro/intra	within, into, in	introduction, intravenous, intrastate
micro	small	microscope, micromanage, microprocessor
mis	wrong	misleading, mismanage, misdirected
mono	one	monologue, monofilament, monopoly
multi	many	multipurpose, multiracial, multistage
non	not	nonfiction, nonstandard, nonverbal
poly	many	polygon, polysyllabic, polytheism
post	after	posttest, postwar, postoperative
pre	before	premarital, prewriting, prepackage
pseudo	false	pseudonym, pseudopregnancy, pseudoscience
re	back, again	repeat, rekindle, relapse
retro	backward	retrospect, retroactive, retrorocket
semi	half	semicircle, semisoft, semiprivate
sub	under, below	submarine, subplot, subway
super	above, extra, above average	supercharge, superpower, superstar
tele	far	telescope, telecommute, telebanking
trans	across, over	transcontinental, transport, transplant
un	not	unskilled

Table 3.2   Common Roots

Root	Meaning	Sample Word
aster/astro	star	astronaut, asteroid
aud/audit	hear	audible, audition
bio	life	biosphere, biochemist
cap	take, seize	captive, capacity
chron(o)	time	chronograph, chronicle
corp	body	corpse, corporation
cred	believe	incredible, credibility
dict/dic	tell, say	predict, dictum
duc/duct	lead	introduce, deduction
fact/fac	make, do	factory, facile
geo	earth	geophysics, geosphere
graph	write	telegraph, graphics
log/logo/logy	study, thought	psychology, theologian
mit/miss	send	dismiss, transmit
mort/mor	die, death	immortal, morbid
path	feeling	sympathy, pathetic
phono	sound/voice	telephone, phonics
photo	light	photosensitive, photocopy
port	carry	transport, portable
scop	seeing	microscope, telescope
scrib/script	write	inscription, scribble
sen/sent	feel	insensitive, sentiment
spec/spect/spic	look, see	retrospect, spectacle
terr/terre	land, earth	territory, terrain
theo	god	theology, theocracy
ven/vent	come	convention, convene
vert/vers	turn	invert, versus
vis/vid	see	invisible, video
voc	call	vocation, vocal

Table 3.3   Common Suffixes

Suffix	Sample Word	Suffix	Sample Word
Suffixes that refer to a state, condition, or quality		-ty	loyalty, admiralty
-able	touchable, capable	-y	creamy, tasty
-ance	assistance, sufferance	*Suffixes that mean "one who"*	
-ation	confrontation, termination	-ee	employee, referee
-ence	reference, interference	-eer	engineer, auctioneer
-ic	aerobic, chronic	-er	teacher, preacher
-ible	tangible, sensible	-ist	activist, chemist
-ion	discussion, intermission	-or	editor, tutor
-ity	superiority, captivity	*Suffixes that mean "pertaining to" or "referring to"*	
-ive	permissive, assertive	-al	autumnal, choral
-ment	amazement, enjoyment	-ship	friendship, authorship
-ness	kindness, happiness	-hood	brotherhood, nieghborhood
-ous	jealous, anxious	-ward	homeward, earthward

**EXERCISE
3-11**

DIRECTIONS: From a chapter of one of your textbooks, select at least five new words made up of two or more word parts. For each word, identify those parts, list the meaning of each part, and then write a brief definition of the word.

A System for Learning Unfamiliar Words

You are constantly exposed to new words in the normal course of your day. However, unless you make a deliberate effort to remember and use these words, many of them will fade from your memory. One of the most practical and easy-to-use systems for expanding your vocabulary is the index card system. It works like this:

1. **Whenever you hear or read a new word that you intend to learn, jot it down in the margin of your notes or mark it in some way in the material you are reading.**

2. **Later, write each new word on the front of an index card, then look up the meaning (or meanings) of the word and write it on the back.** You might also record the word's pronunciation or a sample sentence in which the word is used. Your cards should look like the ones shown in Figure 3.1 below.

3. **Whenever you have a few spare minutes, go through your pack of index cards.** For each card, look at the word on the front and try to recall its meaning on the back. Then check the back of the card to see if you

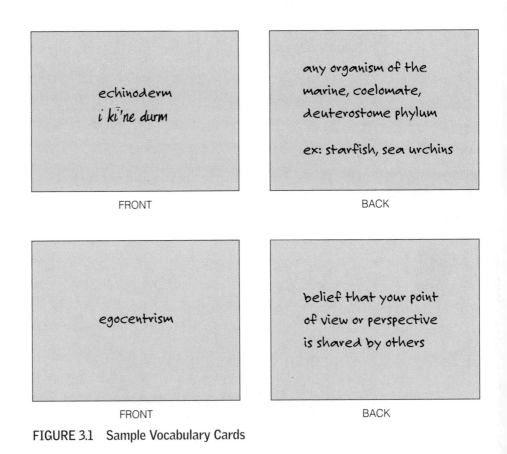

FIGURE 3.1   Sample Vocabulary Cards

were correct. If you were unable to recall the meaning or if you confused it with another word, retest yourself. Shuffle the cards after each use.

4. **After you have gone through your pack of cards several times, sort the cards into two piles;** separate the words you know from those that you have not learned. Then, putting the "known words" aside, concentrate on the words still to be learned. Shuffle the cards to change their order.

5. **Once you have mastered the entire pack of cards, periodically review them to refresh your memory and to keep the words current in your mind.**

6. **If you tend to be a social learner (see Learning Style Questionnaire, page 3 in Chapter 1), arrange to work with a classmate.** Quiz each other and discuss ways to remember difficult or confusing terms.

This word card system of learning vocabulary is effective for several reasons:

- It can be used in the spare moments that are often wasted waiting for a return phone call, waiting for a class to begin, or riding a bus.

- The system enables you to spend time learning what you do *not* know rather than wasting time studying what you already know.

- It prevents you from learning the material in a fixed order.

DIRECTIONS: Prepare a set of vocabulary cards for the new terminology in one chapter of one of your textbooks.

Using Newly Learned Words

A conscious effort is required to learn new words. You must *use* a word for it to remain a part of your vocabulary. The first time you use a new word you may be unsure if you are using it correctly. Don't let this element of risk discourage you from trying new words. The first place to use the new words is in course-related situations. Try to use new words when studying with a friend or participating in a class discussion.

Be conscious of your word choices as you write. Select words that most clearly and accurately convey the meaning you intend. As a general rule, it is best to record your ideas first without thinking about exact choices of words. Then, as you reread what you have written, try to think of words that express your ideas more accurately or that provide more complete information.

Using Vocabulary Reference Sources

To develop a strong vocabulary you need the basic tools with which to work. Just as an artist cannot begin to paint without having a canvas and brushes, you cannot begin to strengthen your vocabulary without owning the necessary reference sources—a dictionary and a thesaurus—and having access to a subject-area dictionary.

The Dictionary

Which Dictionary to Buy?

There are several types of dictionaries, each with its own purpose and use. A pocket or paperback dictionary is an inexpensive, easy-to-carry, shortened version of a standard desk dictionary. It is small enough to carry to classes and costs around $5.

A desk dictionary is a more complete and extensive dictionary. Although a pocket dictionary is convenient, it is also limited in use. A pocket edition lists about 50,000 to 60,000 words; a standard desk edition lists up to 150,000 words. Also, the desk edition provides much more complete information about each word. Desk dictionaries are usually hardbound and cost more than $20.

Several standard dictionaries are available in both desk and paperback editions. These include:

The Random House Dictionary of the English Language
Merriam-Webster's Collegiate Dictionary
The American Heritage Dictionary of the English Language

Standard dictionaries are also available on CD-ROM and online; it may be convenient to access word meanings by using your computer. A third type is the unabridged dictionary. These are found in the reference section of the library. The unabridged edition provides the most complete information on each word in the English language.

Which dictionary should you buy? You should first purchase a pocket dictionary to carry with you regularly. If at all possible, you should also own a desk dictionary, either printed or electronic, preferably a collegiate edition. For most purposes, it is not necessary to have the newest, most current edition; a used dictionary works fine and costs considerably less.

Using the Dictionary

The dictionary is a valuable reference source and an important tool in vocabulary development. Here are a few general principles to keep in mind when using a dictionary:

1. **Never spend time looking up long lists of words, even if you really want to learn each word on the list.** By the time you finish the list, you will have forgotten the first ones you looked up. Instead, look up a few words at a time.

2. **Do not interrupt your reading to check the meaning of a word in the dictionary unless the word is absolutely essential to the meaning of the sentence or paragraph.** Instead, mark unknown words and look them up later.

3. **Whenever you look up a word, be sure to read through all the meanings and choose the meaning that suits the context in which it is used.**

4. **Whenever you do look up a word, be sure to write down the word and its meaning.** (The section of the chapter, "A System for Learning Unfamiliar Words," p. 91, suggests an effective way to do this.)

Types of Information to Find in the Dictionary

Although the dictionary, of course, is a source for definitions of words, it also contains other types of useful information that can significantly expand your vocabulary. Here are some types of information a dictionary provides that we often overlook:

1. **Word pronunciation.** Have you ever been unsure of how to pronounce a word? This situation most commonly arises when you attempt to use a word from your reading vocabulary in speech. Immediately after the word entry in a dictionary, you will find a pronunciation key. Suppose you are trying to figure out how to pronounce the word *deign*, meaning to agree in a condescending manner. After the word you would find the following: (dan). Here the word is spelled phonetically, the way it sounds, and the key at the bottom of the page explains how to interpret

the phonetic symbols. For instance, the *American Heritage Desk Dictionary* lists the following key:

ă pat   ā pay   â care   ä father   ĕ pet   ē be   hw which   ĭ pit   ī tie   î pier   ŏ pot   ō toe   ô paw, for   oi noise
ŏŏ took   ōŏ boot   ou out   th thin   *th* this   ŭ cut   ü urge   zh vision   ə about, item, edible, gallop, circus

From the key you learn that the "a" sound in "deign" rhymes with the word *pay*. An accent mark (´) is included for words with two or more syllables to indicate which part of the word should receive the greatest emphasis.

2. **Part(s) of speech.** A word's part of speech, that part of speech is listed (in abbreviated form) after the word's pronunciation. If a word can function as several different parts of speech, the meanings are often divided according to part of speech. When looking up a word, first see if you know as what part of speech the word is used in the sentence; you can save time by going directly to that part of speech in the dictionary entry.

3. **Key to spelling.** In addition to the basic spelling of a word, the dictionary often shows how spellings change when the word becomes plural or when an ending such as "ing" is added. In the entry below you can see variations of the word "establish" at the end of the entry.

4. **Information on language history.** The dictionary also functions as a brief history of the English language. For each word entry, information is given about the origin of the word. This etymological information tells you the language or languages from which the word evolved. For example, in *Merriam-Webster's Collegiate Dictionary* you can see that the word *establish* is derived from Middle English (ME), Middle French (MF), and Latin (L).

es•ta•blish \i'-sta-blish\ *vt* [**ME** *establissen,* fr. **MF** *establiss-,* stem of *establir,* fr. **L** *stabilire,* fr. *stabilis* stable] (14c) **1** : to institute (as a law) permanently by enactment or agreement **2** *obsolete* : SETTLE **3 a** : to make firm or stable **b** : to introduce and cause to grow and multiply [~ grass on pasturelands] **4 a** : to bring into existence FOUND [~ed a republic] **b** : BRING ABOUT, EFFECT [~ed friendly relations] **5 a** : to put on a firm basis: SET UP [~ his son in business] **b** : to put into a favorable position **c** : to gain full recognition or acceptance of [the role ~ed her as a star] **6** : to make (a church) a national or state institution **7** : to put beyond doubt: PROVE [~ed my innocence]
— es•tab•lish•able \-sh ə -b ə l\ *adjective*
— es•tab•lish•er \-sh ə r\ *noun*

Merriam-Webster's Collegiate Dictionary, Tenth Edition. ©2002

5. **Restrictive meanings.** Restrictive meanings are definitions that apply only when the word is being used in a specific field of study. For example, an entry for the word "curve" lists two restrictive meanings—one for baseball and one for mathematics.

6. **Foreign expressions used in English.** Certain expressions from other languages have become widely used in the English language. These phrases often more accurately express an idea or feeling than do the English translations. The French expression *faux pas,* translated to mean a social blunder, is a good example. Most dictionaries list foreign phrases alphabetically along with English words, although in some dictionaries you may find a separate list of foreign expressions. A few more examples of commonly used foreign expressions that are listed in most dictionaries are: *ad hoc, non sequitur, de facto, tête-à-tête,* and *bona fide.*

7. **Idioms.** An idiom is a phrase that has meaning other than what the common meanings of the words in the phrase mean. For example, the phrase "wipe the slate clean" is not about slates. It means to start over. To find the meaning of an idiom look under the key words in the phrase. To find the meaning of "eat crow" look under the entry for "crow." You will discover that it means to admit you have been wrong.

**EXERCISE
3-13**

DIRECTIONS: Use a dictionary to answer each of the following items. Write your answer in the space provided.

1. What does the abbreviation *e.g.* stand for?

   _____

2. How is the word *deleterious* pronounced? (Record its phonetic spelling.)

   _____

3. From what languages is the word *delicatessen* taken?

   _____

4. Locate one restricted meaning for the word *configuration.*

   _____

   _____

5. What is the history of the word *mascot?*

   _____

_____

_____

_____

6. What is the plural spelling of *addendum?*

_____

7. What type of punctuation is a virgule?

_____

8. List a few words that contain the following sound: ī.

_____

9. Who or what is a Semite?

_____

10. Can the word *phrase* be used other than as a noun? If so, how?

_____

Choosing the Appropriate Meaning

The crucial part of looking a word up in the dictionary is finding the appropriate meaning to fit the context in which the word is used. A dictionary lists all the common meanings of a word, but you are looking for only one definition. For instance, suppose you were to read the following sentence and could not determine the meaning of *isometrics* from its context.

> The executive found that doing isometrics helped him to relax between business meetings.

The dictionary entry (*American Heritage Desk Dictionary*) for *isometrics* is:

> **i•so•met•ric** (īsə-mĕt´rĭk) or **i•so•met•ri[cal]** (-rĭ-kəl) *adj.* **1.** Of or exhibiting equality in dimensions or measurements. **2.** Of or being a crystal system of three equal axes at right angles to one another. **3.** Of or involving muscle contractions in which the ends of the muscle are held in place so that there is an increase in tension rather than a shortening of the muscle: *isometric exercises.* —*n.* **1.** A line connecting isometric points. **2. isometrics** (*used with a sing. verb*). Isometric exercise. [From Greek *isometros,* of equal measure : *isos,* equal + *metron,* measure.]

Notice that the meanings are grouped and numbered consecutively according to part of speech. The meanings of the word when used as an adjective are listed first, followed by two meanings for it as a noun. If you are able to identify the part of speech of the word you are looking up, you can skip over all parts of the entry that do not pertain to that part of speech. For example, in the sample sentence, you can tell that *isometrics* is something the executive does; therefore it is a noun.

If you cannot identify the part of speech of a word you are looking up, begin with the first meaning listed. Generally, the most common meaning appears first, and more specialized meanings appear toward the end of the entry.

Choosing the right meaning is a process of substitution. When you find a meaning that could fit into the sentence you are working with, replace the word with its definition and then read the entire sentence. If the definition makes sense in the sentence, you can be fairly certain that you have selected the appropriate meaning.

EXERCISE 3-14

DIRECTIONS: Write an appropriate meaning for the underlined word in each of the following sentences. Use the dictionary to help you find the meaning that makes sense in the sentence.

1. He <u>affected</u> a French accent.

   _____

2. The <u>amphibian</u> took us to our destination in less than an hour.

   _____

3. The plane stalled on the <u>apron</u>.

   _____

4. We <u>circumvented</u> the problem by calculating in metrics.

   _____

5. Many consumers have become <u>embroiled</u> in the debate over the rising inflation rate.

   _____

EXERCISE 3-15

DIRECTIONS: Explain the meaning of each of the following foreign expressions. Write your answer in the space provided.

1. *non sequitur*

   _____

   _____

   _____

2. *coup d'état*

_____

_____

3. *kowtow*

_____

_____

_____

4. *barrio*

_____

_____

_____

5. *Zeitgeist*

_____

_____

_____ ▬

The Thesaurus

A thesaurus is a dictionary of synonyms. It is available in hardback and paperback, as well as on CD-ROM and online. It is written for the specific purpose of grouping words with similar meanings. A thesaurus is particularly useful when you have a word on the "tip of your tongue," so to speak, but cannot think of the exact word. It is also useful for locating a precise, accurate, or descriptive phrase to fit a particular situation.

Suppose you want to find a more precise term for the expression "told us about" in the following sentence:

My instructor told us about an assignment that would be due next month.

Roget's International Thesaurus lists the following synonyms for the phrase:

.8 VERBS **Inform, tell, speak,** apprise, **advise, advertise,** advertise of, give word, mention to, **acquaint, enlighten,** familiarize, brief, verse, wise up [slang], give the facts, give an account of, give by the way of information; **Instruct** 562.11; possess *or* seize one of the facts; **let know, have one to know, give one to understand;** tell once and for all; notify, give notice *or* notification, serve notice; **communicate** 554.6,7;

bring *or* send *or* leave word; **report** 558.11; **disclose** 556.4-7; put in a new light, shed new *or* fresh light upon.

.9 **post** *or* **keep one posted** [both informal]; fill one in, bring up to date, put one in the picture [Brit.]

.10 **hint, intimate, suggest, insinuate, imply, indicate,** adumbrate, lead *or* leave one to gather, justify one in a supposing, give *or* drop *or* throw out a hint, give an inkling of, **hint at; allude to,** make an allusion to, glance at [archaic]; **prompt,** give the cue; put in *or* into one's head.

Right away you can identify several words that are more descriptive than "told us about." Your next step is to choose a word from the list that most closely suggests the meaning you intend. The easiest way to do this is to test out or substitute various choices in your sentence to see which one is most appropriate. Be sure to choose only those words with which you are familiar and those whose shades of meaning you understand. Remember, a misused word is often worse than a wordy or imprecise expression.

The most widely used thesaurus was originally compiled by Peter Roget and is known today as *Roget's Thesaurus;* inexpensive paperback copies are readily available. When you first use a thesaurus you will have to learn how to use it. First, you have to look up the word in the back. Once you locate the number of the section in the main part of the thesaurus that lists its synonyms, turn to that section.

EXERCISE 3-16

DIRECTIONS: Using a thesaurus, replace the underlined word or phrase with a more precise or descriptive word. You may rephrase the sentence if necessary.

1. The instructor <u>talked about</u> several economic theories.

_____

2. My sisters, who had been apart for three years, were <u>happy</u> to be reunited at the wedding.

_____

3. The professor announced a <u>big</u> test for the end of next week.

_____

4. The student <u>watched</u> the elderly professor climb the stairs.

_____

5. Although it was short, the movie was <u>good</u>.

_____

_____

Subject-Area Dictionaries

Many academic disciplines have specialized dictionaries that index important terminology used in that field. They list specialized meanings and indicate how and when the words are used. For instance, the field of music has *The New Grove Dictionary of Music and Musicians,* which lists and defines specialized vocabulary used in the field. Other subject-area dictionaries include:

Taber's Cyclopedic Medical Dictionary
A Dictionary of Anthropology
A Dictionary of Economics

Find out if there is a subject-area dictionary for your major. Most of these dictionaries are available only in hardbound editions and are likely to be

Critical Thinking Tip #3

Vague Versus Clear Meanings

Word meaning can facilitate or interfere with communication. A word that is exact and specific can help communication. A word whose meaning is vague, relative, or unclear leads to misinterpretation and confusion. Here are a few sentences whose meaning is unclear because the meaning of the underlined word is not specific.

The movie was <u>great</u>!
(What was good about it?)

All <u>drugs</u> should be tightly controlled.
(Which drugs? All drugs? Aspirin too?)

The candidate received a <u>large</u> sum of money.
(How large is large?)

The woman was <u>middle aged</u>.
(How old is middle aged?)

As a critical thinker, be alert for the use of undefined terms and unclear words. Writers may use them to avoid giving specific information ("substantial losses" instead of exact amounts) or to create a false impression.

expensive. Many students, however, find them to be worth the initial investment. Most libraries have copies of specialized dictionaries in their reference section.

EXERCISE 3–17

DIRECTIONS: Visit your college library and discover which subject-area dictionaries are available for the courses you are taking this semester. List the courses you are enrolled in and the subject-area dictionary or dictionaries that would be useful for each.

Summary

1. How can you expand your vocabulary?

You can expand your vocabulary and reap immediate benefits as well as long-term career advantages by
- reading widely.
- deliberately using newly learned words.
- being selective about words to learn.
- using words you already know.
- working on vaguely familiar words.
- learning multiple word meanings.

2. What are the four types of context clues?

The four types of context clues are:
- Definition—a word's meaning is either stated directly or given indirectly.
- Example—the examples used explain or clarify a word's meaning.
- Contrast—a word or phrase opposite in meaning provides a clue to meaning.
- Inference—a word's meaning can be figured out by reasoning about contextual information.

3. What are the three parts from which many English words are formed?

Many words in our language are made up of:
- Prefixes—the beginnings of words
- Roots—the middles of words
- Suffixes—the endings of words

4. Why is it useful to learn about word parts?

When their meanings are added together they can provide strong clues to the meaning of a new word and can unlock the meanings of thousands of English words.

5. What is the index card system?

The index card system is a method for learning unfamiliar words. Write each new word on the front of an index card and its meaning on the back. Study by sorting the cards into two piles—known and unknown words. Review periodically to keep them fresh in your mind.

Reading Selection 5

ARCHAEOLOGY

ARCHAEOLOGICAL SITES
Brian M. Fagan
From *World Prehistory: A Brief Introduction*

What do you think might be left of your town or city in two or three thousand years? What evidence might be left of how you lived? This textbook excerpt describes different sites where archaeologists have discovered evidence of early human activity. Preread and then read the excerpt to discover the six types of sites archaeologists study.

— **·** —

1   World prehistory is written from data recovered from thousands of *archaeological sites, places where traces of human activity are to be found.* Sites are normally identified through the presence of manufactured tools.

2   An archaeological site can consist of a single human burial, a huge rockshelter occupied over thousands of years, or a simple scatter of stone tools found on the surface of a plowed field in the Midwest. Sites can range in size from a huge prehistoric city like Teotihuacán in the Valley of Mexico to a small campsite occupied by hunter-gatherers 100,000 years ago. Sites available for study by archaeologists are limited in number and variety by preservation conditions and by the nature of the activities of the people who occupied them. Some, like Mesopotamian city mounds, were important settlements for hundreds, even thousands, of years. Some small sites were used only for a few hours, others for a generation or two.

3   Archaeological sites are most commonly classified by the activity that occurred there. *Habitation sites* are placed where people lived and carried out a wide range of different activities. Most prehistoric sites come under this category, but habitation sites can vary from a small open campsite, through rockshelters and caves, to large accumulations of shellfish remains (shell middens). Village habitation sites may consist of

a small accumulation of occupation deposit and mud hut fragments, huge earthen mounds, or communes of stone buildings or entire buried cities. Each presents its own special excavation problems.

4   *Burial sites* provide a wealth of information on the prehistoric past. Grinning skeletons are very much part of popular archaeological legend, and human remains are common finds in the archaeological record. The earliest deliberate human burials are between fifty and seventy thousand years old. Individual burials are found in habitation sites, but often the inhabitants designated a special area for a cemetery. This cemetery could be a communal burial place where everyone was buried regardless of social status. Other burial sites, like the Shang royal cemeteries in China, were reserved for nobility alone. Parts of a cemetery were sometimes reserved for certain special individuals in society such as clan leaders or priests. The patterning of grave goods in a cemetery can provide information about intangible aspects of human society such as religious beliefs or social organization. So can the pattern of deposition of the burials, their orientation in their graves, even family groupings. Sometimes physical anthropologists can detect biological similarities between different skeletons that may reflect close family, or other, ties.

5   Burial sites, especially those of important individuals, are among the most spectacular of all archaeological discoveries. Tut-ankh-Amun's tomb, the royal graves of Sumerian and Semitic nobles of Ur-of-the-Chaldees, and the sepulchres of Chinese nobles are justly famous for their remarkable wealth. People have buried their dead in cemeteries under stone pyramids in Egypt and Mexico, in great earthen mass burial mounds in the Midwest, in huge subterranean chambers in China, and in thousands of small, individual earthen mounds in western Europe. In each case, however, the features of the burials and their context in the sepulchre add valuable data to what the skeleton itself can tell us.

6   *Kill sites* consist of bones of slaughtered animals associated with hunting weapons. On the North American Great Plains, for example, the skeletons of eight-thousand-year-old bison are found along with stone spearpoints. The hunters camped by the carcasses while they butchered them, then moved elsewhere, leaving the carcasses, projectile heads and butchering tools where they lay for archaeologists to find thousands of years later.

7   *Quarry sites* are places where people mined prized raw materials such as obsidian (a volcanic glass used for fine knives and mirrors) or copper. Excavations at such sites yield roughed out blanks of stone, or metal ingots, as well as finished products ready for trading elsewhere. Such objects were bartered widely in prehistoric times.

8   *Religious sites* include Stonehenge in southern England, Mesopotamian mudbrick temples, known as *ziggurats,* and the great ceremonial centers of the lowland Maya in Mesoamerica, such as Tikal, Copán, and Palenque. Religious sites may be small shrines or huge public temples. Some are localities where religious ceremonies were conducted, often to the exclusion of any habitation at all.

9   *Art sites* such as the cave of Altamira in northern Spain, or Lascaux in southwestern France, are commonplace in some areas of the world, noticeably southern Africa and parts of North America. Many are caves and rockshelters where prehistoric people painted or engraved game animals, scenes of daily life, or religious symbols. Some French art sites are at least fifteen thousand years old.

10   Each of these site types represents a particular form of human activity, one that is represented in the archaeological record by specific artifact patterns and surface indications found and recorded by the archaeologist.

EXAMINING READING SELECTION 5

Checking Your Vocabulary

Directions: Using context, word parts, or a dictionary if necessary, circle the letter of the meaning for each word as it is used in the reading.

1. accumulations (paragraph 3)
   a. collections
   b. varieties
   c. growths
   d. categories

2. excavation (paragraph 3)
   a. identification of the site
   b. uncovering by digging
   c. altering by uncovering
   d. preservation of the site

3. communal (paragraph 4)
   a. shared
   b. different
   c. unique
   d. special

4. intangible (paragraph 4)
   a. not real
   b. not identifiable
   c. not touchable
   d. not authentic

5. subterranean (paragraph 5)
   a. building-like
   b. beneath the earth
   c. frightening
   d. darkened

Checking Your Comprehension

Directions: Circle the letter of the best answer.

6. Archaeological sites are usually classified by
   a. the people who lived there.
   b. the historical period during which they were occupied.
   c. the type of activity for which they were used.
   d. the degree of civilization of those who lived there.

7. An archaeological site is defined as any place where
   a. some record of human activity is found.
   b. humans bury beloved animals.
   c. evidence of plant or animal life exists.
   d. particular rock formations suggest the patterns of history.

8. All of the following features of graves provide archaeologists with information about a particular society except
   a. the location of the grave.
   b. the goods buried with the person.
   c. the degree of preservation of the body.
   d. the orientation of the body in the grave.

9 Art sites often contain
   a. paintings showing scenes of daily life.
   b. engravings of famous people.
   c. paintings recording the location of burial sites.
   d. tools and primitive devices used for engraving.

10. Quarry sites are places where
   a. game was slaughtered.
   b. prized animals were buried.
   c. raw materials were dug from the earth.
   d. raw materials for burial sites were located.

11. The author explains archaeological sites by
   a. discussing their origin chronologically.
   b. **identifying various types of sites.**
   c. comparing various sites.
   d. listing their contents.

Thinking Critically

12. Which of the following items might you expect to find at a burial site?
   a. tools
   b. jewels
   c. bowls
   d. animal remains

13. The author suggests that different cultural groups
   a. have similar methods of mixing raw materials.
   b. reserve hunting grounds for specific tribes.
   c. have specific sites for celebrations.
   d. have different burial patterns.

14. The author feels that archaeologists
   a. learn a great deal about early history.
   b. locate valuable jewels and art.
   c. disturb natural history by excavating.
   d. prove man's natural superiority.

15. This article was written to
   a. explain the different types of archaeological sites.
   b. discuss archaeological excavation techniques.
   c. explain why archaeology is important.
   d. describe how to identify a habitation site.

Questions for Discussion

1. Prehistoric people are often thought of as apes or monsters. After reading descriptions of their habitation, burial, religious, and art sites, how do you regard them? Were they human?

2. What do you think is the value in studying ancient peoples and their living habits?

3. What kinds of sites do you think future archaeologists might find when studying our civilization?

Selection 5:		794 words
Finishing Time:		
	HR. MIN.	SEC.
Starting Time:		
	HR. MIN.	SEC.
Reading Time:		
	MIN.	SEC.
WPM Score:		
Comprehension Score:		%

Reading Selection 6

Physics

Why the Sky Is Blue, Sunsets Are Red, and Clouds Are White
Paul G. Hewitt
From *Conceptual Physics*

We often tend to accept the physical world around us without questioning why it is as it is. This excerpt from a physics text asks questions about three common characteristics of our physical world. What other questions does this bring to mind?

— **·** —

Why the Sky Is Blue

1   If a sound beam of a particular frequency is directed to a tuning fork of similar frequency, the tuning fork will be set into vibration and will redirect the beam in multiple directions. The tuning fork *scatters* the sound. A similar process occurs with the scattering of light from molecules and larger specks of matter that are far apart from one another—as in the atmosphere. In this scattering process in the atmosphere, light is absorbed and re-emitted at the same frequency.*

2   We know that atoms and molecules behave like tiny optical tuning forks and re-emit light waves that shine on them. Very tiny particles do the same. The tinier the particle, the higher the frequency of light it will scatter. This is similar to the way small bells ring with higher notes than larger bells. The nitrogen and oxygen molecules that make up most of the atmosphere are like tiny bells that "ring" with high frequencies when energized by sunlight. Like sound from the bells, the re-emitted light is sent in all directions. It is scattered. (Figure A)

3   Most of the ultraviolet light from the sun is absorbed by a thin protective layer of ozone gas in the upper atmosphere. The remaining ultraviolet sunlight that passes through the atmosphere is scattered by atmospheric particles and molecules. Of the visible frequency light, violet is scattered the most, followed by blue, green, yellow, orange, and red, in that order. Red is scattered only a tenth as much as violet. Although violet light is scattered more than blue, our eyes are not very sensitive to violet light. The lesser amount of blue predominates in our vision, so we see a blue sky!

4   The blue of the sky varies in different places under different conditions. A principal factor is the water-vapor content of the atmosphere. On clear dry days the sky is a much deeper blue than on clear days with high humidity. Places where the upper air is exceptionally dry, such as Italy

*This type of scattering is called *Rayleigh scattering* (after Lord Rayleigh) and occurs whenever the scattering particles are much smaller than the wavelength of incident light and have resonances at frequencies higher than those of the scattered light.

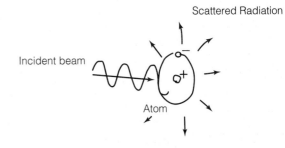

Scattered Radiation

Incident beam

Atom

FIGURE A   A beam of light falls on an atom and increases the vibrational motion of electrons in the atom. The vibrating electrons, in turn, re-emit light in various directions. Light is scattered.

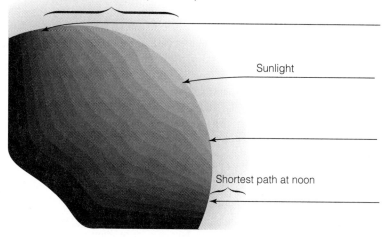

Greatest path of sunlight through
atmosphere is at sunset (or sunrise)

Sunlight

Shortest path at noon

FIGURE B   A sunbeam must travel through more kilometers of atmosphere at sunset than at noon. As a result, more blue is scattered from the beam at sunset than at noon. By the time a beam of initially white light gets to the ground, only the lower frequencies survive to produce a red sunset.

and Greece, have beautifully blue skies that have inspired painters for centuries. Where there are a lot of particles of dust and other particles larger than oxygen and nitrogen molecules, light of lower frequencies is also scattered strongly. This makes the sky less blue; it takes on a whitish appearance. After a heavy rainstorm when the particles have been washed away, the sky becomes a deeper blue.

5   The grayish haze in the skies of large cities is the result of particles emitted by car and truck engines and by factories. Even when idling, a typical automobile engine emits more than 100 billion particles per second. Most are invisible but act as tiny centers to which other particles adhere. These are the primary scatterers of lower frequency light. For the larger of these particles, absorption rather than scattering takes place and a brownish haze is produced. Yuk!

Why Sunsets Are Red

6   Light of lower frequencies is scattered the least by nitrogen and oxygen molecules. Therefore red, orange, and yellow light are transmitted through the atmosphere much more than violet and blue. Red, which is scattered the least, passes

through more atmosphere than any other color. Therefore, when white light passes through a thick atmosphere, higher-frequency light is scattered most while light of lower frequencies is transmitted with minimal scattering. And a thickened atmosphere is presented to sunlight at sunset.

7   At noon the sunlight travels through the minimum amount of atmosphere to reach the earth's surface. Then a relatively small amount of high-frequency light is scattered from sunlight, enough to make the sun somewhat yellow. As the day progresses and the sun is lower in the sky (Figure B), the path through the atmosphere is longer, and more blue is scattered from the sunlight. The removal of blue leaves the transmitted light more reddish in appearance. The sun becomes progressively redder, going from yellow to orange and finally to a red-orange at sunset.*

*Sunsets and sunrises would be unusually colorful if particles larger than atmospheric molecules were more abundant in the air. This was the case all over the world for three years following the eruption of the volcano Krakatoa in 1883, when micrometer-sized particles were spewed out in abundance and spread throughout the world's atmosphere. This occurred to a lesser extent following the 1991 eruption of Mount Pinatubo in the Philippines.

8   The colors of the sunset are consistent with our rules for color mixing. When blue is subtracted from white light, the complementary color that is left is yellow. When higher-frequency violet is subtracted, the resulting complementary color is orange. When medium-frequency green is subtracted, magenta is left. The combinations of resulting colors vary with atmospheric conditions, which change from day to day and give us a variety of sunsets.

Why Clouds Are White

9   Water droplets in a variety of sizes—most of them microscopic—make up clouds. The different-size droplets result in a variety of colors of scattered light: low frequencies from larger droplets and high frequencies from tinier droplets of water molecules. The overall result is a white cloud. The electrons in a tiny droplet vibrate together and in step, which results in the scattering of a greater amount of energy than when the same number of electrons vibrate separately. Hence, clouds are bright!

10   Absorption occurs for larger droplets, and the scattered light intensity is less. The clouds are darker. Further increase in the size of the drops causes them to fall to earth, and we have rain.

11   The next time you find yourself admiring a crisp blue sky, or delighting in the shapes of bright clouds, or watching a beautiful sunset, think about all those ultra-tiny optical tuning forks vibrating away—you'll appreciate these everyday wonders of nature even more!

Writing about Reading Selection 6*

Checking Your Vocabulary

Directions: Complete each of the following items; refer to a dictionary if necessary.

1. Discuss the connotative meanings of the word *sunsets*. (paragraph 8)

2. Define each of the following words:
   a. energized (paragraph 2)

   _____

   b. predominates (paragraph 3)

   _____

   _____

   c. emitted (paragraph 5)

   _____

   d. progressively (paragraph 7)

   _____

   e. intensity (paragraph 10)

   _____

3. Define the word *redirect* (paragraph 1) and underline the word or phrase that provides a context clue for its meaning.

   _____

   _____

   _____

4. Define the word *progressively* (paragraph 7) and underline the word or phrase that provides a context clue for its meaning.

   _____

   _____

   _____

*Multiple-choice questions are contained in Part 6 (page 578).

5. Determine the meanings of the following words by using word parts:

a. optical (paragraph 2)

_____

_____

b. re-emit (paragraph 2)

_____

_____

c. invisible (paragraph 5)

_____

d. transmitted (paragraph 6)

_____

e. complementary (paragraph 8)

_____

_____

Checking Your Comprehension

6. Which of the visible colors is scattered the most? Which is scattered the least?

_____

_____

7. If violet light is scattered more than blue light, why isn't the sky violet?

_____

_____

_____

8. What causes the sky to have a grayish hue in large cities?

_____

_____

_____

9. What are the primary molecular components of our atmosphere?

_____

_____

Thinking Critically

10. Why is the sky more blue in some countries than in others?

_____

_____

11. Why are red, orange, and yellow light more visible in the atmosphere than blue light?

_____

_____

_____

_____

_____

12. What would make sunsets and sunrises even more colorful?

_____

_____

_____

13. Why aren't all sunsets the same color? What causes them to have a variety of shades?

_____

_____

Questions for Discussion

1. How can we solve the problems caused by automobiles emitting particles in the air?

2. Explain the process of rain, then discuss how seeding clouds might affect this process.

3. Describe in nontechnical terms how clouds get to be white.

4. Discuss the probable changes in the earth's atmosphere when the sky changes from one shade of blue to another.

Selection 6:			944 words
Finishing Time:	_____	_____	_____
	HR.	MIN.	SEC.
Starting Time:	_____	_____	_____
	HR.	MIN.	SEC.
Reading Time:		_____	_____
		MIN.	SEC.
WPM Score:			_____
Comprehension Score:		_____	%

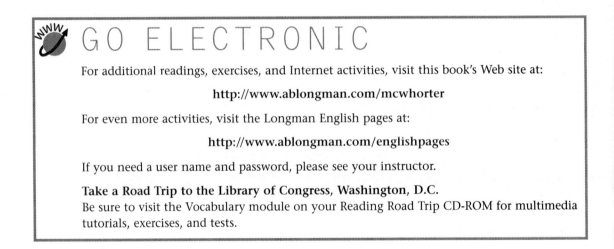

GO ELECTRONIC

For additional readings, exercises, and Internet activities, visit this book's Web site at:

http://www.ablongman.com/mcwhorter

For even more activities, visit the Longman English pages at:

http://www.ablongman.com/englishpages

If you need a user name and password, please see your instructor.

Take a Road Trip to the Library of Congress, Washington, D.C.
Be sure to visit the Vocabulary module on your Reading Road Trip CD-ROM for multimedia tutorials, exercises, and tests.

PART 1
Academic Scenario

The following scenario is designed to assess your ability to use and apply the skills taught in this unit.

THE SITUATION

Assume you are taking an anthropology course this semester. On the first day of class your instructor announced, "If you want to pass this course, you will need to learn to speak its language! You will also have to be able to think about language and its functions."

In class today your instructor returned your first exam; you got an "A," but your best friend got a "D." Your friend asks you what you did to earn such a high grade. When you reply that you heeded your instructor's first-day advice, your friend asks you to show her what you did, using tonight's reading assignment as an example.

THE TASKS

Assume you have been assigned Reading Selection 5 (p. 104) as part of tonight's reading assignment. Complete each of the following tasks as if you were to use them as demonstrations for your friend.

1. Preread Reading Selection 5. Place brackets ([ ]) around everything you read as part of your prereading.

2. Write four guide questions that would be useful to focus your reading.

   _____

   _____

   _____

   _____

3. Prepare a set of vocabulary cards using the index card system. Include at least five words you will need to learn for the next exam.

4. Define each of the following words by using context clues or prefixes, roots, or suffixes.

a. communal (paragraph 4)

_____

b. intangible (paragraph 4)

_____

c. subterranean (paragraph 5)

_____

d. obsidian (paragraph 7)

_____

e. excavations (paragraph 7)

_____

f. *ziggurats* (paragraph 8)

_____

CHAPTER 4

Main Ideas and Paragraph Structure

IN THIS CHAPTER YOU WILL LEARN:

1. To identify the topic of a paragraph.
2. To identify the main idea and topic sentence of a paragraph.
3. To develop expectations about the writer's ideas.
4. To recognize supporting details and understand their relationship to the main idea.
5. To use transitions to see the connections between ideas.

When you shop you expect to find all types of cereal displayed on the same shelf and all size 34 pants hung together on a rack. All items of the same type are grouped together for convenience. Similarly, ideas expressed in written form are grouped together into paragraphs for the reader's convenience. Notice what happens when ideas are *not* grouped together, as in the following sentences:

> Willow trees provide a great deal of shade, but it is difficult to mow the lawn underneath them. Outdoor barbecues or corn roasts are enjoyable ways to entertain during the summer. When beginning college, many students are worried about whether or not they will know someone in each of their classes. The income tax structure in our country has been changed so that it does not discriminate against married couples who are both employed. Most people do not realize that tea and cola drinks contain as much caffeine as coffee.

This so-called paragraph is confusing because the train of thought is impossible to follow. It is not clear which idea or ideas are important and which are not. You have no sense of whether or not the ideas are connected to each other and, if they are, how they are related.

To avoid the confusion demonstrated in the example paragraph and to express written ideas in a clear, understandable way, writers follow a general pattern in developing paragraphs. You need to recognize this structure in order to read paragraphs efficiently. You will then be able to follow the author's train of thought more easily, anticipate ideas as they are about to be developed, and recall more of what you read.

A paragraph is structured around three essential elements: the topic, the main idea, and the supporting details that are often connected by transitional words or phrases. The function of each of these elements is discussed in this chapter.

Identifying the Topic

A paragraph can be defined as a group of related ideas. The sentences relate to one another in the sense that each is about a common person, place, thing, or idea. This common subject or idea is called the *topic*. Simply defined, the topic is what the entire paragraph is about. As you read the following paragraph, notice that each sentence discusses mortgages.

> One of the largest components of debt is the mortgage, the debt owed on real estate. In speaking of the mortgage market it is important to distinguish between real estate mortgages and mortgages as a type of security for a debt obligation. In one sense, one mortgages a car to secure a car loan. Any time an asset is pledged to secure a loan, a mortgage is created. Since real estate loans are so typically secured by a pledge of real estate, such loans are themselves called mortgages. Mortgage borrowing exceeds the combined borrowing of corporations and municipalities by a wide margin.
>
> Kolb, *Investments.*

In this paragraph you can see that each sentence defines, explains, or provides examples of mortgages.

To identify the topic of a paragraph, ask yourself this question: "Who or what is the paragraph about?" Your answer to this question will be the topic of the paragraph. Now, try using this question as you read the following paragraph.

> The characteristic of speed is universally associated with computers. Power is a derivative of speed as well as of other factors such as memory size. What makes a computer fast? Or, more to the point, what makes one computer faster than another? Several factors are involved, including microprocessor speed, bus line size, and the availability of cache. A user who is concerned about speed will want to address all of these. More sophisticated approaches to speed include flash memory, RISC computers, and parallel processing.
>
> Capron, *Computers: Tools for an Information Age.*

In this paragraph, the question leads you directly to the topic—computer speed. Each sentence in the paragraph discusses computer speed or approaches to it.

Now, try to identify the topic in the following paragraph.

> Next time you fill up your tank, look at the price schedule on the pump. There you will see that several cents of each gallon's price is a federal tax. (In addition, most states—and some cities—charge a tax on gasoline.) Most of these federal tax collections flow into highway trust funds, on the assumption that motorists should pay for the construction and repair of the nation's highways. (If you own a boat, you still pay the tax for gasoline. But you can receive a rebate of the federal tax proceeds at the end of the year. The reason, of course, is that boats don't need highways.)
>
> Chisholm and McCarty, *Principles of Economics.*

The topic of this paragraph is gasoline taxes. Each sentence discusses a type of or use for gasoline tax.

EXERCISE
4-1

DIRECTIONS: Read each of the following paragraphs and then select the topic of the paragraph from the choices given.

1. An estimated 6 percent of Americans suffer from seasonal affective disorder (SAD), a type of depression, and an additional 14 percent experience a milder form of the disorder known as winter blues. SAD strikes during the winter months and is associated with reduced exposure to sunlight. People with SAD suffer from irritability, apathy, carbohydrate craving and weight gain, increases in sleep time, and general sadness. Researchers believe that SAD is caused by a malfunction in the hypothalamus, the gland responsible for regulating responses to external stimuli. Stress may also play a role in SAD.

    Donatelle, *Access to Health.*

    a. hypothalamus malfunction
    b. winter blues
    c. seasonal affective disorder
    d. depression

2. Each year, thousands of people get sick from largely preventable diseases such as that caused by E. coli as well as other bacteria such as Salmonella and Listeria. In response to these illnesses, in February 2000, the USDA approved large-scale irradiation of beef, lamb, poultry, pork, and other raw animal foods. Food irradiation is a process that involves treating foods with gamma radiation from radioactive cobalt, cesium, or other sources of X-rays. When foods are irradiated, they are

exposed to low doses of radiation, or ionizing energy, which breaks chemical bonds in the DNA of harmful bacteria, destroying the pathogens and keeping them from replicating. The rays essentially pass through the food without leaving any radioactive residue.

Donatelle, Health: The Basics.

a. food irradiation
b. preventable diseases
c. harmful bacteria in meat
d. salmonella and listeria

3. Today, the formal educational standard for lawyers is 2 to 3 years of graduate study beyond the bachelor's degree. The most common career path for modern lawyers is to complete a bachelor's degree followed by law school. Law schools do not require a specific undergraduate curriculum for admission but recommend a good liberal arts background with emphasis on writing, comprehension, and analytical thinking. In addition to an undergraduate degree, nearly all law schools require the student to take the Law School Aptitude Test (LSAT). The LSAT is a standardized test that measures the student's analytical thinking and writing abilities. The LSAT does not measure the student's knowledge of the law.

Fagin, Criminal Justice.

a. completing law school
b. general liberal arts background
c. the LSAT
d. educational preparation for law school

**EXERCISE
4-2**

DIRECTIONS: Read each of the following paragraphs and then select the topic of the paragraph from the choices given.

1. Because conflict is inevitable, an essential relationship skill involves fighting fair. Winning at all costs, beating down the other person, getting one's own way, and the like have little use in a primary relationship or family. Instead, cooperation, compromise, and mutual understanding must be substituted. If we enter conflict with a person we love with the idea that we must win and the other must lose, the conflict has to hurt at least one partner, very often both. In these situations the loser gets hurt and frequently retaliates so that no one really wins in any meaningful sense. On the other hand, if we enter a conflict

to achieve some kind of mutual understanding, neither party need be hurt. Both parties, in fact, may benefit from the clash of ideas or desires and from the airing of differences.

DeVito, *Messages: Building Interpersonal Communication Skills.*

a. relationships
b. airing differences
c. fighting fair
d. conflicts

2. Both potential and kinetic energies can take many different forms. For example, a car battery has potential electrical energy. (We might also refer to it as chemical energy.) When the electrical energy is released to turn the starter, it becomes mechanical energy. As the parts of the starter move, friction causes some of the initial energy from the battery to be dissipated as heat energy. Thus, we see that not only can energy exist in different forms, it can also be converted from one form to another.

Wallace, *Biology: The World of Life.*

a. forms of energy
b. energy in batteries
c. potential and kinetic energy
d. mechanical energy

3. Different species forage in different ways. Basically, animals can be described as either generalists or specialists. Generalists are those species with a broad range of acceptable food items. They are often opportunists and will take advantage of whatever is available, with certain preferences, depending on the situation. Crows are an example of feeding generalists; they will eat anything from corn to carrion. Specialists are those with narrow ranges of acceptable food items. Some species are extremely specialized, such as the Everglade kite, or snail kite, which feeds almost exclusively on freshwater snails. There is a wide range of intermediate types between the two extremes, and in some species an animal will switch from being one type to being another depending on conditions, such as food availability or the demands of offspring.

Ferl, Wallace, and Sanders, *Biology: The Realm of Life.*

a. species of animals
b. generalists
c. demands of offspring
d. types of foragers

4. Much as we touch and are touched, we also avoid touch from certain people and in certain circumstances. Researchers in nonverbal communication have found some interesting relationships between touch avoidance and other significant communication variables. For example, touch avoidance is positively related to communication apprehension; those who fear oral communication also score high on touch avoidance. Touch avoidance is also high with those who self-disclose little. Both touch and self-disclosure are intimate forms of communication; thus, people who are reluctant to get close to another person by self-disclosing also seem reluctant to get close by touching.

    DeVito, *Messages: Building Interpersonal Communication Skills.*

    a. nonverbal communication
    b. self-disclosure
    c. touch avoidance
    d. communication apprehension

5. The current high divorce rate in the United States does not mean, as common sense would suggest, that the institution of marriage is very unpopular. On the contrary, people seem to love marriage too much, as suggested by several pieces of evidence. First, our society has the highest rate of marriage in the industrial world despite having the highest rate of divorce. Second, within the United States, most of the southeastern, southwestern, and western states have higher divorce rates than the national average but also have higher marriage rates. And third, the majority of those who are divorced eventually remarry. Why don't they behave like Mark Twain's cat, who after having been burned by a hot stove would not go near any stove? Apparently, divorce in U.S. society does not represent a rejection of marriage but only a specific partner.

    Thio, *Sociology.*

    a. the marriage rate
    b. popularity of marriage
    c. high divorce rates
    d. rejection of marriage

EXERCISE 4–3

DIRECTIONS: Read each of the following paragraphs and identify the topic by writing it in the space provided.

1. We know that changes in sea level have occurred in the past. In some instances, however, these were not related to changes in the volume of water, as was caused by melting or forming of glaciers. Rather, sea level shifted in response to changes in the shape of the ocean basin itself. Reducing the dimensions of the ocean basin (especially depth) by increasing the rates of subduction or seafloor spreading could cause a rise in sea level worldwide. An increase in the size of the ocean basin could cause a drop in sea level.

   Ross, Introduction to Oceanography.

   Topic: _____

2. Every culture has its theories about dreams. In some cultures, dreams are thought to occur when the spirit leaves the body to wander the world or speak to the gods. In others, dreams are thought to reveal the future. A Chinese Taoist of the third century B.C. pondered the possible reality of the dream world. He told of dreaming that he was a butterfly flitting about. "Suddenly I woke up and I was indeed Chuang Tzu. Did Chuang Tzu dream he was a butterfly, or did the butterfly dream he was Chuang Tzu?"

   Wade and Tavris, Psychology.

   Topic: _____

3. All surfaces have textures that can be experienced by touching or through visual suggestion. Textures are categorized as either actual or simulated. *Actual* textures are those we can feel by touching, such as polished marble, wood, sand, or swirls of thick paint. *Simulated* (or implied) textures are those created to look like something other than paint on a flat surface. A painter can simulate textures that look like real fur or wood but to the touch would feel like smooth paint. Artists can also invent actual or simulated textures. We can appreciate most textures even when we are not permitted to touch them, because we know, from experience, how they would feel.

   Preble et al., Artforms: An Introduction to the Visual Artist.

   Topic: _____

4. The spread of desert in Saharan Africa is not new. During the last ice age and the early post–ice-age period, the Sahara supported woodlands and grasslands. Rivers flowed northward through this land to the Mediterranean Sea, and the region was home to early agriculturists. Progressive climatic change over the last 6000 years has steadily reduced

rainfall in the region, and the desert has spread to cover the cities and once-fertile lands. The climatic cycles of the last several thousand years have minor wetter and drier phases superimposed on a general drying trend. Thus, the spread of the Saharan desert is basically a natural phenomenon. The most recent drought in northern Africa has caused a further expansion of the desert into the marginal semidesert areas at its edge, and actions of humans trying to survive in these areas have hastened the degradation of the land.

Bush, *Ecology for a Changing Planet.*

Topic: _____

5.   People in the United States have an abiding faith in the value of education. They see education as necessary for participating in democracy, for righting injustices, and for attaining personal happiness (Brint 1998, Davis and Smith 1987). Belief in education transcends the social divisions of race, class, and gender: Whites and nonwhites, women and men, the poor and the wealthy all believe that education is vital for the survival of a free people and for the individual's social and economic advancement. This belief has led the United States to spend more than $500 billion a year on education and to develop the most comprehensive educational system in the world.

Curry et al., *Sociology for the Twenty-First Century.*

Topic: _____

Finding the Main Idea

When you make phone calls have you found it helpful to state the general purpose of your call as you begin your conversation? Have you found that in answering a help-wanted ad, it is useful to begin by saying, "I'm calling about your ad in . . ."? Or, when calling a doctor's office to make an appointment, you might say, "I'm calling to make an appointment to see Dr. —." Beginning with a general statement such as these helps your listener understand why you are calling and what you want. It also allows the listener time to focus his or her attention before you begin to give the details of your situation. The general statement also gives the listener a chance to organize himself or herself or to get ready to receive the information.

Writers also need to help the reader understand the purpose and organization of a written message. Readers, like listeners, sometimes need assistance in focusing and organizing their thoughts and in anticipating the development of the message. Writers, therefore, often provide a general, organizing statement of the main idea of each paragraph. The sentence that most clearly states this main idea is called the *topic sentence.*

Depending on its placement within the paragraph, the topic sentence provides the reader with different clues. In this section, several of the most common placements of topic sentences and the clues that each offers the reader about paragraph development and organization are discussed. Each type has been diagrammed to help you visualize how it is structured.

Topic Sentence First

The most common location of the topic sentence is the beginning of the paragraph. It may appear as the very first sentence or after an introductory or transitional sentence (one that connects this paragraph to the preceding paragraph). In cases with the topic sentence first, the author states his or her main idea and then moves on to specifics that explain and develop that idea, as in the following paragraph.

> <u>Americans even differ in their preferences for "munchies."</u> The average consumer eats 21 pounds of snack foods in a year (hopefully not all at one sitting), but people in the West Central part of the country consume the most (24 pounds per person) whereas those in the Pacific and Southeast regions eat "only" 19 pounds per person. Pretzels are the most popular snack in the Mid-Atlantic area, pork rinds are most likely to be eaten in the South, and multigrain chips turn up as a favorite in the West. Not surprisingly, the Hispanic influence in the Southwest has influenced snacking preferences—consumers in that part of the United States eat about 50 percent more tortilla chips than do people elsewhere.
>
> Solomon, *Consumer Behavior.*

Notice that the author begins by stating that Americans differ in their preferences for "munchies" or snack foods. Then, throughout the remainder of the paragraph, he explains how they differ in the amounts and types of snacks they eat. When the topic sentence appears first in the paragraph, it announces what the paragraph will be about and what to expect in the remainder of the paragraph.

Topic Sentence Last

The second most likely place for a topic sentence to appear is the end of the paragraph. However, on occasion you may find that it is expressed in the second-to-last sentence, with the last sentence functioning as a restatement or as a transition to connect the paragraph with what follows. When the topic sentence occurs last, you can expect the writer to build a structure of ideas and offer the topic sentence as a concluding statement. Commonly used in argumentative or persuasive writing, this structure uses sentences within the paragraph as building blocks that support the topic sentence. Notice in the following paragraph that the author leads up to the main idea and states it at the end of the paragraph.

> We can measure the radioactivity of plants and animals today and compare this with the radioactivity of ancient organic matter. If we extract a small, but precise, quantity of carbon from an ancient wooden ax handle, for example, and find it has one-half as much radioactivity as an equal quantity of carbon extracted from a living tree, then the old wood must have come from a tree that was cut down or made from a log that died 5730 years ago. <u>In this way, we can probe into the past as much as 50,000 years to find out such things as the age of ancient civilizations or the times of the ice ages that covered the earth.</u>
>
> Hewitt, *Conceptual Physics.*

In this paragraph the author begins by explaining that radioactivity of plants and animals can be measured and can be compared with older organic matter. Then he uses an example describing how the radioactivity of an ancient ax handle can be measured and how its age can be determined. In the last sentence the author states the main idea, that this procedure can be used to learn about the past.

Topic Sentence in the Middle

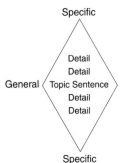

If it is neither first nor last the topic sentence will, of course, appear somewhere in the middle of the paragraph. In this case, the topic sentence splits the paragraph into two parts: those sentences preceding it and those that follow it. The sentences that precede the topic sentence often lead up to or introduce the main idea. At other times, the preceding sentences may function as a transition, connecting the ideas to be expressed in the paragraph with ideas in previous paragraphs. The sentences that follow the topic sentence usually explain, describe, or provide further information about the main idea. Notice the placement of the topic sentence as you read the following paragraph.

> Unlike people in the United States, who believe that different individuals have different abilities, the Japanese believe that all students have much the same innate ability and that differences in academic performance must be due to differences in

effort. <u>Therefore, the key to superior performance is hard work, which begins at an early age.</u> Before most Japanese children even enroll in school, their parents—usually their mothers—have taught them numbers, the alphabet, and some art skills. By age four, more than 90 percent of Japanese children are attending preschool in order to receive a head start on their education. The typical Japanese student spends six to seven hours a day in school, five full days a week and a half-day on Saturday.

Curry et al., Sociology for the Twenty-First Century.

The paragraph begins by offering some statistics that compare Japanese and American beliefs about academic performance. In the middle of the paragraph the writer makes a general statement about what Japanese believe is the key to superior performance. This is the topic sentence of the paragraph. The author then offers additional facts that support the topic sentence.

Topic Sentence First and Last

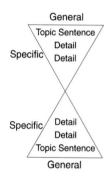

Occasionally you may find a paragraph in which the main idea is stated at the beginning and again at the end. This structure is often used for emphasis or clarification. If a writer wants to emphasize an important idea, he or she may repeat it at the end of the paragraph. Or, a writer who thinks an idea needs to be said another way to ensure that the reader understands it may repeat it at the end of the paragraph. In the following paragraph notice that both the first and last sentences state, in different words, the same idea.

<u>The study of prehistoric humans is, of necessity, the study of their fossil remains.</u> To begin to understand who our ancestors were and what they were like, we must be able to interpret the fragments of them that are coming to the surface in increasing numbers. Given fairly reliable methods to determine their age, we can now turn with more confidence to primate fossils for an answer to the all-important question: How do we tell monkeys, apes, and humans apart? For present-day species this is no problem; all have evolved sufficiently so that they no longer resemble one another. But since they all have a common ancestor, the farther back we go in time, the more similar their fossils begin to look. There finally comes a point when they are indistinguishable. <u>The construction of a primate fossil family tree is essential if we are ever going to discover the line of descent from early hominid to modern human.</u>

Campbell and Loy, Humankind Emerging.

In the preceding paragraph, both the first and last sentences state that the study of fossils enables us to study prehistoric man. The other sentences explain why fossils are important and how they can be used to distinguish stages in the development of man.

DIRECTIONS: Read the following paragraphs and underline the topic sentences in each.

1. People are affected by various elements of climate. The number of hours of sunshine in a day and the degree of cloudiness are important to anyone who is active out of doors—gardeners, farmers, hunters, builders, vacationers at the beach—and residents of homes heated by solar energy. Amounts of rainfall and snowfall make great differences in how we build our homes and roads from place to place. The windiness of a place is important in designing structures and harnessing wind power. Pollutants in the air can have both short-term and long-term effects on human and animal health. Counts of pollen and mold spores are important to those who suffer allergies.

   Bergman and Renwick, *Introduction to Geography.*

2. Manners or etiquette are the rules of a society and different societies have different manners. For example, in Great Britain, parts of Canada, and several European countries, it is customary to hold the knife in the right hand and use it to push food around the plate and onto the fork. This is called the "Continental style" while the "American style" of table manners prohibits pushing food onto the fork with a knife. In general, European-based cultures have similar rules of etiquette. Asian and Arab cultures tend to be very different from Western cultures in their manners.

   Adapted from Cook, Yale, and Marqua, *Tourism: The Business of Travel.*

3. When you're in debt, you speak of being "in the red"; when you make a profit, you're "in the black." When you're sad, you're "blue"; when you're healthy, you're "in the pink"; when you're jealous, you're "green with envy." To be a coward is to be "yellow" and to be inexperienced is to be "green." When you talk a great deal, you talk "a blue streak"; when you're angry, you "see red." As revealed through these timeworn cliches, language abounds in color symbolism.

   DeVito, *The Interpersonal Communication Book.*

4. Suppose a friend holds up her hand, palm flattened, to signal "stop" to someone standing across the room from her. A basketball coach may motion "time out" with his hands to communicate to a player on the court that the player should signal the referee to stop play so that the team can discuss a new strategy. Both of these situations demonstrate the use of emblems—body motions that take the place of words. In order for emblems to be an effective form of nonverbal communica-

tion, both parties must readily understand the motions being used. A spectator unfamiliar with sports might not understand the "time out" motion used by those involved in the game and therefore might question why the referee officially signaled time out. Emblems also can be used effectively when there are obstacles to verbal communication. The example of the basketball game applies here as well; the coach may signal to a player to call for time out because the crowd is generating too much noise for the coach to be heard by the player.

Adapted from Dunn and Goodnight, Communication.

5. At Steelcase, Inc. <u>www.steelcase.com</u>, the country's largest maker of office furniture, two very talented women in the marketing division both wanted to work only part-time. The solution: They now share a single full-time job. With each working 2.5 days a week, both got their wish and the job gets done—and done well. In another situation, one person might work mornings and the other afternoons. The practice, known as work sharing (or job sharing), has improved job satisfaction among employees.

Adapted from Ebert and Griffin, Business Essentials.

EXERCISE 4-5

DIRECTIONS: Read each of the following paragraphs and then select the main idea of each from the choices given.

1. If legislation can compel people to give up discrimination, what about their prejudice? It is true, as many lawmakers believe, that we cannot legislate against prejudice because such legislation is practically unenforceable. That is probably why we do not have any antiprejudice law. But by legislating against discrimination, we can gradually eliminate prejudice. Sample research has long established that people tend to change their attitude if it has been inconsistent for some time with their behavior. This usually involves changing their attitude so that it becomes consistent with their behavior. Thus, people can be expected to gradually change their prejudicial attitude into an unprejudicial one after they have been legally forced to develop the habit of behaving nondiscriminatorily. Indeed, since 1954 a series of civil rights laws and court rulings have caused many whites to stop their discriminatory practices and to reevaluate their attitude toward blacks. Today fewer whites are prejudiced. They do not express their prejudice in the traditional stereotypical "redneck" way but in a more indirect, subtle manner.

Thio, Sociology.

a. Prejudice can be defeated by passing laws against discrimination.
b. Civil rights laws have stopped whites from discriminating against blacks.
c. Most white Americans are prejudiced.
d. We cannot legislate against prejudice.

2. The major benefit of steroids seems to be to allow muscles to recover more quickly from exercise, so that the athlete can train harder. As athletes were reporting remarkable results with steroids, the medical community began testing the effects of the drugs and the drugs were soon banned. Medical researchers reported a variety of serious side effects of steroid use, including liver cancer, heart disease, and kidney damage. One problem with the drugs is that, along with tissue building, they also "masculinize." The masculinization is particularly acute for women, who may grow facial hair as their voices deepen and their breasts decrease in size. They may, indeed, gain muscle mass, but the masculinizing effects may be impossible to reverse. In adolescents, steroids hasten maturation and may cause growth to stop and the loss of hair in boys. Strangely, in men, the high levels of steroids in the body may cause the body's own production of male hormone to cease, resulting in enlarged breasts and shrunken testes.

Wallace, *Biology: The World of Life.*

a. Muscle recovery from exercise is aided by steroids.
b. The medical community recently began testing the results of steroids.
c. There are a number of serious side effects from steroid use.
d. Some women grow facial hair as a result of steroids.

3. In addition to expressing their feelings toward others through consumption, people commonly find (or devise) reasons to give themselves something as well. It is common for consumers to purchase **self-gifts** as a way to regulate their behavior. This ritual provides a socially acceptable way of rewarding themselves for good deeds, consoling themselves after negative events, or motivating themselves to accomplish some goal. Indeed, retailers report that it is becoming increasingly common for people to treat themselves while they are ostensibly searching for goodies for others. As one shopper admitted recently, "It's one for them, one for me, one for them."

Solomon, *Consumer Behavior.*

a. People express feelings toward others through gift giving.
b. Retailers promote self—gift giving.

c. Gift giving is socially acceptable.

d. People use gifts to themselves to regulate their behavior.

4. Assertive people are willing to assert their own rights. Unlike their aggressive counterparts, however, they do not hurt others in the process. Assertive people speak their minds and welcome others doing likewise. Robert Alberti and Michael Emmons (1970), in *Your Perfect Right,* the first book on assertiveness training, note that "behavior which enables a person to act in his own best interest, to stand up for himself without undue anxiety, to express his honest feelings comfortably, or to exercise his own rights without denying the rights of others we call assertive behavior." Furthermore, "The assertive individual is fully in charge of himself in interpersonal relationships, feels confident and capable without cockiness or hostility, is basically spontaneous in the expression of feelings and emotions, and is generally looked up to and admired by others." Surely this is the picture of an effective individual.

DeVito, *Messages: Building Interpersonal Communication Skills.*

a. Assertive people stand up for themselves without hurting others.

b. Aggressive individuals do not care if they hurt other people.

c. Alberti and Emmons wrote the first book on assertiveness training.

d. Effective individuals are the result of assertiveness training.

5. Like all the topics covered in this text, power too has an important cultural dimension. In some cultures power is concentrated in the hands of a few and there is a great difference in the power held by these people and by the ordinary citizen: These are called high power distance cultures; examples include Mexico, Brazil, India, and the Philippines. In low power distance cultures, power is more evenly distributed throughout the citizenry; examples include Denmark, New Zealand, Sweden, and to a lesser extent, the United States. These differences impact on communication in a number of ways. For example, in high power distance cultures there is a great power distance between students and teachers; students are expected to be modest, polite, and totally respectful. In the United States, on the other hand, students are expected to demonstrate their knowledge and command of the subject matter, participate in discussions with the teacher, and even challenge the teacher, something many African and Asian students wouldn't even think of doing.

DeVito, *Messages: Building Interpersonal Communication Skills.*

a. Low power distance cultures distribute power evenly.

b. African and Asian students would never challenge the teacher.

      c. How power is distributed in a culture determines people's
        behaviors.

      d. Only a few people possess power in Mexico, Brazil, India, and the
        Philippines.

**EXERCISE
4-6**

DIRECTIONS: Read the following paragraphs and underline the topic sentence in each.

1. Many Americans with disabilities have suffered from both direct and indirect discrimination. They have often been denied rehabilitation services (a kind of affirmative action), education, and jobs. Many people with disabilities have been excluded from the workforce and isolated without overt discrimination. Throughout most of American history, public and private buildings have been hostile to the blind, deaf, and mobility-impaired. Stairs, buses, telephones, and other necessities of modern life have been designed in ways that keep these individuals out of offices, stores, and restaurants. As one slogan said: "Once, blacks had to ride at the back of the bus. We can't even get on the bus."

                          Edwards et al., *Government in America.*

2. A few years ago it was said that a biologist is one who thinks that molecules are too small to matter, a physicist is one who thinks that molecules are too large to matter, and anyone who disagrees with both of them is a chemist. Many biologists, though, are in fact chemists, and vice versa. Perhaps it is true that the biologist whose scope is limited to molecules must periodically be convinced of the existence of the platypus, but no one else has been able to tell us how tiny hummingbirds are able to make it across the Gulf of Mexico. Fortunately, the sharp lines of division between such disciplines are becoming blurred and indistinct as scientists become more broadly trained and able to handle more kinds of ideas in their continuing effort to solve the "Great Puzzle of Life."

                          Wallace, *Biology: The World of Life.*

3. When frustrations arising from nonproductive behaviors are kept to a minimum, groups can function in an efficient and effective manner. There are, however, times when a group's task and social needs come into direct conflict. If, for example, a group becomes unhappy with its leadership, task-related activities may grind to a halt while members concentrate on the social atmosphere. The group may need to reorganize by appointing new leaders or reassigning responsibilities in

order to refocus its attention on task issues. A group also may assume a "know nothing" attitude, in which it despairs of ever having enough information to make a decision (hence relieving it of the responsibility for acting). In this social atmosphere the group may appoint ad hoc study groups to gain new information or postpone consideration of an issue until new information is forthcoming from outside the group. In both cases, task activities are inhibited by a negative social atmosphere that promotes apathy and indifference at the expense of involvement and commitment.

Benjamin and McKerrow, Business and Professional Communication: Concepts and Practices.

4. This basic division of labor has been accompanied by many popular stereotypes—oversimplified mental images—of what women and men are supposed to be, and to some extent these stereotypes persist. Women are supposed to be shy, easily intimidated, and passive; men, bold, ambitious, and aggressive. Women should be weak and dainty; men, strong and athletic. It is not bad form for women, but it is for men, to worry about their appearance and aging. Women are expected to be emotional, even to cry easily, but men should hold back their emotions and must not cry. Women are expected to be sexually passive and naive; men, aggressive and experienced. Women are believed to be dependent, in need of male protection; men are supposed to be independent, fit to be leaders. Women are expected to be intuitive and inconsistent; men, logical, rational, and objective.

Thio, Sociology.

5. If you are a member of an ethnic group, the assumption of a company that all employees are the same and are treated the same may not hold true in your experience. The fact, for example, that there are associations solely for the support of African-American employees suggests that we still have a ways to go in removing obstacles. In reacting to issues, companies employ a variety of strategies, based on face-to-face communication. Mobil Oil Corporation, for example, did not sit on the assumption that all was well. Instead, it formed two sets of training programs, with one expressly for minority professionals. This gave the minority employees a forum in which to air their perceptions and a means of using communication positively to arrive at solutions. Other companies initiate informal group discussions to ascertain the nature of problems. Out of these, as in the case of Michigan Bell, can come more formalized groups that meet to consider issues that have an impact on ethnic relations.

Benjamin and McKerrow, Business and Professional Communication: Concepts and Practices.

DIRECTIONS: The following excerpt is taken from a biology textbook chapter titled "Bioethics, Technology, and Environment." Read the excerpt and underline the topic sentence in each paragraph.

POLLUTION BY PESTICIDES

Pesticides are biologically rather interesting substances. Most have no known counterpart in the natural world, and most didn't even exist fifty years ago. Today, however, a metabolic product of DDT, called DDE, may be the most common synthetic chemical on earth. It has been found in the tissues of living things from polar regions to the remotest parts of the oceans, forests, and mountains. Although the permissible level of DDT in cow's milk, set by the U.S. Food and Drug Administration, is 0.05 parts per million, it often occurs in human milk in concentrations as high as five parts per million and in human fat at levels of more than twelve parts per million.

Pesticides, of course, are products that kill pests. But what is a pest? Biologically, the term has no meaning. The Colorado potato beetle, for example, was never regarded as a pest until it made its way (carried by humans) to Europe, where it began to seriously interfere with potato production. Perhaps this episode best illustrates a definition of a pest: it is something that interferes with humans.

It seems that the greatest pesticidal efforts have been directed at insects and, clearly, much of it has been beneficial. The heavy application of DDT after World War II decreased malaria and yellow fever in certain areas of the world. But DDT and other chlorinated hydrocarbons have continued to be spread indiscriminately any place in which insect pests are found. The result of course, is a kind of (is it artificial or natural?) selection. The problem was that some insects had a bit more resistance to these chemicals than did others. These resistant ones then reproduced and, in turn, the most resistant of their offspring continued the line. The result is that we now have insects that can almost bathe in these chemicals without harm, and malaria is again on the rise.

There are also other risks involved in such wide use of insecticides. For example, most are unselective in their targets; they kill virtually *all* the insect species they contact. Many insects, of course, are beneficial and may form an important part of large ecosystems. Also, some chemical insecticides move easily through the environment and can permeate far larger areas than intended. Another particularly serious problem with pesticides is that many of them persist in the environment for long periods. In other words, some chemicals are very stable and it is difficult for natural processes to break them down to their harmless components. Newer chemical pesticides are deadly in the short run, but quickly break down into harmless by-products.

In the past, the tendency of DDT to be magnified in food chains has been particularly disastrous for predators that fed high on the food pyramid. This is because as one animal eats another in the food chain, the pesticide from each level is added to the next. Thus, species high on the food chain, the predators, tend to accumulate very high levels of these chemicals. In this light, recall that humans are often the top predator in food chains. Before it was banned in the United States, the effects of accumulated DDT on predatory birds was substantial. Reproductive failures in peregrine falcons, the brown pelican, and the Bermuda petrel have been attributed to ingesting high levels of DDT. The problem is that the pesticide interferes with the birds' ability to metabolize calcium. As a result, they were laying eggs with shells too thin to support the weight of a nesting parent. With the decline in the use of the pesticide, many bird populations have recovered.

Wallace, *Biology: The World of Life.*

EXERCISE 4-8

DIRECTIONS: Read each of the following paragraphs, and then, in the space provided, write a statement that expresses the main idea of the paragraph.

1. Many flowers pollinated by birds are red or pink, colors to which bird eyes are especially sensitive. The shape of the flower may also be important. Flowers that depend largely on hummingbirds, for example, typically have their nectar located deep in a floral tube, where only the long, thin beak and tongue of the bird are likely to reach. As a hummingbird flies among flowers in search of nectar, its feathers and beak pick up pollen from the anthers of the flowers. It will deposit the pollen in other flowers of the same shape, and so probably of the same species, as it continues to feed.

Campbell et al., *Biology: Concepts and Connections.*

Main Idea: _____

2. People migrate for two broad reasons. The first, called *push factors,* are the reasons for leaving a place. Although there may be any number of personal reasons for leaving, the underlying reasons are mostly political and economic. For instance, during the nineteenth century the failure of the potato crop in Ireland "pushed" thousands of Irish to the United States. *Pull factors,* on the other hand, are the forces that attract migrants to a place, such as a congenial government or good weather conditions. Push and pull factors work together. People being pushed from one place will, if they have a choice, go to places that have many pull factors.

Curry et al., *Sociology for the Twenty-First Century.*

Main Idea: _____

3. A consumer's overall evaluation of a product sometimes accounts for the bulk of his or her attitude. When market researchers want to assess attitudes, it can be sufficient for them to simply ask consumers, "How do you feel about Budweiser?" However, as we saw earlier, attitudes can

be composed of many *attributes*, or qualities—some of these may be more important than others to particular people. Another problem is that a person's decision to act on his or her attitude is affected by other factors, such as whether it is felt that buying a product would be met with approval by friends or family. As a result *attitude models* have been developed that try to specify the different elements that might work together to influence people's evaluations of attitude objects.

Solomon, *Consumer Behavior.*

Main Idea: _____

_____

4. The head muscles are an interesting group. They have many specific functions but are usually grouped into two large categories—facial muscles and chewing muscles. Facial muscles are unique because they are inserted into soft tissues such as other muscles or skin. When they pull on the skin of the face, they permit us to smile faintly, grin widely, frown, pout, deliver a kiss, and so forth. The chewing muscles begin the breakdown of food for the body.

Marieb, *Essentials of Human Anatomy and Physiology.*

Main Idea: _____

_____

5. The Internet began as a transmitter of data a generation ago. More recently, it has begun to expand into audio and video services. This is done through a technical process known as streaming, which makes possible real-time delivery of digitized audio and video on computer screens. The data arrives in a PC buffer (temporary storage) and is available for viewing a few seconds later. Once a viewer starts watching, the data continues to arrive. The result is a constant flow of video or audio programming thanks to a continuous filling of the buffer. The process is not always smooth, but it provides a reasonable facsimile of a conventional TV program, albeit one that is limited, for the present, to a small part of the computer's screen.

Dizard, *Old Media, New Media: Mass Communications in the Information Age.*

Main Idea: _____

_____

Specific

Detail
Detail
Detail

Specific

Paragraphs Without a Topic Sentence

Although most paragraphs do have a topic sentence, occasionally you will encounter a paragraph without one sentence that clearly expresses the main idea. This structure is used most commonly in descriptive or narrative writing. In these paragraphs you must form your own statement or impression of the main idea. Although the paragraph contains numerous clues, the reader must piece together the information to form a generalized statement.

Here is a paragraph that does not contain a topic sentence:

> The process of becoming hypnotized begins when the people who will be hypnotized find a comfortable body position and become thoroughly relaxed. Without letting their minds wander to other matters, they focus their attention on a specific object or sound, such as a metronome or the hypnotist's voice. Then, based on both what the hypnotherapist expects to occur and actually sees occurring, she or he tells the clients how they will feel as the hypnotic process continues. For instance, the hypnotist may say, "You are feeling completely relaxed" or "Your eyelids are becoming heavy." When people being hypnotized recognize that their feelings match the hypnotist's comments, they are likely to believe that some change is taking place. That belief seems to increase their openness to other statements made by the hypnotist.
>
> Uba and Huang, *Psychology.*

This paragraph discusses the steps that occur in the process of hypnosis. The first sentence tells how the process begins (with relaxation and a comfortable body position) and the second presents what happens next (focusing the mind) and so forth. Each sentence is concerned with a different step on the way to being hypnotized. Although this paragraph lacks a topic sentence that explains what the paragraph is about, the main idea is quite clear: "The process of being hypnotized follows several steps."

Here is another example:

> The word *biologist* may cause some to conjure up the image of a little old man with a squeaky right shoe, padding through aisles of dusty books on the trail of some ancient description of an extinct lizard. Others may visualize a butterfly chaser with thick glasses, net poised, leaping gleefully through the bushes. Others may think of a biologist as a bird-watcher in sensible shoes, peering through field glasses in the cold, wet dawn in hope of catching a glimpse of the rare double-breasted sapsucker. Maybe such images do fit some biologists, but there are others who search for the mysteries of life in other places, such as in clean, well-lit laboratories amid sparkling glassware.
>
> Wallace, *Biology: The World of Life.*

The paragraph describes various images of what biologists do. Each sentence contributes a different image. Taken together, these descriptions indicate that biologists are engaged in a wide range of activities that include, but also extend beyond the popular images.

From these examples you can see that in some paragraphs the topic sentence is not necessary—the reader can easily "add up" the facts and arrive at his or her own statement of the main idea. If you encounter a paragraph in which the main idea is unstated and not immediately evident, first identify the topic, then ask yourself this question: "What does the writer want me to know about the topic?" In most cases, your answer will be a statement of the writer's main idea.

Once you have identified the main idea in a paragraph in which it is unstated, it may be useful to make a marginal note that summarizes the main idea of that paragraph. Then, when you are reviewing the material, it will not be necessary to reread the entire paragraph.

EXERCISE 4-9

DIRECTIONS: Each of the following paragraphs lacks a topic sentence. Read each paragraph and select the statement that best expresses the main idea of the paragraph.

1. Movies from the United States are seen worldwide. Consumer products made in the United States are sold in most countries throughout the world. Many clothing styles that become popular in foreign countries first begin in the U.S. American restaurant chains like McDonald's exist even in Communist countries. U.S. television shows are routinely translated and broadcast in non-English speaking countries. American music is played by radio stations across the globe and American pop stars enjoy fame on other continents.

   a. American products and trends have a broad impact on the rest of the world.
   b. Foreign countries are not as familiar with American culture.
   c. Communist countries are most resistant to the influence of American culture.
   d. American culture can be used to affect the views and opinions of the people of other countries.

2. Stockholders in a corporation each own shares of the corporation and share in the profits. However, stockholders don't communicate with each other or cooperate to control the corporation. The stockholders do vote and their votes elect a board of directors. The directors have overall control of the company and make decisions about how to raise money,

spend money and pay dividends to shareholders. The directors select the president, vice president, treasurer, secretary and other officers who handle day to day decisions and operations for the corporation.

a. Shareholders stand to profit the most from their stake in a corporation.

b. A corporation's board of directors has the most power.

c. Shareholders own a corporation, but the board of directors controls it.

d. Dividends are profits earned by the corporation, paid out by the board of directors and owned by the shareholders.

3. On January 9, 1991, the Foreign Minister of Iraq, Tariq Aziz, met with the American Secretary of State, James Baker, to discuss Iraq's invasion of Kuwait. Seated next to Aziz was the half-brother of Iraq's president, Saddam Hussein. Baker said, "If you do not move out of Kuwait we will attack you." A clear statement, right? But his nonverbal language was that of an American diplomat—moderate and restrained. He did not shout, stamp his feet, or wave his hands. Saddam Hussein's brother, for his part, behaved like a normal Iraqi. He paid attention to Baker's nonverbal language, which he considered the important form of communication. He reported to Saddam Hussein that Baker was "not at all angry. The Americans are just talking, and they will not attack." Saddam therefore instructed Aziz to be inflexible and to yield nothing. The misunderstanding contributed to the outbreak of a bloody war [the Persian Gulf War] in which thousands of people died.

Wade and Tarvis, *Psychology.*

a. The Persian Gulf War was caused by James Baker.

b. Cultural differences in nonverbal communication can drastically affect how a message is interpreted.

c. Saddam Hussein's brother had little training in interpreting body language.

d. Diplomats should use interpreters to avoid miscommunication.

4. Until the early 1990s, no television network would air a paid condom commercial. Today, three of the six major networks allow condom companies to advertise on their airwaves, with some limitations on topic, tone, and time of day. Fox began accepting condom ads in 1991, CBS in 1998, and NBC in 1999. ABC, UPN, and The WB continue to prohibit paid condom ads. ABC airs ads for prescription birth control pills, and The WB says it would consider ads for the pill as well. Several cable companies have allowed condom advertising for years, and some

broadcasters that restrict paid condom ads accept public service ads referencing condoms or safe sex.

Shehan, Marriages and Families.

    a. Public service ads are the best way to get safe sex information to the viewing audiences of all television networks.
    b. Television networks are gradually becoming more liberal about permitting advertising for condoms and other birth control.
    c. Television networks restrict condom advertising out of a fear of insulting viewers.
    d. If advertisers of birth control products offered higher compensation, more networks would carry their ads.

5.   High rollers are gamblers who spend more and play games that require skill. They also are the gamblers with the highest incomes or assets, allowing them to bet more than other gamblers. Day-trippers are mostly retirees who enjoy playing slots. They spend more than most gamblers, but not as much as high rollers. Low stakes gamblers are those who are just beginning to discover gambling close to home and view it as a form of entertainment. Family vacationers make up the other category of gamblers. For these, gambling is a small part of a vacation.

    a. Gambling is done mostly by retirees.
    b. High rollers spend the most and play games of skill.
    c. Gambling is an important part of vacation plans for many people.
    d. There are four main types of gamblers with distinctive characteristics.

EXERCISE 4-10

DIRECTIONS: Read the following paragraphs, which contain no topic sentences, and then select the main idea of each from the choices given.

1.   Much like others form images of you based on what you do, you also react to your own behavior; you interpret it and evaluate it. For example, let us say you believe that lying is wrong. If you lie, you will evaluate this behavior in terms of your internalized beliefs about lying. You will thus react negatively to your own behavior. You may, for example, experience guilt because your behavior contradicts your beliefs. On the other hand, let's say that you pulled someone out of a burning building at great personal risk. You would probably evaluate this behavior positively; you will feel good about this behavior and, as a result, about yourself.

DeVito, Messages: Building Interpersonal Communication Skills.

    a. If you feel good about your behavior you will feel good about yourself.

    b. How you react to your own behavior helps you to form a self-concept.

    c. You feel guilt when your behavior contradicts your beliefs.

    d. You need to take risks to feel good about yourself.

2. If you are using an object, bring it into view as it becomes the "center" of your speech, and then take the time to remove it from view. Otherwise, your audience's attention both before and after the demonstration will be focused on the object rather than the message. If your speech concerns steps in a process, and using objects helps clarify the methods employed, bring samples of finished stages with you. Do not attempt to work through a complex procedure on a single object. If you need to pass the object around the room, realize that as it moves from person to person less attention will be focused on your message. If you have the time and can continue discussing features of the object as it is passed around, you can focus the listeners' attention on your comments. You will find this approach makes it easier to move on to other phases of your message as you retrieve the object and place it out of sight. If this approach is impractical, and you have to leave the object in plain view, you can refocus attention by using other visual aids.

    Benjamin and McKerrow, *Business and Professional Communication: Concepts and Practices.*

    a. When giving a speech about a physical object, pass it around the room.

    b. Use objects when giving speeches about steps in a process.

    c. Use other visual aids to refocus attention during speeches involving objects.

    d. When giving a speech involving an object, plan how you will use it in advance.

3. People's acceptance of a product is largely determined by its package. The very same coffee taken from a yellow can was described as weak, from a dark brown can too strong, from a red can rich, and from a blue can mild. Even our acceptance of a person may depend on the colors worn. Consider, for example, the comments of one color expert "If you have to pick the wardrobe for your defense lawyer heading into court and choose anything but blue, you deserve to lose the case. . . ." Black is so powerful it could work against the lawyer with the jury. Brown lacks sufficient authority. Green would probably elicit a negative response.

    DeVito, *Messages: Building Interpersonal Communication Skills.*

a. Colors have an influence on how we think and act.
b. A product's package largely determines how we accept it.
c. How effective lawyers are depends on their wardrobe colors.
d. Color experts rank blue as the most influential to be worn.

4. Bonds hold atoms together, forming molecules. An ionic bond, due to the attractive force between two ions of opposite charge, is formed when electrons are transferred from one atom to another. A covalent bond is formed when atoms share electrons. In some molecules shared electrons are more strongly attracted to one of the atoms, polarizing the molecule. A hydrogen bond is a weak bond formed when the positive end of a hydrogen atom that is covalently bonded to one molecule is attracted to the negative end of another polar molecule. Hydrogen bonding between water molecules gives water some of its unusual characteristics.

Wallace, *Biology: The World of Life.*

a. Ionic bonds involve the transfer of electrons between atoms.
b. A number of bonds can be involved in molecule formation.
c. The attraction between electrons and atoms causes bonds.
d. Covalent bonds are formed when atoms share electrons.

5. The United States, Western European countries, and Japan are core countries, the world's upper class, the most industrialized and richest societies, popularly known as industrial or developed countries. They have highly diversified economies, producing practically anything from corn to microchips. They also have a very high standard of living, stable governments, and a great deal of individual freedom. Countries with the least influence in the world are called peripheral countries—the world's lower class, relatively poor societies, popularly known as developing countries. These are the predominantly agricultural countries in Africa, Asia, and Latin America. Their economies are highly specialized, producing and exporting to core countries only a few raw materials or foodstuffs, such as oil, copper, sugar, or coffee. Their governments tend to be unstable.

Thio, *Sociology.*

a. The United States, Western Europe, and Japan are the world's upper class.
b. The developing countries are known as peripheral countries.
c. There are many differences between core and peripheral countries.
d. The core countries are also known as industrialized or developed countries.

**EXERCISE
4-11**

DIRECTIONS: Read each of the following paragraphs, none of which has a topic sentence. For each, write your own statement of the main idea of the paragraph.

1. Some agricultural and business interests, eager to exploit this supply of cheap labor, have opposed strict enforcement of immigration laws. Others have pointed out that ending illegal immigration could have negative effects: It might lead even more industries to relocate to foreign countries where labor is cheap, cause the rate of inflation to rise, and damage diplomatic relations. Labor unions, on the other hand, fearing a possible loss of jobs for Americans, have favored a crackdown on illegal immigration. And population-minded groups have insisted that the influx of immigrants is canceling out the benefits that have accrued from recent declines in the U.S. birth rate.

    Popenoe, *Sociology.*

    Main Idea: _____

    _____

2. Imagine that you have filled a glass up to its rim with water. Carefully adding a few more drops of water or dropping in some pennies does not cause the water to overflow. Instead the water seems to adhere to itself, forming a dome that rises slightly above the rim of the glass. This effect is the result of the polarity of water. Throughout the liquid in the glass, water molecules are attracted in all directions by surrounding water molecules. However, the water molecules on the surface are pulled like a skin toward the rest of the water in the glass. As a result, the water molecules on the surface become more tightly packed, a feature called **surface tension.** Because of surface tension, a needle floats on the top of water, certain water bugs can travel across the surface of a pond or lake, and drops of water are spherical.

    Timberlake, *Chemistry: An Introduction to General, Organic and Biological Chemistry.*

    Main Idea: _____

    _____

    _____

3. Polls can be found indicating strong support for a woman's right to choose, whereas other polls indicate strong majorities opposing unlimited abortion. Proponents of choice believe that access to abortion is

essential if women are to be fully autonomous human beings. Opponents call themselves pro-life because they believe that the fetus is fully human; therefore, an abortion deprives a fetus of the right to life. These positions are irreconcilable, making abortion a politician's nightmare. Wherever a politician stands on this divisive issue, a large number of voters will be enraged.

Edwards et al., Government in America: People, Politics and Policy.

Main Idea: _____

_____

4. Most hospitals, designed to handle injuries and acute illness that are common in the young, do not have the facilities or personnel to treat the chronic degenerative diseases of the elderly. Many doctors are also ill-prepared to deal with such problems. As Fred Cottrell points out, "There is a widespread feeling among the aged that most doctors are not interested in them and are reluctant to treat people who are as little likely to contribute to the future as the aged are reputed to." Even with the help of Medicare, the elderly in the United States often have a difficult time paying for the health care they need.

Coleman and Cressey, Social Problems.

Main Idea: _____

_____

5. In 1950, only two cities, London and New York, had populations over 8 million; today there are 20 of these huge cities, 14 of them in developing countries. At present, the total urban population of the developing countries is an estimated 1.3 billion people—more than the total populations of Europe, Japan and North America combined. At a growth rate of 50 million new urbanites every year, due both to natural increases in resident populations and immigration from rural areas, over half the people in the developing world will live in cities by the year 2020 (Bradford and Gwynne 1995;13).

Hicks and Gwynne, Cultural Anthropology.

Main Idea: _____

_____

EXERCISE 4-12

DIRECTIONS: From a chapter of one of your textbooks, select a headed section of at least five substantial paragraphs and for each paragraph, identify the topic sentence. If there is no clear topic sentence, write your own statement of the main idea of the paragraph.

Developing Expectations as You Read

To be an effective reader you must become mentally active as you read. Rather than just taking in facts and ideas as you encounter them, you should be reacting to and thinking about what you are reading. In fact, there are certain mental activities that should occur almost automatically as you read. For instance, you should be thinking about what you have just read, following the author's pattern of thought, and trying to relate the ideas. Also, as you read a paragraph you should be developing expectations about how the writer will develop his or her ideas and what will come next in the paragraph. In other words, you should not only keep up with the writer, you should try to stay one jump ahead.

At the beginning of a conversation you can often predict in what direction the conversation is headed. If a friend starts a conversation with "I can't decide whether I can afford to quit my part-time job at Sears," you can guess what you will hear next. Your friend will discuss the pros and cons of quitting the job as it relates to his financial situation.

Similarly, as you begin to read a paragraph, often you will find sufficient clues to enable you to know what to expect throughout. The topic sentence, especially if it appears first in the paragraph, will often suggest how the paragraph will be developed. Suppose a paragraph were to begin with the following topic sentence:

The unemployment rate in the past several years has increased due to a variety of economic factors.

What do you expect the rest of the paragraph to include? It will probably be about the various economic factors that cause unemployment. Now, look at this topic sentence:

Minorities differ in racial or cultural visibility, in the amount of discrimination they suffer, in the character of their adjustment, both as individuals and as groups, and in the length of time they survive as identifiable populations or individuals.

This sentence indicates that the paragraph will contain a discussion of four ways that minority groups differ. This topic sentence also suggests the order in which these differences will be discussed. The factor mentioned first in the sentence (visibility) will be discussed first, the second idea mentioned will appear next, and so forth.

DIRECTIONS: Assume that each of the following statements is the topic sentence of a paragraph. Read each sentence, then decide what you would expect a paragraph to include if it began with that sentence. Summarize your expectations in the space provided after each sentence. In some cases, more than one correct set of expectations is possible.

1.   Conventional musical instruments can be grouped into three classes.

    _____

    _____

2.   The distinction between storage and retrieval has important implications for memory researchers.

    _____

    _____

3.   When Charles Darwin published his theories of evolution, people objected on scientific and religious grounds.

    _____

    _____

4.   Narcotics such as opium, morphine, and heroin are derived from different sources and vary in strength and aftereffects.

    _____

    _____

5.   Not all factors that contribute to intelligence are measurable.

    _____

Major and Minor Supporting Details

In conversation, you can explain an idea in a number of ways. If you were trying to explain to someone that dogs make better pets than cats, you could develop your idea by giving examples of the behaviors of particular dogs and cats. You could also give the basic reasons why you hold that opinion, or you could present facts about dogs and cats that support your position. As in conversation, a writer can explain an idea in many ways. In a paragraph a writer includes details that explain, support, or provide further information about the main idea.

Once you have identified the topic sentence, you should expect the rest of the paragraph to contain supporting information. Not all details are equally important, however. For example, in the following paragraph the underlined ideas provide very important information about the main idea. As you read the paragraph notice how these ideas directly explain the topic sentence

> <u>There are potential disadvantages to group therapy. Many psychologists feel that the interactions in group situations are too superficial to be of much benefit.</u> A patient with deep-seated conflicts may be better treated by a psychotherapist in individual therapy; the therapist can exert consistent pressure, refusing to let the patient avoid the crucial issues, and she or he can control the therapeutic environment more effectively. <u>Another criticism of groups is that they are too powerful.</u> If the group starts to focus on one individual's defense mechanisms—which are used for a reason, remember—that individual might break down. If no trained therapist is present—which is often the case in encounter groups—the result can be disastrous.
>
> Geiwitz, *Psychology: Looking at Ourselves.*

Each of the underlined details states one of the disadvantages of group therapy. These are called *major details* because they directly explain and support the main idea. Now look back at the details that were not underlined. Can you see that they are of lesser importance in relation to the main idea? You can think of these as details that further explain details. These details are called *minor details*. They provide information that qualifies, describes, or explains the major details. For example, the third sentence further explains the disadvantage described in the second sentence. Also, the sentences that follow the second underlined sentence explain what may happen as a result of a group becoming too powerful.

Especially if you are a visual learner, it may be helpful to visualize a paragraph as organized in the following way.

Main Idea
   Major Detail
      minor detail
      minor detail
   Major Detail
      minor detail
   Major Detail

To find the most important, or major, supporting details, ask yourself this question: "Which statements directly prove or explain the main idea?" Your answer will lead you to the important details in the paragraph. Now apply this question to the following paragraph. As you read it, first identify the main idea, then try to locate three major details that *directly* explain this idea.

> Today American women and men have similar levels of education. Although this might suggest that full equality has been achieved in education, some notable differences remain. First, the highest levels of education (such as Ph.D.s) are dominated by men. Second, fields of study in higher education are gender labeled, and female and male students are segregated by major. Women cluster in the humanities, health sciences, and education, while men cluster in the physical sciences. Third, the highest levels within a field tend to be male dominated. For instance, while men were awarded 49 percent of the bachelor's degrees in international relations, they received 79 percent of the doctoral degrees in that field. A similar pattern holds for mathematics. The fields of study chosen by women seem to reflect stereotyped ideas about women's and men's interests and abilities; that is, women are nurturant and emotional and more highly skilled in verbal areas, whereas men are rational, and more highly skilled in mathematics. Research shows that such differences are quite small, and not always in the expected direction.
>
> Shehan, *Marriages and Families.*

In this paragraph you should have identified the three ways that inequality exists in education between men and women. Other sentences in the paragraph further explain each reason and can be considered less important.

EXERCISE
4-14

DIRECTIONS: Each of the following statements could function as the topic sentence of a paragraph. After each statement are sentences containing details that may be related to the main idea statement. Read each sentence and put a check mark beside those with details that do not directly support the main idea statement.

1. *Topic Sentence:*
   From infancy to adulthood, women demonstrate marked superiority in verbal and linguistic abilities.

Details:

_____ a. Girls begin to talk at an earlier age than boys and also learn to speak in sentences earlier.

_____ b. Males excel in the area of arithmetic reasoning as evidenced by their higher test scores.

_____ c. Women learn foreign languages much more rapidly and are more fluent in them than men.

_____ d. The incidence of reading disabilities is much lower for girls than for boys.

2. *Topic Sentence:*
   Employment opportunities for college graduates are plentiful in the technical and business fields, but prospects are bleak for the liberal arts areas.

   Details:

   _____ a. Career counseling is provided too late in their college careers to assist students in making effective career decisions.

   _____ b. The competition for jobs in journalism and sociology is highly aggressive and can be characterized as frantic.

   _____ c. Over the last year, the demand for accountants and computer programmers and technicians has increased by more than 16 percent.

   _____ d. There is only one position available for every ten job applicants in the liberal arts field.

3. *Topic Sentence:*
   Quality and content are not the only factors that determine whether a book can achieve best-seller status.

   Details:

   _____ a. Name recognition of the author exerts a strong influence on sales.

   _____ b. The timing of a book's release during the appropriate season or in conjunction with major news events plays a major role.

   _____ c. Readers appreciate well-crafted books that are both literate and engaging.

   _____ d. The book-buying public clearly responds well to well-conceived advance publicity.

4. *Topic Sentence:*
   Showing how a theory can be developed may be the best way to describe one.

Details:

_____ a. Careful testing of a hypothesis leads to more confidence being placed in the idea.

_____ b. After an idea has been carefully described and its premises defined, it becomes a hypothesis.

_____ c. One first comes up with an idea that could explain something that can be observed in nature.

_____ d. A hypothesis is a provisional statement or possible explanation to be tested.

5. *Topic Sentence:*

The vibrations of objects produce longitudinal waves that result in sounds.

Details:

_____ a. Infrasonic and ultrasonic waves cannot be detected by human hearing.

_____ b. Sound travels more slowly in more dense mediums, such as water, than it does in less dense ones like air.

_____ c. Plucking the strings of a guitar or striking a piano's sounding board are good examples.

_____ d. The vibration of the vocal cords is what produces human voice.

EXERCISE 4-15

DIRECTIONS: Read the following paragraphs and select the answer that best completes each statement.

The Abkhasians (an agricultural people who live in a mountainous region of Georgia, a republic of the former Soviet Union), may be the longest-lived people on earth. Many claim to live past 100—some beyond 120 and even 130. Although it is difficult to document the accuracy of these claims, government records indicate that an extraordinary number of Abkhasians do live to a very old age. Three main factors appear to account for their long lives. The first is their diet, which consists of little meat, much fresh fruit, vegetables, garlic, goat cheese, cornmeal, buttermilk and wine. The second is their lifelong physical activity. They do slow down after age 80, but even after the age of 100 they still work about four hours a day. The third factor—a highly developed sense of community—goes to the very heart of the Abkhasian culture. From childhood, each individual is integrated into a primary group, and remains so throughout life. There is no such thing as a nursing home, nor do the elderly live alone.

Adapted from Henslin, *Sociology.*

1. The sentence that begins "The Abkhasians (an agricultural" is
   a. the topic sentence.
   b. a major detail.
   c. a minor detail.
   d. a transitional sentence.

2. The sentence that begins "The second is their lifelong" is
   a. the topic sentence.
   b. a major detail.
   c. a minor detail.
   d. a transitional sentence.

3. The sentence which begins "They do slow down" is
   a. the topic sentence.
   b. a major detail.
   c. a minor detail.
   d. a transitional sentence.

   Small group discussions progress through four phases. The first is orientation, when the members become comfortable with each other. Second is the conflict phase. Disagreements and tensions become evident. The amount of conflict varies with each group. The third phase is known as emergence. The members begin to try to reach a decision. The members who created conflict begin to move towards a middle road. The final phase is the reinforcement phase when the decision is reached. The members of the group offer positive reinforcement towards each other and the decision.

4. The sentence that begins "Small group discussions" is
   a. the topic sentence.
   b. a major detail.
   c. a minor detail.
   d. a transitional sentence.

5. The sentence that begins "The third phase" is
   a. the topic sentence.
   b. a major detail.
   c. a minor detail.
   d. a transitional sentence.

6. The sentence that begins "The amount of conflict" is
   a. the topic sentence.
   b. a major detail.
   c. a minor detail.
   d. a transitional sentence.

A person's personality type can determine how he or she creates and reacts to self-imposed stress. The first kind of personality is known as Type A. Type A personalities work hard, are anxious, competitive, and driven and often create high expectations for themselves. Type A's are more likely to have heart attacks. Type B is the second personality type. Type B's tend to be relaxed, laid back and noncompetitive. A third type of personality type is Type C. Type C's are Type A's who thrive under stress, achieve things and experience little or no stress-related health problems. The more stress Type C's experience, the more productive they become.

7. The sentence that begins "A person's personality type" is
   a. the topic sentence.
   b. a major detail.
   c. a minor detail.
   d. a transitional sentence.

8. The sentence that begins "Type A's are more likely" is
   a. the topic sentence.
   b. a major detail.
   c. a minor detail.
   d. a transitional sentence.

9. The sentence that begins "A third type" is
   a. the topic sentence.
   b. a major detail.
   c. a minor detail.
   d. a transitional sentence.

10. The sentence that begins "The more stress" is
    a. the topic sentence.
    b. a major detail.
    c. a minor detail.
    d. a transitional sentence.

EXERCISE 4-16

DIRECTIONS: Place brackets around the topic sentence in each of the following paragraphs. Then underline the major supporting details in each. Underline only those details that directly explain or support the main idea.

1. Using money costs money, as anyone who's ever taken out a mortgage or a college loan understands. When a firm borrows money, it must pay interest for every day it has the use of the money. Conversely, if a firm has excess cash, it is able to invest that cash and make money from its money. The bottom line: Having cash is an advantage. For this reason many firms try to entice their customers to pay their bills

quickly by offering *cash discounts*. For example, a firm selling to a retailer may state that the terms of the sale are "2 percent 10 days, net 30 days." This means that if the retailer pays the producer for the goods within 10 days, the amount due is cut by 2 percent. The total amount is due within 30 days, and after 30 days, the payment is late.

Solomon and Stuart, *Marketing: Real People, Real Choices.*

2. By regularly rewarding good actions and punishing bad ones, the agents of social control seek to condition us to obey society's norms. If they are successful, obedience becomes habitual and automatic. We obey the norms even when no one is around to reward or punish us, even when we are not thinking of possible rewards and punishments. But human beings are very complicated and not easily conditioned, as animals are, by rewards and punishments alone. Thus, sanctions are not sufficient to produce the widespread, day-to-day conformity to norms that occur in societies all over the world.

Thio, *Sociology.*

3. The skin itself is the largest organ of the body, is composed of epithelial and connective tissue components, and forms a pliable protective covering over the external body surface. It accounts for about 7 percent of the body weight and receives about 30 percent of the left ventricular output of blood. The term protective, as used here, includes not only resistance to bacterial invasion or attack from the outside, but also protection against large changes in the internal environment. Control of body temperature, prevention of excessive water loss, and prevention of excessive loss of organic and inorganic materials are necessary to the maintenance of internal homeostasis and continued normal activity of individual cells. In addition, the skin acts as an important area of storage, receives a variety of stimuli, and synthesizes several important substances used in the overall body economy.

Crouch and McClintic, *Human Anatomy and Physiology.*

4. Assume you are an industrial/organizational psychologist hired by a company to help select a manager for one of its retail stores in a local shopping center. You could begin to tell your employers what sort of person they were looking for until you had a complete description of the job this new manager was to do. You would have to know the duties and responsibilities of a store manager in this company. Then, you could translate that job description into measurable characteristics a successful store manager should have. That is, you would begin with

a job analysis, "the systematic study of the tasks, duties, and responsibilities of a job and the knowledge, skills, and abilities needed to perform it."

Gerow, *Psychology: An Introduction.*

5. Climate is the most influential control of soil formation. Just as temperature and precipitation are the climatic elements that influence people the most, so too are they the elements that exert the strongest impact on soil formation. Variations in temperature and precipitation determine whether chemical or mechanical weathering predominates. They also greatly influence the rate and depth of weathering. For instance, a hot, wet climate may produce a thick layer of chemically weathered soil in the same amount of time that a cold, dry climate produces a thin mantle of mechanically weathered debris. Also, the amount of precipitation influences the degree to which various materials are removed (leached) from the soil, thereby affecting soil fertility. Finally, climatic conditions are important factors controlling the type of plant and animal life present.

Tarbuck and Lutgens, *Earth Science.*

EXERCISE 4-17

DIRECTIONS: Select a section of five or more paragraphs from one of your textbooks and place brackets around the topic sentence in each paragraph. If there is no topic sentence, write a brief statement of the main idea in the margin. Then underline only the major supporting details in each paragraph.   ▬

Types of Supporting Details

A writer can use many types of details to explain or support a main idea. As you read you should notice the type of details a writer uses and be able to identify the details that are most important. As you will see in later chapters on evaluating and interpreting, the manner in which a writer explains and supports an idea may influence how readily you will accept or agree with the idea. Among the most common types of supporting details are illustrations and examples, facts and statistics, reasons, and descriptions. Each is discussed briefly.

Illustrations and Examples

One way you will find ideas explained is through the use of illustrations or examples. Usually a writer uses examples to make a concept, problem, or process understandable by showing its application in a particular situation. In the following paragraph, numerous examples are provided that explain how different languages have different phonemes.

> Every language has its own set of phonemes. English, for example, contains about 21 vowel sounds and 24 consonant sounds; Cantonese, a Chinese dialect, has 8 vowel sounds and 17 consonant sounds; South African Khoisan or "Bushman" has 7 vowel sounds and 41 consonant sounds (So & Dodd, 1995). Native speakers recognize and produce phonemes from their own language as distinct sounds. For instance, babies in English-speaking communities begin to recognize the sound of the letter *r* as the same sound in *run* and *tear*. Meanwhile, babies in Arabic-speaking communities learn their own set of phonemes, which do not include the same short vowel sounds used in English. Thus, to a native speaker of Arabic, the English words *bet* and *bit* sound the same (Wilson, 1996).
>
> Uba and Huang, *Psychology.*

In this paragraph the author uses examples from different languages—English, Catonese, Khoisan and Arabic—to show how phonemes differ among languages. As you read illustrations and examples, try to see the relationship between the illustration or example and the concept or idea it illustrates.

Facts and Statistics

Another way a writer supports an idea is by including facts or statistics that further explain the main idea. Notice how, in the following paragraph, the main idea is explained by the use of statistics.

> In capitalist societies, medicine generates huge amounts of money, and American physicians are among the most highly paid workers in the nation. The typical physician earns $182,000 after expenses, a sum more than five times the earnings of the average worker. Specialists earn even more—obstetricians and gynecologists average $200,000 per year, and orthopedic surgeons $292,000 per year. Family practitioners, on the other hand, average "only" $121,000 per year (U.S. Bureau of the Census 1997).
>
> Curry et al., *Sociology for the Twenty-First Century.*

These authors used income statistics to indicate that physicians are among the most highly paid workers in the U.S. When reading paragraphs developed by the use of facts and statistics, you can expect that these details will answer questions such as what, when, where, or how about the main idea.

Reasons

Certain types of main ideas are most easily explained by giving reasons. Especially in argumentative and persuasive writing, you will find that a writer supports an opinion, belief, or action by discussing *why* the thought or action is appropriate. In the following paragraph the writer provides reasons why so few women become involved in quantitative fields.

> What accounts for the scarcity of women in quantitative fields? In early grades, girls show about the same mathematical aptitude as boys, but by high school they score lower than boys on standardized tests. Evidently, mathematical and other quantitative subjects have been labeled "masculine." As a result, girls are not eager to excel in these areas, because such an achievement would make them appear unusual and perhaps unattractive to their peers. Another factor is unconscious bias on the part of teachers and guidance counselors. Despite increased sensitivity to minority and women's issues, counselors still steer women away from college preparatory courses in mathematics and the sciences. Finally, many fields contain so few women that they supply no role models for younger women.
>
> Curry et al., *Sociology for the Twenty-First Century.*

You can see that the writers offer numerous reasons for the scarcity of women in these professions, including peer influences, bias in the schools, and a lack of role models.

Descriptions

If the purpose of a paragraph is to help the reader understand or visualize the appearance, structure, organization, or composition of an object, then descriptions are often used as a means of paragraph development. Descriptive details are facts that help you visualize the person, object, or event being described. The following paragraph describes the eruption of Mount St. Helens, a volcano in Washington state.

> The slumping north face of the mountain produced the greatest landslide witnessed in recorded history; about 2.75 km³ (0.67 mi³) of rock, ice, and trapped air, all fluidized with steam, surged at speeds approaching 250 kmph (155 mph). Landslide materials traveled for 21 km (13 mi) into the valley, blanketing the forest, covering a lake, filling the rivers below. The eruption continued with intensity for 9 hours, first clearing out old rock from the throat of the volcano and then blasting new material.
>
> Christopherson, *Geosystems: An Introduction to Physical Geography.*

Notice how each detail contributes to the impression of a tremendously forceful landslide. Details such as "rock, ice, and trapped air, all fluidized with steam" help you visually recreate a picture of the eruption. In reading descriptive details, you must pay close attention to each detail as you try to form a visual impression of what is being described.

EXERCISE 4-18

DIRECTIONS: For each of the following topic sentences, indicate what types of supporting details you would expect to be used to develop the paragraph.

1. It is much easier to sell a product to a buyer who possesses complete purchasing authority than to sell to one who has little authority.

   Type of Detail: _____

2. The concept of insurance is an ancient one, beginning with the Babylonians.

   Type of Detail: _____

3. It was cold in the fall in Rome, and the evening fell suddenly and with great importance.

   Type of Detail: _____

4. Government documents indicate that the total number of Americans living in poverty has decreased, but the definition of the poverty line has also been changed.

   Type of Detail: _____

5. A sudden explosion at 200 decibels can cause massive and permanent hearing loss.

   Type of Detail: _____

Using Transitions

Have you ever tried to find your way to an unfamiliar place without any road signs to guide you? Do you remember your relief when you discovered one sign post and then another and finally realized you were being led in the right direction? Like road signs, transitions in written material can help you find your way to a writer's meaning. *Transitions* are linking words or phrases writers use to lead the reader from one idea to another. If you get in the habit of recognizing transitions, you will see that they often guide you through a paragraph, helping you read it more easily.

In the following paragraph, notice how the italicized transitions lead you from one important detail to the next.

> As a speaker, you should consider the dominant attitudes of your listeners. Audiences may have attitudes toward you, your speech subject, and your speech purpose. Your listeners may think you know a lot about your topic, and they may be interested in learning more. This is an ideal situation. *However,* if they think you're not very credible and they resist learning more, you must deal with their attitudes. *For example,* if a speaker tells you that you can earn extra money in your spare time by selling magazine subscriptions, you may have several reactions. The thought of extra income from a part-time job is enticing. *At the same time,* you suspect that it might be a scam and you feel uncomfortable because you don't know the speaker well. These attitudes toward the speech topic, purpose, and speaker will undoubtedly influence your final decision about selling subscriptions.
>
> Gronbeck et al., *Principles of Speech Communication.*

Not all paragraphs contain such obvious transitions, and not all transitions serve as such clear markers of major details. Transitions may be used to alert you to what will come next in the paragraph. If you see the phrase *for instance* at the beginning of a sentence, then you know that an example will follow. When you see the phrase *on the other hand,* you can predict that a different, opposing idea will follow. Table 4.1 lists some of the most common transitions used within paragraphs and indicates what they tell you. In the next chapter you will see that these transitional words also signal the author's organization.

EXERCISE 4-19

DIRECTIONS: Select the transitional word or phrase from the box below that best completes each of the following sentences. Two of the transitions in the box may be used more than once.

on the other hand	for example	because	in addition
similarly	later	next	however

1. In order to sight-read music, you should begin by scanning it. _____ you should identify the key and tempo.

2. Many fruits are high in calories; vegetables, _____ _____ are usually low in calories.

Figure 4.1   Common Transitions

Type of Transition	Examples	What They Tell the Reader
Time—Sequence	first, later, next, finally, then	The author is arranging ideas in the order in which they happened.
Example	for example, for instance, to illustrate, such as	An example will follow.
Enumeration	first, second, third, last, another, next	The author is marking or identifying each major point (sometimes these may be used to suggest order of importance).
Continuation	also, in addition, and, further, another	The author is continuing with the same idea and is going to provide additional information.
Contrast	on the other hand, in contrast, however	The author is switching to an idea that is different from, opposite to, or in contrast to an idea that was previously discussed.
Comparison	like, likewise, similarly	The writer is showing how the previous idea is similar to what follows.
Cause-Effect	because, thus, therefore, since, consequently	The writer is showing a connection between two or more things, how one thing caused another, or how something happened as a result of something else.
Addition	furthermore, additionally also, besides, further, in addition, moreover, again	The writer indicates that additional information will follow.

3. Many rock stars have met with tragic ends. _____, John Lennon was gunned down, Buddy Holly and Ritchie Valens were killed in a plane crash, and Janis Joplin died of a drug overdose.

4. The Internet provides easy access to a lot of information and makes doing research fast. _____, a lot of the information on Web sites can be inaccurate and outdated, so it is always wise to pay attention to the source.

5. As a young poet, e. e. cummings was traditional in his use of punctuation and capitalization. _____, he began to create his own grammatical rules.

6. AIDS is often thought of as the biggest killer, but in fact there are many diseases that take a higher toll on human life. _____, cancer and heart disease kill more Americans than does AIDS.

7. _____ there was no centralized government in Europe in the Middle Ages, feudal lords were in charge of creating order within the lands that were within their control.

8. Decisions by the Supreme Court cannot be overruled by any other court. _____, Congress can pass a law changing a law that the Supreme Court has upheld.

9. The roots of mass tourism are clear. Tourism became an important industry during the first half of the 20th century when paid vacations were created. _____, World War II had made distant places seem closer, and many soldiers and their families made journeys after the war to explore them.

Critical Thinking Tip #4

Recognizing Your Own Bias

In this chapter you are sharpening your skills in understanding an author's message—recognizing topic, main idea, and supporting details. Did you know that research studies suggest you will more easily comprehend and recall a message you agree with than one with which you disagree? Suppose you are reading a section in your biology book about the need for tighter controls on industrial pollution. Suppose you once lived next to a factory and feel strongly that tighter controls are needed. You are more likely to understand and recall the information than another student who is opposed to tighter controls. In fact, readers who disagree with an idea tend to miss or overlook ideas that do not support their beliefs.

How do these findings affect the way you read? You need to take extra care when reading ideas with which you think you disagree. Try the following suggestions:

1. Keep an open mind until you've read what the author has said and have evaluated the evidence provided.
2. Work harder than usual to follow the writer's development and reasoning process.
3. Outline the writer's main points so you don't overlook anything.

Then, once you've grasped the writer's ideas, feel free to evaluate these ideas and disagree with them.

10. Silence permits the speaker time to collect his or her thoughts and prepare for what he or she is going to communicate next. _____, silence allows the listener time to absorb what is being said and prepare for the next phase of the conversation.

DIRECTIONS: Underline the transitional words or phrases used in each paragraph in Exercise 4–16.

DIRECTIONS: Circle the transitional words or phrases used in each paragraph of the text selection you chose for Exercise 4–12.

Summary

1. What is a paragraph?

A paragraph is a group of related sentences about a single topic. It explains, supports, or gives information about a main idea related to that particular topic.

2. What are the essential elements of a paragraph?

A paragraph has three essential parts:
- Topic: the subject of the paragraph.
- Main Idea: the most important idea expressed about the topic.
- Details: the information that explains or supports the main idea.

3. Where is the topic sentence most likely to be found?

The topic sentence expresses the main idea of the paragraph. It may be located anywhere in the paragraph, but the most common positions are first and last.

4. How can you identify main ideas that are not stated in a topic sentence?

Sometimes you will encounter a paragraph that has no single sentence stating the main idea. In this case, it is up to the reader to figure out the main idea. To find an unstated main idea, ask yourself: What does the writer want me to know about the topic?

5. What are the most common types of details used to explain or support a main idea?

Both major details that directly support the main idea and minor details that provide less essential information are of four types:
• illustrations and examples
• facts and statistics
• reasons
• descriptions

6. What clues in paragraphs can help you anticipate the writer's ideas?

Clues to a writer's direction are often evident in the topic sentence, which can suggest how the paragraph will be developed. Further clues can be seen in transitional words or phrases that signal what will come next in the paragraph.

Reading Selection 7

PSYCHOLOGY

THE APPRECIATION OF HUMOR
Mary J. Gander and Harry W. Gardiner
From *Child and Adolescent Development*

Even very young children love to laugh. Taken from a psychology textbook, this reading explores the development of humor in children. Read it to discover the four stages through which children pass in the development of humor.

— • —

1   One example of the growing thinking capacity in middle childhood is children's appreciation of humor. Consider the joke: "Mr. Jones went into a restaurant and ordered a whole pizza for dinner. When the waiter asked if he wanted it

cut into six or eight pieces, Mr. Jones said: 'Oh you'd better make it six! I could never eat eight!'"

2   Why do first graders who have just attained conservation of substance find this joke funnier than do nonconserving first graders or fifth graders who mastered this ability several years before? McGhee believes it is because this joke provokes a moderate amount of cognitive challenge, perfect for the conserving first graders.

3   Although many researchers have investigated children's humor, only Paul McGhee has conducted a longitudinal study of the development of humor. In his work at the Fels Institute, McGhee has proposed a fairly comprehensive theory of humor as part of his ongoing research on child development.

4   McGhee proposes that some incongruity (for example, something unexpected, absurd, inappropriate, or out of context) is usually the basis for humor. However, an incongruity in itself is insufficient; children must know enough about a situation so that the incongruity can be recognized, and they must be in a playful frame of mind. Incongruous events are funny to children precisely because these events are at odds with reality and they know it! Therefore, the kind of humor children appreciate depends on their underlying cognitive development.

5   When the father of three-year-old Paul put on a beard, glasses, and a large plastic nose, the child became frightened and began to cry, but his nine-year-old brother considered the disguise hilarious. The older boy had reached the concrete operational level and could imagine his father as he was; moreover, he knew that the disguise had not really changed him.

6   Precursors of humor may be observed early. Laughter may be induced in four-month-old infants by tactile stimulation such as blowing against the baby's belly; at eight months, peek-a-boo; and at one year, Dad pretending to cry over a "hurt" finger.

7   McGhee proposes that true humor begins during the second year, or after the child has begun to be capable of fantasy and make-believe. It develops in an invariant sequence of stages related to cognitive development.

Stage 1: Incongruous Actions Toward Objects

8   Sometime between the ages of one and two years, toddlers begin to pretend that one object is another. Object number 1 somehow evokes their scheme for Object number 2, and they act on number 1 with the number 2 scheme, though fully aware that number 1 is *not* number 2. In a playful mood they find it funny. For example, eighteen-month-old Sally put one of her blocks to her ear as if it were a phone, then "hung up" and laughed. She laughed too when her mother "ate" her toes and found their "taste" terrible.

Stage 2: Incongruous Labeling of Objects, Events, People

9   This stage usually begins around two years of age, or after children have developed some vocabulary. In it, the commonest type of humor consists of simply giving the wrong names to familiar objects, events, people, and parts of the body. A two-and-a-half-year-old girl told a visitor that she was going to a Winnie-the-Pooh movie. The visitor, trying to be funny, said, "Oh, Winnie-the-Pooh is an elephant, isn't he?" The child collapsed in laughter.

10   Stages 1 and 2 humor do not disappear as the next stage begins, but become incorporated into it in more sophisticated ways.

Stage 3: Conceptual Incongruity

11   This stage may begin sometime between the ages of three and four and is heavily influenced by development of language and concepts. A distortion of a reality that children conceptually understand as a distortion is funny at this age; accordingly children may point and laugh at handicapped or deformed individuals because

their strong egocentrism prevents consideration for others' feelings. Rhyming and creating nonsense words (Billy, pilly, dilly, silly, gilly) are considered great fun at this stage. So are puppets, such as a talking frog and a monster that devours cookies. Children also begin to find humor in taboo subject matter concerning toilets and physical differences between girls and boys. Within the context of a joke, such topics can release tension and excite much laughter in preschoolers as well as older children.

Stage 4: Multiple Meanings and the Beginnings of Adult-Type Humor

12   This stage usually comes around ages seven and eight, when concrete operations and other cognitive skills permit appreciation of more sophisticated jokes. Concrete operational children can keep two ideas in mind at once and thus have no problem with double or multiple meanings, as long as they are familiar with the concepts involved. For example, eight- to ten-year-olds find this funny: "What did the man do when he stubbed his toe and broke it?" Answer: "He called a tow truck!" Riddles and "knock-knock" questions also gain popularity. According to McGhee, stage 4 humor can extend into adolescence and adulthood, although it usually becomes more complex and abstract.

Examining Reading Selection 7

Checking Your Vocabulary

Directions: Using context, word parts, or a dictionary if necessary, circle the letter of the meaning for each word as it is used in the reading.

1. incongruity (paragraph 4)
   a. unexpected happenings
   b. lack of energy
   c. unacceptable events
   d. lack of decisiveness

2. precursors (paragraph 6)
   a. causes
   b. beginnings
   c. types
   d. uses

3. invariant (paragraph 7)
   a. unchanging
   b. inconsistent
   c. unrealistic
   d. forceful

4. egocentrism (paragraph 11)
   a. self-preservation
   b. sense of right and wrong
   c. inability to make exceptions
   d. self-centeredness

5. taboo (paragraph 11)
   a. sexual
   b. controversial
   c. forbidden
   d. unappealing

Checking Your Comprehension

Directions: Circle the letter of the best answer.

6. Children's appreciation of humor
   a. is an area of child development that has not been studied.
   b. develops along with their thinking ability.
   c. does not occur until age 7 or 8.
   d. occurs earlier for girls than for boys.

7. When children pass to stage 3 of humor, what they found to be funny in stage 2
   a. is no longer funny.
   b. becomes incorporated into stage 3.
   c. remains just as funny for them.
   d. is forgotten.

8. The basis for humor is usually
   a. one's fear of injury.
   b. unusual sounding words.
   c. a situation that is incongruous.
   d. other people's weaknesses.

9. "True humor" usually begins in the
   a. fourth month.
   b. second year.
   c. fourth year.
   d. ninth year.

10. Around the age of 3 or 4, children would most appreciate humor based on
    a. "knock-knock" jokes.
    b. cartoon characters and animals.
    c. double meanings.
    d. nonsense words and rhymes.

11. The authors explain childhood humor primarily by
    a. describing its development.
    b. citing research.
    c. giving examples.
    d. comparing it to adult humor.

Thinking Critically

12. A child who pretends that his or her dresser is a refrigerator is at least
    a. 1 year old.
    b. 6 years old.
    c. 8 years old.
    d. 12 years old.

13. A child who enjoys calling his or her dog "Tommy Turtle" is operating at
    a. Stage 1: Incongruous Actions Toward Objects.
    b. Stage 2: Incongruous Labeling.
    c. Stage 3: Conceptual Incongruity.
    d. Stage 4: Multiple Meanings.

14. The joke "What did the father chimney say to his son? You're too young to smoke!" would probably be funniest to a
    a. 2-year-old.
    b. 4-year-old.
    c. 8-year-old.
    d. 16-year-old.

15. The information in this passage is presented by
    a. describing the stages in their order of occurrence.
    b. comparing and contrasting the stages with one another.
    c. presenting the stages in the order of their importance.
    d. listing problems and solutions with each stage.

Questions for Discussion

1. Why is humor important? What does it do for us?

2. Does humor serve the same functions for adults and children?

3. Think of an adult joke. Analyze it and describe its incongruity or multiple meanings.

4. How does the article confirm the statement that the truest test of your knowledge of a foreign language is your ability to understand and tell jokes in that language?

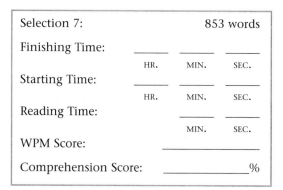

Selection 7:			853 words
Finishing Time:	_____	_____	_____
	HR.	MIN.	SEC.
Starting Time:	_____	_____	_____
	HR.	MIN.	SEC.
Reading Time:		_____	_____
		MIN.	SEC.
WPM Score:			_____
Comprehension Score:			_____%

Reading Selection 8

Computer Technology

Privacy on the Web

Wendy G. Lehnert

From *Light on the Internet*

Can anyone read your e-mail? How can Web servers track the sites you visit on the Web? Read this article to find out how your privacy may be violated on the Web.

— · —

1   A lot of publicly available information has always been there for the taking, but only with some effort. Before the Internet, a court record from a divorce proceeding was public but available only if you visited the courthouse at which it was stored. Copies of old newspapers might have been available on microfiche, but you had to travel to the newspaper publisher or to a regional library and spend time in front of a microfiche reader. Private investigators doing background checks know their way around all the public resources, as well as a few back-door tricks of the trade. Whatever sources they used, the job always involved some amount of footwork. Hence information that was technically free extracted a very real price in terms of time and energy.

2   The Internet is changing many of the hidden costs associated with "free" information. When a court places its records online, no one has to travel to the courthouse to see them. When phone listings for the entire United States are available online, you can research ten cities as easily as one. The Internet isn't giving people anything they couldn't get before; it simply makes many information-gathering tasks much easier. In other words, the convenience factor is shifting. In a legal sense, nothing has changed with respect to the availability of information. But in a practical sense, nothing will ever be the same. Not only is the work of the private investigator facilitated, but people who would never have taken the time to learn about resources in a public library are now surfing the Web and learning about all sorts of information sources online. Rank amateurs are barging in where only professionals used to tread.

Is Anything Private on the Internet?

3   People are used to thinking about degrees of privacy. Absolute privacy is difficult to attain, but relative privacy may be a reasonable goal. For example, a message posted to a mailing list is public relative to that list but private with respect to the world at large. Most e-mail messages are read and discarded or sometimes just discarded without even being read. Even when mailing lists are archived by listservs, the business of locating and searching a mailing list archive isn't terribly easy. So, as long as the convenience factor is low, mailing list participants enjoy some degree of privacy.

4   But with computers, tasks that used to be difficult often become effortless. The Web is a case in point. All those difficult-to-read mailing list archives can now be placed on Web pages, where they are suddenly fairly easy to find. Before you know it, search engines are pointing to e-mail messages sent seven years ago. Archives that were relatively private in 1990 can suddenly pop up in search engine hit lists for all the world to see. Just because something was inconvenient at one time doesn't mean that it's going to stay inconvenient forever. If it's digital, the potential for public distribution is unimaginable.

5   Everyone needs to think about whether the benefits of the Internet outweigh the possible indignities of reduced privacy. For some people, the ability to communicate freely and openly on a global scale is well worth it. For others, any loss of privacy is an unsettling prospect requiring careful consideration.

How Much Data Are Being Collected Surreptitiously?

6   The amount of data being collected surreptitiously is hard to pin down, but many companies seem to be changing their data collection practices so that users have more control. One of the most controversial data collection practices on the Web involves the use of "cookies." A **cookie** is a file created by a Web server and stored on your host machine. It's a small file that patiently awaits your next visit to the Web. Any Web server can check to see if you have a cookie file and, if so, whether it has any useful information about you. For example, suppose that the last time you visited a particular site, you spent all your time on two particular pages. A cookie can record this information so that the next time you visit the site, the server might greet you with a page display that makes it especially easy to navigate to those pages again.

7   Cookies allow Web servers to create a profile about you and your prior activities. Parts of this profile may have been collected with your assistance (e.g., you have to tell it your name if you want a personal greeting). Other parts may be deduced from your past interactions with the server.

8   How can you tell if you've got cookies on your hard drive? You can find yours by searching your hard drive for a file involving the string "cookie." It might be called cookies.txt or MagicCookie. Once you've located a cookie file, you can open it up and look at it—it's just a text file. It will contain separate entries from different Web sites. . . .

9   The names of the sites responsible are given, so you can always tell where the cookies came from. Each of these sites will check for a cookie file the next time you drop by. If a site finds one of its own cookies on the hard drive, it can handle the visit a little differently than it would if no information had been found.

10   Cookie files can be used to make life easier for a Web user. Amazon.com tracks the books you browse when you visit its pages so that the company can offer recommendations next time you visit its site. The more time you spend looking at books, the better these recommendations are likely to be. The *New York Times* on the Web is free but requires visitors to register with a name and a password. Once you've registered yourself at the site, a cookie can be installed, which checks for your name and password each time you return to the site. This means that you can enter the site automatically without having to enter your name or password, as though the site were unrestricted. This is particularly convenient for people who have a lot of passwords and also have a lot of trouble remembering them.

11   Cookies are also used to target potential customers with banner ads. For example, if you visit the Netly News at pathfinder.com, the site will record any of your mouse clicks that reveal an interest in specific technologies. A resulting cookie may be used the next time you visit Pathfinder in order to show you an ad about a product that reflects your apparent interests.

12   On the one hand you might feel that cookies provide a useful service. Maybe you would like to hear about products and promotions that might be of interest to you. On the other hand, you might also want to be reassured that all this information about your reading habits, consumer spending, recreational activities, and so on, is not being sold to information brokers and marketing companies. At the very least, you might want to be informed if a Web site is going to put a cookie on your hard drive.

Examining Reading Selection 8*

Checking Your Vocabulary

Directions: Complete each of the following items; refer to a dictionary if necessary.

1. Discuss the connotative meanings of the word *privacy.*

2. Define each of the following words:
   a. facilitated (paragraph 2)

   _____

   b. rank (paragraph 2)

   _____

   c. indignities (paragraph 5)

   _____

   _____

   d. surreptitiously (paragraph 6)

   _____

   e. brokers (paragraph 12)

   _____

   _____

3. Define the word *extracted* (paragraph 1) and underline the word or phrase that provides a context clue for its meaning.

   _____

   _____

   _____

4. Define the word *profile* (paragraph 7) and underline the word or phrase that provides a context clue for its meaning.

   _____

   _____

   _____

5. Determine the meanings of the following words by using word parts:
   a. unimaginable (paragraph 4)

   _____

   _____

   b. unsettling (paragraph 5)

   _____

   c. interactions (paragraph 7)

   _____

   d. unrestricted (paragraph 10)

   _____

   e. reassured (paragraph 12)

   _____

Checking Your Comprehension

6. How has the Web changed access to publicly available information?

   _____

   _____

   _____

7. What is a "cookie?"

   _____

   _____

   _____

   _____

8. What are the major advantages and the major disadvantages of cookies?

   _____

   _____

   _____

_____
*Multiple-choice questions are contained in Part 6 (page 579).

_____

_____

_____

_____

_____

_____

_____

_____

9. In what ways might one's privacy be violated on the Internet?

_____

_____

_____

Thinking Critically

10. Describe the tone of the selection.

_____

11. Describe the author's attitude toward the use of cookies.

_____

_____

_____

12. Evaluate the amount and type of supporting evidence the author provides in support of his contention that one's privacy is threatened on the Web.

_____

_____

_____

_____

_____

Questions for Discussion

1. In paragraph 2, the author states, "The Internet isn't giving people anything they couldn't get before; it simply makes information-gathering tasks much easier." Do you agree or disagree with the author? Justify your answer.

2. One of the major points in the selection focuses on the issue of whether the benefits of the Web outweigh the "indignities of reduced privacy." Do you think the pluses of the Web outweigh the minuses? Why or why not?

3. In your opinion, what kinds of privacy laws, if any, do you think should be in effect for Web users?

Selection 8:		1191 words
Finishing Time:	_____ _____ _____	
	HR. MIN. SEC.	
Starting Time:	_____ _____ _____	
	HR. MIN. SEC.	
Reading Time:	_____ _____	
	MIN. SEC.	
WPM Score:	_____	
Comprehension Score:	_____ %	

GO ELECTRONIC

For additional readings, exercises, and Internet activities, visit this book's Web site at:

http://www.ablongman.com/mcwhorter

For even more activities, visit the Longman English pages at:

http://www.ablongman.com/englishpages

If you need a user name and password, please see your instructor.

Take a Road Trip to the Maine Woods and to the St. Louis Arch
Be sure to visit the Main Idea and Supporting Details module on your Reading Road Trip CD-ROM for multimedia tutorials, exercises, and tests.

CHAPTER 5

Patterns: Relationships Among Ideas

IN THIS CHAPTER YOU WILL LEARN:

1. To recognize common organizational patterns
   to improve recall.
2. To use patterns to aid in comprehension.
3. To use transitional words to understand relationships
   within and among sentences.

Many of our personal daily activities involve following a pattern or an organizing principle. For instance, when you change a flat tire, bake a batch of cookies, assemble a toy, or write a term paper, you use some organized approach or method. Community activities are also organized. Think of a television talk show, a football game, or a meal in a restaurant. Things happen in a particular order, and at any point you can predict with some confidence what is going to follow.

Why do so many activities and events have a pattern? Many things, of course, won't work unless a particular order is followed. In changing a flat tire, for instance, you cannot put on the new tire until you take the flat tire off, you cannot take the flat tire off until you remove the hubcap, and so forth. Other events, however, have no inherent order, yet they also follow a pattern. Religious services or ceremonies are examples; they proceed in a predictable, systematic way. In these situations, the order often allows participants or spectators to know what to do or expect next. Humans have a basic need to make sense out of things and to understand how things are done.

Written language often follows a pattern for similar reasons. Many ideas or events have a natural order, and this order is often followed as the idea is explained. For example, in describing how to change a flat tire, the simplest way to arrange the details is in the order in which the task is performed. In other more abstract cases, a pattern allows the reader to follow the ideas more easily, to remember them more easily, and to see the relationship among the ideas. In this chapter you will look at the most common organizational patterns and see how recognizing these patterns can improve recall. You will also discover how transitional words can help you understand relationships within and among sentences.

How Recognizing a Pattern Improves Recall

Which of the following phone numbers would be easier to remember?

876–5432
792–6538

Which of the following sets of directions would be easier to remember?

After you pass two signals, turn left. Then pass two more signals, and turn right. Next, pass two more signals, and turn left.
After you pass two streets, turn left. Then after you pass three more streets, turn right. Next, pass one more street, and turn right.

Which of the following shopping lists would be easier to remember if you forgot your list?

paint, brushes, paint remover, drop cloth
milk, deodorant, nails, comb

In each example, you probably selected the first choice as easier to remember. Now, let us consider *why* each is easier to remember than the other choice. The first choices each had a pattern. The items were connected in some way that made it possible to remember them together. The phone number consists of consecutive digits in reverse order; the directions consist of two left, two right, two left; the shopping list contains items related to a particular task—painting. From these examples you can see that items are easier to remember if they are related in some way.

Lists A and B each contain five facts. Which would be easier to learn?

List A

1. Cheeseburgers contain more calories than hamburgers.

2. Christmas cactus plants bloom once a year.

3. Many herbs have medicinal uses.

4. Many ethnic groups live in Toronto.

5. Fiction books are arranged alphabetically by author.

List B

1. Effective advertising has several characteristics.

2. An ad must be unique.

3. An ad must be believable.

4. An ad must make a lasting impression.

5. An ad must substantiate a claim.

Most likely, you chose list B. There is no connection between the facts in list A; the facts in list B, however, are related. The first sentence made a general statement, and each remaining sentence gave a particular characteristic of effective advertising. Together they fit into a pattern.

The details of a paragraph, paragraphs within an essay, events within a short story, or sections within a textbook often fit a pattern. If you can recognize the pattern, you will find it easier to remember the content. You will be able to remember a unified whole rather than independent pieces of information.

You will find that patterns are useful in other academic situations in addition to reading textbooks.

- Professors use patterns to organize their lectures. If you can recognize the pattern of a lecture, note taking will become an easier task.

- Patterns will help you write stronger papers and class assignments.

- Essay exams often contain questions that require you to use one or more patterns.

- Patterns will help you organize your speech, both in formal presentations and in classroom discussions.

Common Organizational Patterns

The most common organizational patterns are chronological order, definition, classification, comparison-contrast, cause-effect, and enumeration. For each of these patterns we give examples and list frequently used transitional words. To help you visualize these patterns, a diagram called a *map* is presented for each. You will see that these maps are useful ways to organize information for study and review, especially if you are a visual learner. If you are an applied learner, you may find that maps make abstract ideas more tangible and concrete. In learning and working with these organizational patterns, focus your attention on the relationships among the ideas, rather than on naming the pattern correctly. As you will see in the section titled Mixed Patterns (on p. 198), patterns sometimes overlap.

Chronological Order/Process

One of the most obvious patterns is time order, also called sequence of events or chronological order/process. In this pattern, ideas are presented in the order in which they occur in time. The event that happened first appears first in the paragraph, the event that occurred next in time appears next, and so on. The chronological order/process pattern can be visualized or mapped as follows:

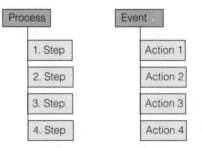

Chronological order is used frequently in reporting current events and appears commonly in news articles and magazines. Directions and instructions are often written using this pattern. It is also used to recount historical events or to provide a historical perspective, and can be found in textbooks and reference sources. The following paragraph, taken from an American government text, is organized using chronological order:

> Ours is an ethnically, religiously, and racially diverse society. The white European Protestants, black slaves, and Native Americans who made up the bulk of the U.S. population when the first census was taken in 1790 were joined by Catholic immigrants from Ireland and Germany in the 1840s and 1850s. In the 1870s, Chinese migrated to America drawn by jobs in railroad construction. Around the turn of the twentieth century, most immigration was from Eastern, Central, and Southern Europe, with its many ethnic, linguistic, and religious groups. Today, most immigration is from Asia and Latin America.
>
> Greenberg and Page, *The Struggle for Democracy.*

This excerpt could be mapped by using a time line:

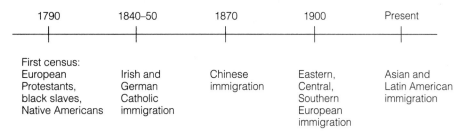

Entire passages and chapters, or even books, may be organized using the chronological order pattern. Here are the section headings from a chapter in an advertising textbook. Notice how the topics proceed in order by time.

THE HISTORY OF ADVERTISING
Early History
How the Advertising Agency Grew Up
Early Twentieth-Century Advertising
Advertising Today

Cohen, Advertising.

A chronological order pattern is often evident within each section. For example, the following subheadings appear in one section:

ADVERTISING TODAY
Advertising in the Seventies
Advertising in the Eighties
Advertising in the Nineties

One of the clearest ways to describe how to do something is to use steps that follow the order in which it is to be done. This is why chronological order is often used to describe the steps in a process or to outline a method or procedure. The following excerpt from a visual arts text describes the process of etching.

> The process of making an *etching* begins with the preparation of a metal plate with a *ground*—a protective coating of acid-resistant material that covers the copper or zinc. The printmaker then draws easily through the ground with a pointed tool, exposing the metal. Finally, the plate is immersed in acid. Acid "bites" into the plate where the drawing has exposed the metal, making a groove that varies in depth according to the strength of the acid and the length of time the plate is in the acid bath.

Preble et al., Artforms: An Introduction to the Visual Arts.

Materials organized in chronological order use signal words or phrases to connect the events or steps in the process. Examples of such transitional words and phrases include:

CHRONOLOGICAL ORDER/PROCESS TRANSITIONAL WORDS/PHRASES

in the Middle Ages . . .
the *final* stage . . .
before the Civil Rights Act . . .
on December 7 . . .
the *last* step

Other transitional words/phrases are:

first, second, later, next, as soon as, after, then, finally, meanwhile, last, during, when, by the time, until

When you realize that a piece of writing is organized using time order, you can expect that whatever event appears next will have happened next. You will find it easier to remember facts, details, dates, or events because they are organized and connected by their occurrence in time.

EXERCISE
5-1

DIRECTIONS: Using chronological order/process, put each of the following groups of sentences in the correct order. In the space provided for each sentence, write a number from 1 to 4, beginning with the topic sentence.

A.

_____ Finally, the completed Voter Guides were distributed to libraries throughout the region one month prior to election day.

_____ Two months before the election, we asked each candidate to submit answers to preselected questions.

_____ The document was then sent out to be printed.

_____ The answers were edited over the course of the next two weeks and compiled into the Voters Guide.

B.

_____ On October 22, this situation was revealed by President Kennedy.

_____ In the fall of 1962, the Soviet Union began setting up missile bases in Cuba with weapons that could easily strike the United States.

_____ Six days later, after a U.S. Naval barricade was established to prevent more shipments of military equipment, Kennedy and Soviet Premier Kruschev resolved the crisis.

_____ On November 2, the president assured Americans that the Cuban missile crisis was over.

C.

_____ During the Ming Dynasty (1368–1644), the wall reached completion.

_____ In 210 B.C., these parts were unified into the first major section.

_____ The very first parts of the Great Wall of China were built in the 4th century B.C.

_____ Today, two main visitor centers provide tourists with access to this human-made marvel.

EXERCISE 5-2

DIRECTIONS: Which of the following topic sentences suggest that their paragraphs will be developed by using chronology? Circle their numbers.

1. The human brain is divided into two halves, each of which is responsible for separate functions.

2. Advertising has appeared in magazines since the late 1700s.

3. The life cycle of a product is the stages it goes through from when it is first created to when it is no longer produced.

4. There are really only two ways to gather information from human beings about what they are currently thinking or feeling.

5. To determine whether you will vote for a particular presidential candidate, you should first examine his or her philosophy of government.

EXERCISE 5-3

DIRECTIONS: Read the following excerpt from a political science textbook and answer the questions that follow.

POLITICAL BACKGROUND OF SEGREGATION

The end of the Civil War and the emancipation of the slaves did not give blacks the full rights of citizenship, nor did the passing of the Thirteenth Amendment in 1865 (which outlawed slavery), or the Fourteenth Amendment in 1868 (which extended "equal protection of the laws" to all citizens), or the Fifteenth Amendment in 1870 (which guaranteed the right to vote to all male citizens regardless of "race, color, or previous condition of servitude"). Between 1866 and 1877 the "radical Republicans" controlled Congress. Although the sometimes corrupt period of *Reconstruction* partly deserves the bad name it has gotten in the South, it was a time when blacks won a number of political rights. In 1875 Congress passed a civil rights act designed to prevent any public form of discrimination—in theaters, restaurants, transportation, and the like—against blacks. Congress's right to forbid a *state* to act contrary to the Constitution was unquestioned. But this law, based on the Fourteenth Amendment, assumed that Congress could also prevent racial discrimination by private individuals.

The Supreme Court disagreed. In 1883 it declared the Civil Rights Act of 1875 unconstitutional. The majority of the Court ruled that Congress could pass legislation only to correct *states'* violations of the Fourteenth Amendment. Congress had no power to enact "primary and direct" legislation on individuals; that was left to the states. This decision meant the federal government could not lawfully protect blacks against most forms of discrimination. In other words, white supremacy was beyond federal control.

Wasserman, *The Basics of American Politics.*

1. Draw a map of the major events discussed in this article in the order in which they occurred.

2. List the transitional words used in this excerpt.

_____

_____ ▬

Definition

Each academic discipline has its own specialized vocabulary. One of the primary purposes of introductory textbooks is to introduce students to this new language. Consequently, definition is a commonly used pattern throughout most introductory-level texts.

Suppose you were asked to define the word *comedian* for someone unfamiliar with the term. First, you would probably say that a comedian is a person who entertains. Then you might distinguish a comedian from other types of entertainers by saying that a comedian is an entertainer who tells jokes and makes others laugh. Finally, you might mention, by way of example, the names of several well-known comedians who have appeared on television. Although you may have presented it informally, your definition would have followed the standard, classic pattern. The first part of your definition tells what general class or group the term belongs to (entertainers). The second part tells what distinguishes the term from other items in the same class or category. The third part includes further explanation, characteristics, examples, or applications.

Here are two additional examples:

Term	General Class	Distinguishing Characteristics
Stress	Physiological reaction	A response to a perceived threat
Mutant	Organism	Carries a gene that has undergone a change

You can map the definition pattern as follows:

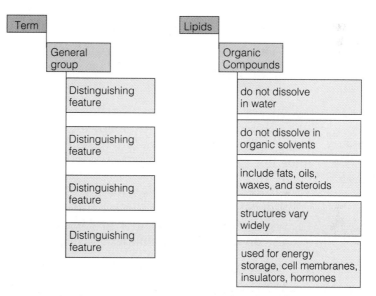

In the following excerpt, the writer defines the term *lipids*:

The **lipids** are a diverse group of energy-rich organic compounds whose main common feature is that they do not dissolve in water. They do, however, dissolve in various organic solvents such as ether, chloroform, and benzene. They include the fats, oils, waxes, and steroids. Their structures vary widely, and they are employed as energy storage molecules (especially in animals), components of cell membranes, insulators for the nervous system, and hormones—just to mention a few. We will focus next on two of the major lipid categories.

Rischer and Easton, *Focus on Human Biology.*

In this paragraph, the general class of lipids is "organic compounds." Their distinguishing feature is that they do not dissolve in water but do dissolve in organic solvents. The remainder of the paragraph gives examples and explains their structure and use.

Writers often use the transitional words shown here to indicate that a definition is to follow.

DEFINITION PATTERN TRANSITIONAL WORDS/PHRASES

nepotism *is* . . .
classical conditioning *refers to* . . .
acceleration *can be defined as* . . .
empathy *means* . . .

Other transitional words/phrases are:

consists of, is a term that, involves, is called, is characterized by, that is, occurs when, exists when, are those that, entails, corresponds to, is literally

**EXERCISE
5-4**

DIRECTIONS: For each of the following brief definitions, circle the term being defined. Then place a box around the class to which it belongs and underline the distinguishing features.

1. Partnership is a form of ownership used by small businesses. A partnership has two or more owners. The partners establish their own rules for the operation of the business and for how money is spent. The partners also divide up responsibilities and decision-making authority.

2. Natural selection refers to a theory developed by Charles Darwin in the 1850s. Also called "survival of the fittest," this theory postulates that over time, living things best suited to their environment tend to survive.

3. A very strong man-made material is concrete. This mixture of sand, stones, cement, and water creates a compact and very hard building material once it is completely set.

4. The troposphere—one of the layers of air that surround our planet—is the lowest and most dense layer and the one in which the most weather occurs.

5. Jainism is thought to be the oldest religion in the world from which many other religions have developed. Jains believe in strict noninterference with other living things and therefore follow a vegetarian diet.

EXERCISE 5–5

DIRECTIONS: From the following textbook chapter headings select those that are most likely to use the definition pattern.

1. The Nature of Culture
2. What Is Conditioning?
3. Stressors: The Roots of Stress
4. The Origin of Life
5. Second Law of Thermodynamics

EXERCISE 5–6

DIRECTIONS: Read the following excerpt from a geography textbook and answer the questions that follow.

SHIFTING CULTIVATION

The native peoples of remote tropical lowlands and hills in the Americas, Africa, Southeast Asia, and Indonesia practice an agricultural system known as **shifting cultivation.** Essentially, this is a land-rotation system. Using machetes or other bladed instruments, farmers chop away the undergrowth from small patches of land and kill the trees by cutting off a strip of bark completely around the trunk. After the dead vegetation has dried out, the farmers set it on fire to clear the land. These clearing techniques have given shifting cultivation the name of "slash-and-burn" agriculture. Working with digging sticks or hoes, the farmers then plant a variety of crops in the clearings, varying from the corn, beans, bananas, and manioc of American Indians to the yams and nonirrigated rice grown by hill tribes in Southeast Asia. Different crops are typically planted together in the same clearing, a practice called **intertillage.** This allows taller, stronger crops to shelter lower, more fragile ones from the tropical downpours and reveals the rich lore and learning acquired by shifting cultivators over many centuries. Relatively little tending of the plants is necessary until harvest time, and no fertilizer is applied to the fields. Farmers repeat the planting and harvesting cycle in the same clearings for perhaps four or five years, until the soil has lost much of its fertility. Then these areas are abandoned, and the farmers prepare new clearings to replace them. The abandoned fields lie unused and recuperate for 10 to 20 years before farmers clear and cultivate them again. Shifting cultivation is one form of **subsistence agriculture**— that is, involving food production mainly for the family and local community rather than for market.

Jordan, Domosh, and Rowntree, *The Human Mosaic: A Thematic Introduction to Cultural Geography.*

1. In your own words, write a definition for each of the three terms defined in the paragraph (see **boldface print**).

_____

_____

_____

_____

_____

_____

2. For each definition, identify the general class and distinguishing characteristics as given in the passage.

_____

_____

_____

_____

_____

3. Underline any transitional words used in the passage.

Classification

If you were asked to describe types of computers, you might mention mainframes, minicomputers, and microcomputers. By dividing a broad topic into its major categories, you are using a pattern known as *classification*.

This pattern is widely used in many academic subjects. For example, a psychology text might explain human needs by classifying them into two categories: primary and secondary. In a chemistry textbook, various compounds may be grouped and discussed according to common characteristics such as the presence of hydrogen or oxygen. The classification pattern divides a topic into parts that are based on common or shared characteristics.

Here are a few examples of topics and the classifications or categories into which each might be divided:

trees: deciduous, evergreen
motives: achievement, power, affiliation, competency
communication: verbal, nonverbal

You can visualize the classification pattern by drawing a map like this:

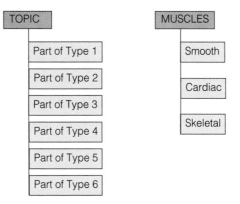

Read the following paragraph to discover how the author classifies muscles:

TYPES OF MUSCLES IN HUMANS

Human muscles can be divided into three groups according to their structure and the nerves that activate them. **Smooth muscle** is found in a number of internal structures, such as the walls of the digestive tract, around some blood vessels, and in certain internal organs. **Cardiac muscle** is found in the walls of the heart. Both of these are involuntary, since they function without conscious control. Thus, you don't have to lie awake nights keeping your heart beating. There is some fascinating evidence that "involuntary" responses can be voluntarily controlled to a degree . . . . **Skeletal muscles** are the voluntary muscles.

Wallace, *Biology: The World of Life.*

This paragraph classifies muscles into three types: smooth, cardiac, and skeletal. The classification is based on their structure and the nerves that activate them.

Transitional words commonly used to signal this pattern are shown here.

CLASSIFICATION PATTERN TRANSITIONAL WORDS/PHRASES

There are *several types of* bones . . .
An S-corporation *is composed of* . . .
Another kind of memory is . . .
Societies can be *classified as* . . .

Other transitional words/phrases are:

comprises, one type, a second class of, another group, several varieties of, kinds, divisions, categories

EXERCISE 5-7

DIRECTIONS: Each item below consists of a topic and several subtopics into which it can be classified. For each word group, fill in the missing information.

1. Topic: Literature

   Types of literature: poems, short stories, _____

2. Topic: Armed Forces

   Branches of the armed forces: Army, Navy, _____

   _____

3. Topic: Deaths

   Leading causes of death: heart disease, diabetes, _____

   _____

4. Topic: Taxes

   Types of taxes: sales, property, _____

5. Topic: Art

   Art movements: modern, abstract, Baroque, _____

6. Topic: Natural disasters

   Types of natural disasters: earthquakes, hurricanes,

   _____

7. Topic: Geography

   Geographic features: mountains, lakes, _____

8. Topic: Federal government

   Departments of the federal government: Health and Human Services, FBI, _____

9. Topic: Medicine

Medical specialties: pediatrics, orthopedics, _____

10. Topic: Pollution

Types of toxic emissions: sulfur dioxide, lead, _____

_____

DIRECTIONS: Identify and circle the topics listed that might be developed by using the classification pattern.

1. Types of utility

2. The staffing process

3. Growth of plant life

4. Functions of dating

5. Theories of evolution

6. The discovery of DNA

7. Formal organizations

8. Animal tissues

9. Effects of negative feelings

10. Classifying emotions

DIRECTIONS: Read the following excerpt from a biology textbook and answer the questions that follow.

ANGIOSPERMS

All plants that develop a *true flower* are classified as **angiosperms.** The angiosperms vary with respect to their number of floral parts, but all **flowers** are reproductive structures that contain both male and female reproductive parts, and their seeds develop within fruits. More than 300 families of angiosperms are separated into two major classes, monocots and dicots.

Monocots

Monocots develop from germinated seeds that have a single embryonic leaf (called a cotyledon) and grow into plants with parallel leaf venation and floral parts that occur in threes or multiples of three. The vascular tissues in cross sections of monocot stems appear as scattered bundles of cells.

Monocots include most species that are cultivated as food crops by humans. The grass family is by far the largest and most important; it includes rice, wheat, barley, oats, other grains, and the grasses on which most animal *herbivores* feed [. . . .] The largest monocot species belong to the pineapple, banana, and palm families.

Many spring wildflowers are monocots in the lily, iris, and orchid families. The orchid family has the largest number of flowering plants, over 20,000 species, most of which grow in tropical or subtropical regions of the world.

Dicots

Dicots develop from germinated seeds that have two cotyledons, grow into plants with nested leaf venation, and produce flowers with parts in fours or fives or multiples of four or five. The vascular tissue in the dicot stem forms a circular pattern when viewed in cross section.

Mix, Farber, and King, *Biology: The Network of Life.*

1. What is the subject of the classification?

   _____

2. How is it divided?

   _____

3. Circle the transitional words used in this excerpt.

EXERCISE 5-10

DIRECTIONS: Select a brief section from a textbook chapter you are currently studying that uses either the chronological, definition, or classification pattern. State which pattern is being used and list the transitional words or phrases that provided you with clues to the type of pattern.

Comparison-Contrast

Often a writer will explain an object or idea, especially if it is unfamiliar to the reader, by showing how it is similar to or different from a familiar object or idea. At other times, it may be the writer's purpose to show how two ideas, places, objects, or people are similar or different. In each of these situations a writer commonly uses a pattern called comparison-contrast. In this pattern the material is organized to emphasize the similarities or differences between two or more items. There are several variations on this pattern: a paragraph may focus on similarities only, differences only, or both. The comparison pattern can be visualized and mapped as follows:

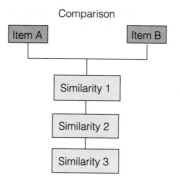

For material that focuses on differences, you might use a map like this:

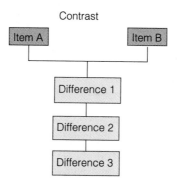

The following passage contrasts two types of advisory groups: councils and committees.

Councils and committees are advisory groups found in many different kinds of societies. We have briefly mentioned **councils** among the Shavante, Tetum, and Qashgai. They meet in public and are usually made up of informally appointed elders. **Committees** differ from councils in that they meet privately. Moreover, whereas councils are typical of simpler political organizations, committees are more characteristic of states. But the two kinds of groups can and often do coexist within the same political organization. When this occurs, councils are superior to committees, whose tasks and powers are delegated to them by councils.

Councils tend to be consensus-seeking bodies, while committees are more likely to achieve agreement by voting (although either kind of body may reach decisions in either way). Consensus seeking is typical of small social groups whose members have frequent personal interaction. Once a council or committee increases to more than about 50 members, decision by consensus is no longer possible. Voting is typical of larger groups whose members do not see much of one another in daily life and who owe their main allegiance not to other group members but to people (perhaps many millions) outside the council or committee. Members may in fact represent these outside people, as is the case with the U.S. Congress.

Hicks and Gwynne, Cultural Anthropology.

A map of the passage could look like this:

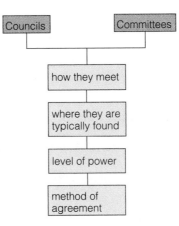

Once you become aware of the comparison-contrast pattern, look for both similarities and differences. First establish what is being compared or contrasted to what. Next determine whether similarities, differences, or both are presented. Often the title, heading, or topic sentence will express the basic relationship between the items or ideas discussed. A topic sentence that states, "It is important to make a distinction between amnesia and forgetting," indicates that the paragraph is primarily concerned with differences. On the other hand, a heading such as "Two Compatible Proposals for Economic Development" emphasizes similarities. Finally, decide whether the comparison or the contrast is the author's central purpose or whether it is used only as a means of support for the main idea.

You will find that transitional words help you identify the pattern. They also help you decide whether the paragraph focuses on similarities, differences, or both.

Comparison-Contrast Transitional Words/Phrases

Comparison	Contrast
both Faulkner and Williams . . .	*unlike* primary groups, secondary groups . . .
values, norms, and ethics *share* . . .	a drive *differs from* a need in that . . .

Other transitional words/phrases are

Comparison: likewise, in comparison, to compare, resembles, is similar, in the same way, correspondingly, as well as, like

Contrast: in contrast, on the contrary, although, even though, similarly, however, on the other hand, as opposed to, whereas, instead, in spite of

**EXERCISE
5-11**

DIRECTIONS: In each of the following sentences, underline the two items that are being compared.

1. Humans are complex organisms made up of many sophisticated systems. Yet humans share several characteristics with primates such as gorillas and New World Monkeys.

2. Students of education need to learn about human behavior in order to become perceptive teachers. Courses in sociology and psychology will provide a strong foundation since both these subjects deal with how people act under certain circumstances.

3. Face-to-face communication and electronic communication share a common goal—the transmission of information.

4. Microbiology deals with a broad range of scientific subjects. Two of these, immunology and virology, are of particular interest to medical researchers who study infectious diseases.

5. Flame retardant and flame resistant fabrics each provide a degree of protection to the person wearing them.

**EXERCISE
5-12**

DIRECTIONS: In each of the following sentences, underline the two items that are being contrasted.

1. Educators differ in their approaches to teaching reading. One method, whole language, applies a holistic model to literacy. The other main approach, seen as old-fashioned by some, is phonics, where children learn to read by "sounding out" letters and letter combinations.

2. To find engineering articles, use one of our databases. "Widget Abstracts" covers a large number of technology journals but does not contain any full text. However, "All Articles" is completely full text but has only the core journals relevant to this field.

3. Internet filters work in different ways. The screening type looks at each Web site being downloaded and determines whether there is offensive content. On the other hand, the list type of filter blocks certain pre-selected sites that are stored in a database. The user can add or remove sites from the list.

4. Most scientists believe in a Darwinian view of evolution. However, there are some in the scientific community who sympathize with the Creationist point of view and would like to meld the two theories together.

5. Many actors believe that stage acting requires more overall skill than movie acting. Unlike filmmaking, where actors can make mistake after mistake, knowing that the scene will just be shot again and again until it is right, live theater demands more concentration and preparation since retakes are not possible.

EXERCISE 5-13

DIRECTIONS: Which of the following topic sentences suggest that its paragraph will be developed by using comparison-contrast?

1. Sociology and psychology both focus on human behavior.

2. The category of mammals contains many different kinds of animals.

3. Two types of leaders can usually be identified in organizations: informal and formal.

4. Interpersonal communication is far more complex than intrapersonal communication.

5. The first step in grasping a novel's theme is to read it closely for literal content, including plot and character development.

EXERCISE 5-14

DIRECTIONS: Read the following excerpt and answer the questions that follow.

Social institutions are often confused with social groups and social organizations, which are described in the next chapter. They are not the same, however. Like institutions, groups and organizations exist to meet some goals, but groups and organizations are deliberately constructed bodies of individuals, whereas institutions are systems of norms. Thus education is an institution; the University of Vermont is an organization. Religion is an institution; the Baptist church is an organization.

The confusion between institutions and organizations stems in part from the fact that the names of institutions can often be used to describe concrete entities as well. In its abstract sense, for example, the word *family* is used to refer to an institution. Using the word in this way, we might say, "During the 1980s, the family in the United States began to undergo important changes." We can also use the word *family* to refer to an actual group of people, however. Using the word in this concrete sense, we might say, "I am going to spend my vacation with my family." The speaker is referring to an existing group of individuals—mother, father, sisters, and brothers. The two meanings of the word are closely related but nevertheless distinct. The word *institution* is an abstraction; the word *organization* refers to an existing group. The distinction should become clearer as we discuss social groups and social organizations in the next chapter and specific institutions in Chapters 12 through 17.

Eschelman et al., *Sociology: An Introduction.*

1. Identify two topics that are discussed in the excerpt. Does the excerpt compare, contrast, or compare *and* contrast these two topics?

    _____

    _____

2. Draw a map of the similarities or differences between the two topics.

3. List any transitional words used in the selection.

    _____

    _____

Cause-Effect

The cause-effect pattern describes or discusses an event or action that is caused by another event or action. Four possible relationships are described by the cause-effect pattern:

1. **Single Cause–Single Effect.** One cause produces one effect.

    Example: Omitting a key command will cause a computer program to fail.

2. **Single Cause–Multiple Effects.** One event produces several effects.

Example: The effects of inflation include shrinking real income, increasing prices, and higher interest rates.

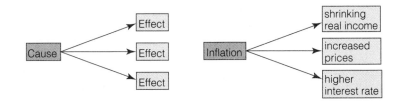

3. **Multiple Causes–Single Effect.** Several events work together to produce a single effect.

Example: Attending class regularly, reading assignments carefully, and taking good lecture notes produce good exam grades.

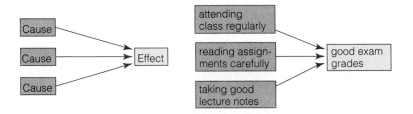

4. **Multiple Causes–Multiple Effects.** Several events work together to produce several effects.

Example: Because you missed the bus and couldn't get a ride, you missed your first class and did not stop at the library.

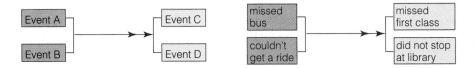

Read the following excerpt and determine what type of cause-effect relationship it illustrates.

EXTERNAL FACTORS IN OBESITY

The external cue theory holds that environmental cues prompt us to eat. This means that rather than relying on internal physical hunger cues, we respond to sight, color, and availability of food or to the time of day when we are programmed to eat. This is further complicated by the fact that food is available around the clock—at home, at work, in restaurants and grocery stores (some restaurants even offer home delivery!).

Other factors that may contribute to people's attitudes toward food are the way in which individual families perceive food. Some families are "food centered," which means they tend to overeat at mealtime, eat rapidly, snack excessively, eat for reasons other than hunger, or eat until all their dishes are empty. Unwittingly, family members may become involved as codependents in the exercise of overeating, and serve as enablers for a person whose eating habits are out of control. Overeating by children may be an imitation of overeating by parents. Obese children, over a given time interval, tend to take more bites of food and chew their food less thoroughly than nonobese children. Some parents preach the "clean plate ethic" by which they praise their children for eating all the food on their plates as a token of thanks for having enough food to eat.

Some people eat in response to stress, boredom, insecurity, anxiety, loneliness, or as a reward for being good. Parents who console a child with food may be initiating a life-long behavior pattern. Some people use food as an inappropriate response to psychological stimuli. As you experience pain, anxiety, insecurity, stress, arousal, or excitement, the brain responds by producing substances that soothe pain and lessen arousal. Another effect of these substances is that they enhance appetite for food and reduce activity. If, in addition, you are unusually sensitive to stress, you are likely to eat to compensate for stress, whether negative or positive. Eating may be an appropriate response to all of these stimuli on occasion, but the person who uses them to overeat creates a whole new set of emotional problems relating to his or her overeating. They may get caught in a vicious cycle—depression causing overeating and vice versa.

Byer and Shainberg, *Living Well: Health in Your Hands.*

The first paragraph discusses environmental cues that may stimulate people to eat. The second paragraph examines how a family's perceptions of food can contribute to overeating. The third paragraph explains how some people eat in response to emotional stimuli. It could be mapped as follows:

External Factors in Obesity

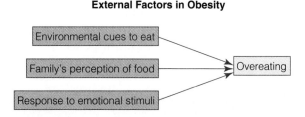

When reading material is organized in the cause-effect pattern, pay close attention to the topic sentence. It usually states the cause-effect relationship that is detailed throughout the paragraph. As you read through the paragraph, read to find specific causes and specific effects. Determine the connection between causes and effects: Why did a particular event or action occur? What happened as a result of it?

Transitional words can help you identify the pattern as well as determine the exact nature of the cause-effect relationship. The following list contains transitional words that most commonly indicate a cause-effect pattern.

CAUSE-EFFECT TRANSITIONAL WORDS/PHRASES

hypertension *causes* . . .
Napoleon was defeated at Waterloo: *consequently* . . .
an interest rate increase *resulted in* . . .
hatred *breeds* . . .

Other transitional words/phrases are:

therefore, hence, for this reason, since, leads to, creates, yields, stems from, produces, for, because, as a result, due to, thus

**EXERCISE
5-15**

DIRECTIONS: In each of the following paragraphs, circle the cause(s) and underline the effect(s).

1. Research has shown that mental illnesses have various causes, but the causes are not fully understood. Some mental disorders are due to physical changes in the brain resulting from illness or injury. Chemical imbalances in the brain may cause other mental illnesses. Still other disorders are mainly due to conditions in the environment that affect a person's mental state. These conditions include unpleasant childhood experiences and severe emotional stress.

2. Many regions are experiencing high levels of unemployment. Unfortunately, widespread job loss affects more than household income levels. Household tensions and even domestic violence rise. Indeed, some communities see an increase in all crimes. Loss of self-esteem and hope are some of the more personal ways unemployment hurts.

3. Government leaders need to look harder at the true reasons our violent crime rates have risen. What they will see are people living in poverty, desperately trying to survive. Add to that rampant drug use and you

have the perfect conditions for violent gang activity. Furthermore, budget cuts have lessened the police presence and done away with special police programs that were working to keep neighborhoods safe.

4. The Earth is always moving in one way or another. When there is volcanic activity, an earthquake can occur. Also, shifting plates of the Earth's crust along faults will make the ground shake beneath us. Most earthquakes cannot be felt but are measured by sensitive equipment at seismic centers around the globe.

5. Low standardized test scores among minorities caused by biased questions leads teachers to "teach to the test." These same students may improve their performance on the next standardized test but do not receive the well-rounded education needed to succeed in school as a whole and ultimately in life.

EXERCISE 5-16

DIRECTIONS: Circle the textbook chapter headings that are most likely to use the cause-effect pattern.

1. The Nature of the Judicial System
2. Why Bureaucracies Exist
3. Explaining the Increase in Homelessness
4. How Walt Whitman Uses Imagery
5. Types of Special Interest Groups

EXERCISE 5-17

DIRECTIONS: Read the following excerpt and answer the questions that follow.

One of the most intriguing hormones is melatonin, which is secreted by the pea-sized pineal gland nestled at the base of the brain. We have known for decades about its role in our daily rhythms, such as our sleep-awake cycles. As night draws near and less light reaches the retina, melatonin levels surge in our blood, only to dwindle as dawn brings the first light. In recent years, melatonin has been taken as a safe, effective sleeping aid, but researchers now tell us that perhaps the hormone has other, more far-reaching effects as well. For example, it "sops up" free radicals, those disruptive parts of oxygen molecules that contribute to aging and diseases. Other antioxidants (such as Vitamins C, E, and beta carotene) may only function in certain cells, but melatonin can reach all cells, including those protected areas of the brain. Researchers also suggest that melatonin may boost immune function, retard aging, prevent or retard cancer, prevent pregnancy (in large doses), prevent heart attacks, and extend life. The hormone can also be used to combat jet lag.

Wallace, *Biology: The World of Life.*

1. Underline the sentence that states the central cause-effect relationship discussed throughout this excerpt.

2. List or draw a map of the various effects of melatonin.

_____

_____

_____

3. List any transitional words used in this excerpt.   ▬

Enumeration/Simple Listing

The enumeration pattern is a list of information. The order of named or listed items is not important. For example, a section in an anthropology text may list and describe characteristics of an ancient culture, or a psychology text may present facts about aggressive behavior.

Often the writer chooses to present the items in a way that is easiest to explain or that is easiest for the reader to understand. Even so, there is still no obvious pattern that will help you organize and remember the information. The following excerpt is an example of a paragraph that lists information.

Social networks perform several important functions. For one, many decisions and preferences are influenced by networks of friends, family, and co-workers. Networks are also a primary source of information and advice, whether for an immigrant searching for a place to live, a student seeking a summer job, or a parent looking for a good day-care center. Networks can also provide individuals with companionship.

Popenoe, *Sociology.*

As you can see, the paragraph listed information about the functions of social networks.

The listing pattern can be visualized and mapped as follows:

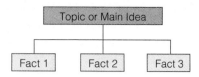

The brief sample paragraph on social networks could be mapped like this:

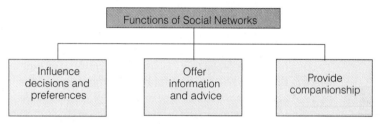

Transitional words are extremely useful in locating items in the list. Usually, as a writer moves from one item in the list to another, he or she will indicate the change. The following list contains common examples of transitional words for lists.

ENUMERATION PATTERN TRANSITIONAL WORDS/PHRASES

there are *several* characteristics of . . .
one feature of families is . . .
Government serves *the following* functions . . .

Other enumeration pattern transitional words/phrases are:

first, second, third, numerals (1., 2., 3.), letters (a., b., c.), another, also, too, finally

EXERCISE 5-18

DIRECTIONS: Each of the following paragraphs lists information. Circle the topic, and underline each item in the list.

1. Audiences favor speakers who communicate in a personal rather than an impersonal style, who speak *with* them rather than *at* them. There are several ways to develop a personal style. First, use personal pronouns, such as *I, me, he, she,* and *you*, which will create bridges to the audience. Using personal pronouns is better than using impersonal expressions such as "One is lead to believe … ." In addition, try to involve the audience by asking questions. When you direct questions to your listeners, they feel that they are part of the public speaking experience. You should

also try to create immediacy—a sense of connectedness—with your audience. You can do this in numerous ways, such as by using personal examples, complimenting the audience, or referring to what you and the audience have in common.

DeVito, *Elements of Public Speaking.*

2. The U.S. deposit-insuring agencies have serious design flaws. First, the price of deposit insurance to individual depository institutions was until recently relatively low; the depository institutions are subsidized by the depository insurers. Second, the insurance premium is the same percentage of total deposits for all depository institutions, regardless of the riskiness of the institution's portfolio. Also, until recently, all deposit-insuring agencies charged a depository institution about .25 percent of the institution's total (not just insured) deposits. For example, federally insured commercial banks pay a flat fee for the FDIC guarantee of the first $100,000 of each deposit account in the bank. The flaw in this pricing structure is that an individual depository institution's premium is set without regard to its probability of failure, the riskiness of its portfolio, or the estimated cost to the insurer should the institution fail.

Miller, *Economics Today.*

3. Beginning teachers have a great deal of preparation before that all-important first day of school. Creating a classroom atmosphere conducive to learning is one of the most crucial elements of this preparation. The new teacher should first consult resources about classroom environment, such as books and articles. After all, other teachers have already created wonderful spaces! Then, measure and draw your classroom so you can start to make real plans. Once you have your ideas down on paper, put them into action. Arrange your classroom a few weeks before school starts in case you need to make adjustments. Finally, and most importantly, be open to changes once your students arrive. You may find that your design performs differently when the room is full of people!

EXERCISE 5-19

DIRECTIONS: Identify and circle the topics listed below that might be developed by using the enumeration pattern.

1. Freud's versus Jung's theories

2. Consumer research technology

3. Varieties of theft

4. Purposes of legal punishment

5. The process of gene splicing

6. Learning theories

7. Hormones and reproduction

8. Pastoral society

9. How acid rain occurs

10. The impact of environment on intelligence

EXERCISE 5–20

DIRECTIONS: Read the following excerpt and answer the questions that follow.

THE STIMULUS FOR HEARING: SOUND

The stimulus for vision is light; for hearing, the stimulus is sound. Sound consists of a series of vibrations (carried through air or some other medium, such as water) beating against our ear. We can represent these pressures as sound waves. As a source of sound vibrates, it pushes air against our ears in waves. As was the case for light waves, there are three major physical characteristics of sound waves: amplitude, frequency (the inverse of wavelength), and purity. Each is related to a different psychological experience. We'll briefly consider each in turn.

The amplitude of a sound wave depicts its intensity—the force with which air strikes the ear. The intensity of a sound determines the psychological experience we call loudness. That is, the higher the amplitude, the louder we perceive the sound. Quiet, soft sounds have low amplitudes.

Measurements of the physical intensity of sound are given in units of force per unit area (or pressure). Loudness is a psychological characteristic. It is measured by people, not by instruments. The decibel scale of sound intensity reflects perceived loudness. Its zero point is the lowest intensity of sound that can be detected, the absolute threshold. Our ears are very sensitive receptors and respond to very low levels of sound intensity. Sounds louder than those produced by jet aircraft engines or fast-moving subway trains (about 120 decibels) are experienced more as pain than as sound. Prolonged exposure to loud sounds causes varying degrees of deafness.

The second physical characteristic of sound to consider is wave frequency, the number of times a wave repeats itself within a given period. For sound, frequency is measured in terms of how many waves of pressure are exerted every second. The unit of sound frequency is the hertz, abbreviated Hz. If a sound wave repeats itself 50 times in one second, it is a 50-Hz sound; 500 repetitions is a 500-Hz sound, and so on.

The psychological experience produced by sound wave frequency is pitch. Pitch is our experience of how high or low a tone is. The musical scale represents differences in pitch. Low frequencies correspond to bass tones, such as those made by foghorns or tubas. High-frequency vibrations give rise to the experience of high-pitched sounds, such as musical tones produced by flutes or the squeals of smoke detectors.

A third characteristic of sound waves is wave purity, or wave complexity. You'll recall that we seldom experience pure, monochromatic lights. Pure sounds are also uncommon in our everyday experience. A pure sound would be one in which all waves from the sound source were vibrating at exactly the same frequency. Such sounds can be produced electronically, and tuning forks produce approximations, but most of the sounds we hear every day are complex sounds consisting of many different sound wave frequencies.

The psychological quality or characteristic of a sound, reflecting its degree of purity, is called timbre. For example, each musical instrument produces a unique variety or mixture of overtones, so each type of musical instrument tends to sound a little different from all others. If a trumpet, a violin, and a piano were to play the same note, we could still tell the instruments apart because of our experience of timbre. In fact, any instrument can display different timbres, depending on how it is constructed and played.

Gerow, *Psychology: An Introduction.*

1. Underline the sentence that states what the entire passage will discuss.

2. Explain in your own words the three major physical characteristics of sound waves and their related psychological experiences.

_____

_____

_____

_____

3. List the transitional words or phrases used in this excerpt.

_____

Mixed Patterns

Many texts contain sections and passages that combine one or more organizational patterns. For instance, in listing characteristics of a newly developed computer program, an author may explain it by comparing it with similar existing programs. Or, in describing an event or process, the writer may also include the reasons (causes) an event occurred or explain why the steps in a process must be followed in the prescribed order.

Read the following paragraph about stalking, and determine what two patterns are used.

Stalking is defined differently in different states. A typical definition is "willful, malicious, and repeated following and harassing of another person." However, three states include "lying in wait," and seven include "surveillance." Many states require a pattern of behavior, and some require that victims have a "reasonable" fear for their safety. Texas requires that the victim continue to be stalked *after* law enforcement officials have been notified. A model definition of stalking developed by the National Institute of Justice is as follows: "a course of conduct directed at a specific person that involves repeated visual or physical proximity, nonconsensual communication, or verbal, written or implied threats, or a combination thereof that would cause a reasonable person fear." Applying this definition, a national survey of 8,000 men and 8,000 women estimated that 1 in 12 American women and 1 in 45 American men had been stalked at some time in their lives.

Barlow, *Criminal Justice in America.*

In this paragraph the textbook author is defining the term "stalking." He is also, however, as the topic sentence (first sentence) of the paragraph states, considering how "stalking is defined differently in different states." Specifically, the author compares what various states, including Texas, require in the definition and quotes a model definition from the National Institute of Justice. Thus, two patterns, definition and comparison-contrast are used in the paragraph.

When reading mixed patterns, focus on one of the patterns and use it to guide your reading. Whenever possible, choose the predominant or most obvious pattern. However, regardless of which pattern you choose, it will serve to organize the author's thoughts and make them easier to recall.

Because more than one pattern is evident in mixed patterns, you can expect a mix or combination of transitional words as well.

EXERCISE 5-21

DIRECTIONS: For each of the following topic sentences, anticipate what pattern that paragraph is likely to exhibit. Write the name of the pattern in the space provided.

1. _____ Unlike Japan and the Western European countries, Canada has been relatively removed from the balance of terror debate.

2. _____ The sections of a comprehensive medical history are introduction, chief concern, history of present illness, past medical history, family medical history, and review of symptoms.

3. _____ Consumers' buying decisions influence the prices farmers receive for their products.

4. _____ The battle for women's suffrage was carried out in the late 1800s and the early 1900s.

5. _____ The majority of Americans will be better off in the year 2025 than they are today.

6. _____ A mild stimulant, such as caffeine, appears to change a person's ability to maintain attention and concentration.

7. _____ The GNP (gross national product) is an economic measure that considers the total value of goods and services that a country produces during a given year.

8. _____ Managers experience a number of different personnel problems that must be solved before a department can work effectively.

9. _____ A health maintenance organization is a medical corporation that takes care of the medical needs of its members.

10. _____ Geomorphology, the study of landforms and the events and processes that create them, has three major branches of study.

EXERCISE 5-22

DIRECTIONS: Read the following excerpt and answer the questions that follow.

VIRUS RISKS AND SAFEGUARDS

Computer viruses are a serious problem for everyone online. Like their medical namesake, some computer viruses are barely noticeable but others are hideous killers. If you plan to download software from the Internet, you need to know how to protect yourself. This is one place where you don't want to learn things the hard way. You never have to be hurt by a computer virus if you take some simple precautions.

A computer virus is a piece of code that someone inserts in an otherwise legitimate computer program for the purpose of causing mischief. Some viruses are just annoying. For example, one may cause a political message or animation display to pop up on your screen, and that's all it does. Other viruses can do considerable damage. A particularly malicious one might erase every file on your hard drive. Viruses are also designed to spread from one machine to another through shared files. A user can unknowingly infect his or her own computer and then spread that virus to others without realizing it.

Some viruses are visible and obvious, whereas others are subtle and devious. A virus that quietly operates behind the scenes might cause a gradual slow-down in the performance of your computer over a long period of time. You wouldn't notice anything right away, and you may never figure out what happened to your machine. The only way to know if a virus is present on your computer is with special software designed to detect viruses hiding in your files.

Virus detection software locates known viruses by watching for identifying signatures that give them away. A good detection program will look for thousands of viruses, and periodic software updates are released to keep up with new viruses. The bad news is that there are more computer viruses than ever before and that the number of known viruses will likely only rise. The good news is that computer users have become educated about viruses and are taking appropriate precautions. So, the amount of serious virus damage is probably decreasing even as the number of viruses in circulation continues to grow.

Lehnert, Light on the Internet.

1. What patterns are evident in this excerpt? Which do you think is predominant?

   _____

2. Underline the transitional words that suggest these patterns.

3. Draw a map of this excerpt.

4. Explain in your own words what viruses are and what can be done to guard against them.

   _____

   _____

   _____

EXERCISE 5-23

DIRECTIONS: Read each of the following paragraphs and identify the predominant organizational pattern used. Write the name of the pattern in the space provided. Choose from among the following patterns: chronological order, definition, classification, comparison-contrast, cause-effect, and enumeration. Draw a map of each paragraph.

1. Erik Erikson (1902–1994) was heavily influenced by Freud. However, because he modified Freud's theories, he is commonly referred to as a "neo-Freudian." Freud emphasized the drives of the id; Erikson's main concern was the more "rational" world of the ego. Erikson saw self-development as proceeding through eight *psychosocial* stages that involve the way we respond to the changing demands made on us as we go through life. Freud focused on childhood; Erikson's stages continue into old age. Thus Erikson believed that the personality is molded throughout life, not just in childhood.

   Popenoe, Sociology.

   Pattern: _____

2. The impact of international migration is even greater than the numbers might suggest. Immigrants are often greeted with apprehension, and immigration has become an explosive political issue in many receiving countries. This is for several reasons. First, official statistics substantially underestimate actual numbers; undocumented migration

is rising everywhere. Second, migrants are usually in the peak years of fertility. Therefore, they are playing an increasing role in the total population growth in the rich target countries. Third, migrant settlements are generally concentrated in a few places within a country. This usually adds to the immigrants' visibility and increases the perception of cultural differences.

Bergman and Renwick, *Introduction to Geography: People, Places and Environment.*

Pattern: _____

3. The technologies for both printing and papermaking came to Europe from China. By the ninth century, the Chinese were printing pictures; by the eleventh century, they had invented (but seldom used) movable type. Printmaking was developed in Europe by the fifteenth century—first to meet the demand for inexpensive religious icons and playing cards, then to illustrate books printed with the new European movable type. Since the fifteenth century, the art of printmaking has been closely associated with the illustration of books.

Preble et al., *Artforms: An Introduction to the Visual Arts.*

Pattern: _____

4. The patterns of stars seen in the sky are usually called constellations. In astronomy, however, the term constellation refers to a *region* of the sky. Any place you point in the sky belongs to some constellation; familiar patterns of stars merely help locate particular constellations. For example, the constellation Orion includes all the stars in the familiar pattern of the hunter, *along with* the region of the sky in which these stars are found.

Bennett, *The Cosmic Perspective.*

Pattern: _____

5. The suburbs developed in response to several social forces. The multi-lane freeways that go around the perimeter of the city (the outerbelts) spurred the development of suburban places along the city's rim. Now, rather than going from the suburb to the central city to work, to shop, to see a doctor, or to enjoy the movies, suburbanites can obtain the same services by driving along the outer belt from one suburban community to another. Another factor has been the decentralization of jobs. Faster transportation and communications have encouraged manufacturing plants and distribution centers to relocate from the central city to the outer rings of the city—that is, to the suburbs. Yet another factor has been the aging of the central city. Facilities in many down-

town areas are simply worn out or obsolete. Parking is expensive and inconvenient; buildings are dirty and run-down. In contrast, suburban shopping malls and industrial centers typically have bright new facilities and ample parking.

Curry et al., *Sociology for the Twenty-First Century.*

Pattern: _____

DIRECTIONS: Turn to Reading Selection 9 or 10 at the end of the chapter. Read the selection and answer the questions. Then review the selection and identify the organizational pattern of each paragraph. In the margin next to each paragraph, write the name of the pattern. Underline any transitional words that you find.

DIRECTIONS: Suppose your instructor asked you to write a paper on one of the following topics. Identify which organizational pattern(s) might be useful in developing and organizing a paper on each topic.

1. Types of hairstyles worn by African-American women

_____

2. How a child's brain develops

_____

3. A study of what is "cool"

_____

4. An explanation of extreme sports

_____

5. An explanation of attention deficit disorder

_____

DIRECTIONS: Choose a section from one of your current textbook chapters. Identify the organizational pattern used in each paragraph by writing CO (Chronological Order), CC (Comparison-Contrast), D (Definition), CL (Classification), or CE (Cause-Effect), or E (Enumeration) in the margin beside each paragraph. Underline the transitional words in each paragraph.

Other Useful Patterns of Organization

The patterns presented in the preceding section are the most common. Table 5.1 below presents a brief review of those patterns and their corresponding transitional words. However, writers do not limit themselves to these six patterns. Especially in academic writing, you may find one or more of the patterns listed in Table 5.2 (p. 205). Here is a brief review of each of these additional patterns.

Statement and Clarification

Many writers make a statement of fact and then proceed to clarify or explain that statement. For instance, a writer may open a paragraph by

Table 5.1   A Review of Patterns and Transitional Words

Pattern	Characteristics	Transitional Words
Chronological order	Describes events, processes, procedures	first, second, later, before, next, as soon as, after, then, finally, meanwhile, following, last, during, when, until, on (date), in (date)
Definition	Explains the meaning of a word or phrase	is, refers to, can be defined as, means, consists of, involves, is a term that, is called, is characterized by, occurs when, are those that, entails, corresponds to, is literally
Classification	Divides a topic into parts based on shared characteristics	classified as, is comprised of, is composed of, several varieties of, one type, a second class of, another group, kinds, divisions, categories
Comparison-contrast	Discusses similarities and/or differences among ideas, theories, concepts, objects, or persons	*Similarities:* both, also, similarly, like, likewise, too, as well as, resembles, correspondingly, in the same way, to compare, in comparison, share *Differences:* unlike, differs from, in contrast, on the contrary, on the other hand, instead, despite, nevertheless, however, in spite of, whereas, as opposed to, although, even though
Cause-Effect	Describes how one or more things cause or are related to another	*Causes:* because, because of, for, since, stems from, one cause is, one reason is, leads to, causes, creates, yields, produces, due to, breeds, for this reason *Effects:* consequently, results in, one result is, therefore, thus, as a result, hence
Enumeration/ simple listing	Items are named of listed where the order of them is not important	the following, several, one, another, also, too, first, second, numerals (1., 2.), letters (a., b.), finally

stating that "The best education for you may not be the best education for someone else." The remainder of the paragraph would then discuss that statement and make its meaning clear by explaining how educational needs are individual and based on one's talents, skills, and goals. Directional words associated with this pattern are listed in Table 5.2.

Here is a sample paragraph. Notice that the author makes a statement in the first sentence and then explains it throughout the remainder of the paragraph. Notice, too, the underlined transitional phrase.

> Sex ratios in the poor countries do not show a consistent pattern. In some poor countries men outnumber women, but in others, in tropical Africa, for example, women outnumber men. <u>In fact</u>, variations in sex ratios can be explained only by a combination of national economic and cultural factors. In the countries of North America and Europe and in Japan, women may suffer many kinds of discrimination, but they are not generally discriminated against when it comes to access to medical care.
>
> Bergman, *Introduction to Geography.*

Summary

A summary is a condensed statement that provides the key points of a larger idea or piece of writing. The summaries at the end of each chapter of this text provide a quick review of the chapter's contents. Often writers summarize what they have already said or what someone else has said. For example, in a psychology textbook you will find many summaries of

Table 5.2   Additional Patterns and Transitional Words

Pattern	Characteristics	Transitional Words
Statement and clarification	Indicates that information explaining an idea or concept will follow	In fact, in other words, clearly, evidently, obviously
Summary	Indicates that a condensed review of an idea or piece of writing will follow	In summary, in conclusion, in brief, to summarize, to sum up, in short, on the whole
Generalization and example	Provides examples that clarify a broad, general statement	For example, for instance, that is, to illustrate
Addition	Indicates that additional information will follow	Furthermore, additionally, also, besides, further, in addition, moreover, again
Spatial order/location	Describes physical location or position in space	Above, below, besides, next to, in front of, behind, inside, outside, opposite, within, nearby

research. Instead of asking you to read an entire research study, the text-book author will summarize the study's findings. Other times a writer may repeat in condensed form what he or she has already said as a means of emphasis or clarification. Transitional words associated with this pattern are listed in Table 5.2.

Here is a sample paragraph in which the author summarizes changes in the magazine industry. Notice that he moves from idea to idea without providing detailed explanation of each idea.

> In summary, the magazine industry is adapting to the new world of electronic multimedia information and entertainment, with formats that will be quite different from the familiar ones. Computer-generated publishing has become the norm in the magazine business, expanding beyond its uses in producing newsletters and other specialized publications. Most general circulation magazines already rely heavily on desktop computers, interacting with other electronic equipment to produce high-quality, graphics-filled products.
>
> Dizard, *Old, Media, New Media.*

Generalization and Example

Examples are one of the best ways to explain something that is unfamiliar or unknown. Examples are specific instances or situations that illustrate a concept or idea. Often writers may give a general statement, or generalization, and then explain it by giving examples to make its meaning clear. In a social problems textbook, you may find the following generalization: Computer theft by employees is on the increase. The section may then go on to offer examples from specific companies in which employees insert fictitious information into the company's computer program and steal company funds. Transitional words associated with this pattern are listed in Table 5.2.

In the following paragraph about dreams, the writer makes a general statement about dreams and then gives examples to explain his statement.

> Different cultures place varying emphases on dreams and support different beliefs concerning dreams. For example, many people in the United States view dreams as irrelevant fantasy with no connection to everyday life. By contrast, people in other cultures view dreams as key sources of information about the future, the spiritual world, and the dreamer. Such cultural views can influence the probability of dream recall. In many modern Western cultures, people rarely remember their dreams upon awakening. The Parintintin of South America, however, typically remember several dreams every night and the Senoi of Malaysia discuss their dreams with family members in the morning.
>
> Davis, Psychology.

Addition

Writers often introduce an idea or make a statement and then supply additional information about that idea or statement. For instance, an education textbook may introduce the concept of home schooling and then provide in-depth information about its benefits. This pattern is often used to expand, elaborate, or discuss an idea in greater detail. Transitional words associated with this pattern are listed in Table 5.2.

In the following paragraph about pathogens, the writer uses addition.

> Some pathogens [disease-causing organisms] evolve and mutate naturally. <u>Also</u>, patients who fail to complete the full portion of their antibiotic prescriptions allow drug-resistant pathogens to multiply. The use of antibiotics in animal feed and sprayed on fruits and vegetables during food processing increases opportunities for resistant organisms to evolve and thrive. <u>Furthermore</u>, there is evidence that the disruption of Earth's natural habitats can trigger the evolution of new pathogens.
>
> Bergman, *Introduction to Geography.*

Notice that the writer states that some pathogens mutate naturally and then goes on to add that they also mutate as a result of human activities.

Spatial Order/Location

Spatial order is concerned with physical location or position in space. Spatial order is used in disciplines in which physical descriptions are important. A photography textbook may use spatial order to describe the parts of a camera. An automotive technology textbook may use spatial order to describe disk brake operation. Transitional words associated with this pattern are listed in Table 5.2. Here is a sample paragraph in which the author's description of blood circulation uses spatial order.

> Pulmonary circulation conducts blood <u>between</u> the heart and the lungs. Oxygen-poor, CO_2-laden blood returns through two large veins (venae cavae) from tissues within the body, enters the <u>right</u> atrium, and is then moved into the <u>right</u> ventricle of the heart. From there, it is pumped into the pulmonary artery, which <u>divides into two branches,</u> each leading to one of the lungs. In the lung, the arteries undergo extensive branching, giving rise to vast networks of capillaries where gas exchange takes place, with blood becoming oxygenated while CO_2 is discharged. Oxygen-rich blood then returns to the heart via the pulmonary veins.
>
> Mix et al., *Biology: The Network of Life.*

EXERCISE 5-27

DIRECTIONS: For each of the following statements, identify the pattern that is evident and write its name in the space provided. Choose from among the following patterns: statement and clarification, summary, generalization and example, addition, and spatial order/location.

1. _____ Short fibers, dendrites, branch out around the cell body and a single long fiber, the axon, extends from the cell body.

2. _____ When faced with a life-threatening illness, people tend to deny its existence. In addition family members may also participate in the denial.

3. _____ If our criminal justice system works, the recidivism rate—the percentage of people released from prison who return—should decrease. In other words, in a successful system, there should be a decrease in the number of criminals who are released from prison that become repeat offenders.

4. _____ Students who are informed about drugs tend to use them in greater moderation. Furthermore, they tend to help educate others.

5. _____ A successful drug addiction treatment program would offer free or very cheap drugs to addicts. Heroin addicts, for example, could be prescribed heroin when under a physician's care.

6. _____ In conclusion, it is safe to say that crime by women is likely to increase as greater numbers of women assume roles traditionally held by men.

7. _____ The pollutants we have just discussed all involve chemicals; we can conclude that they threaten our environment and our well-being.

8. _____ A residual check valve that maintains slight pressure on the hydraulic system is located in the master cylinder at the outlet for the drum brakes.

9. _____ Sociologists study how we are socialized into sex roles, the attitudes expected of males and females. Sex roles, in fact, identify some activities and behaviors as clearly male and others as clearly female.

10. _____ Patients often consult a lay referral network to discuss their medical problems. Cancer patients, for instance, can access Internet discussion groups that provide both information and support.   ▬

Using Transitional Words

As you learned earlier in the chapter, transitional words can help you identify organizational patterns. These words are also called *directional words* because they reveal the author's direction of thought, or *clue words* because they provide readers with clues about what is to follow. Transitional words are also helpful in discovering or clarifying relationships between and among ideas in any piece of writing. Specifically, transitional words help you grasp connections between and within sentences. Transitional words can help you predict what is to come next within a paragraph. For instance, if you are reading along and come upon the phrase *in conclusion,* you know that the writer will soon present a summary. If you encounter the word *furthermore,* you know that the writer is about to present additional information about the subject at hand. If you encounter the word *consequently* in the middle of a sentence (The law was repealed; consequently, . . .), you know that the writer is about to explain what happened as a result of the repeal. Tables 5.1 (p. 204) and 5.2 (p. 205) list the transitional words that correspond to the patterns discussed in this chapter.

**EXERCISE
5-28**

DIRECTIONS: Each of the following beginnings of paragraphs uses a transitional word or phrase to tell the reader what will follow in the paragraph. Read each, paying particular attention to the underlined transitional word or phrase. Then, in the space provided, describe as specifically as you can what you would expect to find next in the paragraph.

1. Many Web sites on the Internet are reliable and trustworthy. <u>However,</u> . . . _____

_____

2. One advantage of using a computer to take notes is that you can rearrange information easily. <u>Another</u> . . .

_____

_____

3. There are a number of ways to avoid catching the cold virus. <u>First of all,</u> . . . _____

_____

4. Jupiter is a planet surrounded by several moons. <u>Likewise</u> . . .

_____

5. When planning a speech, you should choose a topic that is familiar or that you are knowledgeable about. <u>Next,</u> . . .

_____

6. Following a high-protein diet may be rewarding because it often produces quick weight loss. <u>On the other hand,</u> . . .

_____

Critical Thinking Tip #5

Analyzing Cause-Effect Relationships

Cause and effect relationships are complex and often can be misleading. Here's a sample situation:

Sarah earned her bachelor's degree in three years instead of four by attending summer sessions. Since she graduated, she has never held a job for longer than three weeks. Obviously, condensing her studies was not a good idea.

In this situation, the writer assumed that a cause-effect relationship existed: Sarah cannot hold a job *because* she condensed her studies. Although education and job skills may be related, one is not necessarily the cause of the other. Sarah may not be able to hold a job because she is lazy, frequently late, or cannot get along with other employees.

A common reasoning error is to assume that because two events are related or occur close in time, one event caused the other. Some advertising encourages this type of erroneous thinking. For example, an ad may show a happy family eating a particular brand of breakfast cereal. It implies that you will have a happy family if you buy that particular brand.

Always analyze cause-effect relationships; look for evidence that one event or action is the direct cause of another.

7. The iris is a doughnut-shaped portion of the eyeball. <u>In the center</u> . . .

_____

8. Price is not the only factor consumers consider when making a major purchase. They <u>also</u> . . . _____

9. Asbestos, a common material found in many older buildings in which people have worked for decades, has been shown to cause cancer. <u>Consequently,</u> . . .

_____

10. Many Web sites provide valuable links to related sites. <u>To illustrate,</u> visit . . . _____

_____

Summary

1. Why is it helpful to recognize the organizational pattern of a paragraph or passage you are reading?

When you recognize the specific pattern of the material you are reading, you will be better able to follow the ideas being presented and to predict what will be presented next. You will find that you have made connections among the important ideas so that recalling one idea will help you to recall the others. As a result, you will find it easier to learn and remember them.

2. What are the six common organizational patterns?

The six common organizational patterns are
- Chronological Order/Process: events or procedures are described in the order in which they occur in time.
- Definition: an object or idea is explained by describing the general class or group to which it belongs and how the item differs from others in the same group (distinguishing features).
- Classification: an object or idea is explained by dividing it into parts and describing or explaining each.

- Comparison-Contrast: a new or unfamiliar idea is explained by showing how it is similar to or different from a more familiar idea.
- Cause-Effect: connections between events are explained by showing what caused an event or what happened as a result of a particular event.
- Enumeration: information is organized into lists on the basis of characteristics, features, or parts, or according to categories.

3. What other patterns do writers use?

Writers also use statement and clarification, summary, generalization and example, addition, and spatial order/location.

4. What are transitional words and how are they useful?

Transitional words or phrases guide you from one important idea in a paragraph or passage to another. These linking words or phrases are signals or clues to the way a piece of writing is organized and allow you to more easily follow a writer's thoughts. They also reveal relationships between and within sentences.

Reading Selection 9

Careers: Criminal Justice

Electronic Monitoring: An Alternative to Imprisonment
Hugh D. Barlow
From *Criminal Justice in America*

Do all criminals need to be imprisoned? Millions of dollars are spent each year housing convicted criminals. This reading explores electronic monitoring, a means of keeping track of criminals while they are under confinement in their own homes.

— · —

1   Electronic monitoring is part of a "new age of surveillance," according to one criminologist (Lilly, 1990). It is a means by which criminal justice personnel can monitor the movements of offenders who have been released into the community with severe restrictions—the most

restrictive being *house arrest,* also called *home confinement.* Offenders under house arrest are confined to their homes when they are not working or engaged in activities preapproved by their probation officer. Their movements are monitored through electronic devices described in the following section.

2   The rules of confinement vary, but in some jurisdictions every adult in the offender's house is expected to abide by them. "No alcohol, no parties, and no weapons" is one such rule in Cook County, Illinois (Turnbaugh, 1995a:7).

How Electronic Monitoring Works

3   The origins of electronic monitoring are traced back to the 1960s, when researchers at Harvard University constructed a belt-worn transmitter and a series of repeater stations in the Boston area that were linked to a central monitoring station (Renzema, 1992). Signals from the transmitter allowed the wearer to be tracked over several blocks.

4   The most widespread application today consists of a number of computer terminals, or monitoring towers, linked via phone lines to a receiver that resembles a cable TV box in the offender's home. The offender wears a non-removable ankle band holding a transmitter that sends a signal to the receiver. Beyond a certain range, from 100 to as much as 750 feet, the signal fades and the receiver triggers a violation report, which is printed out at the monitoring station. In the Cook County program mentioned

House arrest with electronic monitoring is an intermediate sanction that combines control and restraint with freedoms that promote responsibility and enable offenders to make a living or improve their skills. It is growing in popularity as a low-cost alternative to imprisonment but its overall impact on recidivism and public safety is uncertain.

earlier, the monitoring towers are manned by six technicians who constantly check the activity of 180 to 200 individuals under house arrest.

5   One company, called Sentencing Alternatives, markets both single-offender and multiple-offender systems—which are capable of monitoring up to 40 offenders with one telephone line and one receiver. They offer "full services" such as free officer safety devices, free expert court witnesses, and 24-hour monitoring done on a sophisticated, powerful mainframe computer system, not a PC. The company claims that "only you will know when or where the offender will be subject to being checked, and at the same time the officer never has to leave the comfort and safety of the automobile" (Sentencing Alternatives, 1997, http://www.sentalt.com).

Support for Electronic Monitoring of Offenders

6   In 1986, there were only 95 offenders on electronic monitoring in the entire country (Renzema, 1992:41). By 1995 there were an estimated 70,000 people under some kind of electronic monitoring (Lilly, 1995). In Florida alone, more than 13,000 offenders were on house arrest in 1993 (Blomberg, Bales, and Reed, 1993).

7   Home confinement with electronic monitoring is appealing because it promises so much. Its supporters usually cite four distinct benefits: (1) it protects society; (2) it punishes offenders; (3) it allows offenders to work and to improve their future prospects through counseling and education; and (4) it reduces prison overcrowding and correctional costs. A 1994 national survey of criminal justice professionals found widespread support for electronic monitoring (McEwen, 1995:51–52). One of the few studies of public attitudes toward electronic house arrest found strong yet conditional support for the practice (Brown and Elrod, 1995). Most respondents felt that house arrest was appropriate for low-risk, nondangerous offenders. However, some officials have expressed concern over the

criteria for selecting offenders for monitoring. Individual jurisdictions have largely followed a trial-and-error process, with mixed results.

8   In Mississippi, for example, electronic monitoring was restricted at first to a "very select group" of nonviolent offenders (Gowen, 1995). As time passed, several high-risk offenders with backgrounds of violence, mental illness, or severe drug abuse slipped by the screening yet successfully completed the program. However, that decision meant an increase in the need for supervision and greater risks to probation officers. The officers adapted by using two-way mobile radios, cellular pagers, and bulletproof vests—and many began carrying firearms as well.

Attitudes of Offenders

9   The attitudes toward electronic house arrest among offenders are mixed. Not surprisingly, offenders like being close to their families and loved ones, and those who work or attend school appreciate the rehabilitative possibilities of this community-based sanction. But some have reacted negatively to the constant surveillance. In an English study, a relative of someone under house arrest emphasized the humiliation associated with wearing the device: "[S]he would not use tagging [a British term for electronic monitoring] on a dog as it was so demeaning" (Mair and Mortimer, 1996:20). In contrast, however, when offenders under electronic surveillance in Indianapolis were asked if they would recommend electronic monitoring to "somebody in your situation," nearly 75 percent said they would (Baumer and Mendelsohn, 1989).

How Successful Is Home Confinement with Electronic Monitoring?

10   Electronic monitoring is still a new practice, and there have been few comprehensive studies of its use. In the earlier days, technological problems compromised its use, and while there is more confidence in the technology today,

defects will surface from time to time. Some have come to light as a result of lawsuits filed by citizens who have been robbed, raped, or assaulted by offenders under electronic surveillance (Christianson, 1995).

11   Concerning the two other promised benefits of electronic monitoring—reduction of correctional costs and offender recidivism—most case studies show considerable cost savings over imprisonment, even with the increased probation costs associated with electronic monitoring (Gowdy, n.d.). Evidence on recidivism is more mixed. Not surprisingly, the few studies that have been conducted show more success with low-risk offenders, particularly those convicted of drunk driving. However, some experts remain skeptical of the incapacitative benefits of house arrest (Tonry, 1996:120). Electronic monitoring does not prevent offenders from committing domestic crimes, and motivated offenders can steal from the workplace or commit crimes by enlisting the help of others. More research will reveal the benefits and limitations of electronic house arrest. As things stand today, it remains a popular alternative to traditional imprisonment for nonviolent offenders.

Examining Reading Selection 9

Checking Your Vocabulary

Directions: Using context, word parts, or a dictionary if necessary, circle the letter of the meaning for each word as it is used in the reading.

1. jurisdictions (paragraph 2)
   a. circle of friends
   b. families
   c. neighborhoods
   d. areas of authority

2. origins (paragraph 3)
   a. beginnings
   b. popularity
   c. mechanics
   d. values

3. cite (paragraph 7)
   a. read
   b. refer to
   c. promote
   d. see

4. conditional (paragraph 7)
   a. full
   b. qualified
   c. acceptable
   d. rational

5. respondents (paragraph 7)
   a. relatives of the accused
   b. friends of the offender
   c. people who respond
   d. those who have broken the law

Checking Your Comprehension

Directions: Circle the letter of the best answer.

6. The subject of this selection is
   a. support for lawbreakers.
   b. electronic monitoring of offenders.
   c. different types of electronic devices.
   d. how far technology has come in dealing with prisoners.

7. Why did the author write this selection?
   a. to persuade the reader that using a monitoring device for any lawbreaker is very risky
   b. to argue that nonviolent offenders should have the option of house arrest
   c. to examine various important aspects of using electronic monitoring for offenders
   d. to illustrate the safety features of electronic monitoring devices for prisoners

8. The main point of paragraph 7 is to
   a. highlight the ways in which electronic monitoring can be used.
   b. demonstrate that electronic monitoring does not have sufficient benefits to warrant its use.
   c. show that electronic monitoring does not work.
   d. present the benefits of electronic monitoring.

9. Which statement best describes how electronic monitoring works?
   a. The offender wears an ankle band with a transmitter that sends signals to the responsible party when the offender moves beyond a certain range.
   b. The arresting officer and the offender both wear transmitters that track the movement of the offender.
   c. The offender is hooked up to a computer that sends signals to a local precinct every time he leaves his home.
   d. The offender's family members wear monitors that police can use to trace their location and activities.

10. Most case studies show that
    a. electronic monitoring saves money over imprisoning the offender.
    b. almost all offenders under house arrest do not have repeated arrests in the future.
    c. prisoners view electronic monitoring as having the same lack of freedom as prison.
    d. violent offenders usually switch to nonviolent offenses after being monitored electronically.

11. The author develops his ideas by
    a. contrasting the conditions of electronic monitoring with the conditions of imprisonment.
    b. presenting in-depth studies of several prisoners' use of electronic monitoring.

c. citing research, surveys, and case studies.
d. arguing that electronic monitoring is superior to imprisonment.

Thinking Critically

12. The writer creates interest in his subject by
    a. examining the mechanical conditions of electronic monitoring.
    b. arguing that it is better for offenders to be electronically monitored than to be imprisoned.
    c. discussing people's attitudes about the topic as well as explaining how electronic monitoring of offenders works.
    d. citing statistical research on why electronic monitoring is not a viable alternative to imprisonment.

13. The author's attitude toward electronic monitoring can best be described as
    a. biased.
    b. excited.
    c. angry.
    d. objective.

14. Based upon information in the selection, one can draw the following conclusion about rules regarding house arrests:
    a. Each offender under house arrest in this country is obligated to live under the same set of rules.
    b. Rules for house arrests vary from area to area.
    c. The specific rules for house arrest are decided by each offender's probation officer.
    d. Each prison has its own rules regarding house arrests.

15. The last sentence of the selection is used to
    a. define
    b. summarize
    c. contrast
    d. argue

Questions for Discussion

1. The author cites protecting society as one of the benefits of house arrest. Does house arrest truly "protect society"?

2. What do you think are the important considerations to be taken into account when deciding whether an offender should be placed on house arrest or be imprisoned?

3. For the offender, what are the disadvantages of electronic monitoring (why might an offender refuse house arrest?)

4. Do you think electronic monitoring violates a family's right to privacy when a family member participates in house arrest?

Selection 9:		1062 words
Finishing Time:		
	HR.	MIN.	SEC.
Starting Time:		
	HR.	MIN.	SEC.
Reading Time:		
	MIN.	SEC.
WPM Score:		
Comprehension Score:		%

READING SELECTION 10

EDUCATION

HOW STUDENTS GET LOST IN CYBERSPACE
Steven R. Knowlton
From *The New York Times*

The Internet contains a wealth of information, but as this article explains, it is easy to get lost. Preread and then read this article from the Education Life *issue of* The New York Times *to answer the following questions.*
1. Why is it easy to get lost on the Internet?
2. What precautions should students take to be sure they obtain reliable information?

— · —

1   When Adam Pasick, a political science major at the University of Wisconsin at Madison, started working on his senior honors thesis this fall, he began where the nation's more than 14 million college students increasingly do: not at the campus library, but at his computer terminal.

2   As he roamed the World Wide Web, he found journal articles, abstracts, indexes and other pieces of useful information. But it wasn't until he sought help from his professor, Charles H. Franklin, that he found the mother lode.

3   Dr. Franklin steered Mr. Pasick to thousands of pages of raw data of a long-term study of political attitudes, information crucial to Mr. Pasick's inquiry into how family structure affects political thinking.

4   The Web site containing all this data is no secret to political scientists, Dr. Franklin said, but can be hard for students to find.

5   "It is barely possible that if you did a Web search, you would show it up," he said. "Whether the average undergraduate could is

another question." It would be even harder for the uninitiated to find their way around the site, he said. "One of the things you're missing on the Web is a reference librarian."

6   It is just such difficulties that worry many educators. They are concerned that the Internet makes readily available so much information, much of it unreliable, that students think research is far easier than it really is. As a result, educators say, students are producing superficial research papers, full of data—some of it suspect—and little thought. Many of the best sources on the Web are hard to find with conventional search engines or make their information available only at a steep price, which is usually borne by universities that pay annual fees for access to the data.

7   Mr. Pasick, 21, of Ann Arbor, Mich., whose conversation is filled with computer and Web search terms, admits that he would have never found the site, much less the data, on his own.

8   "All the search engines are so imprecise," Mr. Pasick said. "Whenever I have tried to find something precise that I was reasonably sure is out there, I have had trouble."

9   Dr. David B. Rothenberg, a philosophy professor at the New Jersey Institute of Technology, in Newark, said his students' papers had declined in quality since they began using the Web for research.

10   "There are these strange references that don't quite connect," he said. "There's not much sense of intelligence. We're indexing, but we're not thinking about things."

11   One way to improve the quality of students' research is to insist that students be more thorough, said Elliot King, a professor of mass communication at Loyola College of Maryland and author of "The Online Student," a textbook for on-line searching.

12   "Because information is so accessible, students stop far too quickly," he said. If a research

Adam Pasick, a political science major at the University of Wisconsin at Madison, with Dr. Charles H. Franklin, as he used the Internet to research his thesis.

paper should have 15 sources, he said, the professor should insist students find, say, 50 sources and use the best 15. When Dr. King assigns research papers in his own classes, he insists that students submit all the sources they did not use, along with those they finally selected.

13   The jumble in Web-based student papers mirrors the information jumble that is found on line, said Gerald M. Santoro, the lead research programmer at the Pennsylvania State University's Center for Academic Computing in State College, Pa.

14   The Internet, he said, is commonly thought of as a library, although a poorly catalogued one, given the limitations of the search engines available. But he prefers another analogy.

15   "In fact, it is like a bookstore," Dr. Santoro said, explaining that Web sites exist because someone wants them there, not because any independent judge has determined them worthy of inclusion.

16   Dr. William Miller, dean of libraries at Florida Atlantic University in Boca Raton, and the immediate past president of the Association of College and Research Libraries, cautioned that free Web sites were often constructed "because somebody has an ax to grind or a company wants to crow about its own products." And he said that the creators of many sites neglect to keep them up to date, so much information on the Web may be obsolete.

17   "For the average person looking for what is the cheapest flight to Chicago this weekend, or what is the weather like in Brazil, the Web is good," Dr. Miller said. But much of its material, he added, is simply not useful to scholars.

18   Yet despite the Web's limitations, educators like Dr. King still see it as a way to "blast your way out of the limitations of your own library."

19   Some of the most valuable information comes from home pages set up by the government and universities. One example, said Dr. King, was research conducted by a student trying to find information on cuts in financing for the Corporation for Public Broadcasting. The relevant books in the college's library were few and outdated, he said, but, with his help, the student found full texts of Congressional hearings about public broadcasting's budget.

20   "Her essay no longer consisted of relying on books or magazines," he said, "but in getting raw data on which the books and magazines are based."

21   On the Web, students can also find electronic versions of the most popular academic journals, the mainstay of research for faculty and advanced students. Most university libraries now have electronic subscriptions to a few hundred journals. Dr. Miller warned, however, that while that may be a tenth of the journals in the library of a small liberal arts college, it is a tiny fraction of the journals subscribed to by a large research university, which may order more than 100,000. The trend is clearly toward electronic versions of academic journals, he added, but most are still not on line and the ones that are tend to be expensive. On-line subscriptions, for instance, can often run into thousands of dollars a year.

22   The time will surely come, Dr. Miller said, when most academic journals are on line, "but you'll need either a credit card number or a password" from an institution that has bought an electronic subscription. "And if you don't have one or the other, you won't get in," he said.

23   When Mr. Pasick turned to Dr. Franklin for help, the professor's expertise was only one of the necessary ingredients for success. The other was the University of Wisconsin's access to the Web site, as one of 450 research institutions that pay up to $10,000 a year for the privilege. (The site is operated by the Interuniversity Consortium for Political and Social Research, at http://www.icpsr.umich.edu.)

24   Even at an institution with the resources to take full advantage of cyberspace, there are some forms of assistance that the Web will never provide, some educators say.

25   Dr. Santoro describes academic research as a three-step process: finding the relevant information, assessing the quality of that information and then using that information "either to try to conclude something, to uncover something, to prove something or to argue something." At its best, he explained, the Internet, like a library, provides only data.

26   In the research process, he said, "the Internet mainly is only useful for that first part, and also a little bit for the second. It is not useful at all in the third."

WRITING ABOUT READING SELECTION 10*

Checking Your Vocabulary

Directions: Complete each of the following items; refer to a dictionary if necessary.

1. Discuss the connotative meanings of the word *Internet* (paragraph 6).

2. Define each of the following words:
   a. mirrors (paragraph 13)

   _____

   b. analogy (paragraph 14)

   _____

   c. obsolete (paragraph 16)

   _____

   d. mainstay (paragraph 21)

   _____

   e. consortium (paragraph 23)

   _____

3. Define the word *superficial* (paragraph 6) and underline the word or phrase that provides a context clue for its meaning.

   _____

   _____

   _____

4. Define the word *inclusion* (paragraph 15) and underline the word or phrase that provides a context clue for its meaning.

   _____

   _____

   _____

   _____

5. Determine the meanings of the following words by using word parts:
   a. undergraduate (paragraph 5)

   _____

   _____

   b. uninitiated (paragraph 5)

   _____

   _____

   c. unreliable (paragraph 6)

   _____

   _____

   d. expertise (paragraph 23)

   _____

   _____

   e. Interuniversity (paragraph 23)

   _____

   _____

_____
* Multiple-choice questions are contained in Part 6 (page 580).

Checking Your Comprehension

6. How did Adam Pasick finally find the information he needed on the Internet?

_____

_____

_____

7. What are the major problems with students doing research on the Internet?

_____

_____

_____

_____

_____

8. One professor complained that because "information is so accessible, students stop far too quickly" when doing research. How did this professor solve this problem?

_____

_____

_____

_____

9. This reading discusses online subscriptions to academic journals. According to the reading, why are most journals not available online at many colleges?

_____

_____

_____

_____

Thinking Critically

10. Should students rely on the Internet exclusively to do academic research? Why or why not?

_____

_____

_____

_____

_____

_____

_____

_____

11. How can a student tell if information on the Internet is reliable?

_____

_____

_____

_____

_____

_____

12. Explain what Dr. Santoro means when he states that the Internet is more "like a bookstore" than a library.

_____

_____

_____

_____

_____

_____

_____

_____

_____

_____

_____

_____

13. Do you agree with the author's advice about the best place to begin a research project? Why?

_____

_____

_____

_____

Questions for Discussion

1. In the reading, Dr. Santoro states that one of the reasons students do academic research is to "prove something or to argue something," and he goes on to state that the Internet "is not useful at all" to this end. Do you agree or disagree with Dr. Santoro? Justify your answer.

2. The reading suggests that in many ways the Internet is not useful for academic research. Are there better alternatives to the Web? What are they?

3. How would you proceed with a research project on "solutions to homelessness" for a sociology class? Would you use the Internet? How would you begin the project? What search engines might you use to find the information you need? At what point might you use the library and for what specific reason(s)?

Selection 10:			1219 words
Finishing Time:	_____	_____	_____
	HR.	MIN.	SEC.
Starting Time:	_____	_____	_____
	HR.	MIN.	SEC.
Reading Time:		_____	_____
		MIN.	SEC.
WPM Score:			_____
Comprehension Score:			_____%

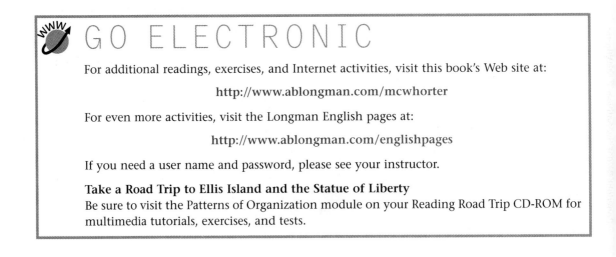

GO ELECTRONIC

For additional readings, exercises, and Internet activities, visit this book's Web site at:

http://www.ablongman.com/mcwhorter

For even more activities, visit the Longman English pages at:

http://www.ablongman.com/englishpages

If you need a user name and password, please see your instructor.

Take a Road Trip to Ellis Island and the Statue of Liberty
Be sure to visit the Patterns of Organization module on your Reading Road Trip CD-ROM for multimedia tutorials, exercises, and tests.

CHAPTER 6

Reading Essays and Articles

IN THIS CHAPTER YOU WILL LEARN:

1. To recognize the parts of formal essays.
3. To read popular press articles.
4. To read scholarly journal articles.
5. To critically analyze essays and articles.

While textbooks are your primary source of information in a college course, they are by no means your only source. Many instructors assign supplemental readings, often in the form of essays and articles. They may be from current popular magazines and may illustrate concepts, principles, or issues you are studying. They may be readings from scholarly journals assigned to update you on new research or to acquaint you with current issues. You also need to read essays and articles when you research a topic for a research paper, prepare for a panel discussion, or provide support for your own ideas in your essays. In English and literature classes you will read a wide variety of essays and be expected to respond to them in discussions and to react to them in writing.

This chapter discusses how to read essays and articles. The information you learn in this chapter will also be helpful to you in your own writing. For example, as you learn the structure of an essay, you can use that structure to write more effective essays. As you learn the structures of various types of articles, you will enhance your ability to write them.

Comparing Essays and Articles

Essays differ from articles in that essays present the personal views of an author on a subject. They are more subjective than articles because they frequently emphasize the author's individual feelings and perceptions about a particular topic. Articles, on the other hand, are generally more objective. When writing an article the author assumes the role of a reporter. He or she avoids expressing personal feelings or viewpoints and concentrates on directly stating the facts. This does not mean that essays are not factual or accurate. Essays simply provide a personal approach to the information presented. Essays allow a writer to describe things as he or she pictures them, to tell a story as if he or she were there, or to present information as he or she understands it. In short, essays and articles differ mainly in their viewpoints.

Reading Essays

Essays usually have a different structure than articles. Understanding how they are organized will help you read them more effectively and efficiently. This section will examine how essays are organized and will help you become aware of their common parts and what is contained in each part. We will then look at three types of essays and how to read them.

Examining the Structure of Essays

Essays are short pieces of writing that examine a single topic and focus on a single idea about that topic. They may be encountered in anthologies, newspapers, and magazines of all types. Essays follow a standard organization and have the following parts:

- title
- introduction
- thesis statement
- supporting information
- summary or conclusion

The structure of an essay is similar to that of a paragraph. Like a paragraph, an essay has a topic. It also explores a single idea about the topic; in an essay this is called the thesis statement. Like a paragraph, an essay provides ideas and details that support the thesis statement. However, unlike a paragraph, an essay deals with a broader topic and the idea that it explores is often more complex. You can visualize the structure of an essay as follows:

The Structure of an Essay

PARTS		FUNCTIONS

Title

1. Can suggest the subject.

2. Can create interest.

Introduction   Thesis Statement

1. Identifies the topic.

2. Presents the thesis statement.

3. Interests the reader.

4. Provides background.

5. Defines terms.

Supporting Idea
(Paragraph 2)

Supporting Idea
(Paragraph 3)

Body

1. Supports and explains the thesis statement.

2. Presents each main supporting point in a separate paragraph.

Supporting Idea
(Paragraph 4)

3. Provides, in each paragraph, details that make each main point understandable.

Supporting Idea
(Paragraph 5)

Conclusion   Final Paragraph

1. Reemphasizes the thesis statement (does not merely restate it).

2. Draws the essay to a close.

Note: There is no set number of paragraphs that an essay contains. This model shows six paragraphs, but in actual essays, the number will vary greatly.

Let's examine the function of each of these parts of an essay in greater detail by referring to an essay titled "Citizenship or Slavery? How schools take the volunteer out of volunteering." It was written by Andrea Martin and first appeared in the *Utne Reader*.

CITIZENSHIP OR SLAVERY?

HOW SCHOOLS TAKE THE VOLUNTEER OUT OF VOLUNTEERING

introduction

"Service-learning" is a new buzzword for sending high school students into the community to do volunteer work. Service-learning isn't really volunteering, though, when it is required for high school graduation—and there's the rub. Americans generally applaud community

}*definition*

thesis statement

introduction

service, but make that service mandatory and sizzling controversy erupts. George Bush promoted the notion of mandatory youth services as a means of reinvigorating responsible citizenship. The hotly debated issue of a national community service draft was finally settled in 1993 with the creation of the voluntary AmeriCorps. Locally, though, requirements for mandatory community service are on the increase, and they're being met with sturdy opposition.

Community service as an adjunct to classroom education is not new. Elective programs began to draw attention about 10 years ago, and both educators and students are generally pleased with them. Students develop new skills, greater self-esteem, and more enthusiasm for school. Communities benefit as energetic young people help in nursing homes and day care centers, lend a hand in nonprofits, and plant trees and pick up roadside trash. Noting these benefits, some enthusiasts began to make the case for required service.

background information

body

authority

The National Service-Learning Cooperative Clearinghouse estimates that more than a million high school students did community work through their schools in 1993, reports Suzanne Goldsmith in the liberal political journal *The American Prospect* (Summer 1995). Some of that is voluntary, but one quarter of America's public schools now impose a service requirement, according to Educational Research Service findings cited by Eric Felten in a critical article in the conservative newsweekly *Insight on the News* (Aug. 15, 1994). Washington, D.C., for example, requires 100 hours of service for high school graduation.

statistics & sources

authority

Before service-learning entered the schools, community service was an individual undertaking or was organized by scouts, churches, and other groups for their members. Many question the intrusion of education into what should be a private matter. Amitai Etzioni, a noted communitarian and a vocal advocate of volunteerism, argues in *Insight on the News* that the "public schools have moved beyond their mission by requiring community service." Politics becomes entangled in the educational process when schools encourage lobbying for specific causes or approve some forms of service and exclude others. (For example, in one community, service to Planned Parenthood was approved but service to an anti-abortion group was not.) As Goldsmith notes, opposition to an educational system perceived as setting a social agenda may ultimately be the most serious threat to service-learning.

fact
supporting idea
authority
quote

example

indirect quote

There are also legal objections to mandatory service. Three high school students in Bethlehem, Pennsylvania, sued the school board on the grounds that the service requirement violated the constitutional prohibition of slavery. The students were represented by the Institute for Justice, a libertarian group that also represented students in similar cases in Mamaroneck, New York, and Chapel Hill, North Carolina. All three cases have failed in the courts. In denying the North Carolina slavery

supporting idea

descriptions & facts

<table>
</table>

case, U.S. District Judge Frank W. Bullock cited the argument made by the American Alliance for Rights and Responsibilities that service-learning is an educational initiative that prepares students for participation in society.

Whether or not mandatory service is moral or legal, some educators question its merit. In the short run, it diverts diminishing resources from teaching basic skills to covering the costs of administering programs and transporting students to their work sites. When they work after the school day is over, students who live in far-flung rural areas are at a disadvantage, as are those who have after-school jobs or whose parents can't provide transportation. In the long run, making volunteer work just one more demand imposed on students may create a backlash, prejudicing them against future volunteer work. Critics of education often point out that schools diminish the joy of learning. Now they run the risk of diminishing the joy of community service too.

[body] *[supporting idea]* *[reasons]*

Writing in the National Civic Review (Summer/Fall 1995), Matthew Moseley describes the enormous resurgence of volunteerism among American youth—a movement that, as witnessed and supported by magazines such as *Who Cares* is proving to be a major social force. And Goldsmith, in *The American Prospect*, holds up as models schools that have made community service an appealing elective course; these programs usually generate enthusiasm and plenty of participation. It all suggests that communities should urge their schools to stimulate young people's natural urge to be useful by ensuring that service remains a genuine choice.

[conclusion] *[authority]* *[authority]* *[further direction, refers back]*

Martin, "Citizenship or Slavery" *Utne Reader.*

The Title

The title usually suggests the subject of the essay and is intended to capture the reader's interest. Some titles are highly descriptive and announce exactly what the essay will be about. For example, an essay titled "Television Addiction" announces the subject of the essay. Other titles are less directly informative. The title "It Begins at the Beginning" reveals little about the subject matter and only becomes meaningful within the context of the essay itself. (It is an article about differences in how males and females communicate and how those differences begin in childhood years.)

Some essays have both a title and a subtitle. In these essays, the subtitle usually suggests the subject matter more directly. In the sample essay, the title "Citizenship or Slavery?" is mainly intended to capture your interest rather than to directly announce the subject. The subtitle "How schools take the volunteer out of volunteering" focuses you more clearly on what the essay will be about.

**EXERCISE
6-1**

DIRECTIONS: What would you expect to be discussed in essays with each of the following titles?

1. Animal Rights: Right or Wrong

   _____

2. Firearms, Violence, and Public Policy

   _____

   _____

3. The Price of Power: Living in the Nuclear Age

   _____

4. The Nature and Significance of Play

   _____

5. Uncivil Rights—The Cultural Rules of Anger

   _____

   _____

**EXERCISE
6-2**

DIRECTIONS: Read the following title and subtitle of an essay. Predict what the essay will discuss.

"Attention Must Be Paid—New Evidence for an Old Truth: Babies Need Love That Money Can't Buy"

_____

_____

The Introduction

The introduction, usually one or two paragraphs long, sets the scene for the essay and places the subject within a framework or context. The introduction may

- present the thesis statement of the essay

- offer background information (explain television addiction as an issue, for example)

- define technical or unfamiliar terms (define addiction, for example)

- build your interest (give an instance of an extreme case of television addiction)

Notice how the sample essay "Citizenship or Slavery?" accomplishes these goals in its first two paragraphs. It opens by defining "service-learning," the topic of the essay, and then in the second sentence states its thesis—that service-learning isn't true volunteerism when it is required. The remainder of the first two paragraphs provides background for the controversy over mandatory community service programs.

EXERCISE 6-3

DIRECTIONS: Read only the first two paragraphs of the essay "Attention Must Be Paid" by Mortimer Zuckerman. What types of information do they provide?

_____

_____

_____ ▬

ATTENTION MUST BE PAID

1   Later than I might have expected, I have begun learning about parenthood first-hand. On July 7, Abigail Jane Zuckerman was born. Now I understand what all the excitement has been about.

2   Looking at a newborn in her crib, anyone must have a sense of the many things that have been determined about her life, by genes and circumstances, but also of the countless decisions and shaping experiences that lie ahead. Parents of every era have worried about making these choices in the right way. Recent scientific findings give new reason for concern—in particular, about whether children can thrive under the modern belief that parents can contract out their basic responsibilities for care.

facts

3   Every day a newborn baby's brain is developing with phenomenal speed. Billions of nerve cells—neurons—are growing and specializing. By age 2, the number of synapses, or connections among the neurons, approaches adult levels, and by age 3 a child's brain has 1 quadrillion such connections. The synapses are the basic tools of processing within the brain.

facts

4   Is inherited ability the main factor in establishing these connections? Apparently not. Interactions with an attentive adult—in most cases, a mother—matter most. The sight, sound, touch, smell, and especially, the intense involvement, through language and eye contact, of parent and child affect the number and sophistication of links within the brain. These neural patterns—again, set by age 3—seem to be

expert authority

more important than factors we usually emphasize, such as gender and race. In their book *Meaningful Difference in the Everyday Experience of Young American*

Children, professors Todd Risley and Betty Hart say that the number of words an infant hears each day may be the single most important predictor of later intelligence and economic and social success.

statistical comparisons

body

5   This should be hopeful news, for it suggests that rich possibilities are open to every child. But the same research shows that verbal stimulation differs by income and education. On average, the child of professional parents hears about 2,100 words an hour; of working-class parents, 1,200 words. Parents on welfare speak about 600 words an hour. Professional parents give their children emotional encouragement 30 times an hour—twice as often as the working-class baby and five times as often as the welfare baby. This word play is so important that those left behind at age 2 may never catch up.

facts

6   These findings come when many subscribe to the notion that there is no harm in a mother's leaving her baby in someone else's care and returning to work. More than half of all mothers are back at work before their baby is 1. The working mother is a fundamental feature of this era. But what will parents do when they learn that absence in the first three years may have a significant effect on their baby's future? Most working parents know in their hearts that "quality time" is no substitute for quantity time—the time that a child requires for emotional and, it now seems, intellectual development.

author's personal observation

7   What children need is the touching, holding, cooing, rocking, and stimulation that come traditionally from a mother. In some households a stay-at-home father will fill the role of the absentee mother, but that is rare. In most families, if it is not the mother spending those three years with an infant, it will be a baby sitter or day-care worker. Often there are class, educational, and—increasingly—language differences between the parents and the hired caretaker. Parents are therefore going to be challenged to find a better balance between raising their children and working, especially parents who are too tired and emotionally drained to give children the stimulus and engagement they need. When babies are cared for by caring adults, they become much better learners and are much more confident to take over the world. Attention is the greatest gift that parents can bestow.

The Thesis Statement

The thesis statement of an essay is its main point. All other ideas and paragraphs in the essay support this idea. Once you identify an essay's thesis, you have discovered the key to its meaning. The thesis is usually stated in a single sentence and this sentence appears in the introductory paragraphs. It often follows the background information and the attention-getter. In our sample essay "Citizenship or Slavery?" the thesis is stated early in the first paragraph and is followed by background information. Occasionally, an author will first present evidence in support of the thesis and finally state the thesis at the end of the essay. This organization is most common in argumentative essays (see Chapter 11). You may also find, on occasion, that an author implies rather than directly states the thesis; the thesis is revealed through the supporting paragraphs. When you cannot find a clear state-ment of the thesis, ask yourself this question: "What is the one main point the author is making?" Your answer is the implied thesis statement.

Here are a few sample thesis statements.

- Due to its negative health effects, cigarette smoking is once again being regarded as a form of deviant behavior.

- Career choice is influenced by numerous factors including skills and abilities, attitudes, and life goals.

- Year-round school will provide children with a better education that is more cost effective.

DIRECTIONS: Read the entire essay "Attention Must Be Paid" (pp. 229–230) and identify its thesis statement.

_____

_____

Body

The body of the essay contains sentences and paragraphs that explain or support the thesis statement. This support may be in the form of

- examples
- descriptions
- facts
- statistics
- reasons
- anecdotes (stories that illustrate a point)
- personal experiences and observations
- quotations from or references to authorities and experts
- comparisons

Most writers use various types of supporting information. In the sample essay "Citizenship or Slavery?" (pp. 225–227) the author uses sev-eral types of information in her supporting paragraphs. Notice how she uses *facts* and *statistics* in the third paragraph to show how widespread community service requirements are. Her fourth paragraph refers to *author-ities* and *quotes* them directly and indirectly. She also includes an *example* of politics at work in these programs. The fifth paragraph concentrates on *descriptions* of and facts about legal cases on required community service programs and the results of these cases. The final paragraph of the body of this essay provides *reasons* against mandatory service.

EXERCISE 6-5

DIRECTIONS: Review the essay "Attention Must Be Paid" and mark where the body begins and ends. Then, in the margin beside each supporting paragraph, label the type(s) of supporting information the author used.

Conclusion

An essay is brought to a close with a brief conclusion, not a summary. (A summary provides a review of the key ideas presented in an article. Think of a summary as an outline in paragraph form. The order in which the information appears in the summary reflects the order in which it appears in the article itself.) A **conclusion** is a final statement about the subject of the essay. A conclusion does not review content as a summary does. Instead, a conclusion often refers back to, but does not repeat, the thesis statement. It may also suggest a direction of further thought or introduce a new way of looking at what has already been said. The sample essay "Citizenship or Slavery?" (pp. 225–227) ends with a conclusion that strengthens the case in favor of volunteerism and elective courses rather than required community service courses. It refers back to the thesis statement by encouraging communities to allow service-learning to be a matter of choice.

EXERCISE 6-6

DIRECTIONS: Explain how the conclusion of "Attention Must Be Paid" draws this essay to a close.

_____

_____

_____

_____

_____

EXERCISE 6-7

DIRECTIONS: The essay "How to Brag About Yourself to Win and Hold a New Job" (Reading Selection 1, pp. 23–24) is an example of an essay. Read or review the essay and answer the following questions.

1. What is the purpose of the essay?

    _____

2. To what extent does the essay include the author's opinions and interpretations?

    _____

3. Do you feel Challenger is qualified to write an essay on the subject? Why?

    _____

    _____

4. Write a list of job-seeking and job-holding advice that summarizes Challenger's suggestions.

    _____

Reading and Evaluating Essays

An **essay** usually presents information on a specific topic from a particular writer's point of view.

Essays are often organized using one or more of the thought patterns described in Chapter 5, "Patterns: Relationships among Ideas." Depending on a writer's purpose, he or she may choose a specific pattern, as shown here.

If a Writer's Purpose Is To	The Pattern Used Is
Trace the history or sequence of events	Chronological order
Explain how something works	Chronological order
Explain a subject by describing types or parts	Classification
Explain why something happened	Cause-Effect
Explain what something is	Definition
Emphasize similarities or differences between two or more things	Comparison-Contrast

When reading essays, use the following guidelines.

1. **Establish the authority of the author whenever possible.** In order to trust that the author presented accurate, reliable information, make sure he or she is knowledgeable about or experienced with the subject.

2. **Pay attention to background information the author provides.** Especially if the subject is one with which you are unfamiliar, you must fill in gaps in your knowledge. If the background supplied is insufficient, consult other sources to get the information you need.

3. **Identify the author's thesis.** Determine exactly what information the author is presenting about the subject. Test your understanding by expressing it in your own words.

4. **Pay attention to new terminology.** Mark or underline new terms as you read them. If some are not defined and you cannot determine their meaning from context, be sure to look them up.

5. **Highlight as you read.** Mark the thesis statement and each major supporting detail.

6. **Outline, map, or summarize the essay.** To ensure recall of the information, as well as to test your understanding of it, use some form of writing.

Reading Articles

Articles can tell a story, describe, or inform. Unlike essays, they do this with little personal involvement of the author. Also, they have structures that are somewhat different from that of an essay. Two types of articles are discussed in this section: popular press articles and scholarly articles. The structure of an article depends upon its type. Each has special features that will help you to locate the information you want more efficiently.

Reading Popular Press Articles

Articles that appear primarily in magazines and newspapers assume a different style and format from most essays. While popular press articles examine a topic and focus on an aspect of it, they tend to be more loosely or informally structured than most essays and scholarly journal articles. The title is usually eye-catching and descriptive. The introductory section may be less fully developed, and a formal paragraph conclusion may not be used.

The two most common types of popular press articles found in both newspapers and magazines are hard news articles and feature articles. They have essentially the same form, consisting of a beginning, called the *lead;* the story itself, called the *body or development;* and sometimes a formal *conclusion* as an ending.

Hard News Articles

Articles that directly report serious news are known as hard news articles. They are stories about conflict, death, and destruction as well as items of interest and importance in government, politics, science, medicine, business, and the economy. Articles of this type may be organized in one of two ways.

Inverted Structure   The traditional structure used in newspaper articles is known as the *inverted pyramid* because the article moves from general to more specific information. It contains the following parts:

- *Title.* Titles, or headlines, used in hard news stories are brief and directly informative about the article's content. They are usually expressed in active language, somewhat in the form of a telegraph message: "President Threatens Veto over Budget" or "Diet Drug Thought to Be Health Risk." Reading the title is usually sufficient to help you decide whether to read the article.

- *Datelines*, *Credit Lines*, and *Bylines.* These follow the title and come just before the summary lead. *Datelines* appear on all but local news stories and generally only give the place where the story came from; occasionally the date will be given. *Credit lines* may also appear before the lead and supplement datelines. They give the name of the wire service or newspaper from which the story was taken, such as "Associated Press" or *Washington Post*. *Bylines* name the writer of the article and are sometimes also included between the title and the lead.

- *Summary Lead.* This opening paragraph contains a summary of the most essential information in the story. It is similar to the *thesis statement* in an essay and the *abstract* in a scholarly article. Reading this lead alone may provide you with all the information you need from the article and will help you to determine whether you need to read further to get the information you want.

- *Body or Development.* The supporting facts are presented here—arranged in descending order of importance or interest. The most important details are placed first, followed by those second in importance or interest, and so on, until those facts most easily dispensed with are placed at the end of the story. If the lead paragraph doesn't contain the information you need, this type of organization will permit you to locate it easily. Since the *inverted pyramid* structure contains no conclusion there is no need to skip to the end of the article when prereading it.

Look at the following news article and note where its parts are located.

title or _____   **LAWSUITS SEEK HEART MONITORING**
headline   **FOR USERS OF WITHDRAWN DIET DRUGS**

byline ———————— By Beth Powell

credit line ———————— *Associated Press*

dateline

summary lead

WASHINGTON—Class-action suits demanding payment for heart monitoring for former diet drug users have been filed in five states against the makers of prescription drugs pulled off the market a week ago.

body

The suits were filed last week in New York, Utah, Colorado and Hawaii and earlier in California on behalf of patients who might have been injured by using fen-phen, the popular name for a combination of prescription diet drugs, attorney Gary Mason said.

After studies linked the diet pills to serious heart damage, drug makers withdrew from the market fenfluramine and dexfenluramine, sold under the brand names Pondimin and Redux, respectively.

The Food and Drug Administration urged millions of dieters to stop taking both drugs immediately.

The FDA said phentermine, which combined with fenfluramine made the once-popular fen-phen combination, appears safe when used by itself. But doctors said phentermine has only mixed results when taken alone.

The lawsuits seek medical monitoring, emergency notification and updated patient warnings for class members, Mason said. Some suits seek specific monetary damages for individuals.

Mason, whose law firm Cohen, Milstein, Hausfeld & Toll is coordinating the class-action suits, said similar actions would be filed in all 50 states within the next few weeks.

The nine defendants in the suits are Wyeth-Ayerst Laboratories Co., division of American Home Products Corp.; Interneuron Pharmaceuticals; Gate Pharmaceuticals, a division of Teva Pharmaceuticals, USA; Smithkline Beecham Corp.; Abana Pharmaceuticals; Richwood Pharmaceutical Co.; Ion Laboratories; Medeva Pharmaceuticals; and A. H. Robins Co.

body

Action Story   A second common format for hard news articles is the *action story*. It contains all the parts of the inverted pyramid with a few variations. It also begins with a telegraphic title that can be followed by a byline, credit line, and dateline. Its opening paragraph is also in the form of a summary lead. However, its body presents the events in chronological order of their occurrence, rather than in order of importance or interest. Furthermore, this format includes a conclusion that contains additional information that does not fit within the chronology used in the body.

**EXERCISE
6-8**

DIRECTIONS: Locate a hard news article in a newspaper or magazine. Determine which format is used, the inverted pyramid or the action story. Then label the article's parts.

Feature Articles

A second type of popular press article is the feature article. Found in both newspapers and magazines, the feature article is longer and goes into greater depth than the usual hard news article. It usually deals with larger issues and subjects. Because of its length, this type of article requires a different structure from hard news articles.

It also begins with a *title* that is often in the form of a complete sentence and may contain a byline, credit line, and dateline. Its other parts may differ, though.

- *Feature Lead.* The lead in a feature article does not usually summarize its contents. Instead, it is intended to spark your interest in the topic being presented. It may begin with an interesting anecdote, present some highlight of the article, or offer an example of something you will learn more about later. Since the feature lead is primarily an interest builder, you may be able to skim through it quickly when reading the article.

- *Nut Graph.* The nut graph explains the nature and scope of the article. Depending upon the length of the article it may be one paragraph, or it may run to several paragraphs. When reading feature articles, read this section carefully. It will offer clues to the organization and content of the article and help you to grasp its main points.

- *Body or Development.* This is where the detailed information of the article is presented. Unlike hard new stories, the information can be organized in more than one way. Each paragraph or section may use a different thought pattern to develop its ideas, much like the expository essay. Mark and annotate this section as you read it, sifting through the main and secondary points.

- *Conclusion.* Feature articles often end with a conclusion, which, like the conclusion of a formal essay, makes a final statement about the subject of the article. Rather than summarizing the information presented, it may refer back to the nut graph, introduce a new way of looking at the information, or suggest a direction for further thought.

Refer to the following feature article to see an example of this structure.

title ———————————

WHY DO DOGS BARK?

byline ———————————

By Richard Folkers

feature lead

Dogs can be pretty good communicators. A yelp is easy to recognize as a sound of distress. Growls are obvious. A whine, coupled with a scratch at the door, may just keep the carpet clean and dry.

nut graph

But what about barking? Is a dog sounding an alarm? Defining its territory? Just playing? The principles of evolution dictate that animals retain traits through natural selection. They hang on to functions that contribute to their survival, and that applies to making sounds no less than anything else. Scientists believe male birds sing, for example, to mark their territory, to attract mates, to maintain pair relationships, and to warn of impending predatory doom. But barking seems to defy all the rules of biological necessity.

body or development

Biologists Raymond Coppinger and Mark Feinstein, who have studied this puzzle, say dogs often seem to bark extravagantly and for no apparent reason at all. The two Hampshire College scientists once spent the night in a Minnesota field listening to a guard dog bark continuously for seven hours. There were no other dogs around, no humans responding, no predators lurking. It just barked. Feinstein recently came upon two dogs in a hot car. "One was barking like crazy, the other staring out the window. They were under the same conditions," he says. "They've got this capacity which doesn't play any necessary function in their lives."

Those dogs, like all domestic dogs, are descended from the wolf, and wolves don't bark much. But their puppies do, and Coppinger and Feinstein believe that may help explain the mystery of barking. Early dogs (wolves really) were scavengers, hanging around human habitations—and their plentiful heaps of garbage. Humans, in turn, tended to tolerate the tamer ones; it was they that became the sires of what would become the domestic dog. Experiments in a number of animals have shown that breeding for tameness breeds animals that are, in effect, perpetual adolescents, displaying many youthful traits into adulthood. "You get an animal more like a juvenile wolf," says Feinstein.

body or development

So why do juveniles bark? Feinstein and Coppinger believe wolf pups are in a transition period; a bark is acoustically halfway between an infantile attention-seeking whine and an adult, hostile growl.

Adult dogs do find ways to use their barks to communicate; they might be asking to go in or out, defending territory, or just playing. But as Feinstein notes, precisely because barking has no biological necessity for dogs, "they can adapt it to use under almost any circumstance."

conclusion

Ultimately, science's best answer may be the punch line of the old joke about why dogs chase their tails and lick themselves: because they can.

DIRECTIONS: Select a feature article from the periodicals available to you. Label its parts, then mark and annotate it.

EXERCISE 6-9

Reading Articles from Scholarly Journals

Scholarly journals are publications by professional societies or college and university presses that report developments and research in a particular academic discipline. For example, in the field of psychology, scholarly journals include *American Journal of Psychology, Journal of Abnormal Psychology,* and *Psychological Bulletin.* Articles published in scholarly journals are usually peer reviewed. That is, before an article is published, other professionals in the field read the article and confirm that it is legitimate, accurate, and worthwhile.

You need to read articles from scholarly journals when you research a topic for a paper or write a research paper. Some professors distribute a reading list each semester, of which scholarly articles are a part. Others supplement text assignments by assigning articles and placing copies of them on reserve in the library. Many scholarly articles, especially those that report research conducted by the author, follow a similar format and often include the following parts, although different journals use different headings to organize their articles, or may not label all sections with headings.

- **Abstract.** An abstract is a brief summary of the article and its findings and is sometimes labeled as "Summary." It usually appears at the beginning of the article following the title and author. Read the abstract to get an overview of the article, and when doing research, to determine if the study or report contains the information you need.

- **Summary of Related Research.** Many research articles begin by summarizing research that has already been done on the topic. Here authors will cite other studies and briefly report their findings. This summary brings you up to date on the most current research and suggests a rationale for why the author's study or research is necessary and appropriate. In some journals, this rationale may appear in a section called *Statement of the Problem.*

- **Description of Research.** In this section, which may also be labeled "Method," the author describes his or her research or explains his or her ideas. For experimental research, you can expect the author to present the research design, including the purpose of the research, description of the population involved, sample size, methodology, and statistical tests applied.

- **Results.** Results of the research are presented in this section.

- **Implications, Discussion, and Conclusions.** Here the author explains what the results mean and draws possible implications and conclusions.
- **Further Research.** Based on their findings, some authors end the article by suggesting additional research that is needed to further explain the problem or issue being studied.

Here is a sample scholarly article from *Psychological Reports*. Read the article and study the annotations.[*]

SEX DIFFERENCES IN HUMOR[1]

Scott A. Myers

Barbara Lorene Ropog,
R. Pierre Rodgers

Department of Speech and Theatre Arts
McNesse State University

School of Communication Studies
Kent State University

abstract

Summary—This study examined how 48 men and 88 women at a small southern university differed in their orientation toward and their uses of humor. They completed two self-report scales with reference to their general use of humor. Analysis indicated that the men reported a greater frequency of attempts at humor than women; men perceived these attempts as more effective than did the women; and the men reported using humor for negative affect more often than women.

what studied

results

summary of related research

Humor provides utility of communication in everyday interactions (Graham, Papa, & Brooks, 1992), in part because everyday conversation thrives on wordplay, sarcasm, anecdotes, and jokes (Norrick, 1993). And as noted by Booth-Butterfield and Booth-Butterfield (1991), a sense of humor is highly valued in American society; however, some research suggests that men and women differ in their approach to the use of humor. In general communicative interactions, men's humor is characterized by aggression, hostility, and competition (Palmer, 1994; Walker & Dresner, 1988) that often targets women for disparagement (Cantor; 1976, Crawford & Gressley, 1991; Palmer, 1994). Women, on the other hand, are more inclined to use understatement, irony, and self-deprecation (Walker & Dresner, 1988) as forms of humor.

Studies of humor in general and men's humor in particular have provided a large body of data regarding how and why humor is used (e.g., Morris, 1994; Walker & Dresner, 1988) but is incomplete regarding the humor used by women and the difference in use of humor by men and women (e.g., Crawford & Gressley, 1991). Therefore, we were interested in whether men and women differ in their frequency and effec-

purpose of study

---

[*] Reproduced with permission of authors and publishers from Myers, S.A., Ropog, B.L., and Rodgers, R.P., "Sex Differences in Humor." *Psychological Reports*, 1997, 81, 221–222. © Psychological Reports 1997.

[1] An earlier version of this paper was presented at the 1997 Central States Communication Association meeting in St. Louis, Missouri. Address enquires to S. A. Myers, Ph.D., Department of Speech and Theatre Arts, POB 90420, McNesse State University, Lake Charles, LA 70609–0420 or e-mail (symers@acc.mcnesse.edu).

tiveness of attempted humor and in their uses of humor for positive affect, expressiveness, and negative affect.

purpose of study

Method.—Participants were 136 undergraduate students (48 men and 88 women) from a small southern university. The ages of the respondents ranged from 17 to 43 years ($M = 20.7$, $SD = 4.4$). Participants were asked to complete two self-report scales in reference to their general use of humor, the Humor Orientation Scale (Booth-Butterfield & Booth-Butterfield, 1991) and the Uses of Humor Index (Graham *et al.*, 1992). Responses for all items were solicited using a 5-point rating scale anchored by strongly agree (5) and strongly disagree (1).

sample population & size

how data was obtained

description of research

The Humor Orientation Scale is a 17-item measure that asks respondents to assess both the perceived frequency, i.e., the rate at which humor attempts are made—"I regularly tell jokes and funny stories when I am with a group," and the perceived effectiveness, i.e., whether the actor believes the attempt was perceived as humorous—"People usually laugh when I tell a joke or story," of the attempts. A coefficient alpha of .80 ($M = 32.0$, $SD = 5.7$) was reported for the frequency dimension and also for the effectiveness dimension ($M = 29.0$, $SD = 4.8$).

description of scales used

data reliability

The Uses of Humor Index is an 11-item measure on which respondents report their reasons for use of humor across three dimensions: (a) positive affect, i.e., prosocial use—"I use humor to make light of a situation," (b) expressiveness, i.e., self-disclosure, emotional expression—"I use humor to let others know my likes and dislikes," and (c) negative affect, i.e., anti-social use—"I use humor to demean and belittle others." A coefficient alpha of .78 was reported for the positive affect dimension ($M = 12.2$, $SD = 2.0$), of 4.7 for the expressiveness dimension ($M = 15.5$, $SD = 3.1$), and .84 for the negative affect dimension ($M = 6.9$, $SD = 3.0$).

data reliability

Results.—Three significant findings emerge from the study. First, men ($M = 33.4$) reported more frequent attempts at humor than women ($M = 31.2$, $F_{1,134} = 5.16$, $p < .05$) Second, men ($M = 30.6$) perceived their humor as more effective than women ($M = 28.1$; $F_{1,134} = 8.86$, $p < .01$). Third, men ($M = 7.7$) reported using humor for negative affect more often than women ($M = 6.5$; $F_{1,134} = 5.45$, $P < .05$). No significant sex difference was evident for either positive affect ($F_{1,134} = 1.39$, ns) or expressiveness ($F_{1,134} = .06$, ns).

moderately significant

highly significant

Moderately significant

results

Because the data were gathered using self-report ratings rather than behavioral or objective measures, the results should be interpreted with caution. However, the findings indicate that not only do men engage in more frequent attempts at humor than women, but that they perceive these attempts as more effective and use humor for expression of negative affect. These findings support the notion advanced by Crawford and Gressley (1991) that perhaps women do not incorporate humor into their repertoire of interpersonal communication behaviors as readily as men. White (1988) posited that women do not use humor regularly due to the social norms that govern communication. Because women

conclusion

conclusions, implications, discussion

why this may be so

conclusions,
implications,
discussion

are conditioned to not complain, to accept existing social norms, and to not express objections to male attitudes (Rowe, 1995), women may be reluctant to violate social norms against being negative, which may naturally contribute toward a reluctance to use humor. In addition, Walker and Dresner (1988) posited that women are conditioned to accept subordinate and passive roles, which subsequently affects the situations in which they use humor.

why this
may be so

References

BOOTH-BUTTERFIELD, S., & BOOTH-BUTTERFIELD, M. (1991) Individual differences in the communication of humorous messages. *Southern Communications Journal,* 56, 205–218.

CANTOR, J. R. (1976) What is funny to whom? The role of gender. *Journal of Communication,* 26, 110–118.

CRAWFORD, M., & GRESSLEY, D. (1991) Creativity, caring, and context; women's and men's accounts of humor preferences and practices. *Psychology of Women Quarterly,* 15, 217–231.

GRAHAM, E. E., PAPA, M. J., & BROOKS, G. P. (1992) Functions of humor in conversation: conceptualization and measurement. *Western Journal of Communication,* 56, 161–183.

MORRIS, L. A. (Ed.) (1994) *American women humorists.* New York: Garland.

NORRICK, N. R. (1993) *Conversational joking: humor is everyday talk.* Bloomington, IN: Indiana Univer. Press.

PALMER, J. (1994) *Taking humor seriously.* New York: Routledge.

ROWE, K. (1995) *The unruly woman: gender and the genres of laughter.* Austin, TX: Univer. of Texas Press.

WALKER, N., & DRESNER, Z. (Eds.) (1988) *Redressing the balance: American women's literary humor from colonial time to the 1980s.* Jackson, MS: Univer. Press of Mississippi.

WHITE, C. L. (1988) Liberating laughter: an inquiry into the nature, content, and functions of feminist humor. In B. Bate & A. Taylor (Eds.), *Women communicating: studies of women's talk.* Norwood, NJ: Ablex. pp. 75–90.

Accepted June 9, 1997.

When reading scholarly journals, keep the following tips in mind.

1. **Be sure you understand the author's purpose.** Determine why the study was conducted.

2. **Highlight as you read.** You may need to refer back to information presented earlier in the article.

3. **Use index cards.** If you are reading numerous articles, keep a 4 × 6 index card for each. Write a brief summary of the purpose and findings.

4. **Use quotations.** If you take notes from the article, be sure to place in quotations any information you copy directly from the article. If you fail to do so, you may inadvertently plagiarize. Plagiarism, presenting someone else's ideas as your own, carries stiff academic and legal penalties.

Analyzing Essays and Articles

Essays and articles require close analysis and evaluation. While textbooks usually present reliable, unbiased factual information, essays and even some articles often express opinions and represent particular viewpoints; consequently, you must read them critically. Use the following questions to guide your analysis.

1. **Who is the author?** Check to see if it is a name you recognize. Try to discover whether or not the author is qualified to write about the subject.

2. **What is the author's purpose?** Is the writer trying to present information, convince you of something, entertain you, or express a viewpoint?

3. **What does the introduction or lead add to the piece of writing?** Does it interest you or supply background information, for example?

4. **What is the author's thesis?** Try to express it in your own words. By doing so, you may find bias or discover a viewpoint you had not previously recognized.

5. **Does the author adequately support the thesis?** Is a variety of supporting information provided? An article that relies entirely upon the author's personal experiences, for example, to support a thesis may be of limited use.

6. **Does the author supply sources, references, or citations for the facts and statistics presented?** You should be able to verify the information presented and turn to those sources should you wish to read more about the subject.

For more information on thinking critically about essays and articles, refer to Chapters 10, 11, and 12 in Part Four, "Reading Critically."

**EXERCISE
6–10**

DIRECTIONS: Evaluate the essay "How to Brag About Yourself to Win and Hold a New Job" (pp. 23–24) by answering each of the questions listed above.

1. _____

_____

2. _____

_____

3. _____

_____

4. _____

_____

5. _____

_____

6. _____

_____

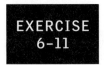

EXERCISE
6-11

ELECTRONIC
APPLICATION

DIRECTIONS: Use an Internet source to locate an article or essay. Try to locate one from an electronic magazine, rather than from an electronic version of a print magazine. Then answer the following questions.

1. Answer questions 1–6 for analyzing essays and articles.

2. In what ways is the article similar to print magazine articles and in what ways is it different?

3. What are the advantages of electronic magazines over print magazines?

Critical Thinking Tip #6

Evaluating Research Sources

When you conduct research, you will read a variety of articles and essays, as well as other source material. Not all sources you encounter while preparing a research paper are equally worthwhile or appropriate. Therefore, it is essential to critically evaluate all sources when conducting research. The following suggestions will help you to evaluate reference sources:

1. Check your source's copyright date. Make certain you are using a current source. For many papers, such as those exploring controversial issues or scientific or medical advances, only the most up-to-date sources are useful.
2. Be sure to use an authoritative source. The material should be written by a recognized authority or by someone who is working within his or her field.
3. Choose sources that provide the most complete and concrete information.
4. Select first-hand accounts of an event or experience rather than second- or third-hand accounts whenever possible.
5. Avoid using sources that present biased information, and be wary of those that include personal opinion and reactions.

EXERCISE 6-12

DIRECTIONS: Compile a list of articles and essays that you have been assigned to read this semester. For each assignment indicate its source: popular press, scholarly journal, or in-text reading.

Summary

1. How do essays and articles differ?

Essays and articles differ mainly in viewpoint. Essays are written from a personal perspective, while articles are more objective in their presentation of information.

2. What are the parts of an essay?

Essays have five essential parts with different functions:
- Title: suggests the subject and attracts the reader.
- Introduction: offers background, builds interest, defines terms, and states the thesis.
- Thesis Statement: clearly and sufficiently expresses the main point of the essay.
- Body: presents, in a number of paragraphs, information that supports or explains the thesis.
- Conclusion: brings the essay to a close by making a final statement of the subject.

3. What can you do to improve your reading of essays?

When reading essays you should
- check that the author can be trusted to present the facts fairly and accurately
- be sure the background information given is complete
- get the writer's thesis clearly in mind
- focus on new terminology used
- mark and highlight the thesis statement and important terms
- make an outline, map, or summary to ensure your recall

4. How are popular press articles organized?

Articles found in magazines and newspapers have a different style and format than essays. Hard news stories, action stories, and feature articles have some differences in format but can contain the following parts:

- Title—often eye catching and descriptive.
- Dateline—the location and date of the story.
- Credit Line—the wire service or newspaper the story came from.
- Byline—the name of the writer.
- Lead—an opening paragraph that either summarizes major information (news stories) or sparks interest in the topic (feature stories).
- Nut Graph—one or more paragraphs that define a feature article's nature and scope.
- Body or Development—the section that presents the supporting facts.
- Conclusion—the final statement about the subject of the article.

5. What are the parts of most scholarly journal articles?

Professional societies publish journals that report research and developments in their fields. They often contain the following six parts, which may or may not be labeled:

- Abstract or Summary—follows the title and author and summarizes the article's content.
- Summary of Related Research—reviews current research on the topic.
- Description of Research—also called "Method," tells how the research was carried out or explains the author's ideas, including the purpose of the study.
- Results—states the outcomes of the study.
- Implications, Discussion, and Conclusions—explains the meaning and implications of the study's results.
- Further Research—suggests additional studies needed.

6. How can you read essays and articles critically?

To closely analyze and evaluate essays and articles, ask these questions:
- Who is the author?
- What is his or her purpose?
- What does the introduction or lead add to the piece of writing?
- What is the thesis?
- Is it adequately supported?
- Are sources, references, or citations given for the facts and statistics used?

READING SELECTION 11

ECOLOGY

WILL WE CONTROL THE WEATHER?
J. Madeleine Nash
From *Time* magazine

Can or should we attempt to affect the weather? This article claims that we have already done so and that the results have been damaging to our environment. Read the article to find out what actions have already negatively affected the climate.

— · —

1   A tropical storm quickly takes shape over the Atlantic Ocean, a furiously whirling dervish with a skirt of thunderstorms. But just as quickly the storm is challenged by dozens of National Weather Service planes, which sally forth from East Coast airstrips like fighters on the tail of an enemy bomber. Attacking from above and below, the planes fire off a barrage of esoteric weapons that sap the strength of the raging winds in the developing eye wall.

2   Ammunition expended, the lead pilot flashes a thumbs-up, confident that once again she and her team of veteran storm chasers have prevented a hurricane from forming.

3   Could something like this really happen? Probably not. Such fanciful scenarios are period pieces. They belong to the 1950s and '60s, when scientists harbored an almost naive faith in the ability of modern technology to end droughts, banish hail and improve meteorological conditions in countless other ways. At one point, pioneering chemist Irving Langmuir suggested that it would prove easier to change the weather to our liking than to predict its duplicitous twists and turns. The great mathematician John von Neumann even calculated what mounting an effective weather-modification effort would cost the U.S.—about as much as building the railroads, he figured, and worth incalculably more.

4   At the start of the 21st century, alas, all that remains of these happy visions are a few scattered

Copyright © 2005 by Kathleen T. McWhorter

cloud-seeding programs, whose modest successes, while real, have proved less than earth-shaking. In fact, yesterday's sunny hopes that we could somehow change the weather for the better have given way to the gloomy knowledge that we are only making things worse. It is now clear that what the world's cleverest scientists could not achieve by design, ordinary people are on the verge of accomplishing by accident. Human beings not only have the ability to alter weather patterns on local, regional and global scales, but they are already doing it—in ways that are potentially catastrophic.

5   Consider the billions of tons of carbon dioxide that are emitted every year in the course of our daily life. Driving a car, switching on a light, working in a factory, fertilizing a field all contribute to the atmosphere's growing burden of heat-trapping gases. Unless we start to control emissions of CO_2 and similar compounds, global mean temperatures will probably rise somewhere between 2°F and 7°F by the end of the next century; even the low end of that spectrum could set the stage for a lot of meteorological mischief. Among other things, the higher the temperature, the more rapidly moisture can evaporate from the earth's surface and condense as rain droplets in clouds, substantially increasing the risk of both drought and torrential rain. There could also be a rise in the number of severe storms, such as the tornado-spawning monsters that hit Texas last week.

6   Human activity is modifying precipitation in other dramatic ways. Satellite images show that industrial aerosols—sulfuric acid and the like—emitted by steel mills, oil refineries and power plants are suppressing rainfall downwind of major industrial centers. In Australia, Canada and Turkey, according to one study, these pollution patterns perfectly coincide with corridors within which precipitation is virtually nil. Reason: the aerosols interfere with the mechanism by which the water vapor in clouds con-

denses and grows into raindrops big enough to reach the ground.

7   This creates an additional conundrum. Because a polluted cloud does not rain itself out, notes University of Colorado atmospheric scientist Brian Toon, it tends to grow larger and last longer, providing a shiny white surface that bounces sunlight out to space. Indeed, one reason the earth has not yet warmed up as much as many anticipated may be due to the tug-of-war between industrial aerosols like sulfuric acid (which reflect heat) and greenhouse gases like carbon dioxide (which trap it). Ironically, then, the cost of reducing one kind of pollution may come at the price of intensifying the effects of the other.

8   Deforestation has a similarly broad range of impact. One thing trees do is lock up a lot of carbon in their woody tissues, thereby preventing it from escaping into the atmosphere. Trees are also important recyclers of moisture to the atmosphere. In some parts of the Amazon basin, deforestation has reached the point where it is altering precipitation patterns. This is because so much of the moisture entrained by clouds comes from the canopy of the forest below; as large tracts of trees disappear, so do portions of the aqueous reservoir that feeds the local rainmaking machine.

9   Shrubs, grasses and other vegetative covers act in much the same way, trapping water, feeding moisture into the atmosphere and providing shade that shields the surface of the land from the drying rays of the sun. Large-scale land-clearing efforts under way around the world wipe all that out. The ongoing development of South Florida, for instance, has filled in and paved over much of the Everglades wetlands, which have long served as an important source of atmospheric moisture. As a consequence, says Colorado State University atmospheric scientist Roger Pielke Sr., South Florida in July and August has become significantly drier and hotter than it

would have been a century ago under the same set of climactic conditions.

10   To complicate matters further, we are changing the landscape in ways that increase our exposure to meteorological extremes, so that even if weather patterns in coming decades were to turn out to be identical to those of the past century, the damage inflicted would be far worse. To appreciate what happens when vegetative cover is removed, one need look no further than the 1930s Dust Bowl in the U.S. and the 1970s famine in Africa's Sahel. In both cases, a meteorological drought was exacerbated by agricultural and pastoral practices that stripped land bare, exposing it to the not so tender mercies of sun and wind.

11   Removal of vegetative cover also worsens the flooding that occurs during periods of torrential rain. Riverine forests serve as sponges that soak up excess water, preventing it from rushing all at once into rivers and tributaries. In similar fashion, estuarine wetlands and mangrove forests help shield human settlements from the storm surges that accompany tropical cyclones and hurricanes. Biologists estimate that 50% of the world's mangrove forests have already been replaced by everything from shantytowns to cement plants and shrimp farms. Stir in the expectation that rising temperatures will trigger a rise in sea level, and you have a recipe for unprecedented disaster.

12   Scientists are just beginning to disentangle the myriad levels on which human beings and the natural climate system interact, which only increases the potential for surprise. For example, we now realize that not all the aerosols we are pumping into the atmosphere exert a cooling effect. A notable exception is soot, which is produced by wood fires and incomplete industrial combustion. Because of its dark color, soot absorbs solar energy rather than reflecting it. So when a recent scientific excursion to the Indian Ocean established that big soot clouds were circulating through the atmosphere, a number of scientists speculated that their presence might be raising sea-surface temperatures, potentially affecting the strength of the monsoon.

13   The monsoon is not the only climate cycle that human activity could alter. Atmospheric scientist John M. Wallace of the University of Washington believes that rising concentrations of greenhouse gases are already beginning to have an impact on another important cycle, known as the North Atlantic or Arctic Oscillation. In this case it's not the warming these gases create in the lower atmosphere that is key, but the cooling they cause in the stratosphere, where molecules of carbon dioxide and the like emit heat to space rather than trapping it in the upper atmosphere. This stratospheric cooling, Wallace and others speculate, may have biased prevailing wind patterns in ways that favor a wintertime influx of mild marine air into Northern—as opposed to Southern—Europe.

14   Is Wallace right about this? No one yet knows. We are tampering with systems that are so complex that scientists are struggling to understand them. Climatologist Tom Wigley of the National Center for Atmospheric Research, for one, fervently believes the answer to our problems lies not just in improved knowledge of the climate system but in technological advances that could counter—and perhaps reverse—present trends. In other words, the farfetched dreams that prominent scientists like von Neumann once harbored have not died. Rather they have been transformed and, in the process, become more urgent.

EXAMINING READING SELECTION 11

Checking Your Vocabulary

Directions: Using context, word parts, or a dictionary if necessary, circle the letter of the meaning for each word as it is used in the reading.

1. barrage (paragraph 1)
   a. few
   b. rapid discharge
   c. average number
   d. definite count

2. duplicitous (paragraph 3)
   a. deceptive
   b. predictable
   c. certain
   d. general

3. incalculably (paragraph 3)
   a. definitely
   b. suitably
   c. immeasurably
   d. timelessly

4. myriad (paragraph 12)
   a. obvious
   b. important
   c. incomplete
   d. many

5. fervently (paragraph 14)
   a. justifiably
   b. clearly
   c. passionately
   d. partially

Checking Your Comprehension

Directions: Circle the letter of the best answer.

6. This selection is primarily concerned with
   a. the fact that scientists have controlled weather in the past.
   b. the idea that the weather cannot be altered.

   c. the presumption that weather is always unpredictable.
   d. the ways in which our actions can alter the weather.

7. The selection supports which of the following ideas?
   a. We have never been able to control the weather and we never will be able to control it.
   b. We should not want to control the weather.
   c. We have controlled the weather in negative ways, and now we need to control it in positive ways.
   d. We cannot expect meteorologists to ever be able to predict the weather.

8. According to the selection, which of the following is a result of moisture evaporating from the earth's surface and condensing in clouds as rain?
   a. thunderstorms only
   b. light rain only
   c. drought only
   d. both drought and torrential rain

9. One of the major ways in which we have negatively altered the weather is by
   a. creating more rivers and streams.
   b. placing carbon dioxide into the atmosphere.
   c. seeding clouds.
   d. creating landfills.

10. One effect of industrial aerosols is
    a. tornadoes.
    b. hurricanes.
    c. drought.
    d. thunderstorms.

11. This selection focuses on
   a. historical events in weather control.
   b. causes and effects of weather.
   c. comparisons among regional weather systems.
   d. classifications of weather systems.

Thinking Critically

12. Which of the following actions is the writer likely to oppose?
   a. building reservoirs in Africa
   b. creating new resorts in South Florida
   c. mining in Arizona
   d. creating landfills in the Dust Bowl

13. The author's tone is one of
   a. casualness.
   b. anger.
   c. confrontation.
   d. danger.

14. The writer refers to the Everglades wetlands to show that
   a. when we alter an environment that acts as a controller of precipitation, the weather will become hotter and dryer.
   b. if we create an area of wetlands, we may alter the weather conditions in that area.
   c. Florida continues to receive an increased amount of rain over the years.
   d. the Everglades area is a good example of how and why severe thunderstorms, without warning, can become tornadoes and hurricanes.

15. Which of the following is a generalization?
   a. A satellite image can show areas affected by industrial aerosols.
   b. Vegetative removal caused famine in Africa's Sahel.
   c. Ordinary people are on the verge of changing the weather.
   d. Carbon dioxide is emitted into our atmosphere by factories.

Questions for Discussion

1. Do you think greater regulation of activities, such as deforestation, is justifiable? Why?

2. Have you noticed recent climatic changes in the area in which you live? If so, describe them.

3. The author states that "we are only making things worse." In what areas, other than the weather, do you feel humans have made matters worse?

Selection 11:			1419 words
Finishing Time:	_____	_____	_____
	HR.	MIN.	SEC.
Starting Time:	_____	_____	_____
	HR.	MIN.	SEC.
Reading Time:		_____	_____
		MIN.	SEC.
WPM Score:			_____
Comprehension Score:			_____ %

READING SELECTION 12

BIOLOGY/HEALTH

ALTERNATIVE DRUG TESTING UPDATE

Lance C. Presley

From *Occupational Health & Safety*

1   It has only been a few years since laboratory-based oral fluid drug screening first appeared on the menu of choices for employers' substance abuse testing programs. In the beginning, some in the employer drug-testing market were skeptical of the new screening. Not everyone was convinced that something so simple could be as reliable and accurate as traditional urine testing. However, as each year of use passed, statistics and satisfied employers have turned the skepticism into acceptance. Today, this once "alternative" method is going mainstream and proving itself as a viable and desirable drug-testing option for small businesses and large corporations everywhere.

The Early Days of Oral Fluid Screening

2   Laboratory-based oral fluid screening is not a new technology. Studies using oral fluid to detect drugs of abuse were published more than 20 years ago, and the methodology has been used in the risk assessment business to test for HIV, cotinine, and cocaine metabolites for almost 10 years. However, it wasn't until 2000 that laboratory-based oral fluid testing became commercially available to the employer drug-testing market.

3   Suddenly, employers had a new option for trying to create and maintain drug-free work environments. Oral fluid drug screening could be used for the most common tests requested by workplace drug testing including the SAMHSA* 5-panel of marijuana, cocaine, opiates, amphetamines, and PCP (Recently, oral fluid screens have also been expanded to detect Ecstasy [MDMA].)

Plus, the alternative method seemed to be as simple and convenient as it had been marketed.

4   Benefits of oral fluid screening quickly began to emerge. Anyone who used urine for non-federally mandated testing programs or administered an alcohol- and drug-testing program for non-regulated employers was a candidate to take advantage of the new option. A survey of more than 1,000 oral fluid employer sites revealed that employers ranked ease of collections, quality, accuracy, and turnaround times as their main reasons for choosing oral fluid testing. Surveyed employers said oral fluid testing was "fast and a very simple test to perform." Others commented on the applicants' positive reaction to the screening: "Applicants were not uncomfortable with the process. They liked the fact that there was no cup, and no embarrassing situations."

Why Oral Fluid Went Mainstream

5   From the beginning, one of the most visible and discussed benefits of oral fluid testing was its less invasive collection method. Employers and donors alike praise it as a more "dignified" collection process than traditional urine testing.

Ease of collection

6   Most oral fluid collection devices are also simple and easy to use. The collection pad is placed between the lower cheek and gum for two to five minutes. The collection pad is then sealed. The entire collection process is easy and quick. Collections are conducted "on site" and

---

* The Substance Abuse and Mental Health Services Administration (SAMHSA—an agency of the U.S. Department of Health & Human Services

are observed, eliminating concerns of adulteration or dilution of the specimen. Once the oral fluid specimen has been collected, it is sent to a laboratory for testing.

7   Georgia-Pacific, one of the world's leading manufacturers and distributors of tissue, pulp, paper, packaging, building products, and related chemicals, has utilized oral fluid for all non-DOT drug testing since the beginning of 2002. "We not only appreciate the ease of collection, but the cost savings of oral fluid screening. By not having to send a donor to a collection site for testing, we expedite the process and save time and money," said Donald Barnard, Industrial Relations coordinator.

Quality and accuracy

8   Once a specimen has been collected, it enters the analysis process at a laboratory. Laboratory-based oral fluid testing adheres to the same high forensic standards as the traditional urine testing method. Samples are first screened using enzyme immunoassay technology, proven reliable for routine drug testing. Any samples that test positive in the screening process are then subjected to gas chromatography/mass spectrometry/mass spectrometry (GC/MS/MS), the highest standard in drug confirmation technology. This tandem "MS," as it is called, provides the most unique fingerprint of the drug in question. This strict methodology ensures the accuracy and reliability associated with urine screening.

9   Just like traditional urine testing, the window of detection in oral fluid testing is different for each drug. Urine testing relies on drug metabolites retained in the body's waste supply and may detect some drugs for a longer period than in oral fluid. However, only oral fluid testing can identify very recent usage—which can be missed by urine testing. (For most drugs, the window of detection in oral fluid is about one to three days.) In a recent analysis of THC (marijuana) testing, among all oral fluid devices

available, only a laboratory-based oral fluid test was sensitive enough to detect THC at a level equivalent to screening results from urine THC screening.

10   Note: 80.2 percent of oral fluid THC positives had a concentration below 50 ng/mL. A device using a 50 ng/mL cutoff would have missed four out of five results.

Turnaround Time

11   Oral fluid testing allows employers to speed up their hiring process. Specimens can be collected on site immediately after an offer is made to a candidate, often eliminating the 24-hour period that is allowed to report to a clinic for a test. Negative results are reported within 24 hours and positive results within 72 hours after receiving the specimen at the lab. Employers indicate that using oral fluid testing reduces their overall hiring time compared to the urine drug testing process.

A Program Enhancement

12   LabOne tested more than 100,000 oral fluid drug screens in 2001. It became the first lab to compile statistical data for presentation to the Drug Testing Advisory Board (DTAB). This group, comprised of government officials, academic researchers, and laboratory personnel, guides SAMHSA* in its rulemaking process. Oral fluid testing data was submitted to DTAB several times throughout the year. As a result, the proposed guidelines include oral fluid pre-employment, random, postaccident, reasonable cause, and follow-up testing.

13   The 2001 statistics continue to show that laboratory-based oral fluid is a viable alternative to traditional urine testing. Today, the consensus is that oral fluid drug testing enhances the employment drug-testing program for many employers. Fast, accurate, and convenient, it is a welcome addition to the menu of drug testing alternatives.

WRITING ABOUT READING SELECTION 12*

Checking Your Vocabulary

Directions: Complete each of the following items; refer to a dictionary if necessary.

1. Discuss the connotative meanings of the phrase "drug testing."

2. Define each of the following words:
   a. skeptical (paragraph 1)

   _____

   b. viable (paragraph 1)

   _____

   c. invasive (paragraph 5)

   _____

   d. adulteration (paragraph 6)

   _____

   e. expedite (paragraph 7)

   _____

3. Define the word "specimen(s)" (paragraph 11) and underline the word or phrase that provides a context for its meaning.

   _____

   _____

   _____

4. Where could you look to find the meanings of technical words such as *cotinine, metabolites, and enzyme immunoassay technology?*

   _____

5. Determine the meaning of the following words by using word parts:
   a. Mainstream (paragraph 1)

   _____

   _____

   _____

   b. pre-employment (paragraph 12)

   _____

Checking Your Comprehension

6. What is the basic purpose of this article?

   _____

   _____

7. Why were companies skeptical of oral fluid testing?

   _____

   _____

   _____

8. What information came from the survey of oral fluid employer sites?

   _____

   _____

   _____

   _____

9. How does the author conclude the article?

   _____

   _____

   _____

_____

* Multiple-choice questions are contained in Part 6 (page 582).

Thinking Critically

10. Why do employers prefer quick hiring times?

11. Who is the intended audience? Support your answer.

12. Why is it important for labs to submit data to the Drug Testing Advisory Board?

Questions for Discussion

1. Do you believe in employer-sponsored drug testing? Why or why not? Can you think of some occupations where drug testing is more justifiable than others?

2. What other sorts of tests should employers give their potential employees? Identify three occupations and discuss the types of tests that would help identify candidates suitable for the job.

3. Discuss the different ways in which someone might react when told that he or she failed a drug test.

Selection 12:		1012 words
Finishing Time:		
	HR. MIN.	SEC.
Starting Time:		
	HR. MIN.	SEC.
Reading Time:		
	MIN.	SEC.
WPM Score:		
Comprehension Score:		%

GO ELECTRONIC

For additional readings, exercises, and Internet activities, visit this book's Web site at:

http://www.ablongman.com/mcwhorter

For even more activities, visit the Longman English pages at:

http://www.ablongman.com/englishpages

If you need a user name and password, please see your instructor.

PART 2
Academic Scenario

The following scenario is designed to assess your ability to use and apply the skills taught in this unit.

THE SITUATION

Assume you are taking a child and adolescent psychology course. This week you are studying the stages of cognitive development in children. Your instructor has assigned Reading Selection 7, "The Appreciation of Humor," (p. 160) as an outside reading. Your next exam will be next week, and you suspect it will include a question on this reading. Read this article carefully before completing the following tasks.

THE TASKS

1. State the thesis of this article.

   _____

   _____

2. Identify the *overall* organization (thought) pattern used in this reading.

   _____

3. Underline the topic sentences of paragraphs 8, 9, 11, and 12.

   _____

   _____

4. Identify four transitional words or phrases in paragraphs 4 through 8.

   _____

   _____

   _____

   _____

   _____

Techniques for Learning Textbook Material

IN THIS CHAPTER YOU WILL LEARN:

1. To use highlighting effectively.
2. To make marginal annotations.
3. To paraphrase text.
4. To use outlining to organize ideas.
5. To draw concept maps.
6. To summarize information.

As a college student, you are expected to learn large amounts of textbook material. Rereading to learn is *not* an effective strategy. Writing *is* an effective strategy. In fact, writing is an excellent means of improving both your comprehension and your retention. Many successful students almost always read with a pen in hand ready to highlight, mark, annotate, or paraphrase ideas. Some students use writing to study and review the material after reading. They outline to organize information, write summaries to condense ideas, or draw maps to show relationships.

Writing during and after reading has numerous advantages:

1. **Writing focuses your attention.** If you are writing as well as reading, you are forced to keep your mind on the topic.
2. **Writing forces you to think.** By highlighting or writing you are forced to decide what is important and understand relationships and connections.
3. **Writing tests your understanding.** One of the truest measures of understanding is your ability to explain an idea in your own words.

257

When you have understood an idea, you will be able to write about it, but when an idea is unclear or confusing, you will be at a loss for words.

4. **Writing facilitates recall.** Research studies indicate that information is recalled more easily if it is elaborated on. Elaboration involves expanding and thinking about the material by drawing connections and associations, seeing relationships, and applying what you have learned. As you will see throughout the chapter, writing is a form of elaboration.

This chapter describes six learning strategies that use writing as a learning tool: highlighting, annotating, paraphrasing, outlining, mapping, and summarizing.

Highlighting Techniques

When reading factual material, the easiest and fastest way to mark important facts and ideas is to highlight them using a pencil, pen, or marker. Many students are hesitant to mark their texts because they want to sell them at the end of the semester. However, highlighting makes the book more useful to you, so try not to let your interest in selling the book prevent you from reading and studying in the most efficient manner.

How to Highlight Effectively

Your goal in highlighting is to identify and mark those portions of an assignment that are important to reread when you study that chapter. Here are a few suggestions on how to highlight effectively:

1. **Read a paragraph or section first and then go back and highlight what is important.** If you highlight as you read, you run the risk of highlighting an idea that you think is important, only to find out later in the passage that it is less important than you originally thought.

2. **Use your knowledge of paragraph structure to guide your highlighting.** Try to highlight important portions of the topic sentence and any supporting details that you want to remember. Use signal words to locate changes or divisions of thought.

3. **Use headings to guide your highlighting.** Earlier in this book you learned that headings could be used to establish a purpose for reading. You can also use headings to help you identify what to highlight. Turn the headings into questions. Then, as you read, look for the answers to your questions; when you find information that answers the questions, highlight it.

4. **Use a system for highlighting.** You can use a number of systems. They include

- using two or more colors of ink or highlighters to distinguish between main ideas and details or more and less important information.
- using single underscoring for details and highlighting for main ideas.
- placing brackets around the main idea and using a highlighter to mark important details.

Because no system is the most effective for everyone, develop a system that works well for you. Once you develop that system, use it consistently. If you vary systems, your chances for confusion and error while reviewing are greater.

5. **Highlight just enough words to make the meaning clear when rereading.** Avoid highlighting a whole sentence. Usually the core parts of the sentence, along with an additional phrase or two, are sufficient. Notice that you can understand the meaning of the following sentence by reading only the highlighted parts.

Fad diets disregard the necessity for balance among the various classes of nutrients.

Now, read only the highlighted parts of the following paragraph. Can you understand what the paragraph is about?

PLEA BARGAINING

When a plea agreement is made, for whatever reason, most states now require that the agreement be in writing and signed by all parties involved. This protects the lawyers, the judge, and the defendant, and ensures that there is a record that can be produced in court should the agreement be denied or contested. In signing the agreement, the defendant is also attesting to the fact that he or she entered a guilty plea voluntarily and knowingly.

Barlow, *Criminal Justice in America.*

Most likely you were able to understand the basic message by reading only the highlighted words. You were able to do so because the highlighted words were core parts of each sentence or modifiers that directly explained those parts.

6. **Be sure that your highlighting accurately reflects the content of the passage.** Incomplete or hasty highlighting can mislead you as you review the passage and cause you to miss the main point. As a safeguard against this, occasionally test your accuracy by rereading only what you have highlighted. Does your highlighting tell what the paragraph or passage is about? Does it express the most important idea in the passage?

Highlighting the Right Amount

If you highlight either too little or too much, you will defeat its purpose. If you highlight too little, you will miss valuable information and your review and study of the material will be incomplete. If you highlight too much, you are not identifying and highlighting the most important ideas. The more you highlight, the more you will have to reread when studying, and the less of a time-saver the procedure will be.

Here is a passage highlighted in three ways. Read the entire passage and then examine each version of the highlighting. Try to decide which version would be most useful if you were rereading it for study purposes.

Version 1

THE FUNCTIONS OF EYE MOVEMENTS

With eye movements you can serve a variety of functions. One such function is to seek feedback. In talking with someone, we look at her or him intently, as if to say, "Well, what do you think?" As you might predict, listeners gaze at speakers more than speakers gaze at listeners. In public speaking, you might scan hundreds of people to secure this feedback.

A second function is to inform the other person that the channel of communication is open and that he or she should now speak. You see this regularly in conversation when one person asks a question or finishes a thought and then looks to you for a response.

Eye movements may also signal the nature of a relationship, whether positive (an attentive glance) or negative (eye avoidance). You can also signal your power through "visual dominance behavior." The average speaker, for example, maintains a high level of eye contact while listening and a lower level while speaking. When people want to signal dominance, they may reverse this pattern—maintaining a high level of eye contact while talking but a much lower level while listening.

By making eye contact you psychologically lessen the physical distance between yourself and another person. When you catch someone's eye at a party, for example, you become psychologically close, though physically far apart.

DeVito, *Messages.*

Version 2

THE FUNCTIONS OF EYE MOVEMENTS

With eye movements you can serve a variety of functions. One such function is to seek feedback. In talking with someone, we look at her or him intently, as if to say, "Well, what do you think?" As you might predict, listeners gaze at speakers more than speakers gaze at listeners. In public speaking, you might scan hundreds of people to secure this feedback.

A second function is to inform the other person that the channel of communication is open and that he or she should now speak. You see this regularly in conversation when one person asks a question or finishes a thought and then looks to you for a response.

Eye movements may also signal the nature of a relationship, whether positive (an attentive glance) or negative (eye avoidance). You can also signal your power through "visual dominance behavior." The average speaker, for example, maintains a high level of eye contact while listening and a lower level while speaking. When people want to signal dominance, they may reverse this pattern—maintaining a high level of eye contact while talking but a much lower level while listening.

By making eye contact you psychologically lessen the physical distance between yourself and another person. When you catch someone's eye at a party, for example, you become psychologically close, though physically far apart.

Version 3

THE FUNCTIONS OF EYE MOVEMENTS

With eye movements you can serve a variety of functions. One such function is to seek feedback. In talking with someone, we look at her or him intently, as if to say, "Well, what do you think?" As you might predict, listeners gaze at speakers more than speakers gaze at listeners. In public speaking, you might scan hundreds of people to secure this feedback.

A second function is to inform the other person that the channel of communication is open and that he or she should now speak. You see this regularly in conversation when one person asks a question or finishes a thought and then looks to you for a response.

Eye movements may also signal the nature of a relationship, whether positive (an attentive glance) or negative (eye avoidance). You can also signal your power through "visual dominance behavior." The average speaker, for example, maintains a high level of eye contact while listening and a lower level while speaking. When people want to signal dominance, they may reverse this pattern—maintaining a high level of eye contact while talking but a much lower level while listening.

By making eye contact you psychologically lessen the physical distance between yourself and another person. When you catch someone's eye at a party, for example, you become psychologically close, though physically far apart.

This passage on eye movements lists five functions of eye movements and briefly explains each. In evaluating the highlighting done in Version 1, you can see that it does not contain enough information. Only four of the five functions are highlighted and practically none of the explanations are highlighted.

Version 2, on the other hand, has too much highlighting. Although all of the important details are highlighted, many less important details are also highlighted. For instance, in the first paragraph, the first function and an explanation are highlighted (though using more text than is necessary), but also additional information about how often speakers and listeners gaze at each other. In fact, nearly every sentence is highlighted, and for review purposes it would be almost as easy to reread the entire passage as it would be to read only the highlighting.

Version 3 is an example of effective highlighting. If you reread only the highlighting, you will see that each of the five functions of eye movements and brief explanations of them have been highlighted.

As a general rule of thumb, try to highlight no more than 20 to 30 percent of the passage. Once you exceed this range, you begin to lose effectiveness. Of course, if a particular section or passage is very factual or detailed it may require more detailed highlighting. However, if you find that an entire assignment or chapter seems to require 60 to 70 percent highlighting, you should consider using one of the other note-taking methods suggested later in this chapter.

EXERCISE 7-1

DIRECTIONS: Read and highlight the following excerpt from a zoology textbook using the guidelines for highlighting. When you have finished, compare your highlighting to that in the sample on page 263.

Excerpt

RODS AND CONES OF THE EYE

Among the most complex receptor cells are the photoreceptor cells of vertebrates. These are called rods or cones, depending on their shapes (Fig. 1). Rods have cylindrical outer segments that contain approximately 2000 disc-shaped membranes bearing light-absorbing pigments. This pigment is rhodopsin, a yellow substance that absorbs a broad range of wavelengths. Rhodopsin combines a vitamin-A derivative called **retinal** with a protein called **opsin**. Cones are similar, except that their outer segments are cone-shaped, and the opsins differ. Vertebrates typically have several types of cones with different opsins that enable them to perceive different colors. In addition, lungfishes, many reptiles, and birds have colored drops of oil in the cones, which narrow the color sensitivity. Mammals have cones with three different opsins, each of which absorbs light most effectively at a different wavelength from the other two. In humans these three wavelengths are perceived as red, blue, and green. Although we have only three kinds of cones, any color can be perceived from the combination of cones it stimulates. For example, stimulation of both red-sensitive and blue-sensitive cones would indicate the color purple.

Rods and cones also differ in their sensitivity. Rods are so sensitive that they can respond to individual photons, but they become blinded in bright daylight. They are therefore useful mainly at night and in heavy shadow. Cones are not sensitive enough to work in darkness, but the different color sensitivities enable them to transmit information about color in bright light. Good vision in the dark requires a large number of rods, while color vision in daylight requires numerous cones. The retinas of most mammals, especially nocturnal ones, have primarily rods. The retinas of humans and other primates have a mixture of rods and cones in peripheral areas and have only cones in the center of focus, called the fovea. Humans have a total of about 100 million rods and 3 million cones.

Harris, *Concepts in Zoology.*

Sample Highlighting

RODS AND CONES OF THE EYE

Among the most complex receptor cells are the photoreceptor cells of vertebrates. These are called rods or cones, depending on their shapes (Fig. 1). Rods have cylindrical outer segments that contain approximately 2000 disc-shaped membranes bearing light-absorbing pigments. This pigment is rhodopsin, a yellow substance that absorbs a broad range of wavelengths. Rhodopsin combines a vitamin-A derivative called **retinal** with a protein called **opsin**. Cones are similar, except that their outer segments are cone-shaped, and the opsins differ. Vertebrates typically have several types of cones with different opsins that enable them to perceive different colors. In addition, lungfishes, many reptiles, and birds have colored drops of oil in the cones, which narrow the color sensitivity. Mammals have cones with three different opsins, each of which absorbs light most effectively at a different wavelength from the other two. In humans these three wavelengths are perceived as red, blue, and green. Although we have only three kinds of cones, any color can be perceived from the combination of cones it stimulates. For example, stimulation of both red-sensitive and blue-sensitive cones would indicate the color purple.

Rods and cones also differ in their sensitivity. Rods are so sensitive that they can respond to individual photons, but they become blinded in bright daylight. They are therefore useful mainly at night and in heavy shadow. Cones are not sensitive enough to work in darkness, but the different color sensitivities enable them to transmit information about color in bright light. Good vision in the dark requires a large number of rods, while color vision in daylight requires numerous cones. The retinas of most mammals, especially nocturnal ones, have primarily rods. The retinas of humans and other primates have a mixture of rods and cones in peripheral areas and have only cones in the center of focus, called the fovea. Humans have a total of about 100 million rods and 3 million cones.

EXERCISE 7-2

DIRECTIONS: Choose one of the reading selections at the end of this chapter. Assume that you are reading it as part of a class reading assignment on which you will be tested. As you read, highlight the important ideas. Tomorrow, reread what you have highlighted and then answer the multiple-choice questions that follow the selection.

Annotating and Making Marginal Notations

If you were reading the want ads in a newspaper in search of an apartment to rent, you would probably mark certain ads. As you phoned for more information, you might make notes about each apartment. These notes would help you decide which apartments to visit. Similarly, in many types of academic reading, making notes, or *annotating,* is a useful strategy. Annotating is a means of keeping track of your impressions, ideas, reactions, and questions as you read. Then, after reading, reviewing your annotations will help you form a final impression of the work. If a writing assignment accompanies the reading, your annotations will serve as an excellent source of ideas for a paper. Annotating should be used in conjunction with highlighting. Highlighting is a means of identifying important information; annotating is a method of recording *your* thinking about these key ideas.

There are no fixed rules about how or what to annotate. In general, try to mark or note any ideas about the assignment that come to mind as you read or reread. Write your annotations in the margins. Use annotations to

- write questions about the material
- condense important points
- identify ideas with which you disagree or that are inconsistent
- mark good or poor examples of supporting data
- locate key terms or definitions
- summarize arguments
- identify the author's viewpoints or feelings

Several methods of annotation are discussed in the following sections.

Using Symbols to Annotate

Symbols can be used to distinguish different types of information, to emphasize material to be studied, or to show relationships among ideas. They can be very convenient, for instance, in calling attention to examples or definitions, portions of an assignment that you feel are particularly important to study, or contrasting ideas and opinions.

Develop your own set of symbols and use them consistently. Here is a sample list of commonly used symbols and their meanings.

Symbol	Meaning
ex	an example is included
def	an important term is defined
☐	unknown word to look up in dictionary later
T	good test question
?	confusing idea
*	very important
sum	summary statement
⤴	relates to another idea

Now read the following passage, paying particular attention to the use of symbols.

3 factors   Three key factors are commonly subsumed within the concept of modernization: industrialization, urbanization, and bureaucratization. ① **Industrialization** refers

def   to a shift from human to nonhuman sources of energy and the rise of the factory system of economic production. An example would be the process by which

ex   shoes, previously made by hand in small shops, came to be manufactured in factories by electrically powered machines. ② **Urbanization** means the movement of

def   people from rural areas into towns and cities (where factories tend to be located).

def   ③ **Bureaucratization** refers to the rise of large-scale formal organizations. These three

°∘°   components of modernization, in turn, lead to changes in such social institutions as religion, politics, and the family.

Popenoe, *Sociology.*

Annotating to Condense Information

Annotating is a helpful technique to use when you work through complicated or lengthy explanations. Often a few marginal notes can be used to summarize an entire paragraph, as shown in the following example.

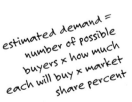

The first step in estimating demand for a particular product is to identify demand for an entire product category in the markets that the company serves. PepsiCo, for example, will estimate the entire demand for soft drinks in domestic and international markets. A small business, such as a start-up premium coffee supplier, will estimate demand only in markets it expects to reach. Marketers predict total demand by first identifying the number of buyers or potential buyers and then multiplying that estimate times the average amount each member of the target market is likely to purchase. For example, the coffee entrepreneur may estimate that there are 10,000 consumer households in his market who would be willing to buy his premium coffee and that each household would purchase approximately 25 pounds of coffee a year. The total annual demand for the product is 250,000 pounds.

Once the marketer estimates total demand, the next step is to predict what the company's market share is likely to be. The company's estimated demand is then its share of the whole (estimated) pie. In our coffee example, the entrepreneur may feel that he can gain 5 percent of this market, or 12,500 pounds or about 1,000 pounds a month—not bad for a new start-up business. Of course, such projections need to take into consideration other factors that might affect demand, such as new competitors entering the market, the state of the economy, and changing consumer tastes.

Solomon and Stuart, *Marketing.*

You can see that annotations are a useful time-saving device when ideas are complicated and cannot be reviewed quickly by highlighting.

Annotating to Record Reactions

Annotations are particularly useful when reading literature, essays, controversial articles, arguments, or persuasive material. Because each type of work is intended to provoke a reader's response, record your reactions and feelings as you read.

The poem "Anecdote of the Jar" follows. Read the poem first, then study the annotations. Notice how the annotations reveal the reader's thinking about the poem.

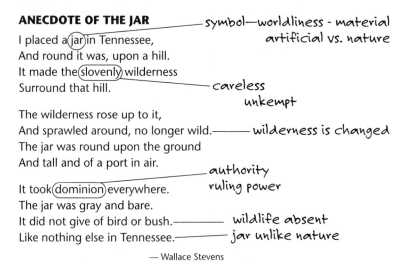

ANECDOTE OF THE JAR ——— symbol—worldliness - material
artificial vs. nature
I placed a (jar) in Tennessee,
And round it was, upon a hill.
It made the (slovenly) wilderness ——— careless
Surround that hill.   unkempt

The wilderness rose up to it,
And sprawled around, no longer wild.——— wilderness is changed
The jar was round upon the ground
And tall and of a port in air.
——— authority
It took (dominion) everywhere.   ruling power
The jar was gray and bare.
It did not give of bird or bush.——— wildlife absent
Like nothing else in Tennessee.——— jar unlike nature

— Wallace Stevens

EXERCISE 7–3

DIRECTIONS: Refer to the same reading selection used for Exercise 7–2. Review your highlighting and add annotations that clarify or summarize content or record your reactions. Add at least two annotations that reflect your thinking.

EXERCISE 7-4

DIRECTIONS: Highlight and annotate a section from a current chapter in one of your textbooks using the suggestions for effective highlighting and annotating presented in this chapter.

Paraphrasing

A paraphrase restates a passage's ideas in your own words. You retain the author's meaning, but you use your own wording. In speech we paraphrase frequently. For example, when you relay a message from one person to another, you convey the meaning but do not use the person's exact words. A paraphrase makes a passage's meaning clearer and often more concise.

Paraphrasing is a useful technique in several situations.

1. **Paraphrasing is a means of recording information from reference sources in note form for later use in writing a research paper.**

2. **Paraphrasing is also useful when dealing with material for which exact, detailed comprehension is required.** For instance, you might paraphrase the steps in solving a math problem or the procedures for a lab set-up in chemistry.

3. **Paraphrasing is also helpful for understanding extremely difficult or complicated passages that must be worked out word by word.**

4. **Paraphrasing is useful when reading material that is stylistically complex, or with an obvious slant, bias, strong tone, or detailed description.**

Study the following example of a paraphrase of the stylistically complex preamble of the United States Constitution. Notice that it restates in different words the intent of the preamble.

PREAMBLE

We the people of the United States, in order to form a more perfect union, establish justice, insure domestic tranquillity, provide for the common defense, promote the general welfare, and secure the blessings of liberty to ourselves and our posterity, do ordain and establish this Constitution of the United States of America.

PARAPHRASE

The citizens of the United States established the Constitution to create a better country, to provide rightful treatment, peace, protection, and well-being for themselves and future citizens.

Notice first how synonyms were substituted for words in the original—*citizens* for *people, country* for *union, protection* for *defense,* and so forth. Next, notice that the order of information was rearranged.

Use the following suggestions to paraphrase effectively:

1. **Read the entire material before writing anything.** Read slowly and carefully.

2. **As you read, focus on both exact meanings and relationships between ideas.**

3. **Read each sentence and identify its core meaning.** Use synonyms, replacing the author's words with your words. Look away from the original sentence and write in your own words what it means. Then reread the original and add any additional or qualifying information.

4. **Don't try to paraphrase word by word.** Instead, work with clauses and phrases (idea groups). If you are unsure of the meaning of a word or phrase, check a dictionary to locate a more familiar meaning.

5. **You may combine several original sentences into a more concise paraphrase.** It is also acceptable to present ideas in a different order than in the original.

6. **Compare your paraphrase with the original for completeness and accuracy.**

EXERCISE 7-5

DIRECTIONS: Provide synonyms for the underlined words or phrases in the following excerpt from Sartre's essay on existentialism. Discuss and compare choices in a class discussion.

The existentialist, on the contrary, thinks it very <u>distressing</u> that God does not exist, because all possibility of finding values in a heaven of ideas disappears along with Him; there can no longer be an *a priori* Good, since there is no <u>infinite</u> and perfect consciousness to think it. Nowhere is it written that the Good exists, that we must be honest, that we must not lie; because the fact is we are on a <u>plane</u> where there are only men. Dostoievsky said, "If God didn't exist, everything would be possible." That is the very <u>starting point</u> of existentialism. Indeed, everything is <u>permissible</u> if God does not exist, and as a result man is <u>forlorn</u>, because neither within him nor without does he find anything to cling to. He can't start making excuses for himself.

Sartre, *Existentialism.*

**EXERCISE
7-6**

DIRECTIONS: Write a paraphrase of the second paragraph of the following selection from a sociology text.

_____

_____

_____

_____

_____

_____

_____

_____

THE HOME SCHOOLING MOVEMENT

It is difficult to estimate the number of youngsters involved in **home schooling,** *where children are not sent to school and receive their formal education from one or both parents.* Legislation and court decisions have made it legally possible in most states for parents to educate their children at home, and each year more people take advantage of that opportunity. Some states require parents or a home tutor to meet teacher certification standards, and many require parents to complete legal forms and affidavits to verify that their children are receiving instruction in state-approved curricula.

Supporters of home education claim that it is less expensive and far more efficient than mass public education. Moreover they cite several advantages: alleviation of school overcrowding, added curricular and pedagogical alternatives not available in the public schools, strengthened family relationships, lower dropout rates, the fact that students are allowed to learn at their own rate, increased motivation, higher standardized test scores, and reduced discipline problems. Proponents of home schooling also believe that it provides the parents with the opportunity to reinforce their moral values through education—something they are not satisfied that the public schools will do.

Critics of the home schooling movement contend that it creates as many problems as it solves. They acknowledge that, in a few cases, home schooling offers educational opportunities superior to those found in most public schools, but few parents can provide such educational advantages. Some parents who withdraw their children from the schools in favor of home schooling have an inadequate educational background and insufficient formal training to provide a satisfactory education for their children. Typically, parents have fewer, not more, technological resources at their disposal than do schools. However, . . . the relatively inexpensive computer technology that is readily available today is causing some to challenge the notion that home schooling is in any way inferior to more highly structured classroom education.

Finally, a sociological concern is the restricted social interaction experienced by children who are educated at home. Patricia Lines, a U. S. Department of Education policy analyst, believes that the possibilities provided by technology and the promise of home schooling are greatly exaggerated and insisted that "technology will never replace the pupil-teacher relationship." Also, while relationships with parents and siblings may be enhanced, children taught at home may develop a distorted view of society. Children who live in fairly homogeneous neighborhoods, comprising people of the same race, socioeconomic status, and religious background, do not experience the diversity that can be provided in the social arena of the schools. They may be ill equipped to function successfully in the larger multicultural world.

Thompson and Hickey, *Society in Focus: An Introduction to Sociology.*

EXERCISE 7-7

DIRECTIONS: Write a paraphrase of the excerpt on page 265 ("The first step . . .). When you have finished, compare your paraphrase with that of another student.

_____

_____

_____

_____

_____

_____

_____

_____

_____

_____

_____

_____

_____

_____

_____

Outlining

Outlining is an effective way to organize information and discover relationships between ideas. It forces you to select what is important from each paragraph and determine how it is related to key ideas in other paragraphs. Outlining enables you to learn and remember what you read because the process of selecting what is important and expressing it in your own words requires thought and comprehension and provides for repetition and review. Outlining is particularly effective for pragmatic learners who can learn material that is orderly and sequential.

Outlining is particularly useful in the following situations:

- When reading material that seems difficult or confusing, outlining forces you to sort ideas, see connections, and express them in your own words.

- When you are asked to write an evaluation or a critical interpretation of an article or essay, it is helpful to outline the factual content. The outline reflects development and progression of thought and helps you analyze the writer's ideas.

- In subject matter where order or process is important, an outline is particularly useful. For example, in a data processing course in which various sets of programming commands must be performed in a specified sequence, an outline is a good way to organize the information.

- In the natural sciences, in which classifications are important, outlines help you record and sort information. In botany, for example, one important focus is the classification and description of various plant groups. An outline enables you to list subgroups within each category and to keep track of similar characteristics.

Developing an Outline

To be effective, an outline must show the relative importance of ideas and the relationship between ideas. The easiest way to achieve this is to use the following format:

I. **First Major Topic**
   A. First major idea
      1. First important detail
      2. Second important detail

B. Second major idea

    1. First important detail

        a. Minor detail or example

        b. Minor detail or example

    2. Second important detail

II. **Second Major Topic**

A. First major idea

Notice that the more important ideas are closer to the left margin, and less important details are indented toward the middle of the page. A quick glance at an outline indicates what is most important and how ideas support or explain one another.

Use the following suggestions to write effective outlines:

1. **Read a section completely before writing.**

2. **Be brief and concise; do not write in complete sentences.** Unless the outline is to be submitted to your instructor, use abbreviations, symbols, or shorthand words as you would in lecture note taking.

3. **Use your own words rather than those in the text.**

4. **Be certain that all information beneath a heading supports or explains it.**

5. **Make sure every heading that is aligned vertically is of equal importance.**

To illustrate further the technique for outlining, read the following passage and then study the outline that follows it.

NONBIODEGRADABLE POLLUTANTS

Heavy metals, such as mercury, cadmium, and arsenic, and manufactured chemicals, such as PCBs and some pesticides, are examples of nonbiodegradable pollutants. These chemicals are highly toxic, so that low levels of exposure or low concentrations of these compounds are poisonous. Such chemicals are so foreign to living organisms that they are not metabolized and remain in the ecosystem basically unchanged. Worse than that, if eaten, they may be stored within the body. Each time chemicals such as PCBs, mercury, or dioxin are taken into the body they are added to the existing stock. If this accumulation continues, a toxic level is reached. The Romans were great poisoners, and they knew the toxic value of gradually administering poisons such an antimony or arsenic. Each meal was safe to eat, but the steady diet of a little poison time after time led to the death of the victim. Even though nonbiodegradable pollutants may be relatively rare, they are stored in the bodies of an organism and passed on up the food chain in a process called **biological amplification** (also referred to as biological magnification). A predator absorbs all the stored pollutants in the hundreds or thousands of prey items that it eats, and each meal provides a dose of the toxin. The chemical is stored in the body of the predator, where the successive doses accumulate and become more concentrated. If the predator then falls prey to a larger carnivore, the entire dose of toxicity is taken to the next step in the food chain. Thus, the concentration of the toxin is amplified at each link in the food chain.

Bush, *Ecology of a Changing Planet.*

Here is the outline for the above selection:

I. Nonbiodegradable Pollutants
   A. examples
      1. heavy metals
         a. mercury
         b. cadmium
      2. manufactured chemicals
         a. PCBs
         b. pesticides
   B. highly toxic
      1. poisonous at low exposure and concentrations
      2. not metabolized; remain in ecosystem unchanged
   C. stored within body when eaten
      1. added to existing stock in body
      2. can eventually reach toxic level
   D. biological amplification (magnification)
      1. predator eats many prey with stored pollutants
      2. doses accumulate and become more concentrated
      3. carnivore eats predator
      4. toxicity taken up food chain

By reading the passage and then reviewing the outline, you can see that it represents, in briefest form, the contents of the passage. Reading an outline is an effective way to reacquaint yourself with the content and organization of a chapter without taking the time that reading, highlighting, or marginal notation requires.

How Much Information to Include

Before you begin to outline, decide how much information to include. An outline can be very brief and cover only major topics, or at the other extreme, it can be very detailed, providing an extensive review of information.

The purpose of your outline should determine how much detail you include. For example, if you are outlining a reading assignment for which your instructor asked that you be familiar with the author's viewpoint and general approach to a problem, little detail is needed. On the other hand, if you are outlining a section of an anatomy and physiology text for an upcoming objective exam, a much more detailed outline is needed. To determine the right amount of detail, ask yourself: "What do I need to know? What type of test situation, if any, am I preparing for?"

EXERCISE 7-8

DIRECTIONS: Read the following excerpt from Brian Fagan's *People of the Earth: An Introduction to World Prehistory,* an archaeology textbook, and write a brief outline.

For hundreds of thousands of years, *Homo erectus* flourished in the tropical and temperate regions of the Old World. Except for an overall increase in brain size, *H. erectus* remained remarkably stable in evolutionary terms for more than a million years, until less than 500,000 years ago. Eventually, *H. erectus* evolved into early *H. sapiens,* but we do not even know when the gradual transition began or how it took place. Some researchers believe it began as early as 400,000 years ago; others, much later, sometime around or after 200,000 years ago.

For hundreds of thousands of years, both *H. erectus* and early *H. sapiens* survived and evolved with the aid of what Steven Mithen calls multiple intelligences separated by walls analogous to those dividing the chapels of a medieval cathedral. As Mithen says (1996), the thoughts in one chapel could barely be heard in another. Archaic humans lacked one vital component of the modern mind: cognitive flexibility, the ability to bridge the walls between their many intelligences. Such flexibility appears to have been the prerogative of modern humans, *Homo sapiens sapiens.*

Homo sapiens sapiens means "wise person," and the controversies surrounding the origins of modern humanity—of ourselves—rank among the most vigorous in archaeology. What is it that separates us from earlier humans, scientists wonder? First and foremost must be our ability to speak fluently and articulately. We communicate, we tell stories, we pass on knowledge and ideas—all through the medium of language. Consciousness, cognition, self-awareness, foresight, and the ability to express oneself and one's emotions—these are direct consequences of fluent speech. They can be linked with another attribute of the fully fledged human psyche: the capacity for symbolic and spiritual thought, concerned not only with subsistence and technology but also with defining the boundaries of existence and the relationship among the individual, the group, and the universe.

EXERCISE 7-9

DIRECTIONS: Write an outline of "The Home Schooling Movement" on page 269. ▬

Mapping to Show Relationships

Mapping is a process of drawing diagrams to describe how a topic and its related ideas are connected. It is a means of organizing and consolidating information by using a visual format. Maps facilitate learning because they group and consolidate information. Although mapping appeals to visual learners, verbal learners will also find it to be effective in organizing information. This section discusses two types of maps: concept maps and thought pattern maps.

Concept Maps

Concept maps are visual outlines; they show how ideas within a passage are related. Maps can take different forms. You can draw them in any way that shows the relationships among the ideas. Sketching rather than exact, careful drawing is appropriate. When drawing maps feel free to abbreviate, add lines to show relationships, add notes, or redraw to make changes. Figure 7.1 shows two sample maps. Each was drawn to show the organization of Chapter 2 of this text. Refer to Chapter 2, pages 31–72, then study each map.

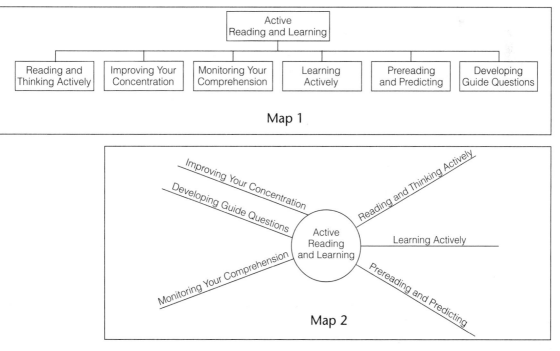

FIGURE 7.1   Two Sample Concept Maps of Chapter 2

Think of a map as a diagram that shows how ideas are connected. Maps, like outlines, can vary in the amount of detail included, ranging from very general to highly specific. The maps shown in Figure 7.1 only provide an overview of the chapter and reflect its general organization. A more detailed map of one of the topics, prereading, included in Chapter 2 (p. 46) is shown in Figure 7.2. Use the following steps in drawing a map.

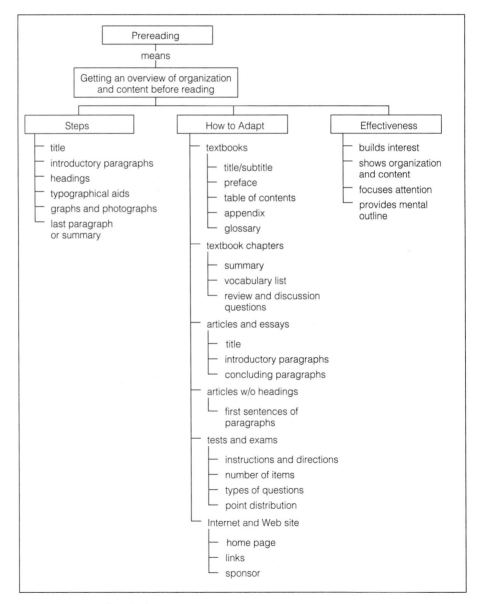

FIGURE 7.2   A detailed concept map

1. **Identify the overall subject and write it in the center or at the top of the page.** How you arrange your map will depend on the subject matter and its organization. Circles or boxes are useful but not absolutely necessary.

2. **Identify the major supporting information that relates to the topic.** State each fact or idea on a line connected to the central topic.

3. As you discover details that further explain an idea already mapped, **draw a new line branching from the idea it explains.**

DIRECTIONS: Draw a map that reflects the overall organization of this chapter.

DIRECTIONS: Draw a map that reflects the organization of one of the end-of-chapter readings in this book that you have read this semester.

DIRECTIONS: Select a section from one of your textbooks. Draw a concept map that reflects its organization.   ▄▄

Thought Pattern Maps

When a particular organizational thought pattern is evident throughout a passage, you may wish to draw a map reflecting that pattern. Maps for each common organizational pattern are shown in Chapter 5. Now that you are familiar with the idea of mapping, review Chapter 5, paying particular attention to the diagrams shown for each pattern. When reading a history text, for example, you may find it helpful to draw time lines (see p. 173) to organize events within historical periods. Or, when reading a text that compares two works of philosophy or two key political figures, you may find one of the maps shown on pages 185–186 helpful in distinguishing similarities and differences.

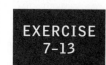

DIRECTIONS: Draw a concept map showing the overall organization of Chapter 8, "Learning and Retention Strategies."

DIRECTIONS: Conduct an experiment to see whether you prefer outlining or mapping to show relationships between ideas. Choose and read a substantial section from one of your textbooks. Write a brief outline of it, then draw a map of this same section. Which of these two methods was easier for you to do? Which of these will be most useful for you? Why?

Summarizing Information

A summary is a compact restatement of the important points of a passage. You might think of it as a shortened version of a longer message. Unlike a paraphrase, a summary does not include all information presented in the original. Instead, you must select what to include. A summary contains only the gist of the text, with limited background, explanation, or detail. Although summaries vary in length, they are often one quarter or less of the length of the original.

Summaries are useful in a variety of reading situations in which a condensed overview of the material is needed. You might summarize information in preparation for an essay exam, or key points of news articles required in an economics class. Some class assignments also require summarization. Lab reports for science courses include a summary of results. A literature instructor may ask you to summarize the plot of a short story.

Use the following steps as a guide when writing a summary.

1. **Read the entire original work first.** Do not write anything until you understand it completely and have a complete picture of the work.

2. **Reread and highlight key points.** Look in particular for topic sentences and essential details.

3. **Review your highlighting.** Cross out all but vital phrases. Eliminate repetitious information.

4. **Write sentences to include all remaining highlighted information.** Condense and combine information wherever possible.

5. **Present ideas in the summary in the same order in which they appeared in the original**, unless you are purposely regrouping ideas.

6. **Revise your summary.** Try to make your summary more concise by eliminating repetition and combining ideas.

Read this selection by Joyce Cary, and study the sample summary.

ART AND EDUCATION

A very large number of people cease when quite young to add anything to a limited stock of judgments. After a certain age, say 25, they consider that their education is finished.

It is perhaps natural that having passed through that painful and boring process, called expressly education, they should suppose it over, and that they are equipped for life to label every event as it occurs and drop it into its given pigeonhole. But one who has a label ready for everything does not bother to observe any more, even such ordinary happenings as he has observed for himself, with attention, before he went to school. He merely acts and reacts.

For people who have stopped noticing, the only possible new or renewed experience, and, therefore, new knowledge, is from a work of art. Because that is the only kind of experience which they are prepared to receive on its own terms, they will come out from their shells and expose themselves to music, to a play, to a book, because it is the accepted method of enjoying such things. True, even to plays and books they may bring artistic prejudices which prevent them from seeing *that* play or comprehending *that* book. Their artistic sensibilities may be as crusted over as their minds.

But it is part of an artist's job to break crusts, or let us say rather that artists who work for the public and not merely for themselves, are interested in breaking crusts because they want to communicate their intuitions.

Carey, *On the Function of the Novelist.*

Sample Summary

> Many people consider their education to be complete at an early age and, at that time, cease to observe and react to the world around them. Art forces people to think and react. For some people, their artistic sensibility may be as stagnant as their minds. It is the artist's responsibility to intervene in order to communicate.

EXERCISE 7-15

DIRECTIONS: Read and summarize the following essay by James Thurber.

A DOG'S EYE VIEW OF MAN

If Man has benefited immeasurably by his association with the dog, what, you may ask, has the dog got out of it? His scroll has, of course, been heavily charged with punishments: he has known the muzzle, the leash, and the tether; he has suffered the indignities of the show bench, the tin can on the tail, the ribbon in the hair; his love life with the other sex of his species has been regulated by the frigid hand of authority, his digestion ruined by the macaroons and marshmallows of doting women. The list of his woes could be continued indefinitely. But he has also had his fun, for he has been privileged to live with and study at close range the only creature with reason, the most unreasonable of creatures.

The dog has got more fun out of Man than Man has got out of the dog, for the clearly demonstrable reason that Man is the more laughable of the two animals. The dog has long been bemused by the singular activities and the curious practices of men, cocking his head inquiringly to one side, intently watching and listening to the strangest goings-on in the world. He has seen men sing together and fight one another in the same evening. He has watched them go to bed when it is time to get up, and get up when it is time to go to bed. He has observed them destroying the soil in vast areas, and nurturing it in small patches. He has stood by while men built strong and solid houses for rest and quiet, and then filled them with lights and bells and machinery. His sensitive nose, which can detect what's cooking in the next township, has caught at one and the same time the bewildering smells of the hospital and the munitions factory. He has seen men raise up great cities to heaven and then blow them to hell.

Thurber, *Thurber's Dogs.*

_____

_____

_____

_____

DIRECTIONS: Write a summary of "The Home Schooling Movement" on page 269. Use the outline you constructed in Exercise 7–9 to guide your writing.

_____

_____

_____

_____

_____

_____

_____

_____

_____

Critical Thinking Tip #7

Annotating and Critical Thinking

Annotating is a way of identifying and summarizing key information. It is also a way to facilitate critical thinking. Annotating helps you record your reactions as you read. You might

- jot down questions
- highlight emotionally charged words
- note opposing ideas
- mark ideas you question or disagree with
- note places where you feel further information is needed
- mark sections you feel are particularly strong or weak

Here is a sample annotation in which a reader recorded her thinking about the passage:

HATE SPEECH ON CAMPUS

definition?

why?   In recent years, a rise in (verbal abuse and violence) directed at people of color, lesbians and gay men, and other historically persecuted groups has plagued the United States. Among the settings of these expressions of intolerance are college and university campuses, where bias incidents have occurred sporadically since the mid-1980s. Outrage, indignation and demands for change have greeted such incidents—understandably, given the lack of racial and social diversity among students, faculty and administrators on most campuses.

guidelines or rules?   Many universities, under pressure to respond to the concerns of those who are the objects of hate, have adopted (codes or policies) prohibiting speech that offends any group based on race, gender, ethnicity, religion or sexual orientation.

opinion   That's the wrong response, well-meaning or not. The First Amendment to the United States Constitution protects speech no matter how offensive its content. Speech codes adopted by *isn't some* government-financed state colleges and universities amount to *response necessary?* government censorship, in violation of the Constitution. And the ACLU [American Civil Liberties Union] believes that all campuses should adhere to First Amendment principles because academic freedom is a bedrock of education in a free society.

Tischler, ed., *Debating Points: Race and Ethnic Relations.*

As you learn more about critical thinking throughout the text, you will get more ideas about what to mark and annotate.

DIRECTIONS: Select a section of at least five substantial paragraphs from one of your current textbook chapters. Write a paraphrase of its first paragraph; then write a summary of the entire section.

DIRECTIONS: Choose one of the reading selections at the end of this chapter. Read the selection, highlight it, and annotate it. Then write a brief outline and summary of its content. Be sure to show the relationships between ideas as well as record the most important ideas.   ▬

Summary

1. Why is writing during and after reading an effective learning strategy?

Writing during and after reading enhances both your comprehension and recall. Writing activities such as highlighting, annotating, paraphrasing, outlining, summarizing, and mapping can
- focus your attention
- force you to think
- test your understanding
- aid your recall

2. How can you highlight more effectively?

To make highlighting an efficient means of identifying what is important within each paragraph you should
- read first, then highlight
- use paragraph structure to guide you
- use headings as a guide
- develop your own highlighting system
- highlight as few words as possible
- reread your highlighting to test its accuracy

3. Why should you annotate and make marginal notations in conjunction with your highlighting?

Annotating involves recording ideas, reactions, impressions, and questions as you read. Using symbols and brief phrases as marginal notes is useful in condensing, supplementing, and clarifying passage content because you are adding your own thinking to the highlighted material.

4. Why is paraphrasing a useful study strategy?

Paraphrasing is the restatement of a passage's ideas in your own words. It is a particularly useful strategy for recording the meaning and checking your comprehension of detailed, complex, precise, difficult, or unusually written passages. Using your own words rather than the author's expresses the meaning of the passage more clearly and concisely, thereby making study and review easier.

5. What is an outline and what are its advantages?

Outlining is a form of organizing information that provides you with a structure that indicates the relative importance of ideas and shows the relationships among them. When done well, it helps you sort out ideas, improves your concentration, and aids your recall.

6. What is mapping?

Mapping is a process of drawing diagrams to show the connection between a topic and its related ideas. Both concept maps and thought pattern maps enable you to adjust to both the type of information being recorded and its particular organization. Grouping and consolidating information in this way makes it easier to learn and remember.

7. What is involved in summarizing?

Summarizing involves selecting a passage's most important ideas and recording them in a condensed abbreviated form. A summary provides a brief overview of a passage that can be useful in completing writing assignments and reports, preparing for class participation, or reviewing for exams.

READING SELECTION 13

POLITICAL SCIENCE

THE SUPREME COURT IN ACTION

Edward S. Greenberg and Benjamin I. Page

From *The Struggle for Democracy*

The Supreme Court of the United States is an important and powerful part of our democratic system. Read this excerpt from an American government textbook to learn the traditions and rules the court follows and how it decides which cases to hear.

— · —

1   The Supreme Court meets from the first Monday in October (set by statute) until late June or early July, depending on the press of business. Let's see how it goes about deciding cases.

Norms of Operation

2   The Court is a tradition-bound institution defined by many rituals and long-standing norms. Brass spittoons still stand next to each justice's chair; quill pens and inkwells still grace the desks of competing counsel. Pages only gave up knickers in 1963; required formal wear (with tails) for lawyers was only recently abandoned. When the justices meet in public session to hear oral arguments or to announce decisions, they enter the courtroom in the same way: the chief justice is the first to emerge from behind the curtain that is draped behind the bench; the remainder enter in order of seniority.

3   More important than rituals are norms, unwritten but clearly understood ways of behaving. One norm is *secrecy,* which keeps the conflicts between justices out of the public eye and elevates the stature of the Court. Justices do not grant interviews very often. Reporters are not allowed to stalk the corridors for a story. Clerks are expected to keep all memos, draft opinions, and conversations with their justices confidential. Justices are not commonly seen on the frantic Washington, D.C., cocktail party circuit. When meeting in conference to argue and decide cases, the justices meet alone, without secretaries or clerks. While a breach of secrecy has occurred on occasion, allowing "insider" books like *The Brethren* to be published, they are the exceptions. As a result, we know less about the inner workings of the Court than about any other branch of government.

4   *Courtesy* is another norm. Though justices may sometimes express their displeasure and distaste for each other in private, in public they treat each other with great formality and respect. The justices shake hands before court sessions and conferences. They refer to each other as "my brother" or my "dissenting brother." Differences of opinion are usually respected; justices are allowed every opportunity to make their case to their fellow justices.

5   *Seniority* is another important norm. Seniority determines the assignment of office space, the seating arrangements in open court (the most junior are at the ends), the order of speaking in conference (the chief justice, then the most senior, etc.), and the order of voting (the most junior goes first).

6   Finally, the justices are expected to stick very closely to *precedent* when they are reaching a decision. When the Court departs from precedent, it is essentially overruling its own past actions, exercising judicial review of itself. In most cases, departure from precedent comes in only very small steps over many years, for example, several decisions chipped away at the "separate but equal" doctrine of *Plessy* v. *Ferguson* before it was decisively reversed in *Brown* v. *Board of Education.* If there is a significant ideological

Oral argument and the announcement of decisions happen here in the main courtroom of the Supreme Court building.

turnover on the court, however, change can come more quickly. The Rehnquist Court has been particularly aggressive in overturning precedents on the civil rights, criminal justice, and abortion fronts.

Controlling the Agenda

7　The Court has a number of screening mechanisms to control its agenda and to focus its attention on cases that involve important federal or constitutional questions.

8　Several technical rules help keep down the numbers. Cases must be real and adverse, meaning that they must involve a real dispute between two parties. The Court will not provide "advisory" opinions to guide the other branches. Disputants in a case must have standing, meaning that they must have a real and direct interest in the issues that are raised. The Court sometimes changes the definition of *standing* to make access easier or more difficult. The Warren Court favored a broad definition of *standing,* inviting litigation. The Rehnquist Court tightened the definition, making it harder for people suing in the name of some larger group of affected people—consumers, racial minorities, and so

on—to bring cases. Cases must also be ripe, meaning that all other avenues of appeal have been exhausted and that injury has already taken place (it will not accept hypothetical or predicted injury cases). Appeals must also be filed within a specified time limit, paperwork must be proper and complete, and a filing fee of $200 must be paid. The fee can be waived if a petitioner is indigent and files an affidavit *in forma pauperis* (in the manner of a pauper). One of the most famous cases in American history, *Gideon* v. *Wainwright* (1963), which established the right to counsel in criminal cases, was submitted *in forma pauperis* on a few pieces of lined paper by a Florida State Penitentiary inmate named Clarence Earl Gideon.

9　The most powerful tool that the Court has for controlling its own agenda is the power to grant or not to grant a **writ of certiorari.** A grant of cert is a decision of the Court that an appellate case raises an important federal or constitutional issue that it is prepared to consider. Law clerks in the chief justice's office prepare a brief summary of each petition for the justices, along with a recommendation on whether or not to grant cert. The clerks, in consultation with the chief justice, prepare a "discuss list" of cases that they are recommending for cert. Under the **rule of four,** petitions are granted cert if at least four justices vote in favor. There are several reasons why a petition may not command four votes, even if the case involves important constitutional issues: it may involve a particularly controversial issue that the Court would like to avoid, or the Court may not yet have developed a solid majority and wishes to avoid a split decision. Few petitions survive all of these hurdles. Of the 5,000 or so cases that are filed in each session, the Court grants cert for only a little more than 200. For cases denied cert, the decision of the lower court stands.

10   Deciding how freely to grant "cert" is tricky business for the Court. Used too often, it threatens to inundate the Court with cases. Used too sparingly, it leaves in place the decisions of 12 different circuit courts on substantial federal and constitutional questions.

EXAMINING READING SELECTION 13

Checking Your Vocabulary

Directions: Using context, word parts, or a dictionary if necessary, circle the letter of the meaning for each word as it is used in the reading.

1. seniority (paragraphs 2 and 5)
   a. length of service
   b. degrees held
   c. importance
   d. age

2. precedent (paragraph 6)
   a. a judicial decision that came before
   b. a judicial decision that was overruled
   c. a judicial decision that is in question
   d. a judicial decision that follows another

3. mechanisms (paragraph 7)
   a. machines that screen or sort
   b. people who make decisions
   c. rules that are followed without variance
   d. process to accomplish something

4. indigent (paragraph 8)
   a. unfamiliar with court procedures
   b. poor
   c. without an attorney
   d. unqualified

5. inundate (paragraph 10)
   a. to mystify
   b. to separate
   c. to overwhelm
   d. to cause ruin financially

Checking Your Comprehension

Directions: Circle the letter of the best answer.

6. This reading focuses on
   a. how justices behave.
   b. how the Supreme Court operates under a code of secrecy.
   c. how the Supreme Court selects cases.
   d. the operations of the Supreme Court.

7. The Supreme Court could best be described as
   a. self-regulating and efficient.
   b. innovative and adaptable.
   c. independent and tradition bound.
   d. eccentric and self-interested.

8. Little is known about the functioning of the Court because
   a. books like *The Brethren* are inaccurate.
   b. the justices maintain secrecy.
   c. the press does not consider the Court's operation newsworthy.
   d. the justices never meet in public session.

9. When cert is granted, the court
   a. reverses a lower court decision.
   b. agrees to consider an important federal or constitutional issue.
   c. recommends whether or not to consider an important issue.
   d. prepares a discuss list.

10. An adverse case is one
    a. that has exhausted all appeals.
    b. for which a cert has been denied.
    c. to which the rule of four does not apply.
    d. that involves a real dispute.

11. Which statement best describes the organization of this reading selection?
    a. The writers focus on causes and effects of court decisions.
    b. The writers emphasize differences among the justices.
    c. The writers present the court's operation chronologically.
    d. The writers list norms and operating procedures.

Thinking Critically

12. What would you expect the attitude of the justices to be toward the author of the book *The Brethren,* which gave "inside" information about the workings of the court?
    a. respect and admiration
    b. disapproval
    c. hate
    d. indifference

13. Which one of the following cases would the Supreme Court most likely consider?
    a. a convicted murderer just about to file an appeal in federal court
    b. a case in which a woman requests that a law be written that prohibits all pregnant women from smoking to prevent possible injury to fetuses
    c. a racial discrimination case that has not yet come to trial
    d. a personal injury case in which the victim has exhausted all appeals

14. The tone of this reading could best be described as
    a. distant.
    b. informational.
    c. argumentative.
    d. critical.

15. Which of the following statements can be inferred from the reading?
    a. The Court at times has chosen to avoid controversial issues.
    b. The justices frequently have personality disputes.
    c. The court is unwilling to try cases for which appeals have been exhausted.
    d. The court welcomes theoretical cases that concern possible injury.

Questions for Discussion

1. Identify and discuss a current legal issue leading to a hypothetical case in which you believe the court might seriously consider departing from a precedent. On what do you base your hypothetical case?

2. The article states that "the Court sometimes changes definition of standing to make access easier or more difficult." What is the definition of standing? Do you think it is fair for the Court to change this definition seemingly at random? Support your position.

3. Why do you think that granting "cert"—a writ of certiorari—places the Supreme Court in a particularly precarious position?

4. Why do you think the Court will hear only cases that are "ripe" as opposed to predicted or hypothetical cases?

Selection 13:		1029 words	
Finishing Time:	_____	_____	_____
	HR.	MIN.	SEC.
Starting Time:	_____	_____	_____
	HR.	MIN.	SEC.
Reading Time:		_____	_____
		MIN.	SEC.
WPM Score:		_____	
Comprehension Score:		_____	%

READING SELECTION 14

ASTRONOMY

ARE WE ALONE IN THE UNIVERSE?

Jeffrey Bennet et al.

From *The Cosmic Perspective*

Is life on earth unique, or does life exist on other planets? This reading reports efforts to answer these long-standing questions and describes plans for our continuing quest to locate those like ourselves.

— · —

1   The study of the Earth can teach us much about other worlds. In particular, it teaches us about the conditions for life and may help us answer what is surely one of the deepest philosophical questions of all time: Are we alone in the universe? . . .

2   In the time between the Copernican revolution and the space age, many people expected the other planets in our solar system to be Earth-like and to harbor intelligent life. In fact, a reward was supposedly once offered for the first evidence of intelligent life on another planet *other than Mars.* Venus, a bit closer to the Sun than Earth, was often pictured as a tropical paradise. Such expectations were dashed by the bleak images of Mars returned by spacecraft and the discovery of the runaway greenhouse effect on Venus. Many scientists began to believe that only Earth has the right conditions for life, intelligent or otherwise. Recently, the pendulum has begun to swing the other way, spurred primarily by two developments. First, biologists are learning that life thrives under a much wider range of conditions than once imagined. Second, planetary scientists are developing a much better understanding of conditions on other worlds. It now seems quite likely that conditions in at least some places on other worlds might be conducive to life.

The Hardiness, Diversity, and Probability of Life

3   Even on Earth, biologists long assumed that many environments were uninhabitable. But recent discoveries have found life surviving in a remarkable range of conditions. The teeming life surviving at temperatures as high as 125°C near underwater volcanic vents and in hot springs is only one of many surprises. Biologists have found microorganisms living deep inside rocks in the frozen deserts of Antarctica and inside basaltic rocks buried more than a kilometer underground. Some bacteria can even survive radiation levels once thought lethal—apparently, they have evolved cellular machinery that repairs mutations as fast as they occur. The newly discovered diversity of microscopic life has forced scientists to redraw the "tree of life," crowding familiar plants and animals into one corner. The majority of these microorganisms need neither sunlight, oxygen, nor "food" in the form of other organisms. Instead, they tap a variety of chemical reactions for their survival.

4   The new view of terrestrial biology forces us to rethink the possibility of life elsewhere. First, life on Earth thrives at extremes of temperature, pressure, and atmospheric conditions that overlap conditions found on other worlds. The Antarctic valleys, for example, are as dry and cold as certain parts of Mars, and the conditions found in terrestrial hot springs may have been duplicated on a number of planets and moons at certain times in the past. Second, life harnesses energy sources readily available on other planets.

The basalt-dwelling bacteria, for example, would probably survive if they were transplanted to Mars. Third, life on Earth has evolved from a common ancestor into every imaginable ecological niche (and some unimaginable ones as well). The diversification of life on Earth has basically tested the limits of our planet, and there is no reason to doubt that it would do so on other planets. Thus, if life ever had a foothold on any other planet in the past, some organisms might still survive in surprising ecological niches today even if the planet has undergone substantial changes. The only real question is whether life ever got started elsewhere in the first place.

5   What is the probability of life arising from nonliving ingredients? This is probably the greatest unknown in exobiology. The fact that we exist and are asking the question does not tell us the probability; it merely tells us that it happened once. But the rapidity with which life arose on Earth may provide a clue. As we've discussed, we find fossil evidence for life dating almost all the way back to the end of the period of early bombardment in the solar system, suggesting that life arises easily and perhaps inevitably under the right conditions. Some people even speculate that primitive life arose many times during the heavy bombardment, only to be extinguished by violent impacts just as many times. If life indeed arises easily given the right conditions, we must search the solar system for those conditions, past or present.

6   **Time Out to Think** *The preceding discussion implies that the rapid appearance of life on Earth means that life is highly probable. Do you agree with this logic? What alternative conclusions could you reach?*

Life in the Solar System

7   Speculation about life in the solar system usually begins with Mars, for good reason. Before it dried out billions of years ago, its early atmo-sphere gave the surface hospitable conditions that rivaled those on Earth, with ample running water, the necessary raw chemical ingredients for life, and a variety of familiar energy sources. Many of Earth's organisms would have thrived under early Martian conditions, and some could even survive in places in today's Martian environment. Our first attempt to search for life on Mars came with the Viking missions to Mars in the 1970s, which included two landers equipped to search for the chemical signs of life. No life was found. But the landers sampled only two locations on the planet and tested soils only very near the surface. If life once existed on Mars, it either has become extinct or is hiding in other locations.

8   Today, a renewed debate about Martian life is under way, thanks in part to the study of a Martian meteorite found in Antarctica in 1984. The meteorite apparently landed in Antarctica 13,000 years ago, following a 16-million-year journey through space after being blasted from Mars by an impact. The rock itself dates to 4.5 billion years ago, indicating that it solidified shortly after Mars formed and therefore was present during the time when Mars was warmer and wetter. Painstaking analysis of the meteorite reveals indirect evidence of past life on Mars, including layered carbonate minerals and complex molecules (called polycyclic aromatic hydrocarbons), both of which are associated with life when they are found in Earth rocks. Even more intriguing, highly magnified images of the meteorite reveal eerily lifelike forms (Figure A). These forms bear a superficial resemblance to terrestrial bacteria, although they are about a hundred times smaller—about the same size as recently discovered terrestrial "nanobacteria" and viruses. Nevertheless, many scientists dispute the conclusion that these features suggest the past existence of life on Mars, claiming that nonbiological causes can also explain many of the meteorite's unusual features.

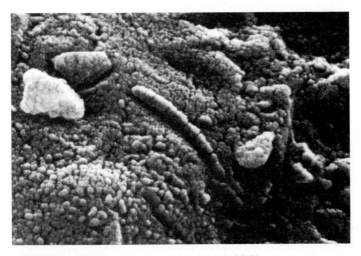

FIGURE A   Microscopic view of seemingly lifelike structures in a Martian meteorite.

Life Around Other Stars

9   Only a few places in our solar system seem hospitable to life, but many more hospitable worlds may be orbiting some of the hundred billion other stars in the Milky Way Galaxy or stars in some of the billions of other galaxies in the universe. Might some of the stars be orbited by planets that are as hospitable as our own Earth?

10   The bottom line is that, according to our theories of solar system formation, planets with all the necessities for life should be quite common in the universe. The only major question is whether these ingredients combine to form life.

The fact that life arose very early in Earth's history suggests that it may be very easy to produce life under Earth-like conditions, but we will not know for sure unless and until we find other life-bearing planets. NASA is currently developing plans for orbiting telescopes that may be able to detect ozone in the spectra of planets around other stars—and, at least in our solar system, substantial ozone implies life. In addition, radio astronomers are searching the skies in hopes of receiving a signal from some extraterrestrial civilization. Perhaps, in a decade or two, we will discover unmistakable evidence of life. On that day, if it comes, we will know that we are not alone.

11   **Time Out to Think** *Consider the following statements: (1) We are the only intelligent life in the entire universe. (2) Earth is one of many planets inhabited by intelligent life. Which do you think is true? Do you find either philosophically troubling?*

Looking outward to the blackness of space, sprinkled with the glory of a universe of lights, I saw majesty—but no welcome. Below was a welcoming planet. There, contained in the thin, moving, incredibly fragile shell of the biosphere is everything that is dear to you, all the human drama and comedy. That's where life is; that's where all the good stuff is.

Loren Acton, U.S. Astronaut

Writing about Reading Selection 14*

Checking Your Vocabulary

Directions: Complete each of the following items; refer to a dictionary if necessary.

1. Discuss the connotative meanings of the phrase *extraterrestrial civilization.*

2. Define each of the following words:
   a. harbor (paragraph 2)

   b. conducive (paragraph 2)

   c. lethal (paragraph 3)

* Multiple-choice questions are contained in Part 6 (page 583).

d. niche (paragraph 4)

_____

_____

e. renewed (paragraph 8)

_____

3. Define the word *dashed* (paragraph 2) and underline the word or phrase that provides a context clue for its meaning.

_____

_____

4. Define the word *hospitable* (paragraphs 7 and 9) and underline the word or phrase that provides a context clue for its meaning.

_____

_____

_____

5. Determine the meanings of the following words by using word parts:
   a. planetary (paragraph 2)

   _____

   b. uninhabitable (paragraph 3)

   _____

   c. microorganisms (paragraph 3)

   _____

   d. terrestrial (paragraph 4)

   _____

   e. nonbiological (paragraph 8)

   _____

Checking Your Comprehension

6. Why does the author believe that life may have once existed on Mars?

_____

_____

7. How does the new view of terrestrial biology support the possibility of life elsewhere in the universe?

_____

_____

_____

_____

_____

8. Describe the evolution of thought regarding the belief in life elsewhere in our solar system.

_____

_____

_____

_____

_____

_____

_____

_____

9. What chemical in the atmosphere of a planet implies life?

_____

10. What indirect evidence of past life was found in the Martian meteorite found in Antarctica in 1984?

_____

_____

Thinking Critically

11. Describe the authors' purpose.

_____

_____

_____

12. What assumptions do the writers of this selection make about life on other planets?

_____

_____

_____

13. Based on the information presented in this selection, what type of studies could scientists undertake to try to prove or disprove that life exists elsewhere besides Earth?

_____

_____

_____

_____

_____

_____

_____

Questions for Discussion

1. Are you convinced by the author's arguments that life exists elsewhere in the universe? Give evidence to support your position.

2. If you were an explorer on Mars, where would you begin your search for life on the planet?

Selection 14:			1209 words
Finishing Time:	_____	_____	_____
	HR.	MIN.	SEC.
Starting Time:	_____	_____	_____
	HR.	MIN.	SEC.
Reading Time:		_____	_____
		MIN.	SEC.
WPM Score:			_____
Comprehension Score:			_____ %

GO ELECTRONIC

For additional readings, exercises, and Internet activities, visit this book's Web site at:

http://www.ablongman.com/mcwhorter

For even more activities, visit the Longman English pages at:

http://www.ablongman.com/englishpages

If you need a user name and password, please see your instructor.

Take a Road Trip to Spring Break! (Florida)
Be sure to visit the Outlining, Summarizing, Mapping, and Paraphrasing module on your Reading Road Trip CD-ROM for multimedia tutorials, exercises, and tests.

CHAPTER 8

Learning and Retention Strategies

IN THIS CHAPTER YOU WILL LEARN:

1. To use textbook structure to guide your reading.
2. To increase your retention and recall using new techniques and systems.
3. To read scientific and technical material more efficiently.

The purpose of this chapter is to help you understand the structure and distinguishing features of textbooks and how to use them to your advantage in reading and recalling information. A textbook is a unique, highly specialized information source. It is very different from any other type of printed material. One feature distinguishes it from all other forms of written expression: It is designed to teach.

A textbook also has a consistent, tight organization not always found in other types of factual material. The first section of this chapter shows you how to use this structure and the learning aids associated with it to guide your learning. The second section discusses a number of strategies for improving your ability to retain information. Next, this chapter presents SQ3R, an effective system for reading and studying factual material. The last section offers suggestions for reading scientific and technical material.

Using the Organization of Textbook Chapters

Have you ever entered a large new discount store or supermarket and felt confused and disoriented? If you are an efficient shopper, you look for the signs that hang over the aisles and indicate what products are shelved in that section so you can quickly find what you need. It is just as easy to

293

become confused and disoriented when reading a textbook chapter unless you identify its organization and follow the signs the author gives you to locate what you need. You will find the headings to be essential guideposts that lead you through each chapter, especially if you are a pragmatic learner who appreciates order and systems.

Headings

The signs used in textbooks are the headings that organize each chapter by dividing it into topics. Headings are labels that indicate the contents of the material that follows. Most chapters use several types of headings, each distinguished by a different size and style of print. Heading positions can also vary.

The various kinds and positions of headings suggest differing degrees of importance. Figure 8.1 shows an excerpt from a chapter on atmospheric and oceanic circulations in an introductory physical geography textbook. Much of the material between headings has been deleted in order to emphasize the function of the headings.

In Figure 8.1 you can see three levels of headings, each distinguishable by its size and location:

1. The largest heading announces a broad, general subject—atmospheric patterns of motion.

2. The headings at the next level are more detailed and announce topics into which the subject has been divided.

3. The third level of headings provides subtopics—in this excerpt a listing of Earth's various pressure areas.

When headings are considered together, they form an outline of the chapter content as shown here:

Atmospheric Patterns of Motion
   Primary High-Pressure and Low-Pressure Areas
      Equatorial Low-Pressure Trough (ITCZ): Clouds and Rain
      Subtropical High-Pressure Cells: Hot, Dry, Desert Air
      Subpolar Low-Pressure Cells: Cool and Moist Air
      Polar High-Pressure Cells: Frigid, Dry Deserts
   Upper Atmospheric Circulation

Often in a text, the table of contents provides a listing of headings and more important subheadings. Develop the habit of using headings as

FIGURE 8.1   The Function of Headings

major heading   Atmospheric Patterns of Motion

With these forces and motions in mind, we are ready to build a general model of total atmospheric circulation. The warmer, less-dense air along the equator rises . . .

minor heading   *Primary High-Pressure and Low-Pressure Areas*

The following discussion of Earth's pressure and wind patterns refers often to Figure 6-11, isobaric maps show . . .

Four broad pressure areas cover the Northern Hemisphere . . .

subtopic   *Equatorial Low-Pressure Trough (ITCZ): Clouds and Rain*

Figure 6-12 is a satellite image showing the equatorial low-pressure trough. Its presence is revealed by the broken band of clouds . . .

subtopic   *Subtropical High-Pressure Cells: Hot, Dry, Desert Air*

Between 20 degrees and 35 degrees latitude in both hemispheres, a broad high-pressure zone of hot, dry air is evident across the globe . . .

subtopic   *Subpolar Low-Pressure Cells: Cool and Moist Air*

January, two low-pressure cyclonic cells exist over the oceans around 60 degrees N latitude, near their namesakes: the North Pacific Aleutian low and the North Atlantic Icelandic low (Figure 6-11a) . . . .

subtopic   *Polar High-Pressure Cells: Frigid, Dry Deserts*

Polar high-pressure cells are weak . . .

Of the two polar regions, the Antarctic high is . . .

minor heading   *Upper Atmospheric Circulation*

Circulation in the middle and upper troposphere is an important component of the atmosphere's general circulation . . .

Christopherson, *Geosystems: An Introduction to Physical Geography.*

guideposts to understanding the organization and important contents of a chapter. Use the following suggestions before reading a chapter:

1. **Study the entry for a chapter in the table of contents before beginning to read the chapter.** Notice how the topics are connected and how the author proceeds from topic to topic.

2. **Preread the chapter to get a more detached picture of its structure and focus.**

3. **Use the chapter's headings to identify its overall organizational pattern (see Chapter 5).** For example, does the chapter follow a time sequence?

DIRECTIONS: Study the following outlines of chapter headings and answer the questions that follow each.

I. Text: *Sociology: An Introduction*

   A. Chapter: **Deviance and Social Control**

      1. Major Heading: **What is Deviance?**

         a. Minor Heading: **Traditional Views of Deviance and Deviants**

            (1) Subtopic: **The Absolutist View**

            (2) Subtopic: **The Moral View**

            (3) Subtopic: **The Medical and Social Pathological View**

            (4) Subtopic: **The Statistical View**

         b. Minor Heading: **The Relative Nature of Deviance**

            (1) Subtopic: **Variation by Time**

            (2) Subtopic: **Variation by Place**

            (3) Subtopic: **Variation by Situation**

            (4) Subtopic: **Variation by Social Status**

1. What is the main purpose of the portion of the chapter summarized by the headings shown?

_____

2. According to what factors does the meaning of deviance vary?

_____

3. What organizational pattern(s) does this chapter seem to reflect?

_____

II. Text: *The Basics of American Politics*

   A. Chapter: **Who Wins, Who Loses: Pluralism versus Elitism**

      1. Heading: **Pluralism**

      2. Heading: **Power Elite**

      3. Heading: **The Debate**

      4. Heading: **Wrap Up**

4. What organizational pattern does this chapter title suggest?

_____

5.   What content do you predict the section titled "Wrap Up" will contain?

_____ ▬

Textbook Learning Aids

Because a textbook is intended to help you learn, it contains various features designed to help you learn its content in the most efficient and effective way. Table 8.1 provides a brief review of common textbook learning aids and their uses.

Table 8.1   Textbook Learning Aids

Feature	Use
Learning Objectives	Focus your attention on what is important in the chapter
Chapter Outline	Enables you to see the sequence and organization of ideas
Chapter Overview	Explains purpose and focus of the chapter
Special Interest Boxes	Provide perspectives or application of important concepts
Marginal Notations	Offer commentary, pose questions, provide illustrations and examples, identify key terms
Summary	Condenses and consolidates chapter content
Vocabulary Lists	Identify terminology to learn
Review Questions	Test your knowledge of key concepts and ideas
Discussion Questions	Provoke thought; enable you to think critically
Suggested Readings or References	Provide additional sources of information
Glossary	Offers easy-to-use mini-dictionary of key terminology
Appendix	Contains useful additional materials

EXERCISE 8-2

DIRECTIONS: Review one of your textbooks to discover the learning aids it contains. Make a list of the "Textbook Learning Aids" from Table 8.1 that it contains. ▬

Applying Effective Recall Strategies

Using Review to Increase Recall

Review refers to the process of going back over something you have already read. There are two types of review: immediate and periodic. Both types can greatly increase the amount you can remember from a printed page.

Immediate Review

When you finish reading an assignment, your first inclination may be to breathe a sigh of relief, close the book, and go on to another task. Before you do this, however, take a few minutes to go back over the material. Briefly review the overall organization and important ideas presented. Think of review as a postreading activity, similar to prereading. In reviewing you should reread the parts of the article or chapter that contain the most important ideas. Concentrate on titles, introductions, summaries, headings, graphic material, and depending on the length of the material, topic sentences. Also review any notes you made and any portions of the text that you highlighted.

Considerable research has been conducted on how individuals learn and remember. These experiments have shown that review immediately following reading greatly improves the amount remembered. However, the review must be *immediate;* it will not produce the same effects if you do it after a ten-minute break or later in the evening. To get the full benefit, you must review while the content of the article or chapter is still fresh in your mind. Review before you have had a chance to forget and before other thoughts and ideas interfere or compete with what you have read.

Periodic Review

Although immediate review is very effective and will increase your ability to recall information, it is not sufficient for remembering material for long periods. To remember facts and ideas permanently, you need to review them periodically, going back and refreshing your recall on a regular basis. For example, suppose you are reading a chapter on criminal behavior in your sociology text, and a midterm exam is scheduled in four weeks. If you read the chapter, reviewed it immediately, and then did nothing with it until the exam a month later, you would not remember enough to score well on the exam. To achieve a good grade, you need to review the chapter periodically. You might review the chapter once several days after reading it, again a week later, and once again a week before the exam.

Why Review Is Effective

Immediate and periodic reviews are effective for two reasons:

1. **Review provides repetition.** Repetition is one important way that you learn and remember information. Think about how you learned the multiplication tables or why you know the phone numbers of your closest friends. In both cases, frequent use enables you to remember.

2. **Review consolidates, or draws together, information into a unified whole.** As you read a chapter, you are processing the information piece by piece. Review, both immediate and periodic, provides a means of seeing how each piece relates to each other piece and to the material as a whole.

DIRECTIONS: Read one of the selections at the end of the chapter and review it immediately. Highlight the parts of the selection that you reread as part of your immediate review. Then answer the questions that follow the selection.

DIRECTIONS: Plan a periodic review schedule for one of your courses. Include both textbook chapters and lecture notes.   ▄

Other Aids to Recall

Review and repetition are primary methods of increasing retention. Other aids or methods for increasing your recall include the following:

Building an Intent to Remember

Very few people remember things that they do not intend to remember. Do you remember what color of clothing a friend wore last week? Can you name all the songs you heard on the radio this morning? Can you remember exactly what time you got home last Saturday night? If not, why not? Most likely you cannot remember these facts because at the time you did not see the importance of remembering them. Of course, if you had known that you would be asked these questions, you would most likely have remembered the items. You can see, then, that you must intend to remember things to be able to do so effectively. The same principle holds true for reading and retention. To remember what you read, you must have a clear and strong intent to do so. Unless you have defined what you intend to remember before you begin reading, you will find that it is difficult to recall specific content.

In Chapter 2 you saw how guide questions can help you keep your mind on what you are reading. Now you can see that they also establish an intent to remember.

Before you begin to read an assignment, define as clearly as possible what you intend to remember. Your definition will depend on the type of material, why you are reading it, and how familiar you are with the topic. For instance, if you are reading an essay assigned in preparation for a class discussion, plan to remember not only key ideas but also points of controversy, application, and opinions with which you disagree. Your intent might be quite different in reviewing a chapter for an essay exam. Here you would be looking for important ideas, trends, guiding or controlling principles, and significance of events.

As you read a text assignment, sort important information from that which is less important. Ask and continually answer questions such as:

1. **How important is this information?**
2. **Will I need to know this for the exam?**
3. **Is this a key idea or is it an explanation of a key idea?**
4. **Why did the writer include this?**

Organizing and Categorizing

Information that is organized, or that has a pattern or structure, is easier to remember than material that is randomly arranged. One effective way to organize information is to *categorize* it, to arrange it in groups according to similar characteristics. Suppose, for example, that you had to remember the following list of items to buy for a picnic: cooler, candy, 7-Up, Pepsi, napkins, potato chips, lemonade, peanuts, paper plates. The easiest way to remember this list would be to divide it in groups. You might arrange it as follows:

Drinks	Snacks	Picnic Supplies
7-Up	peanuts	cooler
Pepsi	candy	paper plates
lemonade	potato chips	napkins

By grouping the items into categories, you are putting similar items together. Then, rather than learning one long list of unorganized items, you are learning three shorter, organized lists.

Now imagine you are reading an essay on discipline in public high schools. Instead of learning one long list of reasons for disruptive student behavior, you might divide the reasons into groups such as peer conflicts, teacher-student conflicts, and so forth.

Associating Ideas

Association is a useful way to remember new facts and ideas. It involves connecting new information with previously acquired knowledge. For instance, if you are reading about divorce in a sociology class and are trying to remember a list of common causes, you might try to associate each cause with a person you know who exhibits that problem. Suppose one cause of divorce is lack of communication between the partners. You might remember this by thinking of a couple you know whose lack of communication has caused relationship difficulties.

Suppose you are taking an introductory physics course and are studying Newton's Laws of Motion. The Third Law states: To every action there is always opposed an equal reaction. To remember this law you could associate it with a familiar everyday situation such as swimming that illustrates the law. When you swim you push water backward with your feet, arms, and legs, and the water pushes you forward.

Association involves making connections between new information and what you already know. When you find a connection between the known and the unknown, you can retrieve the new information from your memory along with the old.

Using a Variety of Sensory Modes

Your senses of sight, hearing, and touch can all help you remember what you read. Most of the time, most of us use just one sense—sight—as we read. However, if you are able to use more than one sense, you will find that recall is easier. Activities such as underlining, highlighting, note taking, and outlining involve your sense of touch and enable you to reinforce your learning. If you are having particular difficulty remembering something, try to use your auditory sense as well. You might try repeating the information out loud or listening to someone else repeat it. Most of us tend to rely only on our strengths. Visual learners tend to rely on visual skills and auditory learners tend to depend on their auditory skills, for example. To become a more efficient learner, try to engage additional sensory modes, even if they are not your strengths.

Visualizing

Visualizing, or creating a mental picture of what you have read, often aids recall. In reading descriptive writing that creates a mental picture, visualization is an easy task. In reading about events, people, processes, or procedures, visualization is again relatively simple. However, visualization of abstract ideas, theories, philosophies, and concepts may not be possible. Instead, you may be able to create a visual picture of the relationship of ideas in your mind or on paper. For example, suppose you are reading about the invasion of privacy and learn that there are arguments for and against the storage of personal data about each citizen in large computer banks. You might create a visual image of two lists of information—advantages and disadvantages.

Using Mnemonic Devices

Memory tricks and devices, often called mnemonics, are useful in helping you recall lists of factual information. You might use a rhyme, such as the one used for remembering the number of days in each month: "Thirty days hath September, April, June, and November. . . ." Another device involves making up a word or phrase in which each letter represents an item you are trying to remember. If you remember the name Roy G. Biv, for example, you will be able to recall the colors in the light spectrum: red, orange, yellow, green, blue, indigo, violet.

EXERCISE
8-5

DIRECTIONS: Five study learning situations follow. Decide which of the retention aids described in this section—organization-categorization, association, sensory modes, visualization, and mnemonic devices—might be most useful in each situation and list that aid after each.

1. In a sociology course, you are assigned to read about and remember the causes of child abuse. How might you remember them more easily?

    _____

2. You are studying astronomy and you have to remember the names of the nine planets: Mercury, Venus, Earth, Mars, Jupiter, Saturn, Uranus, Neptune, and Pluto. What retention aid(s) could help you remember them?

    _____

3. You are taking a course in anatomy and physiology and must learn the name and location of each bone in the human skull. How could you learn them easily?

    _____

4. You have an entire chapter to review for a history course, and your instructor has told you that your exam will contain 30 true/false questions on Civil War battles. What could you do as you review to help yourself remember the details of various battles?

_____

5. You are taking a course in twentieth-century history and are studying the causes of the Vietnam War in preparation for an essay exam. You find that there are many causes, some immediate, others long-term. Some have to do with international politics; others, with internal problems in North and South Vietnam. How could you organize your study for this exam?

_____

EXERCISE 8-6

DIRECTIONS: Find a classmate or group of classmates who are taking one of the same courses you are. (If no one is taking the exact same course, join a group of classmates who are taking a similar course: another social science course, another English course, and so forth.) Discuss how you could use each of the recall strategies described in this section to improve your performance in that course.

EXERCISE 8-7

DIRECTIONS: Read the following excerpt. Then decide which retention aid(s) you might use to learn the four types of groups discussed in the material.

SOCIAL GROUPS

. . . In our discussion, we will focus chiefly on social groups—those in which people physically or socially interact. Several other types are also recognized by most sociologists, however, and deserve to be mentioned.

Statistical groups, or more accurately, statistical groupings, are formed not by the group members but by sociologists and statisticians. In 1990, for example, there were 66,090,000 families in the United States with an average size of 3.17 people per family (*Current Population Reports,* Series P–20, No. 447, 1990). The group of women between 5 feet 1 inch and 5 feet 5 inches tall would be another statistical group.[. . .]

Another type of group is the *categorical group* in which a number of people share a common characteristic. Teenagers, the handicapped, unwed mothers, interracial couples, millionaires, redheads, students, women, senior citizens, and virgins are all categorical groups.[. . .]

A third type of group is the *aggregate.* An aggregate is a social group comprising a collection of people who are together in one place. You may join a group of this sort buying an ice cream cone, riding a bus, or waiting to cross a street.[. . .]

A fourth type is the *associational* or *organizational group,* which is especially important in complex industrialized societies. Associational groups consist of people who join together in some organized way to pursue a common interest, and they have a formal structure.[. . .]

Eschleman, Cashion, and Basirico, *Sociology: An Introduction.*

Reading and Learning with the SQ3R System

Throughout this chapter you have become familiar with devices and techniques to improve your ability to remember what you read. You may be wondering how you will be able to use all these techniques and how to combine them most effectively. Many students have asked similar questions. As a result, systems have been developed and tested that combine some of the most useful techniques into a step-by-step procedure for learning as you read.

The SQ3R Reading-Study System

Developed in the 1940s, the SQ3R system has been used successfully for many years. Considerable experimentation has been done, and the system has proven effective in increasing students' retention. It is especially useful for studying textbooks and other highly factual, well-organized materials. Basically, SQ3R is a way of learning as you read. Each of the steps in the system will be briefly summarized, and you will then see how it can be applied to a sample selection.

1. **Survey.** Become familiar with the overall content and organization of the material. You have already learned this technique and know it as prereading.
2. **Question.** Formulate questions about the material that you expect to be able to answer as you read. As you read each successive heading, turn it into a question. This step is similar to establishing guide questions as discussed in Chapter 2.
3. **Read.** As you read each section, actively search for the answers to your guide questions. When you find the answers, highlight or mark portions of the text that concisely state the information.

4. **Recite.** Probably the most important part of the system, "recite" means that you should stop after each section or after each major heading, look away from the page, and try to remember the answer to your question. If you are unable to remember, look back at the page and reread the material. Then test yourself again by looking away from the page and "reciting" the answer to your question.

5. **Review.** Immediately after you have finished reading, go back through the material again and read titles, introductions, summaries, headings, and graphic material. As you read each heading, recall your question and test yourself to see if you can still remember the answer. If you cannot, reread that section again.

Now, to give you a clear picture of how the steps in the SQ3R method work together to produce an efficient approach to reading-study, the method will be applied to a textbook chapter. Suppose you have been assigned to read the following excerpt, "Meanings and Messages," taken from *Human Communication* by Joseph DeVito for a class that is studying verbal and nonverbal communication. Follow each of the SQ3R steps in reading the selection.

1. **Survey.** Preread the article, noticing introductions, headings, first sentences, and the last paragraph. From this prereading you should have an overall picture of what this article is about and what conclusions the author draws about the listening process.

2. **Question.** Using the headings as a starting point, develop several questions that you might expect the article to answer. You might ask questions such as these:

   How are meanings and messages related?
   How can meanings be "in people"?
   What besides words and gestures makes up meanings?
   What makes meanings unique?
   What is the difference between denotative and connotative meanings?
   How does context affect meaning?

3. **Read.** Now read the entire selection, keeping your questions in mind as you read. Stop at the end of each major section and proceed to step 4.

4. **Recite.** After each section, stop reading and check to see if you can recall the answers to your questions.

5. **Review.** When you have finished reading the entire article, take a few minutes to reread the headings and recall your questions. Check to see that you can still recall the answers.

MEANINGS AND MESSAGES

Meaning is an active process created by cooperation between source and receiver—speaker and listener, writer and reader. Here are a few important corollaries concerning meaning.

Meanings Are in People

Meaning depends not only on messages (whether verbal, nonverbal, or both) but on the interaction of those messages and the receiver's own thoughts and feelings. You do not receive meaning; you create meaning. You construct meaning out of the messages you receive combined with your own social and cultural perspectives (beliefs, attitudes, and values, for example). Words do not mean; people mean. Consequently, to discover meaning, you need to look into people and not merely into words.

An example of the confusion that can result when this relatively simple fact is overlooked is provided by Ronald D. Laing, H. Phillipson, and A. Russell Lee in *Interpersonal Perception* and analyzed with insight by Paul Watzlawick in *How Real Is Real?* A couple on the second night of their honeymoon are sitting at a hotel bar. The woman strikes up a conversation with the couple next to her. The husband refuses to communicate with the couple and becomes antagonistic toward his wife as well as the couple. The wife then grows angry because he has created such an awkward and unpleasant situation. Each becomes increasingly disturbed, and the evening ends in a bitter conflict in which each is convinced of the other's lack of consideration. Eight years later, they analyze this argument. Apparently the idea of honeymoon had meant very different things to each of them. To the husband it had meant a "golden opportunity to ignore the rest of the world and simply explore each other." He felt his wife's interaction with the other couple implied there was something lacking in him. To the wife, honeymoon had meant an opportunity to try out her new role as wife. "I had never had a conversation with another couple as a wife before," she said. "Previous to this I had always been a 'girlfriend' or 'fiancée' or 'daughter' or 'sister.'"

One very clear implication of this principle is that meaning is always ambiguous to some extent. Each person's meaning is somewhat different from each other person's, therefore you can never know precisely what any given word or gesture means. Nonverbal gestures—with the obvious exception of emblems—are usually more ambiguous than verbal messages.

Meanings Are More Than Words and Gestures

When you want to communicate a thought or feeling to another person, you do so with relatively few symbols. These represent just a small part of what you are thinking or feeling, much of which remains unspoken. If you were to try to describe every feeling in detail, you would never get on with the job of living. The meanings you seek to communicate are much more than the sum of the words and nonverbal behaviors you use to represent them.

Because of this, you can never fully know what another person is thinking or feeling. You can only approximate it on the basis of the meanings you receive, which, as already noted, are greatly influenced by who you are and what you are feeling. Conversely, others can never fully know you; they too can only approximate what you are feeling. Failure to understand another person or to be understood are not abnormal situations. They are inevitable, although you should realize that with effort you can always understand another person a little better.

Meanings Are Unique

Because meanings are derived from both the messages communicated and the receiver's own thoughts and feelings, no two people ever derive the same meanings. Similarly, because people change constantly, no one person can derive the same meanings on two separate occasions. Who you are can never be separated from the meanings you create. As a result, you need to check your perceptions of another's meanings by asking questions, echoing what you perceive to be the other person's feelings or thoughts, and seeking elaboration and clarification—in general, practicing all the skills identified in the discussion on effective interpersonal perception and listening.

Also recognize that as you change, you also change the meanings you created out of past messages. Thus, although the message sent may not have changed, the meanings you created from it yesterday and the meanings you create today may be quite different. Yesterday, when a special someone said, "I love you," you created certain meanings. But today, when you learn that the same "I love you" was said to three other people or when you fall in love with someone else, you drastically change the meanings you perceive from those three words.

Meanings Are Both Denotative and Connotative

To understand the nature of denotative and connotative meaning, consider a word such as *death*. To a doctor this word might mean, or denote, the point at which the heart stops beating. To doctor, *death* is a word signifying an objective description of an event; the word is basically denotative. To a mother whose son has just died, the words mean much more. It recalls the son's youth, his ambitions, his family, his illness, and so on. To her the word is emotional, subjective, and highly personal. These emotional, subjective, and personal reactions are the word's connotative meanings.

Nonverbal behaviors may also be viewed in terms of their denotation and connotation. Some nonverbal behaviors are largely denotative (for example, a nod signifying yes) while others are primarily connotative (for example, a smile, raised eyebrows, or a wink).

Another distinction between the two types of meaning has already been implied: the denotative meaning of a message is more general or universal; most people would agree with the denotative meanings and would give similar definitions. Connotative meanings, however, are extremely personal, and few people would agree on the precise connotative meaning of a word or nonverbal behavior. Test this idea by trying to get a group of people to agree on the connotative meanings of such words as *religion, racism, democracy, wealth,* and *freedom* or of such nonverbal behaviors as raised eyebrows, arms folded in front of one's chest, or sitting with one's legs crossed. Chances are very good that it will be impossible to reach an agreement.

Meanings Are Context-Based

Verbal and nonverbal communications exist in a context, and that context to a large extent determines the meaning of any verbal or nonverbal behavior. The same words or behaviors may have totally different meanings when they occur in different contexts. For example, the greeting, "How are you?" means "Hello" to someone you pass regularly on the street but means "Is your health improving?" when said to a friend in the hospital. A wink to an attractive person on a bus means something completely different from a wink that signifies a put-on or a lie. Similarly, the meaning of a given signal depends on the behaviors it accompanies or is close to in time. Pounding a fist on the table during a speech in support of a politician means something quite different from that same gesture in response to news of a friend's death. Divorced from the context, it is impossible to tell what meaning was intended just from examining signals. Of course, even if you know the context in detail, you still may not be able to decipher the meaning of the verbal or nonverbal message.

DeVito, *Human Communication.*

How SQ3R Improves Your Reading Efficiency

The SQ3R system improves your reading efficiency in three ways: It increases your comprehension, increases your recall, and saves you valuable time by encouraging you to learn as you read.

Your comprehension is most directly improved by the S and Q steps. By surveying or prereading you acquire an overview of the material that serves as an outline to follow as you read. In the "Question" step, you are focusing your attention and identifying what is important to look for as you read.

Your recall of the material is improved through the "Recite" and "Review" steps. By testing yourself while reading and immediately after you have finished, you are building a systematic review pattern that will provide the necessary repetitions to ensure learning and recall.

Finally, because you are learning as you are reading, you will save time later when you are ready to study the material for an exam. Because you have already learned the material through recitation and review, you will find that you need much less time to prepare for an exam. Instead of learning the material for the first time, all you need to do is refresh your memory and review difficult portions.

EXERCISE 8-8

DIRECTIONS: Divide the class into two groups. Your instructor will assign a reading selection from the text. One group should read the selection using the SQ3R method. The other group should only read the selection once, *without* using any parts of the SQ3R system. Neither group should highlight or annotate. When both groups have finished, groups may question one another to determine which group learned and recalled more information or compare their scores on the comprehension test that accompanies the reading.

Adapting the SQ3R System

As mentioned previously, SQ3R is a very popular, well-researched reading-study system. However, to make the best use of SQ3R, you need to adjust and adapt the procedure to fit the material you are studying and your learning style.

Adapting SQ3R to Suit the Material

Your texts and other required readings vary greatly from course to course. For example, a mathematics text is structured and written quite differently from a sociology text. A chemistry text contains numerous principles, laws, formulas, and problems, whereas a philosophy text contains mostly reading selections and discussions. To accommodate this wide variation in your textbooks and other assigned readings, use the SQ3R system as a base or model. Add, vary, or rearrange the steps to fit the material. For example, when working with a mathematics text, you might add a "Study the Sample Problems" step in which you analyze the problem-solving process. When reading an essay, short story, or poem for a literature class, add a "React" step in which you analyze various features of writing, including the writer's style, tone, purpose, and point of view. For textbooks with a great deal of factual information to learn, you might add "Highlight," "Take Notes," or "Outline" steps.

EXERCISE 8-9

DIRECTIONS: Read one of the selections at the end of the chapter using the SQ3R system and follow each of the steps listed here. Add to or revise the system as necessary. After you complete the "Review" step, answer the multiple-choice questions that follow the selection.

1. **Survey.** Preread the article to get an overview of the organization and content of the article.

2. **Question.** Write the questions you expect to be able to answer when you read the article.

   _____

   _____

3. **Read.** Read the selection, looking for the answers to your questions. As you find them, write them in this space.

_____

_____

_____

4. **Recite.** After each boldface heading, stop and recall your questions and their answers.

5. **Review.** After finishing the article, quickly go back through the article reviewing the major points.

Adapting SQ3R to Suit Your Learning Style

Throughout this text you have probably found that some techniques work better for you than others. This is perfectly natural and consistent with learning theory. You may also have noted that you learn somewhat differently from others. Both findings are due to variations in personal learning style. Each person finds certain methods for learning easier than others. Just as everyone's personality is unique, so is everyone's learning style. Some students, for example, learn best visually. Seeing charts, diagrams, drawings, or pictures—rather than reading or listening—appeals to them. Other students are auditory learners—they learn best by listening. Such students, for instance, would learn more quickly from an instructor's lecture than from a textbook chapter on the same topic.

As part of the process of developing your own reading-study system, consider your learning style. Ask yourself the following questions:

1. Does repeating things out loud help me to learn?
2. Do organizational charts, lists, and diagrams help me to learn?
3. Is writing and rewriting information a good way for me to learn?
4. Does asking challenging questions and answering them help me to learn?
5. Does writing summaries or outlines help me to remember information?

When you have discovered some features of your own learning style, you can adapt the SQ3R system to suit it. For instance, if writing outlines helps you recall the idea structures, replace the "Recite" step with an "Outline" step and make the "Review" step a "Review of Outline" step. Or, if you have discovered that you learn well by listening, replace the "Recite" and "Review" steps with "Tape Record" and "Listen" steps, in which you dictate and record information to be learned and review it by listening to the tape.

As you are no doubt beginning to see, there are numerous possibilities for developing your own reading-study system. The best approach is to test variations until you find the most effective system for you.

DIRECTIONS: List the courses you are taking this semester in the spaces provided. Next to each, indicate what modification(s) in the SQ3R system you would make to suit each course's content and learning requirements:

_____

_____

_____

_____

Reading Scientific/Technical Material

If you are taking courses in the sciences, technologies, engineering, data processing, or health-related fields, you are working with a specialized type of textbook. In this section you will see how scientific and technical textbooks differ from those used in other classes. You will also learn several specific approaches to reading technical material. The key to reading technical material efficiently is to recognize how it differs from other types of material. You must adapt your reading and study methods to accommodate these differences.

Each of the following paragraphs describes early prediction of earthquakes. Read each and decide how they differ.

PARAGRAPH 1

ISAIAH
Information on Seismic Activity, In A Hurry

ISAIAH (Information on Seismic Activity, In A Hurry) is a modular real-time automatic earthquake analysis system. It produces picks, locations, and magnitudes, generally within 40 seconds of origin time.

ISAIAH consists of three primary real-time modules:

- **PICKLE**—makes phase picks in real-time

- **FALX**—takes the picks, associates them into earthquakes, determines the type of phase (e.g. P, S and others as defined by the site manager). It then calculates a solution using HYPOINVERSE and optionally places the results in a random access catalog file.

- **WART**—first calculates a P-wave magnitude using amplitude data from PICKLE. It then defines windows about the likely location of P-wave and S-wave arrivals and searches those slices of time series for peak amplitude. It then calculates P- and S-wave magnitudes using these amplitudes.

http://www-social.wr.usgs.gov/given/isaiah.html

PARAGRAPH 2

Quake Warning Before the Shaking

Exciting progress is being made in *real-time earthquake warnings*. It's an old idea, that you could hook up a radio to a seismograph and have it send you a message when it feels a quake. You'd have a useful amount of time to react—even five seconds would be enough for a classroom of kids to get under their desks, or for you to save that file you're working on. And with 30 seconds' warning, you could pull a fire engine out of its garage, start your hospital's emergency power, do quick computer backups and prepare in many other ways.

http://geology.about.com/science/geology/library/weekly/aa011198.html

Did you notice that the first paragraph presents only precise, factual information? The words used have very exact meanings. Some words have technical meanings (S-wave magnitude, P-wave magnitude). Others are everyday words used in a specialized way ("pickle," "windows"). Abbreviations, ("ISAIAH, HYPOINVERSE") are also used. Because of the language, the paragraph does not allow for interpretation or expression of opinion. You do not learn whether the author is excited about ISAIAH, or whether he feels it is a worthwhile system. The purpose of the paragraph is to give clear, detailed information about ISAIAH.

The second paragraph is written quite differently; it presents fewer facts and more examples. Words such as "exciting progress" and "useful" reveal the writer's attitude toward the subject. This paragraph helps you imagine how advance notice can help people prepare for an earthquake.

Paragraph 1 is an example of scientific/technical writing. It is very precise, exact, and factual. This section discusses the particular features of scientific/technical material and gives suggestions for reading this type of writing.

Fact Density

Scientific and technical writing is highly factual, dense, and concise. A large amount of information is closely packed together into a relatively small space on the page. Compared to many other forms of writing, technical writing may seem complicated and difficult. Here are a few suggestions for handling densely written material:

1. **Read technical material more slowly and carefully than other textbook content.** Plan to spend more time on a technical reading assignment than on other assignments.

2. **Plan on rereading certain sections several times.** Sometimes it is useful to read a section once rather quickly just to learn what main ideas it contains. Then read it carefully a second time, fitting together all the facts that explain the important ideas.

3. **Keep a notebook of significant information.** In some textbooks you can highlight what is important to remember. (This method is discussed in Chapter 7.) However, because technical books are so highly factual, highlighting is usually not effective. Students who have tried this report that it seems like everything is important and that they end up with most of the page highlighted. Instead, try using a notebook to record information you need to remember. Recording this information in your own words is a useful way of checking whether or not you have really understood it and will increase your retention. Figure 8.2 shows an excerpt from a nursing student's notebook. Notice that this student included definitions and diagrams as well as detail.

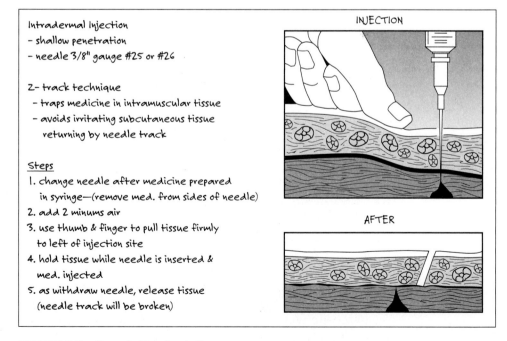

FIGURE 8.2   Sample Notebook Page

The Vocabulary of Technical Writing

Scientific/technical writing in each subject area is built on a set of very precise, exact word meanings. Each field has its own language, and you must learn the language in order to understand the material. Here are a few sentences taken from textbooks in several technical fields. As you read, notice the large number of technical words used in each.

AUTOMOTIVE TECHNOLOGY

A vacuum modulator is used to convert engine manifold vacuum into a signal pressure that increases as engine vacuum decreases.

Halderman and Mitchell, *Automotive Technology.*

MEDICAL ASSISTING

The inflammatory process produces dilation of blood vessels due to an increased blood flow, production of watery fluids and materials (exudate), and the invasion of monocytes (white blood cells) and neutrophils into the injured tissues to produce phagocytosis.

Fremgen, *Essentials of Medical Assisting.*

ENVIRONMENTAL TECHNOLOGY

Glucuronosyltransferases represent one of the major enzymes that carry out the reactions of exogenous and endogenous compounds to polar water-soluble compounds.

Ostler et al., *Health Effects of Hazardous Materials.*

In these examples, some words are familiar ones with new, unfamiliar meanings (*reactions, polar*). Others are words you've probably never seen (*phagocytosis, endogenous*).

In scientific/technical writing you'll encounter two types of specialized vocabulary. First, everyday words with which you are familiar are given entirely new, technical meanings. Here are a few examples.

1. Institution (sociology): a cluster of values, norms, statuses, and roles that develop around a basic social goal

2. Pan (photography): to follow the motion of a moving object with a camera

3. Cabinet (government): a group of presidential advisers who head executive departments

A second type of specialized vocabulary uses words you may have never heard or seen. These also have very exact, precise meanings. Several examples are listed:

Field	Technical Word	Meaning
computer science	modem	an interface (connector) that allows the computer to send and receive digital signals over telephone lines or through satellites
astronomy	magnetosphere	the magnetic fields that surround the earth or other magnetized planets
biology	cocci	spherically shaped bacteria

Tips for Learning Specialized Vocabulary

There are a number of tips that may make it easier for you to learn specialized vocabulary:

1. **Keep a notebook or a notebook section for listing new words in each course.** Add words to the list as they appear in the text.

2. **Use context clues to try to discover the definition of a new term.** (Refer to Chapter 3 for more information.) A definition clue is often provided when the word is introduced for the first time. As each new word is introduced, mark it in your text and later transfer it to your notebook. Organize this portion of your notebook by chapter. Refer to your notebook for review and reference. Use the card system (see Chapter 3) to learn words you are having trouble remembering.

3. **Prefix-root-suffix learning is a particularly useful approach for developing technical vocabulary.** In many fields, the technical words use a particular set of prefixes, roots, and suffixes that are meaningful in that area. For example, fields related to medicine use a set of prefixes, roots, and suffixes in many words. Here are several examples using prefixes:

Prefix	Meaning	Example	Definition
cardi-	heart	cardiogram	test that measures contractions of the heart
hem-/hema-	blood	hematology	study of the blood
hypo-	under	hypodermic needle	needle that goes under the skin
osteo-	bone	osteopath	doctor who specializes in treatment of the bones

In most scientific/technical fields you will find a core of commonly used prefixes, roots, and suffixes. Keep a list of common word parts in your notebook. Add to the list as you work through the course. For those word parts you have difficulty remembering, use a variation of the word card system. Write the word part on the front of the card and its meaning, pronunciation, and an example on the back.

4. **Learn to pronounce each new term you come across.** Pronouncing the word is a good way to fix it in your memory and make you feel confident in its use.

5. **Use the glossary in the back of your text.** A glossary is more useful than a dictionary because it gives the meanings of the words as used in the field you are studying; you won't have to waste time sorting through numerous meanings to find the appropriate one.

6. **If you are majoring in a technical field, consider purchasing a subject-area dictionary.** Many academic disciplines have a specialized dictionary that indexes commonly used terminology particular to that field. Nursing students, for example, often buy a copy of Taber's *Cyclopedic Medical Dictionary*.

Abbreviation and Notation Systems

Many scientific/technical fields use a set of abbreviations and notations (signs and symbols extensively). These are used as shortcuts to writing out complete words or meanings and are used in formulas, charts, and drawings. Here are a few examples:

Field	Symbol	Meaning
chemistry	C	carbon
	H	hydrogen
	O	oxygen
biology	X	crossed with
	♂	male organism
	♀	female organism
physics	M	mass
astronomy	D	diameter
	Δ	distance

To read scientific/technical material efficiently, learn the abbreviation and notation systems as soon as possible. You will save time and avoid interrupting your reading to look up a particular symbol. Check to see if lists of abbreviations and symbols are included in the appendix (reference section) in the back of your text. Also, make a list in your notebook of those symbols you need to learn. Make a point of using these symbols in your class notes whenever possible; regular use is the key to learning them.

Illustrations

Most scientific/technical books contain numerous drawings, charts, tables, and diagrams. Although these make the text appear difficult and complicated, they actually make things easier to understand. Illustrations give you a visual picture of the idea or process being explained. The following figure is a diagram taken from an environmental technology text that explains how sewage effluent diffuses in seawater. The accompanying text is given here:

> Treated sewage effluent from cities and towns is discharged directly into the ocean in many coastal areas. The pipes that carry the wastewater into the ocean are called *outfalls*. These are often large-diameter conduits that may extend far off-shore. For example, the outfall from the Deer Island Treatment Plant in Boston is 12.5 km (7.5 mi) long.
>
> When sewage flows out of the open end of an outfall pipe, it forms a rising column because it is warmer and less dense than seawater. This is illustrated in Figure A. When it reaches the surface, the column of sewage forms a large bubble or *boil*, which moves in the direction of the surface currents. As the current carries the boil, the plume of diluted wastewater forms, similar to a plume from a smoke-stack. Unfortunately, the plume is sometimes carried toward shore, raising the coliform counts near recreational areas. Occasionally, beaches must be closed for swimming because of excessive coliform counts.

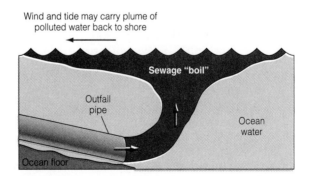

FIGURE A   Diffusion of Sewage in Seawater

> The effectiveness of ocean disposal of sewage effluent depends on how well the effluent is dispersed and spread out in the ocean when it exits the outfall. Sufficient dispersion of the effluent will facilitate the natural purification process, reduce bacteria concentrations, and prevent pollution at shore areas.
>
> Nathanson, *Basic Environmental Technology.*

Here are a few suggestions on how to learn from illustrations:

1. **Refer back and forth between the text paragraphs and the illustrations.** Illustrations are intended to be used with the paragraphs that refer to them. You may have to stop several times while reading the text to refer to an illustration. For example, when "outfall pipe" is mentioned in the example, you should stop reading and check the diagram to see where it is located. You may also have to reread parts of the explanation several times.

2. **Study each illustration carefully.** Notice its title or caption. This tells you what the illustration is intended to show. Then look at each part and try to see how they connect. Note any abbreviations, symbols, arrows, or labels. In the diagram of sewage effluents, the arrows are important. They indicate the direction in which the sewage flows after it is discharged.

3. **Test your understanding of an illustration by drawing and labeling your own illustration without looking at the one in the text.** Then compare your drawing with the text. If you left anything out, continue drawing and checking until your drawing is complete and correct. Make a final drawing in your notebook and use it for review and study.

Examples and Sample Problems

Technical books include numerous examples and sample problems. Use the following suggestions when working with examples and problems.

1. **Pay more attention to examples than you normally do in other textbooks.** Often, examples or sample problems in technical books help you understand how rules, principles, theories, or formulas are actually used. Creative learners who usually prefer experimentation and avoid rules and examples may find that sample problems simplify an otherwise complex process. Think of examples as connections between ideas on paper and the practical, everyday use of those ideas.

2. **Be sure to work through sample problems.** Carefully make sure that you understand what was done in each step and why it was done. For particularly difficult problems, write a step-by-step list of how to solve that type of problem in your notebook. Refer back to sample problems as guides or models when working problems at the end of the chapter or others assigned by your instructor.

3. **Use the problems at the end of the chapter as a self-test.** As you work through each problem, keep track of rules and formulas that you didn't

know and had to look up. Also, notice the types of problems you could not solve without looking back at the sample problems. You'll need to do more work with each of these types.

DIRECTIONS: Read the following excerpt from *Conceptual Physics,* an introductory physics textbook by Paul Hewitt, and answer the questions that follow.

REFLECTED LIGHT AND COLOR

Roses are red and violets are blue; colors intrigue artists and physics types too. To the physicist, the colors of objects are not in the substances of the objects themselves or even in the light they emit or reflect. Color is a physiological experience and is in the eye of the beholder. So when we say that light from a rose is red, in a stricter sense we mean that it appears red. Many organisms, including people with defective color vision, will not see the rose as red at all.

The colors we see depend on the frequency of the light we see. Different frequencies of light are perceived as different colors; the lowest frequency we detect appears to most people as the color red, and the highest as violet. Between them range the infinite number of hues that make up the color spectrum of the rainbow. By convention these hues are grouped into the seven colors of red, orange, yellow, green, blue, indigo, and violet. These colors together appear white. The white light from the sun is a composite of all the visible frequencies.

Except for light sources such as lamps, lasers, and gas discharge tubes, most of the objects around us reflect rather than emit light. They reflect only part of the light that is incident upon them, the part that gives them their color.

SELECTIVE REFLECTION

A rose, for example, doesn't emit light; it reflects light. If we pass sunlight through a prism and then place a deep-red rose in various parts of the spectrum, the rose will appear brown or black in all parts of the spectrum except in the red. In the red part of the spectrum, the petals will appear red, but the green stem and leaves will appear black. This shows that the red rose has the ability to reflect red light, but it cannot reflect other kinds of light; the green leaves have the ability to reflect green light and likewise cannot reflect other kinds of light. When the rose is held in white light, the petals appear red and the leaves green, because the petals reflect the red part of the white light and the leaves reflect the green part of the white light. To understand why objects reflect specific colors of light, we must turn our attention to the atom.

Light is reflected from objects in a manner similar to the way sound is "reflected" from a tuning fork when another that is nearby sets it into vibration. A tuning fork can be made to vibrate even when the frequencies are not matched, although at significantly reduced amplitudes. The same is true of atoms and molecules. Using the spring model of the atom we discussed in the previous chapter, we can think of

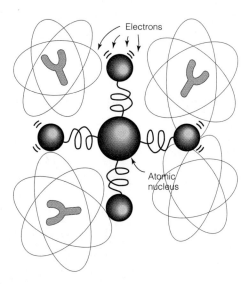

FIGURE A The outer electrons in an atom vibrate as if they were attached to the nucleus by springs. As a result, atoms and molecules behave somewhat like optical tuning forks.

atoms and molecules as three-dimensional tuning forks with electrons that behave as tiny oscillators that vibrate as if attached by invisible springs (Figure A). Electrons can be forced into vibration (oscillation) by the vibrating (oscillating) electric fields of electromagnetic waves.* Once vibrating, these electrons send out their own electromagnetic waves just as vibrating acoustical tuning forks send out sound waves.

Atoms (and molecules) have their own natural frequencies; electrons of one kind of atom can be set into vibration at frequencies that are different from the frequencies for other atoms. At the resonant frequencies where the amplitudes of oscillation are large, light is absorbed. But at frequencies below and above the resonant frequencies, light is re-emitted. If the material is transparent the re-emitted light can travel through the material. For both opaque and transparent materials, the light re-emitted back into the medium from which it came is the reflected light.

Usually a material will absorb some frequencies of light and reflect the rest. If a material absorbs most visible frequencies and reflects red, for example, the material appears red. If it reflects all the visible frequencies, like the white part of this page, it will be the same color as the light that shines on it. If a material absorbs all the light that shines on it, it reflects none and is black.

When white light falls on a flower, some of the frequencies are absorbed by the cells in the flower and some are reflected. Cells that contain chlorophyll absorb most of the frequencies and reflect the green part of the light that falls on it. The petals of a red rose, on the other hand, reflect primarily red light, with a lesser amount of blue. Interestingly enough, the petals of most yellow flowers, like daffodils, reflect red and green as well as yellow. Yellow daffodils reflect a broad band of frequencies. The reflected colors of most objects are not pure single-frequency colors, but are composed of a spread of frequencies.

---

*We use the words oscillate and vibrate interchangeably. Also, the words oscillators and vibrators have the same meaning.

FIGURE B   Color depends on the light source.

An object can only reflect frequencies that are present in the illuminating light. The appearance of a colored object therefore depends on the kind of light used. A candle flame emits light that is deficient in blue; its light is yellowish. An incandescent lamp emits light that is richer toward the lower frequencies, enhancing the reds. In a fabric with a little bit of red in it, for example, the red will be more apparent under an incandescent lamp than when illuminated with a fluorescent lamp. Fluorescent lamps are richer in the higher frequencies, so blues are enhanced under them. With various kinds of illumination, it is difficult to tell the true color of objects. Colors appear different in daylight than they appear when illuminated by either kind of lamp (Figure B).

SELECTIVE TRANSMISSION

The color of a transparent object depends on the color of the light it transmits. A red piece of glass appears red because it absorbs all the colors that compose white light, except red, which it *transmits*. Similarly, a blue piece of glass appears blue because it transmits primarily blue and absorbs the other colors that illuminate it. The piece of glass contains dyes or *pigments*—fine particles that selectively absorb certain frequencies and selectively transmit others. From an atomic point of view, electrons in the pigment molecules are set into vibration by the illuminating light. Some of the frequencies are absorbed by the pigments, and others are re-emitted from molecule to molecule in the glass. The energy of the absorbed frequencies increases the kinetic energy of the molecules and the glass is warmed. Ordinary window glass is colorless because it transmits all visible frequencies equally well.

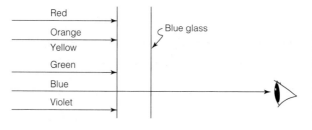

FIGURE C   Only energy having the frequency of blue light is transmitted; energy of the other frequencies is absorbed and warms the glass.

QUESTIONS

1. When red light shines on a red rose, why do the leaves become warmer than the petals?
2. When green light shines on a rose, why do the petals look black?
3. If you hold a match, a candle flame, or any small source of white light in between you and a piece of red glass, you'll see two reflections from the glass: one from the front surface and one from the back surface. What color of reflections will you see?

1. How does this excerpt compare with the psychology textbook excerpt (pp. 325–327) for each of the following characteristics?

   a. fact density _____

   b. number of technical terms _____

   c. number and use of illustrations _____

   _____

   d. number of examples _____

2. Underline terminology you would need to learn to pass an exam based on this chapter.

   _____

3. Explain the purpose of each of the following figures:

   a. Figure A _____

   b. Figure B _____

   c. Figure C _____

4. Answer the questions that appear at the end of the excerpt.

   1. _____

   _____

   2. _____

   _____

   _____

   3. _____

   _____

   _____

Critical Thinking Tip #8

Using Your Background Knowledge and Experience

Your familiarity with a topic can influence how easily you can remember information about it. A brand new topic is more difficult to learn than one you already know something about. In fact, the more familiar a topic, the more easily you can learn new information about it. Your brain establishes connections or links between old and new information. By tying your new learning to the old, you will find you can remember the new information more easily.

When you read the title of a chapter, you may think you know nothing about it, but often you will discover you know more about it than you originally thought. For example, suppose you are ready to begin reading a section of a chapter in your psychology book titled "Aggressive Behavior." At first you may say you know nothing about aggression. However, aggression is something we all witness daily: A man kicks a soda machine when he loses his money; a child slaps another child; a phone salesperson aggressively pursues a conversation until you hang up. Once you realize that you are familiar with aggression, reading the chapter section will become both easier and more interesting.

Sometimes you have to work a bit to discover what you already know. Try the following techniques:

1. Ask yourself: What have I already read or seen that is related to this topic?
2. Brainstorm. Spend two or three minutes thinking about or writing anything that comes to mind about your topic.
3. Try to think of situations or examples from your own experiences that relate to the topic.

Then, apply your prior knowledge. If you are reading about types of aggression, for example, decide which type the soda machine example fits into. Connecting new to old learning will pay off in increased retention and recall!

Summary

1. How are textbook chapters organized to help you learn?

Textbooks are unique information sources and vehicles for learning. Textbook chapters use a system of headings and subheadings to organize information and show what is

important. They also use other aids to help you learn, including
- chapter previews
- special interest inserts
- marginal notations
- summaries
- lists of new terminology
- review questions
- discussion questions
- chapter outlines
- suggested readings or references

2. Describe the two types of review that you can use to increase retention.

Immediate review is done right after reading while the information is still fresh in your mind. Periodic review is done at a later time to refresh your recall of the material.

3. What other aids or methods can be used to increase your recall?

Other aids to retention include
- intent to remember
- organization/categorization
- association
- use of sensory modes
- visualization
- mnemonic devices

4. What is the SQ3R system for reading and learning?

The SQ3R system is a method for increasing reading efficiency and flexibility that directly enhances your retention. The steps are
- survey
- question
- read
- recite
- review

5. What should be considered when adapting the SQ3R system?

To make the best use of the SQ3R method, you should adapt it to suit both the material you are reading and how you learn best. You should consider the reading material's structure and content when adapting SQ3R. Also, you should make adjustments that incorporate the methods for learning that work best for you.

6. How does writing in the scientific/technical fields differ from that in other areas of study?

Textbooks in scientific/technical fields are highly specialized and differ from other texts in that technical material

- is factually dense
- uses technical vocabulary
- uses abbreviations and notation systems
- uses a large number of illustrations and examples
- contains sample problems

READING SELECTION 15

PSYCHOLOGY

PROBLEM SOLVING
Josh R. Gerow
From *Essentials of Psychology*

This psychology textbook excerpt discusses problem-solving strategies. Activate your thinking by pre-reading and answering the following questions.

1. *How would you define a problem? What are its characteristics?*
2. *What steps do you follow in working through a problem?*

— · —

1   Sometimes our goals are obvious, our present situation is clear, and how to get from where we are to where we want to be is obvious. In these cases, we really don't have a problem, do we? Say you want to have a nice breakfast. You have butter, eggs, bacon, and bread. You also have the implements needed to prepare these foods, and you know how to use them. You know that, for you, a nice breakfast would be two eggs over easy, three strips of fried bacon, and a piece of buttered toast. With little hesitation, you can engage in the appropriate behaviors to reach your goal.

2   A problem exists when there is a discrepancy between one's present state and one's perceived goal, *and* there is no readily apparent way to get from one to the other. In situations where the path to goal attainment is not clear or obvious, you need to engage in problem-solving behaviors.

3   A problem situation has three major components: (1) an *initial state,* which is the situation as it is perceived to exist at the moment; (2) a *goal state,* which is the situation as the problem solver would like it to be; and (3) *routes or strategies* for getting from the initial state to the goal state.

4   In addition, psychologists make a distinction between well-defined and ill-defined problems. Well-defined problems are those in which both the initial state and the goal state are clearly defined. "What English word can be made from the letters *teralbay?*" We recognize this question as presenting a problem. We understand the question, have some ideas about how we might go about answering it, and surely we'll know when we have succeeded. "How do you get home from campus if you discover that your car won't start?" We know our initial state, we'll know when we have reached our goal (when we are at home), but we have to undertake a new or different way to get there.

5   Most of the problems that we face every day, though, are of the ill-defined variety. We don't have a clear idea of what we are starting with, nor are we able to identify a ready solution. "What should my college major be?" Many high school seniors (and some college seniors) do not even know what their options are. They have few ideas about how to find out about possible college majors. And once they have selected a major, they are not at all sure that their choice was the best one—which may be why so many college students change their majors so often.

6   Because ill-defined problems usually involve many variables that are difficult to define, much less control, psychologists tend to study problems that are at least reasonably well-defined.

Problem Representation

7   Once we realize that we're faced with a problem, the first thing we need to do is to put it in a form that allows us to think about it in terms that we can work with. We need to come up with a way to *represent* the problem in our own minds, interpreting it so that the initial state and the goal state are clear to us. We also need to note if there are restrictions on how we can go about seeking solutions. In short, we need to understand the nature of the problem. We need to make the problem meaningful, relating it to information we have available in our memories.

8   Finding the best way to represent a problem is not a simple task. Very often, problem representation is *the* stumbling block to finding a solution (Bourne et al., 1983). Once you realize that you are faced with a problem, your first step should be to represent it in a variety of ways. Eliminate any inessential information. Relate the problem to other problems of a similar type that you have solved before. Having done so, if the solution is still not obvious, you may have to develop some strategy to find a solution. We now turn to how one might go about generating possible solutions.

Problem-Solving Strategies

9   Once you have represented the initial state of a problem and have a clear idea of what an acceptable goal might be, you still have to figure out how to get to your goal. Even after you have adequately represented a problem, how to go about solving it may not be readily apparent. You might spend a few minutes guessing wildly at a solution, but soon you'll have to settle on some strategy. In this context, a strategy is a systematic plan for generating possible solutions that can be tested to see if they are correct. The main advantage of cognitive strategies appears to be that they permit the problem solver to exercise some degree of control over the task at hand. They allow individuals to choose the skills and knowledge that they will bring to bear on any particular problem (Gagné, 1984). There are several possible strategies that one might choose. In this section, we'll consider two different types of strategies—algorithms and heuristics.

10   An algorithm is a problem-solving strategy that guarantees that you will arrive at a solution. It will involve systematically exploring and evaluating all possible solutions until the correct one is found. It is sometimes referred to as a *generate-test* strategy because one generates hypotheses about potential solutions and then tests each one in turn. Because of their speed of computation, most computer programs designed to solve problems use algorithmic strategies.

11   Simple anagram problems (letters of a word presented in a scrambled fashion) can be solved using an algorithm. "What English word has been scrambled to make *uleb?*" With sufficient patience, you systematically can rearrange these four letters until you hit on a correct solution: *leub, lueb, elub, uleb, buel, beul, blue!* There it is, *blue*. With only four letters to deal with, finding a solution generally doesn't take long—there are only 24 possible arrangements of four letters $(4 \times 3 \times 2 \times 1 = 24)$.

12   On the other hand, consider the anagram composed of eight letters that we mentioned ear-

lier: *teralbay*. There are 40,320 possible combinations of these eight letters—$8 \times 7 \times 6 \times 5 \times 4 \times 3 \times 2 \times 1 = 40{,}320$ (Reynolds & Flagg, 1983). Unless your system for moving letters around just happens to start in a good place, you could spend a lot of time before finding a combination that produces an English word. If we were dealing with a 10-letter word, there would be 3,628,800 possible combinations to check.

13   Imagine that you go to the supermarket to find just one item: a small jar of horseradish. You're sure the store has horseradish, but you have no idea where to find it. One plan would be to systematically go up and down every aisle of the store, checking first the top shelf, then the second, then the third, until you spied the horseradish. This strategy will work *if* the store really does carry horseradish *and if* you search carefully. There must be a better way to solve such problems. We could use some heuristic strategy.

14   A heuristic strategy is an informal, rule-of-thumb method for generating and testing problem solutions. Heuristics are more economical strategies than algorithms. When one uses a heuristic, there is no guarantee of success. On the other hand, heuristics are usually less time-consuming than algorithm strategies and lead toward goals in a logical, sensible way.

15   A heuristic strategy for finding horseradish in a supermarket might take you to different sections in the store in the order you believed to be most reasonable. You might start with spices, and you'd be disappointed. You might look among the fresh vegetables. Then, upon recalling that horseradish needs to be refrigerated, you go to the dairy case, and there you'd find the horseradish. You would not have wasted your time searching the cereal aisle or the frozen food section—which you might have done if you tried an algorithmic search. Another, more reasonable, heuristic would be to ask an employee where the horseradish is kept.

16   If you have tried the *teralbay* anagram problem, you probably used a heuristic strategy. To do so, you rely on your knowledge of English. You seriously consider only those letter combinations that you know occur frequently. You generate and test the most common combinations first. You just don't worry much about the possibility that the solution may contain a combination like *brty*. Nor do you search for a word with an *aae* string in it. You explore words that end in *able,* because you know these to be fairly common. But that doesn't work. What about *br* words? No, that doesn't work either. How about words with the combination *tray* in them? *Traybeal?* No. *Baletray?* No. "Oh! Now I see it: betrayal."

Examining Reading Selection 15

Checking Your Vocabulary

Directions: Using context, word parts, or a dictionary if necessary, circle the letter of the meaning for each word as it is used in the reading.

1. discrepancy (paragraph 2)
   a. condition
   b. option
   c. signal
   d. disagreement

2. components (paragraph 3)
   a. difficulties
   b. road blocks
   c. routes
   d. parts

3. variables (paragraph 6)
   a. differences
   b. solutions
   c. factors
   d. restrictions

4. inessential (paragraph 8)
   a. critical
   b. descriptive
   c. unimportant
   d. inaccurate

5. cognitive (paragraph 9)
   a. mental
   b. physical
   c. random
   d. representational

Checking Your Comprehension

Directions: Circle the letter of the best answer.

6. This reading is primarily concerned with
   a. types of problems.
   b. the heuristics of problem solving.
   c. the process of problem solving.
   d. algorithms and heuristics.

7. The main point of this reading is that problem solving
   a. depends largely on intuition.
   b. is a random process.
   c. is a systematic, logical process.
   d. varies according to an individual's cognitive style.

8. According to the reading, a problem can best be defined as
   a. being unable to make reasonable choices.
   b. an unresolved or undefinable issue.
   c. a conflict among strategies.
   d. a discrepancy between present state and goal state.

9. An algorithmic strategy is a process of
   a. brainstorming possible solutions.
   b. generating and testing all possible solutions.
   c. distinguishing initial state from goal state.
   d. devising a systematic plan for problem solving.

10. Ill-defined problems
    a. cannot be represented.
    b. have no solutions.
    c. are always solved in a similar way as well-defined problems.
    d. usually involve many variables.

11. This textbook excerpt focuses primarily on
    a. differences.
    b. processes.
    c. solutions.
    d. causes.

Thinking Critically

12. A heuristic strategy differs from an algorithmic solution in that
    a. an algorithmic solution does not guarantee a solution.
    b. a heuristic system explores fewer possible solutions.
    c. a heuristic strategy is more systematic.
    d. an algorithmic strategy is less time-consuming.

13 Searching for your lost car keys by checking places where you usually place them is an example of
    a. problem representation.
    b. an ill-defined problem.
    c. an algorithmic solution.
    d. a heuristic solution.

14. Which of the following words best describes the author's attitude toward his subject?
    a. casual
    b. respectful
    c. indifferent
    d. serious

15. The writer relies on which of the following to explain his ideas to the reader?
    a. examples
    b. comparisons
    c. statistics
    d. personal experiences

Questions for Discussion

1. Give an example of a well-defined problem faced by the government today. Explain a strategy that could be used to resolve it.
2. Discuss why a heuristic solution to a problem you currently have is more economical than an algorithmic solution.
3. Think about a problem you've had with transportation. How could it have been solved using an algorithmic strategy? How could it have been solved using a heuristic strategy?

Selection 15:			1514 words
Finishing Time:	___	___	___
	HR.	MIN.	SEC.
Starting Time:	___	___	___
	HR.	MIN.	SEC.
Reading Time:		___	___
		MIN.	SEC.
WPM Score:			___
Comprehension Score:			___ %

READING SELECTION 16

CAREERS: ANIMAL MANAGEMENT

THE VALUE OF PET OWNERSHIP

H. Stephen Damron

From *Introduction to Animal Science*

Why do people keep pets? To many people, pets are companions. Read this selection to learn the added benefits of pet ownership and to discover new uses of service dogs.

— · —

1   Parents often use pets as a tool in child rearing. Pets provide a mechanism for teaching children about basic biology as well as the larger lessons about life and death. Children learn responsibility by caring for the animal. In addition, the affection of a pet helps children cope with the stresses of life. With the high divorce rate of modern life, pets can help relieve the loneliness that comes from absent parents and siblings. Pets also provide children with willing play-acting partners in their games of fantasy. There is surely a special place in the hereafter for the dog or cat that allows itself to be dressed in doll clothes and pushed around in a baby stroller, or dressed in an army helmet and dragged across the yard in a tank (little red

wagon). In such games, children learn to express feelings, act out conflicts, and practice their imaginations. Although it is difficult to prove cause and effect, studies reveal that adults who had pets as children are less likely to become criminals.

2   Medical studies have verified the benefits of pet ownership. The reasons appear to be physical, emotional, and social. The animals themselves provide companionship. However, multiple studies have demonstrated that pets provide a means for people to meet and interact, helping to alleviate loneliness and depression that is often a result of isolation. Pets help people to be more active because they need daily care. If the pet is a dog, this care often includes walks for the dog, which exercise the owner as well. Pet owners (both children and adults) have lower blood pressure than people who don't own pets. Studies on the aged have confirmed that pet owners have increased longevity and live more satisfying lives compared to their peers without

pets. Elderly pet owners visit the doctor less often and use fewer medications. Pets give some elderly individuals the opportunity to nurture, to touch and be touched, and a sense of safety and security. Interestingly, even birds are successful in making people feel safer. There is increasing interest in the ways that animals can be used to improve the physical and emotional health of the elderly. Studies suggest that animal visitation and full-time residence of pets with their owners in nursing homes and retirement communities should be more the norm than the exception.

3   The use of service animals is one of the most exciting of the developing interests in pet species, predominantly dogs. Nearly 9% of the population of the United States has a disabling handicap. Over half of these people are disabled due to serious visual impairment or blindness, loss or lack of physical mobility, or hearing impairment or complete deafness. Service animals can help people with these handicaps. Dogs have been trained as seeing-eye dogs in the United States in a serious, formal way at least since the 1929 founding of The Seeing Eye Inc., of Morristown, New Jersey. Dogs for the Deaf is a hearing-dog training and placement service that began in 1978. This group takes unwanted dogs from animal shelters and trains them to alert their partners to such sounds as telephones, doorbells, smoke alarms, and other important sounds. Canine Companions for Independence, with national headquarters in Santa Rosa, California, and regional offices across the United States, is perhaps the best-known of several groups that train service, hearing, and social dogs. The dogs help physically disabled individuals in wheelchairs by carrying packages, pulling wheelchairs, turning electric switches on and off, opening doors, and performing other chores to allow independent living for their human companions.

4   Animals are being increasingly used in mental and emotional therapy. Emotionally disturbed children and adults are often more willing to talk in the presence of an animal, often directing responses to questions by the therapist to the

Parents often provide pets to help teach their children responsibility.

animal. This phenomenon is being expanded to help abused children, autistic children, the mentally ill, dysfunctional families, and adult victims of violence. Rehabilitation centers use pets to provide motivation to patients to improve their strength, coordination, and mobility. Therapeutic riding programs have been started all across the country. These programs have developed into a legitimate health profession with special training, formal certification procedures, and a growing body of research findings to support their value.

5   In prisons, innovative programs have been started that aim at improving the behavior and outlook of inmates, as well as providing benefit to broader society. Two programs associated with prisons have been established with the encouragement of Sister Pauline Quinn. The Wisconsin Correctional Liberty Dog Program is located at the Sanger B Powers Correctional Facility in Oneida, Wisconsin. One goal of the Liberty Dog Program is to meet the needs of physically challenged people by providing them with a service dog to help them live more independent lives. The other goal is to allow the prisoners the opportunity to serve their community. The Prison Pet Partnership Program, located at the Washington State Corrections Center for Women, helps inmates learn how to train, groom, and board dogs within the prison walls. Animals are placed with handicapped and disabled individuals and families. Other programs are found across the country. Inmates at 20 different Ohio prisons work with Pilot Dogs Inc., a Columbus-based organization that provides guide dogs for the blind. The inmates raise and socialize the dogs prior to their training as seeing-eye dogs. A program called Friends for Folks at the Lexington Correctional Facility in Oklahoma trains dogs as companions. These programs benefit both inmate and ultimate recipient of the animal.

WRITING ABOUT READING SELECTION 16*

Checking Your Vocabulary

Directions: Complete each of the following items; refer to a dictionary if necessary.

1. Discuss the connotative meanings of the word *pet.*

2. Define each of the following words:
   a. mechanism (paragraph 1)

   _____

   b. confirmed (paragraph 2)

   _____

   _____

   c. longevity (paragraph 2)

   _____

   d. nurture (paragraph 2)

   _____

   e. certification (paragraph 4)

   _____

3. Define the word *alleviate* (paragraph 2) and underline the word or phrase that provides a context clue for its meaning.

   _____

   _____

4. Define the word *regional* (paragraph 3) and underline the word or phrase that provides a context clue for its meaning.

   _____

   _____

____

* Multiple-choice questions are contained in Part 6 (page 585).

5. Determine the meanings of the following words by using word parts:

   a. verified (paragraph 2)

   _____

   b. interact (paragraph 2)

   _____

   c. impairment (paragraph 3)

   _____

   _____

   d. mobility (paragraph 3)

   _____

   e. therapeutic (paragraph 4)

   _____

Checking Your Comprehension

6. What is the main purpose of this selection?

   _____

   _____

7. Name two ways in which pets are helpful to the growth of children.

   _____

   _____

   _____

   _____

8. What three conditions account for the disabilities of more than half of the people with disabling handicaps?

   _____

   _____

9. Describe the medical benefits of pet ownership.

   _____

   _____

   _____

   _____

Thinking Critically

10. What types of evidence does the author provide to support his main points?

    _____

11. Why is it difficult to prove that children who own pets are less likely to become criminals?

    _____

    _____

    _____

    _____

    _____

    _____

12. Identify one statement of opinion in this selection.

    _____

    _____

    _____

    _____

    _____

13. Describe the tone of this selection.

    _____

Questions for Discussion

1. Of all the benefits of animals mentioned in the reading selection, which one benefit do you think is *most* useful to society and why?

2. Can you think of any benefits of pet ownership not mentioned in the reading?

3. How would you study this selection in preparation for a multiple-choice test?

4. If your child were emotionally disturbed, would you consider pet ownership? Why or why not?

Selection 16:			948 words
Finishing Time:	_____	_____	_____
	HR.	MIN.	SEC.
Starting Time:	_____	_____	_____
	HR.	MIN.	SEC.
Reading Time:		_____	_____
		MIN.	SEC.
WPM Score:	_____		
Comprehension Score:	_____%		

GO ELECTRONIC

For additional readings, exercises, and Internet activities, visit this book's Web site at:

http://www.ablongman.com/mcwhorter

For even more activities, visit the Longman English pages at:

http://www.ablongman.com/englishpages

If you need a user name and password, please see your instructor.

Take a Road Trip to Mount Rushmore
Be sure to visit the Memorization and Concentration module on your Reading Road Trip CD-ROM for multimedia tutorials, exercises, and tests.

CHAPTER 9

Graphic and Visual Literacy

IN THIS CHAPTER YOU WILL LEARN:

1. To read graphics effectively.
2. To integrate text and graphics.
3. To interpret and evaluate graphic and visual sources.

Today's textbooks and other academic sources are enhanced with a larger number of graphics than ever before. To read a textbook effectively, you must read not only the prose material, but also graphs, charts, tables, cartoons, photographs, and flowcharts. All of these learning sources require skills in reading and interpreting visual and graphic material and in integrating this material with the accompanying text. The purpose of this chapter is to equip you with visual and graphic literacy skills that will improve your reading of textbook and research materials.

Why Graphics Are Used

Graphics are typically included in textbooks, resource materials, and class instruction in order to clarify complex information and to help you further interpret it. They serve a number of important functions that enhance your reading and learning efficiency. Graphics can consolidate information, explain and illustrate ideas, dramatize information, or display trends, patterns, and variations.

Graphics Consolidate Information

Most graphics display information in a condensed, more easily accessible form than written material. Try this experiment. Look at Figure 9.1 and imagine presenting the information contained in it in sentence and paragraph form. The result might be as follows:

Among college students in the United States, 12.1 percent plan to major in arts and humanities; 6.6 percent plan to major in the biological sciences. Business is the expected major for 16.7 percent of students, while 11 percent plan to major in education. Engineering will be the major for 8.7 percent of students. Physical sciences will be the major for 2.6 percent of students. Eleven and six-tenths percent of students plan to choose a professional major, while 10 percent of students plan to select social sciences as a major. Technical majors will be chosen by 2.1 percent of students. The remaining students will chose other fields (9.9 percent) or are undecided (8.3 percent).

You probably found this paragraph to be repetitious and tedious to read. Certainly reading this paragraph is more time-consuming than studying the pie chart in Figure 9.1. Moreover, the pie chart presents the same information more concisely and in a form that clearly shows the relationships between the individual pieces of information. To determine these relationships from the paragraph alone would require you to read closely and reread frequently.

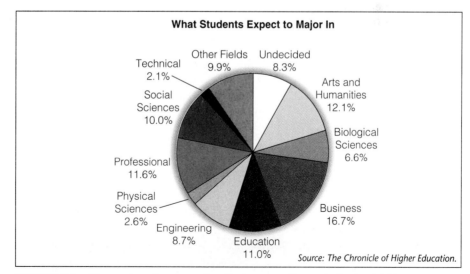

FIGURE 9.1   Planned major areas for first year college students, 2001

Graphics Explain and Illustrate

Imagine trying to set up a computer system or assemble a ten-speed bicycle without a schematic diagram. In a human biology course, imagine trying to understand the digestive system without diagrams to assist you. The purpose of some graphics, especially drawings, diagrams, and flowcharts, is to explain an unfamiliar and complex object or process by showing the relationships among the various parts.

Graphics Dramatize Information

What could more dramatically illustrate the differences in salaries between males and females and between high school and college graduates than the following graph (Figure 9.2)?

This visual representation of salary differences is much more powerful than simply presenting in prose form the annual earnings of male and female, high school and colllege graduates. The difference between the sizes of bars in this graphic makes an immediate visual impact on the reader.

Graphics Display Trends, Patterns, and Variations

Graphics make it easy to see differences and changes. As a result, trends and patterns become clearer and more noticeable. For example, in Figure 9.3 on the next page, you can clearly see that the more hours children watch TV per week, the lower their school achievement is. The steady descent of the trend line in this line graph after 15 hours of viewing time makes obvious this pattern of declining school achievement.

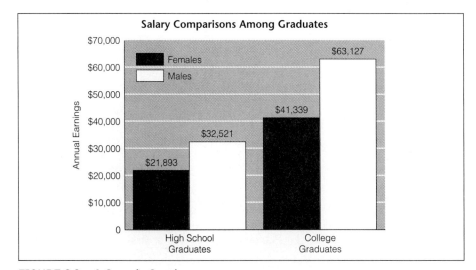

FIGURE 9.2   A Sample Graph.   *Source: Statistical Abstract 1998:* Table 754.

EXERCISE 9-1

DIRECTIONS: Locate one graphic in one of your textbooks or in a newspaper (*USA Today* frequently includes numerous graphics). Identify which function the graphic fulfills.

A Strategy for Reading Graphics

When trying to read an assignment quickly, many students skip over or quickly glance at the graphics. You may tend to rely on the text that accompanies a graphic to convey its meaning, especially if you are a verbal rather than spatial learner. Doing so usually costs more time than it saves. Because graphics clarify, summarize, or emphasize important facts, concepts, and trends, you need to study them closely. Here are some general suggestions that will help you get the most out of graphic elements in the material you read:

1. **Read the title or caption and legend.** The title tells you what situation or relationship is being described. The legend is the explanatory caption that may accompany the graphic. The legend may also function as a key, indicating what particular colors, lines, or pictures mean.

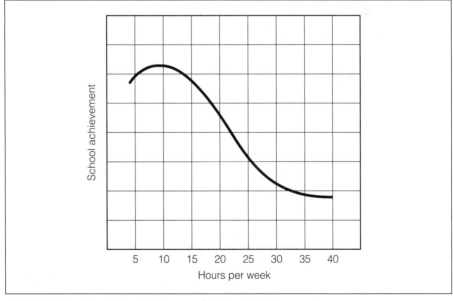

FIGURE 9.3   Television Viewing and School Achievement

2. **Determine how the graphic is organized.** If you are working with a table, note the column headings. For a graph, notice what is marked on the vertical and horizontal axes (top to bottom and left to right lines).

3. **Determine what variables the graphic is concerned with.** Identify the pieces of information that are being compared or the relationship that is being shown. Note any symbols and abbreviations used.

4. **Determine the scale or unit of measurement.** Note how the variables are measured. For example, does a graph show expenditures in dollars, thousands of dollars, or millions of dollars?

5. **Identify the trend(s), pattern(s), or relationships the graphic is intended to show.** The following sections discuss this step in greater detail.

6. **Read any footnotes and identify the source.** Footnotes, printed at the bottom of a graph or chart, indicate how the data were collected, explain what certain numbers or headings mean, and describe the statistical procedures used. The source of data is usually cited at the bottom of the graph or chart. Unless the information was collected by the author, you are likely to find a research journal or publication from which the data were taken. Identifying the source is helpful in assessing the reliability of the data.

7. **Make a brief summary note.** In the margin, jot a brief note about the trend or pattern the graphic emphasizes. Writing will crystallize the idea in your mind, and your note will be useful when you review.

Integrating Text and Graphics

In both textbooks and reference sources, most graphics do not stand alone; they have corresponding printed text that may explain, summarize, or analyze the graphic. Be sure to consider the text and the graphic together to get their complete meaning.

Here are some guidelines for integrating text and graphics.

1. **Notice the type and number of graphics included in the material as you preread the chapter (see Chapter 2).**

2. **Refer to the graphic when the author directs you to.** Writers tell you when they want you to look at the graphic by saying, "See Figure 17.2" or by introducing the graphic, "Table 9.7 displays . . . ."

3. **Read the graphic, using the previously listed steps.**

4. **Move back and forth between the text and graphic.** As you study the graphic, especially if it is a diagram or illustration, refer back to the text as needed, checking the meaning or function of particular terms or parts.

5. **Determine why the text writer included the graphic.** Ask these questions:

   • What am I supposed to learn from this graphic?

   • Why was it included?

   • What new information does the graphic contain?

   • On what topic does the graphic provide more detail or further explanation?

Let's look at an example. The following passage and its corresponding graphic were taken from an anatomy textbook chapter on accessory organs of the skin. Read the passage and study the corresponding diagram using the suggested techniques.

Hairs or *pili* are variously distributed over the body. Their primary function is protection. Hair on the head guards the scalp from injury and the sun's rays; eyebrows and eyelashes protect the eyes from foreign particles; hair in the nostrils protects against inhaling insects and foreign particles.

Each hair is a thread of fused, keratinized cells that consists of a shaft and a root [Figure A]. The *shaft* is the superficial portion, most of which projects above the surface of the skin. The *root* is the portion below the surface that penetrates into the dermis and even into the subcutaneous layer. Surrounding the root is the *hair follicle,* which is composed of two layers of epidermal cells: external and internal root sheaths surrounded by a connective tissue sheath.

The base of each follicle is enlarged into an onion-shaped structure, the *bulb.* This structure contains an indentation, the *papilla of the hair,* which contains many blood vessels and provides nourishment for the growing hair. The bulb also contains a region of cells called the *matrix,* which produces new hairs by cell division when older hairs are shed.

Each hair follicle goes through a *growth cycle,* which consists of a *growth stage* and a *resting stage.* During the growth stage, a hair is formed by cells of the matrix that differentiate, become keratinized, and die. As new cells are added at the base of the hair root, the hair grows longer. In time, the growth of the hair stops and the resting stage begins. During this time, the matrix is inactive and the hair follicle shortens. After the resting stage, a new growth cycle begins in which a new hair replaces the old hair and the old hair is pushed out of the hair follicle. In general, scalp hair grows for about three years and rests for about one to two years.

Associated with hairs is a bundle of smooth muscle called *arrector pili.* It is located along the side of the hair follicle. These muscles contract under stresses of

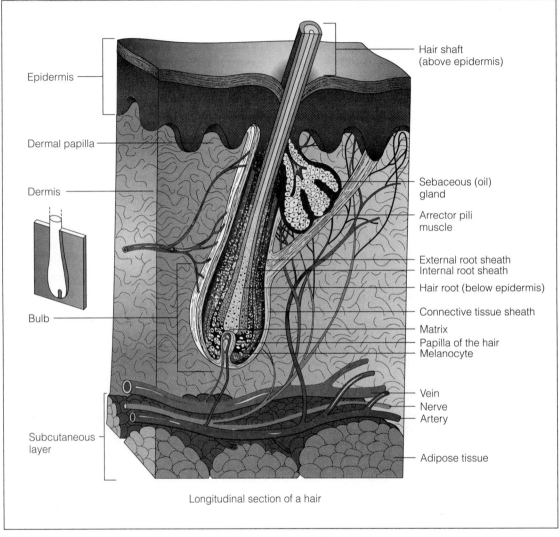

FIGURE A   Principal Parts of a Hair Root and Associated Structures

fright and cold, pulling the hairs into a vertical position and resulting in "goose-bumps" or "gooseflesh."

Tortora, *Introduction to the Human Body.*

Did you find yourself going back and forth frequently between the text and the diagram? This text excerpt and diagram illustrate the back-and-forth reading that is often necessary when reading detailed information.

<table>
<tr><td>

**EXERCISE
9-2**

</td></tr>
</table>

DIRECTIONS: Answer the following questions in reference to the text "Hair" and its corresponding diagram.

1. What was the purpose of the diagram?

   _____

2. What did you learn from it that was not stated in the text?

   _____

   _____

   _____

3. What ideas stated in the text did the diagram make easier for you to understand?

   _____

Types of Graphics

Many types of graphics are used in textbooks. Besides describing some type of relationship, each type achieves particular purposes for the writer.

Photographs

Photographs are included in texts for a variety of reasons. A writer may include photographs to add interest or to help you visualize an event, concept, or feeling. Photographs may provide an example of a concept. Photographs in a biology textbook may be used to illustrate variation among species, for instance. Photographs may be used to create emotional responses. For example, in discussing the problem of poverty and famine in developing countries, a writer may include a photograph of a malnourished child to help readers visualize those conditions and sympathize with the victims. Or, to create an appreciation of the intricate and beautiful carvings discovered at an archaeological site, a photograph of the carvings may be included. Take time to study photographs to determine what ideas or concepts they illustrate. These visual aids provide important clues to what the author considers to be important.

When studying photographs, read the caption. It may provide clues to the importance or meaning of the photograph. The pair of photographs in Figure 9.4 could be confusing without the caption. This caption helps you to visualize the dramatic contrast between what different cultures regard as normal dress.

FIGURE 9.4   What is considered abnormal or deviant in one culture may be viewed as quite normal and acceptable in another. One simple example is how people of various cultures dress.

EXERCISE 9-3

DIRECTIONS: Study the photograph shown in Figure 9.5 on page 343 and answer the questions that follow.

1. What is this photograph intended to illustrate?

_____

_____

2. What does it show that a verbal description could not?

_____

_____

Maps

There are two types of maps: locational and thematic. Locational maps are intended to show the exact positions of physical objects: countries, cities, states, rivers, mountains, and so forth. You will find these maps in history, astronomy, geography, archaeology, and anthropology texts. To

FIGURE 9.5   Children can inherit the debts of their parents and be forced to work alongside them in debt slavery. This Pakistani child will spend his life in fields of mud, making bricks.

read these types of maps, concentrate on each item's position in relation to other objects. For instance, when referring to a map of our galaxy in an astronomy text, concentrate on the locations of planets relative to each other, of the planets to the sun and moon, and so forth.

Thematic maps provide statistical or factual information about a particular area or region. A color coded map of the United States may be used to show mean income levels within each state. A map of Africa may be coded to represent each country's form of government.

When reading thematic maps, look for trends or patterns. When studying a map of the United States showing mean income levels, you should look for regional clusters or patterns. Are incomes higher in the North or South? Are they higher in highly populated states such as New York and California or in lower-population states such as Montana or Idaho? When reading the map of Africa showing types of government, you should look for most and least common forms and try to discover regional similarities. Do the northern or eastern countries, for example, have similar forms of government?

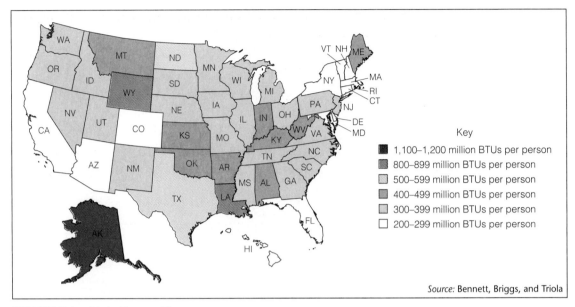

FIGURE 9.6   State Energy Use

EXERCISE
9-4

DIRECTIONS: Study the map shown in Figure 9.6 and answer the questions that follow.

1. What is the purpose of this map?

   _____

2. What type of map is this?

   _____

3. Which states use the largest amount of energy? Which use the least?

   _____

Tables

A table displays facts, figures, statistics, and other data in a condensed orderly sequence for convenience of reference and clarity. The information in tables is classified or organized so that the data can easily be compared.

Use the following steps when reading tables:

1. Determine how the data are classified or divided.
2. Make comparisons and look for trends.
3. Draw conclusions.

Figure 9.7 below, a table taken from a health and wellness text, displays data about infectious diseases for six time periods. By scanning the table, you can easily see what new diseases have evolved and which are no longer common among U.S. citizens.

Pruitt and Stein, *Decisions for Healthy Living.*

DIRECTIONS: Answer the following questions based on the table shown in Figure 9.7.

1. How are the data in this table organized?

FIGURE 9.7 Infectious Disease Trends: Reported Cases in the United States, 1950–2000

Disease	1950	1960	1970	1980	1990	2000
Acquired immune deficiency Syndrome (AIDS)	–	–	–	–	41,595	40,758
Chlamydia	NA	NA	NA	NA	323,663	702,093
Diphtheria	5,796	918	435	3	4	1
Gonorrhea	286,746	258,933	600,072	1,004,029	690,042	358,995
Hepatitis A	NA	NA	56,797	29,087	31,441	13,397
Hepatitis B	NA	NA	8,310	19,015	21,102	8,036
Hepatitis C	–	–	–	–	2,553	3,197
Legionnaires' disease	–	–	–	475	1,370	1,127
Malaria	–	72	3,051	2,062	1,292	1,560
Measles	NA	NA	47,351	3,124	27,786	86
Mumps	NA	NA	104,963	8,576	5,292	338
Pertussis (whooping cough)	102,718	14,809	4,249	1,730	4,570	7,867
Polio	33,300	2,525	31	8	7	0
Smallpox	Last documented case occurred in 1949					
Syphilis (primary and secondary)	217,558	122,538	91,382	68,832	135,043	31,575
Toxic shock syndrome (TSS)	–	–	–	–	322	135
Tuberculosis	121,742	55,494	37,137	27,749	25,701	16,377

NA: Not Available (not previously nationally notifiable)

Note: AIDS, hepatitis C, and TSS data reflect post-1980 discoveries of an infectious agent. Legionellosis (legionnaires' disease) data reflect post–1970 discovery of an infectious agent. Polio data reflect reported cases in the wild only (not vaccine-induced cases).

Source: U.S. Centers for Disease Control and Prevention

2. What does N/A mean?

    _____

3. What three diseases have shown a consistent, steady decrease from 1950 to 2000?

    _____

4. In 2000, which disease infected the largest number of people? Which infected the fewest?

    _____

5. Which diseases have shown an increase between 1990 and 2000?

    _____

Graphs

A graph clarifies the relationship between two or more sets of information. A graph often reveals a trend or pattern that is easily recognizable in visual form but is not as obvious when the data appear in list or paragraph form. Several types of graphs are described in the following sections.

Bar graphs

A bar graph is often used to compare quantities or amounts. It is especially useful in showing changes that occur over time. Bar graphs are often included in texts to emphasize differences. The graph shown in Figure 9.8 displays the most common causes of death in the United States for the year 2002. By glancing at the chart you can quickly determine that heart disease and cancer are the leading causes of death.

When reading bar graphs, pay particular attention to differences in amount between the variables. Notice which variables have the largest and smallest differences and try to think of reasons that account for the differences.

EXERCISE
9-6

DIRECTIONS: Study the bar graph shown in Figure 9.9 and answer the following questions.

1. What is the purpose of this graph?

    _____

    _____

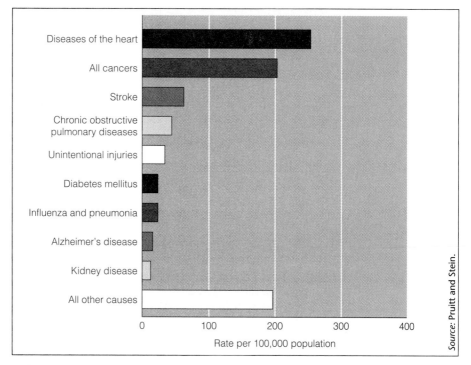

FIGURE 9.8   Most Common Causes of Death, United States, 2002
Chronic diseases are the leading cause of death in the United States, and are a major source of disability, pain, and discomfort.

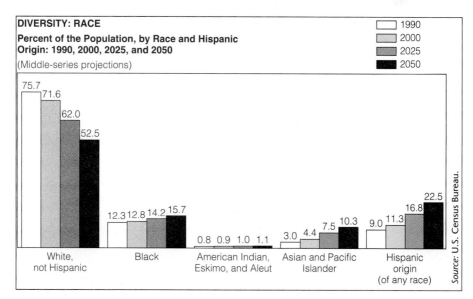

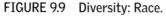

FIGURE 9.9   Diversity: Race.

2. Which group will decrease in percent of the U.S. population between 1990 and 2050?

———

3. Which group will show the largest percentage increase over these years?

———

4. Which group will have the smallest percentage increase over these years?

———

Stacked Bar Graphs

In a stacked bar graph, instead of being arranged side by side, bars are placed one on top of the other as shown in Figure 9.10 below.

The stacked bar graph is often used to emphasize whole/part relationships. That is, it shows the component parts that make up a total. In Figure 9.10 the whole represents all households in the United States in the years 1970, 1980, 1990, and 2000, while the parts are the six categories of households, divided into family and nonfamily households.

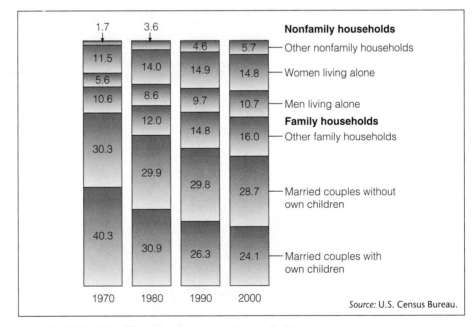

FIGURE 9.10   The Changing American Household.
Over the past thirty years, there has been a decrease in the percent of households with married couples and an increase in other types of families.

Because stacked bar graphs are intended to make numerous comparisons, study the graph carefully to be sure you "see" all possible relationships. For example, in Figure 9.10 be sure you see the decline in married couples with own children category as well as the increase in both men and women living alone.

Line Graphs

In line graphs, information is plotted along a vertical and a horizontal axis, with one or more variables plotted on each. A line graph connects points along these axes. A line graph usually includes more data points than a bar graph. Consequently, it is often used to present detailed and/or large quantities of information. If a line graph compares only two variables, then it consists of a single line. More often, however, line graphs compare two or more variables, and multiple lines are used. The line graph in Figure 9.11 compares four categories of expenditures in the United States budget.

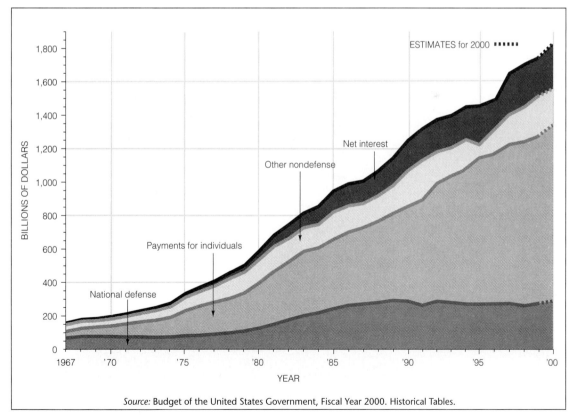

Source: Budget of the United States Government, Fiscal Year 2000. Historical Tables.

FIGURE 9.11   Federal Expenditures

Line graphs are often used to display data that occurs in a sequence. You can see this in Figure 9.11, which displays the levels of expenditures from 1967 to 2000.

Line graphs can display one of three general relationships: positive, negative, or independent. Each of these is shown in Figure 9.12.

Positive relationships. When the variables increase or decrease at the same time, the relationship is positive and is shown by a line that climbs up from left to right. In graph A, as years in school increase, so does income.

Inverse (or negative) relationships. When one variable increases and the other decreases, the relationship is inverse or negative. In graph B, as the years of education increase, the number of children decreases.

Independent relationships. When the variables have no effect on each other, the relationship is independent. In graph C, years in school have no effect on number of house pets. Once you discover the trend and the nature of the relationship a linear graph describes, jot them down in the margin for review later.

To read line graphs, look for upward or downward trends and positive or negative relationships. Notice when the line(s) begin to rise or fall and try to think of reasons that may account for the increase or decline.

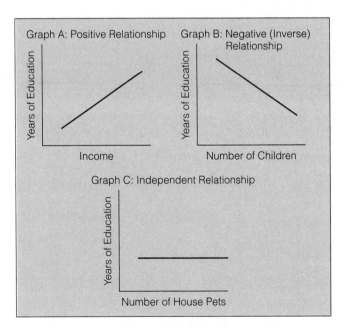

FIGURE 9.12   Line Graph Relationships

EXERCISE 9-7

DIRECTIONS: What type of relationship (positive, inverse, or independent) would each of the following line graphs show?

1. a graph plotting effective use of study time versus college course grades

    _____

2. a graph plotting time spent reading versus time spent playing tennis

    _____

3. a graph plotting time spent checking a dictionary for unknown words versus reading speed

    _____ ▬

Circle Graphs

A circle graph, also called a pie chart, is used to show whole/part relationships or to show how parts of a unit have been divided or classified. They illustrate what part of a total a particular variable represents. Circle graphs often emphasize proportions or emphasize the relative size or importance of various parts. The whole circle represents 100 percent or the total amount of something. The pieces of the pie show the relative size or proportion of particular parts of that whole. The larger the piece of the pie, the larger portion of the total it represents.

Figure 9.13 on page 352 shows the function of federal grants in 2000. It shows the percentage of federal grants received by each of four different policy areas, as well as the percentage going to other areas.

Diagrams

A diagram is a drawing that explains an object, idea, or process by outlining, in visual form, parts or steps or by showing the item's organization. The purpose of a diagram, as with tables and charts, is to simplify and clarify the writer's explanation and to help you visualize the item diagrammed. For example, the diagram from a biology text in Figure 9.14 on page 352 describes the structure of two common viruses. This diagram clearly explains their structures while showing their differences.

To read a diagram, focus on its purpose. What is it intended to illustrate? Why did the author include it? To study a diagram, cover the diagram and try to draw it and label its parts without referring to the text. This activity will provide a good test of whether or not you truly understand the process or concept illustrated.

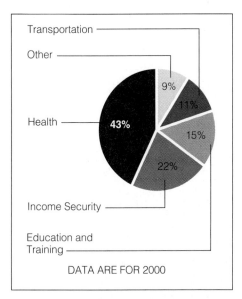

DATA ARE FOR 2000

FIGURE 9.13   Functions of Federal Grants

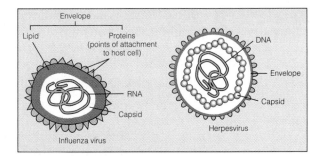

FIGURE 9.14   **The Structure of Viruses.** Viruses are extremely small particles that infect cells and cause many human diseases. Their basic structure includes an outer envelope, composed of lipid and protein, a protein capsid, and genetic material that is enclosed within the capsid.

EXERCISE 9-8

DIRECTIONS: Study the diagram shown in Figure 9.15 and answer these questions.

1. What is the purpose of the diagram?

_____

2. Into what layer of tissue is the medication injected?

_____

3. Why is this diagram more useful than a verbal description?

_____

_____

EXERCISE 9-9

DIRECTIONS: Draw a diagram that illustrates one of the following.

a. the registration process at your college

b. a process explained in one of your textbooks

c. the floor plan of your library's reference section

d. an object described in one of your textbooks

Charts

Three types of charts are commonly used in college textbooks: organizational charts, flowcharts, and pictograms. Each is intended to display a relationship, either quantitative or cause-effect.

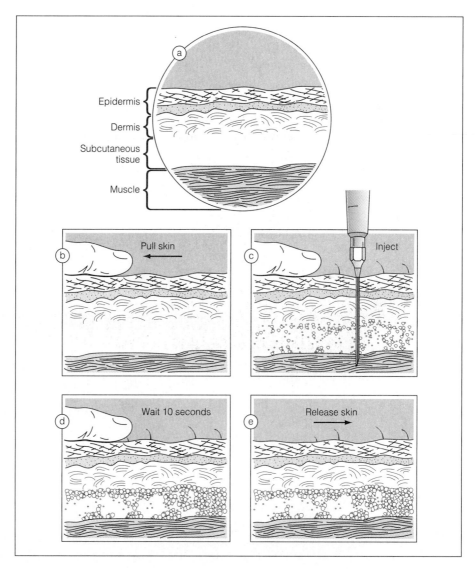

FIGURE 9.15   An Example of the Z-track Method of Injection

Organizational Charts

An organizational chart divides an organization, such as a corporation, hospital, or university, into its administrative parts, staff positions, or lines of authority. Figure 9.16 shows a particular type of corporate departmental organization called matrix departmentalization. It shows levels of authority from the level of general manager to department heads and finally to project managers. It depicts how authority flows in this type of organization.

Flowcharts

A flowchart is a specialized type of chart that shows how a process or procedure works. Lines or arrows are used to indicate the direction (route or routes) through the procedure. Various shapes (boxes, circles, rectangles) enclose what is done at each stage or step. You could draw a flowchart, for example, to describe how to apply for and obtain a student loan or how to locate a malfunction in your car's electrical system. The flowchart shown in Figure 9.17 on page 356, taken from a business information systems textbook, shows a procedure to calculate sales commissions and produce a

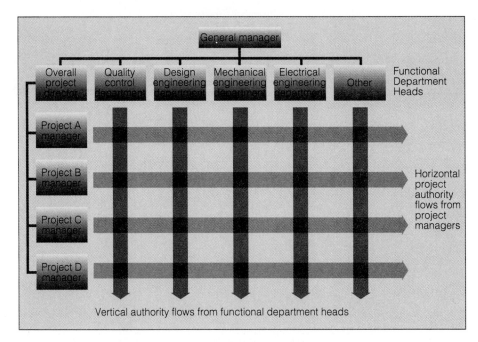

FIGURE 9.16   Example of Matrix Departmentalization

commission report. The chart provides you with a map of the procedure and details the steps to be followed.

To read flowcharts effectively, use the following suggestions:

1. Decide what process the flowchart shows.

2. Next, follow the chart, using the arrows and reading each step. Start at the top or far left of the chart.

3. When you've finished, describe the process in your own words. Try to draw the chart from memory without referring to the text. Compare your drawing with the chart and take note of anything you forgot or misplaced.

Pictograms

A pictogram is a combination of a chart and graph, and uses symbols or drawings (such as books, cars, or buildings) instead of or in addition to lines, bars, or numbers to present information. This type of chart tends to be visually appealing, makes statistics seem realistic, and may carry an emotional impact. For example, a chart that uses stick figure drawings of children to indicate the infant mortality rate per country may have a more significant impact than statistics presented in table form. Imagine a pictogram that uses a section of a globe to indicate that world statistics are being presented and adds stick figures of people to indicate population statistics. Such a pictogram would be eye catching and dramatic.

Cartoons

Cartoons are included in textbooks to make a point quickly or simply to lighten the text by adding a touch of humor about the topic at hand. Cartoons usually appear without a title or legend and there is usually no reference within the text to the cartoon.

Cartoons can make abstract ideas and concepts concrete and real. Pay close attention to cartoons, especially if you are a visual learner. They may help you recall ideas easily by serving as a recall clue that triggers your memory of related material.

The cartoon shown in Figure 9.18 on page 357 appears in a United States history textbook chapter titled "A Global Nation for the New Millennium." It appears in a text section that discusses the growth of the Internet. The cartoon effectively makes the point that you cannot always be sure who you are communicating with on the Internet.

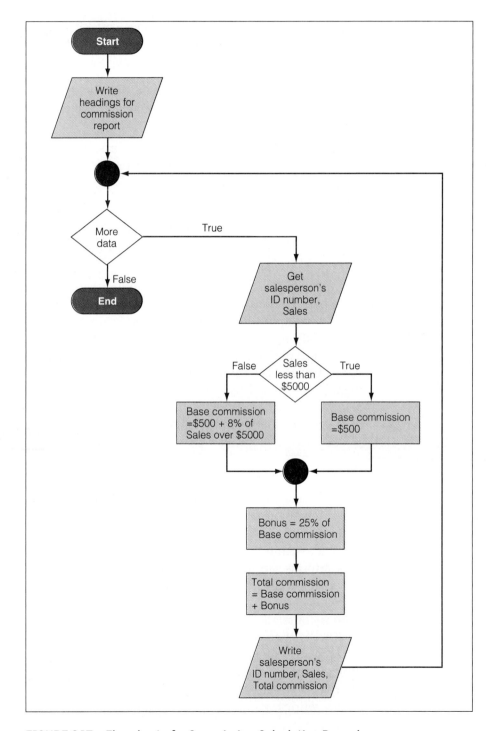

FIGURE 9.17   Flowchart of a Commission-Calculation Procedure

"On the Internet, nobody knows you're a dog."

FIGURE 9.18   A Sample Cartoon

EXERCISE
9-10

DIRECTIONS: Indicate what type of graphic(s) would be most useful in presenting each of the following sets of information.

1. the effects of flooding on a Midwestern town

2. the top five soft drink brands by percent of market share

3. changes in yearly per capita income from 1980 to 2000 in Germany, France, Japan, and the United States

4. the suicide rates for various age groups

5. the top 20 places to live in the United States and their average income, cost of housing, quality of schools, level of taxes, amount of crime, and availability of cultural and recreational activities

6. government spending in 1996 and 2000 for payments to individuals, defense, interest on debt, grants to state and local governments, and all other spending

_____

7. the basic parts of a solar powered automobile

_____

Critical Thinking Tip #9

Analyzing Statistics

The purpose of many graphs, charts, and tables, whether in electronic or print sources, is to display statistics in an easy-to-read format. A critical reader should look as closely at statistics as at any other type of information. Although statistics may seem like "hard facts," they can be misleading and deceiving.

Here is an example: Many graphics report averages—average salaries, average costs, average weights, or average educational levels. Did you know that an average can be computed three different ways with, at times, three very different results? The terms *median, mode,* and *mean* are all used to report averages. Let's say you want to report the average temperature for one week in your town or city. The daily temperatures are 67, 70, 70, 94, 95, 96, and 97.

The mean temperature is 84.1.
The median temperature is 94.
The mode is 70.

These are very different numbers. Here's how they are calculated:

Mean: total the daily temperatures and divide by 7.
Median: arrange the temperatures from low to high and take the middle temperature (the one with three higher and three lower temperatures).
Mode: choose the temperature that occurs most frequently.

This is just one example of why caution is needed when interpreting statistics. There are many others. (In the example, for instance, how was the daily temperature calculated? Was it the daily high, daily low, 24-hour "average"?)

Because statistics are subject to manipulation and interpretation, study graphics with a questioning and critical eye.

8. a description of how acid rain affects the environment

_____

9. the main areas of earthquakes and volcanic activity throughout the world

_____

10. book sales in each of 10 categories for the years 1996 through 2000

_____

Summary

1. Why are graphics included in your courses?

Graphics serve a number of different functions in your courses. They are used to
• consolidate information
• explain and illustrate ideas
• dramatize information
• display trends, patterns, and variations

2. What steps should you take to read graphics more effectively?

To get the most from all types of graphics you should begin by reading the title or caption and determining how the graphic is organized; what symbols, abbreviations, and variables are presented; and what scale, values, or units of measurement are being used. You should then study the data to identify trends, patterns, and relationships within the graphic. Note any explanatory footnotes and the source of the data. Finally, making marginal notes will aid your further reading or review.

3. How can you integrate graphics with their corresponding printed text?

To integrate text and graphics:
• Be alert to the graphics as you preread chapters.
• Refer to each graphic when you are directed to.
• Read the graphic carefully.
• Move back and forth between text and graphic frequently.
• Find out why the graphic was included.

4. What types of graphics are commonly used in textbooks and academic sources?

Many types of graphics are used in conjunction with print materials. They include photographs, maps, tables, graphs, diagrams, charts, pictograms, and cartoons.

READING SELECTION 17
BIOLOGY

HOMEOSTASIS
Carl E. Rischer and Thomas A. Easton
From *Focus on Human Biology*

How does the human body regulate itself? This reading, taken from a biology textbook, explains the principle of homeostasis. Read the excerpt to discover what homeostasis is and how it controls bodily functioning.

— · —

1   The basic principle of homeostasis has made it possible to understand a great deal about how the body works. **Homeostasis is the balance maintained when several systems operate to keep the conditions inside the body roughly constant.** That is, the body maintains its temperature and levels of mineral salts, nutrients, wastes, oxygen, and water within the narrow limits that support human life.

2   Many different diseases can result when various aspects of homeostasis fail. For instance, the human body uses the sugar glucose as its main fuel. Thus, it is extremely important to keep just enough sugar in circulation so that the cells can draw on it to power their own activities; normally that is 90 milligrams (mg) of glucose in each 100 milliliters (ml) of blood. If a person's blood sugar falls too low, he or she suffers from *hypoglycemia* (*hypo* = under, beneath; *glyc* = sweet) and lack of energy. If, on the other hand, the blood sugar is too high, the problem is *hyper-glycemia* (*hyper* = over, above) or diabetes mellitus (sugar diabetes). Excess blood sugar is excreted in the urine; in severe cases, the body's cells lose water, the brain stops working, and the patient goes into a coma.

Negative Feedback and Homeostatic Control

Controlling Sugar Level in the Blood

3   How does the body prevent hypo- and hyper-glycemia? After a meal, when sugar is being absorbed from the digestive system, specific cells in a gland called the pancreas sense the rising sugar level in the blood and secrete *insulin*. Insulin causes cells in the muscles and liver to quickly absorb this excess sugar from the blood, reducing its level back to the normal 90 mg/100 ml [Figure A].

4   Between meals, the blood sugar level falls as the cells use the sugar for energy. The pancreas responds by secreting another substance called *glucagon*, which signals the liver to release some of the extra sugar stored there. This hormone raises the sugar level back up to the normal level (see Figure A).

5   This type of control mechanism is called **negative feedback.** Such feedback mechanisms use

the level of the substance or the physical condition being controlled as the indicator for turning off or on the homeostatic response. Negative-feedback mechanisms measure the level of whatever is being controlled against some "set point," or specific level determined in advance. When the variable departs from the set point, the mechanism switches on to counteract the change, returning the variable to the set point [Figure B].

6   In contrast, *positive feedback* acts in the opposite way: it increases the departure of some variable from its starting point. Once activated, positive-feedback systems are often destructive. An example is the positive-feedback squeal, of increasing intensity, produced by public address systems when a microphone is placed in front of the speaker. (Why does such a situation produce louder and louder squeals?)

7   Why is it hard to think of any examples of positive-feedback systems existing in a living body?

Mechanical Negative-Feedback Controls

8   A simple example of a negative-feedback mechanism is the thermostat that controls room temperature by turning a heater off and on. As the temperature goes up, a temperature-sensitive

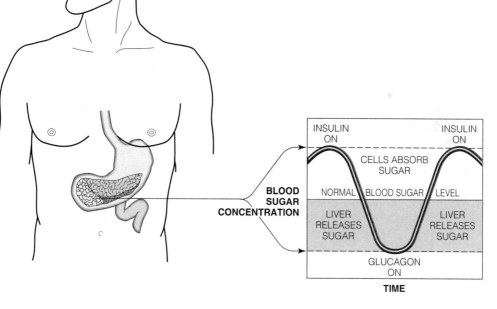

FIGURE A   Homeostatic control of blood sugar concentration. Many of the body's systems are controlled by feedback systems. In this oversimplified diagram, the level of sugar circulating in the blood is regulated by the pancreas. When the sugar level drifts far enough above the normal set point, it stimulates the pancreas to release insulin, which causes many of the body's cells to take up and use or store the excess sugar, causing the level to decline back toward the set point. When the sugar level drops below the set point, the pancreas releases glucagon, which encourages cells that store sugar to release some of their reserve into the blood, raising the level back toward the set point.
Question: Which hormone—insulin or glucagon—will be secreted after you eat a candy bar?

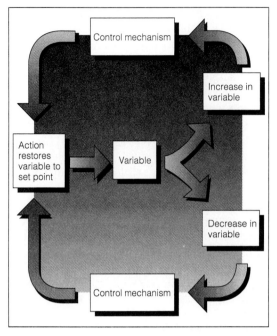

FIGURE B   In negative-feedback systems, "effects" feed back on their cause to keep variation within a narrow range around a "set point."
Question: "To negate" means to undo. Relate this definition to "negative feedback."

switch opens, turning off the heater. As the room temperature cools again, the temperature sensor changes until it turns the heater back on. Thus, by alternately turning the heater off and on, the thermostat keeps the room temperature fairly constant.

Body Temperature Control

9   A similar thermostat works to control human body temperature. Located in the brain, it acti-

vates sweating, panting, and rerouting the blood to the superficial vessels of the skin when the body is overheated. In light-complexioned people, this change in blood flow results in a reddening (flushing) of the skin and quickly dissipates the excess heat. When the body is chilled, it routes the blood away from the skin, conserving the body heat, and activates shivering—releasing small pulses of heat as the tiny muscle fibers quiver (raising the body's temperature).

Negative Feedback in Other Body Systems

10   Negative-feedback mechanisms also work to maintain blood pressure, heart rate, fluid volume, and blood levels of oxygen, carbon dioxide, calcium, sodium, and other substances. The composition of the blood thereby remains constant (within limits) and the body cells remain in an environment that allows them to survive. Extreme changes in blood composition, the availability of nutrients (food molecules), body temperature, or heart function can be fatal.

11   The principle of homeostasis helps us to understand how various aspects of body functions are interrelated. It also tells us that whenever we find a substance or activity in the body that maintains a steady level, we can then expect to find a control mechanism. The concept of homeostasis, therefore, serves both as an organizing principle for our knowledge of the body and as a guide to further research.

1. Explain homeostasis and how it contributes to survival.

2. Diagram and explain how a negative-feedback mechanism operates.

EXAMINING READING SELECTION 17

Checking Your Vocabulary

Directions: Using context, word parts, or a dictionary if necessary, circle the letter of the meaning for each word as it is used in the reading.

1. excreted (paragraph 2)
   a. discharged
   b. neutralized
   c. decreased
   d. distributed

2. glucagon (paragraph 4)
   a. insulin secretion
   b. extra blood sugar
   c. hormone
   d. fluid secreted by the liver

3. counteract (paragraph 5)
   a. distribute
   b. work against
   c. release
   d. initiate

4. rerouting (paragraph 9)
   a. controlling the temperature of
   b. altering the composition of
   c. constricting the flow of
   d. changing the course of

5. fatal (paragraph 10)
   a. dangerous
   b. deadly
   c. threatening
   d. harmful

Checking Your Comprehension

Directions: Circle the letter of the best answer.

6. This reading is primarily about
   a. controlling blood sugar.
   b. how the body maintains balanced conditions.
   c. how negative feedback is beneficial.
   d. the human body's feedback mechanisms.

7. The principle of homeostasis
   a. explains why people suffer strokes.
   b. describes how the body reacts to disease.
   c. describes how the body evolved to its present state.
   d. explains how the body reacts to and survives changes in its environment.

8. Negative feedback is a system in which the body
   a. absorbs excess substances.
   b. regulates overproduction of chemicals.
   c. increases its functioning in response to disease.
   d. restores its functioning to a set level.

9. The author compares the body's regulation of temperature to a
   a. heater.
   b. thermometer.
   c. thermostat.
   d. fuel.

10. When a person's blood sugar decreases,
    a. the pancreas alerts the liver.
    b. the pancreas overproduces sugar.
    c. the pancreas releases glucagon.
    d. the pancreas releases insulin.

11. The author explains homeostasis primarily by
    a. establishing an order of importance.
    b. classifying bodily fluids.
    c. explaining processes.
    d. making comparisons.

Thinking Critically

12. Which of the following statements can be assumed to be true based on information presented in the reading?
    a. Negative feedback regulates the production of hormones.
    b. Negative feedback is responsible for coronary disease.
    c. Body temperature control is an example of positive feedback.
    d. Hyperglycemia is caused by water loss.

13. It is reasonable to assume that
    a. the body uses few or no positive-feedback systems.
    b. The body continually exists in a static, unchanging state.
    c. the principle of homeostasis can explain why cancer spreads.
    d. a positive-feedback system operates in a similar way to a negative-feedback system.

14. Homeostasis explains which of the following?
    a. organ growth
    b. lung collapse
    c. pain
    d. perspiration

15. If your blood pressure were regulated by a positive-feedback system, once your blood pressure fell and the system was activated, your blood pressure would
    a. return to a normal level.
    b. fall to a dangerous level.
    c. rise to a dangerous level.
    d. decrease.

Questions for Discussion

1. Do all people who suffer from sugar diabetes need to take insulin? If not, why not?

2. The author implies that the body uses few or no positive feedback systems. Explain why this is so.

3. Explain how certain extreme changes in the body can be fatal. Give a specific example.

4. How useful are the diagrams included in this reading?

Selection 17:			999 words
Finishing Time:	_____	_____	_____
	HR.	MIN.	SEC.
Starting Time:	_____	_____	_____
	HR.	MIN.	SEC.
Reading Time:		_____	_____
		MIN.	SEC.
WPM Score:		_____	
Comprehension Score:		_____	%

READING SELECTION 18

GEOGRAPHY

PANGAEA: THE SUPERCONTINENT AND THE EFFECTS OF ITS BREAKUP

Edward F. Bergman and William H. Renwick

From *Introduction to Geography*

What are the causes of earthquakes and volcanoes? Read this geography textbook excerpt to discover how events that occurred millions of years ago affect our lives today.

— · —

1   If you were to view Earth from a great distance, as we sometimes view other planets through telescopes, the most distinctive topographic features would be the enormous mountain ranges arranged in linear patterns that extend for thousands of kilometers. Three especially prominent mountain ranges on Earth's land surface include the Rockies of North America, connecting through Central America to the Andes of South America; the Himalayas, extending across Asia; and the north-south system of mountains in Eastern Africa. Large as these highly visible mountain ranges are, none rank as the world's longest. That title belongs to a mountain system beneath the oceans, the interconnecting midocean ridges that are more than 64,000 kilometers (40,000 miles) long.

2   For millennia, people believed that Earth's continents and oceans were fixed in place for all time, and that Earth was only a few thousand years old. This notion of a "fixed Earth" was challenged early in this century by German earth scientist Alfred Wegener. He argued that Earth's land areas once had been joined in a single "supercontinent," now known as Pangaea, and that over thousands of years the continents had moved apart (Figure A). Because Wegener could not explain why the continents moved, his ideas were rejected at the time. But researchers in the 1960s vindicated Wegener by working out an explanation, called **plate tectonics theory**. Since that time, plate tectonics theory has provided us with explanations of the origins of Earth's great mountain chains, volcanoes, and many other important phenomena.

Earth's Moving Crust

3   Earth resembles an egg with a cracked shell. Earth's crust is thin and rigid, averaging 45 kilometers (28 miles) in thickness. Beneath this rigid crust the rock is like a very thick fluid and is slowly deformed by movements within Earth. While far from the free-flowing substances we know as the **mantle**, it is fluid enough to move slowly along in convection currents, driven by heat stored within Earth's core. These currents are analogous to winds in the atmosphere, which carry heat away from Earth's surface. Geologists believe that this motion of the mantle causes Earth's rigid crust to move in pieces, called **tectonic plates**. This is the plate tectonics theory. Movement of the plates causes earthquakes to rumble, volcanoes to erupt, and mountains to be built.

Earthquakes

4   Thousands of **earthquakes**—sudden movements of Earth's crust—occur every day. Figure B shows major earthquake zones around the world, notably clustered where two plates meet. The place where Earth's crust actually moves is the **focus** of an earthquake. The focus is generally near the surface, but can be as deep as 600 kilometers (372 miles) below Earth's surface. The point on the surface directly above the focus is

the **epicenter.** The tremendous energy released at the focus travels worldwide in all directions, at various speeds through different layers of rock.

5   Most earthquakes are too small for people to feel, and they are detectable only with a **seismograph**, a device that records the quake's **seismic waves**, or vibrations. Earthquake intensity is measured on a 0-to-9 logarithmic scale developed by Charles F. Richter in 1935. Magnitude 3 to 4 earthquakes on the Richter scale are minor; magnitude 5 to 6 quakes can break windows and topple weak buildings, and magnitude 7 to 8 quakes are devastating killers if they affect populated areas.

6   Earthquake prediction is unreliable. Potential movement zones are closely monitored, and computer models attempt to replicate conditions along plate boundaries. But predicting an earthquake is like trying to forecast the weather several months from now. It just cannot be done accurately with current technology.

Volcanoes

7   Like earthquakes, volcanoes are clustered along boundaries between **tectonic plates** (Figure B). Movement within Earth and between the plates generates magma (molten rock). Being less dense than the surrounding rock, **magma** migrates

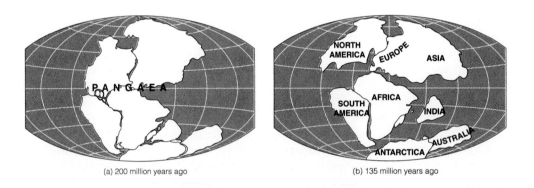

(a) 200 million years ago

(b) 135 million years ago

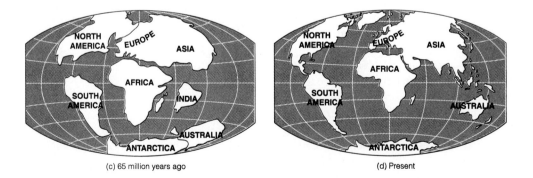

(c) 65 million years ago

(d) Present

FIGURE A   Past plate movements. Two hundred million years ago (a) Earth's continents were all joined in one supercontinent known as Pangaea. This continent gradually broke apart, beginning with the opening of the Atlantic Ocean from south to north and the movement of India away from Antarctica toward Asia (b and c). The world of today is shown in (d).

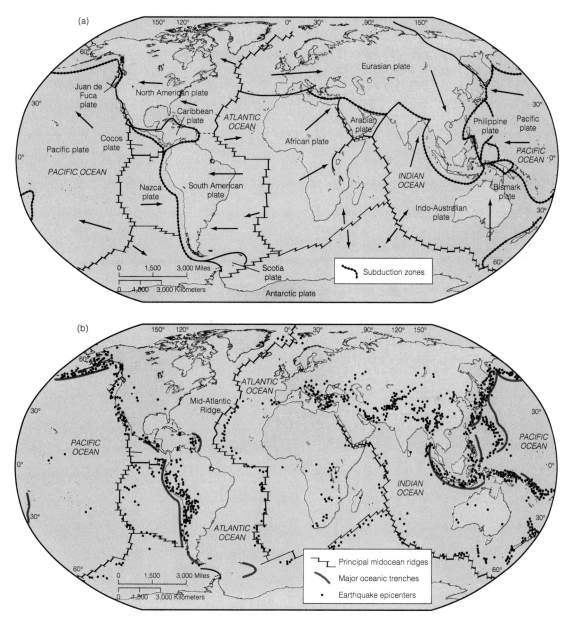

FIGURE B   Earth's Tectonic Plates. (a) The major plates of Earth's crust move relative to one another, generally at rates of a few millimeters per year. (b) These motions cause earthquakes that are concentrated along plate boundaries. Ridges with rift valleys at their centers are formed where plates are moving away from each other, generally in ocean areas. Mountain ranges are created where plates converge, sometimes with deep ocean trenches on the seaward side of the convergence area.

toward the surface. Some reaches the surface and erupts, and it then is called **lava**. A **volcano** is the surface vent where lava emerges. The magma may flow over the surface, forming a plain of volcanic rock, or it may build up to form a mountain. The chemistry of the magma/lava determines its texture, and therefore the type of landform it builds.

8   **Shield volcanoes** erupt runny lava that cools to form a rock called basalt. They are called shields because of their shape (Figure C). Each of the Hawaiian Islands is a large shield volcano, although the only currently active one is Mauna Loa, on the island of Hawaii (the "Big Island"). These generally sedate volcanoes make news on the rare occasions when they grow more active, and flows of lava threaten settlements. The mid-ocean ridges are formed of similar basaltic lava.

9   Explosive volcanoes that cause death and destruction are more likely to be **composite cone volcanoes** (Figure D). Composite cones are made up of a mixture of lava and ash. Their magma is thick and gassy, and it may erupt explosively through a vent. The eruption sends

ash, glassy cinders (called pyroclasts), and clouds of sulfurous gas high into the atmosphere. It may also pour lethal gas clouds and dangerous mudflows down the volcano's slopes. Repeated eruptions build a cone-shaped mountain, made up of a mixture of lava and ash layers.

10   Eruptions of composite cone volcanoes have killed tens of thousands of people at a time, but such disasters are much less frequent than severe earthquakes. One of the greatest volcanic explosions in recorded history was the 1883 eruption of the island of Krakatau in present-day Indonesia. Two-thirds of the island was destroyed, and the event killed about 36,000 people, most of whom died in a flood triggered by the eruption. Ash discharged into the atmosphere by Krakatau significantly blocked sunlight and caused noticeable cooling of Earth's climate for a couple of years.

11   Thousands of volcanoes stand dormant (inactive, but with the potential to erupt) around the world. About 600 are actively spewing lava, ash, and gas—some daily—but they rarely cause damage. Others, however, have not erupted in

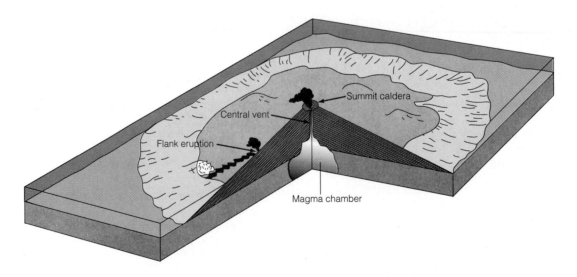

FIGURE C   Shield volcano. Gentle shield volcanoes, exemplified by the Hawaiian islands, are the largest volcanoes on Earth. Lava may erupt on the flank of the volcano or from the crater-like caldera at the top of the mountain. (*Source:* Tarbuck and Lutgens, *Earth Science.*

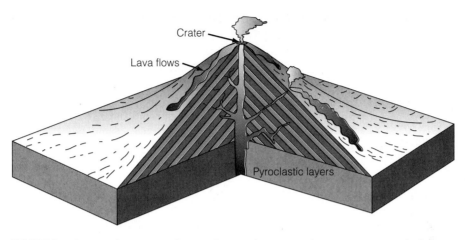

Crater

Lava flows

Pyroclastic layers

FIGURE D   Composite cone volcano. Composite cone volcanoes, composed of alternating lava and ash, are relatively explosive. (*Source:* Tarbuck and Lutgens, *Earth Science.*

hundreds of years, and people have settled nearby. When warnings are not available the danger can be great. The 1985 eruption of Nevado del Ruiz, in Colombia, triggered giant mud slides that buried most of a town, killing 23,000 people. In general, predicting volcanic eruptions is more accurate than predicting earthquakes, because volcanoes give many warnings before erupting.

WRITING ABOUT READING SELECTION 18*

Checking Your Vocabulary

Directions: Complete each of the following items; refer to a dictionary if necessary.

1. Discuss the connotative meanings of the word *earthquake.*

2. Define each of the following words:
   a. topographic (paragraph 1)

   _____

   b. millennia (paragraph 2)

   _____

   c. monitored (paragraph 6)

   _____

   d. replicate (paragraph 6)

   _____

   e. migrates (paragraph 7)

   _____

3. Define the word *phenomena* (paragraph 2) and underline the word or phrase that provides a context clue for its meaning.

   _____

   _____

   _____

____
* Multiple-choice questions are contained in Part 6 (page 587).

4. Define the word *intensity* (paragraph 5) and underline the word or phrase that provides a context clue for its meaning.

_____

_____

5. Determine the meanings of the following words by using word parts:

a. linear (paragraph 1)

_____

b. interconnecting (paragraph 1)

_____

c. supercontinent (paragraph 2)

_____

d. epicenter (paragraph 4)

_____

e. seismograph (paragraph 5)

_____

Checking Your Comprehension

6. How did the present configuration of the continents develop over the past 200 million years?

_____

_____

_____

_____

_____

7. Where are volcanoes and earthquakes located and why are they situated there?

_____

_____

_____

_____

_____

8. Contrast shield and composite cone volcanoes in regard to shape, internal structure, and type of eruptions.

_____

_____

_____

_____

_____

_____

_____

_____

_____

_____

9. What is the Richter scale?

_____

_____

Thinking Critically

10. You are looking down on the Earth from an orbiting space shuttle and see long mountain ranges. Where are they located and what principle is accountable for their formation?

_____

_____

_____

_____

_____

_____

_____

11. The longest mountain systems are actually beneath the oceans, along the midocean ridge. What is the mechanism that produced them?

_____

_____

_____

_____

12. In what different ways can volcanoes cause destruction of nearby towns and subsequent loss of life?

_____

_____

_____

_____

_____

Questions for Discussion

1. If you had the choice of living near a shield volcano or a composite cone volcano, which would you choose? Explain why.

2. Do you think that more government funds should be spent on earthquake prediction research? Are other types of research higher priorities? If so, describe them.

3. At the time Wegener developed the notion of the supercontinent, his theory was rejected. In the 1960s it was accepted. Can you identify other scientists or researchers whose ideas were first rejected and then later accepted?

Selection 18:			1150 words
Finishing Time:	_____	_____	_____
	HR.	MIN.	SEC.
Starting Time:	_____	_____	_____
	HR.	MIN.	SEC.
Reading Time:		_____	_____
		MIN.	SEC.
WPM Score:			_____
Comprehension Score:			_____ %

GO ELECTRONIC

For additional readings, exercises, and Internet activities, visit this book's Web site at:

http://www.ablongman.com/mcwhorter

For even more activities, visit the Longman English pages at:

http://www.ablongman.com/englishpages

If you need a user name and password, please see your instructor.

Take a Road Trip to Wall Street, New York City
Be sure to visit the Graphics and Visual Aids module on your Reading Road Trip CD-ROM for multimedia tutorials, exercises, and tests.

PART 3
Academic Scenario

The following scenario is designed to assess your ability to use and apply the skills taught in this part of the book.

THE SITUATION

Assume you are taking a course in geography. You have been directed to read a geography textbook chapter titled *Landforms*. Your instructor gives tests each month on the assigned chapters. The tests include both multiple-choice and essay questions. Assume that Reading Selection 18, page 365, is from the assigned chapter. Read this selection completely before beginning any of the following tasks. Reread the selection as often as necessary.

THE TASKS

1. Highlight and annotate the reading.
2. Write a one-paragraph summary of this reading.
3. Draw a map that shows the relationship of ideas presented in the reading.

PART 4
Reading Critically

C H A P T E R 1 0

Critical Analysis

IN THIS CHAPTER YOU WILL LEARN:

1. To grasp connotative meanings.
2. To make inferences.
3. To distinguish fact from opinion.
4. To recognize generalizations.
5. To identify tone.
6. To identify an author's purpose.
7. To recognize bias.
8. To understand figurative language.

U p to this point, we have primarily been concerned with the literal meanings of writing. Each chapter has discussed techniques that enable you to understand what the author says and to retain the literal, factual content. However, you often need to go beyond what authors *say* and be concerned with what they *mean*. Through choice of words, descriptions, facts, arrangement of ideas, and suggestions, an author often means more than he or she says. The purpose of this chapter is to present skills that will enable you to interpret and evaluate what you read. These processes require critical reading and thinking skills—the careful and deliberate evaluation of ideas for the purpose of making a judgment about their worth or value. This chapter presents numerous strategies to help you respond to academic reading assignments that demand critical reading.

Many skills are involved in interpreting what you read. Eight of the most useful are discussed in this chapter: grasping connotative meanings, making inferences, distinguishing fact from opinion, recognizing generalizations, identifying tone, identifying the author's purpose, recognizing bias, and understanding figurative language.

Grasping Denotative and Connotative Meanings

If you were asked whether you would rather be the victim of a hoax, a fraud, or a flam, what would you say? If you were to look these words up in a dictionary, you might find that each involves some sort of deception; however, they suggest varying degrees of seriousness. A *hoax* is often a joke or trick; a *flam* is a deceptive trick or lie; a *fraud* often suggests a deception in which someone gives up property or money. Next, suppose you owned a jacket that looked like leather but was not made of real leather. Would you prefer someone to describe your jacket as fake, artificial, or synthetic? Most likely, you would prefer *synthetic*. *Fake* suggests that you are trying to cover up the fact that it is not real leather and *artificial* suggests, in a negative way, that something was made to look like something else. *Synthetic,* however, refers to a product made by a chemical process. You can see that, in addition to their dictionary meanings, words may *suggest* additional meanings.

The meaning of a word as indicated by the dictionary is known as its *denotative* meaning, whereas its *connotative* meaning consists of the additional meanings a word may take on. As an example, think of the word *walk*. Its denotative or primary dictionary meaning is to move forward by placing one foot in front of the other. Here are a few words that also, according to the dictionary, mean to move forward. As you read each word in a sentence, the connotative meaning will become clear to you.

The newlyweds *strolled* down the streets of Paris.
(*Stroll* suggests a leisurely, carefree walk.)

The wealthy businessman *swaggered* into the restaurant and demanded a table.
(*Swagger* suggests walking in a bold, arrogant manner.)

The overweight man *lumbered* along, breathing heavily and occasionally tripping.
(*Lumber* connotes a clumsy, awkward movement.)

From these examples you can see that it is possible to create very different impressions simply by selecting words with certain connotations. Often writers communicate subtle messages or lead you to respond a certain way toward an object, action, or idea by choosing words with positive or negative connotations.

EXERCISE 10-1

DIRECTIONS: For each word listed, write another word that has the same denotative meaning but a different connotative meaning.

Example: to drink   *guzzle*

1. to eat   _____

2. to talk   _____

3. fair   _____

4. famous   _____

5. group   _____

6. to take   _____

7. ability   _____

8. dog   _____

9. fast   _____

10. to fall   _____

EXERCISE 10-2

DIRECTIONS: For each word listed, write a word that has a similar denotative meaning but a negative connotation. Then write a word that has a positive connotation. Consult a dictionary if necessary.

Example: clean decontaminate polish

	Negative	*Positive*
1. to show	_____	_____
2. to leave	_____	_____
3. to ask	_____	_____
4. to task	_____	_____
5. to forget	_____	_____
6. look at	_____	_____
7. unable	_____	_____
8. weak	_____	_____
9. car	_____	_____
10. mistake	_____	_____

DIRECTIONS: Read each of the following statements, paying particular attention to connotative meanings. In each statement, underline at least one word or phrase with a strong connotative meaning. Decide whether it is positive, negative, or neutral and justify your answer. Then suggest a substitute word with a different connotation that changes the meaning of the statement.

1. Educating the electorate about the nature and actual perils of nuclear weapons is a frightening task.

    _____

    _____

    _____

2. Recently, the anti-gun forces throughout the nation were trumpeting that crimes of violence decreased in cities with strict gun-control laws.

    _____

    _____

3. What I want to get rid of is the human garbage that willfully perpetrates outrages against the rest of humanity and whom we have come to call terrorists. (Rivers)

    _____

    _____

    _____

4. Not unlike drugs or alcohol, the television experience allows the participant to blot out the real world and enter into a pleasurable and passive state. (Winn)

    _____

    _____

5. I found Simon Wheeler dozing comfortably by the bar-room stove of the dilapidated tavern in the decaying mining camp of Angel's, and I noticed that he was fat and bald-headed, and had an expression of winning gentleness and simplicity upon his tranquil countenance. (Twain)

    _____

    _____

Making Inferences

Suppose you are ten minutes late for your psychology class, and you find the classroom empty. After a moment of puzzlement and confusion you might remember that your instructor has been ill and decide that your class has been canceled. Or you might recall that your instructor changed classrooms last week and, therefore, you decide that he or she has done so again. In this situation you used what you did know to make a reasonable guess about what you did not know. This reasoning process is called an *inference.* An inference is a logical connection that you draw between what you observe or know and what you do not know. All of us make numerous inferences in daily living without consciously thinking about them. When you wave at a friend and he or she does not wave back, you assume that he or she didn't see you. When you are driving down the highway and see a police car with its lights flashing behind you, you usually infer that the police officer wants you to pull over and stop.

Although inferences are reasonable guesses made on the basis of available information, they are not always correct. For instance, though you inferred that the friend who did not wave did not see you, it may be that he or she did see you, but is angry with you and decided to ignore you. Similarly, the police car with the flashing lights may only want to pass you on the way to an accident ahead. Basically, an inference is the best guess you can make given the available information and circumstances.

If you are a pragmatic or applied learner, you may tend to concentrate on the facts at hand and may overlook their implications. Be sure to question, challenge, and analyze the facts; look for what further ideas the facts, when considered together, suggest.

DIRECTIONS: For each of the following items, make an inference about the situation that is described.

1. A woman seated alone at a bar offers to buy a drink for a man sitting several seats away.

2. A dog growls as a teenager walks toward the house.

_____

3. Your seven-year-old brother will not eat his dinner. A package of cookies is missing from the kitchen cupboard.

_____

4. A woman seated alone in a restaurant nervously glances at everyone who enters. Every few minutes she checks her watch.

_____

5. A close friend invites you to go out for pizza and beer on Tuesday. When you meet her at her home on Tuesday, she tells you that you must have confused the days and that she will see you tomorrow evening.

_____

Making Inferences as You Read

As in many other everyday situations, you make inferences frequently when you are reading. Applied to reading, an inference is a reasonable guess about what the author does *not* say based on what he or she *does* say. You are required to make inferences when an author suggests an idea but does not directly state it. For instance, suppose a writer describes a character as follows:

> In the mirror John Bell noticed that his hair was graying at the temples. As he picked up the morning paper, he realized that he could no longer see well without his glasses. Looking at the hands holding the paper he saw that they were wrinkled.

From the information the author provides, you may infer that the character is realizing that he is aging. However, notice that the author does not mention aging at all. By the facts he or she provides, however, the writer leads you to infer that the character is thinking about aging.

Now, read the following description of an event:

> Their actions, on this sunny afternoon, have been carefully organized and rehearsed. Their work began weeks ago with a leisurely drive through a quiet residential area. While driving, they noticed particular homes that seemed isolated and free of activity. Over the next week, similar drives were taken at different times of day. Finally, a house was chosen and their work began in earnest. Through careful observation and several phone calls, they learned where the occupants worked. They studied the house, noting entrances and windows and anticipating the floor

plan. Finally, they were ready to act. Phone calls made that morning confirmed that the occupants were at work.

What is about to happen in this description? From the facts presented, you probably realized that a daytime home burglary was about to occur. Notice, however, that this burglary is not mentioned anywhere in the paragraph. Instead, using the information provided, you made the logical connection between the known and the unknown facts regarding what was about to occur.

How to Make Inferences

It is difficult to outline specific steps to follow in making inferences. Each inference entirely depends on the situation and the facts provided as well as on your knowledge and experience with the situation. However, here are a few general guidelines for making inferences about what you read.

Be Sure You Understand the Literal Meaning First

Before you can begin any form of interpretation, including inference, you must be sure that you have a clear grasp of the stated facts and ideas. For each paragraph, you should identify the topic, main idea, supporting details, and organizational pattern. Only when you have an understanding of the literal, or factual, content can you go beyond literal meaning and formulate inferences.

Ask Yourself a Question

To be sure that you are making necessary inferences to get the fullest meaning from a passage, ask yourself a question such as:

What is the author trying to suggest from the stated information?

or

What do all the facts and ideas point toward or seem to add up to?

or

For what purpose did the author include these facts and details?

In answering any of these questions, you must add together the individual pieces of information to arrive at an inference. Making an inference is somewhat like putting together a complicated picture puzzle, in which you try to make each piece fit with all the rest of the pieces to form something recognizable.

Use Clues Provided by the Writer

A writer often provides numerous hints that point you toward accurate inferences. For instance, a writer's choice of words often suggests his or her attitude toward a subject. Try to notice descriptive words, emotionally charged words, and words with strong positive or negative connotations. Here is an example of how the choice of words can lead you to an inference:

> Grandmother had been an <u>unusually attractive</u> young woman, and she carried herself with the <u>graceful confidence</u> of a <u>natural charmer</u> to her last day.

The underlined phrases "unusually attractive," "graceful confidence," and "natural charmer" suggest that the writer feels positive about her grandmother. However, in the following example, notice how the underlined words and phrases create a negative image of the person.

> The <u>withdrawn</u> child <u>eyed</u> her teacher with a hostile disdain. When directly spoken to, the child responded in a <u>cold</u>, but carefully respectful way.

In this sentence, the underlined words suggest that the child is unfriendly and that he or she dislikes the teacher.

Consider the Author's Purpose

An awareness of the author's purpose for writing is often helpful in making inferences. If an author's purpose is to convince you to purchase a particular product, such as in an advertisement, you already have a clear idea of the types of inferences the writer hopes you will make. For instance, a magazine ad for a stereo system reads:

> If you're in the market for true surround sound, a prematched system is a good way to get it. The components in our system are built for each other by our audio engineers. You can be assured of high performance and sound quality.

You can guess that the writer's purpose is to encourage you to buy his particular prematched stereo system.

Verify Your Inference

Once you have made an inference, check to be sure that it is accurate. Look back at the stated facts to see that you have sufficient evidence to support the inference. Also, be sure that you have not overlooked other equally plausible or more plausible inferences that could be drawn from the same set of facts.

EXERCISE 10-5

DIRECTIONS: Read each main statement. Put a check mark in front of all the substatements that are reasonable inferences.

1. The students in the nursing program work harder than any other students at our school.

   _____ Nursing students are highly motivated.

   _____ The nursing program requires a great deal of work.

   _____ Students not in the nursing program are lazy.

   _____ Only the best students can become nurses.

2. The moose population on the island was no longer overcrowded once a wolf pack was brought over from the mainland.

   _____ Hunting is not the best way to reduce moose herd populations.

   _____ The wolves are an enemy to the moose.

   _____ Humans introduced the wolf pack to the island.

   _____ A moose cannot kill a wolf in a fight.

3. Many pioneers died on their journey along the Oregon Trail because of illness, diseases, and accidents.

   _____ The Oregon Trail crossed dangerous terrain.

   _____ One in five women was pregnant at some part in their journey along the trail.

   _____ There are many pioneer graves along the Oregon Trail.

   _____ The pioneers could not get the medical attention they needed.

4. Most Americans have tried an alternative health-care product or service without telling their regular primary care physician.

   _____ More and more insurance companies are covering alternative medicine.

   _____ Patients are afraid their regular doctors would not approve of an alternative therapy.

   _____ Everyone likes to try new things.

   _____ Doctors are out of touch with popular attitudes toward the medical field.

5. Small businesses and large corporations are now requiring that their network administrators have a college education, specialized computer training, and even certification.

   _____ Network administrators earn a relatively high wage.

   _____ Companies have had difficulties with young computer wizards who lack specialized training or college degrees.

_____ Employers want highly skilled employees running their computer systems.

_____ The best network administrators have Ph.D.s in computer science.

6. Super strong megathrust earthquakes occur in the Pacific Northwest on average about once every 500 years. The last such earthquake was around 300 years ago.

_____ Residents of the Pacific Northwest need not prepare for earthquakes.

_____ There is no chance of a megathrust earthquake in the Pacific Northwest for at least 200 more years.

_____ The Pacific Northwest is a very dangerous place to live.

_____ Within the next 200 years a mega-thrust earthquake may occur in the Pacific Northwest.

7. Attendance at women's professional basketball games is not as high as attendance at men's professional basketball games even though ticket prices are lower.

_____ Men's basketball is more popular than women's basketball.

_____ The female teams play in smaller arenas.

_____ People do not mind paying higher prices to see men's basketball.

_____ More families attend women's basketball games.

8. Library users oftentimes do not know if they are speaking to a professional librarian, circulation clerk, volunteer, or student worker when they ask a library employee a question.

_____ Library users should avoid asking student workers questions.

_____ All library personnel should know enough to answer all questions.

_____ Only librarians should answer questions.

_____ It would be helpful if library personnel wore name tags with job titles.

9. Many animal shelters are now taking in Vietnamese pot-bellied pigs as more and more people realize that these animals do not indeed make good apartment pets.

_____ These pigs need lots of room.

_____ The public has been misinformed about having these animals as pets.

_____ Pot-bellied pigs have nasty temperaments.

_____ Animal shelters never used to take in any pigs.

10. Young children learn by experiencing and doing. Passive teaching tools such as television and battery-operated toys should be avoided.

_____ Battery-operated toys limit a child's opportunity to experience the real world.

_____ Planting seeds in the garden will teach a child more than watching a video of someone planting seeds.

_____ Children are active learners.

_____ Children are not learning in the best way by watching television.

EXERCISE 10-6

DIRECTIONS: Read each paragraph. Answer the questions that follow.

A. Our county is facing a huge budget crisis, as are many counties across the nation. As would be expected around here from our county leaders who bow down to local corporate leaders, the public-private partnership monster is rearing its ugly head. This time our beautiful parks will be attacked. Swimming pools will now display advertisements along the sides and bottoms. Public ball fields will have billboards. All this revenue will be coming in, but vital services will still be cut. Business leaders would do better by sponsoring a public service instead of a sport. Why shouldn't we see something like "Coca-Cola County Hospital?"

1. What can you infer about the author's attitude toward county government?

_____

_____

2. What inference can you make about the author's feelings toward business?

_____

3. What would the author think about a wealthy business owner donating money to the library system and having the branch named after the company?

_____

_____

B. Modern building techniques and materials have helped make Americans more comfortable and more healthy. We no longer have to live in drafty old houses or work in unpleasant buildings. Today's windows, doors, and insulation keep the cold air out of our homes. Meanwhile, climate-controlled work environments ensure a constant comfortable temperature all year round. Airtight construction keeps us healthy and happy which in turn makes living and working more enjoyable and productive.

1. What inference does the author make about our health and being warm or cold?

   _____

2. How concerned is the author likely to be about "sick building syndrome," an illness that workers get from indoor air pollution?

   _____

   _____

3. How would the author react to someone who believes a window should always be open even just a crack in winter?

   _____

C. Documentary films and films based on true stories do so much more than purely fictional movies to enlighten and educate us. Stories of real life adventures, drama, and successes bring with them hope and inspiration. Through such tales brought to life on the big screen, we can learn and plan and strive for our dreams. These types of films also give our young people the introduction to real accessible heroes about whom they can learn more and perhaps even emulate. With so many great true stories in the word and in history, why watch fiction?

1. What inference can you make about the author's attitude toward fiction?

   _____

2. How would the author respond to someone who said they were inspired by a film such as *Star Wars*?

   _____

   _____

D. Standardized tests measure whether students have learned the basics. Children whose scores are less than the national average should receive special instruction until their scores increase. Through this process teachers will be able to identify children with learning difficulties and put them into the appropriate special education programs. Likewise students who excel on standardized tests can be grouped together for more challenging lessons and work. Everyone can be measured and assessed through the use of standardized tests.

1. What inferences can you make about the author's attitude toward standardized testing?

   _____

2. How would the author respond to a school district's plan to mix high- and low-ability students in each classroom?

   _____

3. What would this author say to someone who worries about teachers "teaching to the test?"

   _____

   _____

   _____

E. People who live in densely populated areas are not as friendly as people living in rural areas. Since most of the world's population now lives in urban centers, that makes the vast majority of the inhabitants of Earth rude and pushy. Living so close to each other makes us edgy and irritable. We need more space to feel comfortable with others and ourselves.

1. What can you infer about the author's feelings toward people who live in the country?

   _____

2. What would the author say to someone who believes densely populated areas build community and develop positive human relationships?

   _____

   _____

**EXERCISE
10-7**

DIRECTIONS: Read the following passage and then answer the questions. The answers are not directly stated in the passage; you will have to make inferences in order to answer them.

One morning I put two poached eggs in front of Charlie, who looked up briefly from his newspaper.

"You've really shaped up, Cassie," he smiled. "A dreadful lady went to the hospital and a very nice Cassie came back. I think you've learned a lesson and, honey, I'm proud of you."

He went to work and I started the dishes, trying to feel thrilled at having shaped up for Charlie. *He sounds as though the hospital performed some sort of exorcism,* I mused, scraping egg off the dish with my fingernail. *Evil is banished, goodness restored. Then why don't I feel transformed?*

The dish slipped out of my hand and smashed into the sink, spraying chips over the counter. I looked down at the mess, then at the cluttered kitchen table, and beyond that to the dust on the television set in the den. I pictured the four unmade beds and the three clothes-strewn bedrooms and the toys in the living room and last night's newspaper on the floor next to Charlie's reclining chair and I yelled at the cat who was licking milk out of a cereal bowl, "What lesson? What goddamn lesson was I supposed to learn?"

I grabbed my coat and the grocery money and was waiting at the liquor store when it opened.

"You find a place where they give it away for free?" the man behind the counter leered. "We haven't seen you for weeks. Where you been?"

"Nowhere," I answered. "I've been nowhere." He gave me my bottle and I walked out thinking that I'd have to start trading at another store where the creeps weren't so free with their remarks.

Rebeta-Burditt, *The Cracker Factory.*

1. What problem is Cassie experiencing?

    _____

2. For what purpose was Cassie hospitalized?

    _____

3. How does Cassie feel about household chores?

    _____

4. What is Cassie's husband's attitude toward her problem? Is he part of her problem? If so, how?

    _____

    _____

    _____

Distinguishing Between Fact and Opinion

The ability to distinguish fact from opinion is an essential critical reading skill. Facts are statements that can be verified—that is, proven to be true or false. Opinions are statements that express feelings, attitudes, or beliefs and are neither true nor false. Here are a few examples of each:

FACTS

1. The average American adult spends 25 hours per week on housework.
2. U.S. military spending has increased over the past ten years.

OPINIONS

1. By the year 2020, tobacco will be illegal, just as various other drugs are currently illegal.
2. If John F. Kennedy had lived, the United States would have made even greater advancements against the spread of communism.

Facts, once verified or taken from a reputable source, can be accepted and regarded as reliable information. Opinions, however, are not reliable sources of information and should be questioned and carefully evaluated. Look for evidence that supports the opinion and indicates that it is reasonable.

Some authors are careful to signal the reader when they are presenting an opinion. Watch for words and phrases such as

it is believed	apparently
in my view	presumably
it is likely that	in my opinion
seemingly	this suggests
one explanation is	possibly

In the following excerpt from a psychology textbook, notice how the author carefully distinguishes factual statements from opinion by using qualifying words and phrases (underlined).

Some research has suggested that day care can have problematic effects on children's development. For example, studies indicate that children who begin day care as infants are more aggressive, more easily distracted, less considerate of their peers, less popular, and less obedient to adults than children who have never attended day care or haven't attended for as long (Bates et al., 1994; Matlock & Green, 1990; Vandell & Corasaniti, 1990).

Other studies have found that day care is associated with adaptive behaviors. For example, researchers have reported that children who attend day care develop social and language skills more quickly than children who stay at home, although the children who don't attend day care catch up in their social development in a few years (Feagans et al., 1995; Mott, 1991). Poor children who go to day care are likely to develop better reading and math skills than poor children who stay at home (Caughy et al., 1994).

Further complicating this picture of day care's developmental effects are <u>additional studies</u> finding no differences between children who attended day care and those who didn't (e.g., Hegland & Rix, 1990; Reynolds, 1995; Roggman et al., 1994; Scarr et al., 1989). What can we conclude about the reasons for these different—and in some cases, contradictory—findings?

Uba and Huang, *Psychology.*

Other authors, however, mix fact and opinion without making clear distinctions. This is particularly true in the case of *informed opinion,* which is the opinion of an expert or authority. Ralph Nader represents expert opinion on consumer rights, for example. Textbook authors, too, often offer informed opinion, as in the following statement from an American government text.

In the early days of voting research, the evidence was clear: voters rarely engaged in policy voting, preferring to rely on party identification or candidate evaluation to make up their minds.

Lineberry and Edwards, *Government in America.*

The author of this statement has reviewed the available evidence and is providing his expert opinion as to what the evidence indicates.

EXERCISE
10-8

DIRECTIONS: Read each of the following statements and decide whether it is fact or opinion. Write "Fact" or "Opinion" in the space provided.

_____ 1. The sexual division of labor in middle-class homes will change in the next 50 years.

_____ 2. An infection is an illness produced by the action of micro-organisms in the human body.

_____ 3. When measured by earning power, the American standard of living has increased steadily since the early 1970s.

_____ 4. Work, or the lack of it, is the primary influence in lifestyle.

_____ 5. Increased job opportunities for women and other minorities depends primarily on the future of the economy.

_____ 6. Parents now spend less time with their children than they did 30 years ago.

_____ 7. Libraries have an obligation to catalog and preserve selected personal Web sites.

_____ 8. Art and music classes are being cut from high school curricula in several states.

_____ 9. Most people believe that Meriwether Lewis (of Lewis and Clark fame) committed suicide.

_____ 10. Being courageous is more important than being clever.

EXERCISE 10-9

DIRECTIONS: Read each topic sentence. Mark the statements that follow as fact (F), opinion (O), or informed opinion (IO).

1. Topic sentence: Cotton farmers use large amounts of fertilizers and pesticides.

    _____ a. Chemical use should be avoided in cotton farming.

    _____ b. Researchers who have studied chemically sensitive individuals state that organically grown cotton is better for them.

    _____ c. Cotton seeds are treated with fungicide.

    _____ d. In some countries, farmers use DDT on cotton fields.

2. Topic sentence: Many universities now offer courses in popular culture.

    _____ a. Students watch films and television shows as homework assignments.

    _____ b. It is wonderful that our young people have the opportunity to study their own culture!

    _____ c. Popular culture studies are vital to sustaining interest in the history department.

    _____ d. Learning specialists acknowledge that students learn better when they are interested in the material; therefore, our students are expected to do very well in these courses.

3. Topic sentence: Noise pollution is becoming a major health issue.

    _____ a. Most of us experience exposure to high levels of noise on a daily basis.

    _____ b. Contractors recommend thick walls and floors to reduce noise from neighbors in apartment buildings.

_____ c. Traffic, construction, and airplanes can contribute to noise pollution.

_____ d. Neighborhood children produce the most annoying type of noise pollution.

4. Topic sentence: Exercise is an important part of maintaining a healthy lifestyle.

_____ a. Regular exercise can improve your grades in school.

_____ b. People who do not exercise are lazy.

_____ c. Aerobic exercise stimulates blood circulation.

_____ d. Every time you exercise, doctors suggest stretching and relaxing.

5. Topic sentence: Water is fundamental to life.

_____ a. Health organizations around the world have studied the availability of fresh water and believe that reforms are necessary to provide equal access to clean drinking water.

_____ b. Most of the Earth's water is sea salt water or ice.

_____ c. Fountains and ponds provide relaxing decoration in city gardens.

_____ d. Water can be used to produce electricity.

6. Topic sentence: Many groups disagree internally on the issue of drilling for oil in the Arctic National Wildlife Refuge.

_____ a. Some native peoples are worried about endangering vital caribou populations.

_____ b. It is not surprising that the politicians do not agree on the drilling issue.

_____ c. Although scientists disagree as to the extent of damage, they all acknowledge there will be an impact upon the region.

_____ d. Some environmentalists have stated that they are not sure whether no development is the best solution.

7. Topic sentence: Thailand's first settlements, made up of farmers, potters and weavers, were located on hillsides.

_____ a. The very first inhabitants of Thailand were wandering hunter-gatherers.

_____ b. The Ban Chiang settlement was founded about 3500 B.C.

_____ c. Scientists have found Ban Chiang artifacts buried with the dead, so they believe these items must have been quite valuable.

_____ d. The craftsmen of Ban Chiang produced their best work from 300 B.C. to 200 A.D.

8. Topic sentence: In America, attitudes toward family have changed over the past one hundred years.

_____ a. Several well-known sociologists report that the immediate family has become more important than the extended family.

_____ b. Divorce is more common now than it was in 1903.

_____ c. Many fathers now stay home with the children while the mothers work full-time.

_____ d. The collapse of the family structure has caused widespread societal chaos.

9. Topic sentence: Mercury, the planet nearest to the sun, has no atmosphere.

_____ a. We know all we need to know about the planet Mercury.

_____ b. Mercury's year equals 88 Earth days.

_____ c. Scientists believe that Mercury is uninhabitable.

_____ d. In 1974, an unmanned spacecraft flew within 460 miles of Mercury.

10. Topic sentence: Many communities now have recycling programs as part of their waste management services.

_____ a. Recycling alone is not enough; people must reuse and reduce as well.

_____ b. People do not like rinsing out bottle and cans and sorting them into different bins.

_____ c. You can avoid extra packaging by buying in bulk.

_____ d. Some environmental scientists believe the process of recycling paper is as harmful as making new paper.

EXERCISE 10-10

DIRECTIONS: Read each of the following passages and underline factual statements in each. Place brackets around clear statements of opinion. In class, discuss the statements about which you are unsure.

PASSAGE 1

Opponents of day care still call for women to return to home and hearth, but the battle is really over. Now the question is: Will day care continue to be inadequately funded and poorly regulated, or will public policy begin to put into place a system that rightly treats children as our most valuable national resource?

More than 50% of the mothers of young children are in the work force before their child's first birthday. An estimated 9.5 million preschoolers have mothers who work outside the home. Most women, like most men, are working to put food on the table. Many are the sole support of their families. They are economically unable to stay at home, although many would prefer to do so.

Phillips, "Needed: A Policy for Children When Parents Go to Work."

PASSAGE 2

Elvis Presley is the king of rock and roll, the best and most famous performer to ever hit the top ten charts. Due to his fame, fans line up outside his former home, Graceland. Fans include teenagers, parents, and the elderly, and they are all waiting to tour his residence. Cash registers are very busy. People with credit card in hand pay outrageous amounts of money for worthless souvenirs and other useless memorabilia. Music plays as people wait. Of course it is songs such as: "Hound Dog" or "Can't Help Falling in Love." The music sets a nostalgic mood and makes people even more willing to waste their hard earned dollars.

PASSAGE 3

Photographers often find that one of the most exciting types of photography is also one of the most difficult. Taking pictures with telephoto lenses is really tough because the laws of photographic physics are against you. With a long-focal-length lens, the magnification is great while the angle of view is very narrow; an image may become blurred or unsharp. The rule of thumb is that when hand-holding a camera and lens, you must use a shutter speed that is equal to, or greater than, the numeric value of your focal length to maintain sharp images. For example, a 300mm lens requires a shutter speed of at least 1/300 to maintain the sharpness equivalent to using a 100mm lens at 1/100.

Adapted from Drafahl and Drafahl, "Films for Long-Lens Photography"

EXERCISE 10-11

DIRECTIONS: For each topic, write a statement of fact and an opinion.

1.   racial and ethnic diversity on college campuses

Fact: _____

_____

Opinion: _____

_____

2. substance abuse

Fact: _____

_____

Opinion: _____

_____

3. airport security

Fact: _____

_____

Opinion: _____

_____

4. reality TV

Fact: _____

_____

Opinion: _____

_____

5. space exploration

Fact: _____

_____

Opinion: _____

_____

EXERCISE 10-12

DIRECTIONS: From a chapter in one of your textbooks, identify two statements that represent an author's informed opinion.

EXERCISE 10-13

ELECTRONIC APPLICATION

DIRECTIONS: Visit a Web site or newsgroup, or choose a print magazine advertisement or newspaper editorial. Identify statements of opinion and/or informed opinion. ▬

Recognizing Generalizations

A generalization is a statement that is made about a large group or a class of items based on observation of or experience with a part of that group or class. Suppose you interviewed a number of students on campus. You asked each why he or she was attending college, and each indicated that he or she was preparing for a career. From your interview you could make the generalization "Students attend college to prepare for a career." Of course, you could not be absolutely certain that this statement is true until you asked *every* college student. Here are a few more generalizations. Some may seem very reasonable; you may disagree with others.

1. All college freshmen are confused and disoriented during their first week on campus.
2. Most parents are concerned for the happiness of their children.
3. Psychology instructors are interested in the psychology of learning.
4. College students are more interested in social life than scholarship.

As you evaluate the evidence a writer uses to support his or her ideas, be alert for generalizations that are used as facts. Remember that a generalization is not a fact and represents the writer's judgment only about a particular set of facts. In the following paragraph, generalizations, not facts, are used to support the main idea:

> The wedding is a tradition that most young adults still value. Most engaged couples carefully plan their wedding and regard it as an important occasion in their life. Couples also are very concerned that their ceremony follow rules of etiquette and that everything is done "just so." Most give a great deal of attention to personalizing their ceremony, including their own vows, songs, and symbols.

Notice that the writer does not use concrete, specific information to develop the paragraph. Instead, the author provides generalizations about how young adults feel about their weddings. If the writer is a sociologist who has studied the attitudes toward and customs of marriage, the generalizations may be accurate. However, if the paragraph was written by a parent and based on experience with his or her children and their friends, then you have little reason to accept the generalizations as facts because they are based on limited experience. Both the expertise of the writer and the method by which he or she arrived at the generalizations influence how readily you should accept them.

When reading material that contains generalizations, approach the writer's conclusion with a critical, questioning attitude. When a generalization is unsubstantiated by facts, regard it as an opinion. Generalizations presented as facts are dangerous and misleading; they may be completely false.

**EXERCISE
10-14**

DIRECTIONS: Indicate which of the following statements are generalizations. Then discuss what type(s) of information or documentation would be necessary for you to evaluate their worth or accuracy.

1. Worker productivity in the United States is rapidly declining.

   _____

2. Government spending on social programs is detrimental to national economic growth.

   _____

3. In 1964 the federal government officially declared a War on Poverty.

   _____

4. Male computer scientists earn more than female computer scientists with similar job responsibilities.

   _____

5. Illegal aliens residing within the United States are displacing American workers and increasing the unemployment rate.

   _____

**EXERCISE
10-15**

DIRECTIONS: Visit a Web site sponsored by a company that is advertising its product, or choose an advertisement from a print magazine. Search and make note of any generalizations made about the product advertised. ▬

ELECTRONIC
APPLICATION

Identifying Tone

A speaker's tone of voice often reveals his or her attitude and contributes to the overall message. Tone is also evident in writing and also contributes to its meaning. Recognizing an author's tone is often important in interpreting and evaluating a piece of writing because tone often reveals feelings, attitudes, or viewpoints not directly stated by the author. The tone of a piece of writing can also suggest the author's purpose. An author's tone is achieved primarily through word choice and stylistic features such as sentence pattern and length.

Tone, then, reveals feelings. Many human emotions can be communicated through tone—disapproval, hate, admiration, disgust, gratitude, forcefulness. Read the following passage, paying particular attention to the feeling it creates.

> Among the worst bores in the Western world are religious converts and reformed drunks. . . . I did give up drinking more than a dozen years ago. This didn't make me feel morally superior to anyone. If asked, I would talk about going dry but, from the first, I was determined to preach no sermons and stand in judgment of no human being who took pleasure in the sauce.
>
> But I must confess that lately my feelings have begun to change. Drinking and drunks now fill me with loathing. Increasingly, I see close friends—human beings of intelligence, wit and style—reduced to slobbering fools by liquor. I've seen other friends ruin their marriages, brutalize their children, destroy their careers. I've also reached the age when I've had to help bury a few people who allowed booze to take them into eternity.
>
> Hamill, "The Wet Drug."

Here the author's disapproval of the use of alcohol is apparent. Through choice of words—slobbering, loathing—as well as choice of detail, he makes the tone obvious.

Tone can also establish a distance or formality between the writer and reader, or can establish a sense of shared communication and draw them together. In the excerpts that follow, notice how in the first passage, a formality or distance is established, and in the second, how a familiarity and friendliness are created.

PASSAGE 1

It's not entirely clear whether party voting differences are caused directly by party affiliation or indirectly by the character of constituencies. Some scholars have found strong independent party effects. Others argue that the tendency of people in the same party to vote together is a reflection of the fact that Democratic lawmakers come from districts and states that are similar to each other and that Republican lawmakers come from ones that are different from those of Democrats. Republicans generally come from higher-income districts than Democrats. Democratic districts, in turn, tend to have more union members and racial minorities in them. The strongest tie, in this line of argument, is between the member of Congress and the constituency and not between the member and the party.

Greenberg and Page, *The Struggle for Democracy.*

PASSAGE 2

Each time I visit my man in prison, I relive the joy of reunion—and the anguish of separation.

We meet at the big glass door at the entrance to the small visitors' hall at Lompoc Federal Correctional Institution. We look at each other silently, then turn and walk into a room jammed with hundreds of molded fiberglass chairs lined up side by side. Finding a place in the crowded hall, we sit down, appalled that we're actually in a prison. Even now, after four months of such clocked, supervised, regulated visits, we still can't get used to the frustrations.

Yet, as John presses me gently to his heart, I feel warm and tender, and tears well up inside me, as they do each weekend. I have seven hours to spend with the man I love—all too brief a time for sharing a lifetime of emotion: love and longing, sympathy and tenderness, resentment and anger.

King, "Love in the Afternoon—In a Crowded Prison Hall."

To identify an author's tone, pay particular attention to descriptive language and connotative meanings. Ask yourself "How does the author feel about his or her subject and how are these feelings revealed?" It is sometimes difficult to find the right word to describe the author's tone. Table 10.1 lists words that are often used to describe the tone of a piece of writing. Use this list to provoke your thinking when identifying tone. If any of these words are unfamiliar, be sure to check their meaning in a dictionary.

Table 10.1   Words Frequently Used to Describe Tone

abstract	condemning	forgiving	joyful	playful
absurd	condescending	formal	loving	reverent
amused	cynical	frustrated	malicious	righteous
angry	depressing	gentle	melancholic	sarcastic
apathetic	detached	grim	mocking	satiric
arrogant	disapproving	hateful	nostalgic	sensational
assertive	disrespectful	humorous	objective	serious
awestruck	distressed	impassioned	obsequious	solemn
bitter	docile	incredulous	optimistic	sympathetic
caustic	earnest	indignant	outraged	tragic
celebratory	excited	indirect	pathetic	uncomfortable
cheerful	fanciful	intimate	persuasive	vindictive
comic	farcical	ironic	pessimistic	worried
compassionate	flippant	irreverent		

**EXERCISE
10-16**

DIRECTIONS: Using Table 10.1 as a reference, choose at least one word that describes the tone of each of the following pieces of writing.

1. An essay that treats a serious subject lightly and casually.

    _____

2. A magazine article that idolizes a motion picture celebrity, describing her amazing talent and beauty while remaining deferential.

    _____

3. A comic strip that makes fun of or ridicules the American expression, "Have a good day!"

    _____

4. A section of a criminal justice textbook titled "The Consequences of Unlawful Searches."

    _____

5. A newspaper editorial that attacks a local mayoral candidate with the intent to injure his reputation and that of his family.

    _____

**EXERCISE
10-17**

DIRECTIONS: Choose a word from the box that expresses the tone of the sentences.

awestruck	cynical	depressing	comic	disapproving
compassionate	forgiving	nostalgic	indirect	cheerful
optimistic	sympathetic	outraged	persuasive	serious

_____ 1. Mark Twain has stated that "Man is the only animal that blushes. Or needs to."

_____ 2. The U.S. economy is bound to turn around sooner than later. It can really only get better at this point!

_____ 3. Road construction is the best way to alleviate traffic. Since people are not going to give up their automobiles, they need the new and bigger highways that can accommodate everyone.

_____ 4. So many nations are scarred by war. Our community sends out support to the innocent people caught in unfortunate circumstances.

_____ 5. Station programmers choose such objectionable programming for children. Our household takes a very dim view of the offerings on any commercial channel.

_____ 6. Back in the good old days, scientists could perform any kind of experiments they wanted. Now there is so much government supervision and regulation.

_____ 7. Our history is full of instances in which people acted in ways that we now consider to be abhorrent. However, these early societies did not understand what we do now about human rights and democracy.

_____ 8. The nursing shortage in our country is reaching a critical stage. We must fill our hospitals with fully qualified and educated nurses to avert a health disaster.

_____ 9. How can people let their homes and neighborhoods fall apart and rot away? It is not acceptable to allow such degradation.

_____ 10. Spring is the absolute perfect time for graduations. As Nature herself is bursting forth with newness, so are the hardworking students blossoming with the flowers of their education.

EXERCISE 10-18

DIRECTIONS: Describe the tone of each of the following passages.

PASSAGE 1   _____

Rude or indifferent waiters and waitresses should be fired. Nothing can ruin a pleasant meal in a restaurant like a snippy waitress or a superior-acting waiter. Part of the cost of any restaurant meal is the service, and it should be at least as good as the food.

PASSAGE 2   _____

Welfare makes you feel like you're nothing. Like you're laying back and not doing anything and it's falling in your lap. But you must understand, mothers, too, work. My house is clean. I've been scrubbing since this morning. You could check my clothes, all washed and ironed. I'm home and I'm working. I am a working mother.

A job that a woman in a house is doing is a tedious job—especially if you want to do it right. If you do it slipshod, then it's not so bad. I'm pretty much of a perfectionist. I tell my kids, hang a towel. I don't want it thrown away. That is very hard. It's a constant game of picking up this, picking up that. And putting this away, so the house'll be clean.

Terkel, *Working.*

PASSAGE 3 _____

Incidence and Types of Schizophrenia

Schizophrenia was originally thought to be confined to North America and Western Europe. We now understand that the disorder (or varieties of the disorder) can be found around the world at the same rate: about 1 percent of the population (Alder & Gielen, 1994; Bloom et al., 1985). People in developing countries tend to have a more acute (intense, but short-lived) course—and a better outcome—of the disorder than do people in industrialized nations. In the United States, schizophrenia accounts for 75 percent of all mental health expenditures. (Carpenter & Buchanan, 1994). Schizophrenia occurs at the same rate for both sexes, but symptoms are likely to show up earlier in males, and males are more likely to be disabled by the disorder (Grinspoon, 1995).

Currie and Skolnick, *America's Problems.*

PASSAGE 4 _____

The most important predictor of student success in school is readiness to learn to read. Unfortunately, many children from high-poverty homes enter school with limited readiness skills. Until we do a more successful job in educating children who have been placed at risk of failure, their communities, and our society in general, will fail to cultivate a substantial reservoir of human talent that will be greatly needed in the years ahead.

From: Center for Research on the Education of Students Placed at Risk,
http://www.csos.jhu.edu/crespar/programs.htm

PASSAGE 5 _____

Alcoholism hurts everyone who is involved with the person afflicted with the disease. Alcoholics may be ill and can get treatment for that, but the damage they do while sick is unforgivable and cannot be fixed. People who abuse alcohol to such a degree that they neglect the basic needs of their own children can never reverse the negative effects upon those innocent, developing personas. Children of alcoholics grow up much faster than they should have to—learning early how to fend for themselves at mealtime, keep secrets from their friends, neighbors, teachers and relatives, make excuses, stay out of the way. Twelve steps will never be enough steps for any alcoholic to cure the pain and injury to a child.

PASSAGE 6 _____

As the former gold-medal-winning Olympic athletes entered the arena, the crowd quieted down into a silence and respect worthy of a great cathedral. While each athlete came forward to receive his or her special honor we listened in awe to their inspiring tales of courage and dedication. Such deep emotion was stirred within us by these remarkable individuals!

PASSAGE 7 _____

I am 33 years old and I just called in sick. I'm not really sick. In fact, I'm not the least bit sick. I am totally faking it. And as I dance around my living room singing, "Sick day, sick day!" I think, "Ah, it's good to be nine!" The call was award-winning. A slightly raspy voice with a hint of fatigue combined with a slow, deliberate delivery. "I started throwing up around 3 A.M.," I told my boss. "I'm exhausted and I can't even keep water down. I must have caught that bug that's going around the office." I was told to stay home, rest, and feel better. Exactly what I had in mind.

McKinnon, "The Magic of a 'Sick Day': Feigning illness can be good for you—
especially when mom's a co-conspirator."

PASSAGE 8 _____

Let's call him "Joe Six Pack." Every Saturday night, he drinks way too much, cranks up the rock 'n roll way too loud, and smacks his girlfriend for acting just a bit too lippy. Or let's call him "Mr. Pillar of the Community." He's got the perfect wife, the perfect kids. But he's also got one little problem: every time he argues with his wife, he loses control. In the past year, she's been sent to the emergency ward twice. Or let's say they're the Tenants from Hell. They're always yelling at each other. Finally a neighbor calls the police. Here is the question. Are the men in these scenarios: (a) in need of help; (b) in need of being locked up; or (c) upholders of the patriarchy?

Satel, "Domestic Violence Laws Are Anti-Male."

PASSAGE 9 _____

Crime victims who survive the ordeals to which they were involuntarily subjected, must be treated with the utmost kindness and helpfulness. No amount of love and caring is too much to gently guide these poor, broken spirits back to healthy, full lives. We must not blame or condemn them for their suffering, but patiently help them through the cloud of pain back to the sunshine of life.

PASSAGE 10 _____

America has entered a great struggle that tests our strength, and even more our resolve. Our nation is patient and steadfast. We continue to pursue the terrorists in cities and camps and caves across the earth. We are joined by a great coalition of nations to rid the world of terror. And we will not allow any terrorist or tyrant to threaten civilization with weapons of mass murder. Now and in the future, Americans will live as free people, not in fear, and never at the mercy of any foreign plot or power.

Bush, "Remarks to the Nation, September 11, 2002,"
http://www.whitehouse.gov/news/releases/2002/09/20020911-3.html.

EXERCISE 10-19

DIRECTIONS: For each topic, write a sentence or two that expresses the given tone.

(Answers will vary; a sample answer is provided for each)

1. **Topic**: Adoption **Tone**: Excited

_____

_____

2. **Topic**: Human rights **Tone**: Tragic

_____

_____

3. **Topic**: Sex education **Tone**: Worried

_____

_____

_____

4. **Topic**: Endangered species **Tone**: Apathetic

_____

_____

5. **Topic**: Poverty **Tone**: Impassioned

_____

_____

_____

EXERCISE 10-20

DIRECTIONS: Choose two of the following end-of-chapter reading selections that appear earlier in the book. Identify the tone of the two that you choose.

1. "How to Brag About Yourself to Win and Hold a New Job" (Sel. 1, p. 23)

_____

2. "Talking a Stranger Through the Night" (Sel. 2, p. 27)

   _____

3. "Just Walk On By" (Sel. 4, p. 68)

   _____

4. "Why the Sky Is Blue, Sunsets Are Red, and Clouds Are White" (Sel. 6, p. 108)

   _____

5. "Will We Control the Weather?" (Sel. 11, p. 247)

   _____ ▬

Identifying the Author's Purpose

Authors write for a variety of purposes: to inform or instruct the reader, to amuse or entertain, to arouse sympathy, to persuade the reader to take a particular action, or to accept a certain point of view. To be an effective reader you must be aware of the author's purpose. Sometimes the writer's purpose will be obvious, as in the following advertisements:

At Hair Design Salons we'll make you look better than you can imagine. Six professional stylists to meet your every need. Stop in for a free consultation today.

Puerto Rican white rum can do anything better than gin or vodka.

The first ad is written to encourage the readers to have their hair styled at Hair Design Salons. The second is intended to encourage readers to use rum instead of gin or vodka in their mixed drinks. In both ads the writer is clearly trying to convince you to buy a certain product. However, in many other types of reading material, even other advertisements, the writer's purpose is not so obvious.

For instance, in an ad for a particular brand of cigarettes, a stylishly dressed woman is pictured holding a cigarette. The caption reads, "You've come a long way, baby." In this case, although you know that all ads are intended to sell a product or service, the ad does not even mention cigarettes. It is left up to you, the reader, to infer that stylish women smoke Virginia Slims.

You will often be able to predict the author's purpose from the title of the article or by your familiarity with the writer. For instance, if you noticed an article titled "My Role in Health-Care Systems," written by Hillary Rodham Clinton, you could predict that the author's purpose is to defend her role in proposing a health care system during the Clinton presidency. An article titled "The President Flexes His Muscles but Nobody Is Watching" suggests that the author's purpose is to describe how the president is attempting to exert power but having little success.

How to Identify the Author's Purpose

To identify the author's purpose when it is not apparent, first determine the subject and thesis of the material and notice how the writer supports the thesis. Then ask the following questions to start thinking critically about the material:

1. **Who is the intended audience?** Try to decide for whom or for what type or group of people the material seems to be written. Often, the level of language, the choice of words, and the complexity of the ideas, examples, or arguments included suggest the audience the writer has in mind. Once you have identified a potential audience, you can begin to consider what the writer wants to communicate to that audience.

   A writer may write for a general-interest audience (anyone who is interested in the subject). Most newspapers and periodicals such as *Time* and *Newsweek* appeal to a general-interest audience. On the other hand, a writer may have a particular interest group in mind. A writer may write for medical doctors in the *Journal of American Medicine,* or for skiing enthusiasts in *Skiing Today,* or for antique collectors in *The World of Antiques.* Also, a writer may intend his or her writing for an audience with particular political, moral, or religious attitudes. Articles in the *Atlantic Monthly* often appeal to the conservative political viewpoint, whereas *The Catholic Digest* appeals to a particular religious group.

2. **What is the tone?** Determine whether the author is serious or whether he or she is trying to poke fun at the subject. If a writer is ridiculing or making light of a subject, he or she will usually offer clues that alert the reader. The writer may use exaggerations, describe unbelievable situations, or choose language and details that indicate that he or she is not completely serious.

3. **What is the point of view?** Point of view is the perspective from which an article or essay is written. An event, for example, may be described from the point of view of someone in attendance or from that of someone who has only heard or read about it. A controversial issue

may be discussed from an objective point of view, examining both sides of the issue, or a subjective one in which one side of the issue is favored. Point of view might be described as the way an author "looks at" or approaches his or her subject. As such, point of view can often suggest the author's purpose in writing.

4. **Does the writer try to prove anything about the subject? If so, what?** Try to determine if the article is written to persuade the reader to accept a certain point of view or to perform a certain action. For instance, a writer may write to convince you that inflation will cause a national disaster, or that abortion is morally wrong, or that the best jobs are available in health-related fields.

To test the use of these questions, read the following passage and apply the critical thinking questions to it.

> I moved to Madison, Wisconsin, from Anchorage, Alaska, in 1987 with my husband and our 18-month-old daughter. Education brought us: My husband had been accepted into a Ph.D. program, and I hoped to finish my undergraduate degree once he began working. In May 1992 I did complete my B.A. in English, but not at all in the way I had planned. From September 1988 until December 1990 my daughter and I received Aid to Families with Dependent Children (AFDC).
>
> Like many women, I was thrown into relative poverty as a result of divorce—my marriage broke up during our first year in Wisconsin. I say *relative* because my daughter and I were never in danger of going without food or shelter. But my financial situation as a single parent was alarmingly precarious. Did I have to go on welfare? No—I chose to. Reaching this decision took time and, having worked since I was 15, I was bothered by it a great deal.
>
> Though I knew I needed help to improve my situation, I had internalized many attitudes our society holds concerning work and public assistance. I was keenly aware that many people would deny that I had any right to hold my hand out, able-bodied citizen that I was. Able-bodied, yes; simpleminded, no. When I reached the point of paying 18 percent interest on credit card cash advances to buy food, I knew I was digging myself into a hole I might never get out of. In the beginning, though, I never considered welfare.
>
> Lovern, "Confessions of a Welfare Mom."

The subject of this excerpt is welfare assistance. The essay seems to be written for an audience familiar with the subject. The tone is serious; the author maintains a reasoned, factual, unemotional tone. The point of view is personal; the author is relating events from her life experience. She seems to be suggesting that receiving welfare assistance can be a reasoned decision and one she does not regret.

EXERCISE 10-21

DIRECTIONS: Identify the author's purpose for two of the reading selections listed in Exercise 10–20.

_____

_____

_____

_____

_____

_____

_____

EXERCISE 10-22

DIRECTIONS: Visit a Web site in an area of interest. Browse through the site, evaluate its purpose, and write a brief statement that summarizes its purpose.

ELECTRONIC
APPLICATION

EXERCISE 10-23

DIRECTIONS: Read each of the excerpts contained in Exercise 10–18. For each, write a statement describing the author's purpose.

_____

_____

_____

Identifying Bias

Bias refers to an author's partiality, inclination toward a particular viewpoint, or prejudice. A writer is biased if he or she takes one side of a controversial issue and does not recognize opposing viewpoints. Perhaps the best example of bias is in advertising. A magazine advertisement for a new car model, for instance, describes only positive, marketable features—the ad does not recognize the car's limitations or faults. In some material the writer is direct and outright in expressing his or her bias; other times the bias is hidden and left for the reader to discover through careful analysis.

Read the following description of the environmental protection group Greenpeace. The author expresses a favorable attitude toward the organization and a negative one toward whale hunters. Notice, in particular, the *underlined* words and phrases.

> Greenpeace is an organization <u>dedicated</u> to the preservation of the sea and its great mammals, notably whales, dolphins, and seals. Its ethic is <u>nonviolent</u> but its aggressiveness in <u>protecting</u> our oceans and the life in them is becoming <u>legendary</u>. In their roving ship, the *Rainbow Warrior*, Greenpeace volunteers have <u>relentlessly hounded</u> the <u>profiteering</u> ships of any nation harming the resources Greenpeace deems to be the property of the world community. Whales, they believe, belong to us all and have a right to exist no matter what the demand for shoe-horns, cosmetics, and machine oil.
>
> Wallace, *Biology: The World of Life.*

To identify bias, apply the following questions:

1. **Analyze connotative meanings.** Do you encounter a large number of positive or negative terms used to describe the subject?
2. **Notice descriptive language.** What impression is created?
3. **Analyze the tone.** The author's tone often provides important clues.
4. **Look for opposing viewpoints.**

EXERCISE 10-24

DIRECTIONS: Read the following passage and underline words and phrases that reveal the author's bias.

> Not unlike drugs or alcohol, the television experience allows the participant to blot out the real world and enter into a pleasurable and passive mental state. The worries and anxieties of reality are as effectively deferred by becoming absorbed in a television program as by going on a "trip" induced by drugs or alcohol. And just as alcoholics are only inchoately aware of their addiction, feeling that they control their drinking more than they really do ("I can cut it out any time I want—I just like to have three or four drinks before dinner"), people similarly overestimate their control over television watching. Even as they put off other activities to spend hour after hour watching television, they feel they could easily resume living in a different, less passive style. But somehow or other while the television set is present in their homes, the click doesn't sound. With television pleasures available, those other experiences seem less attractive, more difficult somehow.
>
> Winn, *The Plug-in Drug.*

EXERCISE 10-25

DIRECTIONS: Choose one of the selections at the end of the chapter and write a one-page paper evaluating the reading. You might:

1. Identify what inferences can be made about the subject.
2. Evaluate statements of opinion.
3. Identify several generalizations.
4. Describe the tone of the article.
5. Summarize the author's purpose.
6. Discuss the author's bias and describe how it is revealed.

EXERCISE 10-26

DIRECTIONS: Visit a Web site or join a newsgroup that concerns a controversial issue. As you browse through the site, look for and make brief notes about any bias you detect.

ELECTRONIC
APPLICATION

Understanding Figurative Language

Figurative language is a way of describing something that makes sense on an imaginative level but not on a literal or factual level. Notice in each of the following sentences that the underlined expression cannot be literally true but that each is understandable and is effective in conveying the author's message.

An overly ambitious employee may find the <u>door to advancement closed</u>. (There is no actual door that may close.)

The federal government is <u>draining</u> taxpayers of any accumulated wealth.

(Nothing is literally being drained or removed from the insides of taxpayers.)

The judge decided to <u>get to the heart</u> of the matter. (Matters do not really have hearts.)

In each of these expressions, one distinct thing is compared with another for some quality that they have in common.

Figurative language is an effective way to describe and limit relationships. By your choice of figurative expressions you can create either a positive or a negative impression. For instance, this first statement is somewhat negative:

> The blush spread across her face like spilled paint.
> (Spilled paint is usually thought of as messy and problematic.)

This second statement, however, creates a more positive image.

> The blush spread across her face like wine being poured into a glass.

> (Wine filling a glass is commonly thought of as a pleasing image.)

Because figurative language involves impressions and judgments, you should regard them as interpretations, as expressions of opinion and judgment rather than as factual statements.

There are two common types of figurative expressions—similes and metaphors. Similes make an explicit comparison by using the words "like" or "as." Metaphors directly equate the two objects. Here are several examples of each:

SIMILES

1. He says the waves in the ship's wake are like stones rolling away. *(Levertov)*

2. When she was here, LiBo, she was like cold summer lager. *(Williams)*

METAPHORS

1. I will speak daggers but use none. (Shakespeare, *Hamlet*)

2. Hope is the thing with feathers—
    That perches in the soul—
    And sings the tune without words—
    And never stops—at all—
    (Dickinson)

EXERCISE 10-27

DIRECTIONS: Explain the meaning of each of the following metaphors or similes.

1. The scarlet of the maples can shake me like the cry of bugles going by. *(Carman)*

    _____

    _____

    _____

2   Every thread of summer is at last unwoven. *(Wallace Stevens)*

_____

_____

_____

Critical Thinking Tip #10

Slanted Writing

Slanted writing is a technique used to persuade. Slanted writing attempts to push or tip the reader in a particular direction—usually toward a particular belief, attitude, or action. Here are two brief news reports. Notice the slant in each.

VERSION 1

The Congressman flapped open his notebook and began his speech in his usual flat tone. He moved mechanically from point to point, dwelling on each longer than necessary.

VERSION 2

The Congressman climbed energetically to the podium and began his speech. He moved methodically from point to point, taking care that each point was well understood before moving to the next.

SLANTED WRITING EMPLOYS TWO TECHNIQUES:

1. The use of words that create a favorable or unfavorable impression. In Version 1, words such as *flat, flapped,* and *mechanically* create a negative impression. In the second version, words such as *energetically, methodically,* and *well understood* create a favorable impression.
2. Selection of detail. Writers select details that create the desired impression and omit details that do not. In Version 1, the writer omitted the detail about how the Congressman climbed to the podium, choosing instead to describe how he opened his notebook. In Version 2, the writer omitted the notebook opening but did include the climbing stairs detail.

Slanted writing is dangerous and can be misleading, and it is easy to miss, especially when reading rapidly or when skimming. Keep this question in mind: What has the writer chosen *not* to tell me? When possible try to read more than one source of information, choosing sources or writers likely to have differing viewpoints. Once you suspect writing is slanted, circle favorable or unfavorable words; write questions about omitted information.

3. What happens to a dream deferred?
    Does it dry up
    like a raisin in the sun?
    or fester like a sore—
    and then run?
    (Langston Hughes)

_____

_____

4. An aged man is but a paltry thing,
    a tattered coat upon a stick, . . .
    (W. B. Yeats)

_____

Summary

1. What is critical analysis?

Critical analysis is the interpretation and evaluation of an author's meaning. By applying the tools of critical reading and thinking, you can analyze a written work deliberately and carefully and make decisions about its worth and value.

2. What are denotative and connotative meanings?

A word's denotative meaning is its literal or dictionary meaning. A word's connotative meaning includes shades of meaning.

3. What is involved in making an inference?

An inference is a reasonable guess made on the basis of available information. To make an inference as you read,
- be sure you understand the literal meaning first
- ask questions about the stated information
- use clues provided by the writer
- consider the writer's purpose
- verify your information

4. How can facts be distinguished from opinions?

Facts can be shown to be true or false; they can be verified and regarded as reliable information. Because opinions express attitudes, beliefs, or feelings, they are not reliable and should be carefully questioned and evaluated.

5. What are generalizations?

Generalizations are statements made about a large group or class of items based on experience with only a part of the group or class. When generalizations are stated as facts, carefully evaluate them before you accept them as true.

6. How can you detect a writer's tone?

The tone of a piece of writing often reveals an author's attitude, feelings, and viewpoints about a subject. Paying attention to the choice of words and the style of writing can reveal a writer's tone.

7. How can you identify an author's purpose?

An awareness of the author's purpose—or reason for writing—is important in evaluating a work. To identify an author's purpose you should ask four questions:
- Who is the intended audience?
- What is the tone?
- What is the point of view?
- What is the writer trying to prove about the subject?

8. How can you detect bias in a piece of writing?

Bias refers to an author's favoring a particular viewpoint on an issue. To detect bias,
- analyze connotative meanings
- notice descriptive language
- analyze the tone
- look for opposing viewpoints

9. What is figurative language?

Figurative language involves the use of expressions that make sense on an imaginative level but not on a literal level.

READING SELECTION 19

LITERATURE: ESSAY

I AM A JAPANESE AMERICAN
Kesaya Noda
From *Making Waves*

The piece that follows is an excerpt from a longer essay that focuses on the author's experiences as a person of color growing up in the United States. In the full essay, the author confronts stereotypes by reflecting on the many aspects of her identity—racial (Japanese), historical/cultural (Japanese American), gender based (Japanese American woman), and finally, human (for her, a spiritual perspective). The essay describes two experiences of identity: the painful experience of having identity imposed from the outside through stereotypes, and the freeing, empowering experience of defining identity oneself from within a rich context of culture, family, and community.

— · —

1   Sometimes when I was growing up, my identity seemed to hurtle toward me and paste itself right to my face. I felt that way, encountering the stereotypes of my race perpetuated by non-Japanese people (primarily white) who may or may not have had contact with other Japanese in America. "You don't like cheese, do you?" someone would ask. "I know your people don't like cheese." Sometimes questions came making allusions to history. That was another aspect of the identity. Events that had happened quite apart from the me who stood silent in that moment connected my face with an incomprehensible past. "Your parents were in California? Were they in those camps during the war?" And sometimes there were phrases or nicknames: "Lotus Blossom." I was sometimes addressed or referred to as racially Japanese, sometimes as Japanese American, and sometimes as an Asian woman. Confusions and distortions abounded.

2   How is one to know and define oneself? From the inside—within a context that is self defined, from a grounding in community and a connection with culture and history that are comfortably accepted? Or from the outside—in terms of messages received from the media and people who are often ignorant? Even as an adult I can still see two sides of my face and past. I can see from the inside out, in freedom. And I can see from the outside in, driven by the old voices of childhood and lost in anger and fear.

3   "Weak." I hear the voice from my childhood years. "Passive," I hear. Our parents and grandparents were the ones who were put into those camps.[1] They went without resistance; they offered cooperation as proof of loyalty to America. "Victim," I hear. And, "Silent."

4   Our parents are painted as hard workers who were socially uncomfortable and had difficulty expressing even the smallest opinion. Clean, quiet, motivated, and determined to match the American way; that is us, and that is the story of our time here.

5   "Why did you go into those camps," I raged at my parents, frightened by my own inner silence and timidity. "Why didn't you do anything to resist? Why didn't you name it the injustice it was?" Couldn't our parents even think? Couldn't they? Why were we so passive?

6   I shift my vision and my stance. I am in California. My uncle is in the midst of the sweet potato harvest. He is pressed, trying to get the

---

[1]During World War II, many Japanese in the United States were placed in camps.

harvesting crews onto the field as quickly as possible, worried about the flow of equipment and people. His big pickup is pulled off to the side, motor running, door ajar. I see two tractors in the yard in front of an old shed; the flat bed harvesting platform on which the workers will stand has already been brought over from the other field. It's early morning. The workers stand loosely grouped and at ease, but my uncle looks as harried and tense as a police officer trying to unsnarl a New York City traffic jam. Driving toward the shed, I pull my car off the road to make way for an approaching tractor. The front wheels of the car sink luxuriously into the soft, white sand by the roadside and the car slides to a dreamy halt, tail still on the road. I try to move forward. I try to move back. The front bites contentedly into the sand, the back lifts at a jaunty angle. My uncle sees me and storms down the road, running. He is shouting before he is even near me.

7   "What's the matter with you," he screams. "What the hell are you doing?" In his frenzy, he grabs his hat off his head and slashes it through the air across his knee. He is beside himself. "Don't you know how to drive in sand? What's the matter with you? You've blocked the whole roadway. How am I supposed to get my tractors out of here? Can't you use your head? You've cut off the whole roadway, and we've got to get out of here."

8   I stand on the road before him helplessly thinking, "No, I don't know how to drive in sand. I've never driven in sand."

9   "I'm sorry, uncle," I say, burying a smile beneath a look of sincere apology. I notice my deep amusement and my affection for him with great curiosity. I am usually devastated by anger. Not this time.

10   During the several years that follow I learn about the people and the place, and much more about what has happened in this California village where my parents grew up. The issei, our grandparents, made this settlement in the

desert. Their first crops were eaten by rabbits and ravaged by insects. The land was so barren that men walking from house to house sometimes got lost. Women came here too. They bore children in 114 degree heat, then carried the babies with them into the fields to nurse when they reached the end of each row of grapes or other truck farm crops.

11   I had had no idea what it meant to buy this kind of land and make it grow green. Or how, when the war came, there was no space at all for the subtlety of being who we were—Japanese Americans. Either/or was the way. I hadn't understood that people were literally afraid for their lives then, that their money had been frozen in banks; that there was a five-mile travel limit; that when the early evening curfew came and they were inside their houses, some of them watched helplessly as people they knew went into their barns to steal their belongings. The police were patrolling the road, interested only in violators of curfew. There was no help for them in the face of thievery. I had not been able to imagine before what it must have felt like to be an American—to know absolutely that one is an American—and yet to have almost everyone else deny it. Not only deny it, but challenge that identity with machine guns and troops of white American soldiers. In those circumstances it was difficult to say, "I'm a Japanese American." "American" had to do.

12   But now I can say that I am a Japanese American. It means I have a place here in this country, too. I have a place on the East Coast, where our neighbor is so much a part of our family that my mother never passes her house at night without glancing at the lights to see if she is home and safe; where my parents have hauled hundreds of pounds of rocks from fields and arduously planted Christmas trees and blueberries, lilacs, asparagus, and crab apples; where my father still dreams of angling a stream to a new bed so that he can dig a pond in the field and fill it with water and fish. "The neighbors already

came for their Christmas tree?" he asks in December. "Did they like it? Did they like it?"

13   I have a place on the West Coast where my relatives still farm, where I heard the stories of feuds and backbiting, and where I saw that people survived and flourished because fundamentally they trusted and relied upon one another. A death in the family is not just a death in a family; it is a death in the community. I saw people help each other with money, materials,

labor, attention, and time. I saw men gather once a year, without fail, to clean the grounds of a ninety-year-old woman who had helped the community before, during, and after the war. I saw her remembering them with birthday cards sent to each of their children.

14   I come from a people with a long memory and a distinctive grace. We live our thanks. And we are Americans. Japanese Americans.

Examining Reading Selection 19

Checking Your Vocabulary

Directions: Using context, word parts, or a dictionary if necessary, circle the letter of the meaning for each word as it is used in the reading.

1. stereotypes (paragraph 1)
    a. unchanging images or attitudes
    b. discriminatory acts
    c. insulting comments
    d. racial slurs

2. incomprehensible (paragraph 1)
    a. uneventful
    b. embarrassing
    c. futile
    d. not understandable

3. passive (paragraphs 3 and 5)
    a. angry
    b. resentful
    c. inactive
    d. frightened

4. harried (paragraph 6)
    a. awkward
    b. rushed
    c. disciplined
    d. commonplace

5. arduously (paragraph 12)
    a. with great effort
    b. in a haphazard, lazy fashion
    c. in a disinterested manner
    d. with little skill

Checking Your Comprehension

Directions: Circle the letter of the best answer.

6. This reading is primarily about Noda's
    a. racial background.
    b. ancestors.
    c. racial identity.
    d. experiences in America.

7. The author's main point is that she
    a. is unsure if she belongs in America.
    b. views herself in two ways.
    c. feels she has rejected her Japanese heritage.
    d. has disappointed her family.

8. During her childhood, Noda thought of her grandparents as
    a. weak.
    b. important.
    c. influential.
    d. stupid.

9. As described in the reading, death in the Japanese community is regarded as
   a. a private family matter.
   b. a religious experience.
   c. a completion of the life cycle.
   d. a community concern.

10. Noda's grandparents willingly went to the camps because they
    a. hated the Germans.
    b. knew they would be treated well.
    c. did not understand where they were going.
    d. wanted to demonstrate their loyalty to America.

11. The author organizes her ideas using
    a. chronology.
    b. classification.
    c. comparisons.
    d. order of importance.

Thinking Critically

12. Which of the following best describes Noda's attitude toward being a Japanese American?
    a. embarrassed
    b. dismayed
    c. angry
    d. proud

13. The author would probably agree with which one of the following statements?
    a. Attitudes are fixed and unchanging.
    b. Ancestors make unfortunate errors in judgment.
    c. Many Americans express stereotyped perceptions of Japanese Americans.
    d. A person's identity is related to his or her ethnic heritage.

14. The author explains her ideas by
    a. analyzing them.
    b. recounting events that illustrate them.
    c. comparing them with those of her parents.
    d. giving reasons.

15. The form of this reading suggests it may have been part of
    a. an argumentative essay.
    b. a newspaper article.
    c. an autobiography.
    d. a novel.

Questions for Discussion

1. Have you ever been stereotyped because of your ethnic background?

2. How is death regarded in your ethnic community? How is this different from the way it is regarded in the Japanese community?

3. What factors other than ethnic origin do you think constitute or define identity?

Selection 19:			1316 words
Finishing Time:	_____	_____	_____
	HR.	MIN.	SEC.
Starting Time:	_____	_____	_____
	HR.	MIN.	SEC.
Reading Time:		_____	_____
		MIN.	SEC.
WPM Score:			_____
Comprehension Score:			_____%

READING SELECTION 20

ART

EARLY ENCOUNTERS WITH THE ARTIST WITHIN

Duane Preble, et al.

From *Artforms*

Did you like to draw or color when you were a child? Read this selection to learn ways that children's artistic expression is discouraged and ways it can be encouraged.

— · —

I'd like to study the drawings of kids. That's where the truth is, without a doubt.

Andre Derain

1   The arts come from innately human needs to create and to communicate. They come from the desire to explore, confirm, and share special observations and insights—a fact readily apparent in nine-year-old Kojyu's *Searching for Bugs in the Park.* The arts are one of the most constructive ways to say "I did it. I made it. This is what I see and feel. I count. My art is me." Unfortunately, the great value of this discover-and-share, art-making process is only rarely affirmed in today's busy homes and schools.

2   We include art by children as the best way—other than actual hands-on artmaking pro-

cesses—to help you reexamine your relationship to your own creative powers and perhaps even to guide you as you prepare to become a parent, a teacher, or a caregiver for children.

3   Children use a universal visual language. All over the world, drawings by children ages two to six show similar stages of mental growth, from explorative mark-making to inventing shapes to symbolizing things seen and imagined. Until they are about six years old, children usually depict the world in symbolic rather than realistic ways. Their images are more mental constructions than records of visual observations.

4   During the second year of life, children enjoy making marks, leaving traces of their movements. Sensitive exploration is visible in *First Lines*, by a one-and-a-half-year-old child. After marking and scribbling, making circles and other shapes fascinates young children. The *house* shape is by a two-year-old. *Hand with Line and Spots* is by a three-year-old, as is the smiling portrait of *Grandma* in which self-assured lines symbolize a happy face, shoulders, arms, body, belly button, and legs.

First Lines.

Kojyu, age 9. Searching for Bugs in the Park.

Alana, age 2. House.

Jeff, age 3. Hand with Lines and Spots.

Alana, age 3. Grandma.

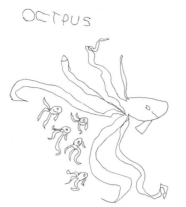

Jason, almost 4. Mother Octopus with Babies.

Yuki, age 8. I Can Ride, I Can Ride My Unicycle.

5   Being the son of a saltwater fish collector, and watching an octopus, gave almost four-year-old Jason the idea for his drawing of a smiling *Mother Octopus with Babies.* The excitement of joyful play with friends on unicycles inspired eight-year-old Yuki's *I Can Ride, I Can Ride My Unicycle.* Notice how she emphasized her own image by greatly exaggerating her size relative to others and how she included important information, such as her right leg seen through the spokes of the wheel.

6   Young children often demonstrate an intuitive sense of composition. Unfortunately, we lose much of this intuitive sense of balanced design as we begin to look at the world from a conceptual, self-conscious point of view. Most children who have been given coloring books, workbooks, and pre-drawn printed single sheets become overly dependent on such impersonal, stereotyped props. In this way, children often lose the urge to invent unique images based on their own experiences. A child's two drawings of *Birds* show this process: The child first interprets the bird in a personal, fresh way, but later adopts the trite forms of a conventional workbook. Without ongoing opportunities for personal expression, children lose self-confidence in their original creative impulses.

7   Children begin life as excited learners. If they are loved and cared for, they soon express enthusiasm for perceiving and exploring the world

Anonymous Child. Birds.

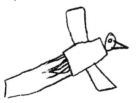

a. This picture shows one child's drawing of a bird before exposure to coloring books.

b. Then the child colored a workbook illustration.

c. After coloring the workbook birds, the child lost creative sensitivity and self-reliance.

around them. Research shows that parents' ability to show interest in and empathy for their child's discoveries and feelings is crucial to the child's brain development. Before the age of one, and well before they talk, babies point tiny fingers at wonderful things they see. Bodies move in rhythm to music. Ask a group of four-year-olds the same questions, and they will too often say "No, we can't." Such an unnecessary loss has ominous implications for the spiritual, economic, social, and political health of society.

8   It is not our inadequacy, but recognizing and taking responsibility for the power of our unique personal voices that we come to fear the most. Almost all of us can tell of painful moments in childhood when someone convinced us that our art was wrong or inadequate. Society's emphasis on art as rare products produced by those with exceptional talent or training causes many of us to fail to discover and sustain our own unique voices.

9   Most abilities observed in creative people are also characteristic of children during interactions with the world around them. What becomes of this extraordinary capacity? According to John Holt, author of *How Children Fail,*

> We destroy this capacity above all by making them afraid—afraid of not doing what other people want, of not pleasing, or of making mistakes, of failing, of being wrong. Thus we make them afraid to gamble, afraid to experiment, afraid to try the difficult and unknown.

10   To ignore or belittle creative expression is like saying, "Your expression is not worthwhile; therefore, *you* are not worthwhile.

11   In the United States, children's dissatisfaction with their own art usually begins around age nine or ten, when they want their pictures to look like photographs or images produced by trained adult artists. Yet, with good coaching, this age group can create such rich documents of experience as *Searching for Bugs in the Park.* Too many preadolescents become frustrated because they feel they cannot draw the kind of realism that they and others expect. Too often this frus-

tration results in a lifetime of blocked creativity, of feeling "untalented."

12   What happens when we are unable to communicate our most significant ideas and experiences? What happens when no one has time to listen to our stories or look at our drawings? When our creativity is not encouraged, we may lose confidence and even interest in our special insights and perceptions. We may lose our sense of wonder and our sense of beauty. Certainly we lose some of our ability to shape our own lives creatively. Sometimes, when natural creative drives are blocked, they can become the source of antisocial, and even destructive, behavior.

13   The best way to learn about art is from the inside, by learning to perceive and think as an artist. Everyone is an artist at birth. What is rare is to stay in touch with such open-minded seeing as one grows up. As preschool children, we had imaginations that wandered freely, unconstrained by the concepts and prejudices of adults.

14   Many artists have been inspired by the creative freedom expressed in children's art. Wassily Kandinsky was one of several leading artists of the early twentieth century who were influenced by children's inventiveness and intuitive sense of design. His imaginary landscape, *With Sun,* is

Wassily Kandinsky. With Sun. 1911. Oil on glass. 12" × 15¾". Stadtische Galerie in Lonbachaus, Munich.

full of the qualify of children's fantasies. Only recently has it been discovered that Kandinsky and other "modern" artists actually collected children's art. And the practice continues. Adult artists, parents, teachers and others are being reawakened by seeing children's art. They are breaking out of old, stereotypical ways of seeing, thinking, and working, encouraged to express their own art, their own insights with greater inventive freedom and directness.

15   Our adult attitudes about art and our own creativity are shaped during childhood. Because artistic efforts are among our most personal endeavors, children tend to be particularly vul-nerable to disinterest, demeaning comparisons, and disparaging remarks about self-expressive efforts. At certain ages and stages of development, children need extra encouragement to be able to express themselves without fear or hesitation. Since artistic endeavors have many equally "correct" solutions, each person—child or adult—has the opportunity to have a right answer, to have his or her own voice heard.

16   Through the arts we can develop personal imagination, critical thinking, self-esteem, the sense of wonder, and the sense of beauty. We can also rediscover the joy of being able to share our personally significant experiences.

Writing about Reading Selection 20*

Checking Your Vocabulary

Directions: Complete each of the following items; refer to a dictionary if necessary.

1. Discuss the connotative meanings of the word *art.*

2. Define each of the following words:
   a. affirmed (paragraph 1)

   _____

   b. depict (paragraph 3)

   _____

   c. intuitive (paragraph 6)

   _____

   d. conceptual (paragraph 6)

   _____

   _____

   e. ominous (paragraph 7)

   _____

3. Define the word *universal* (paragraph 3) and underline the word or phrase that provides a context clue for its meaning.

   _____

   _____

   _____

4. Define the word *preadolescents* (paragraph 11) and underline the word or phrase that provides a context clue for its meaning.

   _____

   _____

   _____

   _____

5. Determine the meaning of the following words by using word parts:
   a. reexamine (paragraph 2)

   _____

_____
* Multiple-choice questions are contained in Part 6 (page 588).

b. pre-drawn (paragraph 6)

_____

c. empathy (paragraph 7)

_____

_____

d. inadequacy (paragraph 8)

_____

e. unconstrained (paragraph 13)

_____

Checking Your Comprehension

6. According to the author, why do many adults feel like failures when it comes to art?

_____

_____

_____

7. What qualities does the author feel can be developed through art?

_____

_____

_____

8. What is the effect on children's artwork when they have used workbooks and other pre-drawn art materials?

_____

_____

_____

9. At what age do children enjoy simply making marks?

_____

Thinking Critically

10. Why is it that most children who use coloring books no longer produce their own "original" art?

_____

_____

_____

11. Predict how the authors would likely view paint-by-number kits, children's cookbooks, and assemble-a-toy kits.

_____

_____

_____

_____

12. What types of evidence do the authors provide to support their thesis?

_____

_____

_____

13. Would the authors agree that self-confidence is important to the creative process? Justify your answer.

_____

_____

_____

_____

Questions for Discussion

1. As a parent or teacher, how can we affirm the artistic ability of children? Discuss some verbal responses as well as facial expressions we might give when presented with a child's work of art.

2. How can you as an adult regain the freedom of expression you once had as a child? What would keep you from trying? Do you think it would be worth the effort to rediscover your innate creativity? How would this enable you to communicate better with others?

3. Recall a piece of artwork you produced as a child that you were very excited about. What was the reaction of the adult to whom you presented it? Was it positive or negative? How did you feel? How did the adult's response affect your future drawings?

4. Some American school systems today believe we should focus on basic academic subjects and think of participating in artistic projects as a frill. Do you agree or disagree? Defend your answer.

Selection 20:			1264 words
Finishing Time:	___	___	___
	HR.	MIN.	SEC.
Starting Time:	___	___	___
	HR.	MIN.	SEC.
Reading Time:		___	___
		MIN.	SEC.
WPM Score:		___	
Comprehension Score:		___	%

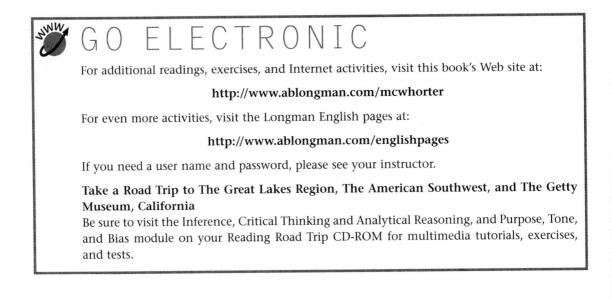

GO ELECTRONIC

For additional readings, exercises, and Internet activities, visit this book's Web site at:

http://www.ablongman.com/mcwhorter

For even more activities, visit the Longman English pages at:

http://www.ablongman.com/englishpages

If you need a user name and password, please see your instructor.

Take a Road Trip to The Great Lakes Region, The American Southwest, and The Getty Museum, California
Be sure to visit the Inference, Critical Thinking and Analytical Reasoning, and Purpose, Tone, and Bias module on your Reading Road Trip CD-ROM for multimedia tutorials, exercises, and tests.

CHAPTER 11

Evaluating Arguments and Persuasive Writing

IN THIS CHAPTER YOU WILL LEARN:

1. To evaluate source and authority.
2. To understand and evaluate arguments.
3. To identify reasoning errors.

A n education professor opens a class discussion on the issue of coeducation by distributing the following statement:

BOYS AND GIRLS HAVE DIFFERENT EDUCATIONAL NEEDS

There are many reasons to think that boys and girls may need different kinds of schooling. First, some have observed that males and females appear to have different aptitudes, or at least different average mixes of aptitudes. Whether these differences are inborn, or a result of family childhood socialization, or both, is hard to say. But it has often been noted that females are less likely to study mathematics, science, or computers at any level of the co-ed school system.

What is also known from research is that females do better in these subjects—show more interest and achieve higher grades, for example—in all-girl schools, particularly where teachers strongly encourage such achievement by girls. Also, some research suggest that a key method of getting girls interested in these subjects is by emphasizing communication and creative problem solving, rather than the theoretical or technical aspects of the topic. Treating girls as if they had the same interests as boys doesn't work.

Tepperman and Blain, *Think Twice!*

She then asks the class to analyze and respond to the statement. An impulsive student responded immediately, saying "The writers oppose coeducation, but I disagree with them." The instructor seems dissatisfied

423

with this response, suggesting she wants more detailed and carefully reasoned responses.

How would you analyze the statement? If you agreed with the writers' position, how would you defend it? If you disagreed, how would you dispute it?

To analyze the statement, you must study the writers' line of reasoning and thought process. You must also evaluate how the writers present ideas, and evaluate their worth. This chapter focuses on techniques to evaluate persuasive writing. Specifically, you will learn to evaluate source and authority, recognize the structure of and evaluate arguments, and identify reasoning errors.

Evaluating Source and Authority

Two very important considerations in evaluating any written material are the source in which it was printed and the authority, or qualifications, of the author.

Considering the Source

Your reaction to and evaluation of printed or electronic material should take into account its source. Obviously, a reader cannot check or verify each fact that a writer provides, but you must assess whether or not the writer has carefully researched and accurately reported the subject. Although many writers are careful and accurate, some are not. Often the source of a piece of writing can indicate how accurate, detailed, and well documented the article is. For example, in which of the following sources would you expect to find the most accurate, up-to-date information on the gas mileage of various cars?

- an advertisement in *Time*
- a research report in *Car and Driver*
- an article in *Reader's Digest* on buying an economical car

The report in *Car and Driver* would be the most likely source for information that is detailed and up-to-date, because it is a magazine devoted to the subject of cars and their performance. *Reader's Digest,* on the other hand, publishes selected articles and condensed writing from other periodicals and may not provide such timely information on a subject. A paid advertisement in *Time,* a weekly news magazine, most likely would not provide completely objective information.

Let's consider another example. Suppose you are in the library trying to find information on sleepwalking for a term paper. You locate the following sources, each of which contains an article on sleepwalking. Which would you expect to be the most factual, detailed, and scientific?

- an encyclopedia entry on sleepwalking
- an article titled "Strange Things Happen While You Are Sleeping," in *Woman's Day*
- an article titled "An Examination of Research on Sleepwalking" in the *Psychological Review*

Again you can see that from the source alone you can make predictions about the content and approach used. You would expect the encyclopedia entry to provide only a general overview of the topic. You might expect the article in *Woman's Day* to discuss various abnormalities that occur during sleep; sleepwalking might be only one of several topics discussed. Also, you might expect the article to relate several unusual or extreme cases of sleepwalking, rather than to present a factual analysis of the topic. The article in *Psychological Review,* a journal that reports research in psychology, is the one that would contain a factual, authoritative discussion of sleepwalking.

In evaluating a source you might ask the following questions:

1. **What reputation does the source have?**
2. **What is the audience for whom the source is intended?**
3. **Are documentation or references provided?**

Considering the Authority of the Author

To evaluate printed or electronic material, the competency of the author also must be considered. If the author lacks expertise in or experience with the subject, the material he or she produces may not meet an acceptable level of scholarship and accuracy.

Depending on the type of material you are using, you have several means of checking the qualifications of an author. In textbooks, the author's credentials may be described in one of two places. The author's college or university affiliation, and possibly his or her title, may appear on the title page beneath the author's name. Second, in the preface of the book, the author may indicate or summarize his or her qualifications for writing the text. In nonfiction books and general market paperbacks, a synopsis of the author's credentials and experiences may be included on the book jacket or the back cover. However, in other types of material, little effort is made to identify the author or his or her qualifications. In newspapers, magazines, and reference books, the reader is given little or no information about the writer. You are forced to rely on the judgment of the editors or publishers to assess an author's authority.

EXERCISE 11-1

DIRECTIONS: Predict and discuss how useful and appropriate each of the following sources would be for the situation described.

1. Using an article from *Working Women* on family aggression for a term paper for your sociology class.

   _____

2. Quoting an article in *The New York Times* on recent events in China for a speech titled "Innovation and Change in China."

   _____

3. Reading an article titled "Bilingual Education in the Twenty-First Century" printed in the *Educational Research Quarterly* for a paper arguing for increased federal aid for bilingual education.

   _____

4. Using an article in *TV Guide* on television's coverage of crime and violence for a term paper on the effects of television on society.

   _____

5. Using information from a book written by former First Lady Nancy Reagan in a class discussion on use and abuse of presidential power.

   _____

Reading Arguments

Argument is a common mode of presenting and evaluating information. It is also used to establish and evaluate positions on controversial issues. In a philosophy course you might read arguments on individual rights, the rights of the majority, or the existence of God. For a literature class you may read a piece of literary criticism that argues for or against the value of a particular work, debates its significance, or rejects an interpretation.

An argument generally refers to a piece of writing that makes an assertion and provides supporting evidence to support that assertion. Two types of arguments are common: inductive and deductive. An inductive argument reaches a general conclusion from observed specifics. For example, by observing the performance of a large number of athletes, you could conclude that athletes possess physical stamina.

A deductive argument, on the other hand, begins with a general conclusion and moves to specifics. For example, from the general conclusion that "Athletes possess physical stamina," you can reason that because Anthony is an athlete, he must possess physical stamina.

Both types of arguments begin with statements that are assumed to be correct. Basically, both follow a general pattern of "If that is so, then this is so. . . ." At times, an argument may be more complex, involving several steps—"If that is so, and this happens, then this should be done." Here are a few examples of arguments:

- Many students have part-time jobs that require them to work late afternoons and evenings during the week. These students are unable to use the library during the week. Therefore, library hours should be extended to weekends.

- Because parents have the right to determine their children's sexual attitudes, sex education should take place in the home, not at school.

- No one should be forced to inhale unpleasant or harmful substances. That's why the ban on cigarette smoking in public places was put into effect in our state. Why shouldn't there be a law to prevent people from wearing strong colognes or perfumes, especially in restaurants, since sense of smell is important to taste?

When reading arguments, use the following steps:

1. **Identify the assertion—what is being argued for.** Determine what position, idea, or action the writer is trying to convince you to accept. Often, a concise statement of this key point appears early in the argument or in the introduction of a formal essay. This point is often restated.

2. **Read the entire article or essay.** Underline important parts of the argument.

3. **Watch for conclusions.** Words and phrases like "since," "thus," "therefore," "accordingly," "it can be concluded," "it is clear that," and "it follows that" are signals that a conclusion is about to be given.

4. **Notice the types of evidence the author provides.**

5. **Identify the specific action or position the writer is arguing for.**

6. **Reread the argument and examine its content and structure.** What is stated? What is implied or suggested? What assertions are made?

7. **Write a brief outline of the argument and list its key points.** Pragmatic learners may find this step especially helpful.

8. **Discuss the argument with a friend or classmate.** Especially if you are a social or auditory learner, you may "hear" yourself summarizing the assertion or evaluating the evidence supplied.

Now, read the following brief article and apply the previous steps.

EQUALITY ISN'T SAMENESS

Soldiers guilty of misconduct must be punished, but let's not sacrifice common sense and our national defense on the altar of feminism and political correctness.

It's unconscionable that military supervisors would take advantage of female subordinates. These officers have violated a special trust. But the Army's scandal raises a very serious question: Does placing men and women in forced intimate settings for extended periods promote or detract from military effectiveness?

Desert Storm commander Gen. Norman Schwarzkopf testified to Congress, "Decisions on what roles women should play in war must be based on military standards, not women's rights."

On the modern battlefield, every soldier is a potential combatant, and all should have equal opportunity to survive. Women don't. That doesn't mean women and men aren't equal. They are, but equality is not sameness. Women are not equally equipped to survive in the violent and physically difficult environment of combat because they have 50% less upper body strength and 70% of a man's aerobic fitness.

The Clinton administration removed many exemptions for women in the military. Congress helped by rescinding laws that precluded their combat service. All without considering the findings of the 1992 President's Commission of the Assignment of Women in the Armed Forces.

Integrating the sexes has become a difficult challenge for commanders. Merely raising the women-in-the-military issue is to jeopardize one's career.

Commanders have the nearly impossible task of fighting the enemy while minimizing the impact of sexual tensions, which creates readiness problems, such as increased fraternization, sex-based rivalries and many unwanted pregnancies. Readiness also suffers because many pregnant soldiers can no longer perform their mission and often must be replaced on short notice with less experienced personnel.

The goal of the military is to protect and defend the United States, but social experiments are weakening the armed forces. Those who engage in sexual improprieties must be prosecuted, but the status of women in the armed services must be reviewed in light of reality instead of some mystical feminist agenda. We have a duty to support those who volunteer to serve us.

Maginnis, "Equality Isn't Sameness."

This article is arguing for reconsidering the place of women in the armed forces. The author makes a four-part argument, offering four reasons why we should rethink women's military roles. The argument can be outlined as follows:

Reasons

1. Women are not equally equipped to survive in combat.

2. Commanders face the added task of controlling sexual tensions and at the same time fighting the enemy.

3. Military readiness suffers because of pregnancies.

4. The armed forces are being weakened by "social experiments" such as placing women in combat roles.

Conclusion

Therefore, the current role of women in the military should be reconsidered.

EXERCISE 11-2

DIRECTIONS: Read the following argument and answer the questions that follow.

"The life of each man should be sacred to each other man," the ancients tell us. They unflinchingly executed murderers. They realized it is not enough to proclaim the sacredness and inviolability of human life. It must be secured as well, by threatening with the loss of their own life those who violate what has been proclaimed as inviolable—the right of innocents to live. Else the inviolability of human life is neither credibly proclaimed nor actually protected. No society can profess that the lives of its members are secure if those who did not allow innocent others to continue living are themselves allowed to continue living—at the expense of the community. To punish a murderer by incarcerating him as one does a pickpocket cannot but cheapen human life. Murder differs in quality from other crimes and deserves, therefore, a punishment that differs in quality from other punishments. There is a discontinuity. It should be underlined, not blurred.

Van Den Haag, "Capital Punishment."

1. What is the author's position on the death penalty?

_____

2. Summarize the argument.

_____

_____

_____

_____

_____

Evaluating Arguments

Once you have understood the article by identifying what is asserted and how it is asserted, the next step is to evaluate the soundness, correctness, and worth of the argument. Specifically, you must evaluate evidence, both type and relevancy, definition of terms, cause-effect relationships, and value systems. You must also recognize counterarguments and identify assumptions.

Types of Evidence

The validity of an inductive argument rests, in part, on the soundness and correctness of the evidence provided to draw the conclusion. The validity of a deductive argument, on the other hand, rests on the accuracy and correctness of the premises on which the argument is based. Evaluating each type of argument involves assessing the accuracy and correctness of statements on which the argument is based. Writers often provide evidence to substantiate their observations or premises. As a critical reader, your task is to assess whether or not the evidence is sufficient to support the claim. Here are a few types of evidence often used:

Personal Experience

Writers often substantiate their ideas through experience and observation. Although a writer's personal account of a situation may provide an interesting perspective on an issue, personal experience should not be accepted as proof. The observer may be biased or may have exaggerated or incorrectly perceived a situation.

Examples

Examples are descriptions of particular situations that are used to illustrate or explain a principle, concept, or idea. To explain what aggressive behavior is, your psychology instructor may offer several examples: fighting, punching, and kicking. Examples should *not* be used by themselves to prove the concept or idea they illustrate, as is done in the following sample:

> The American judicial system treats those who are called for jury duty unfairly. It is clear from my sister's experience that the system has little regard for the needs of those called as jurors. My sister was required to report for jury duty the week she was on vacation. She spent the entire week in a crowded, stuffy room waiting to be called to sit on a jury and never was called.

Statistics

Many people are impressed by statistics—the reporting of figures, percentages, averages, and so forth—and assume they are irrefutable proof. Actually, statistics can be misused, misinterpreted, or used selectively to give other than the most objective, accurate picture of a situation. Suppose you read that magazine X has increased its readership by 50 percent while magazine Y made only a 10 percent increase. From this statistic some readers might assume that magazine X has a wider readership than magazine Y. However, if provided with complete information, you can see that this is not true. The missing, but crucial, statistic is the total readership of each magazine before the increase. If magazine X had a readership of 20,000, and increased it by 50 percent, its readership would total 30,000. However, if magazine Y's readership was already 50,000, a 10 percent increase (bringing the new total to 55,000) would still give it the larger readership despite the fact that it made the smaller increase. Approach statistical evidence with a critical, questioning attitude. (See Critical Thinking Tip #9, p. 358.)

Comparisons and Analogies

Comparisons or analogies (extended comparisons) serve as illustrations and are often used in argument. Their reliability depends on how closely the comparison corresponds or how similar it is to the situation to which it is being compared. For example, Martin Luther King Jr., in his famous letter from the Birmingham jail, compared nonviolent protesters to a robbed man. To evaluate this comparison you would need to consider how the two are similar and how they are different.

EXERCISE 11-3

DIRECTIONS: For the article "Equality Isn't Sameness" on page 428, evaluate whether the author uses adequate evidence to support his claim.

Relevancy and Sufficiency of Evidence

Once you have identified the evidence used to support an argument, the next step is to decide if there is enough of the right kind of evidence to lead you to accept the writer's claim. This is always a matter of judgment; there are no easy rules to follow. You must determine whether the evidence provided directly supports the statement, and whether sufficient evidence has been provided.

Suppose you are reading an article in your campus newspaper that states that Freshman Composition 101 should not be required of all students at your college. As evidence, the writer provides the following:

Composition does not prepare us for the job market. Besides, the reading assignments have no relevancy to modern times.

This argument provides neither adequate nor sufficient evidence. The writer does nothing to substantiate his claims of irrelevancy of the course to the job market or modern times. For the argument to be regarded seriously, the writer needs to provide facts, statistics, expert opinion, or other forms of documentation.

EXERCISE 11-4

DIRECTIONS: Read the following argument, and pay particular attention to the type(s) of evidence used. Then answer the questions that follow.

It is predictable. At Halloween, thousands of children trick-or-treat in Indian costumes. At Thanksgiving, thousands of children parade in school pageants wearing plastic headdresses and pseudo-buckskin clothing. Thousands of card shops stock Thanksgiving greeting cards with images of cartoon animals wearing feathered headbands. Thousands of teachers and librarians trim bulletin boards with Anglo-featured, feathered Indian boys and girls. Thousands of gift shops load their shelves with Indian figurines and jewelry.

Fall and winter are also the seasons when hundreds of thousands of sports fans root for professional, college and public school teams with names that summon up Indians—"Braves," "Redskins," "Chiefs." (In New York State, one out of eight junior and senior high school teams call themselves "Indians," "Tomahawks" and the like.) War-whooping team mascots are imprinted on school uniforms, postcards, notebooks, tote bags and car floor mats.

All of this seems innocuous; why make a fuss about it? Because these trappings and holiday symbols offend tens of thousands of other Americans—the Native American people. Because these invented images prevent millions of us from understanding the authentic Indian America, both long ago and today. Because this image-making prevents Indians from being a relevant part of the nation's social fabric.

Hirschfelder, "It's Time to Stop Playing Indians."

1. What types of evidence are used?

   _____

2. Is the evidence convincing?

   _____

   _____

3. Is there sufficient evidence?

_____

4. What other types of evidence could have been used to strengthen the argument?

_____

Definition of Terms

A clear and effective argument carefully defines key terms and uses them consistently. For example, an essay arguing for or against animal rights should state what is meant by the term, describe or define those rights, and use that definition through the entire argument.

The following two paragraphs are taken from two different argumentative essays on pornography. Notice how in the first paragraph the author carefully defines what he means by pornography before proceeding with his argument, while in the second the term is not clearly defined.

PARAGRAPH 1: CAREFUL DEFINITION

There is unquestionably more pornography available today than 15 years ago. However, is it legitimate to assume that more is worse? Pornography is speech, words, and pictures about sexuality. No one would consider an increase in the level of speech about religion or politics to be a completely negative development. What makes speech about sexuality different?

Lynn, "Pornography's Many Different Forms: Not All Bad."

PARAGRAPH 2: VAGUE DEFINITION

If we are not talking about writing laws, defining pornography doesn't pose as serious a problem. We do have different tastes. Maybe some of mine come from my middle-class background (my mother wouldn't think so!). I don't like bodies presented without heads, particularly female bodies. The motive may sometimes be the protection of the individual, but the impression is decapitation, and I also happen to be someone who is attracted to people's faces. This is a matter of taste.

Rule, "Pornography Is a Social Disease."

Cause-Effect Relationships

Arguments are often built around the assumption of a cause-effect relationship. For example, an argument supporting gun control legislation may claim that ready availability of guns contributes to an increased number of shootings. This argument implies that availability of guns causes increased use. If the writer provides no evidence that this cause-effect relationship exists, you should question the accuracy of the statement. (See Critical Thinking Tip #5, p. 210.)

Implied or Stated Value System

An argument often implies or rests on a value system (a structure of what the writer feels is right, wrong, worthwhile, and important). However, everyone possesses a personal value system, and although our culture promotes many major points of agreement (murder is wrong, human life is worthwhile, and so forth), it also allows points of departure. One person may think that telling lies is always wrong; another person may say it depends on the circumstance. Some people have a value system based on religious beliefs; others may not share those beliefs.

In evaluating an argument, look for value judgments and then decide whether the judgments are consistent with and acceptable to your personal value system. Here are a few examples of value judgment statements:

1. Abortion is wrong.
2. Financial aid for college should be available to everyone regardless of income.
3. Capital punishment violates human rights.

Recognition of Counterarguments

An effective argument often includes a refutation of counterarguments—a line of reasoning that can be used to deny or refute what the writer is arguing for. For example, if a writer is arguing against gun control, he or she may recognize the counterargument that availability of guns causes shootings and refute it by saying "Guns don't kill people: people kill people."

Notice how in the excerpt from an essay advocating capital punishment, the author recognizes the counterargument that everyone has a right to live and argues against it.

Abolitionists [of the death penalty] insist that we all have an imprescriptible right to live to our natural term: if the innocent victim had a right to live, so does the murderer. That takes egalitarianism too far for my taste. The crime sets victim and murderer apart; if the victim died, the murderer does not deserve to live. If innocents are to be secure in their lives murderers cannot be. The thought that murderers are to be given as much right to live as their victims oppresses me. So does the thought that a Stalin, Hitler, an Idi Amin should have as much right to live as their victims did.

Van Den Haag, "Capital Punishment."

Identifying Assumptions

Many writers begin an argument assuming that a particular set of facts or principles is true. Then they develop their argument based on that assumption. Of course, if the assumption is not correct or if it cannot be proven, the arguments that depend on that assumption may be incorrect. For instance, the following passage begins with an assumption (*underlined*) that the writer makes no attempt to prove or justify. Rather, he uses it as a starting point to develop his ideas on the function of cities.

> Given that the older central cities have lost their capacity to serve as effective staging areas for newcomers, the question inevitably poses itself: What is the function of these cities? Permit me to suggest that it has become essentially that of a sandbox.
>
> A sandbox is a place where adults park their children in order to converse, play, or work with a minimum of interference. The adults, having found a distraction for the children, can get on with the serious things of life. There is some reward for the children in all this. The sandbox is given to them as their turf. . . .
>
> Palen, *City Scenes.*

The author offers no reasons or evidence in support of the opening statement: it is assumed to be true. This assumption is the base on which the author builds his argument that the city is a sandbox.

As you read arguments, always begin by examining the author's initial assumptions. Decide whether you agree or disagree with them and check to see whether the author provides any evidence that his or her assumptions are accurate. Once you have identified an assumption, consider this question: If the assumption were untrue, how would it affect the argument?

EXERCISE 11-5

DIRECTIONS: Read the following argument by Luis Rodriguez, and answer the questions that follow.

REKINDLING THE WARRIOR

Over the past year and a half, I have spoken to thousands of young people at schools, jails, bookstores, colleges, and community centers about the experiences addressed in my book *Always Running: La Vida Loca, Gang Days in L.A.*

What stays with me is the vitality and clarity of the young people I met, many of them labeled "at risk." They saw in my experiences and my book both a reflection of their lives and the possibility of transcendence, of change, which otherwise appears elusive. In those faces I saw the most viable social energy for rebuilding the country and realigning its resources. They are the future, but this society has no clear pathway to take them there.

For one thing, today's youth are under intense scrutiny and attack. Schools, for the most part, fail to engage their creativity and intellect. As a result, young people find their own means of expression—music being the most obvious example, but also the formation of gangs.

Despite conventional thinking, gangs are not anarchies. They can be highly structured, with codes of honor and discipline. For many members, the gang serves as family, as the only place where they can find fellowship, respect, a place to belong. You often hear the word love among gang members. Sometimes the gang is the only place where they can find it.

Gabriel Rivera, director of the Transitional Intervention Experience of Bend, Oregon, and a former East Los Angeles gang member, came up with a concept he calls "character in motion" to describe the essence, not the form, of gang participation.

"[Character in motion] is marked by the advertent or inadvertent beginnings of physical, psychological, and spiritual struggle that happens for every young person," writes Rivera. "[It] is what happens when a young person responds to the inevitable inner call to embrace 'the journey,' and chooses to honor that journey above all else with a courage that relies upon connecting with one's 'warrior energy.'"

The warrior needs to be nurtured, directed, and guided—not smothered, crushed, or corralled. This energy needs to be taken to its next highest level of development, where one matures into self-control, self-study, and self-actualization. Most anti-gang measures have nothing to do with any of this. A serious effort would address the burning issue of adolescent rage. It would address a basic need for food, shelter, and clothing, but also needs for expressive creativity and community.

Sociopathic behavior exists within the framework of a sociopathic society. Under these circumstances, gangs are not a problem; they are a solution, particularly for communities lacking economic, social, and political options.

Two examples: Two years ago, I did a poetry reading in a part of eastern Ohio that was once alive with coal mines and industry but now has 50 to 70 percent unemployment in some areas. Many of the young people are selling drugs to survive. In this sense, they could be from the South Bronx or the Pine Ridge Reservation. They are, however, "white." They are listening to their own music ("Wherever kids find obstacles, I find music," an independent record producer recently told Rolling Stone magazine), and establishing ganglike structures to survive.

Soon after the 1992 Los Angeles rebellion, members of the Crips and the Bloods, two of the city's most notorious gangs, circulated a plan. They included proposals to repair the schools and streets and get rid of drugs and violence. At the end of the plan, they wrote: "Give us the hammers and the nails, and we will rebuild the city."

It was a demand to take responsibility, which rose from the inner purpose of Crip and Blood warrior consciousness, and a demand for the authority to carry out the plan. Unfortunately, no one took them up on it.

These young people face great barriers to educational advancement, economic stability, and social mobility—but little or none to criminal activity or violence (as everyone knows, prison is no deterrence; for some youth it is a rite of passage).

Power is the issue here. Without autonomy to make decisions that affect their lives, these young people can only attempt to approximate it, too often with disastrous results.

You want to stop the body count? Empower the youth.

Luis Rodriguez, "Rekindling the Warrior," from the *Utne Reader*

1. Summarize the author's position on gangs.

   _____

   _____

2. What assumptions does Rodriguez make?

   _____

   _____

3. What type(s) of evidence is offered?

   _____

   _____

4. Do you feel the evidence is adequate and convincing?

   _____

5. What values does the author hold?

   _____

   _____

6. Does the author refute counterarguments? If so, describe how he does this.

   _____

   _____

Errors in Logical Reasoning

Errors in reasoning, often called logical fallacies, are common in arguments. These errors invalidate the argument or render it flawed. Several common errors in logic are described on the following page.

Circular Reasoning

Also known as begging the question, this error involves using part of the conclusion as evidence to support it. Here are a few examples:

Cruel medical experimentation on defenseless animals is inhumane.

Female soldiers should not be placed in battle situations because combat is a man's job.

In circular reasoning, because no evidence is given to support the claim, there is no reason to accept the conclusion.

Hasty Generalization

This fallacy means that the conclusion has been derived from insufficient evidence. Here is one example: You taste three tangerines and each is sour, so you conclude that all tangerines are sour. Here is another: By observing one performance of a musical group, you conclude that the group is unfit to perform.

Non Sequitur ("It Does Not Follow")

The false establishment of cause-effect is known as a non sequitur. To say, for example, that "Because my instructor is young, I'm sure she'll be a good teacher" is a non sequitur because youth does not cause good teaching. Here is another example: "Sam Goodwin is the best choice for state senator because he understands the people." Understanding the people will not necessarily make someone an effective state senator.

False Cause

The false cause fallacy is the incorrect assumption that two events that follow each other in time are causally related. Suppose you walked under a ladder and then tripped on an uneven sidewalk. If you said you tripped because you walked under the ladder, you would be assuming false cause.

Either-Or Fallacy

This fallacy assumes that an issue is only two sided, or that there are only two choices or alternatives for a particular situation. In other words, there is no middle ground. Consider the issue of censorship of violence on television. An either-or fallacy is to assume that violence on TV must either be allowed or banned. This fallacy does not recognize other alternatives such as limiting access through viewing hours, restricting the showing of certain types of violence, and so forth.

Emotional Appeal

Also called *ad populum* (to the people), this logical fallacy appeals to the prejudices and emotions of people. For example, an advertisement for a new clothing line may appeal to a reader's sense of patriotism by suggesting that a product is American made using fabrics manufactured made in the U.S. and sewn only by American workers. A writer may use this appeal as a means of omitting evidence that readers need to properly evaluate the writer's claim.

False Analogy

An analogy is an extended comparison between two otherwise unlike things. A sound analogy assumes that two things are alike in some ways. A false analogy compares two things that do not share a likeness. A writer arguing against gun control may say, "Guns are not a major problem in this country. Fatal accidents on the road, in the workplace, and at home kill many more people than do guns." Here the writer is suggesting that death by guns is similar to fatal accidents in the car, on the job, or at home. Yet, accidents and murder are not similar.

Bandwagon Appeal

The bandwagon appeal suggests that readers should accept an idea or take a particular action because everyone else believes or does it. In arguing that an idea or action is popular, and therefore, right or just, the writer evades discussing the issue itself and avoids presenting evidence to support the claim. Here is an example of a bandwagon appeal. "Eighty-five percent of women say they prefer gas ovens and stovetops. Women in the know use gas—so should you."

Ad Hominem

An *ad hominem* (against the man) is an attack on a person rather than on the issue or argument at hand. An *ad hominem* argument may attack the speaker or author of a statement, rather than the statement itself. For example, a bulimic teenager may reject the medical advice of her physician by arguing that her physician knows nothing about bulimia since the physician has never experienced it. Or a politician may attack an opponent's personal characteristics or lifestyle rather than his or her political platform.

Abstract Concepts as Reality

Writers occasionally treat abstract concepts as real truths with a single position. For example, a writer may say, "Research proves that divorce is harmful to children." Actually, there are hundreds of pieces of research on the effects of divorce and they offer diverse findings and conclusions. Some but not all research reports harmful effects. Here is another example: "Criminology shows us that prisons are seldom effective in controlling crime." Writers tend to use this device to make it seem as if all authorities are in agreement with their positions. This device also allows writers to ignore contrary or contradictory opinions.

Red Herring

A red herring is something that is added to an argument to divert attention from the issue at hand. It is introduced into an argument to throw readers off track. Think of a red herring as an argumentative tactic, rather than an error in reasoning. Suppose you are reading an essay that argues for the death penalty. If the author suddenly starts reporting the horrific living conditions of death row prisons and the unjust treatment of prisoners, the writer is introducing a red herring. The living conditions and treatment of prisoners on death row are not relevant to whether the death penalty is just.

EXERCISE 11-6

DIRECTIONS: Identify the logical fallacy in each of the following statements; write your answer in the space provided.

1. All Native American students in my accounting class earned A grades, so Native Americans must excel with numerical tasks.

   _____

2. If you are not in favor of nuclear arms control, then you're against protecting our future.

   _____

3. Linguistics proves that the immersion approach is the only way to learn a second language.

   _____

4. My sister cannot compose business letters or memos because she has writer's block.

   _____

5. People who smoke have a higher mortality rate than nonsmokers. Urban dwellers have a higher mortality rate than suburban dwellers. Now, since we do not urge urban dwellers to move to the suburbs, why should we urge smokers to quit smoking?

_____

6. A well-known senator, noting a decline in the crime rate in the four largest cities in his state, quickly announced that his new "get-tough on criminals" publicity campaign was successful and took credit for the decline.

_____

7. I always order cheesecake for dessert because I am allergic to chocolate.

_____

8. Stricter driving while intoxicated laws are needed in this country. It is a real shame that some adults allow preschool age children to drink sips of wine and to taste beer long before they reach the age of reason. If stricter driving laws were in place, many lives would be saved.

_____

9. Did you know that Dr. Smith is single? How could she possibly be a good marriage counselor?

_____

10. Two million pet owners feed their pets VitaBrite Tabs to keep their dogs healthy and increase longevity. Buy some today for your best friend.

_____

EXERCISE 11-7

DIRECTIONS: The following two essays were written in response to the question "Should animals be used in research?" Read each essay and answer the questions that follow.

ARGUMENT 1: SHOULD ANIMALS BE USED IN RESEARCH?

The use of animals in research has become an extremely emotional as well as legal issue. Very strict federal regulations on the care, maintenance, and use of animals in research now exist. But even though research using animals is closely monitored to identify and eliminate any potential source of pain or abuse of experimental animals, activists still object to the use of animal species, particularly the vertebrates, for research.

Those who oppose the use of animals have become caught up in the developments of the "high tech" world and frequently propose the use of simulators and computer modeling to replace biological research with live animals. Unfortunately, simulators and computer modeling cannot generate valid biological data on their own. Scientific data obtained from experiments using live animals must first provide base data before modelers can extrapolate results under similar conditions.

Simulators and computer modeling do have their place in teaching and research, but they will not and cannot replace the use of animals in many kinds of critical medical research. For example, consider modern surgical procedures in human organ repair and transplanting. The techniques in use today were developed and perfected through the use of laboratory animals. Would you want a delicate operation to be performed by a physician trained only on simulators?

Laboratory animal research is fundamental to medical progress in many other areas as well. Vaccines for devastating human diseases like polio and smallpox and equally serious animal diseases like rabies, feline leukemia, and distemper were all developed through the use of research animals.

The discovery, development, and refinement of drugs that could arrest, control, or eliminate such human diseases as AIDS, cancer, and heart disease all require the use of laboratory animals whose physiological mechanisms are similar to humans.

I have only noted above a few of the many examples where animals have been used in human and veterinary medical research. It's also important to note that studies in behavior, ecology, physiology, and genetics all require the use of animals, in some capacity, to produce valid and meaningful knowledge about life on this planet.

Donald W. Tuff, "Animals and Research" from *NEA Higher Education Advocate*

ARGUMENT 2: SHOULD ANIMALS BE USED IN RESEARCH?

I cannot accept the argument that research on animals is necessary to discover "cures" for humans. Many diseases and medications react very differently in animals than they do in humans. Aspirin, for example, is toxic to cats, and there are few diseases directly transmittable from cats to humans.

I particularly abhor the "research" conducted for cosmetic purposes. The Draise test—where substances are introduced into the eyes of rabbits and then examined to see if ulcers, lesions or other observable reactions take place—is archaic and inefficient. Other alternatives exist that are more accurate and do not cause unnecessary suffering to our fellow creatures.

Household products such as the LD–50 test are also tested needlessly on animals. Animals, in many cases puppies, are force-fed these toxic chemicals to determine the dosage at which exactly 50 percent of them die. These tests are not necessary and do not give very useful information.

Many top medical schools no longer use animals for teaching purposes, but have their medical students practice on models, computer simulations, and then observe techniques on human patients. A medical doctor is expected to honor and revere life, and this approach emphasizes that idea.

If medical students are deliberately taught that animal life is not important, then the next step to devaluing human life is made that much easier. Anatomy and biology classes do not need to use cats for all their students, either. A video of a dissection that is shown to the entire class or a model or computer simulation would be just as effective.

If an experiment using animals is deemed absolutely necessary, then that claim should be fully documented and all previous research should be examined thoroughly to avoid needless replication. In addition, the facility should not be exempt from cruelty laws and should be open to inspection by animal rights advocates not affiliated with the research institution.

Humans have a duty to take care of the earth and to respect all life, for if we poison the earth and annihilate other life on the planet, we are poisoning and annihilating ourselves. We were put on this earth to take care of our earth and the creatures upon it.

Angela Molina,"Animals and Research" from *NEA Higher Education Advocate*

ARGUMENT 1

1. Summarize Tuff's position on the use of laboratory animals.

2. Outline the main points of his argument.

3. What types of evidence does he offer?

4. Evaluate the adequacy and sufficiency of the evidence provided.

5. Does the author recognize or refute counterarguments?

Argument 2

1. Summarize Molina's position.

   _____

2. Outline the main points of her argument.

   _____

   _____

   _____

   _____

   _____

   _____

   _____

3. What types of evidence does she offer?

   _____

   _____

   _____

4. Evaluate the adequacy and sufficiency of the evidence provided.

   _____

   _____

   _____

   _____

5. Does the author recognize or refute counterarguments?

   _____

Both Arguments

1. Which argument do you feel is stronger? Why?

   _____

2. Compare the types of evidence each uses.

   _____

   _____

Critical Thinking Tip #11

Evaluating Emotional Appeals

Emotional appeals attempt to involve or excite readers by appealing to their emotions, thereby controlling the reader's attitude toward the subject. Several types of emotional appeals are described here.

1. **Emotionally Charged or Biased Language** By using words that create an emotional response, writers establish positive or negative feelings. For example, an advertisement for a new line of fragrances promises to "indulge," "refresh," "nourish," and "pamper" the user. An ad for an automobile uses phrases such as "limousine comfort," "European styling," and "animal sleekness" to interest and excite readers.

2. **Testimonials** A testimonial involves using the opinion or action of a well-known or famous person. We have all seen athletes endorsing underwear or movie stars selling shampoo. This type of appeal works on the notion that people admire celebrities and strive to be like them, respect their opinions, and are willing to accept their viewpoints.

3. **Association** An emotional appeal also is made by associating a product, idea, or position with others that are already accepted or highly regarded. Patriotism is already valued, so to call a product "All American" in an advertisement is an appeal to the emotions. A car being named a Cougar to remind you of a fast, sleek animal, a cigarette ad picturing a scenic waterfall, or a speaker standing in front of an American flag are other examples of association.

4. **Appeal to "Common Folk"** Some people distrust those who are well educated, wealthy, highly artistic, or in other ways distinctly different from the average person. An emotional appeal to this group is made by selling a product or idea by indicating that it is originated from, held by, or bought by ordinary citizens. A commercial may advertise a product by showing its use in an average household. A politician may describe her background and education to suggest that she is like everyone else; a salesperson may dress in styles similar to his clients.

5. **"Join the Crowd" Appeal** The appeal to do, believe, or buy what everyone else is doing, believing, or buying is known as crowd appeal. Commercials that proclaim their product as the "Number one best-selling car in America" are appealing to this motive. Essays that cite opinion polls on a controversial issue in support of a position—"sixty-eight percent of Americans favor capital punishment"—are also using this appeal.

EXERCISE 11-8

DIRECTIONS: From among the reading assignments you have completed this semester, choose one that involved persuasive or argumentative writing. Review this piece of writing and then complete the following.

1. Summarize what is being argued for.
2. List the key points of the argument.
3. Indicate what type of evidence the writer uses.
4. Determine whether the evidence is adequate and sufficient to support the author's point.
5. Identify any counterarguments the author recognizes or refutes.

EXERCISE 11-9

ELECTRONIC APPLICATION

DIRECTIONS: Visit a newsgroup that focuses on a controversial issue and either follow or participate in the discussion. What persuasive techniques or emotional appeals (see Critical Thinking Tip #11) did you observe?

Summary

1. What is involved in evaluating arguments and persuasive writing?

Persuasive and argumentative writing urges the reader to take action or accept a particular point of view. To evaluate this type of writing readers must learn to evaluate source and authority, recognize the structure of arguments, and identify logical fallacies in arguments.

2. Why should you consider the source of the material and the author's authority when reading this type of writing?

Evaluating both the source in which material was printed and the competency of its author is essential in evaluating any argument or piece of persuasive writing. Where a piece of writing came from can be an indication of the type of information that will be presented as well as its accuracy and value. The author's qualifications and level of expertise with the subject provide a further indication of the reliability of this information.

3. How can you read arguments more effectively?

Since both inductive and deductive arguments make assertions and give evidence to support them, when reading them it is important to
- identify what is being argued for
- read very closely and carefully
- watch for conclusions
- be alert to the types of evidence given
- reread to examine both content and structure
- underline or outline the key parts

4. How should you evaluate an argument?

Critical readers evaluate the soundness, correctness, and worth of an argument. To do so,
- determine the type of evidence used
- decide whether there is enough evidence and whether it is the right kind
- notice whether key terms are defined and used properly
- be alert to value judgments, assumptions, or cause-effect connections
- look for counterarguments and whether they are adequately refuted

5. What are the common errors in logical reasoning?

Eleven common logical fallacies that can weaken or destroy an argument are:
- circular reasoning
- hasty generalization
- non sequitur
- false cause
- either-or fallacy
- emotional appeal
- false analogy
- bandwagon appeal
- *ad hominem*
- abstract concepts as reality
- red herring

READING SELECTION 21

ARGUMENTATIVE ESSAY

FROM A VEGETARIAN: LOOKING AT HUNTING FROM BOTH SIDES NOW

Timothy Denesha

From *The Buffalo News*

This editorial, originally published in The Buffalo News, *explores the issue of sports hunting. Read the essay to answer the following questions:*

1. *What was Denesha's original position on sports hunting?*
2. *How has his position changed?*

— · —

1   Deer hunting season opened Nov. 18, and as the gunfire resumes in our woodlands and fields so will the perennial sniping between hunters and animal rights supporters. I always feel caught in the cross-fire on this matter, because I have been a vegetarian and animal rights advocate for over 25 years, but I also have friends I respect who are hunters. I've learned the issue is not as black-and-white as I once believed.

2   Growing up with many beloved pets and no hunters in my life, I assumed these people were bloodthirsty animal haters. When, in my 20s, I read the great humanitarian Albert Schweitzer's writings on reverence for life, I became a vegetarian and even more contemptuous of hunters.

3   But I had to revise my opinion after seeing the classic 1981 African film, "The Gods Must Be Crazy." The hero, a good-hearted bushman slays a small gazelle, then tenderly strokes her, apologizing for taking her life. He explains his family is hungry and thanks her for providing food. I was stunned: a hunter practicing reverence for life! Later, I learned that Native American tradition has the same compassionate awareness about life lost so another life may be sustained.

4   My position softened further several years ago when Alex Pacheco, a leading animals-rights activist, spoke here. Detailing inhumane prac-

tices at meat-packing plants and factory farms, he said the most important thing anyone could do to lessen animal suffering was to stop eating meat. I decided to work toward being vegan (eating no animal products) and reluctantly admitted that hunters were not the animal kingdom's worst enemies. However, I still disliked them.

5   What really changed my perspective was getting to know some hunters personally, through my job at a Red Cross blood-donation center. Some of my co-workers and a number of our donors are civic-minded people who donate blood (which most people don't) but also shed animal blood with their guns and arrows. Confronting this paradox brought me some realizations.

6   First, hunters are like any group that differs from me: lacking personal experience of them made it easier to demonize them. They aren't monsters. I don't know if any of them apologizes to or thanks his kill as the hungry bushman did, but I do know they aren't cruel, sadistic or bloodthirsty—quite the opposite, as I later discovered.

7   Second, these people aren't just amusing themselves by ending a life; they are acquiring food. This death that sustains another life has a meaning that, for example, fox hunting does not. To the animal, this distinction may mean little. But it is significant when considering a person's intentions.

8   Also, I was informed that hunters don't "like to kill." They enjoy the outdoors, the camaraderie and the various skills involved. (One of these skills, the "clean kill," is prized precisely because it minimizes suffering.) Like vegetable gardeners,

they enjoy providing food [for] themselves and their families with their own hands. Like those who fish, they enjoy a process of food acquisition that involves an animal's death, but not because it does. Again, this may seem a small point (especially to the prey), but I feel it is meaningful from the standpoint of the hunter's humanity.

9   In addition, I've come to see a certain integrity in hunters as meat-eaters who "do their own dirty work." Packaged cold-cuts and fast-food burgers mask the fact of lives bled out on the killing floor. Hunters never forget this, for they accept personal responsibility for it.

10 Furthermore, were I an animal that had to die to feed a human, I'd rather it happen one-on-one, at the hands of that person in the woods that were my home, than amidst the impersonal mass-production machinery of a meat factory. Either way is death, but one way has more dignity, less fear and less suffering.

11 There are bad hunters who trespass, shoot domestic animals, hunt intoxicated or disregard that cardinal rule of hunting's unwritten code of ethics: wounded prey must not be allowed to suffer. Last Thanksgiving morning in Chestnut Ridge Park, I found a fresh trail of deer tracks in the snow, heavily splashed with blood. It was horrible.

12 One of my hunter co-workers was also upset when I told him about it, and had this story. He himself was able to hunt only one day last season and sighted a small, wounded doe. As a student on a tight budget with a family, he hunts for food and would have preferred to ignore the doe's plight and meet his license limit with a large buck. Instead, he devoted a long, difficult day to trailing her until he was close enough to end her suffering. This was an act of mercy and even self-sacrifice, not the action of a heartless person insensitive to animals. It was reverence for life. He claims many hunters would do and have done the same.

13 And I realized that compassion has many faces, some of the truest the most unexpected.

Examining Reading Selection 21

Checking Your Vocabulary

Directions: Using context, word parts, or a dictionary if necessary, circle the letter of the meaning for each word as it is used in the reading.

1. contemptuous (paragraph 2)
    a. hateful
    b. suspicious
    c. disrespectful
    d. patronizing

2. reverence (paragraph 3)
    a. tenderness
    b. disbelief
    c. respect
    d. honesty

3. inhumane (paragraph 4)
    a. lacking pity or compassion
    b. not respectful
    c. not purposeful
    d. lacking self-awareness

4. paradox (paragraph 5)
    a. evidence
    b. variation
    c. behavior
    d. contradiction

5. camaraderie (paragraph 8)
    a. risk
    b. thrill
    c. companionship
    d. self-sufficiency

Checking Your Comprehension

Directions: Circle the letter of the best answer.

6. This reading is primarily concerned with
   a. the barbarism of hunting.
   b. the reverence hunters have for human life.
   c. the defensibility of hunting.
   d. why people become vegetarians.

7. The main point in this reading is
   a. it is unethical to hunt.
   b. animals suffer as a result of hunting.
   c. hunters have as much integrity and compassion as nonhunters.
   d. most hunters are only interested in killing helpless creatures for sport.

8. It is clear from the article that the author is *not*
   a. a vegetarian.
   b. a health care worker.
   c. a hunter.
   d. an animal rights advocate.

9. According to the article, hunters
   a. have little respect for animal life.
   b. don't eat processed meat.
   c. hunt only to acquire food.
   d. don't enjoy killing.

10. Initially, what made the author begin to change his mind about hunters?
    a. a speech by Alex Pacheco.
    b. the African film "The Gods Must Be Crazy."
    c. the Red Cross blood donation center.
    d. the writings of Albert Schweitzer.

11. The author discusses the issue of sports hunting primarily by
    a. comparing hunters and nonhunters.
    b. classifying types of hunters.
    c. examining his own changing beliefs.
    d. defining sports hunting.

Thinking Critically

12. As used in the first paragraph, a synonym for "sniping" is
    a. shooting.
    b. cutting.
    c. killing.
    d. arguing.

13. Which of the following statements best describes the author's attitude about hunting?
    a. Hunters are aggressive and blood thirsty.
    b. Hunters often take animals' lives with respect and compassion.
    c. Hunting should not be allowed under any circumstances.
    d. Hunting is just a sport like any other sport.

14. From this reading, we can infer that deer hunters' licenses allow them to
    a. kill as many deer as they choose.
    b. hunt on any property where deer can be found.
    c. hunt only one day per season.
    d. kill only a limited number of deer.

15. Which of the following is an example of a deer hunter abiding by hunting's unwritten code of ethics?
    a. He hunts with a bow and arrow instead of a rifle.
    b. He kills a deer that is already wounded.
    c. He brings a wounded deer to the vet for treatment.
    d. He kills only to supply his family with food.

Questions for Discussion

1. Do you think hunting is moral or immoral? Justify your position.

2. Discuss the ways in which hunters prevent animals from suffering.

3. What lessons can be learned from the author's statement that "Hunters are like any group that differs from me: lacking personal experience of them made it easier to demonize them"?

4. When the author refers to hunting he states that "compassion has many faces." What does he mean? Give an example to support your point.

Selection 21:			822 words
Finishing Time:	____	____	____
	HR.	MIN.	SEC.
Starting Time:	____	____	____
	HR.	MIN.	SEC.
Reading Time:		____	____
		MIN.	SEC.
WPM Score:		____	
Comprehension Score:		____	%

READING SELECTION 22

SOCIOLOGY

OUT OF TIME

Alan Weisman and Sandy Tolan

From *Societies: A Multicultural Reader*

Taken from a collection of multicultural readings that accompany a sociology textbook, this essay focuses on the destruction of lands and cultures of primitive societies. Read it to discover what effects such destruction has had and may have in the future.

— · —

1   An old Indian stands in the rain in northern Argentina, amid the charred ruins of his village. His name is Pa'i Antonio Moreira. Over his thin sweater two strings of black beads crisscross his chest like bandoliers, signifying that he is a ñanderú, a shaman[1] of his people. They are among the last few Guaraní Indians in this country, part of a cultural group that once inhabited a forest stretching from Argentina to the Amazon. Now only remnants of that forest and its creatures and people are left.

2   The night before, government men in forest-service uniforms torched the community's village. The 1,500-acre tract of semitropical woodland where they lived is only a few miles from

Iguazú Falls, the biggest waterfall in South America. Once sacred to the Guaraní, Iguazú is now overwhelmed by tourists. Moreira's village was burned to make way for yet another hotel. The next Indian village to the south is also gone, swallowed by the waters of a new reservoir. The villages beyond that are no longer surrounded by black laurel and ceiba trees, which sheltered the deer and tapir the Guaraní once hunted, but by silent forests of Monterey pine, imported from California and planted by a nearby paper company for its superior fiber content.

3   The old shaman's kinsmen huddle around a fire, while the embers of their homes hiss and sizzle in the rain. The people descend from a stubborn band of Guaraní who refused to be evangelized when Jesuits arrived here 400 years ago. Moreira tells us that these ills curse the Guaraní's world because white men ignore the true way of God. Only the Indian, he says, remembers how God intended the world to be.

4   Then why, we ask, has God allowed the white man to triumph, and the Indian to suffer?

____
[1]Spiritual leader

5   He gazes at us from beneath heavy-lidded eyes filled with loss and compassion. "The white man hasn't triumphed," he says softly. "When the Indians vanish, the rest will follow."

6   Throughout the Americas, great changes fueled by visions of progress have swept away the habitats of countless plants and animals. But entire human cultures are also becoming endangered. During the past two years, we traveled to 15 countries, from the United States to Chile, to document this swift, often irreversible destruction.

7   Nations with growing, impoverished populations strike a Faustian[2] bargain with the developed world: to create jobs and electricity for industry, they borrow hundreds of millions of dollars from foreign banks. They build huge dams that flood their richest lands and displace thousands of rural poor. To repay the massive debt, they invite foreign companies to mine their timber, gold, oil, and coal, or convert their farmlands to produce luxury crops for consumers in North America, Europe and Japan. To ease pressures on overcrowded lands, they allow poor settlers to slash and burn their way into virgin forests, where they clash with the indigenous people already living there—including some of the last uncontacted tribes in the hemisphere.

8   For centuries the Yuguí Indians of the Bolivian Amazon roamed naked through jungles so remote they thought no one else existed. Their word for *world* translates simply as *leaves*.

9   "When we first saw the white people, we thought they were the spirits of our dead ancestors," recalled Ataiba, the last of the Yuguí chiefs. He recalled how his people had begun to encounter strange things in the jungle—fresh fish hung from trees, sacks of sugar, cooking pots, machetes—all laid beside new trails. One day, at the end of one of these gift trails, Ataiba saw light-skinned people watching him. After many months, the pale strangers, evangelicals from the Florida-based New Tribes Mission, convinced

Ataiba that they could offer safe haven from the growing violence of confrontations with loggers and settlers. One morning late in 1989, Ataiba led his people out of the forest forever, to become permanent wards of the mission village.

10   Often, on the heels of the missionaries, come the forces of development. In Ecuador during the early 1970s, the government contracted with Texaco to build an oil industry in the Ecuadorian Amazon and help bring the country into the global economy. Until then, many natives there had never even heard of a nation called Ecuador, let alone petroleum.

11   "We didn't know the sound of a motor," explained Toribe, a young Cofán leader. The Cofán, who live along Ecuador's Tío Aguarico, were still hunting peccaries and monkeys with blowguns. "We couldn't figure out what animal could be making those noises." The sounds were Texaco's helicopters. Soon settlers streamed down the oil-company roads, changing life irrevocably for the Cofán.

12   "With the petroleum companies came epidemics," recalled Toribe. "We didn't know flu, measles, and these other illnesses. Many fled from here. Those that stayed were finished. It was all contaminated. There were fifteen thousand of us on this side of the Río Aguarico. Now we are only four hundred."

13   Oil from Ecuador, hardwoods from Bolivia, and from Honduras to Costa Rica to Brazil, beef cattle raised for export where forests once stood; we had stumbled onto another kind of gift trail, this one leading back to the United States. The savanna surrounding Bogotá, Colombia, with some of the finest soil in Latin America, produces not food but bargain-priced roses, chrysanthemums, and carnations to sell on street corners and in supermarkets in the United States and beyond. In Honduras, mangrove forests lining the Gulf of Fonseca's estuaries are threatened by modern mariculture. Huge shrimp farms resist local fishermen's access to the crabs, mollusks, and small fish they have netted for generations.

[2]Faust is a legendary figure who sold his soul to the devil in return for power and knowledge.

14   In Brazil, the biggest dam in the Amazon, Tucurui, has displaced thousands of people and created such mosquito infestations that thousands more are leaving. Tucurui was built to power aluminum smelters owned by U.S., European, and Japanese companies. The ore comes from the Amazon's largest mine, which strips away hundreds of acres of jungle each year to provide foil and cans.

15   On South America's second-biggest river, the Parana, we watched men building the longest dam in the world: Yacyreta, along the Argentina-Paraguay border. More than $1 billion in World Bank and Inter-American Development Bank loans was allegedly diverted from the dam project to finance things like Argentina's Falklands war. Now there's not enough money to relocate the 40,000 people whose cities and farms will be flooded. As much as $30 million was spent, however, on an elevator to carry fish like dorado, a prized local species, upstream to spawn. Unfortunately, the elevator, built by North American dam contractors, was designed for salmon, which go upstream, spawn, and die. Dorado need to return. And there's no down elevator.

16   Our travels did reveal a few signs of hope: a land-recovery program run by villagers in southern Honduras, a proposal to put Kuna Indians in charge of protecting the watershed of Panama's Bayano Dam. But these projects are exceptions. Alone, they are not enough to halve the momentous effects of uncontrolled development. Sustainable development must be contoured to local needs rather than imposed from afar by economic forces.

17   When we reached the Strait of Magellan, residents of southern Chile showed us great inland sounds that soon will be dammed to power yet more aluminum smelters—this time Australian. On Tierra del Fuego, they took us to ancient hardwood rainforests, scheduled to be turned into fax paper by Canadian and Japanese companies.

18   Finally, we stood with Professor Bedrich Magas of Chile's Magellan University at the tip of the Americas, looking out toward the growing polar ozone hole. Magas reminded us that the National Aeronautics and Space Administration had recently discovered destructive chlorine over the northern United States—just like that which was found over Antarctica only a few years earlier. It was a disturbing reminder of the warning of the Guaraní shaman: what we do to the lives and lands of others may ultimately determine the fate of our own.

Writing about Reading Selection 22*

Checking Your Vocabulary

Directions: Complete each of the following items; refer to a dictionary if necessary.

1. Discuss the connotative meanings of the word *endangered* (paragraph 6).

2. Define each of the following words:
   a. evangelized (paragraph 3)

   _____

   b. habitats (paragraph 6)

   _____

   c. wards (paragraph 9)

   _____
   _____

   d. epidemics (paragraph 12)

   _____

   e. allegedly (paragraph 15)

   _____

* Multiple-choice questions are contained in Part 6 (page 590).

3. Define the word *indigenous* (paragraph 7) and underline the word or phrase that provides a context clue for its meaning.

_____

_____

4. Define the word *contoured* (paragraph 16) and underline the word or phrase that provides a context clue for its meaning.

_____

_____

5. Determine the meanings of the following words by using word parts:
   a. semitropical (paragraph 2)

   _____

   b. displace (paragraph 7)

   _____

   c. irrevocably (paragraph 11)

   _____

   _____

   d. mariculture (paragraph 13)

   _____

   e. diverted (paragraph 15)

   _____

Checking Your Comprehension

6. Why is Iguazú no longer sacred to the Guaraní?

   _____

   _____

7. Why were the black laurel and ceiba trees in the Indian villages of Argentina replaced by Monterey pine?

   _____

   _____

   _____

8. Explain why the Yuguí Indians of the Bolivian Amazon referred to "world" as "leaves."

   _____

   _____

   _____

   _____

9. Why were many people from the Cofán in Ecuador forced to leave after the petroleum companies came?

   _____

   _____

   _____

   _____

Thinking Critically

10. What did the authors mean when they said that impoverished populations struck a "Faustian bargain with the developed world . . ."?

    _____

    _____

    _____

    _____

    _____

    _____

11. Why did Ataiba, a Yuguí chief, lead his people from the forest to the mission village? Was this decision in the best interest of his people? Why or why not?

    _____

    _____

_____

_____

_____

12. How has life for the Cofán in Ecuador "irrevocably changed"? Was it changed for the better or for the worse?

_____

_____

_____

_____

13. What do you think Moreira meant by saying "when the Indians vanish, the rest will follow"?

_____

_____

_____

_____

Questions for Discussion

1. How are human cultures becoming an "endangered species"?

2. What are the moral implications of poor nations borrowing huge sums of money from foreign banks to build dams that displace native poor people?

3. According to the passage, Indian villages in Argentina are being systematically destroyed by the government, *without* the permission of the inhabitants, to make way for commercial developments. What does this say about the financial and cultural interests of the government in South America?

Selection 22:			1330 words
Finishing Time:	HR.	MIN.	SEC.
Starting Time:	HR.	MIN.	SEC.
Reading Time:		MIN.	SEC.
WPM Score:			
Comprehension Score:			%

GO ELECTRONIC

For additional readings, exercises, and Internet activities, visit this book's Web site at:

http://www.ablongman.com/mcwhorter

For even more activities, visit the Longman English pages at:

http://www.ablongman.com/englishpages

If you need a user name and password, please see your instructor.

Take a Road Trip to the American Southwest
Be sure to visit the Critical Thinking and Analytical Reasoning module on your Reading Road Trip CD-ROM for multimedia tutorials, exercises, and tests.

CHAPTER 12

Reading and Evaluating
Internet Sources

IN THIS CHAPTER YOU WILL LEARN:

1. To locate electronic sources effectively.
2. To evaluate Internet sources.
3. To read electronic text.
4. To develop new reading and thinking strategies for electronic text.

A student is writing a paper about Amy Tan, a Chinese-American author, for her English class. She decides to work primarily with Internet sources. She chooses to write about Tan's book, *The Joy Luck Club,* and she wants to locate Web sites that discuss this work. She goes to yahoo.com and searches for Amy Tan and Joy Luck Club. After looking through a few of the sites listed, she chooses one (http://www.msu.edu/~shoopsar/joyluck .htm) that is sponsored by an educational institution. She visits the site and finds an essay on Tan's exploration of the self in her book. The essay is three pages long and contains references. At first, the site seems to be reliable. Fortunately, she decides to evaluate the site further before using the information in her paper. Further checking reveals that the essay was written by an undergraduate student for a course on writing, Women Writers in America. Since student papers are not considered suitable reference sources for academic papers, she rejects the site and continues her search. This incident illustrates the potential dangers of using information from Web sites. Unless you carefully evaluate the sources you find, you may end up finding information that is unreliable or inappropriate.

Despite the wealth of materials that appear on the Web, caution is always needed when using the Internet for the following reasons:

- **The Internet is not owned by anyone, and it has no central sponsorship.** Unlike textbooks and much other print material, there is no one to make sure the information contained is accurate and complete. There is no overseeing group or organization that decides what should and should not be placed on the Internet. Consequently, anyone can post anything they want, regardless of whether it is true or false, objective or subjective, biased, opinionated, or even offensive.

- **There is no set of standards by which <u>all</u> material is evaluated before it is published.** Book and magazine publishers have editors and editorial boards that evaluate whether a work is worthy of publication. Many professional journals use a system of peer review whereby an article or research report is read and evaluated by other experts in the same field before it is accepted for publication. While certain Web sites, such as that of the AMA (American Medical Association), do verify all information that appears on their Web sites, many do not. For many Web sites, no such controls exist.

- **Information on the World Wide Web is not organized with the goal of being easy to locate.** Unlike in a library, which organizes books by subject areas and call numbers, information on the Web is not cataloged in any way. One author described the Internet as "like a library with all the books on the floor" (http://www.teacherlibrarian.com/pages/29_4_feature_bonus.html). Although search engines are helpful in locating information, there is no one central organizing system through which all information is categorized.

- **Not all information on a topic is available on the Web.** Due to copyright restrictions, costs, author preferences, and so on, some information is available only in print form.

- **Many materials written prior to the 1980s are not on the Web.** Before the creation of the Internet, most information appeared in print form; much of that information has not been put up on the Web.

Locating Electronic Sources on the Web

Begin by gaining access to the Internet. In addition to a computer, you will need a modem and a browser, such as Microsoft Explorer or Netscape. You will also need an Internet service provider (ISP) to connect your computer to the Internet. Your college's computer center, your telephone or cable company, or a commercial service provider such as America Online can connect you. You will need a name to use online, called a user name, and a password. If you need help getting started, check with the staff in your college's computer lab.

Identifying Keywords

To search for information on a topic, you need to come up with a group of specific words that describe your topic; these are known as **keywords.** It is often necessary to narrow your topic in order to identify specific keywords. Suppose you are looking for information on year-round schools. If you go to yahoo.com and type in those words, you will get more than 240,000 Web sites. By putting the phrase in quotes, you will limit those results to about 11,000. That's still a large number of Web sites. Try narrowing your search—limit it by adding words that home in on your topic, "year-round schools" or "improved test scores," for example. This search will bring your results list down to under 50 hits—a much more manageable group of Web sites to look through. Other ways to limit are by geography (New York State), population (elementary schools), and time (1990s). Before beginning an Internet search, spend some time brainstorming keywords, and try different combinations of words and synonyms. In the preceding example, you could use "year-round education" or "extended school year" or "block scheduling." Finally, if you find a site that is very close to what you want, use the terminology of that site to search again. For example, you might learn from one site that there is an organization called the National Association for Year-Round Education (NAYRE). You could then do another search for the name of this organization.

Using Subject Directories

Subject directories classify Web resources by categories and subcategories. Some offer reviews or evaluations of sites. Use a subject directory when you want to browse the Web using general topics or when you are conducting a broad search. A subject directory would be helpful if you were looking for sites about parenting issues or wanted to find a list of organizations for animal welfare. Two useful subject directories are INFOMINE (http://infomine.ucr.edu) and Yahoo (http://www.yahoo.com).

Using a Search Engine

A **search engine** is a computer program that helps you locate information on a topic. Search engines search for keywords and provide connections to documents that contain the keywords you instruct it to search for. Depending on your topic, some search engines are more useful than others. In addition, each search engine may require a different way of entering the keywords. For example, some may require you to place quotation marks around a phrase ("capital punishment"). Other times, you may need to use plus signs (+) between keywords ("home schooling" + "primary grades" + "California"). The quotation marks around "home schooling" will create a search for those words as a phrase, rather than as single terms. Be sure to use the "help" feature when you use a new search engine to discover the best way to enter keywords.

Using Meta-Search Engines

You can search a number of search engines at the same time and combine all the results in a single listing using a **meta-search engine.** Use this type of engine when you are searching for a very specific or obscure topic or one for which you are having trouble finding information. Table 12.1 on page 460 describes several popular search and meta-search engines.

EXERCISE 12-1

DIRECTIONS: Use one of the search tools listed above to locate three sources on one of the following topics. Then use a different tool or different search engine to search the same topic again. Compare your results. Which engine was easier to use? Which produced more sources?

1. The Baseball Hall of Fame
2. Telecommuting
3 Oil drilling in Alaska
4. Parenting issues

Tips for Locating Reliable Web Sites

Because the Internet contains millions of Web sites, some of possibly questionable value, it is important to be selective and use only sites that contain reliable and accurate information. Use the following tips to help you focus your search:

- **Use the Web only when it is appropriate to do so.** Depending on your research goals, there may be times when print sources are better

Table 12.1   Useful Search and Meta-Search Engines

Name	URL	Description
Google	www.google.com	An extensive and very popular tool. Has basic and advanced (menu-based) searching. Many extra features such as translation, domain/file type searches and filtering. Online help provided.
AltaVista	www.altavista.com	A powerful search engine with basic and advanced (menu-based) searching. Also offers searches for audio, video, and images. Provides news, subject guide, filtering, translation, and Internet portal features. Online help provided.
Yahoo	www.yahoo.com	Biggest subject directory on Web. Pages are organized in a searchable directory. A few advanced features available. Internet portal and site recommendations.
Infomine	http://infomine.ucr.edu/	Academic and research sites compiled, organized, and annotated by college and university librarians. Basic and advanced searching (tips provided). Users can submit sites for inclusion.
Ixquick	www.ixquick.com	A meta-search engine covering at least nine other search tools. Features music, picture, and news searches. Search results are rated.
ProFusion	www.profusion.com	This meta-search tool searches major engines or subject-specific databases and resources. Basic and advanced searching. Results are ranked.

and more convenient to use. If you are searching for specific statistics and basic facts, such as population statistics, biographical or historical information, or background information, it may be easier to use standard print reference books such as an encyclopedia, *World Almanac*, or *Statistical Abstracts of the U.S.*

- **Notice obvious clues that point to lack of credibility.** You should be suspicious of Web sites that seem carelessly designed or that contain grammar and punctuation errors. Writers who have not taken the time to present their information clearly and accurately may also not have taken the time to research or document the information they present on their Web site.

- **Distinguish between original Web material and reprinted material.** Web sites may contain original material designed for the Web. The Web also contains the text of many books, articles, and reports previously published in print. These can be found through databases that are usually available only by subscription. Some publications have Web sites that allow you to access previous issues. *Hispanic Magazine's* Web site, for example, allows users to locate articles and essays previously published in the print magazine. Some may charge for back issues or make them available for only a limited period of time.

- **Recognize that articles put up on the Web (that originally appeared in print) are devoid of many of the usual reliability clues.** When you read an article in a magazine, you have all the surrounding clues that suggest its reliability or the lack of it. In print sources, the table of contents, design, layout, cover content, surrounding article and essays, and type of advertising all provide you with clues as to the trustworthiness of the source. When reading the same article put up on the Web, many of these clues are absent. Although some articles do contain these types of graphics and visual features, many do not. Close scrutiny or further research may be needed to determine reliability.

- **Do not assume that every source contains accurate and reliable information.** Many hoaxes and scams appear on the Internet. For example, in May 1999, there was a GAP Giveaway hoax in which e-mail recipients were led to believe that they could receive free merchandise for forwarding an e-mail to their friends. For each time they forwarded the message to another person, they were to receive a pair of cargo pants; the recipients would, in turn, receive a free Hawaiian T-shirt for each time they passed it on to yet another person, and, finally, the last group would receive a fisherman's hat for each time they sent it to someone else. To learn about other Internet hoaxes, visit the Internet Hoaxes site run by the Department of Energy's Computer Incident Advisory Capability, http://hoaxbusters.ciac.org. Use the suggestions in the remainder of this chapter to help you determine whether a Web site is reliable and trustworthy.

Evaluating the Content of a Web Site

Use the following suggestions to evaluate the content of a Web site.

Evaluate the Appropriateness

To be worthwhile, a Web site should contain the information you need. It should answer one or more of your search questions. If the site only touches upon answers to your questions but does not address them in detail, check the links on the site to see if they will lead you to more detailed information. If they do not, search for a more useful site.

Evaluate the Source

Another important step in evaluating a Web site is to determine its source. Ask yourself "Who is the sponsor?" and "Why was this site put up on the Web?" The sponsor of a Web site is the person or organization who paid for it to be created and placed on the Web. Knowing the sponsor will often help you determine the purpose of a Web site. For example, a Web site sponsored by Nike is designed to promote its products, while a site sponsored by a university library is designed to help students learn to use its resources more effectively.

If you are uncertain who sponsors a particular Web site, check its URL, its copyright, and the links it offers. As you will see below, the ending of the URL often suggests the type of sponsorship. The copyright should indicate the owner of the site. If you cannot determine the owner from the copyright, links may reveal the sponsor. Some links may lead to commercial advertising by the sponsor; others may lead to sites sponsored by non-profit groups, for example.

Another way to check the ownership of a Web site is to try to locate the site's home page. You can do this by using just the first part of its URL—up to the first slash (/) mark. For example, you can trace the Amy Tan Web site mentioned at the beginning of the chapter (http://www.msu.edu/~shoopsar/joyluck.htm) by shortening it to http://www.msu.edu/~shoopsar/. This URL takes you to the author's personal Web site. If you take this a step further and shorten the URL to http://www.msu.edu/, and then search the

Michigan State University Web site for "Joy Luck Club," you will discover the home page for ATL 140 with a link to the student writers.

Evaluate Level of Technical Detail

A Web site should contain a level of technical detail that is suited to your purpose. Some sites may provide information that is too sketchy for your search purposes; others may assume a level of background knowledge or technical sophistication that you lack. For example, if you are writing a short, introductory-level paper on threats to the survival of marine animals, information on the Web site of the Scripps Institution of Oceanography (http://www-sio.ucsd.edu) may be too technical and contain more information than you need, unless you have some previous knowledge in that field.

Evaluate the Presentation

Information on a Web site should be presented clearly; it should be well written. If you find a site that is not clear and well written, you should be suspicious of it. If the author did not take time to present ideas clearly and correctly, he or she may not have taken time to collect accurate information either.

Evaluate Completeness

Determine whether the site provides complete information on its topic. Does it address all aspects of the topic that you feel it should? For example, if a Web site titled "Important Twentieth-Century American Poets" does not mention Robert Frost, then the site is incomplete. If you discover that a site is incomplete, search for sites that provide a more thorough treatment of the topic.

Evaluate the Links

Many reputable sites supply links to other related sites. Make sure that the links work and are current, and check to see if the sites to which you were sent are reliable sources of information. If the links do not work or the sources appear unreliable, you should question the reliability of the site itself. Also determine whether the links provided are comprehensive or only present a representative sample. Either is acceptable, but the site should make clear the nature of the links it is providing.

DIRECTIONS: Visit the following Web sites and evaluate their content. Explain why you would either trust or distrust each site for reliable content.

1. http://www.geocities.com/RainForest/6243/index.html

    _____

    _____

2. http://www.improbable.com

    _____

    _____

Evaluating the Accuracy of a Web Site

When using information on a Web site for an academic paper, it is important to be sure that you have found accurate information. One way to determine the accuracy of a Web site is to compare it with print sources (periodicals and books) on the same topic. If you find a wide discrepancy between the Web site and the printed sources, do not trust the Web site. Another way to determine the accuracy of a site's information is to compare it with other Web sites that address the same topic. If discrepancies exist, further research is needed to determine which site is more accurate.

The site itself will also provide clues about the accuracy of its information. Ask yourself the following questions:

- Are the author's name and credentials provided? A well-known writer with established credentials is likely to author only reliable, accurate information. If no author is given, you should question whether the information is accurate.

- Is contact information for the author included on the site? Often, sites provide an e-mail address where the author may be contacted.

- Is the information complete or in summary form? If it is a summary, use the site to find the original source. Original information has less chance of error and is usually preferred in academic papers.

- If opinions are offered, are they presented clearly as opinions? Authors who disguise their opinions as facts are not trustworthy. (See Distinguishing Between Fact and Opinion, Ch. 10, p. 387.)

- Does the writer make unsubstantiated assumptions or base his or her ideas on misconceptions? (See Identifying Assumptions, Ch. 11, p. 435.) If so, the information presented may not be accurate.

- Does the site provide a list of works cited? As with any form of research, sources used to put information up on a Web site must be documented. If sources are not credited, you should question the accuracy of the Web site.

It may be helpful to determine whether the information is available in print form. If it is, try to obtain the print version. Errors may occur when the article or essay is put up on the Web. Web sites move, change, and delete information, so it may be difficult for a reader of an academic paper you write to locate the Web site that you used in writing it. Also, page numbers are easier to cite in print sources than in electronic ones.

EXERCISE 12-3

DIRECTIONS: Visit the following Web sites and evaluate their accuracy.

1. http://gunscholar.com

_____

_____

_____

2. http://www.theonion.com/onion3102/deathrate.html

_____

_____

_____

Evaluating the Timeliness of a Web Site

Although the Web is well known for providing up-to-the-minute information, not all Web sites are current. Evaluate the timeliness of a site by checking

- the date on which the Web site was mounted (put on the Web)
- the date on which the document you are using was added
- the date on which the site was last revised
- the date on which the links were last checked

This information is usually provided at the end of the site's home page or at the end of the document you are using.

DIRECTIONS: Visit two of the following Web sites and evaluate their timeliness. Follow the directions given below for each site.

1. http://www.state.gov/r/pa/ei/bgn/ Choose a geographic region, such as Africa, and evaluate whether information is up-to-date.

_____

_____

2. http://www.netcat.org/trojan.html Evaluate the timeliness of this paper as a whole and the references within it.

_____

_____

_____

_____

3. http://www.trailmix.ca/parks/parksupdateval.shtml Evaluate whether this site contains up-to-date information and discuss why current information on this topic is crucial.

_____

_____

_____

Evaluating the Purpose of a Web Site

There are five basic types of Web sites: informational, news, advocacy, personal, and commercial. Each has a different purpose, and you should approach each differently. This section summarizes these differences.

Informational Web Sites

The purpose of informational Web sites is to present facts and research data. An informational Web site may offer reference sources, such as directories and dictionaries. It may contain reports, statistical data, scholarly research, presentations of research, and so forth.

The URLs of informational Web sites often end in *.edu* or *.gov*. Many informational Web sites are sponsored by educational institutions or government agencies; however, private individuals or companies may also sponsor informational Web sites. Figure 12.1 on page 467 presents the

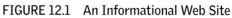

FIGURE 12.1   An Informational Web Site

home page of an informational Web site of FEMA (Federal Emergency Management Agency). Notice that the site reports top news stories, offers a storm watch, and provides information on disaster preparedness, agency news, and so forth.

EXERCISE 12-5

DIRECTIONS: Visit two of the following informational sites. Identify the purpose of each site you visit.

1. http://bioguide.congress.gov/

    _____

    _____

    _____

    _____

2. http://crux.astr.ua.edu/4000WS/4000WS.html

    _____

    _____

    _____

    _____

3. http://www.pcwebopedia.com

    _____

    _____

    _____

    _____

News Web Sites

A news Web site is intended to provide current information of local, national, or international interest. News sites often supplement print newspapers, periodicals, and television news programs. For example, the CNN television network sponsors a news Web site that provides updated news, news analysis, and links to other sources of information. Figure 12.2 (p. 469) shows that the CNN News home page excerpt for July 15, 2003, contains updates on a hurricane threatens Texas, lists other current news stories, provides multimedia links, and offers interactive chat opportunities.

FIGURE 12.2   A News Web Site

The URL of a news Web site usually ends in *.com*. News sites are useful for finding late-breaking news, more detailed information on a news story, photographs, or other interactive information that was not or could not be included in the print media source.

DIRECTIONS: Visit two of the following news Web sites. Identify the purpose of each site.

1. Washington Post Online, http://www.washingtonpost.com

   _____

   _____

   _____

2. PR Newswire, http://prnewswire.com

   _____

   _____

   _____

3. Psycport: Psychology in the News, http://www.psycPORT.com/news

   _____

   _____

   _____

Advocacy Web Sites

Advocacy Web sites are usually sponsored by nonprofit organizations or public service groups (and occasionally for-profit organizations) that wish to promote a particular cause or point of view, often concerning a controversial issue. The purpose of an advocacy Web site is to provide information that supports its cause. The site may also call for action in addition to presenting information. A sample advocacy Web site sponsored by International Wolf Center is shown in Figure 12.3 on page 471. Notice that it provides a center for teaching about wolves, offers information on wolf country adventures, and sponsors a live wolf cam

The URL of an advocacy Web site usually ends with *.org*. When you use an advocacy Web site, you should expect to find only information that supports the cause or viewpoint of that site. Do not expect to find an unbiased examination of both sides of an issue. In the Web site on wolves, you

FIGURE 12.3   An Advocacy Web Site

do learn about wolves' lives and how to support their survival. You do not learn, however, why some cattle ranchers oppose their reintroduction into wild areas and other objections to their survival and proliferation.

EXERCISE 12-7

DIRECTIONS: Visit two of the following advocacy Web sites. For each, identify the issue and the site's position on the issue. Check the site's home page or search for the organization's mission statement if the position is not clear.

1. http://www.scorecard.org

   _____

   _____

2. http://www.amnesty-usa.org/rightsforall

   _____

   _____

   _____

   _____

3. http://www.sierraclub.org

_____

_____

_____

_____ ▪

Personal Web Sites

Personal Web sites are published by individuals who wish to provide information about themselves, their interests, and their accomplishments. Some individuals make their resumes available on their Web site or list their credentials. An author may, for example, list his or her publications or provide links to published articles. Many people who are job hunting publish their resumes on their home page. Still others use their Web site as a means of providing information about themselves and their interests. The Web page of the Dalsemer family (Figure 12.4, p. 473), who have adopted two Vietnamese children, is used to provide information about their family and the adoption process. Notice that the site provides numerous links to other sites and to other pages on their site.

An individual may or may not be affiliated with an organization or institution; consequently, the ending of the URL may vary. The URL may contain *.com* or *.org*; often you may find a tilde (~) included in the URL.

**EXERCISE
12-8**

DIRECTIONS: Visit two of the following personal Web sites and, for each one, answer the questions that follow.

a. http://www.georgetown.edu/tannen/
b. http://www.alexfoundation.org/
c. http://www.hopetillman.com

1. What is the purpose of each Web site?

_____

_____

_____

_____

_____

FIGURE 12.4   A Personal Web Site

_____

_____

_____

2. Describe each person's area of academic expertise.

_____

_____

_____

Commercial Web Sites

Commercial Web sites are sponsored by businesses or corporations whose purpose is to sell or promote goods or services. The sites may provide news and information related to their products. Links to news or informational sites may also be provided. The sponsor may offer public service information, games, contests, and a variety of other gimmicks that are intended to keep readers coming back to the site. Amtrak's Web site in Figure 12.5 below allows users to locate information about its fares and schedules. It also contains numerous special weekly deals, a virtual reality tour, and a description of services.

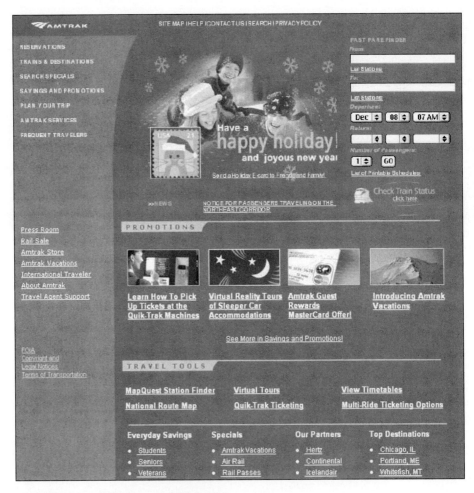

FIGURE 12.5   A Commercial Web Site

The URL of a commercial Web site usually ends in *.com*. Information found on commercial Web sites should be carefully evaluated for use in academic papers. To evaluate a commercial Web site, ask "Why is the information provided?" Look for the connection between the information provided and the product or service the company sells. For example, if you look at the ehow site (http://www.ehow.com) you will notice that for each topic for which information is provided, commercial sources are supplied for purchasing necessary equipment and supplies. If you were to visit a commercial site on how to conduct a market survey, links would be provided for purchasing word processing software and obtaining mailing lists.

EXERCISE 12-9

DIRECTIONS: Visit two of the following commercial Web sites. Identify the purpose and evaluate the usefulness of each site.

1. http://www.chipsahoy.com

    _____

    _____

    _____

    _____

2. http://www.nike.com

    _____

    _____

    _____

3. http://www.amazon.com

    _____

    _____

    _____

    _____

Combination Sites

Some sites combine news and information with commercial product or service marketing. The purpose of such sites may not be obvious. Some sites include advertising as a means of paying for the site. For example, the home page of the American Chemical Society (http://www.acs.org/) has links to numerous commercial sites from which to purchase software, chemicals, and other products. Other times, the advertiser has a vested interest in the content or purpose of the site. If advertising appears on a Web site, you need to determine to what degree, if any, the advertiser has influenced the content and viewpoint of the site. Ask yourself: "What connections, if any, exist between the content of the site and the product or service being sold?"

**EXERCISE
12-10**

DIRECTIONS: Visit two of the following combination Web sites. For each, identify its purpose and determine the degree of influence each of its advertisers exerts.

1. http://www.homefair.com/index.html

    _____

    _____

    _____

2. http://www.medicinenet.com

    _____

    _____

    _____

3. http://www.gallup.com/

    _____

    _____

    _____

Evaluating the Structure of a Web Site

A Web site should be easy to use. You should be able to navigate among pages and links easily, and you should be able to find the information you need quickly, usually within two or three clicks. A complex site should have a site map or directory that visually displays the organization and content of the site. The graphics and art should serve specific functions;

they should be more than simply decoration. Graphics, sound, color, and animation should not detract from the usability of the site.

DIRECTIONS: Evaluate how easy it is to navigate within one of the following Web sites. Consider, for example, whether it has a site map or search capabilities. Does it use graphics, sound, and color?

1. http://www.census.gov/prod/www/statistical-abstract-us.html

   _____

   _____

   _____

   _____

2. http://jobstar.org/

   _____

   _____

3. http://www.recipesource.com/special-diets/vegetarian/

   _____

   _____

   _____

DIRECTIONS: Suppose you are writing a research paper on the effects of television violence on children. You use the search engine Hotbot.com and enter the terms "television violence effect children." Among others, you find the following six Web sites. Visit each site and evaluate its overall usefulness and reliability.

1. http://www.avsands.com/Kids/childtelevision_twd_av.htm

   _____

   _____

   _____

   _____

   _____

   _____

2. http://www.ed.gov/databases/ERIC_Digests/ed414078.html

_____

_____

_____

_____

_____

_____

_____

3. http://gecko.gc.maricopa.edu/~ssburd/tv.htm

_____

_____

_____

_____

_____

_____

_____

4. http://www.aap.org/policy/re0109.html

_____

_____

_____

_____

_____

_____

5. http://www.jeannebeckman.com/page18.html

_____

_____

_____

_____

_____

_____

_____

_____

_____

_____

6. http://www.mediafamily.org/research/report_issbd_2002.shtml

_____

_____

_____

_____

_____

_____

_____

_____

_____

_____

_____

A Checklist for Evaluating Web Sources

Use the following checklist to evaluate Web sites:

1. What is the purpose of the site?
2. Is the site appropriate for your research purpose?
3. Who is the site's sponsor and who is the author?
4. Are the author's name, credentials, and contact information provided?
5. Does the site have an appropriate level of detail?
6. Is the information presented clearly?

7. Is the information complete?

8. Are sources documented?

9. Are opinions distinguished from facts?

10. Is the information available in print form?

11. When was the site last revised?

12. Are the links useful and up-to-date?

13. What role, if any, does advertising play?

Reading Electronic Text

Reading electronic text (also called hypertext) is very different from reading traditional printed text such as textbooks or magazines or newspaper articles. The term *electronic text,* as used in this chapter, refers to information presented on a Web site. It does not refer to articles and essays that can be downloaded from Searchbank or from an e-journal, for example. Because Web sites are unique, they require a different mind-set and different reading strategies. If electronic text is new or unfamiliar to you, you need to change the way you read and the way you think when approaching Web sites. If you attempt to read Web sites the same way you read traditional text, you may lose focus or perspective, miss important information, or become generally disoriented. Text used on Web sites is different in the following ways from traditional print text.

- *Reading Web sites involves paying attention to sound, graphics, and movement, as well as words.* Your senses, then, may pull you in several different directions simultaneously. Banner advertisements, flashing graphics, and colorful drawings or photos may distract you. Some Web sites are available in two formats—graphical and text-only. This is most common for academic sites. If you are distracted by the sound and graphics, check to see if a text-only version of the site is available.

- *Text on Web sites comes in brief, independent screenfuls, sometimes called nodes.* These screenfuls tend to be brief, condensed pieces of information. Unlike traditional text, they are not set within a context, and background information is often not supplied. They do not depend on other pages for meaning either. In traditional print text, paragraphs and pages are dependent—you often must have read and understood a previous one in order to comprehend the one that follows it. Electronic pages are often intended to stand alone.

- *Text on Web sites may not follow the traditional main idea–supporting details organization of traditional paragraphs.* Instead, the screen may appear as a group of topic sentences without detail.

- *Web sites are multidirectional and unique; traditional text progresses in a single direction.* When reading traditional text, a reader usually follows a single direction, working through the text from beginning to end as the author has written. Web site text is multidirectional; each electronic reader creates his or her own unique text by following or ignoring different paths. Two readers of the same Web site may read entirely different material, or the same material in a different order. For example, one user of the National Library of Medicine site in Figure 12.6 might begin by reading "New & Noteworthy"; another user might start by looking for information using MEDLINEplus; a third might begin by clicking on the NIH link.

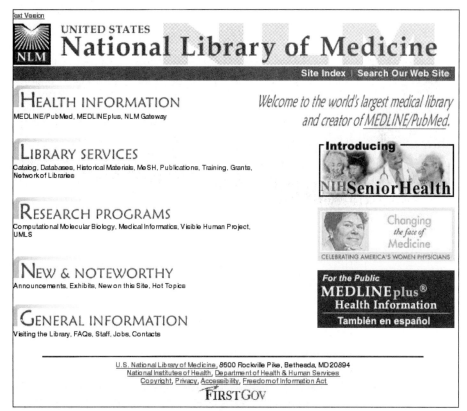

Source; The National Library of Medicine (http://www.nlm.nih.gov/)

FIGURE 12.6   A Multidirectional Web Site

- *Web site text requires readers to make decisions.* Because screens have menus and links, electronic readers must always make choices. They can focus on one aspect of the topic and ignore all others, for example, by following a path of links. Readers of print text, however, have far fewer choices to make.

- *Web sites allow readers the flexibility to choose the order in which to receive the information.* Partly due to learning style, people prefer to acquire information in different sequences. Some may prefer to begin with details and then come to understand underlying rules or principles. Others may prefer to begin in the opposite way. Electronic sources allow readers to approach the text in any manner compatible with their learning style. A pragmatic learner may prefer to move through a site systematically, either clicking or ignoring links as they appear on the screen from top to bottom, for example.

- *Web sites use new symbol systems.* Electronic texts introduce new and sometimes unfamiliar symbols. A flashing or blinking light may suggest a new feature on the site, or an underlined word or a word in a different color may suggest a link.

DIRECTIONS: Locate a Web site on a topic related to one of the end-of-chapter readings in this text. Write a list of characteristics that distinguish it from the print readings.   ▬

Changing Your Reading Strategies for Reading Electronic Text

Reading electronic text is relatively new to the current generation of college students. (This will no doubt change with the upcoming generations who, as children, will learn to read both print and electronic text.) Most current college students and teachers first learned to read using print text. We have read print text for many more years than electronic text; consequently, our brains have developed numerous strategies or "work orders" for reading traditional texts. Our work orders, however, are less fully developed for electronic text. Electronic texts have a wider variety of formats and more variables to cope with than traditional texts. A textbook page is usually made up of headings, paragraphs, and an occasional photo or graphic. Web sites have vibrant color, animation, sound, and music as well as words.

Reading is not only different, but it also tends to be slower on the computer screen than on print sources. One expert estimates reading a screen is

25 percent slower than reading on paper. Your eyes can see the layout of two full pages in a book. From the two pages, you can see headings, the division of ideas, and subtopics. By glancing at a print page, you get an initial assessment of what it contains. You can tell, for example, if a page is heavily statistical (your eye will see numbers, dates, symbols) or is anecdotal (your eye will see capitalized proper names, quotation marks, and numerous indented paragraphs for dialogue, for example). Because you have a sense of what the page contains and how it is organized, you can read somewhat faster. Because a screen holds fewer words, you get far less feedback before you begin to read.

Developing New Ways of Thinking and Reading

Reading electronic sources demands a different type of thinking from reading print sources. A print source is linear—it goes in a straight line from idea to idea. Electronic sources, due to the presence of links, tend to be multidirectional and let you follow numerous paths (see illustration below).

Electronic text also requires new reading strategies. The first steps to reading electronic text easily and effectively are to understand how it differs from print (see preceding section) and realize that you must change and adapt how you read. Some specific suggestions follow.

Focus on Your Purpose

Focus clearly on your purpose for visiting the site. What information do you need? Because you must create your own path through the site, unless you fix in your mind what you are looking for, you may wander aimlessly, wasting valuable time, or even become lost, following numerous links that lead you farther and farther away from the site at which you began.

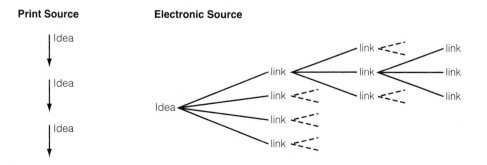

Get Used to the Site's Design and Layout

Each Web site has unique features and arranges information differently.

1. *When you reach a new site, spend a few minutes getting used to it and discovering how it is organized.* Scroll through it quickly to determine how it is organized and what information is available. Ask yourself the following questions.
   • What information is available?
   • How is it arranged on the screen?

2. *Expect the first screen to grab your attention and make a main point.* Web site authors know that many people (up to 90 percent) who read a Web page do not scroll down to see the next screenful.

3. *Get used to the colors, flashing images, and sounds before you attempt to obtain information from the site.* Your eye may have a tendency to focus on color or movement, rather than on print. Because Web sites are highly visual, they require visual as well as verbal thinking. The author intends for you to respond to photos, graphics, and animation.

4. *Consider both the focus and limitations of your learning style.* Are you a spatial learner? If so, you may have a tendency to focus too heavily on the graphic elements of the screen. If, on the other hand, you are a verbal learner, you may ignore important visual elements or signals. If you focus *only* on the words and ignore color and graphics on a particular screen, you will probably miss information or may not move through the site in the most efficient way. Review your learning style (p. 3), and consider both your strengths and limitations as they apply to electronic text.

EXERCISE 12-14

DIRECTIONS: In groups of two or three students, consider at least two aspects of learning style. For each, discuss the tendencies, limitations, and implications these particular learning styles may have for reading electronic text. For example, consider how a pragmatic learner would approach a Web site with numerous links and buttons. Then consider how a creative learner's approach might differ.

EXERCISE 12-15

DIRECTIONS: Locate two Web sites that you think are interesting and appealing. Then answer the following questions.

1. How does each use color?
2. How does each use graphics?
3. Is sound or motion used? If so, how?

Pay Attention to How Information Is Organized

Because you can navigate through a Web site in many different ways, it is important to have the right expectations and to make several decisions before you begin.

Some Web sites are much better organized than others. Some have clear headings and labels that make it easy to discover how to proceed; others do not and will require more thought before beginning. For example, if you are reading an article with 10–15 underlined words (links), there is no pre-scribed order to follow and these links are not categorized in any way. Figure 12.7 shows an excerpt from a Web site discussing the Embodied Conversational Agent research of an associate professor at MIT. Notice that it has numerous links built into paragraphs that lead the reader to supple-mental information.

Use the following suggestions to grasp a site's organization.

1. *Use the site map, if provided, to discover what information is available and how it is organized.* A sample site map, a Web site sponsored by the Better Business Bureau, is shown in Figure 12.8 (p. 487). Notice that the links are categorized according to the types of information (advertising, dispute resolution, news and alerts, etc.)

2. *Consider the order in which you want to take in information.* Choose an order in which to explore links; avoid randomly clicking on link but-tons. Doing so is somewhat like randomly choosing pages to read out of a reference book. Do you need definitions first? Do you want histor-ical background first? Your decision will be partly influenced by your learning style.

3. *Consider writing brief notes to yourself as you explore a complicated Web site.* Alternatively, you could print the home page and jot notes on it.

4. *Expect shorter, less detailed sentences and paragraphs.* Much online com-munication tends to be more brief and concise than in traditional sources. As a result, you may have to mentally fill in transitions and make inferences about relationships among ideas. For example, you may have to infer similarities and differences or recognize cause-and-effect connections.

EXERCISE 12-16

DIRECTIONS: Visit two Web sites on the same topic. Write a few sentences comparing and contrasting the sites' organization and design.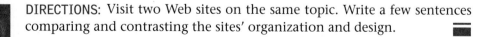

In the newest Embodied Conversational Agent project, <u>Rea</u>, we are working with <u>Matthew Stone</u> to integrate a natural language generation engine (SPUD) and are now generating hand gestures and sentences as one single process, in real time. This work addresses the challenges of specifying an underlying representation of discourse that is capable of driving generation of several modalities. We have also integrated into Rea the ability to engage in social chit-chat as a way of reducing interpersonal distance and increasing trust between the user and the system.

We have also integrated the foundations of the Embodied Conversational Agent work into the design of a 3D graphical online world (<u>BodyChat</u>), an interactive kiosk (<u>MACK</u>), and an animator's tool, <u>BEAT</u>, which allows animators to input typed text that they wish to be spoken by an animated human figure, and to obtain as output appropriate and syncronized nonverbal behaviors and synthesized speech in a form that can be sent to a number of different animation systems.

In studies of these systems at the Gesture and Narrative Language Group, we have shown that these autonomously-generated conversational signals are more important to user satisfaction and efficiency than some simple facial displays of emotion (Cassell & Thorisson 1998), and that the ability to directly manipulate the interface (Cassell & Vihjalmsson, 1998). A recent experiment demonstrated that Rea's social chit-chat significantly increases the trust that people have in the system, particularly for *extroverted users.*

For publications about the Embodied Conversational Agents, see <u>publications</u>. Press clippings about this work may be seen <u>here</u>. By the way, Rea has now made her debut on the world stage as a permanent exhibit at the Deutsche Telekom Future Labs.

Source: http://web.media.mit/edu/~justine/research.html

FIGURE 12.7   A Web Page with Links

Use Links to Find the Information You Need

Links are unique to electronic text. Here's how to use them.

1. *Plan on exploring links to find complete and detailed information.* Links—both remote links (those that take you to another site) and related links within a site—are intended to provide more detailed information on topics introduced on the home page.

2. *As you follow links, be sure to bookmark your original site and other useful sites you come across so you can find them again.* Bookmarking is a feature on your Internet browser that allows you to record Web site addresses and access them later by simply clicking on the site name. Different search engines use different terms for this function. Netscape uses the term *Bookmarks;* Microsoft Explorer calls it *Favorites.* In addition, Netscape has a *GO* feature that allows a user to retrace the steps of the current search.

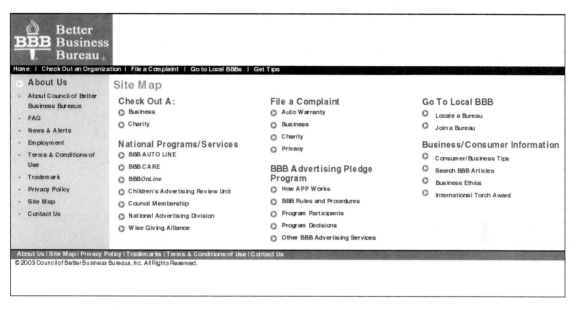

FIGURE 12.8   Website Map

3. *If you use a site or a link that provides many pages of continuous paragraphs, print the material and read it offline.*

4. *If you find you are lacking background on a topic, use links to help fill in the gaps, or search for a different, less technical Web site on the same topic.*

5. *If you get lost, most Internet browsers have a history feature.* It allows you to backtrack or retrace the links you followed in a search. In Netscape, for example, clicking on "Back" takes you back one link at a time; "History" keeps track of all searches over a given period of time and allows you to go directly to a chosen site, rather than backtracking step-by-step.

EXERCISE 12–17

DIRECTIONS: For one of the Web sites you visited earlier in the chapter or for a new site of your choice, follow at least three links and then answer the following questions.

1. What type of information did each contain?

2. Was each source reliable? How do you know?

3. Which was the easiest to read and follow? Why?

Critical Thinking Tip #12

Choosing Between Print and Internet Sources

Much information that is available on the Internet is also available from print sources. Many students incorrectly believe that the Internet is always the quickest and the best source to use to locate whatever information they need. Many librarians who are experts on research agree that in certain situations, a print source is preferable to an Internet source. Here are a few situations in which a print source may be more appropriate than an Internet source.

1. **Use a print source to browse for ideas to begin an open-ended assignment.** Suppose you have been asked to write a two-page paper describing a current trend in education. If you search on the Internet, you will retrieve volumes of information. It would be better to use an education encyclopedia or an educational research journal to browse for ideas. Begin, then, in the reference or current periodical section of your library.

2. **Use a print source to learn the basics about an unfamiliar topic.** Suppose you want to learn more about ear infections. If you type "ear infections" into a search engine, you will receive an overwhelming amount of information. Instead, start with a subject-specific dictionary or encyclopedia to get a basic definition and some fundamental facts and theories. Then, once you have a stronger grasp of your topic, you can search for further information on the Internet more confidently and efficiently.

3. **Use print sources for very in-depth research.** Books can be very important since they represent years of study by the author. You will find hundreds of pages devoted to all aspects of a topic collected in one place and interpreted by an authority on the subject.

4. **Use print sources to locate illustrations, art reproductions, and photographs.** Many of the best graphics are found in print sources.

5. **Use print sources to locate quick facts.** It is often easier to find a single piece of information, such as a population statistic, by picking up a reference book such as an almanac than by researching online.

6. **Use print sources to verify conflicting information that you find in online sources.** Since published materials go through a selective editorial process, they can present a more trustworthy source.

Summary

1. How can you locate electronic sources more effectively?

- Use an appropriate search or meta-search engine.
- Choose keywords carefully to limit your number of hits.

2. How can you locate reliable Web sites?

- Use Web sources only when appropriate.
- Pay attention to obvious clues.
- Recognize that nonoriginal Web material may lack reliability clues.
- Do not assume that every source is reliable and accurate.

3. What factors should you consider when evaluating a Web site?

Evaluate the content: consider the appropriateness of the site, its source, its level of technical detail, its presentation, its completeness, and any links. Also evaluate the accuracy, timeliness, purpose, and structure of the site.

4. What are the five basic types of Web sites?

The five types of Web sites are informational, news, advocacy, personal, and commercial. Combination sites also exist.

5. How does text on Web sites differ from print text?

- Web sites involve graphics, sound, color, and animation.
- Language on Web sites tends to be brief.
- Screens are often independent of one another.
- Web sites are multidirectional, requiring decision making and allowing flexibility.

6. How should you read electronic text?

- Identify the purpose of the site.
- Familiarize yourself with the site's design and layout.
- Pay attention to how the information is organized.
- Use links to find additional information.

READING SELECTION 23

HEALTH

THE SWEET LURE OF CHOCOLATE
From http://www.exploratorium.edu

Have you ever wondered why chocolate tastes so good? This article, taken from the Exploratorium Web site, explains the addictive qualities of chocolate.

— · — · —

The Exploratorium

"Feel Good" Food

1   One of the most pleasant effects of eating chocolate is the "good feeling" that many people experience after indulging. Chocolate contains more than 300 known chemicals. Scientists have been working on isolating specific chemicals and chemical combinations which may explain some of the pleasurable effects of consuming chocolate.

2   Caffeine is the most well known of these chemical ingredients, and while it's present in chocolate, it can only be found in small quantities. Theobromine, a weak stimulant, is also present, in slightly higher amounts. The combination of these two chemicals (and possibly others) may provide the "lift" that chocolate eaters experience.

3   Phenylethylamine is also found in chocolate. It's related to amphetamines, which are strong stimulants. All of these stimulants increase the activity of neurotransmitters (brain chemicals) in parts of the brain that control our ability to pay attention and stay alert.

REALAUDIO
Researcher Daniele Piomelli explains why his group decided to study chocolate.

4   While stimulants contribute to a temporary sense of well-being, there are other chemicals and other theories as to why chocolate makes us feel good. Perhaps the most controversial findings come from researchers at the Neurosciences Institute in San Diego, California. They believe that "chocolate contains pharmacologically active substances that have the same effect on the brain as mari-

REALAUDIO
Daniele Piomelli discusses the pharmacological differences between chocolate and THC.

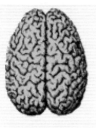

juana, and that these chemicals may be responsible for certain drug-induced psychoses associated with chocolate craving." We talked to Emmanuelle diTomaso, who worked on the original study in San Diego (she's now a researcher at Harvard), and to Daniele Piomelli, who heads the project and continues to do research at the Neurosciences Institute.

5   How does this work? Brain cells have a receptor for THC (tetrahydrocannabinol), which is the active ingredient in marijuana. A receptor is a structure on the surface of a cell that can lock onto certain molecules, making it possible to carry a signal through the cell wall. (diTomaso described it as a "lock-and-key" system.) "The active compound," she told me, "will lock itself to the protein on the membrane of the cell, and that triggers a reaction inside the cell." In the case of THC, that chemical reaction is what would make someone feel "high."

6   THC, however, is not found in chocolate. Instead, another chemical, a neurotransmitter called anandamide, has been isolated in chocolate. Interestingly, anandamide is also produced naturally in the brain. Both diTomaso and Piomelli went to great lengths to explain that this finding doesn't mean that eating chocolate will get you high, but rather that there are compounds in chocolate that may be associated with the good feeling that chocolate consumption provides.

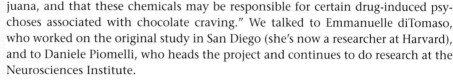

7   Still, the research results made for great newspaper headlines. In 1996, when Piomelli's first study was published and "picked up" by the press, he received a number of phone calls and visits from representatives of the major chocolate companies. "They were worried," he said, "that they would have to put a warning from the Surgeon General on their products."

8   Anandamide, like other neurotransmitters, is broken down quickly after it's produced. Piomelli and his team found other chemicals in chocolate which may inhibit the natural breakdown of anandamide. This means that natural anandamide (or introduced anandamide) may stick around longer, making us feel good longer, when we eat chocolate.

REALAUDIO
Daniele Piomelli explains how "anandamide" works in the brain and how chocolate consumption may affect us.

9   More research needs to be done to understand the effects of chocolate on the brain, and Piomelli's group is currently working on a new study that should be published next year. In the meantime, I'm going to be doing a few experiments of my own. Now that I know more about the captivating confection, I guess I'm going to have to start sampling all the different types and brands of chocolate at my local candy store—one by one.

Back ——————————— Exploring ——————————— Next

© 1998-1999, The Exploratorium

Examining Reading Selection 23

Checking Your Vocabulary

Directions: Using context, word parts, or a dictionary if necessary, circle the letter of the meaning for each word as it is used in the reading.

1. theobromine (paragraph 2)
   a. a chemical affecting taste
   b. a weak stimulant
   c. a form of caffeine
   d. a strong depressant

2. neurotransmitters (paragraph 3)
   a. sections of the brain
   b. strong amphetamines
   c. brain chemicals
   d. types of stimulants

3. receptor (paragraph 5)
   a. perforation in the cell wall
   b. membrane of the cell
   c. molecule within the cell
   d. structure on the surface of the cell

4. anandamide (paragraph 6)
   a. brain chemical
   b. brain receptor
   c. brain protein
   d. brain cell

5. inhibit (paragraph 8)
   a. induce
   b. hold back
   c. encourage
   d. repeat

Checking Your Comprehension

6. This selection is primarily concerned with the
   a. production of chocolate.
   b. effects of chocolate.
   c. origin of chocolate.
   d. chemicals in the brain.

7. Which of the following would be the most accurate subtitle for the selection?
   a. "You Are What You Eat"
   b. "Stay Away from Chocolate and Marijuana"
   c. "Chocolate Contains Dangerous Chemicals"
   d. "Why It Feels Good to Eat Chocolate"

8. The amount of caffeine contained in chocolate is
   a. surprisingly large.
   b. variable.
   c. unknown.
   d. small.

9. The lift that chocolate provides comes from a combination of
   a. sugar and theobromine.
   b. caffeine and sugar.
   c. theobromine and anandamide.
   d. caffeine and theobromine.

10. Piomelli and diTomaso's research suggests that
    a. chocolate craving is chemically based.
    b. chocolate contains unknown substances.
    c. chocolate consumption may lead to marijuana use.
    d. chocolate triggers autoimmune responses.

11. The selection focuses primarily on
    a. events.
    b. definitions.
    c. effects.
    d. differences.

12. After a person has consumed several chocolate candy bars, we could expect that person to be
    a. sleepy.
    b. alert.
    c. hyperactive.
    d. irritable.

13. After Piomelli's first study was released, chocolate companies were probably concerned that
    a. his findings would have a negative effect on the consumption of chocolate.
    b. the government would restrict chocolate consumption for children.
    c. newspapers would distort Piomelli's findings.
    d. chocolate lovers would turn to marijuana.

14. The author of this article is most likely a
    a. researcher who studies the effects of chocolate.
    b. a psychologist who studies brain behavior.
    c. a journalist who has researched the effects of chocolate.
    d. a nutritionist who studies chemicals in food.

15. The author's purpose is primarily to
    a. urge readers to restrict their consumption of chocolate.
    b. report information on the effects of chocolate.
    c. summarize Piomelli's research.
    d. call for further research on the similarities between chocolate and marijuana.

Questions for Discussion

1. Evaluate the source of this Internet reading by visiting the site's home page located at http://www.exploratorium.edu.

2. What other foods, if any, seem to produce a "feel good" or comforting feeling?

3. The effect of chocolate seems to be chemically based. Do you think pleasure from food can also be psychologically based? That is, do you associate certain foods with pleasurable experiences, for example, birthday cakes with birthday celebrations? If so, create a list of foods and the experiences associated with them.

Selection 23:			650 words
Finishing Time:	_____	_____	_____
	HR.	MIN.	SEC.
Starting Time:	_____	_____	_____
	HR.	MIN.	SEC.
Reading Time:		_____	_____
		MIN.	SEC.
WPM Score:			_____
Comprehension Score:			_____%

Reading Selection 24

Business

The Sandman Is Dead—Long Live the Sleep Deprived Walking Zombie

Dorritt T. Walsh

From http://www.hrplaza.com

What happens when you do not get enough sleep? Is your ability to work and function affected? This article describes how sleep deprivation affects on-the-job performance and suggests possible solutions to the problem.

— · — · —

FAST FACTS   SPOTLIGHT SITE   PEOPLE ARE TALKING   LINKS   MEETINGS
HC RECRUITER   NEWSFEED   CAREER CENTER   TOP MSAs   ASSOCIATIONS

HR Plaza
PEOPLE ARE TALKING ABOUT...
BERNARD HODES GROUP

1   Back in 1954, the Chordettes had a number one hit singing the praises of "Mr. Sandman," but today he's dead. It was a slow death; gradually, over a few decades, Americans killed him. Farewell sweet dreams and golden slumbers—we've entered into the age of waking up tired. Don't assume it's not you, either. Here's a quick quiz: do you get less than eight hours of sleep a night? Fall asleep almost as soon as your head hits the pillow? Need an alarm clock to wake up? And sometimes that doesn't even work? A "yes" to any of those questions means you're probably one of the chronically sleep deprived.

2   Before I continue, let me clarify why an article on lack of sleep is on a business Web site. After all, not getting enough sleep is a personal problem, right? Wrong. While it is up to the individual to control his or her sleeping habits, unfortunately, for various reasons that I'll discuss in this article, today more than 100 million Americans are sleep deprived. And this lack of sleep has a direct and substantial effect on American businesses. In 1990 the National Commission on Sleep Disorders put the direct costs of sleep loss at $15.9 billion, and the indirect costs, such as higher stress and diminished productivity, clocked in at $150 billion. One hundred and fifty billion dollars is way more than a "personal problem."

The Basics: Why Sleep Is Important

3   Before going into the facts about why Americans aren't getting enough sleep, or the problems sleep deprivation causes, the first logical step is a brief explanation of exactly why sleep is so important to humans.

4   Contrary to popular belief, sleep isn't just a wasteful state of inertness. In fact, your brain when it's "sleeping" is often more active than when you're awake—neural activity drops by about only 10 percent when we're asleep. Sleeping consists of five cycles, one through four and REM sleep, so depending on how long you sleep at night you may experience anywhere from three to five cycles. The most significant stages are Stage 4, the deepest phase of sleep, and REM or Rapid Eye Movement Sleep. Stage 4 plays a major part in maintenance of our general health, including our natural immune system. REM sleep is when we dream, but more importantly, it's the key player in maintaining the various aspects of memory. It also has a lot to do with how we're able to learn new things and general mental performance.

5   Sleep restores and rejuvenates us, and affects everything from our creativity and communication skills to reaction times and energy levels.

How Much Sleep Do We Need? How Much Are We Getting?

6   The simple answer to this question is: more than we're getting. According to Dr. James B. Maas, Cornell University professor and author of the book *Power Sleep*, the optimal amount of sleep we should be getting nightly is ten hours. Although ten hours of sleep per night may seem high by today's standards, it actually used to be the standard in this country. Before the invention of the electric light in 1879, most people slept ten hours per night. In fact, Einstein said that he could only function well if he had a full ten hours of sleep every night.

7   Since the late 1800s we've gradually cut back the time we sleep each night by a full 20 percent, to eight hours. However, even with a "standard" at two hours less than optimal, according to the National Sleep Foundation's "1998 Omnibus Sleep in America" poll, most Americans now average seven hours (actually only six hours and fifty-seven minutes) of sleep per night during the work week, or 30 percent less than the ideal. Nearly 32 percent only get six hours of sleep during the work week.

8   As far as why we're getting less sleep, there's no one single answer. Part of it's due to increased workloads (since 1977 Americans have added 158 hours annually to our working/commuting time), and then there's the stress that comes from the increased workloads. Or the fact that many people today, especially a number of "motivational speakers" downplay the need for sleep, so we don't want to be perceived as lazy. Or it could be what's on TV, or the book we just "have" to read, or the kids, or whatever.

Effects of Sleeplessness

9   Because many adults have never gotten sufficient sleep, or have gotten so used to getting by on less sleep than they need, many of the effects often go unnoticed. They don't realize that if they got more sleep, they could be in a better mood, be more productive, more creative, and think more clearly.

10   However, there are far reaching, quantifiable consequences that result from not getting enough sleep. Some of the most significant are:

- Thirty-one percent of all drivers say they've fallen asleep at the wheel at least once;

- Accidents resulting from falling asleep at the wheel cost Americans more than $30 billion each year;

- The National Transportation Safety Board cited fatigue as the number one factor detrimentally affecting airline pilots;

- Shiftworkers are particularly affected by lack of sleep. Fifty-six percent of them say they fall asleep on the job at least once a week;

- According to *The Wall Street Journal,* $70 billion is lost annually in productivity, health costs and accidents, a direct result of shiftworkers' not being able to adjust to late-night schedules;

- Forty percent of adults say that they're so sleepy during the day that it interferes with their daily activities, including work (remember, these are only the people who acknowledge or realize that their productivity is lessened).

  - Research done at Leicestershire, England's Sleep Research Center found that not getting enough sleep has noticeable negative effects on our ability to understand situations that change rapidly. They found sleep deprivation also makes us more likely to be distracted, makes us think less flexibly, and hampers our ability to solve problems innovatively.

  - Studies at Loughborough University have shown a direct connection between our abilities to remember and concentrate, and sleep deprivation;

  - The U.S. National Highway Traffic Safety Administration has proven that there's a direct connection between hand-eye coordination (a necessity when you're driving) and lack of sleep.

And according to the National Sleep Foundation survey, an incredible one-third of American adults tested reached levels of sleepiness that are known to be dangerous.

What To Do?

11   Again, there's no one simple answer to this question. Obviously people need more sleep. And one of the problems is that many people simply don't realize how important sleep is to us, or how serious the affects of sleep deprivation are. The National Sleep Foundation's "1998 Omnibus Sleep in America Poll" rated the sleep knowledge of 1,027 Americans, and it showed that Americans are generally ignorant when it comes to sleep and many sleep myths (e.g., that you need more sleep as you get older—you don't; that sleep needs remain the same throughout adulthood).

12   Along with self education, employers could help both by providing the facts about sleep to employees and stressing how important an adequate amount of sleep is to everyday performance. Don't equate sleepiness with laziness; they're two totally different issues. Sleepy workers are more likely to cause accidents, make mistakes, and are more susceptible to heart attacks. Lazy workers, for whatever reason, just don't do their jobs.

13   One thing employers can do is give the okay to napping at work. This doesn't have to be the old kindergarten version with blankets on the floor; just closing the door and sitting in your chair with your eyes closed and trying to sleep for fifteen minutes will help to restore your energy. That's all you need, 15–30 minutes. Besides relieving stress, naps increase your ability to make important decisions and pay sufficient attention to details.

14   If you employ shift workers, realize that shift work simply isn't natural and humans can simply not adapt to just any work cycle. Also, get more information on recommendations (the National Sleep Foundation Web site and/or the book *Power Sleep* are good places to start) on how to help arrange shift working schedules to help your employees stay alert and healthy.

15   It's time that Americans, both as individuals and businesses, start to acknowledge the vital importance sleep plays in our everyday lives and in our society. Although he wrote in the 1600s, Miguel de
Cervantes may have described the importance of sleep best in *Don Quixote de la Mancha*:

> "Now blessings light on him that first invented this same sleep! It
> covers a man all over, thoughts and all, like a cloak; 'tis meat for
> the hungry, drink for the thirsty, heat for the cold, and cold for the
> hot . . . and the balance that sets the kind and the shepherd, the
> fool and the wise man even."*

---

*from *Bartlett's Familiar Quotations*. Little, Brown and Company.

Bibliography:

Hammon, Christopher A. "If You Don't Snooze, You Lose: Getting a Good Night's Sleep Is Critical to
    Productivity and Creativity." The Quanta Dynamics Center for Sleep & Stress Web site.

Maas, Dr. James B. *Power Sleep*. Villard Books, 1998.

National Sleep Foundation. "1998 Omnibus Sleep in America Poll" and accompanying press release.
    The National Sleep Foundation Web site.

National Sleep Foundation. "Sleepiness in America" survey press release. The National Sleep Foundation
    Web site.

National Sleep Foundation. "Strategies for Shift Workers." The National Sleep Foundation Web site.

WRITING ABOUT READING SELECTION 24*

Checking Your Vocabulary

Directions: Complete each of the following items;
refer to a dictionary if necessary.

1. Discuss the connotative meanings of the
   word *sleep*.

2. Define each of the following words:
   a. substantial (paragraph 2)

   _____

   b. diminished (paragraph 2)

   _____

   c. cited (paragraph 10)

   _____

   d. hampers (paragraph 10)

   _____

   e. acknowledge (paragraph 15)

   _____

3. Define the word *clarify* (paragraph 2) and
   underline the word or phrase that provides a
   context clue for its meaning.

   _____

   _____

   _____

* Multiple-choice questions are contained in Part 6 (page 591).

4. Define the word *optimal* (paragraph 6) and underline the word or phrase that provides a context clue for its meaning.

_____

_____

5. Determine the meanings of the following words by using word parts:
   a. chronically (paragraph 1)

   _____

   b. productivity (paragraph 2)

   _____

   _____

   c. quantifiable (paragraph 10)

   _____

   d. detrimentally (paragraph 10)

   _____

   e. innovatively (paragraph 10)

   _____

Checking Your Comprehension

6. State the author's thesis.

_____

_____

_____

_____

7. Name three effects of sleep deprivation.

_____

_____

_____

_____

8. What types of evidence does the author provide to support the thesis?

_____

_____

9. What can employers do to help employees who suffer from sleep deprivation?

_____

_____

_____

Thinking Critically

10. What is the author's purpose?

_____

_____

_____

_____

11. Describe the tone and intended audience.

_____

_____

_____

_____

12. What is the purpose of the Cervantes quotation that concludes the selection?

_____

_____

_____

13. What types of evidence does the author supply to support the thesis?

_____

_____

_____

Questions for Discussion

1. Describe the effects of sleep deprivation that you have experienced.

2. The selection focuses on the effects of and solutions for sleep deprivation in the workplace. How do you think sleep deprivation affects academic performance? What solutions do you recommend for sleep deprived college students?

3. Visit the HR Plaza Web site and evaluate its reliability, content, accuracy, timeliness, and purpose.

Selection 24:		1269 words
Finishing Time:		
	HR. MIN.	SEC.
Starting Time:		
	HR. MIN.	SEC.
Reading Time:		
	MIN.	SEC.
WPM Score:		
Comprehension Score:		%

GO ELECTRONIC

For additional readings, exercises, and Internet activities, visit this book's Web site at:

http://www.ablongman.com/mcwhorter

For even more activities, visit the Longman English pages at:

http://www.ablongman.com/englishpages

If you need a user name and password, please see your instructor.

PART 4
Academic Scenario

The following scenario is designed to assess your ability to use and apply the skills taught in this unit.

THE SITUATION

Assume you are taking an English class and you have been given the assignment of writing a paper analyzing an argument. Your instructor has given you two articles on gun control and expects you to read both articles and then choose one to write about. You are expected to analyze the article and explain the strengths and weaknesses of the arguments. As you read the articles, you are evaluating each argument. In particular, you are looking to see how each author defends his or her position.

THE TASKS

The following two readings discuss gun control. Be sure to read them carefully and completely before beginning any of the tasks listed. You may reread the pieces as often as necessary. Feel free to highlight or write marginal notes.

READING A

Guns don't kill people, people kill people. Gun laws do not deter criminals. (A 1976 University of Wisconsin study of gun laws concluded that "gun control laws have no individual or collective effect in reducing the rate of violent crime.") A mandatory sentence for carrying an unlicensed gun, says Kates, would punish the "ordinary decent citizens in high-crime areas who carry guns illegally because police protection is inadequate and they don't have the special influence necessary to get a 'carry' permit." There are fifty million handguns out there in the United States already; unless you were to use a giant magnet, there is no way to retrieve them. The majority of people do not want guns banned. A ban on handguns would be like Prohibition—widely disregarded, unenforceable, and corrosive to the nation's sense of moral order. Federal registration is the beginning of federal tyranny; we might someday need to use those guns against the government.

Smith, "Fifty Million Handguns."

READING B

People kill people, but handguns make it easier. When other weapons (knives, for instance) are used, the consequences are not so often deadly. Strangling or stabbing someone takes a different degree of energy and intent than pulling a trigger. Registration will not interfere with hunting and other rifle sports but will simply exercise control over who can carry handguns. Ordinary people do not carry handguns. If a burglar has a gun in his hand, it is quite insane for you to shoot it out with him, as if you were in a quick draw contest in the Wild West. Half of all the guns used in crimes are stolen; 70% of the stolen guns are handguns. In other words, the supply of handguns used by criminals already comes to a great extent from the households these guns were supposed to protect.

Smith, "Fifty Million Handguns."

1. In preparing to write your paper, identify each position on gun control and examine the reasons offered for taking that position. Pay particular attention to how each position is supported. Begin by preparing a summary sheet for each reading. Do this by supplying the missing information in the summary sheet below.

READING A

Position on Gun Control: _____

_____

_____

Supporting Information:

a.

b.

c.

READING B

Position on Gun Control: _____

_____

_____

Supporting Information: _____

a.

b.

c.

2. Write a one-page paper in which you evaluate the position in either Reading A or Reading B. State the author's position, examine the evidence, and explain the strengths and weaknesses of the argument. Be sure to evaluate fact versus opinion and give examples. Discuss the author's use of generalizations, again giving examples. Evaluate the relevance and sufficiency of evidence and indicate what further information is necessary.

PART 5
Increasing Your Rate and Flexibility

CHAPTER 13

Skimming and Scanning

IN THIS CHAPTER YOU WILL LEARN:

1. To skim to get an overview of an article.
2. To scan to locate specific information quickly.

M ost students are accustomed to reading everything completely. In fact, in most academic reading, full, complete reading *is* necessary. However, there are times when complete comprehension is not needed. In those situations, skimming and scanning are alternative reading strategies that may save you time.

Skimming

Suppose that you are browsing through Web sites on the Internet, and just before it is time to leave for your next class, you follow a link and find a two- or three-page article that you are interested in reading. You do not want to bother bookmarking the site and returning to it later, and you do not have time to read it before class. What do you do?

One alternative is to forget about the article and go to class. A second alternative is to *skim* the article, reading some parts and skipping others, to find the most important ideas. You would read the parts of the article that are most likely to provide the main ideas and skip those that contain less important facts and details. *Skimming* means reading selectively to get a general idea of what an article is about.

This chapter discusses the purposes and types of skimming, presents a step-by-step procedure for skimming, and shows how to adapt the technique to various types of reading material.

503

Purposes for Skimming

It is not always necessary to read everything completely. In fact, in some circumstances thorough reading may be an inefficient use of your time. Let's take a moment to consider a few examples of material for which skimming would be the most effective technique to use:

1. **A section of a text chapter that reviews the metric system.** If you have already learned and used the metric system, you can afford to skip over much of the material.

2. **A Web site that you are using to complete a research paper.** If you have already collected most of your basic information, you might skim through the list of links, looking only for new sites that you had not previously visited.

3. **A newspaper report of a current political event.** If you are reading the article only to learn the basic information, skimming is appropriate. You can skip sections of the article that give details.

4. **A movie review.** If you are reading the review to decide whether you want to see the movie, you are probably looking for the writer's overall reaction to the movie: Was it exciting? Was it boring? Was it humorous? You can skip in-depth descriptions of characters, particular scenes, and particular actors' or actresses' performances.

Now try to think of some other situations or types of material that might be appropriate for you to skim. List them in the spaces provided.

1. _____

2. _____

3. _____

You can see that skimming is appropriate when complete information is *not* required. Use skimming when you need only the most important ideas or the "gist" of the article. Your *purpose* for reading is crucial in determining when it is appropriate to skim.

How to Skim

In skimming, your overall purpose should be to read only those parts of an article or selection that contain the most important information. Skip what is not important. The type of material you are reading will, in part, determine how you should adapt your reading techniques.

To acquaint you with the process of skimming, a basic, step-by-step procedure is presented and applied to a sample article. Then, adaptations of this general technique to specific types of reading materials are discussed.

As a general guide, read the following items:

The title. The title often announces the subject and provides clues about the author's approach or attitude toward the subject.

The subtitle or introductory byline. Some types of material include a statement underneath the title that further explains the title or is written to catch the reader's interest.

The introductory paragraph. The introductory paragraph often provides important background information and introduces the subject. It may also provide a brief overview of how the subject is treated.

The headings. A heading announces the topic that will be discussed in the paragraphs that follow. When read successively, the headings form an outline or list of topics covered.

The first sentence of each paragraph. Most paragraphs are built around a topic sentence, which states the main idea of the paragraph. The most common position for the main idea is in the first sentence of the paragraph. If you read a first sentence that clearly *is not* the topic sentence, you might jump to the end of the paragraph and read the last sentence. (See Chapter 4 for a more detailed discussion of main ideas and topic sentences.)

Key words. Quickly glance through the remainder of the paragraph. Try to pick out key words that answer who, what, when, where, or how much about the main idea of the paragraph. Try to notice names, numbers, dates, places, and capitalized or italicized words and phrases. Also notice any numbered sequences. This quick glance will add to your overall impression of the paragraph and will confirm that you have identified the main idea of the paragraph.

The title or legend of any maps, graphs, charts, or diagrams. The title or legend will state concisely what the typographical aid depicts and suggest what important event, idea, or relationship it is intended to emphasize.

The last paragraph. The last paragraph often provides a conclusion or summary for the article. It might state concisely the main points of the article or suggest new directions for considering the topic. If it is lengthy, read only the last few lines.

Now that you are familiar with the procedure for skimming, you are probably wondering how fast to skim, how much to skip, and what level of comprehension to expect. Your reading rate should generally be 800 wpm or above for skimming, or about three or four times as fast as you would normally read.

As a general rule of thumb, you should skip more than you read. Although the amount to skip varies according to the type of material, a safe estimate might be that you should skip about 70 to 80 percent of the material. Because you are skipping large portions of the material, your comprehension will be limited. An acceptable level of comprehension for skimming is often 50 percent, although it may vary according to your purpose.

To give you a better idea of what the technique of skimming is like, the following article has been *highlighted* to indicate the portions of the article that you might read when skimming. Of course, this is not the only correct way to skim this article. Depending on their purposes for reading, readers could identify different parts of the article as important. Also, readers might select different key words and phrases while glancing through each paragraph.

ELEMENTS OF RELIGION

Most religions contain four common elements: sacred objects or places, rituals, a system of beliefs, and an organization of believers.

THE SACRED

According to Durkheim, the **profane** consists of all the elements of everyday life that are considered part of the ordinary physical (natural) world. The **sacred**, on the other hand, is anything set apart from everyday life that is capable of evoking deep respect and awe. This sense of awe in the presence of the sacred is the underlying and most basic religious impulse whether one regards the ultimate source of awe as the supernatural or transcendent itself or whether one agrees with Durkheim's theory that it is the subconscious recognition of the power of society over the individual that is the best explanation for the awe experienced by the believer. In any event, when confronted by the sacred, people generally feel in touch with the eternal source of life and believe that they are experiencing a special power that cannot be understood by reason alone. Because the sacred is so supremely desirable, it arouses feelings of great attraction. Because of its power, the sacred also can provoke feelings of dread.

The experience of the sacred is frequently linked with material objects, such as an altar, a statue, or a cross. Almost anything can be considered sacred: certain locations, such as a grove of trees, a spring, or a cave; particular times, such as sunrise or Easter; or animals or plants, such as cows, rattlesnakes, or trees. Sometimes, the sacred is connected with unusual events, such as erupting volcanoes or over-flowing rivers. People with rare abilities and the dates of unusual occurrences may also be regarded as sacred.

RITUAL

A religious **ritual** is an established pattern of behavior closely associated with the experience of the sacred. It is typically performed to express or revive powerful experiences of the sacred or to ask the sacred power for some favor. By holding certain ceremonies along the banks of the Nile, for example, the ancient Egyptians felt that they could bring on, or symbolically participate in, the annual flooding that brought needed water and silt to the fields. Ritual is also a way of protecting the sacred from contamination by the profane. A sacred chalice or cup is not routinely used for drinking water. It may be used only in special ceremonies, when it is filled with special wine and passed from one person to another.

Ritual is a means of organizing the believers of a religion; it brings them together in a group. The repetition of a ritual, psychologists believe, helps to restore people's feeling of integration, identity, and security. By worshiping the crocodile in formal ceremonies, for example, certain African tribes felt that they were protecting themselves from attack by these frightening beasts.

Ritual itself can become sacred through its connection with the sacred. The objects used in ritual—the herbs or potions consumed, the clothes worn by the participants, the place where the ritual is conducted—can all come to be revered. For this reason, a house of worship, the location of religious ritual, is generally considered to be sacred.

A SYSTEM OF BELIEFS

The system of religious beliefs is the element of religion that has undergone more development than any other. In traditional religions, the main function of the belief system was to relate sacred objects to religious rituals and to define and protect the sacred. In the Old Testament, for example, God is portrayed as a superhuman figure who nevertheless can be understood in human terms. The abstract concept of God is transformed into a symbol that people can identify with and relate to.

Belief systems also explain the meaning and purpose of ritual. Muslims, for instance, learn that they must wash before evening prayers because physical cleanliness is a sign of moral cleanliness, and one must always appear morally clean before God. In light of this knowledge, the ritual of washing becomes a meaningful event.

Most modern systems of religious belief go far beyond merely supporting the other elements of religion. They often include moral propositions (such as the equality of all people) that are considered important truths. Although not necessarily considered "holy" by the faithful, these beliefs have a sacred quality. Because they are frequently translated into constitutions, political ideology, and education doctrine, these beliefs are important not only to the religions themselves but also in the nonreligious affairs of a society.

AN ORGANIZATION OF BELIEVERS

An organization of believers is needed to ensure the continuity and effectiveness of the religious experience. Conducting rituals, building places of worship, and choosing specialists such as priests, monks, and ministers to cultivate and safeguard the sacred all call for some kind of organization. For example, the Second Methodist Church of Great Falls, Montana, builds the church building, selects and pays the minister, buys the hymnals and the organ, and recruits the choir. The culmination of these activities is that the believers can go to church on Sunday morning and share their experience of the sacred.

Popenoe, *Sociology.*

EXERCISE 13-1

DIRECTIONS: After you have skimmed the article "Elements of Religion," answer the following questions. For each item, indicate whether the statement is true or false by marking "T" or "F" in the space provided.

_____ 1. The same basic elements are found in most religions.

_____ 2. Ritual serves the purpose of expressing or reviving experiences of the sacred.

_____ 3. The element of religion that has developed the most is ritual.

_____ 4. A system of beliefs often includes moral propositions.

_____ 5. Some type of organization is essential to the religious experience.

EXERCISE 13-2

DIRECTIONS: Skim the following article by Susan Gilbert, from *Science Digest,* on noise pollution. Your purpose for reading is to learn about the causes, effects, and control of noise pollution. Answer the questions following the article when you have finished skimming.

NOISE POLLUTION

THE VOLUME CONTINUES TO RISE, YET THE RESEARCH MONEY DWINDLES

Loud noise is the most pervasive kind of pollution. Scientific studies have shown that it not only harms the ears, it alters moods, reduces learning ability and may increase blood pressure. It doesn't take the earsplitting clatter of a jackhammer for a city dweller to experience, daily, enough noise to cause permanent hearing loss. The screeching of traffic, the din in a crowded restaurant, the roar of airplanes overhead—even music from blaring radios—are enough to exceed the maximum noise the federal government permits in workplaces for an eight-hour day.

The Environmental Protection Agency, once committed to reducing the insidious problem of noise, has been stifled in its attempts to do anything. Its $14-million program to curb noise pollution was eliminated four years ago. Some government agencies, however, have been successful. The Federal Aviation Administration has forced airplanes to cut noise levels by half within two miles of taking off and landing at major airports. New York City adopted the nation's first antinoise code in 1972 and imposes $25 fines for violations, although a majority of cab drivers still lean more on their horns than on their brakes. Chicago, San Francisco and a host of other cities have taken similar measures. In fact, it was such legislation that rallied the forces opposed to the Chicago Cubs playing night baseball at Wrigley Field.

HAZARDOUS HEADPHONES

Many of the most damaging noises, however, are within the power of all of us to control, simply by using a little common sense. Consider the use of stereo head-phones—devices that mask uncomfortable noise with entertaining sound. A study by otolaryngologist Phillip Lee, of the University Hospital in Iowa City, disclosed that teenagers who used stereo headphones for three hours suffered temporary hearing loss. These devices proved to be exceptionally damaging when played at 100 deci-bels or more, the intensity of a chain saw. "People should not turn them up above a normal, conversational level," says Lee.

While stunning and sudden explosions can cause deafness by rupturing an eardrum, hearing can be at least partially restored by surgery. Not so with sustained environmental noises; the damage they cause is often irreversible. As sounds enter the inner ear, they wave hair cells back and forth, causing them to release a chem-ical transmitter to the nerve fibers that carry auditory messages to the brain. This is how we hear. But too much noise can exhaust—even kill—some hair cells. The effect may be a slight temporary hearing loss or a ringing in the ears.

"A few missing hair cells won't damage hearing permanently," says neurobiolo-gist Barbara Bohne, of the Washington University School of Medicine in St. Louis. "But a few lost each weekend will gradually lead to noticeable hearing problems. Once this happens, it's too late to do anything." But some precautions can be taken. Earplugs and muffs, which reduce noise by as much as 25 decibels, can make the difference between hazardous and safe exposure. And, adds Bohne, "If you have to cut wood with a chain saw, do it for an hour one Saturday and another hour the following week, rather than for two hours at once." Separating periods of intense noise with at least a day of relative quiet can allow stunned hair cells time to recover.

Noise certainly makes us angry, but does it increase our blood pressure? Studies have been contradictory. Otolaryngologist Ernest Peterson, of the University of Miami, found that noise makes monkeys' blood pressure rise. But in a letter pub-lished in *The Lancet* last fall, a Swedish doctor reported no such effect on shipyard workers after studying them for eight years.

Noise's impact on the brain has been measured with more certainty. Children in schools located on loud streets score well below their socioeconomic counterparts in quiet schools, according to the California Department of Health Services.

Two British psychologists, reporting last year in the *Journal of the Acoustical Society of America,* found that suburban traffic of about 46 decibels (comparable to the hum of a refrigerator) impairs sleep. When the amount of noise entering subjects' bedrooms was reduced by five decibels (to the level of soft speech), their brains showed an increase in low-frequency, high-amplitude delta waves—a sign of deep sleep.

Audiologist John Mills, of the Medical College of South Carolina, believes that the brain is "the most significant area in need of further study." He reports that in several animal experiments, 65 decibels of sound sustained for 24 hours (the same level as that produced by an air conditioner) were found somehow to damage the brain stem. This, says Mills, is reason enough to investigate whether the same damage occurs in humans. "When does injury to the brain begin?" he asks. "Is it independent of injury to the ear? These are the things we must learn."

1. How does noise pollution affect humans?

    _____

    _____

2. Give several examples of noise pollution.

    _____

3. Has the Environmental Protection Agency been successful in controlling noise pollution?

    _____

4. What questions remain unanswered about the effects of noise pollution on humans?

    _____

Using Skimming Effectively

Now that you are familiar with the steps involved in skimming, you may realize that it is very similar to a technique you learned earlier in this book—prereading. Actually, prereading may be considered one form of skimming. Generally, there are three types of skimming:

1. **Preview skimming.** To become generally familiar with the organization and content of material *before* reading it. This is the type of skimming that is equivalent to prereading. (See Chapter 2.)

2. **Overview skimming.** To get an *overview* of the content and organization without reading the material completely. Often referred to as skim-reading, this form of skimming is used when you do not intend to

return to reading the material for another more thorough reading and when skimming alone meets your needs.

3. **Review skimming.** To go back over material you have already read to *review* the main points. Your purpose is to become reacquainted with the basic content and organization of the material. (Chapter 8 discusses review in detail.)

Limitations of Skimming

Because skimming involves skipping large portions of the material, you should not expect to retain the less important facts and details. As mentioned previously, you can expect a comprehension level of about 50 percent when skimming. Use skimming *only* when your purpose for reading allows you to read for general concepts rather than specific information.

Alternating Skimming and Reading

Many effective readers alternate between skimming and more careful reading. In a given article, for example, you may skim several sections until you come to a section that is of particular interest or that fulfills your purpose for reading. At that point, you may read completely rather than skim, and then continue skimming later sections. At other times, it may be necessary to read completely when you feel confused or when you encounter difficult or unfamiliar ideas.

Skimming Internet Sources

Skimming Internet sources is easily done by scrolling through the document by using the down arrow or the page down key. Soon you'll develop a rhythm that allows you to quickly glance at each screen before moving on to the next.

When you skim an electronic source, you do not have the benefit of the full text in front of you at one time. By paging through a print source, you can pick up initial clues about length, organization, placement of graphics, and relative importance of ideas. To obtain these initial clues, consider scrolling through the entire document very quickly, noticing only major headings, graphics, and length. Then skim the document using the suggestions given.

Skimming Various Types of Material

Effective skimming hinges on the reader's ability to recognize the organization and structure of the material and to locate the main ideas of the selection. The procedure for skimming outlined in the earlier section,

Table 13.1 Adapting Your Skimming Strategy

Type of Material	Focus On
Textbook chapters	1. Chapter objectives and introductions 2. Headings and typographical aids 3. Graphic and visual aids 4. Review and discussion questions
Reference sources	1. Date 2. Organization of the source 3. Topical index
Newspaper articles	1. Title 2. Opening paragraphs 3. First sentences of remaining paragraphs
Magazine articles	1. Title/subtitle/byline 2. Opening paragraphs 3. Photograph/captions 4. Headings/first sentences 5. Last several paragraphs
Nonfiction books	1. Front and back cover of book jacket 2. Author's credentials 3. Table of contents 4. Preface 5. First and last chapters

"How to Skim," is a general guide that must be adapted to the material. Table 13.1 lists suggestions for skimming textbooks, reference sources, newspaper and magazine articles, and nonfiction books.

EXERCISE 13-3

DIRECTIONS: Your communications instructor mentioned in class that different cultures have different concepts of time. You decide you want to learn more about these cultural differences. In your research, you located the following article on the topic. Skim this article and then answer the questions that follow it.

TIME AND CULTURAL DIFFERENCES

Time is another communication channel with great cultural differences. Two types of cultural time are especially important in nonverbal communication: formal and informal. In American culture, **formal time** is divided into seconds, minutes, hours, days, weeks, months, and years. Other cultures may use phases of the moon or the seasons to delineate time periods. In some colleges courses are divided into

50- or 75-minute periods that meet two or three times a week for 14-week periods called semesters. Eight semesters of fifteen or sixteen 50-minute periods per week equal a college education. Other colleges use quarters or trimesters. As these examples illustrate, formal time units are arbitrary. The culture establishes them for convenience.

Informal time refers to the use of general time terms—for example, "forever," "immediately," "soon," "right away," "as soon as possible." This area of time creates the most communication problems because the terms have different meanings for different people.

Another interesting distinction is that between **monochronic** and **polychronic time** orientations. Monochronic people or cultures (the United States, Germany, Scandinavia, and Switzerland are good examples) schedule one thing at a time. Time is compartmentalized; there is a time for everything, and everything has its own time. Polychronic people or cultures (Latin Americans, Mediterranean people, and Arabs are good examples), on the other hand, schedule a number of things at the same time. Eating, conducting business with several different people, and taking care of family matters may all be conducted at the same time. No culture is entirely monochronic or polychronic; rather these are general tendencies that are found across a large part of the culture. Some cultures combine both time orientations; Japanese and parts of American culture are examples where both orientations are found.

Attitudes toward time vary from one culture to another. In one study, for example, the accuracy of clocks was measured in six cultures—Japan, Indonesia, Italy, England, Taiwan, and the United States. Japan had the most accurate and Indonesia had the least accurate clocks. A measure of the speed at which people in these six cultures walked found that the Japanese walked the fastest, the Indonesians the slowest.

Another interesting aspect of cultural time is your "social clock." Your culture and your more specific society maintain a time schedule for the right time to do a variety of important things—for example, the right time to start dating, to finish college, to buy your own home, to have a child. And you no doubt learned about this clock as you were growing up. . . . On the basis of this social clock, you then evaluate your own social and professional development. If you're on time with the rest of your peers—for example, you all started dating at around the same age or you're all finishing college at around the same age—then you will feel well adjusted, competent, and a part of the group. If you're late, you will probably experience feelings of dissatisfaction. Recent research, however, shows that this social clock is becoming more flexible; people are becoming more willing to tolerate deviations from the established, socially acceptable timetable for accomplishing many of life's transitional events.

DeVito, *Messages.*

1. Explain the differences between informal and formal time.

_____

_____

2. Explain monochronic time and indicate at least one country in which it is used.

_____

_____

3. Explain polychronic time and indicate at least one country in which it is used.

_____

_____

4. Define the term "social clock."

_____

_____

EXERCISE 13-4

ELECTRONIC APPLICATION

DIRECTIONS: Locate an article on a topic of interest on the Internet. Skim it and then answer the questions that follow.

1. What is the main point of the article?

_____

2. How did the author support or explain this point?

_____

3. How is skimming an Internet source different from skimming a print source?

_____

EXERCISE 13-5

ACADEMIC APPLICATION

DIRECTIONS: Select a chapter from one of your textbooks, skim-read the first five pages of it, and answer the following questions.

1. What general subject is discussed in the chapter?

_____

2. How is the chapter organized?

_____

3. Write a brief list of ideas or topics that are discussed in the pages you skimmed.

_____

_____

EXERCISE 13-6

DIRECTIONS: Choose one of the reading selections at the end of the chapter. Skim-read the selection and answer the questions that follow the selection. Do not be concerned if you are unable to answer all the questions correctly; you should expect your rate to be higher but your comprehension lower than on most other readings you have completed up to this point.

Scanning

Have you ever searched through a crowd of people for a particular person or looked through a rack of clothing for an item of a particular size, color, or price? Have you ever used a telephone directory to find someone's phone number or address? Have you checked a bus schedule or located a particular book on a library shelf? If so, you used a technique called *scanning*. Scanning is searching for a specific piece of information; your only purpose is to locate that information. In fact, when you scan you are not at all interested in anything else on the page; you have no reason to notice or remember any other information.

Although scanning is a commonly used skill, many people do not know how to scan effectively. Have you ever become frustrated when trying to locate the ad for a particular movie on the entertainment page of a newspaper or when trying to find out at which theater a particular movie is playing? Have you ever had to read a particular article completely to find a particular section or fact? These frustrations probably occurred because you were not scanning in the most effective, systematic manner. That is precisely the focus of this section of the chapter—systematic scanning. Its purpose is to provide you with an organized procedure that will enable you to scan more effectively and efficiently.

How to Scan

Many people do not scan as efficiently as possible because they randomly search through material, hoping to stumble on the information they are seeking. Scanning in this way is time-consuming and frustrating, and it often forces the reader to "give up" and read the entire selection. The key to effective scanning is a systematic approach, described in the following steps:

1. Check the Organization

Before you begin to scan, check to see how the article or material is organized.

For *graphics*, check the title of the item you are scanning and other labels, keys, and legends. They state what the graphic is intended to describe and tell you how it is presented.

For *prose selections*, notice the overall structure of the article so that you will be able to predict where in the article you can expect to find your information.

For *electronic* sources, scroll through the entire document to discover its overall organization.

2. Form Specific Questions

Fix in your mind what you are looking for by forming specific questions about the topic. For example, when scanning for information about abortions in New York State, ask questions such as these:

- How many abortions were performed in a certain year?
- What rules and limitations restrict abortions?
- Where are most abortions performed?

3. Anticipate Word Clues

Anticipate clues that may help you locate the answer more rapidly. For example, if you were trying to locate the population of New York City in an article on the populations of cities, you might expect the answer to appear in digits such as 2,304,710, or in words such as "two million" or "three million." If you were looking for the name of a political figure in a newspaper article, you should expect to find two words, both capitalized. Try to fix the image of your clue words or phrases in your mind as accurately as possible before you begin to scan.

4. Identify Likely Answer Locations

Try to identify likely places where the information you are looking for might appear. You might be able to identify a column or section that contains the needed information. You might be able to eliminate certain sections, or you might be able to predict that the information will appear in a certain portion of the article.

5. Use a Systematic Pattern

Scanning should be organized and systematic. Do not randomly skip around, searching for clues. Instead, rhythmically sweep your eyes through the material. The pattern or approach you use will depend on the material. For material printed in narrow six- or seven-word columns, such as newspaper articles, you might move your eyes straight down the middle, catching the phrases on each half of the line. For wider lines of print, a zigzag or Z pattern might be more effective. Using this pattern, you would move your eyes back and forth, catching several lines in each movement. When you do come to the information you are looking for, clue words may seem to "pop out" at you.

6. Confirm Your Answer

Once you think you have located your information, check to be sure you are correct. Read the sentence that contains the answer to confirm that it is the information you need. Often, headings and key words seem to indicate that you have found your answer when in fact you have located related information, opposite information, or information for another year, country, or similar situation.

Now let us try out this procedure. Assume that you are writing a paper on health care in the United States and you need to find out how extensive at-home health care has become. You have located a section of a textbook titled "The Organization of Health Care" that contains the following subsection. Use each of the steps previously listed to find the answer to your question.

OTHER SOURCES OF PRIMARY CARE

A variety of organizations other than hospitals provide health care. These include nursing homes, hospices, ambulatory-care centers, emergency-care centers, rehabilitation institutes, diagnostic centers, surgical centers, health maintenance organizations and neighborhood health centers.

The *health maintenance organization (HMO),* a prepaid group practice in which members pay a monthly sum for comprehensive health-care services, is one of the most rapidly growing types of providers. Participating physicians are paid annual salaries or fixed amounts per patients. This arrangement gives doctors an incentive to keep patients healthy through the practice of preventive medicine. HMO physicians tend to prescribe fewer unnecessary treatments, which would reduce the organization's profits. In 1997, enrollment in HMOs had reached 67 million, double the enrollment in 1991 (Health, 1998).

Neighborhood health centers are federally funded clinics designed to provide medical care to people living in poor areas. Although they have made medical care more accessible to the poor, their staffs tend to be less well trained than the staffs of other organizations.

In addition to relying on health-care organizations, about 4 million Americans now receive some form of personal health care at home. New technologies have made home health care feasible for patients requiring chemotherapy, kidney dialysis, intravenous antibiotics, or special painkillers or nutrients. Such patients are typically under the care of for-profit home health businesses or nonprofit agencies that charge between 30 and 70 percent less than the average cost of a hospital stay.

Popenoe, *Sociology.*

First, when you assess the organization of this material, you see that it is divided into four paragraphs, with only one heading provided. Next, you find that fixing in your mind what you are looking for is an easy task, if you first form a question such as "How many Americans receive at-home health care?" Then, when you anticipate the form of the answer, you expect that phrases such as *at-home, personal care,* or *home care* will be contained in it. While scanning for the topic of each paragraph, you see that paragraph one is about organizations, paragraph two is about HMOs, and paragraph three focuses on health centers. You then choose the fourth paragraph as the likely location for the answer because it contains the phrase *personal home care.* Finally, suspecting that the answer to your question is "4 million Americans," you read the surrounding context to verify that you have found the correct information. Although scanning in this way may seem complicated when explained step-by-step, it is actually a very rapid procedure for locating information.

Scanning Columnar Materials

Columnar material includes all sorts of information presented in lists, tables, columns, schedules, or charts. Examples of columnar material include dictionaries, plane schedules, TV listings, the *Readers' Guide to Periodical Literature,* and lists of course offerings.

1. **Check to determine the overall organization and then see if it is divided in any particular way.** Notice whether column titles, headings, or any other clues are provided about the material's organization. For instance, you would note that a TV program schedule is organized by day of the week, but that it is also arranged by time. In scanning a zip code directory, you would see that it is arranged alphabetically but that there is a separate alphabetical list for each state.

2. **Scan for a specific word, phrase, name, date, or place name.** For example, in checking the meaning of a term in *Taber's Cyclopedic Medical Dictionary,* you are looking for a specific word. Similarly, in looking up a metric equivalent in the glossary of your physics textbook, your purpose is quite specific.

3. **Use the arrow scanning pattern; it is a straight-down-the-column pattern.**

4. **Focus on the first letter of each line until you reach the letter that begins the word you are looking for.** Then, focus on the first two let-

ters until you reach the two-letter combination you are searching for. Successively widen your focus until you are looking for whole words.

EXERCISE 13-7

DIRECTIONS: Scan the table shown in Figure 13.1 to answer each of the following questions.

1. How is this table organized?

    _____

    _____

2. What countries have the highest and lowest literacy rates for women?

    _____

3. In what countries are the literacy rates for men and women the same?

    _____

4. What is the literacy rate for men in South Africa?

    _____

Adult Literacy and Gender: Literacy Rates in Least Industrialized and Industrializing Nations

Country	Women	Men	Country	Women	Men
Nepal	14%	41%	Ghana	54%	76%
Sierra Leone	18%	45%	Papua New Guinea	63%	81%
Mali	23%	39%	Kenya	70%	86%
Mozambique	23%	58%	Turkey	72%	92%
Ethiopia	25%	46%	Indonesia	78%	90%
Bangladesh	26%	49%	Zimbabwe	80%	90%
Morocco	31%	57%	Dominican Republic	82%	82%
Sudan	35%	58%	South Africa	82%	82%
India	36%	66%	Venezuela	90%	92%
Egypt	39%	64%	Lebanon	90%	95%
Laos	44%	69%	Colombia	91%	91%
Iraq	45%	71%	Thailand	92%	96%
Nigeria	47%	67%	Costa Rica	95%	95%
Guatemala	49%	62%	Cuba	95%	96%
Gabon	53%	74%	Uruguay	98%	97%

Source: UNESCO Institute for Statistics, Assessment Year: July 2002.

FIGURE 13.1   Columnar Material

DIRECTIONS: Using the portion of a book's index shown in Figure 13.2 below, scan to locate the answer to each of the following questions.

1. On what page(s) would you find information on the housing of slaves?

    _____

2. What page contains information on the 1932 election of Herbert Hoover?

    _____

3. On what page can you find information on Hispanic Americans in the Great Depression?

    _____

FIGURE 13.2   Reference Book Index

Source: Goldfield et al., *The American Journey: A History of the United States.*

Scanning Prose Materials

Prose materials are more difficult to scan than columnar material. Their organization is less apparent, and the information is not as concisely or obviously stated. And, unless the headings are numerous and very concise, you may have to scan large amounts of material with fewer locational clues. For prose materials, you must rely heavily on identifying clue words and predicting the form of your answer. It is useful to think of scanning prose materials as a floating process in which your eyes drift quickly through a passage searching for clue words and phrases. Your eyes should move across sentences and entire paragraphs, noticing only clue words that indicate that you may be close to locating the answer.

EXERCISE 13-9

DIRECTIONS: Scan each of the following prose selections to locate the answer to the question indicated. Write your answer in the space provided.

1. What two factors determine how a shopper will react to a store environment?

   _____

It's no secret that people's moods and behaviors are strongly influenced by their physical surroundings. Despite all their efforts to presell consumers through advertising, marketers know that the store environment influences many purchases. For example, consumers decide on about two out of every three of their supermarket product purchases in the aisles. Therefore, the messages they receive at the time and their feelings about being in the store are important influences on their decisions.

Two dimensions, *arousal* and *pleasure,* determine if a shopper will react positively or negatively to a store environment. In other words, the person's surroundings can be either dull or exciting (arousing), and either pleasant or not. Just because the environment is arousing doesn't necessarily mean it will be pleasant—we've all been in crowded, hot stores that are anything but! Maintaining an upbeat feeling in a pleasant context is one factor behind the success of theme parks such as Disney World, which try to provide consistent doses of carefully calculated stimulation to patrons.

The importance of these surroundings explains why many retailers are combining two favorite consumer activities, shopping and eating, into elaborate *themed environments.* According to a recent Roper Starch survey, eating out is the top form of out-of-home entertainment, and innovative firms are scrambling to offer customers a chance to eat, buy, and be entertained all at once. Planet Hollywood, for example, is crammed full of costumes and props, and the chain now grosses over $200 million a year around the world.

Solomon and Stuart, *Marketing.*

2. Where does gas exchange occur in the lungs?

_____

Among mammals, external respiration takes place by means of special pouches called lungs. External respiration is accomplished as oxygen-laden air is brought into the lungs by **ventilation,** or **breathing.** Air passes from the large **trachea** into the branched **bronchi** (singular, *bronchus*) and on into increasingly smaller **bronchioles** that terminate in the many saclike **alveoli,** which is where gas exchange occurs. The alveoli are so numerous that they give a spongelike quality to the lung. The total area of the alveoli in human lungs, by the way, is about equal to the area of a tennis court—a large exchange surface, indeed.

The surface of the lungs is moist, as is the respiratory surface of any animal. The moistness is necessary because oxygen must dissolve before it can cross these delicate membranes of the alveoli and enter the bloodstream. The blood transports the oxygen to the body's tissue, where it diffuses into the cells. In the cells, the oxygen has the humble but critical role of picking up spent electrons from the electron-transport chain, thereby producing metabolic water.

Wallace, *Biology: The World of Life.*

3. What causes both Dutch elm disease and chestnut blight?

_____

For the last 30 years, the composition of European and American deciduous forests has been dramatically changed by disease. Two diseases—Dutch elm disease and chestnut blight—have virtually eliminated large elms and American chestnut trees from the North American landscape. The diseases are caused by fungi that infect and kill mature trees or young trees that are just old enough to reproduce. Very few trees survive infestation, so disease-tolerant strains among the native species of elms or chestnuts have yet to be identified. Consequently, there has been a precipitous decline in the populations of these trees in the forests of the eastern United States. These species were once major components of the forest canopy. As they have died, their replacement by other species has led to continued shifts in forest composition.

Bush, *Ecology of a Changing Planet.*

4. Which of these four distances is appropriate for conducting business?

_____

Edward Hall distinguishes four distances that define the type of relationship between people and the type of communication in which they're likely to engage. In **intimate distance,** ranging from actual touching to 18 inches, the presence of the other individual is unmistakable. Each person experiences the sound, smell, and feel of the other's breath. You use intimate distance for lovemaking, comforting, and protecting. This distance is so short that most people do not consider it proper in public.

Personal distance refers to the protective "bubble" that defines your personal distance, ranging from 18 inches to 4 feet. This imaginary bubble keeps you protected and untouched by others. You can still hold or grasp another person at this distance but only by extending your arms, allowing you to take certain individuals such as loved ones into your protective bubble. At the outer limit of personal distance, you can touch another person only if both of you extend your arms. At this distance you conduct much of your interpersonal interactions, for example, talking with friends and family.

In **Social distance**, ranging from 4 to 12 feet, you lose the visual detail you have at personal distance. You conduct impersonal business and interact at a social gathering at this social distance. The more distance you maintain in your interactions, the more formal they appear. In offices of high officials, the desks are positioned so the official is assured of at least this distance from clients.

Public distance, from 12 to more than 25 feet, protects you. At this distance you could take defensive action if threatened. On a public bus or train, for example, you might keep at least this distance from a drunkard. Although at this distance you lose the fine details of the face and eyes, you're still close enough to see what is happening.

DeVito, *Messages.*

Critical Thinking Tip #13

Anticipating Your Reading Assignments

Skimming can help you to make predictions about the content and organization of your reading assignments. By preview skimming, you can anticipate what an assignment will contain and how it will be presented. Knowing this will enable you to make decisions about how to approach the material and which reasoning and thinking strategies will be needed to learn the material.

To improve your ability to anticipate your reading tasks, keep the following questions in mind when you preview skim:

1. What is the difficulty level of the material?
2. How is it organized?
3. What is the overall subject and how is it approached?
4. What type of material is it (practical, theoretical, historical background, case study)?
5. Are there logical breaking points where you might divide the assignment into portions, perhaps leaving a portion for later study?
6. At what points might you stop and review?
7. What connections are there between this assignment and class lectures?

5. What is the distinction between open and closed societies?

_____

_____

Stratification systems differ in the ease with which people within them can move from one social status to another. A completely *open* society has never existed. But if it did, people could achieve whatever status their natural talents, abilities, and desires allowed them to attain. An open society would not be a society of equals; unequal social positions would still exist, but these positions would be filled solely on the basis of merit. Therefore, such a system could be described as a perfect *meritocracy*.

In a completely *closed* society everyone would be assigned a status at birth or at a certain age. That status could never be changed. No society has ever been completely closed, although some have been fairly close to this extreme.

The chief distinction between relatively open and relatively closed societies concerns the mix of statuses each contains. Open societies are characterized by greater reliance on *achieved* status than are closed societies; closed societies rely more on *ascribed* status. Many studies have shown that industrial, technologically advanced societies such as the United States tend to be relatively open. In contrast, preindustrial societies with economies based on agriculture tend to be relatively closed.

Popenoe, *Sociology.*

EXERCISE 13-10

DIRECTIONS: Make a list of your academic reading tasks for the past week. Indicate which of these tasks involved overview or review skimming and which involved scanning. ▬

Summary

1. What is skimming?

Skimming is a selective reading technique used to obtain important ideas. It is used when complete detailed information is *not* required.

2. What steps should you follow to skim effectively?

Skimming involves reading only those parts of articles or selections containing key ideas, such as

- the title and subtitle
- headings
- the introductory paragraph
- the first sentence of other paragraphs
- key words
- graphic elements
- the last paragraph

3. What are the three types of skimming?

There are three general types of skimming depending upon your purpose:

- Preview: for becoming familiar with the material before reading it thoroughly
- Overview: for getting just the main ideas when you won't read the material completely
- Review: for refreshing your memory about material you have already read

4. What is scanning?

Scanning is a process of rapidly locating information in printed material. It differs from skimming in that scanning involves looking only for a specific piece of information—a word, fact, or statistic—and ignoring the rest of the material.

5. What steps are involved in the process of scanning?

Effective scanning involves the following steps:

- checking the organization
- forming specific questions
- anticipating clue words
- identifying likely answer locations
- using a systematic pattern
- confirming your answer

READING SELECTION 25

BUSINESS

BARRIERS TO EFFECTIVE LISTENING
Norman B. Sigband and Arthur Bell
From *Communication for Business and Management*

Listening is an important part of the communication process. Read this excerpt from a business communication textbook and answer the following questions.

1. What factors interfere with effective listening?
2. What can you do to improve your listening skills?

— · —

1   Perhaps the most important barrier to effective listening results from the fact that most of us talk at about 125 to 150 words per minute, while we can listen to and comprehend some 600 to 800 words per minute. Quite obviously if the sender talks at 125 words and the receiver listens at 600, the latter is left with a good deal of time to think about matters other than the message; and he or she does: illness, bills, cars, the baseball game score, what's for dinner tonight, and so on. This is the **internal competition** for attention.

2   However, there is also the **external competition** to effective listening. These are the distractions caused by ringing telephones, noisy production lines, heated arguments, intriguing smells, captivating sights, and dozens of other factors we all encounter in a busy, complex society.

3   **Time,** or more accurately, the lack of it, also contributes to inefficient listening. Effective listening requires that we give others a block of time so they may express their ideas as well as their feelings. Some individuals require more time than others to do this. If we are—or appear to be—impatient, they will either not express themselves fully or will require more time than usual. And yet the listener possesses a limited amount of time also. In addition, there are some individuals who will monopolize *all* of your listening time. If you begin to listen to such a person at noon, you could still be listening at 3:00 P.M.

4   You must turn off a person like this as tactfully as possible. However, there are others with whom you work or live that you should give time to so that you may listen with undivided attention. Remember, if *you* don't listen to *them*, they will always find someone who *will*.

5   If employees feel their supervisor won't listen to them, they will find other employees or the union representative who will; if young people feel their parents won't or don't listen to them, they may find friends, gang members, or people whose influence might be detrimental. And if customers feel a supplier really isn't listening, they will find a competitor to the supplier who will. There is no such thing as a vacuum in communication.

6   **Conditioning** is still another factor that contributes to poor listening. Many of us have conditioned ourselves not to listen to messages that do not agree with our philosophy or that irritate, upset, or anger us. TV and radio play a role in this conditioning. If the program we see or hear doesn't entertain or intrigue us, we have been conditioned to reach over and simply change channels or stations. And we carry this habit of changing the channel to tune a message out into our daily listening activities.

7   **Evaluating** what we hear may constitute still another barrier. So often we listen and almost immediately evaluate and reject the idea before it is completely voiced. Or we listen and then detour

mentally while the individual is still talking. Of course, it is not possible not to evaluate, but one should continue to listen after evaluating. The problem is that most of us tune out as soon as we hear an idea or point of view that does not agree with ours.

8   **Emotions,** if colored or at a high level, may also get in the way of effective listening. Surely if you hear ideas that are counter to yours, or if you are involved in a confrontation or are emotionally upset because of fear, anger, or happiness, effective listening becomes very difficult.

9   **Lack of training** on how to listen is still another barrier. Most of us have received much instruction on how to write more concisely and clearly, read more efficiently and rapidly, and speak more forcefully and effectively. But few of us have ever received any instruction on how to listen. Perhaps this flaw in our educational system stems from the belief on the part of many educators that if one hears, one is listening. The fact remains that more effective listening can be taught. Fortunately, increasing numbers of schools today are teaching pupils how to listen more effectively, and there are even programs available in many universities.

10   Our **failure to concentrate** is another barrier to effective listening. That may be due to the fact that many of us have not been taught how to listen, or to the fact that we don't work at listening. . . .

Listening for Facts

11   If you are a student, you have probably experienced missing an important class. If you are a manager, you have occasionally missed a meeting. The problem is playing "catch up." As a result, you approach Mitchell and ask about Monday's class and what you've missed.

12   If Mitchell can tell you little more than it was "an interesting class and I really thought the financial analysis of the case was OK," he probably is not very efficient in his attentive listening

for facts. If you continue to press him, he may go on to say, "It was a great case," or, "It emphasized financial aspects of a major corporation." Then you surely know that he doesn't listen very well (or attentively) for facts.

13   On the other hand, you may find Jan's response to the same question on the same class quite different. "Yes," says Jan, "it was a very interesting class. First, Professor Maxwell set the stage by indicating we would look at three aspects of high interest rates and the problem of getting residential mortgages: the trend in home sales, the cost of mortgage money, and the tax benefits secured by the residential purchaser."

14   Jan may then go on to list the specific subpoints under the three items noted and even give you Professor Maxwell's summary statement.

15   What is the difference between Mitchell's ability to listen for facts and Jan's ability? To some extent, Mitchell has not used his class time very well and will surely spend much more time reviewing for his final exam than Jan will. And the real pity is that his store of knowledge doesn't grow as quickly or as efficiently as Jan's.

16   Jan listens and retains facts; Mitchell does not. How do you listen? Like Jan or like Mitchell?

How to Improve Your Ability to Listen for Facts

17   **Catalog Key Words**   In almost every discussion or presentation, several key ideas are presented. Each of these ideas can be retained if a key word is remembered that can be associated with each of the key ideas. In the discussion above, Jan probably remembered "home sales," "cost of money," and "tax benefits." Because she remembered these key words, she was able to discuss intelligently the concepts presented during the class.

18   **Resist Distractions**   A dozen distractions take place while you listen. Whether you are in a group listening to a speaker or having a conversation with one other person, distractions are

present. There are the external ones such as heat and humidity, noise and smell, bickering, illumination, and competing activities. Internally there is our own tendency to daydream, evaluate, and think of other important matters as well as our emotions, values, and the speakers' personality.

19   But we must resist these distractions and focus on the key concepts and words. No one maintains that such concentration is easy. It requires effort, but the task is made easier if we assume a posture of attentiveness and mentally force ourselves to pay attention to the task at hand. Many people find that taking notes during the presentation assists them in resisting distractions. If our friend Jan took notes during the class in question, she possibly wrote and underlined the key words "home sales," "cost of money," and "tax benefits."

20   **Review Key Ideas**   In the course of Professor Maxwell's lecture, both Mitchell and Jan had a good deal of free time. Professor Maxwell spoke at an average pace of about 140 words per minute. Both Mitchell and Jan comprehend approximately 650–700 words per minute. Mitchell used the "extra time" to think about last night's dinner with Betty and the fact that

Chablis might have been a better wine to order than Blanc de Blanc. Jan, on the other hand, used her "extra time" to review the evidence Professor Maxwell cited in relation to home sales, cost of money, and tax benefits. Learning is a constant search for key ideas. As Keith Davis stated in his book, *Human Behavior at Work*, "Hearing is with the ears, but listening is with the mind."

21   **Be Open and Flexible**   The old saw, "Don't bother me with the facts, my mind is made up," may be humorous, but it is also true for many people. Their biases are so strong that they may prefer not to listen. Or perhaps their instant assessment of the speaker's clothes, ethnic background, hair style, accent, or beard is enough for them to fix their opinions.

22   Obviously this attitude is an injustice not only to the speaker but most certainly to the listener as well. It is true that Mitchell had a very unhappy experience in a real estate transaction last year. But is that any reason for him not to listen to Professor Maxwell today?

23   Listen to whatever is being directed to you. Be flexible and receptive. No one suggests that you must accept the ideas and concepts presented by others. However, you should listen to them.

Examining Reading Selection 25

Checking Your Vocabulary

Directions: Using context, word parts, or a dictionary if necessary, circle the letter of the meaning for each word as it is used in the reading.

1. monopolize (paragraph 3)
   a. take control of
   b. eliminate
   c. reverse
   d. dissipate

2. constitute (paragraph 7)
   a. make up
   b. alter
   c. address
   d. eliminate

3. confrontation (paragraph 8)
   a. activity
   b. deception
   c. position
   d. conflict

4. posture (paragraph 19)
   a. angle
   b. degree
   c. reason
   d. attitude

5. receptive (paragraph 23)
   a. anxious to discover
   b. eager to confront
   c. willing to receive
   d. open to change

Checking Your Comprehension

Directions: Circle the letter of the best answer.

6. The reading focuses on
   a. reasons for ineffective listening and how to overcome them.
   b. causes of ineffective listening.
   c. external and internal listening barriers.
   d. techniques for becoming a more effective listener.

7. Internal competition refers to
   a. a vacuum in communication.
   b. environmental distractions.
   c. mental distractions.
   d. dealing with competing messages.

8. If a listener appears impatient, the speaker may
   a. require more time than usual to express himself or herself.
   b. respond to external distractions.
   c. become emotional.
   d. find someone else to talk to.

9. The author cautions against
   a. spending too much time listening to emotional messages.
   b. revealing emotions during speech.
   c. conditioning ourselves not to evaluate.
   d. not listening to those with whom we must work or live.

10. According to the article, if you have difficulty resisting distractions during a class lecture, you should
    a. ask questions to keep your mind focused.
    b. take notes on the lecture.
    c. make a list of distractions.
    d. listen with a purpose.

11. The authors' primary approach to their topic is to
    a. argue that students do not know how to listen.
    b. offer advice and explanations.
    c. compare good and poor listeners.
    d. define the differences between listening and hearing.

Thinking Critically

12. The author includes Jan and Mitchell as examples primarily to
    a. make the article more interesting.
    b. discuss internal competition.
    c. describe listening flexibility.
    d. emphasize the differences between effective and ineffective listeners.

13. A student with strong feelings on the issue of abortion had recently been involved in local antiabortion demonstrations. Her sociology instructor conducted a class discussion on the abortion issue. The student did not hear her instructor ask each student to write a paragraph summarizing the pro-choice position.

    The reason she did not hear the assignment may be best explained by
    a. conditioning.
    b. evaluation.
    c. internal competition.
    d. time.

14. The statement "Hearing is with the ears, but listening is with the mind" was quoted in the article to
    a. suggest a strategy for overcoming distractions.
    b. distinguish types of listening.
    c. emphasize that listening is thinking.
    d. define the terms.

15. The selection uses which of the following methods of organization?
    a. comparison-contrast
    b. cause-effect
    c. enumeration
    d. time order

Questions for Discussion

1. Describe a situation or example in which conditioning functions as a barrier.

2. Which of the barriers to effective listening do you experience when listening to classroom lectures? How have you overcome them?

3. Are there other types of listening besides listening for facts? If so, describe them.

4. What features of this excerpt made it easy or difficult to read?

Selection 25:		1544 words	
Finishing Time:	_____	_____	_____
	HR.	MIN.	SEC.
Starting Time:	_____	_____	_____
	HR.	MIN.	SEC.
Reading Time:		_____	_____
		MIN.	SEC.
WPM Score:		_____	
Comprehension Score:		_____	%

READING SELECTION 26

INTERPERSONAL COMMUNICATION

STRESS MANAGEMENT: PERSONALLY ADJUSTING TO STRESS
Richard L. Weaver

From *Understanding Interpersonal Communication*

Why do we suffer from stress? How can we cope with stress? This reading, taken from an interpersonal communication textbook, addresses these questions. Read the excerpt to find some helpful suggestions to cope with stress.

— · —

1   *Stress is a state of imbalance between demands made on us from outside sources and our capabilities to meet those demands. Often, it precedes and occurs concurrently with conflict. Stress, as you have seen, can be brought on by physical events, other people's behavior, social situations, our*

own behavior, feelings, thoughts, or anything that results in heightened bodily awareness. In many cases, when you experience pain, anger, fear, or depression, these emotions are a response to a stressful situation like conflict.

2   Sometimes, in highly stressful conflict situations, we must cope with the stress before we cope with the conflict. Relieving some of the intensity of the immediate emotional response will allow us to become more logical and tolerant in resolving the conflict. In this brief section, some of the ways we have for controlling our physical reactions and our thoughts will be explained.

3   People respond differently to conflict just as they respond differently to stress. Some people handle both better than others do. Individual differences are not as important as learning how to manage the stress we feel. The goal in stress management is self-control, particularly in the face of stressful events.

4   Stress reactions involve two major elements: (1) heightened physical arousal as revealed in an increased heart rate, sweaty palms, rapid breathing, and muscular tension, and (2) anxious thoughts, such as thinking you are helpless or wanting to run away. Since your behavior and your emotions are controlled by the way you think, you must acquire skills to change those thoughts.

5   Controlling physical symptoms of stress requires relaxation. Sit in a comfortable position in a quiet place where there are no distractions. Close your eyes and pay no attention to the outside world. Concentrate only on your breathing. Slowly inhale and exhale. Now, with each exhaled breath say "relax" gently and passively. Make it a relaxing experience. If you use this method to help you in conflict situations over a period of time, the word "relax" will become associated with a sense of physical calm; saying it in a stressful situation will help induce a sense of peace.

6   Another way to induce relaxation is through tension release. The theory here is that if you tense a set of muscles and then relax them, they will be more relaxed than before you tensed them. Practice each muscle group separately. The ultimate goal, however, is to relax all muscle groups simultaneously to achieve total body relaxation. For each muscle group, in turn, tense the muscles and hold them tense for five seconds, then relax them. Repeat this tension-release sequence three times for each group of muscles. Next, tense all muscles together for five seconds, then release them. Now, take a low, deep breath and say "relax" softly and gently to yourself as you breathe out. Repeat this whole sequence three times.

7   You do not need to wait for special times to practice relaxing. If, during the course of your daily activities, you notice a tense muscle group, you can help relax this group by saying "relax" inwardly. Monitor your bodily tension. In some cases you can prepare yourself for stressful situations through relaxation *before* they occur. Practice will help you call up the relaxation response whenever needed.

8   For other ways to relax, do not overlook regular exercise. Aerobic or yoga-type exercise can be helpful. Personal fitness programs can be tied to these inner messages to "relax" for a complete relaxation response.

9   Controlling your thoughts is the second major element in stress management. Managing stress successfully requires flexibility in thinking. That is, you must consider alternative views. Your current view is causing the stress! You must also keep from attaching exaggerated importance to events. Everything seems life-threatening in a moment of panic; things dim in importance when viewed in retrospect.

10   Try to view conflict from a problem-solving approach: "Now, here is a new problem. How am I going to solve this one?" (A specific problem-solving approach will be discussed in the next section.) Too often, we become stressed because we take things personally. When an adverse event occurs we see it as a personal affront or as a

threat to our ego. For example, when Christy told Paul she could not go to the concert with him, he felt she was letting him know she disliked him. This was a blow to Paul because he had never been turned down—rejected—before. Rather than dwell on that, however, he called Heather, she accepted his invitation, and he achieved his desired outcome—a date for the concert.

11   One effective strategy for stress management consists of talking to ourselves. We become our own manager, and we guide our thoughts, feelings, and behavior in order to cope. Phillip Le Gras suggests that we view the stress experience as a series of phases. Here, he presents the phases and some examples of coping statements:

1. *Preparing for a stressor.* [Stressors are events that result in behavioral outcomes called stress reactions.] What do I have to do? I can develop a plan to handle it. I have to think about this and not panic. Don't be negative. Think logically. Be rational. Don't worry. Maybe the tension I'm feeling is just eagerness to confront the situation.

2. *Confronting and handling a stressor.* I can do it. Stay relevant. I can psych myself up to handle this, I can meet the challenge. This tension is a cue to use my stress-management skills. Relax. I'm in control. Take a slow breath.

3. *Coping with the feeling of being overwhelmed.* I must concentrate on what I have to do right now. I can't eliminate my fear completely, but I can try to keep it under control. When the fear is overwhelming, I'll just pause for a minute.

4. *Reinforcing self-statements.* Well done. I did it! It worked. I wasn't successful this time, but I'm getting better. It almost worked. Next time I can do it. When I control my thoughts I control my fear.

12   The purpose of such coping behavior is to become aware of and monitor our anxiety. In this way, we can help eliminate such self-defeating, negative statements as "I'm going to fail," or "I can't do this." Statements such as these are cues that we need to substitute positive, coping self-statements.

13   If the self-statements do not work, or if the stress reaction is exceptionally intense, then we may need to employ other techniques. Sometimes we can distract ourselves by focusing on something outside the stressful experience—a pleasant memory, a sexual fantasy—or by doing mental arithmetic. Another technique is imaging. By manipulating mental images we can reinterpret, ignore, or change the context of the experience. For example, we can put the experience of unrequited love into a soap-opera fantasy or the experience of pain into a medieval torture by the rack. The point here is that love and pain are strongly subjective and personal, and when they are causing us severe stress we can reconstruct the situation mentally to ease the stress. In both these cases the technique of imaging helps to make our response more objective—to take it *outside* ourselves. The more alternatives we have to aid us in stress reduction, the more likely we are to deal with it effectively.

Writing about Reading Selection 26*

Checking Your Vocabulary

Directions: Complete each of the following items; refer to a dictionary if necessary.

1. Discuss the connotative meanings of the word *stress*. (paragraph 1)

2. Define each of the following words:
   a. concurrently (paragraph 1)

   _____

   b. monitor (paragraph 7)

   _____

   c. adverse (paragraph 10)

   _____

   d. outcome (paragraph 10)

   _____

   e. subjective (paragraph 13)

   _____

   _____

3. Define the word *rejected* (paragraph 10) and underline the word or phrase that provides a context clue for its meaning.

   _____

   _____

   _____

   _____

4. Define the word *stressor* (paragraph 11) and underline the word or phrase that provides a context clue for its meaning.

   _____

   _____

   _____

5. Determine the meanings of the following words by using word parts:
   a. imbalance (paragraph 1)

   _____

   b. precedes (paragraph 1)

   _____

   c. retrospect (paragraph 9)

   _____

   _____

   d. reinterpret (paragraph 13)

   _____

   e. unrequited (paragraph 13)

   _____

   _____

Checking Your Comprehension

6. Define the term *stress*.

   _____

   _____

   _____

7. How are stress reactions characterized?

   _____

   _____

   _____

8. How can physical stress symptoms be controlled?

   _____

   _____

* Multiple-choice questions are contained in Part 6 (page 592).

9. How can thoughts be controlled to manage stress?

_____

_____

_____

10. List the four phases in coping with the stress experience as suggested by Le Gras.

_____

_____

_____

_____

_____

11. Explain the technique of imaging.

_____

_____

_____

Thinking Critically

12. What evidence does the author provide about the effectiveness of the stress management techniques he describes? Does the evidence or lack of it alter your opinion of the techniques?

_____

13. What is the author's purpose in writing?

_____

_____

_____

14. Identify the stress control technique(s) used in the following situation: A student receives an "F" grade on a term paper in psychology. She says to a friend, "Oh well, it is just another grade among many!"

_____

_____

_____

Questions For Discussion

1. What are some of the major causes of stress for college students?

2. How useful do you think the relaxation response is or might be?

3. In what situations, other than those suggested by the author, might imaging be useful?

Selection 26:			1186 words
Finishing Time:	_____	_____	_____
	HR.	MIN.	SEC.
Starting Time:	_____	_____	_____
	HR.	MIN.	SEC.
Reading Time:		_____	_____
		MIN.	SEC.
WPM Score:			_____
Comprehension Score:			_____%

GO ELECTRONIC

For additional readings, exercises, and Internet activities, visit this book's Web site at:

http://www.ablongman.com/mcwhorter

For even more activities, visit the Longman English pages at:

http://www.ablongman.com/englishpages

If you need a user name and password, please see your instructor.

Take a Road Trip to Indianapolis Speedway
Be sure to visit the Reading Rate module on your Reading Road Trip CD-ROM for multimedia tutorials, exercises, and tests.

CHAPTER 14

Techniques for Reading Faster

IN THIS CHAPTER YOU WILL LEARN:

1. To control your eye-movement patterns.
2. To increase and vary your reading rate.

One of the first steps in becoming a more efficient and flexible reader is learning to vary your reading rate. Many adults read everything in the same way: at the same rate with the same level of comprehension. This chapter discusses several methods for increasing and varying your reading rate.

The chapter first describes the physical aspects of reading. Then, a technique for grouping words into meaning clusters is presented as a means of improving both rate and comprehension. Finally, five other methods for increasing your reading rate are discussed—key word reading, cue words, rapid reading drills, pacing, and rereading.

Eye-Movement Patterns

Reading is primarily a thinking process. However, it has physical aspects: your eyes recognize words and transmit them in the form of signals to the brain. These physical aspects of reading are far less important than the cognitive processes. Still, the following brief overview of the physical aspects will help you recognize habits that interfere with rate and comprehension.

What Happens When You Read

Your eyes are highly specialized and complicated instruments. They have the capacity to recognize words rapidly and to transmit them in the form of signals to the brain. Mental processes become involved as your brain attaches meaning to the signals it receives. As these two processes occur, you comprehend what you are reading. To explain what occurs as your eyes move across a line of print, let us look at some physical features of the eye-movement process.

Left-to-Right Progression

Your eyes are already well trained to move in a left-to-right pattern across the page. The speed of this progression, however, is variable and can be significantly increased with practice and training.

Fixation

As your eyes move across a line of print, they move and stop, move and stop. When your eyes are in motion, they do not see anything. When your eyes stop, or focus, this is called a *fixation*. As your eyes move across a line of print, they make a number of stops, or fixations, and the number of fixations you make per line is directly related to your reading efficiency.

Eye Span

As your eyes stop, or fixate, while progressing from left to right across the line, they see a certain number of words or letters. The amount you see during each fixation is called your *eye span*. Some readers see only a part of a word in each fixation; others are able to see a whole word in one fixation. Still others may see several words in each fixation.

You may find that your eye span varies greatly according to the type of material you are reading. For example, if you are reading a children's book to a child, you may be able to see several words at a time. On the other hand, when you read a chemistry textbook, you may need to focus on single words. Occasionally, when identifying an unfamiliar word, you may look at one part of a word and then another part.

Return Sweep

When your eyes reach the end of a line of print, they return to the beginning of the next line. This return motion is called the *return sweep*. Although your eyes are already trained to return automatically, the speed with which they make this return is variable.

Regression

Your eyes normally progress in a left-to-right direction, seeing each word in the order in which it was written. Occasionally, your eyes will move backward, or *regress,* to a word already read instead of moving to the next word. This word may be on the same line or on a previous line. In the following line, each fixation is numbered consecutively to show a sample reader's regression pattern.

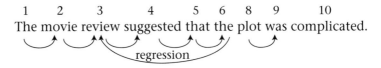

Notice that this reader moved from left to right through the sixth fixation. Then, instead of progressing to the next word, the reader regressed to the word "review" before proceeding with the sentence.

Regression is often unnecessary and slows you down. In fact, regressing may scramble the sentence order. As a result, you may have difficulty comprehending what you are reading.

Observing Eye-Movement Patterns

Most of the processes described so far can be readily observed by watching another person read. To get a better understanding of eye-movement patterns, choose another person to work with and try the following experiments. Be sure to sit so that the other person is facing you, and select sample pages from a book or text neither of you has already read.

EXPERIMENT 1: OBSERVING EYE MOVEMENT

Ask the other person to hold up the book so that you can see his or her eyes as he or she reads. Then direct the person to start reading a paragraph. As he or she reads, notice how the eyes move and stop, move and stop. Also notice the return sweep to the beginning of the next line.

EXPERIMENT 2: COUNTING FIXATIONS

As the person reads, count the number of eye stops or fixations made on each line. By counting the average number of words on the line and dividing it by the average number of fixations per line, you will be able to compute the person's eye span.

EXPERIMENT 3: REGRESSION

When observing the other person reading, ask him or her to deliberately regress to a word on a previous line. Notice the eye movement that occurs. Then have the person continue reading, and notice if he or she unknowingly makes any regressions.

Now allow the other person to try each of these three experiments while you read.

Now that you are familiar with the eye-movement process, you can begin to develop habits and eye-movement patterns that will increase your efficiency.

Reducing Regressions

Although even very good readers occasionally regress, you will find that frequent regression interferes with your comprehension and slows you down. Various mechanical devices can reduce regression, but you can easily get the same results by using one or more of the following techniques:

1. **Be conscious of your tendency to regress, and force yourself to move your eyes only from left to right.** Do not regress in the middle of a sentence. Instead, if the meaning of a sentence is unclear after you have finished reading it, reread the entire sentence.

2. **Use a 5" × 8" index card to prevent regression to previous lines.** As you read, slide the index card down the page so that it covers what you have already read. This technique will help you eliminate regressions, because when you look back to a previous line it will be covered up. If you look back and find the line is not visible often enough, eventually you will stop looking back.

3. **Use a pen, pencil, or finger to guide your eyes in a left-to-right direction across each line as you read.** Move the object or your finger at the speed at which you normally read. You will find that the forward motion of your finger or the pen will force you to continue reading toward the right and will discourage you from regressing.

Vocalization and Excessive Subvocalization

Some ineffective readers actually vocalize or sound out each word on a page by moving their lips and pronouncing each word. Others "hear" each word mentally as they read silently. This process is known as *subvocalization*. Research indicates that while subvocalization may be necessary and, at times, may enhance comprehension, it should not occur continuously as one reads. Mentally hearing each word may help clarify a confusing passage, but when done continuously, subvocalization usually limits the reader to word-by-word reading. Some students vocalize or subvocalize as a habit even though it is unnecessary.

If you find that you vocalize or subvocalize frequently, practice pushing yourself to read so rapidly that it is impossible. Also, if you discover that you move your lips as you read, place your hand or fingers near your lips as you read. You will feel your lips moving and can work to eliminate the habit.

Reading in Meaning Clusters

When you read a paragraph do you read one word and then another word, or do you jump from one group of words to another group of words? Most adult readers concentrate on a single word at a time, as described in the first half of the preceding sentence. Although most are capable of grouping words together, they have not developed the skill of doing so. Word-by-word reading is time-consuming and, in many cases, actually detracts from understanding the meaning of a sentence.

To understand how slow word-by-word reading can be, read the following paragraph. It is written so that you will have to read it from *right to left,* forcing you to read each word separately.

spirits neutral of combination a is Vodka
bring to added is water The .water and
neutral Since .proof final its to vodka
,neutral equally much pretty are spirits
but subtle for makes that water the is it
.differences appreciable

Clustering is the technique of grouping words together. You recall that your eyes move and stop, move and stop, as they proceed across a line of print. Clustering involves widening your eye span so that you see several words in one fixation.

How to Cluster Read

Essentially, clustering involves widening your eye span or point of concentration to encompass two or three words. To cluster most effectively, however, you should try to group words together that naturally fit or go together. In both written and spoken language, words fall into natural groupings. Our language contains many words that carry little meaning alone but, when combined with others, express a thought or idea. For example, the words *in* and *the* have meaning mainly when combined with other words: for example, "in the house." The word grouping "in the house" is a meaningful cluster and could be read as a unit. When you group words together in meaning units, you will find that it is easier to understand what you read. To illustrate this point, read both versions of the following sample paragraph. One version divides the paragraph into meaningful clusters; the other does not. Decide which version is easier to read.

VERSION 1

(Public libraries) (provide access) (to a world) (of information.) (But they also) (contribute to the) (preservation of) (our valuable forests.) (Each library) (saves a forest) (of trees) (by making) (individual purchase) (of books and periodicals) (unnecessary.)

VERSION 2

(Public libraries provide) (access to a) (world of) (information. But they) (also contribute to the) (preservation of our) (valuable forests. Each) (library saves a) (forest of) (trees by) (making individual) (purchase of books) (and periodicals unnecessary.)

You probably decided that the first version is easier to read because the words that are grouped together belong together.

Cluster reading can have a dramatic effect on your reading efficiency. By grouping words together into meaningful clusters, you make sentences easier to understand. Also, by widening your eye span, and thereby reducing the number of fixations per line, you are reducing the time it takes to read a line and are increasing your reading rate.

Learning to Cluster Read

For most students, learning to read in clusters requires considerable practice. It is not a skill that you can develop after a few trial reading sessions. Instead, you may find that it takes several weeks of continued practice to develop the habit. To develop the skill, try to read as many things as possible in clusters. Begin by reading easy material, such as newspaper and magazine articles, in phrases. Later, as you feel more confident about the skill, progress to more difficult types of material.

As you begin cluster reading, you may find that you frequently lapse back into word-by-word reading. This is a natural happening since your attention focuses on the content of the material rather than the technique of reading. Once you realize that you have lapsed into word-by-word reading, just switch back to cluster reading and continue reading. As you become more skilled with phrase reading, you will find that fewer lapses will occur.

EXERCISE 14-1

DIRECTIONS: Read the following passages that have been divided into clusters. They are designed to give you an idea of how it feels to cluster read. As you read, you should feel your eyes moving from cluster to cluster in a rhythmical motion.

1. When you   cluster read   it should feel   like this.
   Your eye should   move and stop,   move and stop.
   Each time   your eye stops   or fixates   it should see
   a meaningful phrase.   Cluster reading   will improve
   your comprehension   and help you   read faster.

2. As a   used car shopper,   your first task is
   to decide   what kind   of car   is going   to fill
   your needs.   Then   shop around   until you
   have a   good feel   for the market value   of that car.
   This way   you'll know   a bargain   when you   see one.
   You can   also check   the National   Automobile Dealers
   Association Used Car Guide   and the   Kelly Blue Book
   for prices   of used cars.   They'll give   you prices
   to work with,   *but they're   only guides.*
   Condition and mileage   will adjust   the price up
   or down.

3. Anytime   you're told   that you   need surgery
   and it's   not an emergency,   it's a good idea
   to get   a second   opinion from   a qualified specialist
   in the appropriate   field.   To find   this specialist,
   ask your   primary care physician   for a recommendation,
   or call   the nearest   teaching hospital   or an accredited
   hospital for   a recommendation.   You can   also consult
   the *Directory   of Medical Specialists.**

4. Actually,   the common cold   is not   as simple
   as it seems.   It can   be caused   by any
   of 200 different   viruses,   and it can   bring misery
   eight ways: sore throat,   sneezing,   runny nose,
   watery eyes,   aches and pains,   mild fever,
   nasal congestion,   and coughing.   Thus
   the thinking behind   "combination" products: they
   supposedly contain   a little something   for each
   different symptom.   One pill   or capsule,
   the advertisers say,   handles the   whole malady.
   A little like   one-stop shopping.**

5. Psychological principles   can be applied   by everyone.
   You can learn   to use   scientific psychology
   to help solve   your own problems.   There are
   a number   of important advantages   of do-it-yourself

---

* George

psychology.   One factor   is manpower.   For most people
the major problem   a few   generations ago
was physical   survival: now it is psychological   survival.
We seem to be tense,   alienated, confused.
Suicide, addiction,   violence, apathy,   neurosis—
are all   problems of   the modern world.
Psychological problems   are accelerating
and there   are not enough   professional psychologists
to go around.   Non-psychologists *must*   practice psychology
if psychology   is to be applied   to our problems.**

**EXERCISE
14-2**

DIRECTIONS: The following material has already been clustered. Practice reading each cluster with only one eye fixation. Move your eyes down each column, making only one fixation per line.

1. There is
    no better way
    to test
    fishing boats
    than under
    actual fishing
    conditions.
    Actual conditions
    provide the

    opportunity to
    try out
    the fishing boat
    under the most
    adverse weather
    conditions and
    the most rapid
    and unexpected
    passenger movements.

2. The purpose of
    life insurance
    is to prevent
    financial difficulty
    for someone else
    in the event
    of your death.
    With that in mind,
    you can determine
    if you need

    life insurance
    by simply
    asking yourself
    if your death
    would put someone
    else in a tough
    financial position.
    If the answer
    is yes,
    you need insurance.

3. The job interview
    is your best chance
    to sell yourself,
    so it pays
    to be well prepared.

    will be impressed
    if you can
    ask intelligent questions
    about their company,
    questions that show

** Holland

First, rehearse
in your mind
the qualifications
that would make
you an asset
to the organization.
Second, learn
something about it.
Most employers

you've done
your homework.
Your local librarian
can direct you
to a number
of reference books
that "profile"
business organizations.

EXERCISE 14-3

DIRECTIONS: Choose one of the reading selections at the end of this chapter. Read the first five paragraphs and, as you read, divide each sentence into meaningful clusters. Separate each cluster by using a slash mark (/) as has been done in the following example.

Studying economics/is difficult/because it requires/careful attention/to facts and figures.

Then, reread the five paragraphs, trying to see each cluster rather than each single word. ▬

Key Word Reading

Read each of the following versions of a paragraph.

VERSION 1

KEY WORD READING NEW TECHNIQUE. FASTER THAN CAREFUL READING. DECREASE FACTUAL COMPREHENSION. WORTH LOSS, DEPENDING PURPOSE TYPE MATERIAL. (18 words)

VERSION 2

Key word reading is a new technique. Although it is faster than most of the careful reading techniques, the reader must expect a decrease in factual comprehension skill. In some situations, it is worth the loss, depending on the reader's purpose and the type of material being read. (48 words)

Were you able to understand the passage conveyed in Version 1? If so, then you are already on your way to mastering the technique of key word reading. You have already read in a manner similar to key word reading.

Compare the number of words in each version. Notice what is deleted in the first version that is included in the second. Did you gain much additional information about key word reading from the complete version that you had not acquired in the first?

What Is Key Word Reading?

From our example, you can see that key word reading involves skipping nonessential words and reading only those words and phrases that carry the primary or core meaning of each sentence.

To further understand key word meaning, read the following paragraph in which the key words have been underlined. Read the paragraph two ways. First, read only the underlined key words in the paragraph. Can you understand the message the paragraph conveys? Second, read the entire passage. How much additional information did you acquire?

America's only nonelected president, Gerald Ford, became chief executive at a time when the nation desperately craved an end to distrust and uncertainty. Ford seemed the right man to initiate the healing process. A stolid legislator who had served in the House for many years without great distinction, he was an open, decent, and generous person, and most Americans seemed to like him.

Unger, *These United States: The Question of Our Past.*

By reading only the key words, you were probably able to understand the basic message of the paragraph. Then, when you read the complete paragraph, you only learned a few additional details about Ford.

In developing skill in key word reading, it sometimes helps to think of the process as similar to that of reading a telegram, a headline in a newspaper, or a news caption that is run across the bottom of a television screen while a program is in progress.

| Telegram: | ARRIVING TUESDAY 6 P.M. AMERICAN FLIGHT 321. LAGUARDIA. |
| TV News Caption: | AIRLINE HIJACKING LOS ANGELES. 52 HOSTAGES. FOUR HIJACKERS. IDENTITY AND PURPOSE UNKNOWN. |

Both of these messages contain only the words that carry the basic meaning. Most frequently, these meaning-carrying words are nouns, action verbs, and important descriptive adjectives and adverbs. They are the words that tell the "who, what, when, and where" and frequently include names, dates, places, numbers, capitalized words, and italicized words.

When to Use Key Word Reading

You will find that key word reading is a valuable and efficient technique for some reading situations. You should expect your comprehension to be 70 percent or lower, usually in the 50–70 percent range. But, as a tradeoff for lower comprehension, you can expect an increase in rate. You actually gain more than you lose because, although you read less than half the material, normally you can expect to get more than 50 percent of the message. You might expect to achieve reading rates of between 600 and 700 words per minute when using key word reading.

Key word reading cannot be used on all types of material. In many situations a comprehension level below 80 percent is not acceptable. Especially when reading textbooks or highly technical material, your goal should be to understand everything, and key word reading is obviously inappropriate. However, in many other situations, a level of comprehension in the 60–70 percent range is adequate. In these situations, key word reading will suit your purposes and enable you to cover the material at a high reading rate.

Here are a few situations in which key word reading might be an appropriate technique:

- when you are visiting a Web site to determine whether the site contains any information you do not already have for a research paper

- when you are reading magazine movie reviews to decide whether you want to see the movie

- when you are reading newspaper articles to find the key ideas and primary details about a recent local event

- when using reference books to gain a general idea of an author's approach and treatment of an event, idea, concept, or theory

- when reading correspondence to determine the writer's purpose and the level and nature of response required

Aids to Key Word Reading

The ability to key word read draws on many comprehension skills and reading techniques. Your knowledge and familiarity with the structure of the English language, which you have acquired naturally throughout your lifetime, to help you locate key words. Although you may not be aware of them, you have learned many rules and patterns of the structure of English.

Using Sentence Structure

Sentences contain core parts that tell you what the sentence is about (the subject), what action occurred (the predicate), and who or what received the action (the object). These parts carry the basic meaning of the sentence. To illustrate this, look at the following paragraph, in which these key parts have been highlighted. Read only the highlighted words and phrases; you will notice that you get the basic meaning of each sentence and the paragraph as a whole.

> And so, by 1968 or 1969, the country found itself caught in a giant whirlpool of anger and change. Nothing from the past, apparently, was sacred any longer. Patriotism was in bad repute: students burned their draft cards and desecrated the American flag. Chastity had become a thing of the past: college students lived in open "sin," and skirts had crawled two-thirds the way up the female thigh. Civility in public life had almost disappeared: every group was demanding "liberation" and would take to the streets, occupy public buildings, attack the police, riot, or even throw bombs to get it. Worst of all, the family was disintegrating: despite parental protest, children dressed the way they wanted, smoked "pot," and abandoned promising careers and futures to become political activists. Wives demanded that husbands share household chores so they could take jobs or go back to school.
>
> Unger, *These United States: The Question of Our Past.*

Now read the complete paragraph. Notice that it fills you in on the details you missed when you read only key words, but also notice that you did not miss any of the key ideas.

EXERCISE 14-4	**DIRECTIONS:** In each of the following sentences, draw a line through the words that do not carry the essential meaning of the sentence. Only key words should remain.

Example: Work ~~should be~~ arranged so ~~there are~~ specific stopping points ~~where you can~~ feel something ~~has been~~ accomplished.

1. In some large businesses, employees are practically strangers to each other and often do not discuss problems or ideas.

2. Criminal law as we know it today is a product of centuries of change.

3. From the standpoint of criminal law, a criminal is an individual who is legally capable of conduct that violates the law and who can be shown to have actually and intentionally engaged in that conduct.

4. By the time Congress assembled on December 4, 1865, the Republican majority—Radicals as well as most moderates—were seething with anger at the Johnson government.

5. During the 1960s the United States attained a level of material well-being beyond anything dreamed of in the past. ▬

Using Punctuation

Punctuation can serve as an aid in locating key words. Punctuation may signal what is to follow, separate nonessential parts of a sentence from the main sentence, or indicate the relationships of various parts of a sentence to one another.

The use of a colon or semicolon indicates that important information is to follow. When you see a colon, you may anticipate a list of items. Often, you can expect to find a separate but closely related idea when a semicolon is used. In both cases you are alerted to look for key words ahead.

Commas, depending on their use, provide several types of clues for the location of key words. When used to separate an introductory phrase from the main sentence, the comma tells you to pay more attention to the main sentence as you look for key words.

When used to separate items in a series, the comma indicates that all items are important and should be read as key words. When a comma is accompanied by a conjunction and is used to join two complete thoughts, expect to find key words on both sides of the comma. The parenthetical use of the comma tells you that the information enclosed within the commas is nonessential to the basic meaning of the sentence and may be skipped when you read key words.

Using Typographical Aids

Most printed material contains typographical features that will help you locate key words and phrases. Typographical aids include boldface print, colored print, italics, capitalization, underlining, enumeration, or lists of information. Most typographical aids emphasize important information; others help the reader organize the information. Italics, underlining, and boldface print are all used to make important information more noticeable.

Using Grammatical Structure

Your knowledge of grammar can also help you read key words effectively. You have learned that certain words modify or explain others. You know that adjectives explain or describe nouns and that adverbs give further information about verbs. Adjectives and adverbs that modify the key parts of the sentence, then, are also important in key word reading.

For example, in the following sentence you see that the adjectives and adverbs (single underlining) make the meaning of the key parts (double underlining) more complete.

The <u>psychology instructor</u> hastily <u>summarized</u> his lecture.

You also know that many words in the English language work very much like glue—they stick other, more important, words together. If classified by parts of speech, these "glue words" are usually prepositions, conjunctions, or pronouns.

In the following sentence, all the glue words have been deleted.

. . . summary, it seems safe . . . say . . . society, . . . whole, believes . . . individuals can control . . . destiny.

Can you still understand the sentence? Most likely you can guess the words that were deleted. Try it. Now, compare the words you supplied with the complete sentence.

In summary, it seems safe to say that society, on the whole, believes that individuals can control their destiny.

You probably guessed some words exactly, and for others you supplied a synonym. In either case, you supplied a word that fit into the meaning of the sentence.

EXERCISE 14-5

DIRECTIONS: Assume you are working on a research paper on the psychological effects of color. You located the following article by Kelly Costigan in *Science Digest,* and you want to see if it presents any new information on the psychology of color that you do not already have. Read the article using the key word reading technique. To help you get started, the first few lines have been shaded so that the key words are emphasized. After reading the article, answer the questions that follow.

How Color Goes to Your Head

Orange Makes You Hungry; Beige Makes You Neat and Efficient

Can simply looking at a color affect your behavior or alter your mood? Although some researchers are skeptical, others suggest that color may have a profound influence on human behavior and physiology.

A recent report in the *International Journal of Biosocial Research* revealed that after a change in the color and lighting scheme at a school in Wetaskiwin, Canada, the IQ scores of some students jumped and absenteeism and disciplinary problems decreased. The study, conducted by visual-arts professor Harry Wohlfarth of the University of Alberta, involved substituting yellow and blue for orange, white, beige and brown and replacing fluorescent lights with full-spectrum ones.

Clinical psychologist Alexander Schauss, director of the American Institute for Biosocial Research in Tacoma, Washington, spearheaded the now widespread use of bubblegum-pink rooms to calm delinquents and criminals in correctional facilities across the country. In 1979, Schauss evaluated the effect on subjects as they looked at this pink shade on a piece of cardboard. He reported later in the *Bulletin of the Psychonomic Society* that the color relaxed the subjects so much that they did not perform simple strength tests as well as they did when viewing other hues. A U.S. Navy brig in Seattle took notice of Schauss's work and permitted him to test his calming-color hypothesis on its inmates. Now hundreds of institutions place individuals in pink rooms when tempers flare.

"We used to have to give them drugs, even use handcuffs," says Paul Boccumini, director of clinical services at California's San Bernardino County Probation Department. "But this works."

Schauss and Wohlfarth are not certain how color can have an impact on biology or behavior. But Schauss conjectures that response to color is determined in the brain's reticular formation, a relay station for millions of the body's nerve impulses. And there have been studies indicating that when subjects look at warm hues, such as red, orange or yellow, their blood pressure rises, brain-wave activity increases, respiration is faster and perspiration greater. In the late 1970s, a UCLA study showed that blue had the opposite effect. Given these data, researchers speculate that the perception of color by the eye ultimately spurs the release of important biochemicals in the body.

The human eye is sensitive to millions of colors. Each is a distinctive wavelength of light that strikes color-sensitive cones on the back of the eye in a unique way. These cells then fire, sending nerve signals to the brain. Wohlfarth and others contend that the release of hormones or neurotransmitters may be triggered during this process, and they in turn influence moods and activities such as heart rate and breathing.

COLORED LIGHT AIDS HEALTH

There is also some evidence that colored light affects health. Baths of light emitting a high concentration of blue wavelengths are now used in many hospitals to cure infants of neonatal jaundice. The light penetrates the skin and breaks down the chemical bilirubin, which causes the condition.

Psychologists and commercial color consultants are already prescribing the use of a variety of hues to elicit certain behaviors. Gradations of blue are used on the walls of a Canadian dental clinic to ease patients' fears; rooms painted in peach, yellow and blue are said to relax residents at Aid for the Retarded in Stamford, Connecticut; and orange, which stimulates the appetite, adorns the walls of fast-food chains. Even machinery is painted light blue or beige instead of battleship gray to inspire neatness and efficiency in workers at a gas-turbine plant in the northeastern United States.

But the idea that color is a legitimate tool for modifying behavior is still being debated. "We need to speak from hard data," says Norman Rosenthal, a psychiatrist at the National Institute for Mental Health. "And how do you get by the cultural bias that might be built into a response, that red is stimulating and blue is connected to depression?"

Costigan, "How Color Goes to Your Head," *Science Digest.*

1. The article mentions numerous effects of color. List as many as you can recall.

   _____

   _____

2. Summarize one theory that explains how color affects behavior.

   _____

   _____

3. What references or sources does the article provide for further research?

   _____

   _____

EXERCISE 14-6

DIRECTIONS: Select a magazine or newspaper article or two or three pages from a nonfiction paperback you are reading. Before beginning to read, underline the key words in the first paragraph and in five to six sentences randomly selected from the remainder of the passage. Use key word reading on the article and record your results in the space provided. (See Chapter 1 for information on how to estimate number of words and your words-per-minute score.)

Source of Material: _____

Finishing Time: _____

Starting Time: _____

Reading Time: _____

Estimated Total Number of Words: _____

WPM Score: _____

Using Transitional Words

You have already learned that not all materials need to be read in the same way or at the same speed. The same principle also applies to reading a single piece of material. Not every sentence, paragraph, or section within a work must be read in the same way. When reading an essay or textbook chapter, for instance, your speed may vary, depending on the content and its relative importance. Fortunately, many materials contain cue words and phrases that indicate when to speed up, when to maintain your pace, and when to slow down. These words and phrases often function as transitions, connecting and leading from one idea to another. These transitions also cue the reader as to what is to follow and indicate its relative importance.

For example, readers often find it necessary to slow down when a new or different idea is presented. One word that signals a change in thought is *however,* as in the following statement.

> Selecting a career to match your interests, skills, and abilities is critically important. *However,* few students are able to find a perfect match. Instead, most students must settle for . . .

In this statement the author is switching from discussing a perfect match to other alternatives.

A decrease in reading speed may also be necessary when the author is presenting key points, emphasizing important information, or concluding or summarizing. Transitional words and phrases for these conditions are listed in Table 14.1 on page 553. A reader can afford to speed up when the material is repetitious, familiar, or unimportant to his or her given purpose. Maintaining the same speed is appropriate when the author is continuing with the same line of thought or presenting information of equal importance. Speed-up and maintain-speed transitional words are also shown in Table 14.1.

DIRECTIONS: Choose a section of a chapter from one of your textbooks and circle the transitional words contained in it. Determine if each cue is a speed-up, slow-down, or maintain-speed cue.

Table 14.1   Reading Rate Transitional Words

Speed-Up Cues	
Repetitious information	Again, in other words, that is
Examples	To illustrate, for example, suppose, for instance, such as
Slow-Down Cues	
Change in thought	However, nevertheless, instead of, despite
Summary	In summary, for these reasons, to sum up, in brief
Conclusion	In conclusion, thus, therefore
Emphasis (above all, indeed)	Most important, it is essential
Maintain-Speed Cues	
Continuation	Likewise, similarly, also, furthermore, and added to, in addition
Enumeration (listing)	First, second . . . , next, then, 1) . . . , 2) . . .

Rapid Reading Drills

Many students read more slowly than is necessary. In fact, some students read so slowly that it interferes with their comprehension. A gap sometimes occurs between rate of intake of information and speed of thought. If information is taken in too slowly, the mind has time to drift or wander, resulting in loss of concentration or weak comprehension.

One effective way to build reading rate is to practice reading various materials at an uncomfortably high rate. Do not be too concerned if at first your comprehension is incomplete. Your first goal is to gain speed—to cover material faster than ever before. Then, as you become more skilled at faster reading, you will find that your comprehension will improve.

You might think of this strategy as similar to stretching a rubber band. A new rubber band is very tight and narrow in length. However, as it is stretched, it loosens and becomes longer and more flexible. A similar change occurs with reading rate: it loosens, stretches, and becomes more flexible.

The following rapid reading drills are intended to stretch your reading rate. Complete each drill as rapidly as possible.

**EXERCISE
14-8**

DIRECTIONS: For each item, read the word in column A. Find a word in column B that means the same, and underline it. Sweep your eye rapidly across each line. Do not reread if you are unable to find a match; go to the next item.

Set I

Begin timing.

Column A	Column B				
1. secure	secret	output	luckiness	improve	possess
2. imprint	bearable	engrave	treaty	flutter	improper
3. fabricate	extra	eyeless	make	façade	tremor
4. disturb	question	review	tremble	interrupt	dilute
5. blush	redden	submit	treasure	social	dim
6. backing	shaken	support	register	grate	obstacle
7. desert	observer	goodness	quarter	typical	abandon
8. authentic	twisting	resign	genuine	stimulate	reasonable
9. dateless	ageless	serving	qualm	permit	perjury
10. cunning	perish	clever	rejoice	grateful	graphic

Time: _____ seconds

Set II

Begin timing.

Column A	Column B				
1. author	query	tread	writer	grave	miracle
2. defect	ministry	grapple	misbehavior	murky	flaw
3. posterior	back	haven	façade	frontal	haul
4. sentiment	shadow	extort	feeling	mirage	extreme
5. equivalent	cheeky	decompose	opposite	equal	declare
6. decrease	historical	flog	bombard	cheat	diminish
7. defer	reign	together	dual	token	delay
8. extract	remove	quarter	hoard	snap	tipple
9. squeal	tread	object	yelp	pester	soar
10. hint	profane	sensual	suggest	taint	uprising

Time: _____ seconds

EXERCISE 14–9

DIRECTIONS: Read as rapidly as possible each of the following passages from *Discovering Mass Communication* by Samuel L. Becker. Time yourself, circle the speed closest to yours, and answer the questions that follow each passage. Try to increase your words per minute (WPM) score on successive passages. Do not hesitate to take risks: read faster than you think you are able to.

Passage A

EXPOSURE TO TELEVISION

A television receiver in the average American household is on for about seven hours a day. Almost every year that figure increases. Just twenty years ago the average time was only five and one-half hours. The viewing of network television, though, is not increasing. In fact, it is dropping. Cable and videotapes are attracting the attention of a larger and larger percentage of the audience each year. Those inroads into the network and station audience are not yet tremendous, but they are sufficient to cause concern by network and station executives.

The reason people in the industry label the evening hours "prime time" is evident if you examine data on the percentage of households using television at each hour of the day. About 10 percent of homes have a television set on between 7:30 and 8:00 in the morning. That percentage rises very slowly during the day until about 4:00 or 4:30 P.M., when somewhat over 30 percent have sets on. At that point, viewing begins to rise sharply and steadily to its peak, which comes between 8:00 and 10:00 P.M. On a winter evening, from 8:00 to 10:00 P.M., a television set is on in more than 60 percent of American households. Somewhat fewer are on during summer evenings.

Words: 210
Timing:

Seconds	WPM
20	630
30	420
40	315
50	252
60	210
70	180

Questions

1. Television watching is (increasing, decreasing). Circle one.
2. Television viewing is highest during the _____ season.

Passage B

IMPLICATIONS FOR THE MEDIA OF SEX ROLE SHIFTS

The combination of sexual revolution and economic need is bringing a far larger percentage of adult American women into the work force and out of the home. This, combined with the increased numbers of males at home, may force [radio and television] broadcasters to rethink totally their daytime programming. By the twenty-first century, female homemakers may no longer dominate the daytime radio, television, and cable audience.

The fact that rapidly increasing numbers of adult women are moving into the work force will probably also affect the readership of books and magazines. Traditionally, women have been the major consumers of light fiction, both in book and magazine form. In good part this has been because they had more leisure time. As they enter the work force, however, and still retain many household duties in most cases, whether married or not, their time for reading fiction will be sharply reduced. Publishers may need to strive harder for older readers to maintain their circulation.

As more women enter the work force, a breakdown is occurring in the sharp division between male and female roles in the home. Men increasingly are sharing in the homemaking tasks, from cooking, caring for children, and cleaning to shopping for household necessities. This change in life-styles will affect mass communication in two ways. It will mean that men have less time to devote undivided attention to the media during prime time and on weekends. Perhaps more important, it will mean that all advertising presently designed to appeal largely to housewives will need to be redesigned to appeal equally to househusbands.

Words: 262
Timing:

Seconds	WPM
20	786
30	524
40	393
50	314
60	262
70	224
80	196

Questions

Directions: Indicate whether the statement is true or false by marking "T" or "F" in the space provided.

_____ 1. In the future men may have less time to watch TV.

_____ 2. Advertising is likely to remain the same in the future as it is now.

Passage C

Much graffiti is simply a safe form of exhibitionism. You can feel bold writing dirty words on the walls of a toilet, for example, without risking the criticism you might receive on saying the words aloud in public. A somewhat different form of exhibitionism is the desire to see your name etched forever on a tree in a public park or on a schoolroom desk. Although they obviously communicate something, these kinds of graffiti hardly qualify as mass communication in any meaningful sense.

Some graffiti, on the other hand, are as much mass communication as the billboards along the highways and as the local newspaper. The scrawled sign on a wall, "Divest now" or "U.S. out of everywhere!" speaks to the concerns of many people today. There is a great range of such messages, from "Gay Rights" to "Beat Illinois." Graffiti obviously are giving voice to the thoughts of many people and reinforcing them; just as obviously, since much graffiti is anti-establishment, such messages are also designed to discomfort those who disagree.

Some societies have tried to institutionalize graffiti, providing special walls where people can write their messages for all to see. The People's Republic of China has had such walls, for example. And some colleges provided similar space for graffiti during the late 1960s and early 1970s when anti-Vietnam feeling was at its height. The colleges hoped that students would use these specially constructed walls instead of painting their antiwar and other messages on buildings and sidewalks where they were costly to remove. Not surprisingly, the ploy did not work. Much of the pleasure from the creation of graffiti clearly comes from putting the messages in forbidden places.

Words: 279

Timing:

Seconds	WPM
20	837
30	558
40	418
50	335
60	279
70	239
80	209

Questions

1. List one function of graffiti.

    _____

2. Are special graffiti walls effective in controlling graffiti?

    _____

Pacing Techniques

An established method of improving reading rate is called *pacing*. Pacing involves forcing yourself to read slightly faster than you normally would and trying to keep up with a preestablished pace. To better understand the concept of pacing, imagine that you are in a crowd of people and suddenly everyone starts walking forward quickly. You are forced along at the pace at which the crowd is moving, regardless of how fast you want to move. Similarly, in reading you can read more rapidly if you are "forced along" by some external means. Pacing is a way of forcing yourself to read faster than your normal speed while maintaining your level of comprehension.

Pacing Methods

There are two easy ways to pace yourself for speed increase. Among the most common are:

1. **Use an index card.** Slide a 3" × 5" card down the page, moving it so that it covers up lines as you read them. This technique will force you along and keep you moving rapidly. Move the card down the page at a fixed pace. How fast you move the card will, of course, depend on the size of the print, the length of the line, and so on, and will then vary for each new piece of material you read. At first you will need to experiment to find an appropriate pace. Try to move at a pace that is slightly uncomfortable and that you are not sure you can maintain. You can also use your hand or index finger, or a pen or pencil in place of an index card.

2. **Use a timer or alarm clock.** Start by measuring what portion of a page you can read in a minute. Then set a goal for yourself: Determine how many pages you will attempt to read in a given period of time. Set your goal slightly above what you measured as your current rate. For example, suppose in a particular book you can read half a page in a minute. You might set as your goal reading five pages in nine minutes (forcing yourself to read a little more than a half page per minute). The next day, try to read five pages in eight or eight and a half minutes. Use an alarm clock or timer to let you know when you have used up your time.

As you begin to use one of these pacing methods, here are several suggestions to keep in mind:

1. **Keep a record of your time, the amount you read, and your words per minute.** A quick way to estimate your speed is given in Appendix A at the end of the book.

2. **Be sure to maintain an adequate level of comprehension.** To test your comprehension, try to summarize what you read. If you are unable to remember enough ideas to summarize what you read, you have probably read too fast.

3. **Push yourself gradually, across several weeks of practice.**

4. **Try to keep your practice material similar from day to day.** Consistently use newspapers, magazine articles, or the same paperback book for practice.

Why Pacing Works

Pacing is effective partly because it establishes a goal to be met, a speed to attain. It is psychologically motivating to work toward a goal, and when you attain a goal it is rewarding and encourages you to keep on working. It also provides a way for you to keep moving, and does not allow you to slow to a more comfortable speed.

EXERCISE 14-10

DIRECTIONS: Select an article from a periodical or use material that you have been assigned to read for one of your courses. Using one of the pacing techniques described in this section, try to increase your current reading speed by approximately 50 wpm. Record your results in the space provided. (See Chapter 1 for information on how to estimate the number of words and your WPM score.)

Material Used: _____

Estimated Level of Comprehension: _____

Finishing Time: _____

Starting Time: _____

Reading Time: _____

WPM Score: _____

Rereading for Rate Increase

Rereading is an effective method to build your reading rate. This technique is similar to pacing in that it involves building your rate gradually by using small increments.

To reread for speed increase, use the following steps:

1. Select an article or passage and read it as you normally would for careful or leisure reading.

2. Time yourself and compute your speed in words per minute after you finish reading.

3. Take a break (five minutes or so). Then reread the same selection. Push yourself to read faster than you read the first time.

4. Time yourself and compute your speed once again. You should be able to reread the selection at a faster rate than you read it initially.

5. Read a new selection, pushing yourself to read almost as fast as you reread the first selection.

You are probably wondering how rereading helps you read new, unfamiliar material faster. Rereading serves as a preparation for reading the new material faster. Rereading establishes the mechanical process of more rapid eye movements and gives you preliminary practice, or a "trial run," with reading at a higher reading rate. It helps you learn things about reading faster while keeping your comprehension in balance. Because you already have a basic understanding of the selection from your first reading, you are free to focus and concentrate on improving your rate.

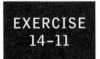

EXERCISE 14-11

DIRECTIONS: For one of the selections at the end of this chapter, apply the technique of key word reading. For the other, use the cluster reading technique. When you have completed both selections, compare your performance by reviewing your rate and comprehension scores. What can you conclude about the relative effectiveness of the two techniques?

Critical Thinking Tip #14

Recognizing Judgments

It is easy to miss nuances and shades of meaning when reading rapidly. Be sure to read articles, essays, and Web-based materials carefully and critically before you accept the information presented. One important critical reading skill is recognizing judgments.

Judgments are reasoned decisions based on evidence. They are decisions about the value or worth of an object, event, person, or idea. Here are a few examples:

Professor Lopez is the best lecturer on campus.

Ronald Reagan was the most politically aware president of the twentieth century.

Sam's serves the tastiest pizza in town.

Writers may make judgments based on factual information and use some standard or set of criteria to make them. As a critical reader, be sure to question the criteria used. For example, what criteria were used to decide that Professor Lopez was the best lecturer? Is she the most interesting, the best organized, or the most understandable? Similarly, what criteria were used to judge political awareness or tastiness?

Judgments often involve personal opinion. It is therefore possible that two authors may make two different judgments about the same topic. (Another writer may state that Professor Hargrave is the best lecturer.)

As a critical thinker, study the standards used to make a judgment before accepting it or agreeing with it. If none are provided, treat the judgment as merely a personal opinion. If standards are provided, evaluate them.

- Are they reasonable?
- Are they comprehensive?
- Does the author justify them?

Summary

1. What are five aspects of eye movement that can directly affect your reading rate?

Reading rate is directly affected by the following physical aspects of eye movement:

- speed of left-to-right progression
- number of fixations or "eye stops"
- size of eye span or amount of print seen in each fixation
- speed of return sweep from the end of one line to the start of the next
- number of regressions or backward eye movements

2. What two reading habits, when taken to excess, can decrease your reading efficiency?

Unnecessary regressions and vocalization/subvocalization can reduce your reading efficiency. Frequent regressions can increase your reading time and interfere with your comprehension. Likewise, your speed and comprehension are decreased by vocalizing (saying every word) and subvocalizing (mentally hearing every word) because they limit you to word-by-word reading.

3. What techniques can you use to read faster?

There are five techniques, which with practice, can help you to read faster.

- Cluster reading: widening your eye span to read words in meaningful groupings
- Key word reading: reading only important words and skipping nonessential words
- Transitional words: knowing how to adjust your rate
- Pacing: forcing yourself to read slightly faster than normal
- Rereading for rate increases: rereading previously read material at a higher speed and then attempting to read new material at the same speed

Reading Selection 27

Interpersonal Communication

Flirtation—The Signals of Attraction Deciphered

Maggie Paley

From *Vogue*

This article, reprinted from Vogue *magazine, explores the courtship ritual known as flirting. Read this article to discover the elements of flirting and how behaviorists study it.*

— · —

1   The art of flirtation is going out of style. I began to think about this the first time I heard Timothy Perper, Ph.D., discuss his work. We were both at his older sister's apartment for dinner. Perper, then a biologist at Rutgers University, with an interest in animal behavior, announced, by way of filling his sister in on his recent activities, that he'd been taking students with him to observe human flirtation at New Jersey singles bars. He'd discovered, he said, that most often women were the ones who chose the men. He hoped to get a grant to study the phenomenon further.

2   "You're going to get a grant to go to bars to prove that women choose men?" said Perper's belligerent sister. "You don't need a grant. Why don't you just ask me? Of course, women do the choosing. Any woman could tell you that."

3   At the time, Perper was thirty-nine and recently separated from his wife. His new line of research struck me as a peculiarly modern solution—in the self-help spirit—to the plight of the single scientist. In the old days, if a man wanted to watch people engage in "the first stages of becoming intimate," as Perper put it, he wouldn't have told anybody. In the old days, I could not have been lured into a singles bar, even to watch a behavioral scientist. Yet this was what, with some enthusiasm, I ended up doing a number of times recently.

4   It was a transition period in the history of the war between the sexes. Those women who'd been brought up to think you batted your eyes, smiled at a man, and then he made all your troubles disappear were beginning to see the flaws in this point of view. There were rumors that men were changing, and that some of them wanted equal relationships with women. These so-called "new men," instead of trying to amuse you, liked to talk about their feelings and health habits ("Can I make you a hamburger?" "I say the faster an animal moves the less fat is on it. I won't eat anything slower than a chicken.") You paid your own way with them, and you were direct instead of demure.

5   To be direct and seductive at the same time took a discouraging amount of energy. I found it hard to flirt at all under these conditions. Everyone was so confused about the things that should be most natural—how to assert themselves, enjoy themselves, be themselves. What *was* correct flirtation behavior? I got tired of trying to decide. I phoned Perper.

6   By ignoring his sister's advice at that dinner four years ago, Perper had become an authority on flirtation behavior and was beginning his third year of research in singles bars supported by a grant from the Harry Frank Guggenheim Foundation.

7   He had now ventured far beyond his sister's area of expertise. As a biologist, he told me, he'd learned to watch people flirt in much the same way he'd once watched rats engage in "copulatory behavior." Using this method, he'd discovered that all human flirtation, like mate selection among rats, took place in the form of body

movement. What others called "chemistry," or "sexual attraction," he referred to as "body-movement compatibility." In his opinion, everyone worried too much about good opening lines and clever conversation with strangers, when what they were really doing when they met was the human equivalent of sniffing each other out. Since no one could control such a process, he wished people would just relax and enjoy it.

8   We sat at a table at the Greenwich Village singles bar, One University Place. "I think there are a lot of unhappy people around," he said, "who don't really know how to make contact. And I would have put myself in that category, before I learned to read signals."

9   Most of the people who didn't know how to make contact, he told me, were men, and he thought it was a matter of training: men were so *ignorant* about behavior that a man could easily be in the middle of a flirtation without even knowing it. Women almost always knew when they were flirting, and it was in this sense that they could be said to be the ones doing the choosing. He had confirmed his observations with interviews; most men didn't notice cues and signals, and they didn't understand what women meant with their languorous looks and graceful gestures, though women assumed they did. A man didn't have to be good-looking or smart to be successful with women under these circumstances, according to Perper; he just had to pay attention to what they were doing.

10   Flirting, which I liked to think of as light, graceful, and easy, Perper had broken down into a sequence with four parts. Every flirtation he'd watched so far, he said, went through "approach" (the couple acknowledge each other's presence and begin talking); "swivel" (they turn gradually to face each other); "synchronization" (their movements begin to match); and "touch." Perper said "synchronization" was the most important step and made people feel, when they reached it, that they had "good vibes" together. I asked him to take me with him to watch this mating dance that I, a lifelong flirt, presumably had many

times performed, smiling, nodding, and batting my eyes, in a semiconscious state.

11   Most of the men and women at the bars Perper showed me appeared to be suffering from a failure of imagination. They were there, but pretending not to be. The men were just lolling around by themselves, drinking beer and watching television. The women, who traveled in pairs, or in packs of three or more, seemed to have dressed up and gone out to have a good gossip with each other. It was as if the courage it took to enter a bar, seeking the company of strangers, had exhausted their supply of enthusiasm for the opposite sex. The men looked frightened and the women exasperated, and no one seemed capable of entering into a flirtation sequence.

12   I spent five nights with Perper, looking for a pickup to watch, and listening to his complaints about men—a welcome change from listening to my women friends' complaints about men. Perper spoke of men affectionately, as a high-school football coach might speak of a promising team that was always dropping the ball. During flirtation, he said, this happened particularly at what he called "escalation points," the moments when one partner, usually the woman, would act to move things forward—by turning to begin a "swivel," for example, or by putting a hand on the table where it could easily be touched. If the other partner, usually the man, didn't respond, the result would be "de-escalation." Perper hated to see a man de-escalate by accident.

13   With some agitation he would point out, say, a woman in a red dress, whom he'd refer to as "Red Dress." Red Dress would be sitting on a bar stool, facing "Check Suit" with adoration in her milk-chocolate eyes while Check Suit stood pivoting nervously back and forth. "That dumb jerk!" Perper would whisper to me. "If he doesn't turn towards her, she'll give up. You'd think he'd figure out that someone who's looking at him that way must like him."

14   Sometimes, Perper said, it was hard to stop himself from rushing to the aid of a floundering couple. "Once again now," he could imagine

himself telling the man, "this time when she does that, take her hand." Check Suit looked to me like a man wracked [*sic*] by ambivalence—which was what most men and women seemed to feel for each other most of the time. Perper said he thought what women did when they flirted was absolutely beautiful, and he felt sorry for the men who couldn't see it.

15   Now, there are male flirts who know perfectly well what women do when they flirt. I can assure you; men who know how to laugh and bat their eyes in return. But few of any sex can have studied, with the absorption Perper has, the entire arsenal of the human gestures of flirtation. These are sure signs that the person using them is flirting—what else could he be doing?—and once Perper was comfortable in a bar, he liked to mimic them. Some of the gestures he showed me were as obvious as the "eye avert"—when a man who's been looking a woman up and down then casts his eyes sideways (Perper mimed looking demure); or "brushing"—when a woman brushes against a man as if by accident ("It's never by accident," Perper said, brushing my left leg). Other gestures were disturbingly indirect, and apparently unconscious. Flirting people, he pointed out, spend a great deal of time preening and caressing themselves: stroking the neck, massaging an arm or leg. Touching the hair is a giveaway. Perper explained this phenomenon as "displacement"—you do to yourself what you'd like to do to the other person.

16   In a bar, Perper was a man in an invisible lab coat. His eyebrows seemed perpetually raised above steel-rimmed spectacles and pale eyes that focused on the middle distance; his high-bridged, beaked nose probed the air as if searching for a decent smell. He wore calculatedly nondescript clothes: the technique he practiced, "participant observation," required that he blend in with his environment. He ordered his drinks according to what bar he was in, and for the sake of appearances, he told me, he always worked as a "mixed-sex couple," and flirted with his partner. At regular intervals, when we were

out together, he would lovingly touch my arm; I'd remind myself this was for the benefit of the people watching us. No one was watching us, but it wasn't my business to disturb his equilibrium.

17   I did worry about the fact that there was nothing happening for us to watch. Then, on our fifth night, I saw synchronization. We were at a back table at The Mad Hatter of Second Avenue in Manhattan, a singles bar as cozy as home, with sawdust floors and mad hats hung from the ceiling beams. Perper had brought one of his regular partners with him, a bouncy anthropology graduate student named Marilyn Frasier.

18   Perper and Frasier were like hunters watching for lions. First they would scan the bar, where twelve men were lined up looking at the Yankees game and two women in jeans were talking to each other near the jukebox. Then they'd turn to the dining room which was crowded with young couples on dates, all of whom, according to Perper, were struggling through the flirtation sequence. Then, for a break, Perper and Frasier would flirt with each other. In the middle of my dinner, they located some action.

19   The couple at the table directly in front of us were engaging, Perper said heatedly, in "synchronization of drink-stirring behavior." This meant they'd stirred their drinks at the same time, and it didn't impress me. I continued to work on my filet of sole when Perper and Frasier gossiped about the couple.

20   "They're clasping their hands in unison."

21   "They're taking a drink. It's hard to see who's leading there."

22   "When you're really attracted to someone, you just seem to come towards each other at the same time, don't you?"

23   I thought something must actually be happening at that table. When I looked, a fluttering movement of the woman's right hand caught my attention. Almost at the same moment, the man made the same gesture with his right hand. Then the heel of his right hand went thoughtfully to his chin, and the heel of her right hand went to her chin, too. Next, he pulled his right

earlobe. She pulled her right earlobe. Their gestures were light and graceful. She clasped both hands under her lower lip, and so did he. Both of them sipped from their drinks, causing Perper and Frasier to chortle. The lifting of glasses was apparently a well-known chorus in the ongoing dance of hands at the table. I felt like a voyeur.

24   No such reverence for privacy inhibited the gleeful Perper. "I'm waiting for the first touch," he said confidentially. "They have to get the ketchup out of the way, and then the drinks, so they can touch by accident."

25   To contemplate manifestations of the unconscious in people I'd never met was an unsettling experience. I thought the sheer amount of energy being concentrated on this couple would cause them to turn around and glare back at us. I looked away from them to find that Perper was in sync with Frasier. The two of them smiled, forearms on the table, right hands grasping left elbows. They didn't know what they were doing. "Sometimes I think this is more fun than sex," Frasier said.

26   That night none of us was to reach a climax. The unfortunate couple couldn't negotiate their next escalation point. When Perper said it was time for them to touch, they didn't. The woman caressed her glass (a "touch invitation"), and the man mistook the signal and lifted his glass to drink ("de-escalation"). The woman dropped her hands to her lap, giving up, and after that they gestured to each other in nervous jabs. They had lost the beat. "Dummy," Perper said in a small pained voice as if he were the one who'd been de-escalated. "She made overtures, he did not respond, and he should have. It has an unhappy ending."

27   "Don't jump to conclusions," Frasier told him, "just relax." But the couple ate their dinner, paid their check, and left without ever synchronizing their body movements again.

28   By this time, the men at the bar were three-deep, watching the Yankees game. Two women in jeans sat on the jukebox. "The more I think about that, the more I think his inability to respond was absolutely classic," Perper said to Frasier.

29   "He got more and more uncomfortable," Frasier agreed. A man at the bar asked the two women to get off the jukebox. They stood by his side while he made his selections, but he didn't talk to them. He wore a T-shirt with a drawing of a molecule on it and the name of the male sex hormone, "testosterone."

30   Perper is writing a book about his findings. He says he thinks everyone should be "comfortable with their biology," and I hope he helps people to take it easy when they flirt. As for me, now that I've seen synchronization I can hardly gesture across a dinner table without checking to see what my partner is doing. I'm not sure all humans were meant to have their consciousness raised.

EXAMINING READING SELECTION 27

Checking Your Vocabulary

Directions: Using context, word parts, or a dictionary if necessary, circle the letter of the meaning for each word as it is used in the reading.

1. languorous (paragraph 9)
   a. dreamy
   b. angry
   c. suspicious
   d. mild

2. synchronization (paragraph 10)
   a. making compatible decisions
   b. working out problems
   c. discovering mutual attraction
   d. working in unison

3. ambivalence (paragraph 14)
   a. multipurpose
   b. mixed feelings
   c. similar feelings
   d. singular purpose

4. mimic (paragraph 15)
   a. insult
   b. disturb
   c. imitate
   d. influence

5. nondescript (paragraph 16)
   a. extremely fashionable
   b. without obvious care
   c. lacking distinctive characteristics
   d. having self-important features

Checking Your Comprehension

Directions: Circle the letter of the best answer.

6. The main idea of this article could be stated as follows:
   a. Men generally prefer women to de-escalate during the flirtation process.
   b. Flirtation is composed of several distinct steps of which most people are not conscious.
   c. In all flirtation situations it is the woman who begins the conversation.
   d. Most people are highly skilled in the flirtation process and practice it at bars.

7. The so-called "new men" would prefer to
   a. have an equal relationship with a woman.
   b. have women be demure.
   c. hide their feelings.
   d. make women inferior to them.

8. During the scene that took place at The Mad Hatter of Second Avenue, the couple being observed had to move the ketchup and the drinks before moving on in the flirtation process because
   a. these items were a barrier to his de-escalation.
   b. she felt intimidated by having a barrier between them.
   c. these items were a barrier to touching accidentally.
   d. the author could not observe them with these obstructions.

9. Men often found themselves in the middle of a flirtation without even knowing it because
   a. women were ignorant of this type of behavior.
   b. men were ignorant of this type of behavior.
   c. women had better opening lines and caught the men off guard.
   d. men did not usually go to bars to flirt.

10. The four parts of flirtation behavior are
    a. approach, swivel, synchronization, touch.
    b. approach, synchronization, swivel, touch.
    c. approach, touch, swivel, synchronization.
    d. approach, swivel, touch, synchronization.

11. The article is organized using
    a. cause and effect arrangement.
    b. spatial arrangement.
    c. chronological arrangement.
    d. comparison and contrast arrangement.

Thinking Critically

12. In the case of the couple being observed at The Mad Hatter, the flirtation was ended due to the fault of the
    a. observers.
    b. bartender.
    c. woman.
    d. man.

13. Perper ignored his sister's advice because he
    a. needed to prove his discovery scientifically.
    b. believed she was wrong.
    c. thought it would be fun to go to bars himself.
    d. needed to spend the grant money.

14. Judging by the author's experience in singles bars, you can conclude that
    a. there are a great many examples of flirtation to be viewed there.
    b. not as much flirtation goes on there as many people think.
    c. men are really experts at flirtation.
    d. women are very clumsy and inept flirters.

15. When the author refers to Perper as "a man
    in an invisible lab coat," she means that
    a. his coat really was invisible.
    b. he wore a coat of clear plastic.
    c. he was being a scientist but nobody knew
       it.
    d. his clothes were nondescript.

Questions for Discussion

1. Does the four-part flirtation sequence accurately describe what you personally have
   observed? Why?

2. Why do you think men are unable to
   respond to flirting as well as women?

3. In what situations, other than flirtation, do
   you think synchronization might occur?

Selection 27:			2528 words
Finishing Time:	___	___	___
	HR.	MIN.	SEC.
Starting Time:	___	___	___
	HR.	MIN.	SEC.
Reading Time:		___	___
		MIN.	SEC.
WPM Score:		___	
Comprehension Score:		___	%

READING SELECTION 28

MASS COMMUNICATION

THE FUNCTIONS AND EFFECTS OF MUSIC
Samuel L. Becker
From *Discovering Mass Communication*

*This excerpt from a mass communication textbook
explores the uses of music. Read the excerpt to answer
these questions.*

1. What are the political uses of music?
*2. What other functions of music does the excerpt
   discuss?*

— · —

1   You are well aware of the fact that books,
newspapers, magazines, motion pictures, radio,
and television have been used for persuasive purposes: to sell beer and soap, ideas and political
candidates; to bring about social change or to
quell a revolution. Few of us think about music
or recordings being used for these purposes, but
they are and have been for a long time.

2   Every war has had its songs that whipped up
patriotic fervor or, in the case of the Vietnam
War, that encouraged protest against it. Some
titles of records popular in this country during
World War II suggest the extent of the mobiliza-
tion of the recording industry for the war effort:
"Remember Pearl Harbor," "Have to Slap That
Dirty Little Jap," "There's a Star Spangled Banner
Waving Somewhere," "Any Bonds Today," and
"'Round and 'Round Hitler's Grave."

3   The anti-Vietnam protests of the sixties and early seventies brought forth quite another kind of song. One was "Big Muddy," about a group of soldiers blindly following their commanding officer into a river where many were drowned. Those who sang and heard the song knew that the "Big Muddy" referred to Vietnam and the commander to President Lyndon Johnson, and their anti-war passions were intensified. "Where Have All the Flowers Gone," "The Times, They Are A-Changin'," and "Give Peace a Chance" were other popular songs whose recordings were widely played and used to build resistance to the war.

4   Music is used not only to add persuasive bits of information for the messages in our heads about war. Persuasive music plays an important role in peacetime also. "We Shall Overcome" was a tremendously important force in the civil rights movement, just as the folk songs of Joan Baez, Pete Seeger, and Woody Guthrie have been important to the peace movement. In recent times, music has been used to raise money as well as consciousness for various causes. The Live Aid, Farm Aid, Band Aid, and U.S.A. for Africa concerts and recording sessions raised funds for such causes as famine relief in Africa and destitute American farmers.

5   Somewhat further back in this country's history, the radical left adopted many old Negro spirituals to communicate its message effectively. "We Shall Not Be Moved," for example, was adopted as the official song of the radical Southern Tenant Farmers Union in the 1930s. In the 1930s also, "Gimme That Old Time Religion" was transformed into "Gimme That New Communist Spirit." That sort of adaptation of songs—giving them new lyrics—has been a favorite tactic of many groups who want to use music for persuasive purposes. The idea is to take a song that people like or that has particular meaning or emotional association for them and use it with new words, hoping that some of the liking, meaning, or emotional associations will transfer to the new ideas being communicated. And it often works.

Threats of Censorship

6   Such political uses of music have never caused much controversy in this country. There has been some pressure at times to keep certain anti-war songs or songs associated with the radical left off the air, but this pressure has been neither strong nor persistent. Far more pressure and controversy has been aroused by the lyrics of some of the popular songs of the last twenty or thirty years. Many critics have charged that certain rock-and-roll songs encourage sexual promiscuity and the use of drugs. Rightly or wrongly, the dress and antics of some of the rock music stars, both on and off the stage, reinforce these beliefs. As a result, a number of community and national groups have applied pressure on stations to keep these songs and performers off the air. These charges also stimulated investigations by the Federal Communications Commission, the regulatory agency charged with overseeing broadcast practices. The FCC has taken the position, unpopular with many broadcasters, that the station licensee has the same public service responsibility in selecting and rejecting music to be played on the station as it has in selecting and rejecting any other content of the station. The FCC position is that the station should exercise the same supervision of what is sung on the station as of what is said. In a general sense, this is a reasonable position and the only one the FCC could take, given present law. A problem arises with the interpretation of this injunction, however. Does it mean a station should permit no language or ideas in a song that it would not permit on the news or in a sports program? Or does it mean the station should recognize that different forms of communication or entertainment, or programs designed for different kinds

of audiences, should have different standards concerning language and ideas? This issue is still far from settled.

7   Having been largely unsuccessful in keeping sexually suggestive songs or songs that seem to be promoting drug use off the air, some parents' groups in recent years have been attempting to force companies to label their recordings in the same way film companies now label motion pictures. The assumption is that such labels will provide parents with information they need to control the kinds of music to which their young children are exposed. One of the major pressure groups involved in this attempt is the Parents Music Resource Center based in Washington, D.C. The leaders in this group include the wives of some powerful congressmen and other government officials, so it is taken seriously by leaders in the music industry. The concern of many people in the music business, though, is that the labeling being advocated could be just a first step toward other forms of control or censorship.

The Impact of Recordings on Our Perceptions

8   Whatever the direct effects of musical recordings on our attitudes and behaviors, they are certainly an ever-present and important part of our communication environment, and they contribute to the realities in our heads. No one who listened to popular music during the '80s could escape the perception that drugs were a major factor in the lives of many people. Popular music of the early '70s contributed to the belief that most people opposed the war in Vietnam. These messages, sneaking into consciousness from the background music around us, formed an important part of our communication mosaics, just as the messages in today's music form an important part of our present communication mosaics.

The Role of Music in Identification and Rebellion

9   Popular music has two other major functions or effects. It provides each generation of young people a common and cherished experience. Years later, the sound of that music can bring strangers together and stimulate memories of that earlier era. Vivid evidence of the meaningfulness of such experiences can be seen by watching the tourists who are attracted to Graceland, Elvis Presley's former home and now the site of his grave in Memphis. A common sight there is the middle-aged married couple bringing their children to see and, they hope, to feel some of the special magic Presley created for them during their courtship and early married years.

10   Another major function popular music serves is the provision of a relatively harmless source of rebellion for the young. Each generation of young has its own music, almost invariably unappreciated by parents, just as parents' favorite music was unappreciated by their parents. This music is important in part because older people do not like it, and in part because demonstrating one's love of it is part of the ritual of affiliation with peers.

11   One author has suggested that popular music also serves a "rite of passage" function for young girls. The teenage singing idols may serve as nonthreatening substitutes for actual boys until boys' maturation catches up with that of girls and some semblance of easy boy-girl relationships can be established.

Writing about Reading Selection 28*

Checking Your Vocabulary

Directions: Complete each of the following items; refer to a dictionary if necessary.

1. Discuss the connotative meanings of the word *music*. (paragraph 1)

2. Define each of the following words:
   a. destitute (paragraph 4)

   b. tactic (paragraph 5)

   c. vivid (paragraph 9)

   d. affiliation (paragraph 10)

   e. semblance (paragraph 11)

3. Define the word *injunction* (paragraph 6) and underline the word or phrase that provides a context clue for its meaning.

4. Define the word *era* (paragraph 9) and underline the word or phrase that provides a context clue for its meaning.

5. Determine the meanings of the following words by using word parts:

a. mobilization (paragraph 2)

b. anti-Vietnam (paragraph 3)

c. regulatory (paragraph 6)

d. licensee (paragraph 6)

e. suggestive (paragraph 7)

Checking Your Comprehension

6. How was music used during World War II? During the Vietnam War?

7. Describe peacetime uses of music.

* Multiple-choice questions are contained in Part 6 (page 594).

8. To what do critics object in current rock-and-roll songs?

_____

_____

_____

9. List the major effects and functions of music.

_____

_____

_____

Thinking Critically

10. Identify the basic issues in the FCC regulatory position.

_____

_____

_____

_____

11. What problems do you foresee in the development of record labeling plans?

_____

_____

_____

12. How does music function as a form of rebellion?

_____

_____

_____

_____

_____

13. What types of evidence does the author use to support his contentions?

_____

_____

_____

Questions for Discussion

1. Adaptation of popular or favorite songs is a persuasive tactic. Where is this technique used today? Cite several examples. (Hint: advertising commercials)

2. If music shapes our perceptions and attitudes, should we be forced to listen to music in public places such as restaurants and shopping malls?

3. Does music have other effects that are not included in this article?

Selection 28:		1291 words
Finishing Time:		
	HR. MIN. SEC.	
Starting Time:		
	HR. MIN. SEC.	
Reading Time:		
	MIN. SEC.	
WPM Score:		
Comprehension Score:		%

GO ELECTRONIC

For additional readings, exercises, and Internet activities, visit this book's Web site at:

http://www.ablongman.com/mcwhorter

For even more activities, visit the Longman English pages at:

http://www.ablongman.com/englishpages

If you need a user name and password, please see your instructor.

Take a Road Trip to Indianapolis Speedway
Be sure to visit the Reading Rate module on your Reading Road Trip CD-ROM for multimedia tutorials, exercises, and tests.

PART 5
Academic Scenario

The following scenario is designed to assess your ability to use and apply the skills taught in this unit.

THE SITUATION

This semester you are working as a tutor for psychology in the Academic Skills Center. One of the students you are tutoring complains that he must spend too much time reading his assignments. On questioning him further, you learn that he reads all information the same way: He uses the same technique on everything and reads all materials slowly. When you tell him that you vary your technique and speed to suit what you are reading and why you are reading it, he asks you if you can help him change his approach.

After consulting with your supervisor, you ask the student to bring samples of the reading he must do. The student brings the following:

1. his psychology textbook, on which his instructor bases multiple choice exams.

2. a sample of the additional readings that are on reserve in the library. The instructor requires students to be familiar with important ideas in each reading in preparation for a class discussion.

3. a research article from the *Journal of Psychology* that describes an experiment conducted to measure aggressive tendencies of young children. The instructor has asked students to read it critically and write a summary of the article.

THE TASK

Make a list of strategies and advice you would give the student that would help him read *each* of the materials effectively and efficiently. Be specific. Suggest the level of comprehension he needs and suggest reading techniques that would help him read at an appropriate speed. Also, suggest what the student should do before, during, and after reading, if anything, to help him achieve his purpose for reading. Describe each technique or strategy that you suggest. You may include any technique you have learned so far (you need not limit yourself to techniques taught in Part Five).

Reading Selection 2 "Talking a Stranger Through the Night"

Checking Your Vocabulary

Directions: Using context, word parts, or a dictionary if necessary, circle the letter of the meaning for each word as it is used in the reading.

1. empathetic (paragraph 2)
   a. compassionate
   b. humanizing
   c. impressive
   d. warm

2. succession (paragraph 3)
   a. challenge
   b. extent
   c. confusion
   d. sequence

3. railed (paragraph 3)
   a. condemned at length
   b. argued about
   c. made fun of
   d. blamed

4. imminent (paragraph 5)
   a. frightening
   b. dangerous
   c. about to happen
   d. complicated

5. dictum (paragraph 7)
   a. cue
   b. rule
   c. message
   d. opportunity

Checking Your Comprehension

Directions: Circle the letter of the best answer.

6. This article is primarily about
   a. how to work a crisis line.
   b. the way the author helped someone and was helped in return.
   c. why hotline volunteers need training.
   d. the downside to working with the public.

7. Why was Sandy so upset?
   a. She had a life full of tragedy and pain.
   b. She lacks religious faith.
   c. Her family did not trust her.
   d. Someone she knew had committed suicide.

8. According to the reading, some people who call Help Line
   a. lie to the volunteer.
   b. want to become phone volunteers.
   c. are repeat callers.
   d. are not interested in what the volunteer has to say.

9. The author was trained to
   a. say whatever the caller wants to hear.
   b. recommend a good psychiatrist, if necessary.
   c. trace phone calls.
   d. listen sympathetically but not to give advice.

10. How did the author help Sandy?
    a. She stayed on the phone for two hours.
    b. She agreed that she had numerous problems.
    c. She consulted her supervisor.
    d. She encouraged her to remember pleasant things about life.

11. How did the author feel after Sandy's call?
    a. pleased that Sandy wanted to talk to her again.
    b. satisfied that she had helped someone.
    c. relieved that Sandy decided to refocus her life and make new friends.
    d. happy to get off the phone.

Thinking Critically

12. The author wrote the article to
    a. emphasize the value helping others.
    b. demonstrate the need for more help lines.
    c. express the joy of life.
    d. reveal the tragedy of suicide.

13. The author supports her ideas on volunteering by
    a. providing statistics.
    b. describing personal experience.
    c. citing research studies.
    d. interviewing Help Line supervisors.

14. From the reading, you can infer that the author
    a. lives alone.
    b. has never experienced the death of a loved one.
    c. leads a very busy and thrilling life.
    d. is a well-to-do New York City resident with a rewarding career.

15. This reading is organized
    a. chronologically, in the order in which events occurred.
    b. using cause-and-effect relationships.
    c. from most to least important ideas.
    d. Spatially, according to where events occurred.

Reading Selection 4 "Just Walk On By: A Black Man Ponders His Power to Alter Public Space"

Checking Your Vocabulary

Directions: Using context, word parts, or a dictionary if necessary, circle the letter of the meaning for each word as it is used in the reading.

1. menacingly (paragraph 1)
   a. strikingly
   b. threateningly
   c. obviously
   d. seriously

2. elicit (paragraph 3)
   a. create
   b. bring out
   c. disturb
   d. draw back

3. avid (paragraph 4)
   a. careful
   b. frightened
   c. fearful
   d. enthusiastic

4. retrospect (paragraph 7)
   a. thinking about the future
   b. thinking about the past
   c. regretting an action or event
   d. dwelling on an action or event

5. episodes (paragraph 9)
   a. incidents
   b. periods
   c. causes
   d. traumas

Checking Your Comprehension

Directions: Circle the letter of the best answer.

6. Which of the following statements best describes the reading?
    a. It is an essay about why white women fear black men.
    b. It is a description of racial tensions in large cities.
    c. It is an argument for greater racial equality.
    d. It is a personal account of a black man's experiences and feelings about the way he is perceived in public places.

7. The author may have been unaware of public reactions to him before age 22 because
    a. he was a member of a gang.
    b. he lived in a small town in Pennsylvania.
    c. he wasn't noticeable among criminals and street gangs.
    d. he was shy and withdrawn.

8. The "mugging literature" the author cites is
    a. writings of other authors about fear of black males.
    b. crime statistics about muggers.
    c. essays that describe muggers and their intentions.
    d. literature describing the role of black men in society.

9. The author regards the attitude that men must be powerful and valiant as
    a. a personal expression.
    b. nonsense.
    c. having historical justification.
    d. legitimate.

10. The "hunch posture" as described by the author, is a(n)
    a. protective, defensive posture.
    b. disrespectful gesture.
    c. aggressive movement.
    d. signal that assistance is needed.

11. Which of the following best defines the word *alienation* as used in paragraph 6?
    a. problems
    b. feeling of separation or aversion
    c. anger or fear
    d. repulsiveness

Thinking Critically

12. The author's primary purpose in writing the article is to
    a. persuade people to alter their public behavior toward blacks.
    b. describe his feelings about reactions to him in public space.
    c. familiarize the reader with problems of large cities.
    d. argue that public space should not be altered.

13. The author whistles Vivaldi to
    a. state his music preferences.
    b. suggest that he is unlike typical muggers.
    c. indicate his level of musical expertise.
    d. announce that he is unafraid.

14. Which of the following best describes the author's attitude about women's fear of black men?
    a. The author thinks their fear is unfounded.
    b. The author regards their fear as exaggerated, as a hallucination.
    c. The author finds their fear understandable but still has difficulty when it is applied to him.
    d. The author is angry and feels he is not understood.

15. To communicate his ideas, the author relies most heavily on
    a. logical reasoning.
    b. statistics and "mugging literature."
    c. personal experience.
    d. fact.

Reading Selection 6 "Why the Sky Is Blue, Sunsets Are Red, and Clouds Are White"

Checking Your Vocabulary

Directions: Using context, word parts, or a dictionary if necessary, circle the letter of the meaning for each word as it is used in the reading.

1. redirect (paragraph 1)
   a. send in a different direction
   b. remove from the atmosphere
   c. eliminate from view
   d. change in composition

2. emitted (paragraph 5)
   a. eliminated
   b. destroyed
   c. taken in
   d. sent out

3. transmitted (paragraph 6)
   a. removed from view
   b. repeatedly changed
   c. sent across a distance
   d. focused and strengthened

4. progressively (paragraph 7)
   a. quickly
   b. decreasingly
   c. obviously
   d. gradually

5. instensity (paragraph 10)
   a. concentration
   b. dimness
   c. scattering
   d. movement

Checking Your Comprehension

Directions: Circle the letter of the best answer.

6. This reading is primarily about
   a. light.
   b. atoms.
   c. sound.
   d. vibrations.

7. The main point of the reading is that
   a. ultraviolet light is absorbed by ozone gas.
   b. a certain frequency of sound causes a similar frequency of sound to vibrate.
   c. the way in which light responds under various conditions affects several natural phenomena.
   d. the color blue scatters with greater frequency than any other color.

8. The blue of the sky varies in color because of
   a. water vapor.
   b. intensity of sunlight.
   c. low-level haze.
   d. high-frequency light.

9. The author uses the ringing of bells to
   a. demonstrate how sound scatters.
   b. explain how light scatters.
   c. explain what particles look like.
   d. show how frequencies change.

10. This textbook excerpt focuses primarily on
    a. order and sequence.
    b. causes and effects.
    c. similarities and differences.
    d. classification and division.

11. The word *progresses* (paragraph 7) as used in the reading means
    a. increases suddenly.
    b. moves forward.
    c. shows improvement.
    d. becomes brighter.

Thinking Critically

12. Which of the following has the lowest frequency?
    a. blue light
    b. yellow light
    c. red light
    d. white light

13. If molecules in the sky scattered low-frequency light instead of high-frequency light, how would sunsets appear?
    a. red
    b. blue
    c. green
    d. yellow

14. Based on information in the reading, which of the following do you think the author would support?
    a. policies restricting research in outer space
    b. laws restricting seeding clouds to control weather
    c. laws limiting automobile pollution
    d. further research on the effects of color

15. Distant mountains appear bluish because
    a. the atmosphere between us and the mountains is blue.
    b. light is reflected from the mountains.
    c. it frequently rains on the mountaintops.
    d. sunlight on the mountains is absorbed.

Reading Selection 8 "Privacy on the Web"

Checking Your Vocabulary

Directions: Using context, word parts, or a dictionary if necessary, circle the letter of the meaning for each word as it is used in the reading.

1. regional (paragraph 1)
    a. large in population size
    b. covering a large geographical area
    c. complete and comprehensive
    d. modern and up-to-date

2. relative (paragraph 3)
    a. public
    b. exclusive
    c. tremendous
    d. comparative

3. archive (paragraph 3)
    a. declaration of intent
    b. arrangement of messages
    c. collection of records
    d. group of listservs

4. digital (paragraph 4)
    a. written down
    b. factual
    c. computerized
    d. told to someone

5. surreptitiously (paragraph 6)
    a. ethically
    b. legally
    c. publicly
    d. secretly

Checking Your Comprehension

Directions: Circle the letter of the best answer.

6. This selection is primarily concerned with
    a. privacy.
    b. selling information.
    c. cookies.
    d. regulations.

7. Which statement best expresses the main point of the selection?
    a. Legal restrictions have been placed on Internet research.
    b. Many people are not concerned about Internet privacy.
    c. The Web has reduced computer users' privacy.
    d. The Web needs some sort of protection against companies seeking consumer information.

8. The main idea in paragraph 5 deals with the issue of
    a. who uses the Internet.
    b. whether the benefits of the Internet outweigh its disadvantages.
    c. whether privacy is truly an issue when it comes to the Internet.
    d. how privacy is actually defined.

9. According to the author
    a. most people are not upset about the idea of lack of privacy on the Internet.
    b. what is thought to be private information on the Web may, in the future, become available to others.
    c. any information that is on the Internet has always been available elsewhere.
    d. only certain computers contain cookies.

10. In reference to the issue of degrees of privacy on the Internet, the author says that
    a. the goal of privacy has already been reached.
    b. privacy of any kind is not a reasonable goal.
    c. absolute privacy is a reasonable goal.
    d. relative privacy is a reasonable goal.

11. To develop her ideas, the author
    a. gives examples.
    b. classifies information.
    c. compares and contrasts.
    d. organizes her material in a sequential fashion.

Thinking Critically

12. It is reasonable to conclude that people probably do *not* use microfiche as much as before because
    a. the Internet contains most information that would be on microfiche.
    b. libraries don't use microfiche anymore.
    c. books are better for storing information than microfiche.
    d. microfiche has been replaced by microfilm.

13. The author would most likely agree with which one of the following statements?
    a. There is no problem with Internet privacy.
    b. Web users should be informed when a cookie is placed on their hard drives.
    c. A watchdog agency should be established to regulate matters of Web privacy.
    d. Nothing should be placed on the Internet unless it is first screened for right-to-privacy violations.

14. One of the major purposes of a cookie is
    a. to record information people have stored on the Internet.
    b. to determine which Web sites most people visit out of curiosity.
    c. to allow the user to trace his own movements on the Internet.
    d. to create a record of a user's visit to a Web site.

15. The tone of this selection is
    a. argumentative.
    b. informative.
    c. persuasive.
    d. entertaining.

Reading Selection 10 "How Students Get Lost in Cyberspace"

Checking Your Vocabulary

Directions: Using context, word parts, or a dictionary if necessary, circle the letter of the meaning for each word as it is used in the reading.

1. superficial (paragraph 6)
    a. shallow
    b. illegal
    c. detailed
    d. descriptive

2. analogy (paragraph 14)
    a. explanation
    b. version
    c. comparison
    d. analysis

3. obsolete (paragraph 16)
   a. false
   b. inaccurate
   c. opinionated
   d. outdated

4. mainstay (paragraph 21)
   a. principle source
   b. topic of research
   c. best direction
   d. best location

5. expertise (paragraph 23)
   a. patience
   b. success
   c. skill
   d. opinion

Checking Your Comprehension

Directions: Circle the letter of the best answer.

6. According to the reading, the World Wide Web is useful for
   a. scholars.
   b. professors.
   c. students at universities.
   d. the average citizen.

7. The Internet is least useful for
   a. focusing information to make a point.
   b. finding information related to a topic.
   c. determining the reliability of sources.
   d. overcoming the limitations of your college library.

8. At what point did Adam Pasick find the information that he needed?
   a. when he first searched the Internet
   b. when he was guided by a reference librarian
   c. when he asked his professor for help
   d. when he decided to use paper journals not on the Internet

9. From the point of view of a professor, the problem with doing research on the World Wide Web is
   a. there is so much information available students don't research an issue thoroughly.
   b. students often plagiarize information from the Internet.
   c. students can't tell the reliable information on the Internet from the unreliable.
   d. students will become unaccustomed to using paper sources in the library when they need to.

10. Students can expect to find the least valuable information for research papers at a home page set up by
    a. an academic publication.
    b. an educational institution or foundation.
    c. an agency of the federal government.
    d. an individual interested in a particular issue.

11. In paragraph 6, the author states that the cost for information is "borne by universities." In this context, "borne" means
    a. created.
    b. paid.
    c. determined.
    d. increased.

Thinking Critically

12. When beginning a research project, you should first
    a. select the most efficient search engine.
    b. browse the Web for useful information.
    c. go directly to a home page.
    d. seek the assistance of a reference librarian.

13. The problem with online subscriptions is that they are
    a. wasteful since the journals are available in paper also.
    b. not reliable sources of information.
    c. too difficult to locate on the Web.
    d. too expensive for many colleges.

14. One form of assistance that the Web will probably never provide in the future is
    a. a wide variety of search engines.
    b. screening for the reliability of information.
    c. a wide range of scholarly journals.
    d. an efficient method to search for information.

15. The best reason for including both Internet and paper sources in a major research paper is to
    a. lend it the variety it needs.
    b. save time doing the research.
    c. produce a more thorough paper.
    d. add interest to it.

Reading Selection 12 "Alternative Drug Testing Update"

Checking Your Vocabulary

Directions: Using context, word parts, or a dictionary if necessary, circle the letter of the meaning for each word as it is used in the reading.

1. viable (paragraph 1)
   a. living
   b. feasible
   c. impractical
   d. advisable

2. invasive (paragraph 5)
   a. intrusive
   b. trespassing
   c. dangerous
   d. popular

3. adulteration (paragraph 6)
   a. corruption, making impure
   b. reversal
   c. making unrecognizable
   d. attacking

4. expedite (paragraph 7)
   a. emerge
   b. put an end to
   c. explain
   d. speed up

5. consensus (paragraph 13)
   a. vote
   b. account
   c. general agreement
   d. coincidence

Checking Your Comprehension

Directions: Circle the letter of the best answer.

6. This article is primarily about the
   a. pros and cons of drug testing.
   b. problems with urine testing.
   c. drawbacks of oral fluid testing.
   d. reasons oral fluid testing has become more popular.

7. Employers could not use the oral test before 2000 because the test
   a. returned too many false positive results.
   b. was not yet invented.
   c. cost too much.
   d. was not commercially available.

8. Which of the following is *not* one of the qualities ranked by employers using oral testing?
   a. price.
   b. quality.
   c. turnaround.
   d. ease of collection.

9. What is one advantage of the oral test over the urine test?
   a. It is cost effective.
   b. Very recent drug usage can be detected.
   c. Employees can take the test at home.
   d. No one objects to oral testing.

10. Paragraph 4 is primarily about
   a. alternatives to oral drug testing.
   b. methodology of oral drug testing.
   c. problems created by oral drug testing.
   d. advantages of oral drug testing.

11. The author's purpose for writing this article is to
   a. change drug testing policy.
   b. convince employers to start oral fluid testing programs.
   c. describe oral fluid drug testing.
   d. sell a product.

Thinking Critically

12. The intended audience for the article is
   a. members of the Drug Testing Advisory Board.
   b. employees who are about to undergo a drug test.
   c. those who are directly engaged in carrying out drug testing, such as human resources managers.
   d. employers who need to explain drug testing procedures to their new employees.

13. The author concludes that oral fluid testing
   a. will become more popular than urine testing.
   b. is still regarded with skepticism.
   c. needs more study.
   d. is a welcome newcomer in the list of drug test choices.

14 Which does the author *not* use to support his ideas?
   a. statistics
   b. firsthand experience
   c. survey results
   d. expert opinion

15. Overall, the article's style is
   a. light and informal.
   b. critical and subjective.
   c. angry and bitter.
   d. serious and informative.

Reading Selection 14 "Are We Alone in the Universe?"

Checking Your Vocabulary

Directions: Using context, word parts, or a dictionary if necessary, circle the letter of the meaning for each word as it is used in the reading.

1. conducive (paragraph 2)
   a. hostile
   b. difficult
   c. favorable
   d. charming

2. uninhabitable (paragraph 3)
   a. not livable
   b. not realistic
   c. under water
   d. unimportant

3. lethal (paragraph 3)
   a. impossible
   b. deadly
   c. premature
   d. feasible

4. diversity (paragraph 3)
   a. confusion
   b. abundance
   c. seriousness
   d. variety

5. resemblance (paragraph 8)
   a. likeness
   b. acceptance
   c. construction
   d. relevance

Checking Your Comprehension

Directions: Circle the letter of the best answer.

6. The selection focuses on which of the following questions?
   a. Did meteorites start life on our planet?
   b. Will the loss of ozone mean the end of life on Earth?
   c. Will man be able to colonize the solar system?
   d. Is there life on other planets?

7. The central thesis of this reading is that
   a. the exploration of other planets is worthwhile.
   b. there is strong evidence that meteorites seeded life on Earth.
   c. it is possible that life exists on other planets.
   d. ozone depletion will mean the end of life on our planet.

8. The main idea of paragraph 7 is that
   a. life might have existed on Mars billions of years ago.
   b. Mars currently has inhospitable conditions for life.
   c. the Viking landers proved beyond doubt that there is no life on Mars.
   d. Mars is a good place to begin to search for life outside the solar system.

9 "Nanobacteria" (paragraph 8) are bacteria that
   a. exist only in meteorites.
   b. are about 100 times smaller than normal bacteria.
   c. have been created artificially by man.
   d. are used by man as miniature robots.

10. According to this selection life has been found on our planet
    a. in crude oil pumped from beneath the ocean floor.
    b. deep inside rocks in the deserts of Saudi Arabia.
    c. in underwater volcanic vents and in hot springs at temperatures up to 125 degrees Celsius.
    d. inside volcanoes formed billions of years ago.

11. The writer supports his thesis by
    a. gathering a consensus from all available scientists.
    b. using a negative argument (asking why something would *not* occur).
    c. conducting his own experiments on the subject.
    d. reporting data and evidence to support it.

Thinking Critically

12. The writer's argument is based on the assumption that life elsewhere in the universe will
    a. be older than life on Earth.
    b. have the same requirements as on Earth.
    c. be newer than life on Earth.
    d. be completely different from life on Earth.

13. To show that life may once have existed on Mars the writer refers mainly to
    a. ozone levels.
    b. a meteorite found in Antarctica.
    c. the results of the Viking missions.
    d. the greenhouse effect on Venus.

14. Which of the following statements expresses an opinion held by the writer rather than a fact?
    a. The Viking missions to Mars found no chemical signs of life.
    b. Newly discovered microscopic life does not require either sunlight, oxygen, or other organisms as food.
    c. Radio astronomers are likely to receive a signal from an extraterrestrial civilization.
    d. Billions of years ago, Mars had running water.

15. Which one of the following judgments is justified by the selection?
    a. There are a number of scientific discoveries that support the contention that life exists elsewhere in the universe.
    b. It is too difficult to infer that life exists elsewhere in the universe at this time due to a lack of scientific evidence.
    c. Life can exist only under highly optimal conditions, and therefore the possibility of life elsewhere is remote.
    d. Life can exist under such inhospitable conditions that it assures that life is in abundance in the universe.

Reading Selection 16 "The Value of Pet Ownership"

Checking Your Vocabulary

Directions: Using context, word parts, or a dictionary if necessary, circle the letter of the meaning for each word as it is used in the reading.

1. mechanism (paragraph 1)
   a. part
   b. means
   c. mechanical device
   d. place

2. alleviate (paragraph 2)
   a. analyze
   b. increase
   c. lessen
   d. pinpoint

3. longevity (paragraph 2)
   a. peace of mind
   b. productivity
   c. happiness
   d. length of life

4. mobility (paragraph 3)
   a. awareness
   b. handicap
   c. movement
   d. functions

5. therapeutic (paragraph 4)
   a. having healing power
   b. demonstrating knowledge
   c. giving exercise
   d. showing expertise

Checking Your Comprehension

Directions: Circle the letter of the best answer.

6. This reading focuses primarily on
   a. how pets make good companions.
   b. the many ways in which pets are beneficial.
   c. research on pet therapy.
   d. how pets help the elderly.

7. The central point the author makes throughout this reading is that animals
   a. can provide many different advantages to many people in society.
   b. are more useful to the elderly than to anyone else.
   c. can be used in therapeutic situations.
   d. should be utilized as companions to people with a handicapping condition.

8. Paragraph 1 illustrates which one of the following ideas?
   a. Children are always kind to animals.
   b. Children instinctively know how to properly care for their pets.
   c. Parents should buy their children at least one pet.
   d. Parents can use pets as a means to teach their children.

9. How are prison inmates helped by dogs?
   a. The dogs assist prison guards and wardens.
   b. Programs involving dogs help inmates to improve their behavior and outlook.
   c. The dogs provide the inmates with unconditional love which they have never had.
   d. Working with the dogs helps the inmates to feel in control of their lives.

10. Pets help people in rehabilitation centers by
    a. helping them to gain perspective on their situation.
    b. calming them down.
    c. providing motivation for patients to improve.
    d. offering a discussion.

11. To develop his idea about how pets can be helpful in mental and emotional therapy, the author
    a. compares how different pets have been useful in this situation.
    b. discusses the details of emotional therapy and how it works.
    c. arranges his information in chronological order.
    d. lists different mental and emotional conditions in which animals have been helpful.

Thinking Critically

12. From the selection you can infer that the use of pets in correctional institutions is
    a. still at the experimental stage.
    b. opposed by most inmates.
    c. outlawed in some states.
    d. unrealistic for certain types of inmates.

13. The author mentions that pet owners generally have lower blood pressure than people who don't have pets to show that
    a. people with low blood pressure are usually good caretakers of pets.
    b. there is scientific evidence to suggest that pets are medically helpful to people.
    c. only healthy people make good pet owners.
    d. people with high blood pressure should not take care of pets.

14. The tone of this passage can best be described as
    a. amusing.
    b. argumentative.
    c. informative.
    d. biased.

15. Which of the following children would most likely benefit from pet ownership?
    a. a child who refuses to play with toys
    b. a child who sleepwalks
    c. a child whose mother recently died of cancer
    d. a child who fights with his older sister

Reading Selection 18 "Pangaea: The Supercontinent and the Effects of Its Breakup"

Checking Your Vocabulary

Directions: Using context, word parts, or a dictionary if necessary, circle the letter of the meaning for each word as it is used in the reading.

1. topographic (paragraph 1)
   a. zones around earthquakes
   b. regarding the surface of the land
   c. concerning ocean currents
   d. involving photography

2. millennia (paragraph 2)
   a. months
   b. decades
   c. ages
   d. example

3. potential (paragraph 6)
   a. possible
   b. active
   c. strong
   d. many

4. replicate (paragraph 6)
   a. copy
   b. control
   c. emphasize
   d. enhance

5. sedate (paragraph 8)
   a. ancient
   b. calm
   c. lethal
   d. unknown

Checking Your Comprehension

Directions: Circle the letter of the best answer.

6. This reading mainly deals with
   a. the formation of the Hawaiian Islands.
   b. plate tectonics theory.
   c. measuring earthquake intensity.
   d. volcanic eruptions.

7. The author's main point in this selection is to
   a. explain why earthquakes occur.
   b. differentiate the types of volcanoes.
   c. show that the major features of our planet are caused by the movement of the Earth's crust.
   d. describe the major land formations of our planet, past and present.

8. Paragraph 6 illustrates which one of these ideas?
   a. Earthquake prediction can be done months in advance with a high degree of accuracy.
   b. Computer models of earthquakes are close to being able to predict seismic events.
   c. By knowing the exact conditions along plate boundaries, earthquakes can be predicted.
   d. Earthquake prediction cannot be done at the present time with any accuracy.

9. The plate tectonics theory was first advanced by
   a. Albert Einstein.
   b. Alfred Wegener.
   c. Sir Isaac Newton.
   d. Charles F. Richter.

10. The Hawaiian Islands are an example of
    a. an earthquake epicenter.
    b. shield volcanoes.
    c. composite cone volcanoes.
    d. Pangaea.

11 In discussing the mantle and plate tectonics, the author arranges his information to show
    a. cause and effect.
    b. comparison and contrast.
    c. problem and solution.
    d. description and examples.

Thinking Critically

12 In this selection the writer refers to Pangaea to demonstrate how
   a. the breakup of the "supercontinent" is the cause of the formation of the Hawaiian Islands.
   b. Antarctica remains as the last piece of the "supercontinent."
   c. plate tectonics has shaped the Earth over the millennia.
   d. before the first earthquake, the Earth's crust did not move.

13. Which of the following statements expresses a true fact?
   a. Volcanic eruption will increase unless drastic action is taken.
   b. Earthquakes will be able to be predicted in the future.
   c. The Earth's continents and oceans are fixed in place for all time.
   d. The movement of tectonic plates causes earthquakes, volcanoes, and mountain formation.

14. Which of the following statements best supports the writer's assertion that earthquakes are due to tectonic plate movement.
   a. Thousands of earthquakes—movements of Earth's crust—occur every day where two plates meet.
   b. The place where Earth's crust actually moves is the focus of an earthquake.
   c. Most earthquakes are detectable only with a seismograph.
   d. Earthquake prediction is unreliable.

15. Excessive rain is to flooding as tectonic plate movement is to
   a. a seismograph.
   b. the mantle.
   c. earthquakes.
   d. continents.

Reading Selection 20 "Early Encounters with the Artist Within"

Checking Your Vocabulary

Directions: Using context, word parts, or a dictionary if necessary, circle the letter of the meaning for each word as it is used in the reading.

1. innately (paragraph 1)
   a. deep
   b. learned
   c. inborn
   d. universal

2. ominous (paragraph 7)
   a. specific and detailed
   b. broad and general
   c. new and unique
   d. negative and threatening

3. sustain (paragraph 8)
   a. recapture
   b. initiate
   c. maintain
   d. discourage

4. belittle (paragraph 10)
   a. admire
   b. treat as unimportant
   c. oppose
   d. praise the value of

5. stereotypical (paragraph 14)
   a. specific to an art form
   b. unusually striking
   c. conforming to a pattern
   d. free-flowing

Checking Your Comprehension

Directions: Circle the letter of the best answer.

6. The selection is primary concerned with
   a. adults viewing children's art.
   b. children's artistic expression.
   c. helping children understand art.
   d. learning to appreciate art.

7. The central thought of this selection is
   a. artistic endeavors of children can be destroyed by lack of interest or by undue criticism by adults.
   b. the best way to learn about art is from the inside.
   c. children use a universal visual language.
   d. young children often demonstrate an intuitive sense of composition and balanced design.

8. The main idea of paragraph 3 is that
   a. most children follow the same process of artistic growth.
   b. young children begin by creating realistic drawings.
   c. for young children, a sense of composition is intuitive.
   d. children should be encouraged to draw by age four.

9. When we first begin to draw, our artwork is
   a. structured.
   b. conceptual.
   c. intuitive.
   d. learned.

10. Children often lose their intuitive sense of composition when they
    a. don't practice enough.
    b. aren't given the proper crayons or paint.
    c. are given coloring books and workbooks.
    d. attempt drawing at too early an age.

11. The writer creates interest in his subject mainly by
    a. explaining techniques for teaching children to draw.
    b. giving historical notes and facts about children and art.
    c. providing research on how art affects children.
    d. discussing and showing examples of young children's drawings.

Thinking Critically

12. The author suggests that adults could benefit from
    a. studying children's art.
    b. changing their attitudes about art that they learned as children.
    c. studying the works of famous artists.
    d. using various art forms.

13. From this passage we can conclude that
    a. the pursuit of arts is attainable for only a few gifted people.
    b. the arts are a means for each of us to communicate our personally significant experiences.
    c. the arts are not as important in our development as is the ability to read.
    d. we cannot develop our ability in arts as an adult if we have not already attained it in our youth.

14. The writer thinks the fact that children learn to produce standard forms of art as they grow older is
    a. natural.
    b. necessary.
    c. unfortunate.
    d. appropriate.

15. The author's descriptions of young children's drawings supports the conclusion that
    a. the younger the children are the more standard their drawings are.
    b. the older the children are the more creative they can be.
    c. most parents encourage their children to follow standard rules when drawing.
    d. most children feel self-conscious when they begin to draw, but they soon outgrow this.

Reading Selection 22
"Out of Time"

Checking Your Vocabulary

Directions: Using context, word parts, or a dictionary if necessary, circle the letter of the meaning for each word as it is used in the reading.

1. remnants (paragraph 1)
   a. clothing pieces
   b. opportunities
   c. remaining parts
   d. destroyed materials

2. habitats (paragraph 6)
   a. dwelling places
   b. water resources
   c. identification labels
   d. native uses

3. impoverished (paragraph 7)
   a. incomprehensible
   b. very poor
   c. strongly independent
   d. very powerful

4. indigenous (paragraph 7)
   a. uncivilized
   b. native
   c. communal
   d. aggressive

5. allegedly (paragraph 15)
   a. knowingly
   b. deliberately
   c. occasionally
   d. supposedly

Checking Your Comprehension

Directions: Circle the letter of the best answer.

6. This reading primarily concerns
   a. technology and innovation.
   b. tribesmen and leaders.
   c. cultures and environments.
   d. a writer's experiences.

7. The main point of this reading is that
   a. native lands and civilizations are being destroyed and endangered.
   b. Indian tribes are losing their leadership.
   c. technology has improved the quality of life of native tribes.
   d. native tribes seek and desire change.

8. When the Yuguí Indians first saw white people, they thought they were
   a. warriors who wanted to fight.
   b. missionaries trying to help.
   c. spirits of dead ancestors.
   d. Indians from a lighter skinned tribe.

9. The elevator that carried the dorado upstream was environmentally harmful because
   a. it replaced valuable forests.
   b. the fish did not use it.
   c. there was no downstream elevator.
   d. its operation used valuable natural resources.

10. The Cofán tribe thought the sounds of helicopters were
    a. wild animals.
    b. spirits.
    c. ancestors.
    d. gifts.

11. As used in the reading, the term *peccaries* (paragraph 11) refers to
    a. a flower species.
    b. unknown tribes.
    c. insects.
    d. a type of animal.

Thinking Critically

12. The author supports his points about the destruction of native cultures and environments by
    a. describing statistical trends.
    b. making comparisons.
    c. recounting his travel experiences.
    d. quoting experts.

13. Based on information given in the reading, you can conclude that the author regards missionaries as
    a. helpful in locating remote tribes.
    b. initiating the destruction of a culture.
    c. the end result of global economics.
    d. necessary for the survival of religion.

14. The attitude of Moreira, the Guaraní shaman, toward the destruction of his village was
    a. resignation.
    b. anger.
    c. disbelief.
    d. sadness.

15. The shaman's warning, "What we do to the lives and lands of others may ultimately determine the fate of our own," means
    a. fate is culturally determined and not within our control.
    b. in a global environment, all events and changes are interrelated.
    c. ozone holes are a threat to the entire civilization.
    d. each culture should preserve its artifacts and traditions.

Reading Selection 24 "The Sandman Is Dead—Long Live the Sleep Deprived Zombie"

Checking Your Vocabulary

Directions: Using context, word parts, or a dictionary if necessary, circle the letter of the meaning for each word as it is used in the reading.

1. chronically (paragraph 1)
   a. continually
   b. typically
   c. uncommonly
   d. unusually

2. optimal (paragraph 6)
   a. unfortunate
   b. pleasing
   c. unlucky
   d. most favorable

3. quantifiable (paragraph 10)
   a. recognizable
   b. disputable
   c. measurable
   d. understandable

4. detrimentally (paragraph 10)
   a. harmfully
   b. obviously
   c. flawlessly
   d. observably

5. acknowledge (paragraph 15)
   a. determine
   b. recognize
   c. dispute
   d. evaluate

Checking Your Comprehension

Directions: Circle the letter of the best answer.

6. This selection is primarily concerned with
   a. myths about sleep.
   b. lack of sleep.
   c. patterns of sleep.
   d. sleep and safety.

7. Which of the following is the best alternative descriptive title for this selection?
   a. Why Americans Can't Sleep
   b. What to Do if You Wake Up Tired
   c. Sleep Deprivation in The Workplace: Effects and Solutions
   d. Loss of Productivity in American Businesses

8. Over the past century, Americans have reduced their amount of sleep by
   a. 5 percent.
   b. 10 percent.
   c. 20 percent.
   d. 30 percent.

9. One reason Americans sleep less is that
   a. they no longer value sleep.
   b. there is too much noise.
   c. they suffer from sleep disorders.
   d. their workloads have increased.

10. According to the author sleepiness and laziness are
    a. inversely related.
    b. different problems.
    c. observed in the same workers.
    d. caused by stress.

11. The main way the writer develops the thesis is by
    a. citing research and statistics.
    b. making contrasts.
    c. classifying sleep related problems.
    d. giving examples.

Thinking Critically

12. The purpose of the quotation by Cervantes is to
    a. emphasize the benefits of sleep.
    b. show that sleep deprivation has been a problem since the 1600s.
    c. make workers realize the effects of sleep deprivation.
    d. lend credibility by quoting an important person.

13. The overall tone of this selection is one of
    a. detachment.
    b. ambivalence.
    c. hopelessness.
    d. concern.

14. After stating that 40 percent of adults are affected by sleepiness, the author says, "remember, these are only the people who acknowledge that their productivity is lessened." The author includes this information to suggest that
    a. 60 percent of adults are unaffected.
    b. the actual number may be less than the 40 percent.
    c. there may be others who are affected but don't recognize it.
    d. there may be other unrecognized effects.

15. A person suffering sleep deprivation is likely to have particular difficulty
    a. watching television.
    b. cooking dinner.
    c. communicating with family.
    d. balancing a checkbook.

Reading Selection 26 "Stress Management: Personally Adjusting to Stress"

Checking Your Vocabulary

Directions: Using context, word parts, or a dictionary if necessary, circle the letter of the meaning for each word as it is used in the reading.

1. elements (paragraph 4)
   a. parts
   b. causes
   c. symptoms
   d. effects

2. induce (paragraph 5)
   a. eliminate
   b. bring about
   c. focus on
   d. enhance

3. simultaneously (paragraph 6)
   a. in sequence
   b. under opposing conditions
   c. in similar situations
   d. at the same time

4. affront (paragraph 10)
   a. opportunity
   b. event
   c. insult
   d. advantage

5. manipulating (paragraph 13)
   a. cleverly adjusting
   b. quickly reducing
   c. slowly eliminating
   d. carefully suggesting

Checking Your Comprehension

Directions: Circle the letter of the best answer.

6. The main point of this reading is that
   a. stress is an imbalance of internal and external demands.
   b. controlling physical reactions and thoughts are effective means of managing stress.
   c. relaxation is the key to successful stress management.
   d. stress management requires a problem-solving approach.

7. Controlling your thoughts always involves
   a. considering the situation from alternative viewpoints.
   b. visualizing yourself managing the stressful situation successfully.
   c. relaxation techniques to eliminate physical symptoms.
   d. a sense of being overwhelmed by the situation.

8. In the tension release method of relaxation, you should tense all your muscles together
   a. after tensing each muscle group separately.
   b. before tensing each muscle group separately.
   c. while thinking relaxing thoughts.
   d. only if you feel tension in each group.

9. Human response to stress is
   a. universal.
   b. variable according to sex.
   c. unchanging.
   d. individual.

10. Talking to ourselves is an effective means of managing stress because
    a. it takes our minds off the conflict.
    b. it releases tension.
    c. it is a means of directing our thoughts and feelings.
    d. it facilitates imaging.

11. Which of the following best defines the meaning of the word *reconstruct* as used in paragraph 13?
    a. refer back to
    b. re-create
    c. reestablish
    d. focus

Thinking Critically

12. The author's primary purpose in writing the selection is to
    a. explain the relationship between stress and conflict.
    b. instruct the reader in how to control stress.
    c. describe relaxation techniques.
    d. persuade the reader to reduce stress through successful management.

13. A basketball player who, before an important game, visualizes himself making every
jump shot in the game instead of missing
each as he did in the last game is using the
technique of
   a. relaxation.
   b. tension reduction.
   c. self-talk.
   d. imaging.

14. Which of the following statements included
in the reading most directly supports the
writer's view that stress is controllable?
   a. Things dim in importance when viewed
      in retrospect.
   b. Stress is an imbalance between outside
      demands and our capabilities to meet
      those demands.
   c. People respond differently to conflict,
      just as they respond differently to stress.
   d. Because your behavior and your emotions
      are controlled by the way you think, you
      must acquire skills to change those
      thoughts.

15. A student who, before taking her final exam
in biology, says to herself "I am just as smart
as everybody else in this class, and I've
worked harder than most, so I should get
an A or B on this," is
   a. confronting and handling the stress.
   b. coping with the feeling of becoming
      overwhelmed.
   c. using imaging.
   d. reconstructing the situation.

Reading Selection 28 "The Functions and Effects of Music"

Checking Your Vocabulary

Directions: Using context, word parts, or a dictionary if necessary, circle the letter of the meaning for each word as it is used in the reading.

1. destitute (paragraph 4)
   a. dissatisfied
   b. uneducated
   c. unreasonable
   d. poor

2. tactic (paragraph 5)
   a. source
   b. rationale
   c. belief
   d. strategy

3. injunction (paragraph 6)
   a. exercise
   b. directive
   c. process
   d. group

4. advocated (paragraph 7)
   a. recommended
   b. formed
   c. written
   d. distributed

5. affiliation (paragraph 10)
   a. separation
   b. difference
   c. association
   d. repetition

Checking Your Comprehension

Directions: Circle the letter of the best answer.

6. The main point of the article is that music
   a. has political, attitudinal, and social
      effects.
   b. is primarily a political tool.
   c. is subject to censorship, as are other
      forms of communication.
   d. distinguishes generations from one
      another.

7. The technique of giving an old familiar song new lyrics is intended to
   a. transfer feelings or associations from old to new.
   b. bring back fond memories.
   c. create new folk heroes.
   d. reestablish familiar environments.

8. From the information presented in this reading, you can infer that the recording industry
   a. prefers to remain politically neutral.
   b. was forced by the public to release patriotic songs.
   c. has remained anti-war throughout the past 50 years.
   d. has taken a political stand in past wars.

9. According to the reading, music has played an important role in the
   a. political campaigns of national leaders.
   b. civil rights movement.
   c. legalization of abortion debate.
   d. socialist propaganda.

10. The Federal Communications Commission's position on censorship of music states that it is
    a. the artist's responsibility.
    b. the station's responsibility.
    c. the disc jockey's and program director's responsibility.
    d. the listener's or parent's responsibility.

11. Which of the following best defines the word *mosaics* as used in paragraph 8?
    a. artistic models
    b. bits of information and perceptions
    c. skills
    d. beliefs

Thinking Critically

12. The author's primary purpose in writing is to
    a. discuss the functions of music in our society.
    b. argue that music has been used by age groups as a form of identification and rebellion.
    c. urge censorship of controversial lyrics.
    d. describe music as a political tool.

13. Which of the following conclusions can be most clearly drawn from this article?
    a. Music will continue to be a form of social and political expression.
    b. The Federal Communications Commission will soon change its position on censorship.
    c. Music will cease to distinguish one generation from another.
    d. Elvis Presley will diminish in popularity with successive generations.

14. From the last paragraph of the reading, it is reasonable to infer that
    a. singing idols are important in the establishment of boy-girl relationships.
    b. boys' emotional maturation is equal to that of girls of the same age.
    c. boys prefer not to become involved with girls.
    d. girls mature more rapidly than boys during early teenage years.

15. The opening paragraph of the reading suggests that the functions of music are
    a. unique.
    b. diverse.
    c. of questionable value.
    d. extraordinary.

APPENDIX A

Words-Per-Minute Conversion Chart

Reading Selection

Reading	1	2	3	4	5	6	7	8	9	10	11	12	13	14
Time (minutes)														
1:00	959	824	1227	1645	794	944	853	1191	1062	1219	1419	1012	1029	1029
1:15	767	659	982	1316	635	755	682	953	850	975	1135	810	823	967
1:30	639	549	818	1097	529	629	569	794	708	813	946	675	686	806
1:45	548	471	701	940	454	539	487	681	607	697	811	578	588	691
2:00	480	412	614	823	397	472	427	596	531	610	710	506	515	605
2:15	426	366	545	731	353	420	379	529	472	542	631	450	457	537
2:30	384	330	491	658	318	378	341	476	425	488	568	405	412	484
2:45	349	300	446	598	289	343	310	433	386	443	516	368	374	440
3:00	320	275	409	548	265	315	284	397	354	406	473	337	343	403
3:15	295	254	378	506	244	290	262	366	327	375	437	311	317	372
3:30	274	235	351	470	227	270	244	340	303	348	405	289	294	345
3:45	256	220	327	439	212	252	227	318	283	325	378	270	274	322
4:00	240	206	307	411	199	236	213	298	266	305	355	253	257	302
4:15	226	194	289	387	187	222	201	280	250	287	334	238	242	284
4:30	213	183	273	366	176	210	190	265	236	271	315	225	229	269
4:45	202	173	258	346	167	199	180	251	224	257	299	213	217	255
5:00	192	165	245	329	159	189	171	238	212	244	284	202	206	242
5:15	183	157	234	313	151	180	162	227	202	232	270	193	196	230
5:30	174	150	223	299	144	172	155	217	193	222	258	184	187	220
5:45	167	143	213	286	138	164	148	207	185	212	247	176	179	210
6:00	160	137	205	274	132	157	142	199	177	203	237	169	172	202
6:15	153	132	196	263	127	151	136	191	170	195	227	162	165	193
6:30	148	127	189	253	122	145	131	183	163	188	218	156	158	186
6:45	142	122	182	244	118	140	126	176	157	181	210	150	152	179
7:00	137	117	175	235	113	135	122	170	152	174	203	145	147	173
7:15	132	114	169	227	110	130	118	164	146	168	196	140	142	167
7:30	128	110	164	219	106	126	114	159	142	163	189	135	137	161
7:45	124	106	158	212	102	122	110	154	137	157	183	131	133	156
8:00	120	103	153	206	-	118	107	149	133	152	177	127	129	151
8:15	116	-	149	199	-	114	103	144	129	148	172	123	125	147
8:30	113	-	144	194	-	111	100	140	125	143	167	119	121	142
8:45	110	-	140	188	-	108	-	136	121	139	162	116	118	138
9:00	107	-	136	183	-	105	-	132	118	135	158	112	114	134

Reading Selection

Reading	1	2	3	4	5	6	7	8	9	10	11	12	13	14
Time (minutes)														
9:15	104	-	133	178	-	102	-	129	115	132	153	109	111	131
9:30	101	-	129	173	-	-	-	125	112	128	149	107	108	127
9:45	-	-	126	169	-	-	-	122	109	125	146	104	106	124
10:00	-	-	123	165	-	-	-	119	106	122	142	101	103	121
10:15	-	-	120	160	-	-	-	116	104	119	138	-	100	118
10:30	-	-	117	157	-	-	-	113	101	116	135	-	-	115
10:45	-	-	114	153	-	-	-	111	-	113	132	-	-	112
11:00	-	-	112	150	-	-	-	108	-	111	129	-	-	110
11:15	-	-	109	146	-	-	-	106	-	108	126	-	-	107
11:30	-	-	107	143	-	-	-	104	-	106	123	-	-	105
11:45	-	-	104	140	-	-	-	101	-	104	121	-	-	103
12:00	-	-	102	137	-	-	-	-	-	102	118	-	-	101
12:15	-	-	100	134	-	-	-	-	-	-	116	-	-	-
12:30	-	-	-	132	-	-	-	-	-	-	114	-	-	-
12:45	-	-	-	129	-	-	-	-	-	-	111	-	-	-
13:00	-	-	-	127	-	-	-	-	-	-	109	-	-	-
13:15	-	-	-	124	-	-	-	-	-	-	107	-	-	-
13:30	-	-	-	122	-	-	-	-	-	-	105	-	-	-
13:45	-	-	-	120	-	-	-	-	-	-	103	-	-	-
14:00	-	-	-	118	-	-	-	-	-	-	101	-	-	-
14:15	-	-	-	115	-	-	-	-	-	-	-	-	-	-
14:30	-	-	-	113	-	-	-	-	-	-	-	-	-	-
14:45	-	-	-	112	-	-	-	-	-	-	-	-	-	-
15:00	-	-	-	110	-	-	-	-	-	-	-	-	-	-
15:15	-	-	-	108	-	-	-	-	-	-	-	-	-	-
15:30	-	-	-	106	-	-	-	-	-	-	-	-	-	-
15:45	-	-	-	104	-	-	-	-	-	-	-	-	-	-
16:00	-	-	-	103	-	-	-	-	-	-	-	-	-	-
16:15	-	-	-	101	-	-	-	-	-	-	-	-	-	-
16:30	-	-	-	-	-	-	-	-	-	-	-	-	-	-
16:45	-	-	-	-	-	-	-	-	-	-	-	-	-	-
17:00	-	-	-	-	-	-	-	-	-	-	-	-	-	-
17:15	-	-	-	-	-	-	-	-	-	-	-	-	-	-
17:30	-	-	-	-	-	-	-	-	-	-	-	-	-	-
17:45	-	-	-	-	-	-	-	-	-	-	-	-	-	-
18:00	-	-	-	-	-	-	-	-	-	-	-	-	-	-
18:15	-	-	-	-	-	-	-	-	-	-	-	-	-	-
18:30	-	-	-	-	-	-	-	-	-	-	-	-	-	-
18:45	-	-	-	-	-	-	-	-	-	-	-	-	-	-
19:00	-	-	-	-	-	-	-	-	-	-	-	-	-	-
19:15	-	-	-	-	-	-	-	-	-	-	-	-	-	-
19:30	-	-	-	-	-	-	-	-	-	-	-	-	-	-
19:45	-	-	-	-	-	-	-	-	-	-	-	-	-	-
20:00	-	-	-	-	-	-	-	-	-	-	-	-	-	-

Reading Selection

Reading	15	16	17	18	19	20	21	22	23	24	25	26	27	28
Time (minutes)														
1:00	1514	948	999	1150	1316	1264	822	1330	650	1269	1544	1186	2528	1291
1:15	1211	758	799	920	1053	1011	658	1064	520	1015	1235	949	2022	1033
1:30	1009	632	666	767	877	843	548	887	433	846	1029	791	1685	861
1:45	865	542	571	657	752	722	470	760	371	725	882	678	1445	738
2:00	757	474	500	575	658	632	411	665	325	635	772	593	1264	646
2:15	673	421	444	511	585	562	365	591	289	564	686	527	1124	574
2:30	606	379	400	460	526	506	329	532	260	508	618	474	1011	516
2:45	551	345	363	418	479	460	299	484	236	461	561	431	919	469
3:00	505	316	333	383	439	421	274	443	217	423	515	395	843	430
3:15	466	292	307	354	405	389	253	409	200	390	475	365	778	397
3:30	433	271	285	329	376	361	235	380	186	363	441	339	722	369
3:45	404	253	266	307	351	337	219	355	173	338	412	316	674	344
4:00	379	237	250	288	329	316	206	333	163	317	386	297	632	323
4:15	356	223	235	271	310	297	193	313	153	299	363	279	595	304
4:30	336	211	222	256	292	281	183	296	144	282	343	264	562	287
4:45	319	200	210	242	277	266	173	280	137	267	325	250	532	272
5:00	303	190	200	230	263	253	164	266	130	254	309	237	506	258
5:15	288	181	190	219	251	241	157	253	124	242	294	226	482	246
5:30	275	172	182	209	239	230	149	242	118	231	281	216	460	235
5:45	263	165	174	200	229	220	143	231	113	221	269	206	440	225
6:00	252	158	167	192	219	211	137	222	108	212	257	198	421	215
6:15	242	152	160	184	211	202	132	213	104	203	247	190	404	207
6:30	233	146	154	177	202	194	126	205	100	195	238	182	389	199
6:45	224	140	148	170	195	187	122	197	-	188	229	176	375	191
7:00	216	135	143	164	188	181	117	190	-	181	221	169	361	184
7:15	209	131	138	159	182	174	113	183	-	175	213	164	349	178
7:30	202	126	133	153	175	169	110	177	-	169	206	158	337	172
7:45	195	122	129	148	170	163	106	172	-	164	199	153	326	167
8:00	189	119	125	144	165	158	103	166	-	159	193	148	316	161
8:15	184	115	121	139	160	153	-	161	-	154	187	144	306	156
8:30	178	112	118	135	155	149	-	156	-	149	182	140	297	152
8:45	173	108	114	131	150	144	-	152	-	145	176	136	289	148
9:00	168	105	111	128	146	140	-	148	-	141	172	132	281	143
9:15	164	102	108	124	142	137	-	144	-	137	167	128	273	140
9:30	159	-	105	121	139	133	-	140	-	134	163	125	266	136
9:45	155	-	102	118	135	130	-	136	-	130	158	122	259	132
10:00	151	-	-	115	132	126	-	133	-	127	154	119	253	129
10:15	148	-	-	112	128	123	-	130	-	124	151	116	247	126
10:30	144	-	-	110	125	120	-	127	-	121	147	113	241	123

Reading Selection

Reading	15	16	17	18	19	20	21	22	23	24	25	26	27	28
Time (minutes)														
10:45	141	-	-	107	122	118	-	124	-	118	144	110	235	120
11:00	138	-	-	105	120	115	-	121	-	115	140	108	230	117
11:15	135	-	-	102	117	112	-	118	-	113	137	105	225	115
11:30	132	-	-	100	114	110	-	116	-	110	134	103	220	112
11:45	129	-	-	-	112	108	-	113	-	108	131	101	215	110
12:00	126	-	-	-	110	105	-	111	-	106	129	-	211	108
12:15	124	-	-	-	107	103	-	109	-	104	126	-	206	105
12:30	121	-	-	-	105	101	-	106	-	102	124	-	202	103
12:45	119	-	-	-	103	-	-	104	-	-	121	-	198	101
13:00	116	-	-	-	101	-	-	102	-	-	119	-	194	-
13:15	114	-	-	-	-	-	-	100	-	-	117	-	191	-
13:30	112	-	-	-	-	-	-	-	-	-	114	-	187	-
13:45	110	-	-	-	-	-	-	-	-	-	112	-	184	-
14:00	108	-	-	-	-	-	-	-	-	-	110	-	181	-
14:15	106	-	-	-	-	-	-	-	-	-	108	-	177	-
14:30	104	-	-	-	-	-	-	-	-	-	106	-	174	-
14:45	103	-	-	-	-	-	-	-	-	-	105	-	171	-
15:00	101	-	-	-	-	-	-	-	-	-	103	-	169	-
15:15	-	-	-	-	-	-	-	-	-	-	101	-	166	-
15:30	-	-	-	-	-	-	-	-	-	-	-	-	163	-
15:45	-	-	-	-	-	-	-	-	-	-	-	-	161	-
16:00	-	-	-	-	-	-	-	-	-	-	-	-	158	-
16:15	-	-	-	-	-	-	-	-	-	-	-	-	156	-
16:30	-	-	-	-	-	-	-	-	-	-	-	-	153	-
16:45	-	-	-	-	-	-	-	-	-	-	-	-	151	-
17:00	-	-	-	-	-	-	-	-	-	-	-	-	149	-
17:15	-	-	-	-	-	-	-	-	-	-	-	-	147	-
17:30	-	-	-	-	-	-	-	-	-	-	-	-	144	-
17:45	-	-	-	-	-	-	-	-	-	-	-	-	142	-
18:00	-	-	-	-	-	-	-	-	-	-	-	-	140	-
18:15	-	-	-	-	-	-	-	-	-	-	-	-	139	-
18:30	-	-	-	-	-	-	-	-	-	-	-	-	137	-
18:45	-	-	-	-	-	-	-	-	-	-	-	-	135	-
19:00	-	-	-	-	-	-	-	-	-	-	-	-	133	-
19:15	-	-	-	-	-	-	-	-	-	-	-	-	131	-
19:30	-	-	-	-	-	-	-	-	-	-	-	-	130	-
19:45	-	-	-	-	-	-	-	-	-	-	-	-	128	-
20:00	-	-	-	-	-	-	-	-	-	-	-	-	126	-

APPENDIX B

Reading Progress Graph

DIRECTIONS: For each reading selection you complete, record the date and selection number. Then place a dot in the appropriate column to indicate the words-per-minute score and the comprehension score you achieved. Connect the consecutive dots to form a line graph.

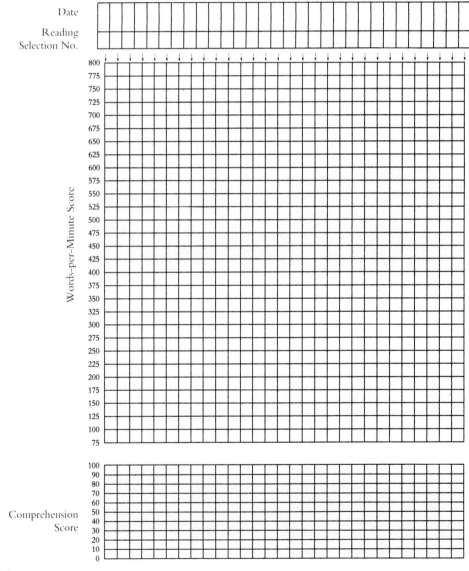

Credits

Reading Is For Everyone

Doctor's Book of Home Remedies: Reprinted from *Doctor's Book of Home Remedies*, © 1990 by Rodale. Permission granted by Rodale, Inc., Emmaus, PA 18098. Available wherever books are sold or visit www.rodalestore.com or call the Publisher at (800) 848-4735.

Fashion Victim: Based on a description of the book *Fashion Victim* at amazon.com.

Knowing Bass: Based on a description of the book *Knowing Bass* at amazon.com.

How to Talk So Kids Will Listen & Listen So Kids Will Talk: From a review of *How to Talk So Kids Will Listen & Listen So Kids Will Talk*, from *The Los Angeles Times*.

How to Rock Climb!: Based on a description of the book *How to Rock Climb!* at amazon.com.

Friendship: Celebration of Humanity: Based on a description of the book *Friendship: Celebration of Humanity* at amazon.com.

The Gift of Fear: Excerpt from a review by Patricia Hassler of *The Gift of Fear*. From *Booklist*, June 1 and 15, 1997. Copyright American Library Association. Used with permission.

Credit Card & Debt Management: Review by Joe Collins of *Credit Card & Debt Management*. From *Booklist*, February 15, 1996. Copyright American Library Association. Used with permission.

Chapter 1

23: James E. Challenger, "How to Brag About Yourself to Win and Hold a New Job." *The Buffalo News*, July 20, 1997. Reprinted by permission of Herbert Rozoff Public Relations, Inc. for James E. Challenger.

27: Sherry Amatenstein, "Talking a Stranger Through the Night." From *Newsweek*, November 18, 2002, p. 16. © 2002 Newsweek, Inc. All rights reserved. Reprinted by permission.

35: Carl E. Rischer and Thomas A. Easton, Focus on Human Biology, Second Edition, p. 141. Copyright © 1995 by HarperCollins College Publishers. Reprinted by permission.

Chapter 2

37: From John C. Merrill, John Lee, and Edward J. Friedlander, Modern Mass Media, Second Edition, p. 139. Copyright © 1994 by HarperCollins College Publishers. Reprinted by permission of Addison-Wesley Educational Publishers, Inc.

43: From Joseph A. DeVito, The Elements of Public Speaking, Seventh Edition. New York: Longman, 2000, p. 109.

43: From Jerry A. Nathanson, Basic Environmental Technology: Water Supply, Waste Management, and Pollution Control, Third Edition, p. 351. Copyright © 2000 by Prentice-Hall, Inc. Reprinted by permission of Prentice-Hall, Inc., Upper Saddle River, NJ.

48: From Richard Weaver II, Understanding Interpersonal Communication, Fifth Edition. Copyright © 1990 by Scott, Foresman and Company. Reprinted by permission.

63: Cindy C. Combs "Profile of a Terrorists." From *Terrorism in the Twenty-First Century*, Third Edition by Cindy C. Combs. Copyright © 2003, 2000, 1997 by Pearson Education, Inc. Reprinted by permission of Pearson Education, Inc., Upper Saddle River, New Jersey.

68: Brent Staples, "Just Walk On By: A Black Man Ponders His Power to Alter Public Space." *Ms.*, September 1986. Reprinted by permission of the author.

Chapter 3

96:    *American Heritage Desk Dictionary*, excerpt from the pronunciation key. Copyright ©
       1981 by Houghton Mifflin Company. Reproduced by permission from The American
       Heritage Desk Dictionary.

96:    *Merriam-Webster's Collegiate Dictionary*, definition of the word "establish" used by
       permission. From *Merriam-Webster's Collegiate Dictionary*, Tenth Edition. © 2002 by
       Merriam-Webster, Incorporated (www.Merriam-Webster.com).

98:    *American Heritage Desk Dictionary*, definition of "isometric." Copyright © 1981 by
       Houghton Mifflin Company. Reproduced by permission from The American Heritage
       Desk Dictionary.

100:   *Roget's International Thesaurus*, excerpt of synonyms for the phrase "told us about"
       from *Roget's International Thesaurus*, Fourth Edition, revised by Robert L. Chapman.
       Copyright © 1977 by Harper & Row, Publishers, Inc. Reprinted by permission of
       HarperCollins Publishers Inc.

104:   Brian M. Fagan "Archaeological Sites," from *World Prehistory: A Brief Introduction*.
       Copyright © 1979 by Brian M. Fagan. Reprinted by permission of Little, Brown and
       Company.

108:   Paul Hewitt, "Why the Sky Is Blue, Sunsets Are Red, and Clouds Are White," from
       Conceptual Physics, Eighth Edition, pp. 478–482. Copyright © 1998 by Paul Hewitt.
       Reprinted by permission of Addison-Wesley Educational Publishers, Inc.

Chapter 4

116:   Excerpt from Robert W. Kolb, *Investments*. Glenview, IL: Scott, Foresman, 1986, p. 59.

116:   H. L. Capron, *Computers: Tools for an Information Age*, Brief Edition. Reading, MA:
       Addison-Wesley Longman, Inc., 1998, p. 82.

117:   Roger Chisholm and Marilu McCarty, *Principles of Economics*. Glenview, IL: Scott,
       Foresman, 1978, pp. 91–92.

117:   Rebecca J. Donatelle, *Access to Health*, Seventh Edition. San Francisco: Benjamin
       Cummings, 2002, p. 53.

117:   Rebecca J. Donatelle, *Health: The Basics*, Fifth Edition. San Francisco: Benjamin
       Cummings, 2003, p. 247.

118:   James A. Fagin, *Criminal Justice*. Boston: Allyn & Bacon, 2003, p. 285.

119:   From Joseph A. DeVito, *Messages: Building Interpersonal Communication Skills, Third
       Edition*, p. 302. Copyright © 1996 by HarperCollins College Publishers. Reprinted by
       permission of Addison-Wesley Educational Publishers, Inc.

119:   From Robert A. Wallace, *Biology: The World of Life*, Seventh Edition, p. 82. Copyright
       © 1997 by Addison-Wesley Educational Publishers, Inc. Reprinted by permission.

119:   From Robert J. Ferl, Robert A. Wallace, and Gerald P. Sanders, *Biology: The Realm of
       Life*, Third Edition, p. 790. Copyright © 1996 by HarperCollins College Publishers.
       Reprinted by permission of Addison-Wesley Educational Publishers, Inc.

120:   DeVito, *Messages: Building Interpersonal Communication Skills*, Third Edition, p. 157.

120:   From Alex Thio, *Sociology*, Fourth Edition, p. 347. Copyright © 1996 by
       HarperCollins College Publishers. Reprinted by permission of Addison-Wesley
       Educational Publishers, Inc.

121:   David A. Ross, *Introduction to Oceanography*. New York: HarperCollins College
       Publishers, 1995, p. 62.

121:   Carole Wade and Carol Tavris, *Psychology*, Sixth Edition. Upper Saddle River, NJ:
       Prentice-Hall, Inc., 2000, p. 153.

121:   From Duane Preble, Sarah Preble, and Patrick Frank, *Artforms: An Introduction to the
       Visual Arts*, Sixth Edition, p. 71. Copyright © 1999 by Addison-Wesley Educational
       Publishers, Inc. Reprinted by permission.

121:   From Mark B. Bush, *Ecology of a Changing Planet*, Second Edition, p. 268. Copyright ©
       2000, 1997 by Prentice-Hall, Inc. Reprinted by permission of Prentice-Hall, Inc.,
       Upper Saddle River, New Jersey.

122: From Tim Curry, Robert Jiobu, and Kent Schwirian, *Sociology for the Twenty-First Century*, Second Edition, pp. 326–327. Copyright © 1999, 1997 by Prentice-Hall, Inc. Reprinted by permission of Prentice-Hall, Inc., Upper Saddle River, New Jersey.

123: Michael R. Solomon, *Consumer Behavior: Buying, Having, and Being*, Fourth Edition. Upper Saddle River, NJ: Prentice-Hall, Inc., 1999, p. 184.

124: From Paul G. Hewitt, Conceptual Physics, Seventh Edition, p. 524. Copyright © 1993 by Paul G. Hewitt. Reprinted by permission of HarperCollins Publishers, Inc.

124: From Curry, Jiobu, and Schwirian, *Sociology for the Twenty-First Century*, Second Edition, p. 330.

125: Bernard Campbell and James B. Loy, *Humankind Emerging*, Seventh Edition. New York: HarperCollins College Publishers, 1996, p. 171.

126: Edward F. Bergman and William H. Renwick, *Introduction to Geography: People, Places, and Environment*, Updated Second Edition. Upper Saddle River, NJ: Prentice Hall, 2003, p. 69.

126: Adapted from Roy A. Cook, Laura J. Yale, and Joseph J. Marqua, *Tourism: The Business of Travel*, Second Edition. Upper Saddle River, NJ: Prentice Hall, 2002, p. 370.

126: Joseph A. DeVito, *The Interpersonal Communication Book*, Ninth Edition. New York: Addison Wesley Longman, 2001, p. 219.

126: Adapted from Daniel M. Dunn and Lisa J. Goodnight, *Communication: Embracing the Difference*. Boston: Allyn & Bacon, 2003, p. 92.

127: Adapted from Ronald J. Ebert and Ricky W. Griffin, *Business Essentials*, Fourth Edition. Upper Saddle River, NJ: Prentice Hall, 2003, p. 208.

127: Thio, *Sociology*, Fourth Edition, pp. 170–171.

128: Wallace, *Biology: The World of Life*, Seventh Edition, p. 49.

128: Solomon, *Consumer Behavior: Buying, Having, and Being*, Fourth Edition, p. 503.

129: DeVito, *Messages: Building Interpersonal Communication Skills*, Third Edition, p. 360.

129: DeVito, *Messages: Building Interpersonal Communication Skills*, Third Edition, p. 338.

130: From George C. Edwards III, Martin P. Wattenberg, and Robert L. Lineberry, *Government in America: People, Politics, and Policy*, Seventh Edition, p. 134. Copyright © 1996 by HarperCollins College Publishers. Reprinted by permission of Addison-Wesley Educational Publishers, Inc.

130: Wallace, *Biology: The World of Life*, Seventh Edition, p. 24.

130: From James Benjamin and Raymie E. McKerrow, Business and Professional Communication: Concepts and Practices, p. 146. Copyright © 1994 by HarperCollins College Publishers. Reprinted by permission of Addison-Wesley Educational Publishers, Inc.

131: Thio, Sociology, Fourth Edition, p. 290.

131: Benjamin and McKerrow, *Business and Professional Communication: Concepts and Practices*, p. 84.

132: "Pollution by Pesticides" from Wallace, *Biology: The World of Life*, Seventh Edition, pp. 567-569.

133: From Neil Campbell, Lawrence Mitchell, and Jane Reece, *Biology: Concepts and Connections*, Third Edition, p. 358. Copyright © 2000 by Benjamin/Cummings, an imprint of Addison Wesley Longman, Inc. Reprinted by permission.

133: Curry, Jiobu, and Schwirian, *Sociology for the Twenty-First Century*, Second Edition, p. 131.

133: Solomon, *Consumer Behavior: Buying, Having, and Being*, Fourth Edition, pp. 218–219.

134: Elaine N. Marieb, *Essentials of Human Anatomy and Physiology*, Sixth Edition. San Francisco: Benjamin/Cummings, 2000, p. 173.

134: Wilson Dizard, Jr., *Old Media, New Media: Mass Communications in the Information Age*, Third Edition. New York: Longman, 2000, p. 101.

135: From Laura Uba and Karen Huang, *Psychology*, p. 148. Copyright © 1999 by Addison-Wesley Educational Publishers. Reprinted by permission of Prentice-Hall, Inc., Upper Saddle River, New Jersey.

135: Wallace, *Biology: The World of Life*, Seventh Edition, p. 24.

137:    Wade and Tavris, *Psychology*, Sixth Edition, pp. 409–410.

137:    Constance Shehan, *Marriages and Families*, Second Edition. Boston: Allyn & Bacon, 2003, p. 170.

138:    DeVito, *Messages: Building Interpersonal Communication Skills*, Third Edition, p. 29.

139:    Benjamin and McKerrow, *Business and Professional Communication: Concepts and Practices*, p. 175.

139:    DeVito, *Messages: Building Interpersonal Communication Skills*, Third Edition, p. 153.

140:    Wallace, *Biology: The World of Life*, Seventh Edition, p. 52.

140:    Thio, *Sociology*, Fourth Edition, p. 245.

141:    From David Popenoe, *Sociology*, Eleventh Edition, p. 444. Copyright © 2000 by Prentice-Hall, Inc. Reprinted by permission of Prentice-Hall, Inc., Upper Saddle River, New Jersey.

141:    Karen C. Timberlake, *Chemistry: An Introduction to General, Organic, and Biological Chemistry*, Seventh Edition. San Francisco: Benjamin/Cummings, 1999, p. 284.

141:    From George Edwards III, *Government in America: People, Politics, and Policy*, Ninth Edition, p. 133. Copyright © 2000 by Addison-Wesley Educational Publishers, Inc. Reprinted by permission.

142:    James W. Coleman and Donald R. Cressey, *Social Problems*, Sixth Edition. New York: HarperCollins College Publishers, 1996, p. 277.

142:    David Hicks and Margaret A. Gwynne, *Cultural Anthropology*, Second Edition. New York: HarperCollins College Publishers, 1996, p. 144.

145:    From James Geiwitz, *Psychology: Looking at Ourselves*, Second Edition, pp. 543–544. Copyright © 1980 by James Geiwitz. Reprinted by permission of Little, Brown and Company.

146:    Shehan, *Marriages and Families*, Second Edition, pp. 79-80.

148:    Adapted from James Henslin, *Sociology: A Down-to-Earth Approach*, Sixth Edition. Boston: Allyn & Bacon, 2003, pp. 380–381.

150:    From Michael Solomon and Elnora Stuart, *Marketing: Real People, Real Choices*, Second Edition, p. 363. Copyright © 2000 by Prentice-Hall, Inc. Reprinted by permission of Prentice-Hall, Inc., Upper Saddle River, New Jersey.

150:    Thio, *Sociology*, Fourth Edition, p. 54.

151:    James E. Crouch and J. Robert McClintic, *Human Anatomy and Physiology*, Second Edition. New York: Wiley, 1976, p. 120.

151:    From Josh R. Gerow, *Psychology: An Introduction*, Fifth Edition, p. 530. Copyright © 1997 by Addison-Wesley Educational Publishers, Inc. Reprinted by permission.

152:    Edward Tarbuck and Frederick Lutgens, *Earth Science*, Ninth Edition. Upper Saddle River, NJ: Prentice-Hall, Inc., 2000, p. 70.

153:    Uba and Huang, Psychology, p. 406.

153:    Curry, Jiobu, and Schwirian, *Sociology for the Twenty-First Century*, Second Edition, pp. 380–381.

154:    Curry, Jiobu, and Schwirian, *Sociology for the Twenty-First Century*, Second Edition, p. 340.

154:    Robert W. Christopherson, *Geosystems: An Introduction to Physical Geography*, Fourth Edition. Upper Saddle River, NJ: Prentice-Hall, Inc., 2000, p. 368.

156:    From Bruce E. Gronbeck, Kathleen German, Douglas Ehninger, and Alan H. Monroe, *Principles of Speech Communication*, Twelfth Brief Edition, pp. 57–58. Copyright © 1995 by HarperCollins College Publishers. Reprinted by permission of Addison-Wesley Educational Publishers, Inc.

160:    From Mary J. Gander and Harry W. Gardiner, "The Appreciation of Humor" from *Child and Adolescent Development*. Copyright © 1981 by Mary J. Gander and Harry W. Gardiner. Reprinted by permission of Little, Brown and Company.

164:    Wendy G. Lehnert, "Privacy on the Web" from *Light on the Internet: Essentials of the Internet and the World Wide Web*, by Wendy G. Lehnert, pp. 93–99. © 1999 Addison Wesley Longman, Inc. Reprinted by permission of Pearson Education, Inc. Publishing as Pearson Addison Wesley.

Chapter 5

172: Edward Greenberg and Benjamin Page, *The Struggle for Democracy*, Brief Version, Second Edition. New York: Longman, 1999, p. 71.

173: Dorothy Cohen, *Advertising*. Glenview, IL: Scott, Foresman, 1988, pp. ii–iii.

173: From Duane Preble, Sarah Preble, and Patrick Frank, *Artforms: An Introduction to the Visual Arts*, Sixth Edition, p. 148. Copyright © 1999 by Addison-Wesley Educational Publishers, Inc. Reprinted by permission.

175: Gary Wasserman, The Basics of American Politics, Eighth Edition. New York: Longman, 1997, pp. 163–164.

177: From Carl E. Rischer and Thomas A. Easton, *Focus on Human Biology*, Second Edition, p. 40. Copyright © 1995 by HarperCollins College Publishers. Reprinted by permission.

179: From Terry G. Jordan, Mona Domosh, and Lester Rowntree, *The Human Mosaic: A Thematic Introduction to Cultural Geography*, Sixth Edition, pp. 87–89. Copyright © 1994 by HarperCollins. Reprinted by permission.

181: From Robert A. Wallace, *Biology: The World of Life*, Sixth Edition, p. 488. Copyright © 1992 by HarperCollins Publishers. Reprinted by permission.

183: From Michael C. Mix, Paul Farber, and Keith I. King, *Biology: The Network of Life*, p. 50. Copyright © 1992 by HarperCollins Publishers. Reprinted by permission.

185: David Hicks and Margaret A. Gwynne, *Cultural Anthropology*, Second Edition. New York: HarperCollins College Publishers, 1996, p. 304.

189: From J. Ross Eschelman, Barbara G. Cashion, and Laurence A. Basirico, *Sociology: An Introduction*, Fourth Edition, p. 109. Copyright © 1993 by HarperCollins College Publishers. Reprinted by permission of Addison-Wesley Educational Publishers, Inc.

190: From Curtis O. Byer and Louis W. Shainberg, *Living Well: Health in Your Hands*, Second Edition, p. 306. Copyright © 1995 by HarperCollins College Publishers. Reprinted by permission of Addison-Wesley Educational Publishers, Inc.

193: From Robert A. Wallace, *Biology: The World of Life*, Seventh Edition, p. 408. Copyright © 1997 by Addison-Wesley Educational Publishers, Inc. Reprinted by permission.

194: From David Popenoe, *Sociology*, Eleventh Edition, p. 109. Copyright © 2000 by Prentice-Hall, Inc. Reprinted by permission of Prentice-Hall, Inc., Upper Saddle River, New Jersey.

195: Joseph A. DeVito, The Elements of Public Speaking, Seventh Edition. New York: Longman, 2000, p. 164.

196: Roger LeRoy Miller, Economics Today, Eighth Edition. New York: HarperCollins College Publishers, 1994, p. 335.

197: "The Stimulus for Healing: Sound," from Josh R. Gerow, *Psychology: An Introduction*, Fifth Edition, pp. 87–89. Copyright © 1997 by Addison-Wesley Educational Publishers, Inc. Reprinted by permission.

198: From Hugh Barlow, *Criminal Justice in America*, p. 19. Copyright © 2000 by Hugh Barlow. Reprinted by permission of Prentice-Hall, Inc., Upper Saddle River, New Jersey.

200: Wendy G. Lehnert, "Virus Risks and Safeguards," from *Light on the Internet: Essentials of the Internet and the World Wide Web*, by Wendy G. Lehnert, pp. 91, 92. © 1999 Addison Wesley Longman, Inc. Reprinted by permission of Pearson Education, Inc. Publishing as Pearson Addison Wesley.

201: Popenoe, *Sociology*, Eleventh Edition, p. 121.

201: From Edward F. Bergman and William H. Renwick, *Introduction to Geography: People, Places, and Environment*, p. 192. © 1999 by Prentice-Hall, Inc. Reprinted by permission of Prentice-Hall, Inc., Upper Saddle River, New Jersey.

202: Preble, Preble, and Frank, *Artforms: An Introduction to the Visual Arts*, Sixth Edition, p. 143.

202: From Jeffrey Bennett, Megan Donahue, Nicholas Schneider, and Mark Voit, *The Cosmic Perspective*, Brief Edition, p. 28. Copyright © 2000 by Addison Wesley Longman. Reprinted by permission of Addison-Wesley Educational Publishers, Inc.

202:    From Tim Curry, Robert Jiobu, and Kent Schwirian, *Sociology for the Twenty-First Century*, Second Edition, p. 148. Copyright © 1999, 1997 by Prentice-Hall, Inc. Reprinted by permission of Prentice-Hall, Inc., Upper Saddle River, New Jersey.

212:    Hugh D. Barlow, "Electronic Monitoring: An Alternate to Imprisonment," from *Criminal Justice in America* by Hugh D. Barlow, pp. 657–659.

217:    Steven R. Knowlton, "How Students Get Lost in Cyberspace." Education Life section, *The New York Times*, November 2, 1997. Copyright © 1997 The New York Times Co. Reprinted with permission.

Chapter 6

225:    Andrea Martin, "Citizenship or Slavery" in *Utne Reader*, May-June 1996, pp. 14, 16. Reprinted with permission from Utne Reader and Andrea Martin.

229:    From Mortimer B. Zuckerman, "Attention Must Be Paid." *U.S. News & World Report*, August 18/25, 1997, p. 92. Copyright 1997 U.S. News & World Report, L.P. Reprinted with permission.

236:    Beth Powell, "Lawsuits Seek Heart Monitoring for Users of Withdrawn Diet Drugs." *The Buffalo News*, September 22, 1997, p. A5. Copyright © 1997 by The Associated Press. Reprinted by permission of the Associated Press.

238:    From Richard Folkers, "Everyday Mysteries: Why Do Dogs Bark?" *U.S. News & World Report*, August 18/25, 1997, pp. 86-87. Copyright 1997 U.S. News & World Report, L.P. Reprinted with permission.

240:    Reproduced with permission of authors and publisher from Myers, S.A., Ropog, B.L., & Rodgers, R.P. Sex differences in humor. Psychological Reports, 1997, 81, 221-222. © Psychological Reports 1997.

247:    J. Madeline Nash, "Will We Control the Weather?" *Time*, April 10, 2000, pp. 98, 100. © 2000 TIME Inc. Reprinted by permission.

252:    Lance C. Presley, "Alternative drug testing update." *Occupational Health & Safety*, January 2003. © Copyright 2003 by Stevens Publishing Corporation. Reprinted with permission.

Chapter 7

259:    From Hugh Barlow, *Criminal Justice in America*, p. 411. Copyright © 2000 by Hugh Barlow. Reprinted by permission of Prentice-Hall, Inc., Upper Saddle River, New Jersey.

260:    From Joseph A. DeVito, *Messages: Building Interpersonal Communication Skills*, Fourth Edition, p. 146. Copyright © 1999 by Addison-Wesley Educational Publishers, Inc. Reprinted by permission.

262:    Leon Harris, *Concepts in Zoology*, Second Edition. New York: HarperCollins College Publishers, 1996, pp. 163–164.

265:    From David Popenoe, *Sociology*, Eleventh Edition, p. 503. Copyright © 2000 by Prentice-Hall, Inc. Reprinted by permission of Prentice-Hall, Inc., Upper Saddle River, New Jersey.

265:    From Michael Solomon and Elnora Stuart, *Marketing: Real People, Real Choices*, Second Edition, pp. 327–328. Copyright © 2000 by Prentice-Hall, Inc. Reprinted by permission of Prentice-Hall, Inc., Upper Saddle River, New Jersey.

266:    Wallace Stevens, "Anecdote of the Jar" from *The Collected Poems of Wallace Stevens* by Wallace Stevens, copyright 1954 by Wallace Stevens and renewed 1982 by Holly Stevens. Used by permission of Alfred A. Knopf, a division of Random House, Inc.

268:    From Jean-Paul Sartre, *Existentialism*. In *The Norton Reader*, Seventh Edition. Edited by Arthur M. Eastman et al. New York: W.W. Norton, 1988, p. 1196. From *Existentialism*, Philosophical Library Publishers. Reprinted by permission of Philosophical Library Publishers.

269: "The Home Schooling Movement" from William E. Thompson and Joseph V. Hickey, *Society in Focus: An Introduction to Sociology*, Second Edition, pp. 352–353. Copyright © by William E. Thompson and Joseph V. Hickey. Reprinted by permission of Addison-Wesley Educational Publishers, Inc.

272: "Nonbiodegradable Pollutants" from Mark B. Bush, *Ecology of a Changing Planet*, Second Edition, p. 278. Copyright © 2000, 1997 by Prentice-Hall, Inc. Reprinted by permission of Prentice-Hall, Inc., Upper Saddle River, New Jersey.

274: Brian M. Fagan, *People of the Earth: An Introduction to World Prehistory*, Ninth Edition. New York: Longman, 1998, pp. 107–108.

279: Joyce Carey, "Art and Education." From *On the Function of the Novelist*. New York: New York Times, 1949. Reprinted by permission of Andrew Lownie, Literary Agent on behalf of the estate of Joyce Carey.

279: James Thurber, "A Dog's Eye View of Man," excerpted from an introduction to *Thurber's Dogs* by James Thurber. Copyright © 1955 Rosemary A. Thurber. Reprinted by arrangement with Rosemary A. Thurber and The Barbara Hogenson Agency. All rights reserved.

Chapter 8

284: "The Supreme Court in Action" from Edward S. Greenberg and Benjamin I. Page, *The Struggle for Democracy*. Copyright © 1993 by HarperCollins Publishers. Reprinted by permission.

288: "Are We Alone in the Universe?" from Jeffrey Bennett, Megan Donahue, Nicholas Schneider, and Mark Voit, *The Cosmic Perspective*, Brief Edition, pp. 230–233. Copyright © 2000 by Addison Wesley Longman. Reprinted by permission of Addison-Wesley Educational Publishers, Inc.

295: Robert W. Christopherson, *Geosystems: An Introduction to Physical Geography*, Fourth Edition. Upper Saddle River, NJ: Prentice-Hall, Inc., 2000, pp. 147, 149, 151, 152.

303: From J. Ross Eschleman, Barbara G. Cashion, and Laurence A. Basirico, *Sociology: An Introduction*, Fourth Edition, p. 118. Copyright © 1993 by HarperCollins College Publishers. Reprinted by permission of Addison-Wesley Educational Publishers, Inc.

306: "Meaning and Messages" from Joseph A. DeVito, *Human Communication: The Basic Course*, Seventh Edition, pp. 108–110. Copyright © 1997 by Addison-Wesley Educational Publishers, Inc. Reprinted by permission.

311: From "ISAIAH: Information on Seismic Activity, In A Hurry," http://www-social.wr.usgs.gov. U.S. Geographical Survey/U.S. Department of the Interior, 2000.

312: From Andrew L. Alden, "Quake Warnings Before the Shaking Starts," at http://geology.about.com/library/weekly/aa011198.htm. Reprinted by permission of the author.

314: Halderman and Mitchell, *Automotive Technology*.

314: From Bonnie Fremgen, *Essentials of Medical Assisting: Administrative and Clinical Competencies*, p. 350. Copyright © 1998 by Prentice-Hall, Inc. Reprinted by permission of Prentice-Hall, Inc., Upper Saddle River, New Jersey.

314: Neal K. Ostler et al., *Health Effects of Hazardous Materials*. Upper Saddle River, NJ: Prentice-Hall, Inc., p. 52.

317: From Jerry A. Nathanson, *Basic Environmental Technology: Water Supply, Waste Management, and Pollution Control*, Third Edition, p. 131. Copyright © 2000 by Prentice-Hall, Inc. Reprinted by permission of Prentice-Hall, Inc., Upper Saddle River, New Jerseyt.

319: "Reflected Light and Color" from Paul G. Hewitt, *Conceptual Physics*, Seventh Edition. Copyright © 1993 by Paul G. Hewitt. Reprinted by permission of HarperCollins Publishers, Inc.

325: "Problem Solving" from Josh R. Gerow, *Essentials of Psychology: Concepts and Applications*. Copyright © 1993 by HarperCollins College Publishers. Reprinted by permission.

329:    "The Value of Pet Ownership" from W. Stephen Damron, *Introduction to Animal Science: Global, Biological, Social, and Industry Perspectives*, pp. 577-579. Copyright © 2000 by Prentice-Hall, Inc. Reprinted by permission of Prentice-Hall, Inc., Upper Saddle River, New Jersey.

Chapter 9

335:    Figure data from *The Chronicle of Higher Education*. In Bennett, Briggs, and Triola, *Statistical Reasoning for Everyday Life*. Boston: Pearson Addison Wesley, 2003, p. 103.

336:    Figure 9.2: A Sample Graph. Data from *Statistical Abstract of the United States, 1998* in Bennett, Briggs, and Triola, Statistical Reasoning for Everyday Life. Pearson Addison Wesley, 2005, p. 311.

337:    Figure from Nora Newcombe, *Child Development: Change Over Time*, Eighth Edition, p. 400. Copyright © 1996 by HarperCollins College Publishers. Reprinted by permission of Addison-Wesley Educational Publishers, Inc.

339:    From Gerard J. Tortora, *Introduction to the Human Body: The Essentials of Anatomy and Physiology*, Third Edition, p. 91. Copyright © 1994 by Biological Sciences Textbooks, Inc. and A & P Textbooks, Inc. Reprinted by permission of Addison-Wesley Educational Publishers, Inc.

340:    Figure of principal parts of a hair root and associated structures. From Tortora, *Introduction to the Human Body: The Essentials of Anatomy and Physiology*, Third Edition, Figure 5.3.

344:    Map of state energy use. From Bennett, Briggs, and Triola, *Statistical Reasoning for Everyday Life*, p. 118. © 2003 Pearson Education, Inc. Reprinted by permission of Pearson Education, Inc. Publishing as Pearson Addison Wesley.

345:    Data in figure: Infectious disease trends. From Centers for Disease Control and Prevention. In B.E. Pruitt and Jane J. Stein, *Decisions for Healthy Living*. Pearson / Benjamin Cummings, 2004, p. 174.

347:    Data in Figure 9.8. From National Center for Health Statistics. In Pruitt and Stein, *Decisions for Healthy Living*, p. 151.

347:    Figure 9.9, bar graph. From Maxine Baca Zinn and D. Stanley Eitzen, *Diversity in Families*, Fourth Edition. Copyright © 1996 by HarperCollins College Publishers. Reprinted by permission of Addison-Wesley Educational Publishers, Inc.

348:    Data in Figure 9.10. From U.S. Census Bureau. In Pruitt and Stein, *Decisions for Healthy Living*, p. 216.

349:    Figure 9.11. Adapted from George C. Edwards III, Martin P. Wattenberg, and Robert L. Lineberry, *Government in America: People, Politics, and Policy*, Ninth Edition, p. 467. Copyright © 2000 by Addison-Wesley Educational Publishers, Inc. Reprinted by permission.

352:    Figure 9.13. Adapted from Edwards III, Wattenberg, and Lineberry, *Government in America: People, Politics, and Policy*, Ninth Edition, p. 88.

352:    Figure 9.14. Adapted From Michael C. Mix, Paul Farber, and Keith I. King, *Biology: The Network of Life*, p. 752. Copyright © 1992 by HarperCollins Publishers. Reprinted by permission.

353:    Figure 9.15. From Bonnie Fremgen, *Essentials of Medical Assisting: Administrative and Clinical Competencies*, p. 737. Copyright © 1998 by Prentice-Hall, Inc. Reprinted by permission of Prentice-Hall, Inc., Upper Saddle River, New Jersey.

354:    Figure 9.16. Adapted from Donald C. Mosley, Paul H. Pietri, and Leon C. Megginson, *Management: Leadership in Action*, Fifth Edition, p. 258. Copyright © 1996 by HarperCollins College Publishers. Reprinted by permission of Addison-Wesley Educational Publishers, Inc.

356:    Figure 9.17. Adapted from Robert C. Nickerson, *Business and Information Systems*, p. 387. Copyright © 1998 by Addison-Wesley Educational Publishers. Reprinted by permission of Prentice-Hall, Inc., Upper Saddle River, NJ.

360:    "Homeostasis." From Carl E. Rischer and Thomas A. Easton, *Focus on Human Biology*, Second Edition. Copyright © 1995 by HarperCollins College Publishers. Reprinted by permission.

365:   "Pangea: The Supercontinent and the Effects of Its Breakup." From Edward F. Bergman and William H. Renwick, *Introduction to Geography: People, Places, and Environment*, pp. 90–95. Copyright © 1999 by Prentice-Hall, Inc. Reprinted by permission of Prentice-Hall, Inc., Upper Saddle River, New Jersey.

Chapter 10

386:   Joyce Rebeta-Burditt, *The Cracker Factory*. New York: Macmillan, 1977, pp. 3, 5.

387:   From Laura Uba and Karen Huang, *Psychology*, p. 323. Copyright © 1999 by Addison-Wesley Educational Publishers, Inc. Reprinted by permission of Prentice-Hall, Inc., Upper Saddle River, New Jersey.

388:   Robert A. Lineberry and George C. Edwards, *Government in America*, Fourth Edition. Glenview, IL: Scott, Foresman, 1989, p. 309.

392:   From Maxine Phillips, "Needed: A Policy for Children When Parents Go to Work." Appeared in the *Los Angeles Times*, December 6, 1987. Reprinted by permission of Maxine Phillips, *Dissent Magazine*.

392:   From Jim Miller, "Forever Elvis." *Newsweek*, August 3, 1987. Copyright © 1987, Newsweek, Inc. All rights reserved. Reprinted by permission.

392:   Jack Drafahl and Sue Drafahl, "Films for long-lens photography: how to get sharp shots when conditions conspire against you." *Petersen's Photographic*, May 2003 v32 i1 p34(4).

396:   Pete Hamill, "The Wet Drug," *San Jose Mercury News*, March 24, 1983.

396:   From Edward S. Greenberg and Benjamin I. Page, *The Struggle for Democracy*, p. 390. Copyright © 1993 by HarperCollins Publishers. Reprinted by permission.

397:   Sarah King, "Love in the Afternoon—In a Crowded Prison Hall." *Los Angeles Times*, November 5, 1976.

399:   Studs Terkel, *Working: People Talk About What They Do All Day and How They Feel About What They Do*. New York: Random House, 1972.

400:   Elliott Currie and Jerome H. Skolnick, *America's Problems*, Second Edition. Glenview, IL: Scott Foresman, 1988, p. 217.

400:   From Center for Research on the Education of Students Placed at Risk, at http://www.csos.jhu.edu/crespar/programs.htm.

401:   From Alison McKinnon, "The Magic of a 'Sick Day': Feigning Illness Can Be Good for You—Especially When Mom's a C-conspirator." *Maclean's*, May 12, 2003, p. 52.

401:   From Sally L. Satel "Domestic Violence Laws Are Anti-Male.". In *Violence Against Women*, James D. Torr, ed. Current Controversies Series. Greenhaven Press, 1999 (first published in Sally L. Satel, "It's Always His Fault." *Women's Quarterly*, Summer 1997).

401:   President George W. Bush, excerpt from "Remarks to the Nation," September 11, 2002. http://www.whitehouse.gov/news/releases/2002/09/20020911-3.html.

405:   Beth Lovern, "Confessions of a Welfare Mom." *Utne Reader*, July/August 1994, pp. 81–82. Reprinted by permission of the author.

407:   From Robert A. Wallace, *Biology: The World of Life*, Sixth Edition, p. 518. Copyright © 1992 by HarperCollins Publishers. Reprinted by permission.

407:   Marie Winn, *The Plug-In Drug*. New York: Viking, 1981.

413:   Kesaya E. Noda, "I Am a Japanese American" from *Making Waves*, edited by Asian Women United of California, 1989. Reprinted by permission of Kesaya E. Noda.

417:   "Early Encounters with the Artist Within." From Duane Preble, Sarah Preble, and Patrick Frank, *Artforms: An Introduction to the Visual Arts*, Sixth Edition, pp. 21–23. Copyright © 1999 by Addison-Wesley Educational Publishers, Inc. Reprinted by permission.

Chapter 11

423:   Lorne Tepperman and Jenny Blain, *Think Twice! Sociology Looks at Current Social Issues*. Upper Saddle River, NJ: Prentice-Hall, Inc., 1999, p. 175.

428:   Robert L. Maginnis, "Equality Isn't Sameness." *USA Today*, November 20, 1996. Reprinted by permission of Robert L. Maginnis.

512:   From Joseph A. DeVito, *Messages: Building Interpersonal Communication Skills*, Fourth Edition, pp. 164-165. Copyright © 1999 by Addison-Wesley Educational Publishers, Inc. Reprinted by permission.

517:   Popenoe, *Sociology*, Eleventh Edition, p. 285.

519:   Figure 13.1—Adult Literacy and Gender: Literacy Rates in Least Industrialized and Industrializing Nations, from UNESCO Institute for Statistics. Assessment Year: July 2002. Reprinted by permission of UNESCO Institute for Statistics.

520:   Figure 13.2—A page of the index from American Journey: A History of the United States, Second Edition, Combined Edition by Goldfield et al. © Reprinted by permission of Pearson Education, Inc., Upper Saddle River, NJ.

521:   From Michael Solomon and Elnora Stuart, Marketing: Real People, Real Choices, Second Edition, pp. 161–162. Copyright © 2000 by Prentice-Hall, Inc. Reprinted by permission of Prentice-Hall, Inc., Upper Saddle River, NJ.

522:   From Robert A. Wallace, *Biology: The World of Life*, Seventh Edition, pp. 365–366. Copyright © 1997 by Addison-Wesley Educational Publishers. Reprinted by permission.

522:   From Mark B. Bush, *Ecology of a Changing Planet*, Second Edition, p. 205. Copyright © 2000, 1997 by Prentice-Hall, Inc. Reprinted by permission of Prentice-Hall, Inc., Upper Saddle River, New Jersey.

523:   DeVito, *Messages: Building Interpersonal Communication Skills*, Fourth Edition, pp. 147–148.

523:   Popenoe, Sociology, Eleventh Edition, p. 204.

526:   "Barriers to Effective Listening" from Norman B. Sigband and Arthur Bell, *Communication for Management and Business*, Fifth Edition, pp. 417–421. Copyright © 1989 Scott, Foresman and Company. Reprinted by permission.

530:   "Stress Management: Personally Adjusting to Stress" from Richard L. Weaver II, *Understanding Interpersonal Communication*, Seventh Edition, pp. 397–400. Copyright © 1996 by HarperCollins College Publishers. Reprinted by permission of Addison-Wesley Educational Publishers, Inc.

541:   From Richard George, *The New Consumer Survival Kit*, p. 69. Copyright © 1978 by the Maryland Center for Public Broadcasting. By permission of Little, Brown and Company.

541:   George, *The New Consumer Survival Kit*, p. 97.

541:   George, *The New Consumer Survival Kit*, p. 103.

541:   Morris K. Holland and Gerald Tarlow, *Using Psychology*, Second Edition. Boston: Little, Brown and Company, 1980, pp. 8-9.

542:   George, *The New Consumer Survival Kit*, p. 219.

542:   George, *The New Consumer Survival Kit*, p. 214.

544:   From Irwin Unger, *These United States: The Question of Our Past*, Second Edition, Vol. 2, p. 871. Copyright © 1982 by Irwin Unger. Reprinted by permission of Little, Brown and Company.

546:   Irwin Unger, *These United States: The Question of Our Past*. Boston: Little, Brown and Company, 1978, p. 897.

546:   Hugh D. Barlow, *Introduction to Criminology*, Second Edition. Boston: Little, Brown and Company, 1984, p. 12.

546:   Barlow, *Introduction to Criminology*, Second Edition, p. 16.

545:   Unger, *These United States: The Question of Our Past*, Second Edition, Vol. 2, p. 421.

547:   Unger, *These United States: The Question of Our Past*, Second Edition, Vol. 2, p. 848.

549:   Kelly Costigan, "How Color Goes to Your Head." *Science Digest*, December 1984. Reprinted by permission of the author.

555:   From Samuel L. Becker, *Discovering Mass Communication*, Second Edition, p. 306. Copyright © 1987 by Scott, Foresman and Company. Reprinted by permission.

555:   Becker, *Discovering Mass Communication*, Second Edition, p. 330.

Chapter 12

556:　Becker, *Discovering Mass Communication*, Second Edition, p. 377.
563:　Maggie Paley, "Flirtation: The Signals of Attraction—Deciphered." *Vogue*, February
　　　1982. Copyright © 1982 by The Condé Nast Publications, Inc. Reprinted by permis-
　　　sion.
568:　From Samuel L. Becker, "The Functions and Effects of Music" from *Discovering Mass
　　　Communication*, Second Edition. Copyright © 1987 by Scott, Foresman and
　　　Company. Reprinted by permission.

Photo Credits

Reading Is For Everyone
Opening page: (top left): Ryan McVay/Getty Images, (top right): Russell Kaye/Getty
Images, (center right): Antonio M. Rosario/Getty Images, (bottom right): David
Young-Wolff/PhotoEdit Inc., (bottom left): Yellow Dog Productions/Getty Images;
second page: (top): Courtsy of Aegis Publishing Group, Ltd., (bottom): Jacket Cover
of THE DOCTORS BOOK OF HOME REMEDIES by Sid Kirchheimer. Used by permission of Bantam Books, a division of Random House, Inc.; **third page:** (top): Jacket
Cover of FASHION VICTIM by Michelle Lee. Used by permission of Broadway Books,
a division of Random House, Inc., (bottom): Courtesy of The Lyons Press, a division
of The Globe Peqout Press; **fourth page:** (top): Book cover from HOW TO TALK SO
KIDS WILL LISTEN AND LISTEN SO KIDS WILL TALK (REPRINT) by ADELE FABER
and ELAINE MAZLISH. Reprinted by permission of HarperCollins Publishers Inc.,
(bottom): Courtesy of the Falcon Press, a division of The Globe Peqout Press; **fifth
page:** (top): Courtesy of the M. I. L. K. Collection and HarperCollins Publishers Inc.,
front cover image © Janice Rubin, (bottom): Jacket Cover of THE GIFT OF FEAR by
Gavin DeBecker. Used by permission of The Dial Press/Dell Publishing, a division of
Random House, Inc.; **sixth page:** (bottom): "Cover Design & Logo", from WHAT'S
SO GREAT ABOUT AMERICA by Dinesh D' Souza, copyright © 2002 by Dinesh D'
Souza. Used by permission of Penguin, a division of Penguin Group (USA) Inc.
Photograph of flag: Blue Lemon Productions/Getty Images; **seventh page:** (top):
Jacket cover of THE COMPLETE TIGHTWAD GAZETTE by Amy Dacyczyn. Used by
permission of Bertelsmann, Random House, Inc., (bottom): Courtesy of Scott Bilker
(DebtSmart.com) and Press One Publishing. Available at DebtSmart.com and
Amazon.com; **eighth page:** (top): "Cover", from THE HARD QUESTIONS by Susan
Piver, copyright © 2000 by Susan Piver. Used by permission of Jeremy P. Tarcher, an
imprint of Penguin Group (USA) Inc., (bottom): From The Worst-Case Scenario
Survival Handbook ™: Parenting by Joshua Piven, David Borgenicht, & Sarah Jordan,
© 2003 by Quirk Productions, Inc. Used with permission of Chronicle Books LLC,
San Francisco. Visit ChronicleBooks.com.

23: John and Guy Productions/Index Stock Imagery, Inc.; **213:** A. Ramey/PhotoEdit
Inc.; **218:** © Andy Manis/ The New York Times; **285:** Floyd Yewell/ Courtesy of the
Supreme Court of the United States; **290:** NASA Headquarters, Media Services Code
PM; **330:** Myrleen Ferguson Cate/PhotoEdit Inc.; **342 (left):** © J.T. Gwynne
Photography; **342 (right):** Glen Allison/Getty Images; **343:** Mark Peters /SIPA Press.

Index